Money Financial Markets and Economic Activity

Norman E. Cameron
University of Manitoba

Addison-Wesley Publishers
Don Mills, Ontario • Reading, Massachusetts
Menlo Park, California • London • Amsterdam • Sydney

DESIGN: Pronk & Associates
EDITORIAL: Valerie Daigen
TECHNICAL ART: Frank Zsigo
COMPOSITION: Trigraph

Canadian Cataloguing in Publication Data
Cameron, Norman E.
Money, financial markets and economic activity

Includes index.
ISBN 1-201-18670-5

1. Money. 2. Money market. 3. Finance. I. Title.

HG173.C35 1984 332 C84-098667-X

ISBN 0-201-18670-5

Printed in the United States of America

A B C D E F -DON- 89 88 87 86 85 84

To Vera Alice Cameron

Contents

PREFACE

There are now several texts about money, banking, and financial markets in Canada. It may help to explain where this one fits relative to the others.

Like the others, this book assumes that readers have had an introductory course in economics. I may have made a little more use of the economic tools developed in an introductory course, so prior exposure to economics will be very helpful to students at certain points.

This text is different from the competition in several ways. First, I have given more consideration than is usual to markets other than that for money. Courses in economics departments tend to focus sharply on the money market because of money's unique importance in macroeconomic theory. Instructors in business schools find this focus too narrow for their students, many of whom will have to make their living in the financial system but outside banks. This text takes the view, derived from the work of James Tobin and others, that money is just an asset like other assets and can in principle be analysed with the same approach used for other assets. True, the approach requires some customizing to fit money, because of special institutional considerations, but there are not two separate compartments labelled "theory of money" and "theory of other assets."

Second, this text approaches seriously the idea of risk in financial markets. Risk is all around us, but it is particularly important in the financial system. The entire insurance and futures market sectors of the financial system owe their existence to the desire of individuals to avoid risk. In order to analyse risk properly, I develop several theoretical tools early in the book — tools that can be applied to any situation involving uncertainty. The student learns how to apply these tools to the standard asset choice of households, to the simultaneous choice of assets and debts by firms, banks, and other financial institutions, and finally to the optimal choice of policy instruments for stabilization policy.

Third, the part of the text dealing with stabilization policy introduces a number of modern features. The macroeconomic model used to assess impacts of stabilization policy gives prominent place to supply considerations, including the probability of both favorable and adverse supply shocks. The model is not cast as necessarily stable. The student learns to consider, in addition to short- and long-run properties, the medium-run dynamic time path likely to follow any disturbance. This sort of analysis is necessary if students are to appreciate the uncertainty in which policy is actually made and thus to appreciate the modern theory of policy making under uncertainty.

The macroeconomic approach used in this book is modern, eclectic, and neo-Keynesian, which is another way of saying middle-of-the-road in the dispute between monetarists and Keynesians. Even though I work in a department thought of by some as a hotbed of radical Keynesians, one reviewer thought he detected a monetarist bias in my discussion of policy, so I must have succeeded in finding the middle ground.

Writing this book has taken more time than I care to measure, but in the process I have accumulated a series of debts that I am happy to count and acknowledge. Useful comments and criticisms on both style and substance have been provided by Beverly Cameron (wife and chief critic), John S. McCallum, Stephen Watson and Robert Mitchell of the University of Manitoba, Christopher A. Sarlo and John C. Evans of York University, Louis N. Christofides of the University of Guelph, Robert L. Comeau of Dalhousie University, David Backus of Queen's University, Pierre L. Siklos of Wilfred Laurier University, Ralph Kolinski of the University of Windsor, S. Bruce Benton of the University of New Brunswick, and M.L. Kliman of McMaster University. These criticisms have caused me a lot of extra work, all of it worthwhile. Frank Burns and Richard Kitowski of Addison-Wesley have been constructive and supportive throughout, a pleasure to work with. Val Daigen has done an excellent job of copy editing to remove ambiguities and to keep the prose consistent. Susan Eidelheit, Rose Shipley, June Renton, Roy Switzer, and especially Joyce Laird have all cheerfully typed parts of various drafts. Maninder Bhatia and Agathe LaFrance provided competent and efficient research assistance, as did the helpful staff of the reference and government documents sections of the University of Manitoba library system. The University of Manitoba and the Social Sciences and Humanities Research Council of Canada between them provided financial support for a sabbatical leave during which this book was finished. St. John's College provided throughout an excellent facility and atmosphere for this kind of work. Finally, Mr. H. Kaslove, Curator of the National Currency Collection at the Bank of Canada, graciously provided the photographs of card money used in chapter 4. To all of you, my sincere thanks and my assurance that I do not hold any of you responsible for any errors that may remain.

My final two debts are for forbearance. First, for the forbearance of past students in my money and banking classes who have had to grapple with previous versions of this manuscript and with material since dropped as obscure, irrelevant, or just plain wrongheaded. Second, for the forbearance of Ewen and Fraser (and often their mother as well) when they would rather have had their father doing something more congenial with his weekends than writing a book.

Norman E. Cameron

PART ONE

Money and Financial Markets

CHAPTER 1

Introduction

Study of a modern financial system at work involves an interesting mixture of institutional description, case study, and analytical theory. It is also more difficult than study of most other sectors of the economy because there are so many parts, interrelated in so many ways and often protected from understanding by so much technical jargon (*butterfly straddles, purchase funds, retractable income debentures*, and the like).

The task of an introductory chapter should therefore be not only to describe what the book covers (done in section 3) and to review why the study of financial systems is topical and fascinating (done in section 1), but also to put in place a few of the key ideas that will help you tie together the various parts of the financial system as described and analysed in this book. Those key ideas are presented in section 2 — a section that will be useful both as an introduction and, later, as a review.

SECTION 1 Introduction to the field of money and finance

The field of money, banking, and finance is both fascinating and arcane. It is arcane only because of the level of jargon used. For instance, in the money market (actually a market for issue and resale of short-term, large-scale, resalable loans), a single type of debt has seven different names, depending on the type of issuer.

Money, banking, and finance are fascinating for several reasons. The first is that they matter to us all. Money itself lubricates the whole economy by making purchases and sales possible. Transfer of money from those who earn more than they spend to those who spend more than they earn determines the size and pattern of real investment (in housing, plant and equipment, and inventories) in the economy. Today's real investment determines tomorrow's output and jobs.

Individuals and families also realize most of their long-range plans through the financial system. It is here that retirement planning starts. It is here that a medical-school education or a new family business may be financed. It is here that families set up a trust for children or buy life insurance to protect all their other financial plans.

Despite the importance of money, banking, and finance to individuals and to the economy, the world's entire financial structure rests on nothing more than public confidence. Every nation's financial system is built on promises to pay money and on the belief that those promises will be kept. Money itself is one of humanity's finest inventions, the prize counterexample to Murphy's law (that if anything can go wrong, it will). Money is money simply because we all agree to accept it as such. If we did not (and only a hyperinflation will ever cause us not to), all the promises to pay in the financial system would be meaningless; the economy would grind to a halt, except for barter transactions.

Changes in the financial system since the 1960s

The field of money, banking, and finance is fascinating for still another reason: because the financial system itself is changing as rapidly as the lead in a good horse race. Consider just the following changes since the 1960s in Canada:

1. Bank credit cards and automated teller machines have spread coast-to-coast.
2. Banks' foreign-currency business grew to become half of their total business by 1981. Banks have become Canada's largest multinationals.
3. Barriers to entry into various kinds of financing business have been lowered throughout the financial system as prohibitions have been relaxed and financial charters made much easier to get. Almost five dozen foreign banks have set up shop in Canada. Even companies still limited by legislation have often found ways around the limits. Banks are even threatening to invade the sheltered, conservative, and profitable stockbrokerage business.
4. Consumer loan companies have seen their business wither away in the face of competition from banks and credit unions.
5. Monetary policy has been recognized as a powerful demand-management tool, and there have been radical changes in the way it is conducted by the Bank of Canada.
6. The international system of pegged exchange rates, established at the Bretton Woods conference in 1944, broke down in 1971 after a lengthy illness and has been replaced with a system of loosely floating exchange rates. Despite an agreement by seven European countries to reinstate pegged exchange rates among themselves (in the European *snake*), and despite exchange-rate management by central banks in other countries, foreign exchange risk in international trade has increased greatly since 1970.

7. High and uncertain inflation has decimated the real values of bonds and deposits. The same inflation has caused huge movements in nominal interest rates, mostly upward — movements that have decimated the market value of long-term bonds even in nominal terms. The level of financial risk has increased for everyone.
8. A whole new international financial market has been created, separate from domestic financial systems and independent of national governments. This Eurocurrency market deals in large-scale deposits and loans in currencies other than that of the host country, in international financial centres such as London, Singapore, Luxembourg, Nassau, and Bahrain (all chosen for their lack of detailed financial regulations). The Eurocurrency market is already larger than the financial systems of most nations and is growing rapidly on a diet of no regulation at all.
9. As a result of the growth of the Eurocurrency market, the large banks of industrialized countries are up to their chins in loans to Third World governments, all of which are having a hard time with both energy prices and the world recession. Parts of the world's financial system are close to the edge of a steep cliff. A few parts of it already lie at the bottom.
10. Whole new financial markets have sprung up in specialized financial instruments such as stock options and financial futures contracts (and gold) to allow people to offset some of the extra risks of today's uncertain financial environment.

There are more changes to come. The financial system is becoming increasingly competitive, and the new technology of the microchip is providing most of its benefits in the financial sector (because its impact is largest in the most information-intensive sectors), so the pace of change is not likely to slow down much in the near future. In the future people will make many payments out of bank deposits merely by pushing buttons at electronic cash-register terminals in stores or on computer terminals in their homes. Lending will be possible in real-term instruments, where a real rather than a nominal return is guaranteed regardless of the rate of inflation. And more that is hard to conceive of today.

Clearly, now is a time when it is of use to understand money, banking, and finance. In the 1950s the field may have been dull, staid, and forgettable, but it is not so in the 1980s.

SECTION 2 The approach of this book

In introductory economics courses, instructors tend to treat the financial system as a complicated device whose inner workings do not matter to the main issues of economic policy. Students therefore receive a greatly truncated and simplified treatment of financial matters. The most common treatment, supposedly derived from Keynes' General Theory of Employment, Interest, and Money, is to lump all nonmoney assets together as a single homogeneous asset, usually called bonds, and then to concentrate on demand and supply of the remaining asset, money.[1]

With that preamble, it will come as no surprise that this book takes a broader approach. We will look at the financial system as a set of many different financial markets, and we will see that the pattern of demand and supply in the different markets is important for economic policy. The truncated approach is acceptable only as a first approximation for introductory courses.

Financial-market behavior

All of the functions of the financial system are best understood by thinking of the financial system as a set of interrelated financial markets. Each financial market has its own demand D and supply S. Some of the demand in financial markets is by families, such as the O'Malleys, some by manufacturing firms, such as Acme Chemical, some of it by financial firms, such as Evermore Insurance and Faithful Trustco Ltd., and some by governments. The same holds for supply of financial assets, which are merely the debts of O'Malley and the others.

There are many different types of financial markets, but just one kind of explanation of their demand and supply behavior. Only the market for money requires special treatment, because of the way that nominal income levels affect the demand for money.

The wealth constraint

Financial markets are interrelated in two ways. The most obvious is that most financial assets are reasonably close substitutes for each other. Stocks and bonds are closer substitutes than shoes and stereo equipment, for instance. Increased desire for stocks is therefore likely to involve reduced desire for bonds.

The second way in which financial markets are interrelated is by the wealth constraint. Each individual has at any point of time a specific level of wealth (W_i). Each individual's net demand for assets (the difference between total demand for assets, D_i, and total debts issued or supplied, D_i)

[1]Axel Leijonhufvud has made it clear that Keynes' actual treatment of financial matters in the General Theory is much more sophisticated than that; see his "Keynes and the Keynesians: A Suggested Interpretation," *American Economic Review*, May 1967, 401–10. The truncation and simplification were done by Keynes' followers, particularly J.R. Hicks in his justly celebrated article "Mr. Keynes and the 'Classics': A Suggested Interpretation," *Econometrica*, April 1937, 147–59, which first developed the *IS–LM* curves to analyse levels of aggregate demand.

cannot ever be different from that individual's total wealth, except by fraud. Algebraically, the wealth constraint is that

$$D_i - S_i = W_i,$$

for all individuals i.

It follows from the wealth constraint that whenever anyone's demand for stocks rises, there must be exactly compensating changes elsewhere. Demand for some other asset must fall, or supply of some debt must rise, or both. It is these changes that "finance" the extra demand for stocks. With time, of course, the individual can also save to add to total wealth as well.

Stocks and flows

Demand and supply are to be understood as *stocks* at a point of time, rather than as *flows* per period of time. *Demand for an asset* refers to the amount of any asset that people are willing to hold at a point of time, rather than to the rate at which they are willing to plough new funds into buying that asset during a year. *Supply of an asset* refers to the quantity in existence. For financial assets, which are called debts by their issuers, supply refers to the amount that issuers are willing to leave outstanding at any point of time. Decisions by assetholders to sell off or redeem their holdings should therefore be thought of as a fall in demand rather than as an increase in supply. Missing this distinction can cause great confusion later, so fix it firmly in mind now.

Demand for an asset

Supply of an asset

Explaining total stock demand and supply of each asset also implies an explanation of flows of buying and selling during each period. Flows of buying and selling represent changes in demand and supply, adjustments of last period's holdings to those desired now. If we know past holdings and can determine desired holdings, we can also determine what current buying and selling will be.

Risks

One of the key determinants of demand and supply of assets is relative risks (the others are total wealth and relative expected yields). Some of the effects of risk are fairly obvious, such as investors' not putting all their eggs in one basket. Some risk-avoiding behavior is not so obvious. Risk is generally hard to observe, because it relates to possible outcomes in the future, and O'Malley's and Evermore's estimates of the future will not necessarily be the same. Even so, the influence of risk is powerful enough that it is worth investigating in detail and at length as in this book. Changes in risk perceptions, for instance, explain such financial upheavals as the reported "death" of the long-term bond market in the early 1980s.

Impacts of financial-market behavior

Explaining the behavior of demand and supply also explains the behavior of financial-market yields, which typically adjust quickly to bring supply and demand into balance. Behavior of financial-market yields is important because it determines the pattern of real investment. For instance, if assetholders are demanding mainly short-term assets, as in the early 1980s, borrowers who want short-term finance will find credit available on easy terms. Short-term real investment projects such as adding equipment or inventories will tend to be carried out. Borrowers wanting to finance long-term assets such as pipelines or new mines will not find suitable credit readily available, and some projects will be delayed or cancelled.

Understanding the behavior of various financial markets also helps to explain the impact of monetary policy on the economy. Essentially, monetary policy works by creating excess demand or supply of money; the real sector is affected only as that disequilibrium causes adjustments in other financial markets and changes relative yields on various assets. Such adjustments can vary a great deal from year to year, depending on what else is happening in financial markets, so the response of real spending to monetary policy can vary a great deal as well.

Techniques used in this book

This book uses several techniques to explain the material. Riffling quickly through the next hundred pages will reveal diagrams; a slower riffle will also reveal some algebra. With very few exceptions, the diagrams are familiar tools used in a slightly different setting — indifference-curve diagrams where the O'Malleys must choose between savings and consumption, or between combinations of expected yield and risk; demand and supply curves to explain shifts in equilibrium yields; *IS* and *LM* curves; aggregate demand and supply curves; and Phillips curves. Some will be familiar from the introductory economics course; others, from an intermediate economics course. For those launching into the study of this subject without intermediate economics, each of these tools is explained before it is pressed into service.

Notwithstanding the reassurances of the preceding paragraph, you are hereby warned that some of the concepts we use to analyse risk are slippery. Unless you apply these concepts frequently to circumstances around you, they will be quickly forgotten. There are thousands of situations, by no means all in the area of finance, in which the concepts of this book can be used to explain behavior or to suggest answers. Choices among traffic routes to follow to class, foods to eat in the cafeteria, courses to take, and even times to set the alarm for can all be analysed with the concepts we develop and use in this book. Some of the questions at the ends of chapters will help stimulate such applications, if inspiration fails you.

SECTION 3 Topics covered in this book

In the first part of the book, I describe and explain the economy's fundamental financial asset, money. Money is fundamental because it is the other half of every financial transaction, because it is the means of payment by which all other assets are transferred. This role of money is taken for granted nowadays, but it was far from automatic in the past. Canada in particular has had colorful and innovative experiments with various moneys, two of which are described in some detail.

Chapter 5 introduces an accounting framework, the national flow of funds and capital accounts, to help us organize our thinking about parts of the financial system. The remainder of part I explains and describes the major flows and stocks of the financial system: first those of households like the O'Malleys, then those of firms and governments.

Risk is introduced in part II. First I offer a measure of risk, explain how assetholders respond to it, and explain how their responses affect the demand for individual assets. Then some of the *hedging* markets are described — the markets for insurance and options and futures contracts, which exist solely to allow reduction of risks. A separate chapter reviews the major theories of the demand for money, as a special but important case of the asset demand theory given earlier. Finally I explain the role of risk in supply decisions and describe past patterns of borrowing.

Part III looks at financial intermediaries in more detail. These firms are both demanders and suppliers of financial assets, but in principle their response as assetholders and as suppliers is no different from that of primary lenders or borrowers like the O'Malleys or Acme Chemical. In practice, the scale of operation of financial intermediaries is so much bigger that they need a special section of their own. Separate chapters discuss the banks, the group of other short-term intermediaries known collectively as near-banks, and the two major long-term intermediaries — life insurers and pension funds.

Part IV brings together the demands and supplies of different groups to describe a general equilibrium in financial markets. Because of extensive arbitrage (shifting of demand and supply) between different financial markets, especially by financial intermediaries, this general equilibrium can be expected to produce certain patterns, or *structures*, of relative yields. The last chapter in part IV discusses the role of governments and points out the remaining problems of greatest social concern in the microeconomic functioning of the financial system.

Part V presents a model with which stabilization policy can be analysed. The model is a modern, neo-Keynesian or post-Keynesian version of aggregate demand theory, with the financial sector more developed than is usual in macroeconomics textbooks. The first four chapters explain the logic of stabilization policy and the behavior of aggregate demand and aggregate supply. The last chapter explains how the preceding chapters imply a business cycle.

Part VI discusses stabilization policy — first the tools available, with emphasis on monetary policy, then what sort of uses of those tools might be socially optimal in a world where policy effects are uncertain and where the public must anticipate as well as react to stabilization policy.

Part VII provides a brief look at those aspects of the international financial system not already included in other parts of the book.

SECTION 4 Summary

The financial system is fascinating for a variety of reasons, including the remarkable rate at which it is changing. This book explains much of the detail of financial markets that is left out of introductory and intermediate economics courses. We will look at the financial system as a set of interconnected markets for different types of assets, all related by patterns of substitutability and by the overall wealth constraint. Each market has its own demand and supply at any point of time, which will be kept in balance by adjustments in relative yields.

Changes in demand and supply are caused by changes in relative yields, relative risks, and total wealth. Changes in relative yields have an important impact on the real, or nonfinancial, sector of the economy by altering the terms for financing various types of real investment projects. The structure and behavior of financial markets are also important determinants of the ability of monetary policy to stabilize the economy.

Questions for discussion

1. When you get fed up with the performance of your Acme stock and want to sell it off, what has changed in the stock market: demand or supply?
2. What compensating change is likely to accompany your sale of Acme stock, as a result of your wealth constraint?
3. In what sense does money lubricate the whole economy? What transactions do not require money?
4. Why do financial professionals tend to be more conservatively dressed than other professionals (doctors, architects, and so on)? Would you expect bankers to be particularly conservative in their choice of clothes? Why?
5. What financial innovations of the last three years have you made use of in the last week? What innovation do you most want to see that has not arrived yet?
6. In what financial markets are you now a demander or supplier? When did you last adjust your demand or supply, and how? What happened to your total wealth at that point?

7. Describe some action you have taken in the last week to avoid what would otherwise be an unacceptable level of risk (not necessarily financial risk). What did you have to give up, if anything, to get rid of that extra risk?
8. What sources of credit are open to you to finance your investment in education? Does availability of these sources affect your demand for that kind of investment? If so, how?

References

Since this chapter does not get into the substance of money, banking, and finance, these references are chosen more for their flavor than for their academic rigor. They are all best-selling paperbacks.

Erdman, Paul. *The Billion-Dollar Sure Thing.* New York: Scribners, 1973. A novel written to while away the time spent in a Swiss jail for a banking misdemeanor.

Hailey, Arthur. *The Moneychangers.* Garden City, N.Y.: Doubleday, 1976. A novel written on the author's estate in the Bahamas.

Sampson, Anthony. *The Moneylenders: Bankers and a World in Turmoil.* New York: Viking Press, 1982.

Smith, Adam [George J.W. Goodman]. *Paper Money.* New York: Dell, 1981. A sequel to *The Money Game* and *Supermoney*.

CHAPTER 2

The Roles of the Financial System

The previous chapter described how we will go about studying the financial system. This chapter describes what the financial system does and how its performance can be evaluated. What the financial system does is fill several roles at once, so each needs to be described. Many of the functions of the financial system involve financial flows in the economy, so the accounting concepts underlying financial flows must be introduced too. You should therefore learn from this chapter:

1. the various functions fulfilled by the financial system,
2. the basic flows of funds through the financial system, and
3. the criteria used to evaluate the performance of the financial system — the same sort of criteria that we use for evaluating all other parts of the economy.

SECTION 1 The roles of the financial system

Aside from providing useful and interesting employment for many graduates in economics and finance, the financial system plays five major roles, as outlined below.

Channelling savings into real investment

Real investment

The financial system accounts for most of the flow of savings into *real investment*. Real investment is defined here, as in introductory economics courses, as the purchase of new durable goods such as housing, plant and equipment, and inventories; in some cases even consumer durables are included. Some savings are directly reinvested by the saver, without any contact with the financial system — for instance, where Acme Chemical Ltd. uses all its undistributed profits to add to its fleet of trucks, or where the O'Malley family ploughs all the family income it can spare into building a summer home at the lake. The rest of total savings each year is recycled into investment spending through the financial system. Savers add to their collections of financial assets while borrowers run up their debts.

Without the financial system to match up (a) savings not directly reinvested with (b) investments not fully self-financed, much of the investment in real capital would not take place. Without that investment, the economy's capital stock would grow more slowly. Without as much capital stock, output and productivity would grow more slowly. We would all be worse off materially.

Some of the matching of savers to investors is just brokerage, as in the stock market: an issuer of new stock is brought together with potential new subscribers by a broker whose role is essentially just to introduce the two parties. More commonly, the assets bought by savers are not the same as the debts issued by the borrowers. In these cases, some financial institution intermediates; *intermediation* is borrowing by selling the kind of asset the saver wants to hold and lending the funds by buying the debt that borrowers want to issue. Such indirect channelling of funds from savers to investors now absorbs about two-thirds of each year's savings flow and explains why financial institutions are so large.

Intermediation

Providing a medium of exchange

The financial system provides a medium of exchange called money, an asset used by all sectors of the economy for buying and selling everything else, a specialized device to save the transactions costs of barter (searching for a trading partner whose wants are exactly the opposite of your own). The financial system also operates the payments mechanism by which money is transferred from one holder to another.

Providing stores of wealth

The financial system provides a wide variety of stores of wealth to complement real assets such as houses, land, and capital equipment. With a well-developed financial system, firms and households can arrange future income streams to match future needs more closely. The O'Malley family needs a level lifetime income stream beginning at retirement. Acme Chemical needs to cover losses during recessions. Others need assets realizable on short notice without significant cost — that is, liquid assets. The stock, bond, and money markets of the financial system provide *liquidity* for many assets that would otherwise be fairly illiquid.

Liquidity

Providing credit facilities

The financial system provides credit facilities for those who want to spend more than they can afford out of current income alone. The O'Malleys might want to finance their summer home partly out of savings and partly by borrowing against future income. Acme Chemical might decide to draw down its line of credit at the bank to finance a larger fleet of trucks than it could afford out of its current profits alone.

Stabilizing the economy

The way our financial system is arranged, the government can use control of chartered-bank cash reserves to exert powerful influence over levels of output, inflation, and unemployment. By controlling the supply of one critical asset with fixed return — money — the government can influence all other yields in the financial system and thereby influence the level of aggregate demand. This influence can be used to stabilize or destabilize economic performance. Experts are still divided on which uses of monetary policy will have which effects, but all are agreed that monetary policy is powerful.

SECTION 2 The flow of funds

Recall from the circular flow diagram used at the start of your introductory or intermediate macroeconomics course that each year the economy generates a flow of savings. Households do not spend all of their disposable income on consumption, governments do not usually spend all of their tax revenues on purchases of current (as opposed to capital) goods and services, and the business sector usually retains for its own use each year most of its after-tax profit as well as all of the flow of revenue set aside as capital consumption allowances. These savings flows are the raw material of the financial system. They appear at the bottom of figure 2–1 as gross saving.

Some of the gross-savings flow is directly reinvested in new real capital goods by the saver. Savings flows not directly reinvested in new real assets are used to buy financial assets instead; the flow is called *primary lending*, and those providing the funds in each year are known as *primary lenders*.

Primary lending

Similarly, the part of gross investment spending not financed internally (that is, out of current profits of the investor) must be financed externally by issuing extra debt or selling off assets. This flow is called *primary borrowing*, and the participants, *primary borrowers*.

Primary borrowing

Primary lending is channelled to primary borrowers either directly or indirectly. When lending is direct, the primary lender ends up holding an obligation of some sort (a loan note, a bond, or a share of common stock, for instance) issued by the primary borrower. When lending is indirect, it goes though one or more financial intermediaries. The primary lender ends up holding a debt of some financial institution, which in turn ends up holding the debt of the primary borrower. An example of such indirect credit is the O'Malleys' lending money to a bank in exchange for a two-year term deposit and then the bank's lending that money to Acme Chemical in exchange for Acme's demand loan note.

FIGURE 2–1 The circular flow of funds in the financial system

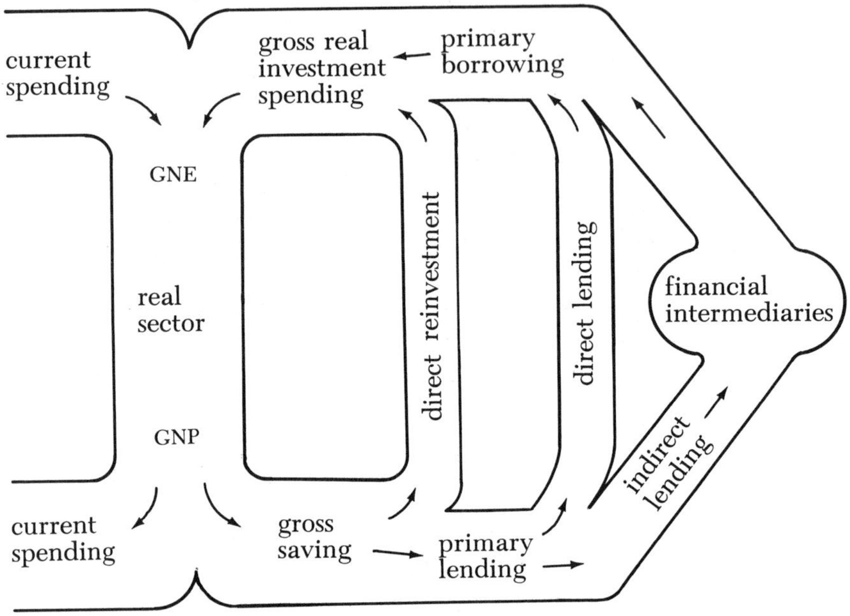

The annual flow of income from the real sector (GNP) is used for current spending or is part of gross saving. Of gross saving, part is reinvested directly in new capital goods by the saver; the rest is held in some form of financial asset — loaned out — as primary lending. Some primary lending is loaned directly to primary borrowers, but most is loaned indirectly via financial intermediaries. Total primary borrowing plus direct reinvestment of savings accounts for all of gross real investment spending, a component of gross national expenditure.

The flow-of-funds identity

Primary lending must always equal primary borrowing, by definition, for exactly the same reason that measured gross savings must always exactly equal measured gross investment in the national accounts. Figure 2–1 shows that primary lending (PL) is gross savings (S) less the part directly reinvested by savers (S_d). Thus, $PL = S - S_d$. Primary borrowing (PB) is gross investment (I) less the part financed internally out of current savings, which is the part of gross savings directly reinvested by savers, S_d. Thus, $PB = I - S_d$. Since measured savings equals measured investment in the national accounts, it follows that measured primary borrowing PB will also exactly equal measured primary lending PL.

You learned in introductory macroeconomics that just because $S = I$ in the national accounts does not mean that the producing sector is always in equilibrium. For exactly the same reason, equality of measured primary borrowing and lending does not imply that financial markets are always in equilibrium.

For instance, if there is excess demand for goods and services, planned savings will be less than planned investment, and planned primary lending will be less than planned primary borrowing. In this situation, the business sector will find its inventories falling, and business customers will find some of their equipment orders unfilled. Both adjustments imply less measured investment but also less measured primary borrowing and possibly more measured primary lending. With less investment to finance because of lower inventories and more unfilled orders, there is less need for borrowing, so primary borrowing will be less than originally planned. If some of the inventory financing would have been done out of current savings, then more of current savings is left for lending elsewhere, and the total of primary lending is greater than planned.

Equality of measured lending and borrowing is not necessarily an equilibrium situation because it will not necessarily persist. If there is excess demand for goods so that inventories are being run down, then in the next period inventory levels will be built back up, so both investment and primary borrowing will change from their current levels. Only if planned savings equals planned investment, so that inventory levels are not changed, is there equilibrium.

SECTION 3 Evaluation of the financial system

Criteria for evaluation of the financial system follow from the roles that the financial system is expected to play.

Static efficiency

Static efficiency refers to use of inputs in such a way as to maximize output. Financial markets employ people and machines to provide a wide range of financial instruments and services. It is always of concern to economists that people and machines not be wasted and that the range of financial instruments and services be wide. In thinking about static efficiency, economists take into account the time spent and the risk borne by customers of financial institutions and markets, as well as the time spent and the risk borne by bankers and brokers.

Static-inefficiency losses mean unnecessary time and expense in making transactions, or unnecessary exposure to risk, or transactions foregone that would have been worthwhile. New kinds of automatic teller services, for instance, reduce banks' labor costs and also the transactions costs of bank deposit and loan customers. New financial-futures-market instruments enable firms to offset much of the risk of fluctuations in market value of their bond holdings.

Dynamic efficiency

Dynamic efficiency refers to choice of real investments to maximize the rate of growth of output. If the financial system does not channel savings into the most productive real investments, output growth in the economy will be slower or in some other way less desirable. Dynamic inefficiency would appear in the Canadian economy if financial institutions were barred from lending to particular groups of firms, such as small firms with no established earnings record, or firms without real estate to use as collateral. Anything that affects an economy's growth rate will be very important in the long run, however small it might appear in the short run, since the effects compound over time.

Equity

The third criterion for evaluation is the *equity* with which the financial system treats savers and borrowers. Society is generally averse to unequal treatment of equals even if it does not have any impact on the efficiency of investment and growth. Women are the most recent group to protest unequal treatment — in particular, the provision of insurance and annuities at different rates for men and women. On occasion governments will use the financial system to create special advantages for particular groups with subsidized loan schemes, to compensate for some inequity elsewhere in the economy. Exporters, home-owners, and farmers are the main beneficiary groups.

Stabilization of output and price levels

In the past, this has been interpreted as how readily the banking system permits tight control of the money supply and how much the impact of monetary policy is weakened by the growth of near-banks. More recently, some economists have come to view discretionary monetary and fiscal policies themselves as sources of instability, so that a stabilizing financial system could also be one that more effectively offsets those discretionary policies.[1]

SECTION 4 Summary

The financial system recycles savings into real investment; provides media of exchange, convenient stores of wealth, and credit facilities; and gives the

[1]For instance, Neil Bruce and Douglas Purvis "take seriously the possibility that stabilization policy has been and can continue to be destabilizing" in "Fiscal Policy and Recovery from the Great Recession," *Canadian Public Policy*, March 1983, 54.

government more room to pursue stabilization policy. The financial recycling of funds from primary lenders to primary borrowers is partly direct but mostly indirect, through financial institutions. By definition, measured primary borrowing is equal to measured primary lending at all times, though planned borrowing will exceed planned lending whenever planned investment exceeds planned saving in the economy.

Performance criteria for the financial system include static and dynamic efficiency, equity in treatment of participants, and contributions to stabilization of national economic performance.

Questions for discussion

1. In the current year, are you likely to be a primary lender or a primary borrower? If you treat spending on education as accumulation of human capital, what proportion of your investment is internally financed?
2. If you or your family were primary lenders during the current year, were the savings loaned directly or indirectly to primary borrowers? If directly, were the services of a broker used at all?
3. What happens to your flow of primary borrowing or lending if the stereo you wanted to buy turns out to be out of stock? Is your new level an equilibrium level?
4. Give an example from your personal experience of some static inefficiency that remains in the financial system.
5. If, because of poor allocation of loan funds, the financial system were to finance investment projects with an average yield 5 percent below what was otherwise available, what would be the loss to society? Can you express this as a share of GNP? How large a loss would it be if this were repeated every year for twenty-five years?

References

Binhammer, H.H., and Jane Williams. *Innovation and the Process of Change: A Study of Deposit-taking Institutions.* Ottawa: Economic Council of Canada, 1976.

Economic Council of Canada. *Intervention and Efficiency.* Ottawa: Economic Council of Canada, 1982, chaps. 2 and 8.

CHAPTER 3

Money and the Payments Mechanism

The centrepiece of any financial system is money. Often the money is not the most flamboyant part, but it is always the most fundamental, simply because all payments in the economy are made with money. In fact, money is so fundamental that it is often taken for granted. It is therefore appropriate to start a description of Canada's financial system with two chapters on money. This chapter describes the current monetary system in Canada; chapter 4 will look at some periods in Canada's monetary history. Canada's past monetary experiments are as interesting as any in the world, and the current monetary system is on the verge of massive change as new electronic payments mechanisms are introduced in the 1980s and 1990s.

You should learn in this chapter:

1. the significance of having a medium of exchange, to avoid having to rely on barter,
2. the other roles money plays,
3. what type of money we use now and why we hold it even though it pays no interest, and
4. how the Canadian payments mechanism works.

The more adventurous among you can also learn how to apply the tools of welfare economics to the question of how much money society ought to have as a matter of static efficiency.

SECTION 1 Barter

All parts of the financial system make their contributions to society, but some contributions are larger than others. Without money and a payments mechanism we would be reduced to *barter*. Barter transactions still occur in modern economies, but they are insignificant in total trade. Skate exchanges held in many neighborhoods in early fall are one example.

Barter transactions are relatively rare because they require a double coincidence of wants: both parties to the transaction must want exactly the commodity offered by the other party, and at exactly the same time. In skate exchanges this occurs. Elsewhere it is very unlikely. For a whole economy the requirements of barter would be a crippling restriction. In the early 1980s, much trade of less-developed countries was of this type, since many of these countries could not pay for imports unless the supplier also arranged for an equal volume of exports. This is a temporary problem, caused by a foreign exchange shortage brought on by a world recession. Such bilateral barter exchange is better than nothing in such circumstances but far inferior to free multilateral trade.

SECTION 2

The roles of money

Money is basically that class of assets that serves as money. We will therefore discuss the roles that money plays before defining what it is.

Money fills three distinct roles in a modern economy. These roles have quite different implications for the class of assets one might define as money, so they need to be kept separate. Money serves as a unit of account and standard of deferred payment, as a medium of exchange, and as a store of value. Each role will be discussed in turn.

Unit of account

In all economies people must choose between different pairs of goods or different pairs of inputs. The choices depend in one way or another on the relative values of each pair of alternatives, such as shoes and bread, or machinists' time and drilling equipment. Some way must be found to express those relative values. One way is to use the exchange rates at which each pair of alternatives will exchange in a market. The difficulty is that there are so many different pairs to be considered, so many different exchange rates. Where there are n different goods, there are $n(n - 1)/2$ different pairs and exchange rates.

Unit of account, or numeraire

The number of exchange rates can be reduced dramatically if all commodities have values expressed in terms of one common good called a *unit of account*, or *numeraire*. The unit of account could be anything: dollar bills, wildcat skins, peanuts, or cowrie shells. In modern economies the basic currency unit serves as unit of account. In international currency markets the unit of account is usually the United States dollar, although it is sometimes the British pound. When a unit of account is used, the exchange rate of any two other goods is simply the inverse ratio of their individual values in terms of the unit of account. If an hour of machinist's time has a value of 15 dollar bills or cowrie shells, and an hour of drilling equipment has a value of 30 dollar bills or cowrie shells, then their exchange rate is 30:15, or 2:1.

The major benefit of having a unit of account accrues only if everybody uses the same unit. It is to secure this benefit to Canadians that the Currency and Exchange Act, after defining the currency of Canada to be dollars, cents, and mills, goes on in finest legalese:

> Every contract, sale, payment, bill, note, instrument and security for money and every transaction, dealing, matter and thing whatever relating to money or involving the payment or the liability to pay any money, that is made, executed or entered into, done or had, shall be made, executed, entered into, done or had according to the currency of Canada, unless it is made, executed, entered into, done or had according to
> (a) the currency of a country other than Canada; or
> (b) a unit of account that is defined in terms of the currencies of two or more countries.

What item serves as unit of account does not make much difference. Usually, the local currency unit is used, but not always. The British government used the pound (really pounds, shillings, and pence) as its unit of account for keeping financial records in the colonies but actually paid its soldiers in Canada mainly with Spanish silver dollars. In Upper Canada, much of the accounting of merchants in outlying areas was done in wildcat skins, or *cats*.[1] Some of the merchants' trade was paid for with wildcat skins, but most was paid for with a hodgepodge of foreign coins from other countries. Not until 1858 was Canada's currency unit also used as its unit of account.

Many recorded values refer to some future period, such as the deferred payments made under a credit contract. There must be some unit of account or standard of value for such deferred payments. It is convenient to use the same standard for all deferred payments, just to simplify comparisons. In modern economies the standard of deferred payments is normally the domestic currency unit — in Canada, the dollar. Occasionally, borrowers and lenders will agree instead on something else, but usually the something else is just Swiss francs or U.S. dollars, the currency unit of some other nation. In Israel, for instance, where the shekel's future purchasing power is very uncertain due to rapid inflation, many future payments are specified in U.S dollars.

The item that serves as unit of account need not have any physical existence or actually be held by anybody. The unit of account is used just to express value measurements in the same way that the light-year is used to express distance measurements in astronomy. For instance, Canada's Currency and Exchange Act specifies that the mill (one-tenth of a cent) is part

---

[1]Sources for historical material in this and later sections are E.P. Neufeld, *The Financial System of Canada* (Toronto: Macmillan of Canada, 1972), chap. 1, and E.P. Neufeld, ed., *Money and Banking in Canada* (Toronto: McClelland and Stewart, 1964: Carleton Library Series 17), part 1, especially chaps. 1–5 and 14.

of the currency of Canada. This designation is useful, even though there is no way of actually paying one or even nine mills for anything. Money balances are demanded (that is, held as assets) because of money's other two functions: as a medium of exchange and as a store of value.

It is easier to appreciate that money is not demanded as an asset because of its unit-of-account function if we look at a kind of economy in which money has only a unit-of-account role. This is the Walrasian exchange economy. The exchange economy is a theoretical economy first developed by Léon Walras in the early nineteenth century, an important tool in the development of our modern value theory in economics.[2]

In an exchange economy, individuals, or *agents*, are initially endowed each year with particular baskets of real goods and services of various sorts, which they are allowed to exchange for more desirable goods in other agents' baskets. The exchange is handled through an elaborate set of simultaneous auction markets run by a single auctioneer with a set of clerks. The auctioneer's job is to find a set of exchanges that will satisfy all agents and that will not leave any excess demand or supply. To find this set of exchanges, the auctioneer first cries out a set of prices for each good, expressed in the unit of account, and asks agents to report to a clerk the amount of each good they would like to buy or sell. The clerks add up the totals for each good and compare demand to supply. If the two do not match, the auctioneer changes the prices and cries out a new set. Agents are asked to submit a new list of amounts demanded and supplied. When a set of prices is found at which demands and supplies match for each good, the auctioneer bangs the gavel and the most recently recorded exchanges actually take place.

All exchanges take place at the same time in a static exchange economy, and there is no excess demand or supply. All suppliers simply put the goods supplied in a pile in the middle of the auction floor, go around to pick up the goods they have contracted to buy, and go home to enjoy their purchases (and tell their families what great deals they made). At the end, there are no goods left on the floor and no buyers without what they wanted at the final set of prices. No money was ever held or ever changed hands. The only role of money was as a unit of account.

In all economies other than the Walrasian exchange economy, money also serves the other two roles, as a medium of exchange and as a store of value.

Medium of exchange

An asset serves as a *medium of exchange* if it is regularly and generally transferable in exchange for other commodities. The definition is not absolute, since some asset may be accepted in exchange only for a certain

---

[2]Léon Walras, *Eléments d'Economie Politique Pure, ou Théorie de la Richesse Sociale*, 4th ed. (Lausanne: Rouge, 1900).

range of commodities or only up to a certain amount. The essential property of a medium of exchange is that it is accepted in exchange not principally for its own intrinsic value (if it has any at all) but for what it can be exchanged for later on. Assets with this property are said to possess liquidity in various degrees. The wider the range of commodities for which a medium of exchange can be exchanged, the more liquid it is. For example, dollar bills and gold bars and bearer bonds can all be used as a medium of exchange for some transactions. Dollar bills can be used for a much wider range of transactions, so dollar bills are more liquid.

Many items can serve as media of exchange at the same time. One of Canada's recurring problems used to be that we had too many kinds of media of exchange. Several colonial acts were passed to clear up what the exchange rates were between the various currencies in use, but the exchange rates still differed between colonies. Through most of the period up to the 1850s our forebears had to make do with a hodgepodge of foreign coinage too worn or defaced to use in foreign trade, or private notes and tokens issued by various merchants and others. Neufeld quotes a complaint sent to the *Acadian Recorder* on October 18, 1820, by an exasperated man who bought sixpence of squash with a twenty-shilling note, lost threepence in discount on the note itself, and received the following in change (at face value):

5 shillings in the note of George Leggett
5 shillings in the note of Wm. Lawson
1 shilling in the team boat note of H.H.Cogswell
1 shilling 3 pence in the note of Adam Esson
1 shilling 3 pence in the note of John A. Barry
three 7½ pence notes of Wm. Smith
7½ pence in silver
3 shillings 6 pence in copper[3]

Astute readers familiar with old-style British accounting will note that the list of change above has a face value of more than twenty shillings, not even counting the squash. The reason is that some of the notes were traded at a discount from their face value, a discount that varied considerably between communities.

Gresham's Law

Where assets that are used as media of exchange can also be used in some other way — as a store of value, as a tooth filling, as wallpaper — the medium of exchange with the most valued other uses will tend to disappear from circulation into those other uses. Only the inferior money with few or low-valued other uses will be left in circulation. This is *Gresham's Law*, that "bad money drives out good."

Gresham's Law

[3]Neufeld, *The Financial System of Canada*, 37.

There are countless examples of Gresham's Law at work. For instance, Roy Radford recounted his monetary experiences in a prisoner-of-war camp in World War II. The camp inmates used cigarettes as both unit of account and medium of exchange. There were several different kinds of cigarettes, made of cigarette tobacco and pipe tobacco, hand made and machine made. The alternative use for all kinds was for smoking pleasure, but some gave more smoking pleasure than others. So "Churchman's No. 1" (a high-quality, machine-made cigarette) "was rarely seen in the shop" (as a medium of exchange).[4]

Another semimilitary example comes from Nova Scotia after 1713, where the British government paid its garrison at Annapolis Royal and at Louisbourg in liquor. Liquor served as a medium of exchange, but obviously it had other uses. Finally the garrison petitioned the Crown "That they be payd in money, or Bills, & not in Rum or Other Liquors, that cause them to be Drunk every days, and Blaspheme the name of God."[5]

The importance of confidence

What any item needs to serve as a medium of exchange is only that holders believe it will be accepted later when they want to spend it — in short, confidence. Confidence in a medium of exchange has all the properties of a self-fulfilling prophecy. If enough people believe a medium of exchange will be accepted, then it will be accepted, precisely because enough people believe it will be accepted.

Store of value

A *store of value* is any asset that can be bought now and converted into something of value in the future. The definition is very general, and the class of assets that can serve as stores of value is very broad. In fact, hopelessly so. All financial and real assets are stores of value, including the assets used as media of exchange. In Africa, the cowrie shells used in market transactions were stored as wealth in the form of necklaces. The same has been true of gold for thousands of years. Modern Canadians regularly hold currency and chequing deposits as part of their total wealth. The key feature of the store-of-value function of money is that it is served by such a multitude of assets. Money is generally the safest, and always the most liquid, of the assets that can be used as a store of value, but it accounts for only a small part of total stores of value for most households.

---

[4]R.A. Radford, "Money in a Prisoner-of-War Camp," in Jonas Prager, ed., *Monetary Economics* (New York: Random House, 1971), 6. Reprinted from *Economica*, Nov. 1945.

[5]R.A. Lester, "The Playing Card Currency of French Canada," in Neufeld, ed., *Money and Banking in Canada*, 9.

SECTION 3

Measuring and explaining the demand for money

Chapter 9 gives a much more thorough survey and explanation of the demand for money than is offered here. This early sketch will give you an idea of how money is defined and a way of thinking about why money is held as an asset.

Measures of money

Narrow money

Broad money

The general rule for defining the class of assets to be included in the category of money is to include all the assets that fulfill money's roles. Of the three roles of money, the unit-of-account role is not useful; it implies no demand for any asset at all. The store-of-value function is only slightly more useful, since the class of assets serving as stores of value is so broad. What is left is the medium-of-exchange function. Almost all measures of money are based on the medium-of-exchange function of money.[6] *Narrow money* definitions try to include all regularly reported assets that have significant roles as media of exchange. *Broad money* definitions also include some close substitutes, not themselves media of exchange but readily convertible into narrow-money assets.

M1

M1A

In Canada there are two official measures of narrow money, called *M1* and *M1A*. M1 is a simple, traditional measure, but it excludes some assets that are used significantly as a medium of exchange, so it has been supplemented by the broader measure M1A since March 1983. M1 contains Canadian currency and coin in circulation outside banks (that is, in wallets and cash registers) and Canadian-dollar demand deposits (non-interest-bearing chequing accounts) in chartered banks excluding those held by other banks and by the federal government. M1A also includes daily interest chequable savings accounts in chartered banks, plus nonpersonal (corporate) notice deposits whether chequable or not.[7]

M2

Broad-money measures in Canada are *M2* and *M3*. M2 includes all M1A assets plus other notice and personal fixed-term deposits in chartered banks. *Other notice* means in this case the nonchequable personal savings

---

[6]See, for example, W.T. Newlyn and R.P. Bootle, *The Theory of Money* (Oxford: Oxford University Press, 1978), 2. Harry Johnson also refers to the medium-of-exchange role of money as "decisive" in the definition of money, in "Recent Developments in Monetary Theory," in David R. Croome and H.G. Johnson, eds., *Money in Britain, 1959–69* (Oxford: Oxford University Press, 1970), 83–114.

[7]In principle, chequable accounts at other institutions should be included in either M1 or M1A, but generally they are not. The reason is that totals of such deposits are not measured as frequently and accurately and quickly in the other institutions (particularly the thousands of local credit unions) as in chartered banks. The exception is for the deposits of those mortgage loan companies wholly owned by chartered banks; their deposits and assets have been consolidated with those of the parent banks for reporting purposes since November 1981, so their deposits do count in the money-supply totals. Very few of their deposits fit the M1 and M1A categories, though.

M3 deposits. M3 includes all M2 assets plus Canadian-dollar nonpersonal fixed-term deposits in chartered banks, plus foreign-currency deposits held by residents in chartered banks in Canada. Government of Canada deposits in chartered banks are excluded from all of these totals, but provincial and local government deposits are included.

As payments habits change, as new types of deposit come into being, and as existing types of deposit come to be used in new ways, these money-supply definitions will gradually change. For instance, nonchequable corporate notice deposits have been included in a narrow-money measure (M1A) only since March 1983. As reliable and timely estimates become possible, chequing accounts in credit unions and trust companies will likely also be included in M1A.

The demand for money: a preliminary sketch

This section provides only a sketch of a modern view of the demand for money, to illustrate how the medium-of-exchange and store-of-value functions both play roles.[8] This explanation fits both the narrow and the broad definitions of money.

Let the O'Malleys be a typical family in this economy. They start the year endowed with a bundle of items (chiefly labor services) that they can sell off during the year to finance their purchases of other goods and services. The O'Malleys' sales and purchases are not naturally synchronized; in other words, sales of labor and purchases of goods do not normally occur in matching amounts on each day. Further, the O'Malleys care about when they supply their labor and when they buy their goods. They actively prefer to spend more before Christmas and during vacations; they actively prefer to work regularly, though not on weekends. It is possible for them to rearrange their earning and spending so they match each other from day to day, but the adjustment is painful (doing their Christmas shopping throughout the year, spending nothing during vacation, and the like).

To avoid such painful adjustment of their spending and working schedules, the O'Malleys must accumulate some excess receipts before vacation and before Christmas, in order to finance later surges of spending. Excess receipts will be held in stores of value, one of which will be money. The O'Malleys' wealth will be equal to the cumulative excess receipts, rising and falling each day as excess receipts are positive or negative. In Niehans' words, "it is the main function of money to permit a more attractive timing of transactions than could be maintained without it."[9]

The exact amount of their total wealth that the O'Malleys will hold as either narrow or broad money depends on how much of their accumulated excess receipts can be more profitably stored elsewhere. That in turn

---

[8]This section is adapted from Jurg Niehans, *The Theory of Money* (Baltimore: Johns Hopkins University Press, 1978).

[9]Niehans, *The Theory of Money*, 25.

depends on how long funds can be left in assets other than money and how much extra interest they will earn per day in those assets. The higher the extra interest rate, the shorter the period over which extra interest earnings will fully offset transactions costs of buying and then selling or redeeming nonmoney assets. The shorter that period, the less of the O'Malleys' wealth will be held as money. Unless transactions costs of buying and selling nonmoney assets are nil, however, some part of the cumulated excess receipts will be held as money at some point in the year where funds are available only for very short periods.

FIGURE 3–1 Cumulative excess receipts for the O'Malleys

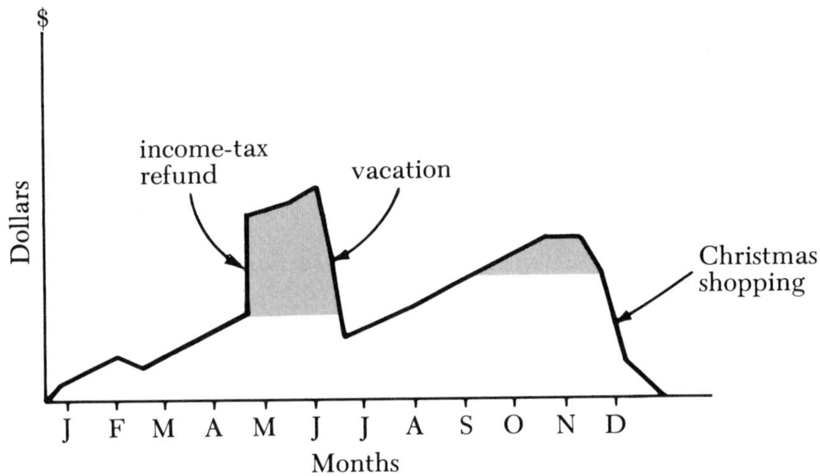

The O'Malleys have chosen a pattern of spending that requires the build-up and rundown of excess receipts over the course of a year (shown by the solid line). They have excess receipts in each pay period except during vacation, Christmas shopping, and a ski weekend in February. Excess receipts are run down in those three periods and built up in all other periods. Excess receipts will be put into nonmoney assets only when they are available for long enough that extra earnings can more than pay for extra transactions costs of buying and then reselling such assets. Otherwise excess receipts will be parked in savings deposits or (for very short periods) in chequing deposits and currency. The latter two uses are shown as the shaded areas.

Figure 3–1 illustrates what the O'Malleys' time path of cumulative excess receipts might look like over a year. Excess receipts in any day increase the cumulative total of excess receipts, while excess spending lowers it. The total of excess receipts therefore rises before vacation and plummets during vacation; it rises gradually toward Christmas and then drops during Christmas shopping and does the same around a February ski break. Like those of most households in Canada, the O'Malleys' financial forecasts include a substantial windfall early in May in the form of an income tax refund that boosts their asset total.

Any dollar that is not needed for long enough to justify the transactions costs will be held in the form of some interest-earning asset other than money. The remainder, dollars available only for shorter periods, will be held as money.

This sketch of the logic behind the demand for money underlies most of the theory and empirical work on money demand that we will be exploring more fully in chapter 9.

SECTION 4

Money and the Payments Mechanism in the 1980s

You have learned so far in this chapter that the medium-of-exchange function of money is an important one. This section will describe in some detail just how Canadian money fulfills that function — how money is transferred to make payments, how long the process takes, and what resources are used up in the process.

Currency

Currency has become steadily less important in making payments over the the last century, as the use of chequing deposits has spread. This decline is despite a growing ratio of currency holdings to M1 totals, which is shown in figure 3–2 for the years 1946 to 1983.

Bearer instrument

Currency is a *bearer instrument* — one of the few in the financial system. The person who bears it is the person who owns it. Almost all other assets are registered as the property of a particular owner, regardless of whose safety deposit box they may be in at any point of time. Currency is therefore risky to carry around, as well as bulky. It is used where payment by cheque or credit card would be inconvenient — in small transactions and in those larger transactions where the participants do not wish to leave a record. Chequing deposits are used for virtually all other payments.

The sharply rising ratio of currency to demand deposits since 1965 is evidence to some observers that illegal transactions now make up a far larger share of total transactions than they did in 1965. Some economists in the United States have attributed the entire rise in the relative size of currency to an increase in the relative importance of illegal transactions — those in what is called the underground economy. Those economists have

Velocity of circulation

used estimates of the *velocity of circulation* of currency (from estimates of how many transactions it takes to wear out a dollar bill, and of how often bills are replaced) to estimate how large the underground economy's transactions total must be.[10] However, there are other explanations for a decline in the size of demand deposits in banks relative to currency holdings. One is the introduction of closer substitutes for bank demand deposits, such as chequing deposits in credit unions and trust companies, and more easily transferable notice deposits. Another explanation may be greater sensitivity of demand-deposit demand than currency demand to higher interest rates, coupled with much higher prevailing levels of interest rates.

FIGURE 3-2 Share of currency in narrow money (M1), 1946–83

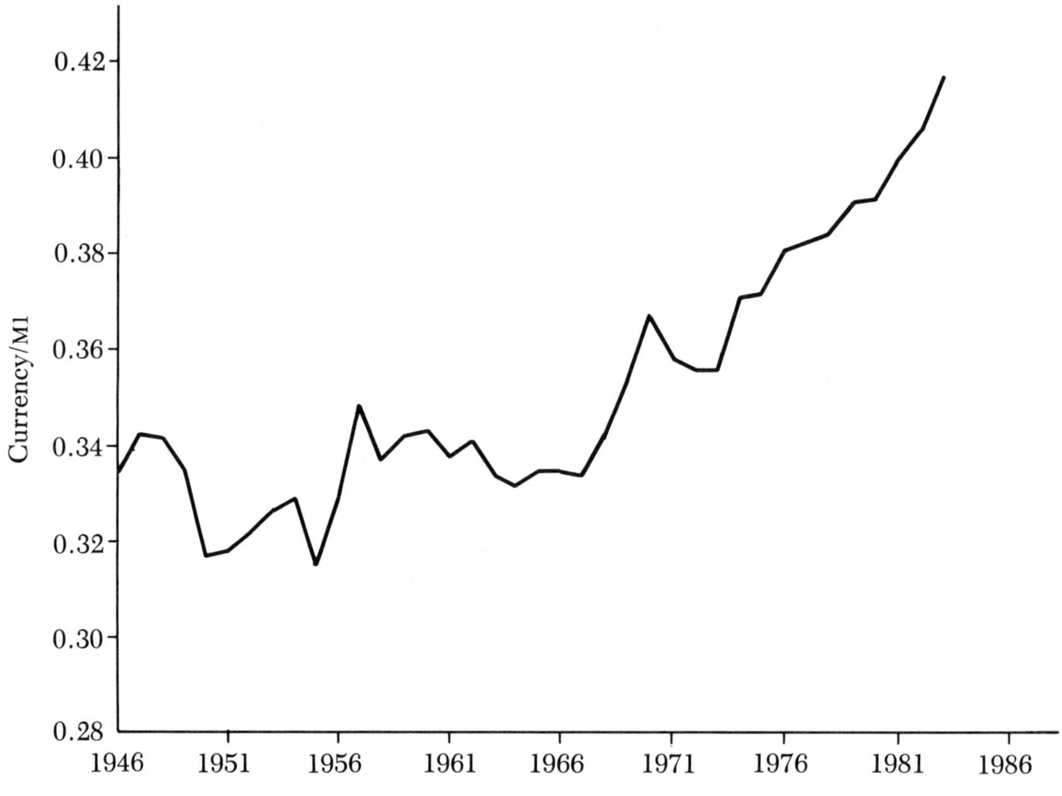

Chequable deposits

Chequable deposits are issued by banks, trust companies, credit unions and caisses populaires, and even some brokerage firms. The largest part of our money supply is in the form of chequing deposits — $22 billion in the banks

[10]This discussion is well summarized in Norman N. Bowsher, "The Demand for Currency: Is the Underground Economy Undermining Monetary Policy?" *Federal Reserve Bank of St. Louis Review*, Jan. 1980, 11–17.

alone as of January 1983. Table 3–1 shows the relative shares of each source of chequable deposits in Canada.

TABLE 3–1 Proportions of chequable deposits by type of issuer (percent)

Banks	
current accounts (business)	44.0
personal chequing accounts	12.1
chequable savings and nonpersonal notice deposits	23.3
total bank deposits	79.6
Local credit unions and caisses populaires	12.7
Trust companies — chequable savings deposits	4.3
Mortgage loan companies — chequable savings deposits	0.3
Quebec savings bank	
chequing accounts	0.1
chequable savings deposits	0.7
Alberta Treasury Branches	0.7
Province of Ontario Savings Office	1.7

Note: Proportions are as of September 1980.

Source: Bank of Canada Review; correspondence with La Banque d'Épargne, with POSO, and with the Alberta Treasury Branches.

New methods of deposit transfer are being developed, but the vast majority of transfers are still by paper cheque. Canadians write five million cheques, worth about $20 billion, every business day. The average dollar of chequing-deposit balance is transferred by cheque over 240 times during a year. Of these cheques, only about 15 percent are drawn on a deposit in the bank branch used by the recipient of the cheque, so all the rest involve a transfer of deposits between banks or between branches.[11]

The cheque transfer mechanism

The cheque transfer mechanism is in transition between manual processing and automated electronic processing. Since February 1983 this mechanism has been operated by the Canadian Payments Association, an association of some 120 deposit-taking institutions, set up to ensure that new deposit transfer technology is not developed in such a way as to favor particular financial institutions at the expense of others.

There are still many steps in transferring money by cheque, each of them costly. To illustrate the transfer process, let us trace two cheques. Both are received by Mr. O'Malley and deposited in his Toronto branch of the Royal Bank. The first cheque is written by Acme Chemical, O'Malley's employer, on Acme's account in the Royal Bank. The second cheque is a

[11]This estimate is derived from results of a 1973 survey done for the Economic Council of Canada, reported in *Efficiency and Regulation* (Ottawa: Supply and Services, 1976), 99.

dividend cheque written by NOVA Corp. on its account in the Bank of British Columbia.

1. O'Malley endorses both cheques on the back for credit to his deposit account and presents them to his favorite teller in the Royal Bank.
2. The Royal Bank takes these and all other cheques it has received to its Toronto-area data centre for overnight sorting and tabulating.
3. During the sorting process the cheque from Acme is recognized as being drawn on a Royal Bank account. The amount is deducted immediately from Acme's account. This would happen even if Acme did its business through a Royal Bank branch elsewhere in the country; the one national computer system handles all of the Royal Bank's accounts, so it does not matter whether the account holder does business with the Royal in Halifax or in Vancouver.
4. The cheque from NOVA is added to a pile of cheques deposited in the Royal Bank's branches in the Toronto area and drawn on the Bank of British Columbia. At the end of the sorting process the B.C. pile is bundled up and exchanged at the Toronto clearing centre for a similar bundle of cheques deposited in the Bank of British Columbia and drawn on the Royal Bank. The clearing officer of whichever bank has the smaller bundle makes out a settlement slip drawn on that bank's deposit account in the Bank of Canada, to cover the difference between the values of the two cheque bundles. That settlement makes the exchange of cheques an even swap.
5. The Bank of British Columbia sorts its bundle of cheques and sends each to the data centre nearest the branch that handles the individual accounts on which the cheques are written. There the cheques are all read by machine again, and the amount of NOVA's cheque is deducted from its account. NOVA's cheque is returned to NOVA with the corporation's monthly statement. The transfer process is complete.

Float

For some out-of-town cheques there is still a lag between the time the cheque is credited to the account of the payee and the time the same amount is deducted from the account of the payor. The lag is getting shorter, but it still exists. During that period the total of bank deposits recorded on banks' books is exaggerated. The amount of exaggeration of

Debit float

total deposits is known as *debit float*. The amount of float varies widely over the course of a year: as of January 5, 1983, it was $2.6 billion, but by May 30 it was estimated to have risen to $4 billion.[12] An estimate of net

[12]Debit float is not inevitable even now. In the United Kingdom, many people use the Post Office Girobank system to make payments to other members of that system. Such payments are made by instructing the Girobank to transfer deposit amounts from one customer to another. The Girobank does its deducting before it does the crediting, so for a while there is exactly the opposite of debit float: recorded deposits are smaller than they should be, rather than larger as in the Canadian cheque-clearing system. The amount of understatement should be called, symmetrically, *credit sink*.

private-sector float (that is, for other than government of Canada deposits and those held by each bank in other banks) is deducted from the recorded demand-deposit measurements used in the official money-supply measures M1, M1A, M2, and M3. Total chequing deposits in banks amounted to only $22 billion, so debit float was over 10 percent of the total in January 1983. Float is still large, even though most cheques clear the same day.

Debit float will become smaller in Canada as the banks' computers become more closely connected. Eventually, if and when all accounts are connected in a single on-line computer system for all chequable deposits, the same entry on a teller's terminal that credits a cheque to a customer's account will also automatically debit it from the payor's account. All the intervening cheque-clearing steps will have been eliminated, and debit float will be zero.

Other forms of cheque transfer

Other forms of cheque transfer are available, and there are certainly more to come. One is automatic transfer via magnetic tape, introduced in Canada in 1976. This system is used for a wide variety of regular payments from one account to many others. Dividend payments, annuity payments, Canada Savings Bond coupon payments, and the payrolls of some 1.5 million Canadians are handled by this method. Also, a range of regular payments from many accounts into one central account are handled this way: prearranged utility-bill payments and house mortgage payments are two examples. Either a bank or a computer service company processes the customer's accounts to prepare magnetic tapes of the necessary deposit transfers, one for each institution involved. When the time for payment or receipt comes, the tapes are fed into each bank's computer, and the necessary transfers are made electronically. No cheques are issued, and there is no debit float. Written statements are sent to each participant just for information. There is no paper to process through a clearing mechanism, since the written statements go directly from payor to payee or vice versa, and not through a bank.

A second form of chequeless transfer of deposit has just arrived but will spread gradually. The debit card was introduced into Canada by credit unions in 1981–82. A debit card is just like a credit card (VISA or MasterCard) except that, in using it to pay merchants' bills, cardholders are authorizing their credit union to deduct (debit) the amount from their chequing account immediately, rather than to add (credit) it to their unpaid credit-card balance for payment at the end of the month. In essence, the debit-card voucher signed by the customer will become just like a cheque written on the customer's account.

The clearing mechanism for debit-card vouchers will look much like the clearing mechanism for regular cheques, but without return of the signed vouchers to card users. Instead, the user receives a descriptive list at the end of the month of all the vouchers presented for payment using his or her card. This is a form of truncated cheque clearing that saves the financial institutions a lot of expensive paper-shuffling.

There are other forms of deposit transfer that so far are used mainly in international transactions. Money orders, bank drafts, wire transfers, and certified cheques are all alternatives to the ordinary cheque. All are used mostly to make payments abroad. For large interbank transfers, there is a Society of Worldwide Interbank Financial Telecommunication (SWIFT), whose members have a computer hookup that permits them to relay funds to each other instantaneously. This sort of service will gradually be made available to first wholesale and then retail customers of banks as computer hookups become more standard.

Transferable savings and notice deposits

Zero-balance banking, or automatic transfer service

Between 1975 and 1977 both U.S. and Canadian banks introduced for their larger clients a service known as *zero-balance banking*, *automatic transfer service*, sweep accounts, or something similar. The key feature of this service is that the bank undertakes to transfer funds automatically from notice deposits into chequing deposits, whenever a cheque is presented that is larger than the remaining balance in the chequing account. With such an arrangement, no rational individual will wish to keep more than a zero balance in the chequing account: with no loss of purchasing power, more interest can be earned on the same funds in a notice deposit. For most of these accounts, the banks agreed to sweep all funds in the chequing account into the notice deposit at the end of each day — hence the name *sweep account*.

More important, the notice deposit used for this sweep arrangement has effectively been made transferable by cheque. Technically, the cheque is still an order to transfer funds only from a chequing account, but practically, once the bank has promised to transfer funds automatically from notice deposits whenever necessary to cover cheques written on the chequing account, the cheque is an order to transfer funds from either the chequing or the notice deposit. There is no relevant distinction as far as the payee is concerned. In recognition of this, the Federal Reserve Board in the United States (the U.S. central bank) revised its narrow-money definition in February 1980 to include sweep accounts.[13] The Bank of Canada followed suit in March 1983.

SECTION 5 Optimal money supply (relatively advanced material)

We can do more in this chapter than discuss the payments mechanism and why people hold money. We can apply the tools of welfare economics to

---

[13]For description and discussion of the changes, see R.W. Hafer, "The New Monetary Aggregates," *Federal Reserve Bank of St. Louis Review*, Feb. 1980, 25–32.

analyse what level of money demand and supply is socially optimal. Milton Friedman was the first to do so, in 1956.[14] His initial approach has been taken up by others.[15] This section gives the gist of their arguments, building on our sketch in section 3 of the logic behind holding money.

Marginal social utility

Marginal social cost

The welfare of society is maximized if money is supplied until its *marginal social utility* just matches its *marginal social cost*. Any more or less is a waste. In the absence of externalities (for example, where one person's money holdings affect the welfare of others), marginal social utility comes from the marginal private utility of those individuals holding the marginal unit of money balances during the year. From the logic of demand-for-money theory presented in section 3 we can infer that the marginal utility of money is the extra pleasure derived from a better scheduling of spending relative to income receipts. Marginal social cost is the opportunity cost of the resources used to create an extra unit of money. Social welfare is maximized, therefore, when the marginal utility of rescheduling consumption during the year just matches the marginal resource cost of producing more money.

Canada's paper money (including bank deposits) is created by a stroke of the pen or a blip of the computer. It is virtually costless to produce, unlike other stores of value such as gold and houses. The marginal social cost of creating money is therefore zero. There are positive social costs of operating the cheque-clearing mechanism and keeping bank records, but let us assume that depositors pay for those marginal social costs in chequing-account charges; the optimal amount of those services is therefore supplied, and their costs can be ignored hereafter.

It follows that social welfare is maximized if individuals hold money to the point where the marginal utility of money (that is, of rescheduling consumption) is close to zero. Such a state is easy to imagine, since there is a limit to the amount of consumption rescheduling anybody would want to do, but is the optimal amount of money holding likely to occur? Individuals will hold the optimal amount of money if and only if the marginal costs of money to them are close to zero. Otherwise their money holdings will fall short of the optimum: resources will be wasted on other, more expensive stores of value, and the pattern of spending will be less desirable than it could have been.

Marginal costs of money

Are the private marginal costs of money holding close to zero? To answer that question we need to look at the ingredients of marginal costs of money

[14]Milton Friedman, "The Optimal Quantity of Money," in Friedman, ed., *The Optimal Quantity of Money and Other Essays* (Chicago: Aldine, 1979).

[15]H.G. Johnson, "Recent Developments in Monetary Theory," in Croome and Johnson, eds., *Money in Britain, 1959–69*; Niehans, *The Theory of Money*, chaps. 2–5. The discussion in this section is derived from Niehans.

for a typical individual. Let's take O'Malley again. First, O'Malley loses some real purchasing power in holding money balances if there is inflation. Inflation can be seen as a negative real yield on money. Second, O'Malley's pleasure is postponed. Building up money balances does require some temporary abstinence from consumption, until the money is spent. If O'Malley values consumption now more than consumption later, simply postponing consumption has a price. That price is the proportional difference between current pleasure and future pleasure (from the same expenditure), known as the *marginal rate of time preference*. O'Malley's marginal cost of money is the sum of inflation and the marginal rate of time preference and is unlikely to be near zero. It is therefore unlikely that O'Malley is holding money balances to the point where the marginal utility of money is zero. O'Malley is likely to be holding too much of his wealth in some more socially expensive asset such as gold, or else foregoing some socially (and personally) desirable rescheduling of consumption.

Marginal rate of time preference

Arranging optimal money holdings

In order to persuade O'Malley to hold the optimal amount of money, society must subsidize money holding in some way. Until recently in the United States, for instance, the Federal Reserve System (the U.S. central bank) used some of its profit from creating money to pay all of the costs of operating the cheque transfer mechanism. This arrangement indirectly subsidizes the holding of money by subsidizing the transactions costs of using money for payments.

Paying interest on money would be more direct. In 1956 Milton Friedman thought that it would be impractical to pay interest on currency, so he suggested providing a positive real yield by arranging steady deflation of the price level; the optimal rate of deflation would be just equal to the marginal rate of time preference. In Canada there are no obstacles to explicit payment of nominal interest on money balances held in chequing deposits. It is still too expensive to pay interest on currency, but if currency and demand deposits are close to perfect substitutes, and neither has significant marginal costs of production, it is sufficient to pay interest on just one of the two assets.

For optimal results, interest on demand deposits should equal inflation plus the marginal rate of time preference. Is that likely? Yes, if there is sufficient competition between financial institutions supplying demand deposits. In fact the Canadian chartered banks started issuing daily-interest chequing deposits in July 1980. These deposits grew to 2.5 percent of the narrow-money measure, M1, by the end of 1981 and are still growing fast. The marginal interest rate on such deposits is often close to money market interest rates, which in turn are usually greater than expected inflation by several percentage points.

SECTION 6 Summary

Money can and does play three distinct roles in modern economies: as a unit of account for recording and calculating values, as a medium of exchange for making payments, and as a store of value for postponing consumption. Money is defined either narrowly, as whatever serves as a medium of exchange, or broadly, as media of exchange plus close substitutes. It is the medium-of-exchange function of money that allows us to get around the severe restriction (double coincidence of wants) that barter would impose on trading.

Money is demanded both as a medium of exchange and as a store of value. Money is held, along with other stores of value, to bridge the gap between receipts and spending, in a world where the two can be synchronized only at significant cost. The proportion of wealth held as money rather than in other assets reflects the transactions costs of buying and selling nonmoney assets and the length of time the funds can be left in nonmoney form to earn interest. Where the available time is short or the extra interest rate is small, wealth will be held as money.

The current payments mechanism in Canada transfers currency and chequable deposits of financial institutions. Transfer of currency is from hand to hand. Transfer of chequing deposits was originally only by cheque, but in the 1970s other methods of transfer began to develop as well, which will be both more convenient for depositors and less expensive for banks.

In the final section of this chapter we reviewed the logical argument about the socially optimal supply of money for an economy. Optimal-money-supply theory recognizes that money as we now know it is virtually costless to create. It follows that society should make use of money where possible in place of other assets that do have significant costs of production or where doing so would allow more convenient scheduling of spending. In order to achieve such a result, individuals must be persuaded, by the prospect of positive real yields on money, to hold large money balances. At one point it was thought that positive real yields on money required a steady rate of price deflation, but in Canada at least, it is quite feasible to pay positive nominal interest at least on the chequing-deposit form of money. Banks are already doing so for their larger customers.

Questions for discussion

1. What barter transactions have you engaged in over the last month? Why were they not cash transactions?
2. What difference would it make to you if we used the Japanese yen as our unit of account, as long as the conversion rate from yen units to Canadian dollars was known and constant?
3. What is the key requirement for a medium of exchange, and why?

4. How long do you hold your typical money balance in currency? In your chequing account? How much consumption rescheduling do you do during the year, relative to your income (what proportion of your income flow is spent the week or month it is received)?

References

Binhammer, H.H. *Money, Banking and the Canadian Financial System*. 4th ed. Toronto: Methuen, 1982, chaps. 1–3.

Boreham, G.F. *Money and Banking*. 2d ed. Toronto: Holt, Rinehart and Winston, 1979, chaps. 1–3.

Canadian Banker & ICB Review. Occasionally contains discussions of changes in bank legislation and in the cheque-clearing mechanism.

Friedman, Milton. *The Optimal Quantity of Money and Other Essays*. Chicago: Aldine, 1969.

Neufeld, E.P., ed. *Money and Banking in Canada*. Toronto: McClelland and Stewart, 1964.

———. *The Financial System of Canada*. Toronto: Macmillan of Canada, 1972.

Newlyn, W.T., and R.P. Bootle. *The Theory of Money*. Oxford: Oxford University Press, 1978.

Niehans, Jurg. *The Theory of Money*. Baltimore: Johns Hopkins University Press, 1978.

"Technical Note: New and Revised Monetary Aggregates." *Bank of Canada Review*. March 1983, 3–33. Also "Notes to the Tables" for the *Bank of Canada Review*. Contain brief discussions of the latest measures of money in Canada.

Vachon, Serge. "The Canadian Payments Association." *Bank of Canada Review*. Nov. 1982.

CHAPTER 4

Monetary Standards Playing Cards and Army Bills

Chapter 3 described the workings of Canada's monetary system. Our sophisticated payments mechanism is about to become much more so as we switch from a paper to an electronic system. The switch to paper money was itself a major innovation with enormous cost savings, and Canada was one of the first regions of the western world to make the switch. This chapter reviews the history of Canada's early experiments with paper money — one experiment in New France after 1685 and one in both Upper and Lower Canada during the War of 1812. In order to provide background for such a historical review, the first section of the chapter outlines the various kinds of monetary system that are possible.

In this chapter you should learn:

1. what kinds of money there are and which properties are necessary, or merely desirable, if an item is to serve as money,
2. how Canada came to have two of the world's more interesting early experiments in the use of paper money, and
3. the bare bones of how Canada developed the monetary system that exists today.

SECTION 1 Monetary standards

Money has taken a huge variety of forms because the only necessary ingredient is that enough people have confidence in it (confidence meaning belief that other people believe in it enough to accept it in payment). Nevertheless, most moneys have certain features in common. Moneys are usually easily portable or transferable, and easily divisible. In the past, the most successful moneys over long periods have also been limited in supply. That still leaves a large range of items as potential moneys.

In fact, the history of the development of moneys in western civilization has followed a logical progression, from less convenient but obviously scarce forms to more convenient but potentially less scarce forms. At each stage, government has become more involved, controlling the money supply more and more. Nowadays that control is essentially complete.

Commodity moneys

Originally, all moneys were simply some particular commodity such as gold nuggets or cattle or wheat or wildcat skins. These commodities were desired for themselves but also because they had the necessary properties to serve as media of exchange. What kept them in limited supply was their cost of production and also, periodically, diversion to their other uses.

We mentioned in section 2 of chapter 3 some examples of diversion of money into other uses. In Roy Radford's prisoner-of-war camp during World War II, the supply of cigarettes available for use as money in the camp store dwindled over the period between Red Cross shipments, because the supply was lit up and burned up by the smokers in the camp. In the British garrisons in Nova Scotia, which were paid in liquor, the soldiers' complaint about being drunk too much of the time suggests that the amount of rum in circulation as money also dwindled between paydays.

Commodity standards

The next stage in development of commodity moneys is reached when the commodity is standardized in the form of minted coins, so that the commodity can be valued by count rather than by weighing or measuring. Since coins typically exchanged for more than the intrinsic value of their ingredients (whether because of the greater convenience of using them in trade, or because their precious-metal content had been reduced), the business of minting coins was profitable. This profit is known as *seigniorage* and has been reserved to the Crown through most of history.

Seigniorage

Commodity standard

The use of standardized commodity items such as gold and silver coins is known as a *commodity standard*. Commodity standards are not necessary if the natural commodity itself comes in homogeneous units rather than in a continuous range of sizes. The cigarettes in Radford's POW camp were homogeneous enough to start with, despite their differences in smoking pleasure. Later on, users had shaken so much of the loose tobacco out of the cigarettes used in trade that this was no longer true. Some of them were too thin to be counted as full cigarettes even for currency purposes. In the Hudson's Bay Company trade, the finished or "made" beaver pelt was also close to homogeneous. The "made beaver" became the fur traders' medium of exchange, until they replaced this bulky item with a made-beaver token that "stood for" a pelt.

The danger in relying on a commodity standard is that everybody has a temptation to cheat, and some may not resist that temptation very hard. If all silver dollars are treated as equal for exchange purposes, then a silver dollar will still be just as valuable in trade if the holder clips a little of the silver off the edges to sell separately. Despite heavy fines and elaborate minting procedures, such as the use of milled edges and fine detail in engraving, the coinage was subject to gradual debasement. The most significant debasers were the minters themselves, the kings. Kings short of funds could always increase their seigniorage by diluting the amount of gold put into a gold coin, without reducing its exchange value. Many kings resorted to this method of finance.

Token money

Token money

The next stage beyond commodity moneys is *token money*. Token money is more convenient to use than commodity money as a rule, and there is no incentive to debase a token money. However, the limits to oversupply are much weaker. Token moneys are notes or certificates with no intrinsic value, accepted in exchange because they are guaranteed by the issuer to be convertible into other money such as gold coins. Where token money is convertible into commodity money, the system is called a commodity standard. Where the token money is convertible only into a commodity that is not money (for example, into a 400-oz. gold bar, as in Canada from 1926 to 1929), the system is known as a *commodity exchange standard*.

Commodity exchange standard

Goldsmiths' receipts were the first form of token money in England, though token moneys had been used much earlier in other countries. For much of the colonial period up to 1763, the French settlers in Canada used token moneys that were convertible (with a lag) into the silver coin of France. We will discuss this period in section 2. From 1820, when private bank notes were introduced in Canada, to 1914, bank notes were convertible into gold coin, known as *specie*.[1]

Specie

Fiduciary money

Fiduciary money

All convertible token money is *fiduciary money* (from the Latin word *fiducia*, meaning trust). The issuer's money is accepted even though it has no intrinsic value, because the issuer guarantees it will be convertible into intrinsic-value money on demand, and the holder trusts the issuer to fulfill this guarantee. The weak link is the issuer. Not all issuers were trustworthy, and some simply overestimated the amount of notes they would be able to redeem. The result was often bankruptcy, and holders of the token money stood to lose the whole value of their token-money holdings.

---

[1]Sources for historical material in this and later sections are E.P. Neufeld, *The Financial System of Canada* (Toronto: Macmillan of Canada, 1972), chap. 1, and E.P. Neufeld, ed., *Money and Banking in Canada* (Toronto: McClelland and Stewart, 1964: Carleton Library Series 17), part 1, especially chaps. 1–5 and 14.

On several occasions in Canadian history the obligation of issuers to convert token moneys into commodity money was suspended. The French government twice suspended redemption of its paper money in New France (and for that matter in France also). The convertibility of private bank notes was suspended in 1837–38; convertibility of government notes was suspended in 1914–25, and permanently after 1929. In all those periods except the last, the result was immediate overissue of token money and general price inflation.

Only while notes were convertible was it possible to exercise some discipline over banks' note issue. In the United States, the Second Bank of the United States (a central bank whose first charter ran only from 1816 to 1836) exercised this discipline by regularly collecting notes of various private banks and presenting them to the issuers for redemption in specie. This practice embarrassed quite a few banks, put some more into bankruptcy, and generally antagonized both banks and their loan customers so much that the Second Bank's first charter was also its last. No other central bank was set up to replace it until 1913.

Fiat money

Fiat money

The final stage in the development of moneys is *fiat money* (from the Latin verb meaning let it be done). Fiat money is not convertible into anything of intrinsic value, but by law, or fiat, the money must be accepted in payment of debts. Our current dollar bill is a fine example. A Canadian dollar bill is money because an Act of Parliament threatens legal penalties for anyone in Canada not accepting Canadian currency in payment of debts. The note itself promises nothing; it merely declares "This note is *legal tender*," and that declaration (with the force of law behind it) makes it a medium of exchange.

Legal tender

The early paper money of New France, discussed in the next section, was a very early form of fiat money: it was not convertible into coin until several months after issue, and in the meanwhile the Governor threatened to fine anyone not accepting it in payment.

Paper standards

Paper standard

In Canada we now have a fiat money (dollar bills and coins) supplemented by a fiduciary money (bank deposits that are convertible into the fiat money on demand). The system as a whole is known as a *paper standard*. Most modern economies have something similar to the Canadian paper standard.

The history of the development of moneys reflects two main endeavors: the search for more convenient forms of payment, and the struggle of governments to control the issue of new money. The first of these efforts has been very successful. We have come a long way from the time when a Queen's dowry, for example, had to be transported in coin and with an armed escort from one country to another. Now millions of dollars are transferred between countries by a touch of a computer key, in milliseconds.

Governments have not completely resolved the second problem, that of controlling the issue of money. Until recently it seemed to be agreed, however, that the government should be given complete control of the size of the money supply. In Canada, the Bank of Canada was explicitly created in 1935 to take on that function. The problem was then reduced to what the government should do with that control. More recently, advocates of a return to the gold standard have come back into the fray; their advocacy of the gold standard is based precisely on the idea that control of the money supply should not be entrusted to governments.[2]

The next two sections provide brief accounts of two of the more successful experiments in world monetary history. Both were conducted in Canada — the first by the French colonial government and the second by the British colonial government.

SECTION 2 Playing-card money in Canada, 1685–1763

In the years up to 1685, the colony of New France suffered from a chronic currency shortage.[3] The colony received an annual injection of coin from France — the Governor's budget allocation — which the Governor used to pay the soldiers of the garrison. Soon after the arrival of the budget funds, the cash went back to France to pay for imports to the colony; much of it went back on the same ship that brought it out. The colonial government had tried several schemes to keep the currency in the economy, but none was very successful.

In 1685 it was the Governor's turn to feel the pinch, and the colonial Intendant's response initiated a very successful, efficient monetary experiment. For some reason the French budgetary system changed in 1684, so that the Governor and Intendant of New France did not receive their appropriations and funds for 1685 in advance, as usual. Instead, the funds for 1685 did not arrive until early September of 1685.

The Intendant had to finance the garrison and meet other expenses for the first eight months. After exhausting his own resources and those of his friends and, as he confided later to a friend, "not knowing to what saint to pay his vows, money being extremely scarce," he decided to issue paper money, redeemable in French silver coin when the funds should arrive.

[2]For a summary of the views of gold-standard advocates, see Rep. John Paul and Lewis Lehrman, *The Case for Gold: A Minority Report of the U.S. Gold Commission* (Washington, D.C.: Cato Institute, 1982).

[3]This section is based on the sources in footnote 1 and on the original documents in Adam Shortt, ed., *Documents Relating to Currency, Exchange, and Finance in French Canada* (New York: B. Franklin, 1968).

FIGURE 4–1 Playing-card money, 1714

Source: National Currency Collection, Bank of Canada.
Photographer: James Zagon.

The paper money consisted of ordinary playing cards cut up into a different shape for each denomination (for the illiterate) and signed by three colonial officials. The Intendant did not have the printing facilities or the paper to make more elaborate paper money, and playing cards were both plentiful and durable.

The Governor used both carrot and stick to ensure the acceptance of the new money as a medium of exchange. The carrot was his pledge to redeem the cards in September either in coin or in bills of exchange drawn on the colonial treasury in Paris — the latter arrangement a very convenient one for merchants with bills to pay in France. The stick was his threat to fine any inhabitant who refused to accept the playing-card money in settlement of debts.

The experiment was popular with everybody except the distant King, who rightly feared loss of control over the expenditures of his colonial officials. When the colony's appropriations finally did come in in September, the playing cards were redeemed as promised and then burned. The King forbade repetition of the experiment, but he was far away, and the same problem caused the Intendant to issue playing cards again in 1686 and then every year from 1690 to 1719. Because the cards were redeemed as promised, the inhabitants gradually developed enough confidence in them that some cards were hoarded rather than presented for redemption in September. The cards began to be used as a long-term store of value within the colony, as well as to make payments within the colony.

The advantages of card money

Playing-card money was not Canada's first fiduciary money. Private merchants had previously issued their own notes to serve as a circulating means of payment, promising redemption in whatever goods the merchant sold. These notes did circulate but were not accepted at par by everybody. Playing-card money was the first fiduciary money accepted by all at par as a medium of exchange. To achieve that status the cards had to be issued by the state and convertible into currency.

Card money turned out to have some quite unexpected advantages over the silver coinage relied on before. First, it did not leave the colony, since it was worthless elsewhere. Second, it soon eliminated any need to ship coin across the Atlantic Ocean and back again, thereby removing some of the incentive for piracy on the high seas. Within the economy, most of the cards ended up in the hands of the merchants by the fall, since the merchants were the major sellers of goods. The merchants in turn had imported most of the goods from France, and therefore had bills to pay in France. The most convenient method of payment to French suppliers was by endorsing bills of exchange drawn on the colonial treasury in Paris. The merchants therefore redeemed their card money holdings in bills of exchange rather than in coin.

The Intendant quickly came to realize that there was little need to send the colony's appropriation out in the form of cash. Mere pieces of paper announcing what total of bills of exchange the Intendant could write would be sufficient. When war broke out between France and England, the shipment of coin was forbidden, and all of the cards without exception were redeemed in bills of exchange. The colony had shifted over entirely to a paper-money system, though the paper was still backed by the exchangeability of bills on the treasury in Paris for silver coin. It was a silver exchange standard.

Third, the use of playing-card money may have had a significant effect on the outcome of the Massachusetts expedition to capture Quebec in 1690. The Massachusetts troops were promised that they would be paid out of the plunder from Quebec. At some point in their expedition it must have dawned on even the most simple-minded soldier that, in a colony that used playing-card money both as a medium of exchange and as a store of value, much of the plunder would be worthless even if Quebec could be taken. All the paper money in Quebec could not buy a single beer in Massachusetts. The expedition returned home empty-handed, and the Massachusetts colony promptly issued its own paper money to pay the troops — the first paper money in the English colonies.

The disadvantages of card money

The system of playing-card money eventually broke down for the reason that most fiduciary-money systems have broken down: overissue. The reasons have more to do with France than with the French colony, however. Louis XIV bankrupted the French government with his wars in Europe, so the card money in the colony could not be redeemed in silver coin. The cards could be redeemed in paper money in France, but that traded at a substantial discount from its face value in silver coin. Since the old card money was not redeemed, and new cards had to be issued each year to finance new and large expenditures for the colony's wartime defences, the amount of card money in existence rose steadily, from 4 livres per head in 1702 to 70 livres per head in 1714 (an average annual growth rate of 27 percent in the per-capita money supply). Even so, the colonists had more confidence in the card money than they did in the French paper money into which it was convertible. The fiduciary money was stronger than its backing.

The second card-money episode

The card money was finally redeemed in coin at half face value in 1720, and the first card-money episode was over. The colony immediately returned to the perennial currency shortage of the years before 1685, and colonists promptly began to plead for a reissue of card money. Their wish was granted in 1730, and card money was reissued each year thereafter until 1763. Blank cards were used this time. Some are reproduced in figure 4–2.

The second card-money experiment worked very well until once again the French government overextended itself and used issue of paper money to finance large wartime spending. In particular, the Army commanders were allowed to issue Army Orders to pay their bills in the field. These were made legal tender in order to circulate as currency, but the amount of issue was not controlled by the Intendant and was not related to the French government's ability to repay. Since the card money issued by the Intendant was subject to a bit more discipline, it became a superior store of value. Gresham's Law came into operation: the superior card money was hoarded, and only the inferior Army Orders remained in circulation. After New France was ceded to the British in 1763, the card money was eventually redeemed at about one-quarter of face value.

Lessons of the card-money experiment

The lesson from the card-money experiment drawn by the British colonial government after 1763 was that paper money was dangerous. Not until 1820 was a private bank chartered with the power to issue notes intended

FIGURE 4–2 Card money, 1733, 1749

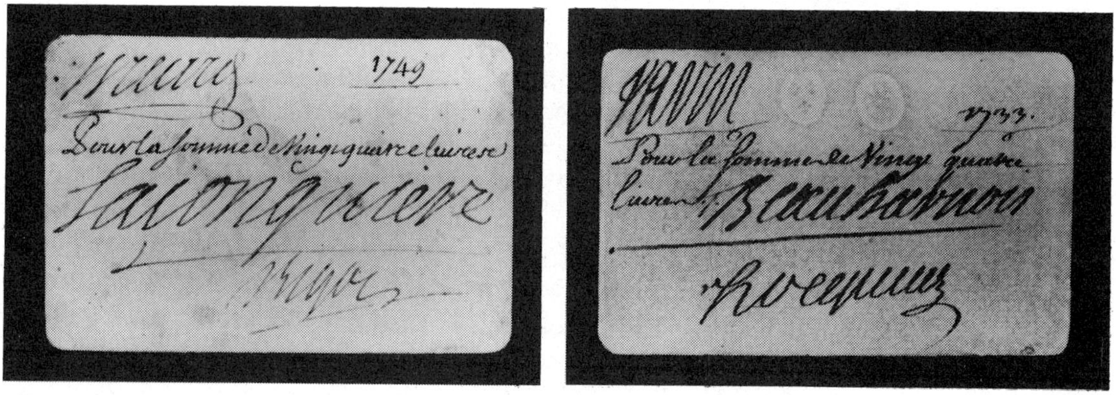

Each of these notes is signed by the Governor, the Intendant, and the Clerk of the Treasury. For the 24-livre note, these are M. Beauharnois, M. Hocquart, and M. Varin, respectively. The seal imprints are the arms of France and of Navarre.

Source: National Currency Collection, Bank of Canada.
Photographer: James Zagon.

for circulation. Even then the notes were to be redeemable on the spot in specie; the card money had been redeemable in the fall, if the ship came in with the colony's appropriations and if the Intendant's bills of exchange were honored in Paris.

In fact, the lesson learned should have been quite different. For most of the sixty-five years in which the card money was used, the colonists had a stable, safe, and very convenient payments mechanism. In particular, the colony and France saved both lives and resources by not having to ship valuable coin across the sea and back, and saved wealth by reducing the number of robberies at sea. The colony's price levels and trading volumes were not subject to unnecessary fluctuations caused by the seasonal flows of currency into and out of the colony.

SECTION 3 Army Bills, 1812–14

After the peace of 1763 the British American colonies once again settled into the pattern of chronic currency shortage. "Good" media of exchange, suitable for payments abroad, were shipped to Europe to make those payments. Only "bad" currency stayed behind. The colonists had to make do with worn and defaced coinage of many countries, and a variety of merchants' notes, redeemable in merchandise of various sorts and subject to varying discounts from face value. Interest was forming in banks as a source of note issue to replace the merchants' note issue. Three Montreal merchant firms therefore put the following notice in the Official Gazette on October 18, 1792:

> The undersigned, having experienced great inconvenience in Canada from the deficiency of specie or some other medium to represent the increasing circulation of the Country, as well as from the variety of money now current, and knowing the frequent loss and general difficulty attending receipts and payments, have formed the resolution of establishing a Bank at Montreal, under the name of the 'Canada Banking Company.'[4]

The scheme fell through for a variety of reasons, and the merchants founded only a bank of deposit rather than a bank of note issue. Twenty years later, however, the British colonial government found itself in the predicament that the French colonial government had been in during its wars. (Incidentally, this was the same predicament that the Canadian government would find itself in during World War I, and the response would be the same.)

The outbreak of the War of 1812–14 meant a huge increase in the government's spending for soldiers, munitions, and fortifications. The British imperial government was unlikely to send the necessary funds, as it was still locked in a very expensive struggle with Napoleon. The Governor took the advice of his executive council and issued a paper money known as Army Bills. The bills were made available in denominations of 1, 2, 3, 4, 5, 10, 16, 20, 25, 50, 100, and 400 dollars. Interest was paid at 4 percent on bills of $25 and over. Smaller bills were redeemable in coin, larger bills in coin or Treasury Bills issued in London, at the discretion of the Governor. The smaller bills were made out to Bearer. The larger bills were made out to individuals but could be transferred by endorsement on the back, like a modern cheque.

The first issue of Army Bills totalled only £250 000, but as the war progressed the amount outstanding grew to £1 249 000 (a rate of increase of 123 percent per year over the period, much larger than for the French card-money experiment). Fortunately the war was short, so the issue did not get out of hand. All the Army Bills were promptly redeemed at full value (plus interest on the larger bills) at the end of the war.

Sequel to the Army Bills episode

The Army Bills proved just as convenient to the colony as had the playing-card money to New France. Furthermore, in both cases the issue of paper money was successfully used to finance government deficits caused

---

[4]Quoted in James Stevenson, "The Canadian Banking Company," in Neufeld, ed., *Money and Banking in Canada*, 28–29.

by wars. The difference is only that the War of 1812 was short and the British government was not bankrupted, whereas the French colony's wars were long and the French government was bankrupted on both occasions. The successful ending to the Army Bills episode served to remove from people's minds the idea that paper moneys inevitably led to overissue and then default. Instead, people remembered the great convenience of a medium of exchange that was easy to use and that would stay in the colony.

SECTION 4 Development of the modern monetary system

Following the Army Bills episode, the pressure for introduction of paper money grew quickly. The proposed means was private banks, which would issue their own bank notes, redeemable on demand in gold coin. Between 1817 and 1822, five such banks opened their doors, including the Bank of Montreal and the Bank of Nova Scotia. The number of note-issuing banks grew steadily throughout the century, reaching a peak of sixty in 1900 before a wave of mergers consolidated the Canadian banking system into only eight banks by 1965.

Strangely enough, the Army Bills episode did not lead quickly to establishment of a government note issue in the provinces of Upper and Lower Canada. This failure was despite provincial notes' having been issued in 1761 in Nova Scotia and in 1790 in Prince Edward Island. Even a domestic Canadian coinage did not appear until 1858. There were several attempts by Governors to take over the private banks' note issues, but all these attempts were stoutly opposed by business and banking interests, which favored both free enterprise and an elastic money supply. The bankers knew a good thing when they saw it; borrowing by issuing bank notes paying zero interest, in order to lend to merchants paying positive interest, was too profitable a business to share with government.

The government persevered, however, and in 1866 introduced Provincial Notes in the Canadian provinces. After Confederation in 1867 these were replaced by Dominion Notes. As these government notes were introduced, the banking legislation was changed to allow private banks' notes to be redeemable in either specie or the government notes. Dominion Notes themselves were redeemable only in specie. It was convenient for the banks to have Dominion Notes as an extra form of cash reserves against their note issue, since (like the French colony's card money) Dominion Notes did not leave the country to pay for imports.

The major disturbances to the three-tier system of chartered bank notes, Dominion Notes, and specie after Confederation came from (a) the spread of chequable deposits among business customers as the main medium-of-exchange asset and (b) the suspension of convertibility of Dominion Notes (and therefore of private bank notes as well) into specie, because of World War I from 1914 to 1925, and then from 1929 on. The first suspension was caused by the urgent needs of war finance; the government used the period to print more money to finance its part in World War I. The second suspension was part of a general breakdown of the international gold standard system in the late 1920s.

Private bank notes continued to be issued until 1935, when the Bank of Canada was established. By then the right to issue bank notes was no longer very important to the banks, as they were relying mainly on the issue of deposits to finance their loan business. By 1935 the payments mechanism of the business sector already depended mainly on cheques written against deposits (current accounts) rather than on the transfer of currency hand to hand. When the Bank of Canada was established it took over responsibility for the remaining note issue of the chartered banks and issued its own Bank of Canada notes to replace the Dominion Notes. Bank of Canada notes were a pure fiat currency, so control of their issue rested (and still rests) with the Governor of the Bank. This power and its use are described fully in part VI of this book.

Since 1935 the drift toward making payments with chequable deposits has continued. In 1958 the chartered banks introduced personal chequing accounts for the first time, tailoring the business current account to the needs of households. The volume of chequing business done by credit unions and trust companies has mushroomed since 1960, before which it was almost nil, so that bank deposits and currency no longer account for all of Canada's medium-of-exchange assets. In 1967 bank charge cards (VISA first, then MasterCard) started their rapid spread, further reducing the need for currency. In December of 1980 the Bank Act revision set up the Canadian Payments Association, which took over responsibility for the payments mechanism from the Canadian Bankers' Association in 1983. The Canadian Payments Association represents not just banks, but also the credit unions, trust companies, and other deposit-taking institutions that do a significant volume of chequing business.

SECTION 5 Summary

The items that have served as money in the past have all been easily portable and divisible. The successful items have also been limited in supply. There has been a steady progression in western civilizations from the precious metals toward lighter and more convenient paper currencies, a progression that has depended on finding methods of limiting the rate of growth of paper currencies. Commodity and gold standards tied paper currency issue to a volume of commodity or gold reserves. Pure paper standards such as we have now are controlled entirely by the government through its central bank.

French Canada's playing-card money, issued in two episodes between 1685 and 1763, was an unplanned but successful early experiment in paper currency, until the excessive wartime needs of the French govenment led to overissue and collapse. The Army Bills of 1812–14 were issued specifically to finance wartime spending, but the war was short and the currency paid off in full immediately afterward, so the experiment was considered highly successful. Private note issue by chartered banks followed shortly thereafter.

Canada's monetary system after the Army Bills episode consisted initially of coin (specie) and bank notes redeemable in specie. Dominion Notes were added in 1868, chequable deposits gradually through the nineteenth century. Redeemability in specie was suspended after 1914, except for a brief resumption in 1926–29. In 1935 the Bank of Canada took over the Dominion Notes issue and also the private note issues of chartered banks, to give itself its current monopoly of the note issue.

Questions for discussion

1. What sort of societies are likely to use cattle as money, and why?
2. Why is there concern about overissue of token moneys and commodity standard moneys but not about commodity moneys themselves?
3. Does a modern government make more seigniorage from paper money than old-style kings used to do from their coinage?
4. Why did playing cards circulate in French Canada as a medium of exchange? Were they also a store of value?
5. How did Gresham's Law make its appearance during the first and second card-money episodes?
6. What limit was there on the issue of private bank notes after 1817? What limit is there on the issue of Bank of Canada notes now?
7. What is the key ingredient necessary for an item to serve as money? Does Monopoly money (from the board game) have that property? Does gold?

References

Binhammer, H.H. *Money, Banking and the Canadian Financial System*. 4th ed. Toronto: Methuen, 1982, chaps. 3–5.

Boreham, G.F. *Money and Banking: Analysis and Policy in a Canadian Context*. 2d ed. Toronto: Holt, Rinehart and Winston, 1979, chaps. 2–3.

Neufeld, E.P., ed. *Money and Banking in Canada*. Toronto: McClelland and Stewart, 1964.

———. *The Financial System of Canada*. Toronto: Macmillan of Canada, 1972.

Shortt, Adam, ed. *Documents Relating to Currency, Exchange, and Finance in French Canada*. New York: B. Franklin reprint, 1968.

CHAPTER 5

Stocks, Flows, and Financial Markets

In this chapter we shift our focus from money to the financial system as a whole. We start the job of analysing the pattern of saving, lending, borrowing, and holding of financial assets.

Analysis of financial flows and stocks is important because they determine the flow of real investment in new plant and equipment. Real investment in turn affects both the output potential of the economy and the aggregate demand for that output. Also, the federal government's monetary policy has its initial, direct impact only on financial flows and stocks. Understanding the subsequent effects of monetary policy on real output, inflation, and growth requires that we first understand the behavior of financial flows and stocks.

This chapter is devoted mainly to familiarizing you with financial markets. To this end, it should teach you:

1. the basic accounting behind the Financial Flow Accounts and their stock counterpart, the National Capital Account,
2. the many different types of financial market that exist, and who frequents them, and
3. the main instruments and operating features of the two big markets for purchase and resale of existing financial assets — the money market and the capital market.

SECTION 1 An accounting framework

Wealth

The basic identity lying behind and connecting financial flows and financial markets is the wealth identity: *wealth* (W) is the difference between total assets demanded (A) and total debts outstanding (D):

$$W = A - D.$$

W, A, and D all refer to stocks outstanding at a point of time, rather than to flows per period of time. Other names sometimes given to this wealth concept are *equity* (for firms) and *net worth*.

Net worth, or wealth, or equity

All debts lead a double life. They are financial liabilities to the issuer, but financial assets to the holder. Issuance of a new debt therefore does not change the economy's total wealth; those holding the debts have larger total assets, but those issuing them have larger debts by exactly the same amount. A frequently used accounting convention that brings out this property of debts is to treat them as negative holdings of assets. If Acme Chemical, for instance, has \$50 million of bond debt outstanding, it would be described by this convention as having bond holdings of −\$50 million. The total Acme Chemical bond holdings of Acme (−\$50 m) and of its bondholders (+\$50 m) would therefore sum to exactly zero.

With debts classified as negative asset holdings, the wealth identity becomes even simpler. Wealth (W) is simply the total of net asset holdings (A), both positive and negative:

$$W = A.$$

The National Capital Account

National Capital Account

Table 5–1 presents an accounting framework that illustrates the wealth identity for the whole economy and for each sector within it. We call this framework the *National Capital Account*. Each column in table 5–1 gives the asset holdings of a particular sector. Theoretically, the table could include a column for each individual and firm, but then the table would not fit on our page. Debts outstanding are recorded in the appropriate row and column (the Loans row and the Household column, for bank loans of households) as negative asset holdings. Only the rest-of-the-world sector is not complete, since that would require an accounting of the entire world's wealth. What appears in the Rest-of-the-world column is only Canadian assets held by foreigners, and foreign assets held by Canadians.

Private domestic wealth

The sum of entries in any one column gives the total wealth of that sector.[1] If a domestic sector's debts were to exceed its assets, its total wealth would be negative.[2] The horizontal sum of the bottom row is national wealth. The horizontal sum of the bottom row for all but the government and foreign sectors is *private domestic wealth*, which we will encounter in the second half of this book as an important link in the transmission of monetary policy to the real sector of the economy. Private domestic wealth will differ from national wealth by (a) the difference

[1]For the rest-of-the-world sector, the column total gives only Canadian wealth — Canadian assets less debts to Canadians.

[2]Human wealth is not included in this wealth total. Human wealth is the present value of current and expected future labor income. If human wealth were included in the calculation of wealth, few individuals would ever have negative total wealth.

between the government's debts and the government's assets and (b) the net debt to foreigners.

TABLE 5–1 The National Capital Account: an accounting framework

Assets	Households	Nonfinancial business firms	Financial institutions	Total private domestic sectors	Govern-ments	Rest of the world	TOTAL
Currency and deposits							0
Loans							0
...							...
...							...
...							...
Inventory							I
Fixed capital							K
Housing							H
Land							L
				Private domestic wealth	Public wealth		NATIONAL WEALTH

Note: I = stock of inventories as at date of table; K = stock of fixed capital; H = housing stock; L = value of land and natural resources.

Source: Adapted from James Tobin, "A General Equilibrium Approach to Monetary Theory," *Journal of Money, Credit, and Banking* 1 (1969), 17.

Each row (other than the bottom row, of course) represents a particular type of asset. The horizontal sum of any row gives the net total of that asset outstanding. For real assets, the horizontal sum is the amount in existence. For financial assets, the horizontal sum is zero. Negative holdings of borrowers (the suppliers of financial assets) must always match exactly the positive holdings of lenders. The last column of the table therefore contains mostly zeroes. Within each row, however, the positive and negative numbers reveal who is borrowing in that market and who is lending; each row is a summary picture of a particular asset market.

It is plausible to identify markets with rows of table 5–1. I should point out, however, that such a concept of financial markets does conflict with the way we sometimes talk about the banking system. It is often said, for instance, that banking is a tight oligopoly. *Oligopoly* describes a market with few sellers, so the implication is that banking is a market. But banking is a subsector in the Capital Account table, part of the financial-institutions sector. Therefore banking is a column rather than a row in table 5–1. Banking is a form of borrowing to invest in financial assets, which involves demanding and supplying in many different financial markets. Some of those markets are dominated by just a few banks; some are not.

The National Capital Account in table 5–1 is just an accounting framework, so far. Statistics Canada does not report all of the asset values that would be needed to fill in table 5–1. However, Statistics Canada does provide estimates of total financial assets held and debts issued by each sector, so the current values of the financial-asset section of table 5–1 can be produced. Table 5–2 presents those figures as of the end of 1981. Though the number at the bottom of each column represents only financial, not total, wealth (because data for sectors' real asset holdings are missing), each row does describe all of the demands and supplies in each financial market, by sector. Since all sectors' demands and supplies are included, and since financial assets are also debts, all the rows add up to zero (discrepancies are due to rounding and measurement errors).

TABLE 5–2 The National Capital Account (excluding real assets), 1981 (billions of dollars)

Financial assets, net	Persons and unincorporated business	Nonfinancial corporations	Banks and near-banks	Other financial institutions	Governments[a]	Rest of the world
Currency and deposits	214	23	−274	7	−1	33
Consumer and trade credit	−58	11	40	9	−2	—
Loans	−42	−86	125	14	1	−12
Treasury Bills and short-term paper	2	−3	12	−9	−20	4
Mortgages	−107	−22	81	44	4	1
Bonds	46	−73	11	48	−102	59
Life insurance and pension funds	109	—	—	−108	−1	—
Stocks and claims on affiliates	105	−197	2	−16	56	47
Foreign investments	2	1	—	5	—	−9
Official international reserves	—	—	—	—	5	−5
Other financial assets	29	−22	1	−8	—	2
TOTAL (NET) FINANCIAL WEALTH[b]	302	−366	−3	−8	−72	119

[a]Includes social security funds and the monetary authorities.

[b]Column totals often do not add up due to both rounding errors and large measurement errors for some sectors (Rest of the world, Corporations, and Governments, particularly).

Source: Statistics Canada, *Financial Flow Accounts*, Cat. 13–002, Fourth Quarter 1981.

Nonfinancial corporations and governments are clearly the main sectors that on balance take funds out of the financial markets. Financial institutions borrow large amounts via deposits and insurance and pension funds, but they lend it all right back out again; they have insignificant holdings of real assets as a group, so their wealth is small. The other two sectors — persons and unincorporated business, and rest-of-the-world — have been the ultimate source of the net financial investment that matches corporations' and governments' net borrowing.

The Financial Flow Accounts

The National Capital Account records stocks of assets and debts at a point in time. For many purposes we also want to know how stocks change over time; that is, about flows. The flow table corresponding to the National Capital Account is the *Financial Flow Accounts*, reported by Statistics Canada for each quarter and year since 1961. The Financial Flow Accounts identify flows of saving, investing, lending, and borrowing in total and for each sector, as well as changes in financial asset holdings for each sector and asset.

Financial Flow Accounts

Changes in asset holdings are calculated simply as the difference between totals at the end of one period and totals at the end of the previous period. Financial assets and debts are broken down into many categories and are shown separately, but real assets are classified only into new assets and previously produced, or *existing*, assets.

The savings-investment identity

Underlying the Financial Flow Accounts is a savings-investment identity derived from the wealth identity. The flow of *savings* in any period (S) is by definition equal to the change in wealth (dW) between the start and the end of the period:

Saving, or net saving

$$S = dW.$$

In this definition, dW reflects not only assets bought and sold and debts incurred or paid off, but also decreases in asset values caused by wear and tear. The amount of wear and tear, known as *depreciation* or *capital consumption*, is estimated crudely with a measure called *capital consumption allowances*. For some purposes a savings concept that ignores wear and tear is more useful; the concept is *gross savings* (S_g), which is defined as net savings (S) plus capital consumption allowances (CCA):

Depreciation, or capital consumption

Capital consumption allowance

$$S_g = S + CCA.$$

Real investment or real capital formation (I) is the name given to the increase in holdings of real assets — plant and equipment, housing, inventories, and stocks of natural resources. Real investment can be measured in net form (I) or in gross form (I_g), where the difference is again measured by capital consumption allowances:

$$I_g = I + CCA.$$

Net real investment
Gross real investment

Net real investment is the net increase in holdings of real assets; *gross (real) investment* is total purchases of assets, ignoring the depreciation of assets already held.

Net real investment is the net change in holdings of real assets. The change in wealth (dW) is the net change in holdings of both real and financial assets. The net change in holdings of financial assets is the difference between purchases of financial assets (dFA) and any increase in debts (dD), or $dFA - dD$. It follows that

$$dW = I + (dFA - dD).$$

Since $S = dW$, the basic savings-investment identity underlying the Financial Flow Accounts is that

$$S = I + (dFA - dD), \text{ or}$$

$$S - I = dFA - dD.$$

$S - I$ corresponds to net lending, so net lending must by definition be equal to the net increase in financial assets.

The Financial Flow Accounts for 1981

The Financial Flow Accounts, reported in table 5–3 for the year 1981, are built around this identity. The top third of table 5–3 records the components of net lending; the bottom two-thirds records the net increase in financial assets. Statistics Canada reports dFA and dD separately, but in table 5–3 we have netted them out against each other for each type of asset or debt.

The Financial Flow Accounts for 1981 refer only to 1981 and can change significantly from year to year, but some major and persistent patterns are worth noting.

First, almost all sectors do some saving, even in a year of recession like 1981. Nonfinancial corporations are especially important in gross saving, which of course includes capital consumption allowances. Governments and nonfinancial corporations are important net borrowers, but only because their gross real investment is even greater than their gross savings.

Second, households and the foreign sector are the main primary lenders of the economy.

Third, the Treasury Bill and short-term-paper market (for large-scale issues of resalable short-term debts) is a relatively small proportion of total flows. The publicity the Treasury Bill market gets is out of proportion to its size.

Fourth, the net figures in table 5–3 mask a lot of borrowing and lending that go on within sectors. Trade credit between firms and loans from parents to subsidiaries (or the other way around) are the most underestimated. When those flows are taken into account, nonfinancial corporations do much of their borrowing outside the impersonal, arm's-length credit markets and also finance most of their real capital formation out of their own savings. They are dependent on the formal credit markets only for a small part of their spending requirements.

TABLE 5–3 Financial flows, 1981

Flows	Persons and unincorporated business	Nonfinancial corporations	Banks and near-banks	Other financial institutions	Governments	Rest of the world
Gross saving (*Sg*)	35	29	1	0	7	8
Gross real capital formation (*Ig*)	18	54	1	—	9	—
Net purchases of existing real assets	−4	2	—	1	—	1
Net lending, or net purchase of financial assets ($S - I = dFA - dD$)	21	−27	0	−1	−2	7
Net increase in financial assets						
Currency and deposits	26	—	−38	1	5	7
Consumer and trade credit	−6	1	4	1	—	—
Loans	−10	−20	34	−1	—	−1
Treasury Bills and short-term paper	−1	−1	2	—	−1	1
Mortgages	−7	−1	4	2	—	—
Bonds	7	−11	1	5	−14	12
Life insurance and pensions	14	—	—	−14	—	—
Stocks and claims on affiliates	−4	4	−7	5	7	−2
Foreign investments	−1	—	—	1	—	—
Official international reserves	—	—	—	—	—	—
Other financial assets	1	−1	4	−1	−2	−1

Source: Statistics Canada, *Financial Flow Accounts*, Cat. 13–002, Fourth Quarter 1981.

Fifth, and finally, households do their lending mainly through financial institutions (indirect lending). The same is becoming true of foreigners; there used to be substantial direct lending to subsidiaries in Canada, but that has tapered off since 1977. Now most foreign lending in Canada is either via bank deposits issued by foreign branches of Canadian banks, or via bonds.

Just as each financial-asset row adds up to zero in the financial-assets section of the National Capital Account (since demand for financial assets equals supply of financial assets), so each row adds up to zero in the Financial Flow Accounts. Changes in demand must equal changes in supply. For instance, all the deposits issued by financial institutions in 1981 must be held by some other sector; a deposit not held by anyone must be a deposit not issued. Where any row total in table 5–3 differs from zero, the difference is due solely to rounding or measurement error.

SECTION 2

Characteristics of financial markets

We have identified the rows of the National Capital Account with individual financial markets. Positive entries record demand; negative entries record supply. Similarly, the financial-asset rows in the Financial Flow Accounts record changes in demand and changes in supply in the same markets.

The rows of tables 5–2 and 5–3 therefore give the range of financial markets in Canada by type of asset, and the relative size of each financial market. In this section we classify financial markets by several different criteria and explain the significance of each for market behavior. For instance, the differences between markets for households and those for large business firms affect the level and volatility of asset yields available and the liquidity and variability of household wealth. These in turn affect households' demand for wealth and therefore the flow of saving and investment each year. Variability and liquidity of wealth also affect the response of consumption demand to changes in interest rates, an important factor in conducting stabilization policy.

Retail versus wholesale markets

Retail markets

Households and small firms borrow and lend in *retail markets*. Retail markets are small in scale and the assets not standardized. Household transactions are usually customized to suit each household. Retail business involves higher processing costs per dollar, so the spreads between lending rates and borrowing rates are larger; households and small business earn less on their savings and pay more on their debts than if they were transacting in *wholesale markets*. Wholesale markets, frequented by larger firms and governments, have larger transactions and more standardized assets.

Wholesale markets

Direct versus indirect lending

Direct lending

Indirect lending

Direct lending is from primary lender (a current saver) directly to a primary borrower (a real investor needing external funds, typically). *Indirect lending* is via one or more intermediaries, which re-lend primary lenders' funds to primary borrowers. Almost all household lending and borrowing is part of indirect lending flows. Savings put into deposits, insurance, pension funds, mutual funds, or trust plans all flow to primary borrowers through financial institutions. The main exception is Canada Savings Bonds, since the government spends the proceeds on its current and capital needs.

In the business sector, by contrast, there is a large flow of direct credit from one firm to another out of retained earnings. This may take the form of loans to affiliates, or trade credit, or the purchase of money-market paper. Household borrowing is almost entirely through financial institutions as well — credit unions, banks, trust companies, mortgage loan companies, and insurance companies. Small-business borrowing not done through trade credit is done indirectly, almost all via banks but some via venture-capital companies, which lend in return for a share of equity in the firm.

Private versus public markets

Private markets
Public markets

In *private markets*, terms of loans are negotiated privately for each customer. In *public markets*, the terms are posted for all to see, or set impersonally in a public auction such as that for Treasury Bills. Interest rates paid to households by banks and near-banks are posted, as a rule, but lending rates to households and small businesses are subject to private negotiation rather than impersonal auction bidding. One result of private negotiation is that lenders can, and do, practise more discrimination among customers.[3] Another result is higher costs, and therefore higher interest spreads.

Competitive versus concentrated markets

Households and small businesses lend and borrow in relatively concentrated markets; that is, markets where relatively few firms do a large share of the total borrowing or lending. The financial institutions facing households and small businesses are usually price setters, whereas in a competitive market they would be price takers. The price setters are usually rivals who recognize their interdependence. One result is that in concentrated markets interest-rate wars are uncommon.[4] Another is that rates in these markets tend to be relatively stable. They adjust with yields available in wholesale markets, but less frequently. When wholesale, market-determined rates are moving rapidly, large differentials can open up between wholesale and retail rates. As a rule, retail financial markets tend to be more concentrated and wholesale markets more competitive.

Some of the concentration of household financial markets is clear from tables 5–4 and 5–5. Table 5–4 shows sources of funds for consumer credit. Almost 90 percent of the funds come from banks and credit unions and

[3]There is nothing to prevent a dissatisfied borrower from shopping around among lenders, but the process is tiresome in private markets. Imagine, for instance, the bother of having ten life insurance agents come to explain the advantages of their companies' products.

[4]An exception occurs in February, just before the deadline for contributions to Registered Retirement Savings Plans. The stakes are large at that point, and the competition fierce.

TABLE 5–4 Major sources of consumer credit, 1977–81 (millions of dollars)

	1977	1979	1981	Percent share of total, 1977–81
Chartered banks	2520	3506	2909	70.6
Sales finance and consumer loan companies	−93	−184	395	0.5
Credit unions and caisses populaires	628	728	178	14.5
Life insurers (policy loans)	59	196	478	4.8
Trust and mortgage loan companies	81	331	328	7.2
Other	82	151	115	2.5
TOTAL	3277	4728	4403	100.0

Notes: "Other" includes Quebec savings banks and department stores. VISA and MasterCard loans are included under the sponsoring organizations (mostly banks).

Source: Bank of Canada Review.

TABLE 5–5 Major sources of mortgage credit, 1977–81 (millions of dollars)

	1977	1979	1981	Percent share of total, 1977–81
Trust and mortgage loan companies	4078	5671	5613	45.1
Chartered banks	2664	2896	−2284	12.8
Credit unions and caisses populaires	2345	2321	682	17.3
Life insurers	1327	1559	1315	11.5
Pension funds	838	576	690	6.9
Mutual funds	323	82	−166	1.0
Sales finance and consumer loan companies	66	89	94	1.1
Real estate investment trusts	172	32	—	—
Other financial institutions	150	141	1360	4.3
Canada Mortgage and Housing Corporation (CMHC)	410	−171	—	—
TOTAL	12 373	13 196	7304	100.0

Notes: Some of the mortgage loan companies are owned by banks (for example, Kinross, Roymor, Scotia Covenants). Such companies accounted for 28 percent of the extra mortgage credit of all trust and loan companies for the period 1977–81. Both residential and other mortgages are included; the bulk of mortgage loans are residential.

Source: Bank of Canada Review.

caisses populaires. True, there are thousands of credit unions and sixty-nine banks, not to mention the number of bank branches, but for each individual consumer borrower, only a very few of those institutions are close enough to be considered as a source of funds. Generally borrowers have an effective choice of only two or three lenders for consumer credit. Rural borrowers may have no choice at all. Lenders therefore have considerable room to discriminate among customers and to keep rates higher than in less concentrated markets.

Table 5–5 shows that the mortgage market is much less concentrated. Discrimination is less likely than in consumer credit markets for this reason and also because the payoff from shopping around for a mortgage loan is much higher.[5] Small savings on the interest rate on a mortgage can amount to hundreds of dollars a year.

Primary versus secondary markets

Primary, or new-issue, markets

Secondary markets

A *primary market* is a new-issue market, one in which every buyer is buying a new issue from the borrower. In *secondary markets*, the seller will be a holder who is adjusting actual holdings downward to a new, lower level of demand (for example, a pension fund selling off some of its holdings of an unpromising stock). Everybody borrows in primary markets, by definition. There are secondary or resale markets for many of the assets and debts of large firms and governments — in particular, for stocks, bonds, Treasury Bills, wholesale deposits, and short-term paper. There is a secondary market for trade credits in the *factoring and acceptance business*, where factors and acceptance companies buy up blocks of trade credits at a discount. There are even markets in which borrowers or lenders can protect themselves from swings in prices of stocks, bonds, and short-term paper — the options and financial-futures markets, which we will deal with in chapter 10.

Factoring and acceptance business

Having a secondary market makes any credit instrument more liquid to the holder. This should give some advantage to the borrower, in lower interest rates or a longer term or both. However, it also exposes the holder to capital-value risk, since the secondary-market price will fluctuate in response to demand or supply shocks. Note that the borrower is not affected by this capital-value uncertainty, since debts are redeemed at maturity and at par value regardless of what market value they may have before then.

There are typically no secondary markets for the debts that households and small business supply.[6] When lenders lend to households, they must

---

[5]Discrimination is more difficult for mortgage loans. The degree of credit risk does not vary as much among borrowers, so any difference in mortgage loan rates is more easily exposed as being discriminatory.

[6]Strictly speaking, households do not supply loan notes to most of their lenders. Banks, for instance, have the loan note forms already. Household borrowers supply only the signature, but that is the part that counts.

generally figure on holding their asset to maturity. Banks, for instance, never sell a household borrower's personal loan note to some third party. Mortgage loans can be resold in large blocks to some financial institutions, but even that market is not well developed.[7] Household and small-business debts are therefore not very liquid assets to the holder.

There is also no secondary market for the resale of households' chequing, savings and term deposits (in banks and elsewhere) before maturity. Household deposits are fully registered and nonnegotiable, as are Canada Savings Bonds. Bank term deposits and all notice deposits are still very liquid, however, because they are redeemable more or less on demand, like Canada Savings Bonds, at close to face value plus accrued interest.[8]

Lack of a secondary market also insulates the values of nonredeemable deposits from changing interest rates. For an outstanding marketable bond with an interest coupon fixed at $100, an increase in yields available on new bonds from 10 to 11 percent will cause demand to shift away from this bond; its price will fall until the $100 coupon provides the same 11 percent yield as on competing assets.

Nonredeemable deposits with fixed interest payments would suffer the same fate if there were a secondary market and if holders were aware of their market price. Since there is no market, holders are not generally aware that their "true value" is less when current interest rates rise. Depositors therefore do not think of their wealth as lower when interest rates rise. Monetary policy affects demand for goods and services partly through the effects of changes in interest rates on the value of wealth, so insulation of wealth values from interest-rate changes is important.

Effective versus nominal interest rates

Interest is usually paid on financial assets more frequently than once per year, but almost universally interest rates are quoted "at annual rates." Each financial market uses one of two different methods of calculating "annual rates": as nominal annual rates, or as effective annual rates. *Nominal annual interest rates* ignore any compounding within the year, whereas *effective annual interest rates* do not. Where interest is paid (and therefore compounded) monthly, for instance, the nominal interest rate is simply $12r$, where r is the monthly interest rate. The effective rate is $(1 + r)^{12} - 1$. The difference is small when both rates are below 6 percent, but the difference can amount to over $\frac{1}{2}$ percent when nominal annual rates

Nominal annual interest rate

Effective annual interest rate

[7]The market is rudimentary in that most of the mortgage loan companies that buy large blocks of mortgages on this secondary market are buying only from their parent banks. Resale of such blocks is rare.

[8]Usually the bank pays only the notice deposit rate as accrued interest on fixed-term deposits withdrawn before maturity.

get up to double digits.[9] Household interest rates are generally quoted in nominal terms, whereas other financial-market participants generally deal with effective rates.

Type of instrument

The main groups of financial markets can be classified by type of financial instrument traded. These instruments include medium-of-exchange assets (moneys); other short-term liquid assets, known collectively by the misleading name *money market* assets; short-term, less liquid assets (trade credit and loans); long-term assets, known collectively as *capital market* assets; and insurance, options, and futures contracts, designed to allow "hedging" against various risks.

We will quickly dispose of the first, third, and fifth of these groups of markets and then concentrate on the money and capital markets.

The market for money is a peculiar one in all economies, in that the secondary market in which money changes hands — in exchange for other goods and services such as groceries — is just the rest of the economy. We described in section 4 of chapter 3 the mechanism by which money changes hands.

The markets for trade credit and loans are only primary markets (in which all transactions involve either new borrowing or else repayment of debt). Transactions are almost always between borrowers and lenders rather than between lenders exchanging assets. Every sale is of a new issue; every purchase is a redemption. The major types of asset in this class are trade credits, consumer credit, and ordinary loans from banks and other institutions. There is not much to tell about the operation of those markets except what is already contained in the circular flow chart in figure 2–1. Borrower meets lender, loan notes are signed and exchanged for money, balance sheets are adjusted, and no other record is kept. The market is just a series of such encounters across the economy.

About the hedging markets there is more to tell, but it requires an understanding of risk behavior that we have not developed yet. Discussion of hedging markets is therefore postponed to the end of chapter 8.

The money and capital markets are both large, impersonal, auction-type, secondary markets into which new issuers can also bring new issues as a way of raising funds. We will deal with the money market first.[10]

---

[9]For instance, the effective annual interest rate on a loan with monthly payment of interest is

6.16 percent for a nominal rate of 6 percent,
12.68 percent for a nominal rate of 12 percent, and
26.82 percent for a nominal rate of 24 percent.

The effective annual interest rates on a deposit with semi-annual compounding are 6.09, 12.36, and 25.4 percent respectively for the nominal rates above.

[10]For a much more detailed discussion than is given in the next section, see S. Sarpkaya, *The Money Market in Canada* (Toronto: Butterworths, 1980).

SECTION 3

The money market

The significance of the money market

The money market is important for two reasons. First, changes in its yields provide a signal for other financial markets. Money-market yield changes serve as signals because the money market is a large auction market reflecting demand and supply from many sectors of the economy. Its rates serve as important guides to rate setters in other, more concentrated markets, where rates are posted; changes in posted rates often follow changes in money-market rates, the most obvious example being the lag of banks' prime loan rates behind the Treasury Bill rate set at the weekly auction in the money market.

The second reason for the importance of the money market is that it is the market in which monetary policy has its first impact, via the chartered banks. The Bank of Canada conducts monetary policy mainly through changing the excess cash reserves of the chartered banks. The banks invest excess cash reserves in liquid assets bought in the money market, so money-market yields are driven down whenever excess cash reserves are increased. Little real investment is financed in the money market, and real assets are not close substitutes for money-market assets, but money-market rates do have an indirect effect on real investment by their effect on other interest rates to which real investment is sensitive.

Borrowers and instruments

The money market is a wholesale market for short-term liquid assets. The minimum amount is $100 000. Maturities are short, from overnight to one year, but concentrated mostly in the thirty- to ninety-day range.[11] Financial instruments are mainly nonredeemable but negotiable (that is, resalable), though overnight deposits and day-to-day loans have terms so short that they are just redeemable on demand.

Table 5–6 shows the relative importance of various borrowers, and some of the instruments used. The major borrowers are financial institutions, particularly banks. The banks issue various types of redeemable deposits to the public, as well as overnight interbank deposits to each other. The finance-company borrowings are done with nonredeemable loans called *finance paper*, for which the finance companies' consumer loans serve as collateral.

Finance paper

Of the nonfinancial users, the federal government is by far the biggest. The federal government taps the money market with its Treasury Bill issues; the short-term government bonds shown in table 5–6 were almost all issued for much longer terms and have become short-term only with the passage of time. Large producing firms with excellent credit ratings can tap

[11]For maturities longer than 180 days, sellers may have trouble finding buyers, except at a substantial discount below prevailing yields.

TABLE 5–6 Outstanding amounts of money-market instruments, December 1981, by type of issuer (millions of dollars)

Governments	
Federal Treasury Bills outside banks	6 191
Provincial Treasury Bills and short-term paper	965
Federal government bonds under three years to maturity, outside government and Bank of Canada	11 200
	18 356
Banks	
Bank of Canada advances	38
Bank bearer deposit notes	9 117
Bank nonpersonal fixed-term deposits[a]	36 455
Bank foreign-currency deposits of residents	8 471
Interbank deposits	2 695
	56 776
Investment dealers	
Day loans	25
Purchase and resale agreements	231
Buybacks	260
Special call loans	1 055
	1 771
Sales finance and consumer loan companies	
Finance paper	3 979
Private nonfinancial corporations	
Commercial paper	2 527
Bankers' acceptances	6 561
	9 088
Private financial corporations	
Commercial paper[b]	7 178
TOTAL, ALL ISSUERS	97 148

[a]Includes an undetermined amount of smaller deposits not part of the money market.
[b]The bulk of the commercial paper outstanding is issued by subsidiaries of foreign banking corporations.

Sources: Bank of Canada Review and Statistics Canada, *Financial Institutions*, Cat. 61–006, Fourth Quarter 1981.

Commercial paper

Bankers' acceptances

the money market with their own loan notes, called *commercial paper*. Smaller firms can tap the market only by transforming some of their trade credits into *bankers' acceptances* and then selling them off; banks arrange the transformation (for an acceptance, or *marking*, fee of $\frac{3}{4}$ of 1 percent per annum) by stamping the trade credit bill as guaranteed by the bank.[12] A bankers' acceptance is therefore effectively a postdated, certified cheque. Some provincial and local governments also use a form of commercial paper, known in their case for obvious reasons as a *tax-anticipation note*.

Tax-anticipation note

Investment dealers provide a small but colorful volume of debts, whose various names reflect various purchasers. Their *day loans* and *purchase and resale agreements* (PRAs) are one-day (extendible) loans from the chartered banks and the Bank of Canada respectively. *Buybacks* are purchase and resale agreements from anyone else. *Special call loans* are short-term, callable loans from the chartered banks.[13] A purchase and resale agreement and a buyback are both loans in which the investment dealer sells some of its security holdings, agreeing at the time of sale to buy them back one or more days later from the purchaser, at a slightly higher price. The price difference is the cost of funds for the intervening period.

Day loan

Purchase and resale agreement (PRA)

Buyback

Special call loans

Lenders in the money market

Table 5–7 shows which groups hold the major money-market assets other than wholesale bank deposits (the Financial Flow Accounts do not break down bank deposits into those that are and those that are not part of the money market). Most money-market lending is done by financial institutions, but some of it is not what we normally think of as voluntary. For instance, roughly two-thirds of the money-market assets held by chartered banks reflect the *secondary reserve requirement*: by law, an amount of assets equal (currently) to 4.5 percent of their total deposits must be held in the form of excess cash reserves or Treasury Bills or day loans to money-market dealers. Only money-market assets over and above that requirement are held voluntarily.

Secondary reserve assets

The Bank of Canada is likewise "forced" to hold Treasury Bills since the Bank of Canada Act sets tight limits on assets that the Bank can hold. The Bank's holdings vary predictably with monetary growth, because it is mostly through the purchase of Treasury Bills that the Bank of Canada increases its outstanding deposits and the cash reserves of chartered banks.

Many groups make voluntary use of the money market, for a variety of purposes. The large household-sector holdings reflect mainly temporary

---

[12]If conversion of a trade credit to a bankers' acceptance is arranged by the holder rather than by the issuer, then the holding firm has merely made its asset more liquid, rather than supplied its own debt to tap the money market. It is the issuing firm that has the outstanding debt.

[13]Investment dealers also borrow from banks with regular call loans. These are not liquid, despite their name, for the same reason that bank demand loans are not liquid. A firm understanding has grown up between bankers and the dealer firms that the banks will not call regular call loans if they can possibly avoid doing so. Regular call loans are therefore not part of the money market even though special call loans are. For full discussion of this part of the market, see "Overnight Financing in Canada: Special Call Loans," *Bank of Canada Review*, May 1983, 3–14.

TABLE 5–7 Holdings of Treasury Bills, finance and other short-term paper by sector, December 1981 (millions of dollars)

	Treasury Bills	Other short-term paper
Households and unincorporated business	2 318	135
Nonfinancial corporations		
private sector	422	3 401
public sector	143	60
Bank of Canada	5 431	0
Chartered banks	8 269	1 748
Credit unions and caisses populaires	48	636
Trust companies	232	1 851
Mortgage loan companies	9	127
Life insurers	281	1 167
Trusteed pension funds	215	3 348
Investment dealers	752	2 475
Other private financial institutions	370	1 314
Public financial institutions	147	68
Federal government	—	14
Provincial and local governments and hospitals	1 010	588
Rest of the world	1 053	3 180
TOTAL	20 700	20 112

Source: Statistics Canada, *Financial Flow Accounts*, Cat. 13–002, Fourth Quarter 1981.

investment of estate, trust, and agency funds by trust companies rather than directly by the households themselves. Financial institutions typically hold money-market assets as their liquid asset reserve against sudden needs. They can and do hold bank deposits as well as other money-market assets for this purpose; it is the threat or prospect of financial institutions' switching back and forth from other money-market assets to bank deposits that keeps money-market deposit yields in line with the rest of the money market.

Money-market asset holdings of pension funds and life insurers are far larger than can be explained by liquidity needs. These institutions also hold short-term money-market assets as a substitute for long-term bonds and stocks, rolling them over into new Treasury Bills and other money-market assets each time they mature. As we will see in chapters 13 and 15, it is mostly through the holdings of pension funds and life insurers that we expect money-market yields to be tied in some way to longer-term yields.

Jobbers

Holdings of investment dealers make up the inventory of the money-market *jobbers* — the investment dealer firms that collectively make the money market operate. It is through investment dealers' traders and telephones that money-market deals are made. The jobbers' inventory is held as a working inventory to keep the market liquid, rather than as a financial investment to store spending power for later periods.

Nonfinancial corporations use the money market to park surplus cash flows not needed for short periods — for example, funds accumulated toward a major asset purchase still months in the future, or excess funds from a large bond flotation that are not needed immediately.

The rest-of-the-world sector's use of the money market includes foreign parent firms' parking their subsidiaries' dividend payments temporarily before converting them to foreign currency, as well as investments attracted from abroad by higher relative yields. Money-market dealers spend considerable time designing investment packages to attract such demand to the Canadian money market, as well as to attract Canadian investors to foreign money markets (through their friendly Canadian broker, of course). It is partly through the dealers' efforts that capital flows between Canada and the rest of the world are as sensitive as they are to relative yields.

Money-market mechanics

The money market is operated, or "made," by eleven Canadian money-market dealers.[14] These firms buy and sell the complete range of money-market assets as principals, covering their costs by the small spread between bid and asked prices. They keep an inventory on hand, just like any storekeeper, and finance it through their own money-market borrowings and other loans. As new-issue underwriters, they also buy up new issues from borrowers and sell them off into the money market just like a village grocer handling local farmers' eggs. In order to keep the money-market dealers liquid and encourage growth of the money market, the Bank of Canada is ready (and has been since 1954) to lend funds to money-market dealers through purchase and resale agreements whenever they wish.

New issues of federal government Treasury Bills are treated differently from issues of other money-market assets. The Bank of Canada handles all of the federal government's borrowing arrangements as its fiscal agent, so money-market dealers do not sell new issues of Treasury Bills. Instead, The Bank of Canada auctions off an issue of Treasury Bills each Thursday by sealed-bid auction.[15] The highest bids are filled first until all the available Bills are gone. There are clearly different yields to different purchasers, but only the average yield from all satisfied bids is reported. The Bank Rate for Bank of Canada advances is currently set $\frac{1}{4}$ of 1 percent above this average yield each week.

[14]As of 1983, these firms were Burns Fry, Dominion Securities Ames, Equitable Securities, Midland Doherty, Merrill Lynch Royal Securities, McLeod Young Weir, Nesbitt Thomson Bongard, Pitfield Mackay Ross, Richardson Greenshields, Walwyn Stodgell Cochran Murray, and Wood Gundy. This is basically a list of the larger bond dealers.

[15]Ninety-one- and 182-day bills are issued each week; 365-day bills are issued every four weeks.

The Treasury Bill auction is quickly and strongly affected by the Bank of Canada's monetary-policy actions. If the Bank of Canada has made available more cash reserve assets than the chartered banks need to meet their cash reserve requirements, the banks will be bidding for larger amounts of Treasury Bills than they currently have maturing. Larger bids will drive up the average price of Treasury Bills, and the average yield will fall. Some of the buyers squeezed out of the Treasury Bill auction by larger bank bids will turn to other money-market assets instead; these asset prices will then rise, and their yields will fall. Soon the whole structure of money-market yields will have fallen. Institutional investors like pension funds and life insurers may also decide that the lower money-market yields make longer-term assets preferable, and they may shift their demand to bond and stock and real estate markets instead.

International connections

Eurodollar, or Eurocurrency market

Canada's money market is not alone. It has strong links with the U.S. money market and with the Eurodollar market. The *Eurodollar market* is a sort of floating world money and loan market operating out of many centres — London, Luxemburg, Bahrain, Singapore, Hong Kong, and the Caribbean, to name only the largest.[16] The Eurodollar market trades in negotiable deposits of the world's largest banks, mainly, but in currencies other than that of the host country (usually in U.S. dollars). The link between Eurodollar markets and national money markets is that investors (prodded by investment dealers, who do the homework involved) will switch their lending from one market to another if expected yields differ significantly. This movement of funds keeps relative yields in world financial markets fairly close, after allowance for expected exchange-rate changes.

SECTION 4 The capital markets

Stocks, bonds, mortgages, term loans, and financial leases are the main forms of long-term borrowing instrument. Stocks and bonds each come in several varieties and have well-developed secondary markets such as the Toronto Stock Exchange. Mortgages are more homogeneous, generally shorter-term or with nominal yields adjustable during the life of the mortgage, and have a very limited secondary market.[17] Term loans generally are for terms of up to ten years and are intended for equipment

---

[16]In 1981 the United States allowed domestic banks to set up subsidiaries in the U.S. to conduct Eurodollar or offshore business, without being subject to domestic U.S. financial regulations. Thus, some Eurodollar business is now conducted out of New York.

[17]The secondary mortgage market is a wholesale market only in Canada, though a retail secondary market is developing in the United States. In Canada, many of the transactions are between banks and their mortgage loan subsidiaries, which keeps the market narrow and illiquid.

financing or for project financing (for large, independent new projects such as new plants) or for venture-capital loans (for startup or expansion of new firms). There is almost no resale market at all for term loans. Financial leases are long-term leases of large pieces of equipment such as ships and airplanes; the terms are almost as long as the useful life of the equipment being leased, in order to protect the lessor from ending up with expensive equipment that might be hard to lease out again. Leases also have no secondary market.[18]

We will look briefly at who participates in the capital markets and then describe how the two large secondary markets for stocks and bonds operate.

Borrowers

Table 5–2 showed which sectors issue stocks, bonds, and mortgages. The rows of table 5–2 for these three assets are repeated in table 5–8. Separate data on term loans and financial leases are not available, but the totals are relatively small. Financial leases are held mostly by specialized financial leasing companies, many of them, such as RoyLease, being subsidiaries of banks. Financial leases are "owed" by nonfinancial corporations. Term loans are included in the loan category of table 5–2 and cannot be separated out from regular short-term loans.

TABLE 5–8 Capital-market borrowers, December 31, 1981 (billions of dollars)

	Nonfinancial corporations	Banks and near-banks	Other financial institutions	Governments
Mortgages	27	—	—	—
Bonds	74	5	14	147
Stocks and claims held by associated firms	258	30	66	7
TOTAL DEBT AND STOCKS	567	356	230	220

Source: Statistics Canada, *Financial Flow Accounts*, Cat. 13–002, Fourth Quarter 1981.

Nonfinancial corporations are the only nonhousehold users of mortgage loans, and for good reason. A mortgage loan is a loan secured by real estate of some sort to protect the lender against default. Financial institutions do

[18]Many of the financial leases held by leasing companies are formally bought in a secondary market, in that they are originally arranged between a lessee and the dealer in the equipment being leased, but such rediscounted leases are rarely resold by the leasing companies.

not own enough real estate as a rule to be able to pledge it as collateral, and governments' credit would not be improved by pledging a national park or a highway as security. Larger nonfinancial corporations other than real estate developers typically use bonds rather than mortgages. Nonfinancial corporations and financial institutions all rely on stock issues from time to time as a source of new funds.

Lenders

Table 5–9 shows the distribution of holdings of mortgages, bonds, and stocks as of December 31, 1981, in more detail than table 5–8. The lenders in capital markets are more diverse than the borrowers. All sectors participate. Households hold mostly Canada Savings Bonds and mutual fund shares when they do hold primary borrowers' instruments at all; most of their long-term investments are made in financial institutions or in trust funds managed by financial institutions. Many of the stocks and bonds shown in table 5–9 as held by households are part of funds owned by households but managed on their behalf by professionals in trust companies. Governments play an active role in the capital markets as lenders, but almost always through one of their legion of financial institutions such as

TABLE 5–9 Holdings of stocks, bonds, and mortgages by sector, December 1981 (billions of dollars)

Sector	Stocks of subsidiaries	Other stocks	Bonds	Mortgages
Households and unincorporated business	—	105	47	9
Nonfinancial corporations				
private	60	2	0.3	5
public	1	0.1	1	0.2
Monetary authorities	—	—	12	—
Chartered banks	20	8	7	18
Near-banks	1	3	9	63
Insurance companies and pension funds	0.4	16	46	25
Other financial institutions				
private	26	5	8	5
public	0.8	1	8	14
Government				
federal	32	0.3	0.2	0.3
other	22	1	24	3
Social security funds	9	—	20	—
Rest of the world	88	5	59	1
TOTAL	261	146	240	144

Source: Statistics Canada, *Financial Flow Accounts*, Cat. 13–002, Fourth Quarter 1981.

the Canada Development Corporation. Governments themselves do very little lending.

In the stock and bond markets, as in the money market, it is possible for issuers to borrow in foreign currency as well as domestic currency. Many stock and bond issues are denominated in U.S. dollars and are actually issued in New York. Provincial governments have been conspicuous borrowers abroad, both in New York and in Europe. Only very large and well-known borrowers have access to the large-scale Eurobond market, but the ability of these borrowers to switch between domestic and Eurobond markets serves to keep domestic bond yields in line with those abroad.

Organization of the stock market

The stock market is largely a secondary market for issues of several types of shares. All are traded through brokers who usually act only as go-betweens rather than as principals and charge an explicit commission fee.[19] In some cases banks act as contacts between the public and the brokers; this is still a small part of the brokerage business, but many brokers are worried it will increase now that brokerage commission rates are unregulated. Stocks of larger companies with many shares outstanding are formally listed on one or more of Canada's five stock exchanges, and trade in them is carried out on the exchange floor. Other stocks trade *over the counter* in brokers' offices (over the telephone these days); this is known as the *OTC market.* Most trading is in listed stocks, traded on the exchange floor itself. The most active listed stocks are still traded "by open outcry" — with shouting and waving of hands — but the 780 less active listed stocks and small-volume trades of the active stocks (*odd-lot* orders) are now handled by interactive computer terminals in brokers' offices across Canada; this is the Computer-Assisted Trading System, or CATS. Eventually all trades are likely to be made over an interactive video computer terminal network, right out of brokers' offices. Stock exchanges as such will be only rule-making bodies. In the United States, the NASDAQ system (for National Association of Securities Dealers Automatic Quotation) is already close to being a complete video terminal market for stocks, operating out of dealers' offices.

Over-the-counter (OTC) market

The stocks traded in the stock market are basically either common or preferred. *Common shares* share in residual profit without limit, though they receive as cash only the amount declared as dividends. *Preferred shares* usually give up voting rights and also accept a ceiling on the dividend rate in exchange for being paid dividends before the common shareholders. Preferred shares are redeemable by the issuer as a rule, so

Common shares

Preferred shares

[19] The commission rates were 3 percent or less under the old, fixed commission schedule. As of April 1983 the Toronto Stock Exchange is on negotiated commissions, so the rates now vary more.

Retractable

Convertible

they are not permanent financing.[20] Some are also *retractable*; that is, redeemable at the discretion of the holder and/or convertible into common stock at a specified price. *Convertibility* gives the holder the protection of a preferred share and still the right to unlimited capital gains (by converting to common stock) if the company is wildly successful.

Trust units

Brokers will also trade over the counter such stocklike assets as *trust units* — basically partnership units in film productions, oil exploration programs, and specialized real estate development or mortgage lending programs. All these special programs provide special tax shelter when financed by trust units, or else they would be financed by shares and debt like all other investments.

New issues in the stock market are usually bought (underwritten) by large groups of brokers acting as principals and then resold to more permanent holders (known as *subscribers* when they buy in the new-issue market).[21] The new-issue mechanism is basically the same as for new money-market and bond-market issues, except that the money market deals only in wholesale amounts. Strangely, new-issue purchases are not handled on the floor of the stock exchange, though they can be resold there later if the stock is listed.

Organization of the bond market

The bond market is basically a long-term version of the money market, with many of the same dealers and customers. Trades are handled by dealers acting as principals and making their revenue from spreads between bid and asked prices.

Indenture agreement

The bonds traded are of two types: mortgage bonds and debentures. All bonds have an elaborate form of promissory note known as an *indenture agreement*, which specifies in great detail all the terms and conditions of the loan. Mortgage bonds have an explicit provision in the indenture agreement that, in event of default, the trustee acting for the bondholders can take possession (ahead of other creditors) of certain specified assets of the borrower to help recover their principal and interest. *Debentures* are just bonds without any special mortgage provision.

Debentures

Sinking fund

Most bonds have *sinking fund* arrangements, whereby the issuer agrees to put aside funds each year to redeem a portion of the bonds in advance of

---

[20]Issuers of preferred shares must usually agree to some restrictions, such as on use of assets or issue of new debts, in order to attract purchasers of their preferred shares. Later such a restriction may become onerous, and redeemability provides an acceptable way out for all concerned. Term preferred shares, widely used in the late 1970s, are redeemable on a fixed schedule, just like bonds.

[21]Occasionally, new issues are underwritten on a "best efforts" basis. The underwriting brokers charge a fixed commission (but smaller than they would expect from their spread in a normal underwriting) and pay the issuer whatever they are able to realize from their selling efforts. The uncertainty is borne by the issuer and not by the underwriter in such new issues.

the final maturity — a kind of instalment payment arrangement. The average term to redemption for such bonds is therefore less than the term to maturity. Some bonds have a purchase fund arrangement instead, which allows the issuer to buy back some of the issue and retire it if the price falls.

In recent years many bond issues have had new features added to make them more attractive and to lower the nominal coupon yield required. Some are convertible into preferred or even common shares at a specified price. Some are retractable (callable at the discretion of the holder) as well as callable at the discretion of the issuer. Some are extendible, which is exactly the opposite of retractable; longer-term issues are often retractable, shorter-term issues extendible. Some bonds, called income debentures, pay interest only if profits are sufficient, just like preferred shares.

New issues of bonds are underwritten by groups of bond dealers in the same way that stocks are. Banks participate as underwriters of some provincial and local government bonds, while the Bank of Canada is the sole underwriter for federal government issues. For larger issues of non-federal bonds, an underwriting group of up to twenty dealers, led by a managing or lead underwriter, agrees to take up the entire new issue at a fixed price. They and members of a larger selling group then try to find buyers for the issue, at a price high enough to leave them a comfortable profit margin. Smaller bond issues may be placed privately and directly with one or more large financial institutions such as pension funds.

SECTION 5 Summary

This chapter has presented an accounting framework, the National Capital Account, for describing and analysing the behavior of financial markets. Summary measures of the capital accounts provide measures of national wealth. Wealth is the difference between assets and debts; for the economy as a whole, wealth consists only of real assets, since financial assets are exactly cancelled out by debts. A flow version of the capital accounts, the Financial Flow Accounts, records changes in wealth, total assets, and total debts. Rows of the National Capital Account and the Financial Flow Accounts correspond to individual financial markets.

Individual financial markets differ in many ways other than by the type of financial instrument. Financial markets can be retail or wholesale, direct or indirect, private or public, competitive or not competitive, primary or secondary.

The money market and the capital markets are the main secondary markets of the financial system. The money market is relatively small, but it is very active and gives important signals to the rest of the economy, where rates are "posted" and adjust more slowly. Both money and capital markets are "made" by specialized investment dealers acting either as principals or (in the stock market) as brokers. The sales forces used in the secondary market are also used to distribute new issues of stocks, bonds, and money-market instruments when groups of dealers agree to underwrite new issues. Federal government Treasury Bills and bonds are the exception: Treasury Bills are issued weekly in a special closed-bid auction that is the centrepiece of the money market, while federal bonds are underwritten entirely by the Bank of Canada.

Questions for discussion

1. What is the equity of Acme Chemical if it has fixed assets that cost \$10 million originally, bonds outstanding of \$3 million, inventories of \$1 million, cash of \$0.5 million, and accumulated capital consumption allowances of \$4 million?
2. What extra information is needed to calculate private domestic wealth from table 5–2?
3. In which financial markets do banks and near-banks participate, according to tables 5–2 and 5–3?
4. Which sectors (taken as a whole) were important primary lenders in 1981? Which were important primary borrowers? Did any of the sectors dissave?
5. Explain the possible meanings of a negative entry in one of the financial-asset rows in the Financial Flow Accounts.
6. What are the characteristics of the typical financial market for household financial business?
7. What is a cumulative, retractable, convertible, term preferred share?
8. How does the activity or presence of the money-market jobbers improve the performance of the money market?

References

Binhammer, H.H. *Money, Banking and the Canadian Financial System*. 4th ed. Toronto: Methuen, 1982, chap. 9.

Boreham, G.F. *Money and Banking: Analysis and Policy in a Canadian Context*. 2d ed. Toronto: Holt, Rinehart and Winston, 1979, chaps. 4, 12, 13.

Neave, G. *Canada's Financial System*. Toronto: Wiley, 1981.

Neufeld, E.P. *The Financial System of Canada*. Toronto: Macmillan, 1972.

Sarpkaya, S. *The Money Market in Canada*. Toronto: Butterworths, 1980.

Shearer, Ronald, John Chant, and David Bond. *The Economics of the Canadian Financial System*. 2d ed. Toronto: Prentice-Hall, 1984.

Statistics Canada. *Financial Flow Accounts*. Cat. 13–002. Quarterly.

CHAPTER 6

Household Wealth Saving and Borrowing Behavior

Chapter 5 has described a rich and varied set of financial flows and stocks. Canadians have been channelling savings into a huge variety of assets, and to buy some of those assets they have supplemented their savings with large amounts of borrowed funds. The result has been an accumulation of large amounts of wealth in various forms, and large outstanding debt totals.

The stocks of assets held and of debts outstanding constitute demand and supply in each financial market, so if we are to understand financial markets we must understand what determines stocks of accumulated wealth and outstanding debts. This chapter is the first of five that will provide that understanding. In this chapter and chapter 7 I explain why some save and others borrow — why some add to their wealth while others add to their debts — and what that behavior depends upon. While this chapter deals with the relatively simple case of households, chapter 7 will deal with the more complicated case of firms — both business firms and financial institutions such as banks.

You will therefore learn in this chapter:

1. the logic of demand for wealth,
2. how a graphical tool can be used to analyse demand for wealth in a simple, two-period situation,
3. how actual Canadian savings and wealth patterns reflect the predictions of sections 1 and 2, and
4. the logic, the analysis, and the actual patterns of household borrowing in Canada.

The explanation is based partly on a look at a rational, typical household and partly on a review of aggregate data on the Canadian household sector. You can (and should) test the explanation for plausibility by seeing whether it fits your own family experience.

SECTION 1

Demand for wealth

Wealth seems so obviously a good thing that it is almost looking a gift horse in the mouth to ask why it should be wanted. Wealth is different from the other parts of a household's income, however: extra wealth gives no direct satisfaction to its holders, unless they are misers. Wealth is desired because it promises greater consumption in the future — either by the holder or by the holder's heirs. To test this idea, consider whether you would ever consider adding to your wealth by buying a condemned building, a defaulted bond, or a debt repayable only in free accommodation in Albania. None of these holdings offers much promise of future benefit.

What savers are buying when they add to their wealth is extra future consumption, in those future periods when the wealth will be sold off and the proceeds spent. More saving now means less current consumption, so the choice savers are making is between current and future consumption.

We will use two methods to develop the logic of consumption choice over time. First we will consider the lifetime consumption problem of a rational individual called Brown. This discussion will of necessity be relatively formal and algebraic. Then we will illustrate the essentials of the argument graphically for the two-period case of a hockey star called Jones.

The lifetime consumption problem of Sarah Brown

Brown chooses her consumption and savings levels over her remaining $n + 1$ years so as to maximize a utility function U that depends on real consumption C in current and future periods. That is, her objective is to choose the flow of current saving to maximize

$$U = U(C_0, C_1, \ldots, C_n),$$

where $C_0, C_1, \ldots, C_n$ are consumption levels in years $0, 1, \ldots, n$. Assume further that all consumption levels have positive but declining marginal utility and that all are normal goods.

Brown makes her decision knowing she will have a pattern of income flow $Y_0, Y_1, \ldots, Y_n$ that she cannot change. She does not have to spend in each future period exactly the income received in that period. She can borrow against future income to raise consumption now, or she can defer spending from now to later periods by adding to her wealth. Brown's spending constraint is that the total cost of her consumption over all periods must equal the total value of her income from all periods.

Total value of income is not just the sum of $Y_0, Y_1, \ldots$ and Y_n; when dollars of consumption and income are spent and received at different points of time, they are not all of equal value. Later income is less valuable to Brown than current income because she has less time left to earn interest on later income. A dollar of current income is better than a dollar of income next year by the amount of its extra potential interest, r per dollar.[1] Therefore next year's income is worth only the fraction $1/(1 + r)$ of the same income today. Let the discount factor D stand for the fraction $1/(1 + r)$. Income two years from now is worth only the fraction $[1/(1 + r)]^2 = D^2$ of the same income today, and so on for later periods. In general, income n years from now is worth only the fraction D^n of the same income today.

The same considerations apply to consumption at different points of time. Earlier consumption is more expensive, because \$1 of consumption deferred now will provide \$1(1 + r) of consumption next year. Next year's consumption therefore costs only $D = 1/(1 + r)$ as much as the same consumption today. Consumption n years from now is only $[1/(1 + r)]^n = D^n$ as expensive as the same consumption today.

When we discount future values to reflect potential interest earnings, Brown's income constraint is that the total *present discounted value* of consumption must equal the total present discounted value of available income; algebraically,

$$C_0 + C_1D + C_2D^2 + \ldots + C_nD^n = Y_0 + \ldots + Y_nD^n.$$

In this equation the discount factors D, D^2, and so on can be thought of as the prices of future consumption in years 1, 2, and so on, relative to consumption now.

The Brown model is abstract and formal so far. It may help to provide an example of her logic at work in our own financial affairs. When a family buys life insurance on the life of its major breadwinner, one of the problems is choosing the amount of insurance coverage to buy. What life insurance is usually designed to do is finance a stream of consumption over time for the survivors in the family. That stream of consumption is the extra consumption made possible by the major breadwinner's extra income. The amount of the death benefit required to provide that consumption stream is precisely the present discounted value of the consumption stream, calculated as on the left-hand side of Brown's spending constraint.

The optimal consumption stream

If Brown maximizes utility in choosing a lifetime consumption stream subject to the income constraint above, we know several things about her chosen consumption pattern. Since saving is income less consumption, and income is given exogenously for each period, then knowing about her consumption stream implies also knowing about her savings patterns and about her demand for wealth.

---

[1]The interest rate is a real rather than a nominal rate. It measures the extra future buying power available from deferring present consumption, not just the extra dollars available. It is also an after-tax rate.

She will choose to consume in any two periods i and j to the point where the relative marginal utilities of different periods' consumption levels (MU_i/MU_j) are just equal to their relative prices in the income constraint[2]—that is, until

$$\frac{MU_i}{MU_j} = \frac{D^i}{D^j} = D^{i-j}.$$

If $j = i + 1$ (that is, if periods i and j are just one year apart), the fraction D^{i-j} is just D^{-1}, or $1 + r$; the marginal utility of consumption in period i is $(1 + r)$ times the marginal utility of consumption a year later. When $j = i + 1$, the ratio MU_i/MU_j is by definition equal to $1 + MRTP$, where $MRTP$ is the *marginal rate of time preference*. Some of you encountered the marginal rate of time preference in section 5 of chapter 3 as a measure of savers' impatience to consume now rather than later. It is the proportional excess of current over future marginal utility from the same extra consumption in each period.

Marginal rate of time preference

Brown's derived demand for wealth

Brown's optimal choice of consumption over time implies that she will defer spending her income in all years where income is relatively high, unless needs (and therefore marginal utilities) are also high in those years. She will run down her accumulated wealth, or run up debts, in years where income is relatively low or where needs are high. The net effect is to smooth out the pattern of lifetime income into a pattern of consumption more closely resembling the pattern of lifetime consumption needs. Essentially she will save in fat years and use up savings plus interest in lean years, just like the ancient Egyptians in the story of Joseph in Egypt. If we, like Joseph, have some idea which years are likely to be fat and which are likely to be lean, we can then predict savings patterns.

For most households, there is a predictable life cycle of fat and lean years of earnings. The one shown in figure 6–1 is typical of many households.[3] For most families the years of peak consumption needs are

---

[2]The optimal conditions for Brown's equilibrium are derived from the first-order conditions for a maximum of $U(C_1, \ldots, C_n)$ subject to the income constraint. The first-order conditions can be found by setting to zero the partial derivatives of the Lagrangean function

$$L = U(C_0, \ \ldots, C_n) - g(C_0 + C_1D + \ldots + C_nD^n - Y_0 - \ \ldots \ - Y_nD^n)$$

with respect to $C_0, \ldots, C_n$ and g. These first-order conditions are

$$MU_i - gD^i = 0, \text{ for } i = 1, \ \ldots, n,$$

and the income constraint.

[3]The life-cycle approach to saving behavior was developed by Franco Modigliani and Richard Brumberg, "Utility Analysis and the Consumption Function: An Interpretation of Cross-section Data," in K.K. Kurihara, ed., *Post-Keynesian Economics* (New Brunswick, N.J.: Rutgers University Press, 1954).

FIGURE 6–1 A typical life cycle

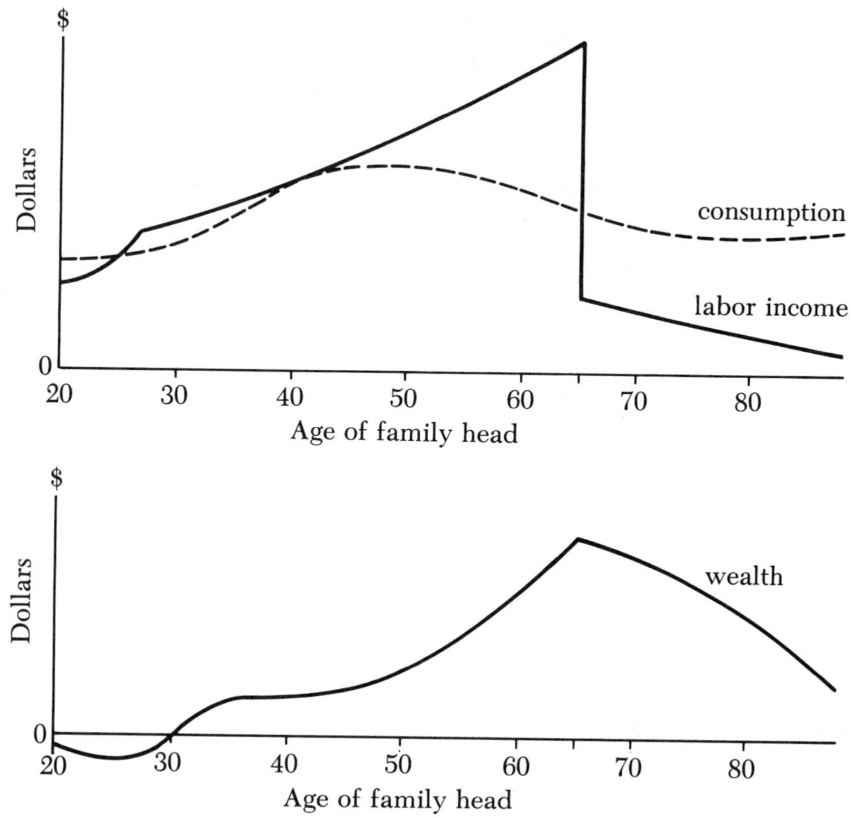

The upper panel shows a typical income pattern: one or both spouses settling into careers, with steadily rising real incomes to retirement, at which point labor income drops abruptly. Consumption needs reflect the family's growth. Gaps between income and consumption represent flows of saving or dissaving. These flows add to or subtract from wealth as shown in the lower panel.

those in which the parents are in their thirties and forties, when children begin to eat more, demand fancier toys, and go to university. When the children leave home, consumption needs drop abruptly. Salary income continues to grow to retirement and then drops to nearly zero.

With that typical profile of needs and incomes, Brown would borrow against future income in the early years and save up in the peak earning years to pay off debts acquired earlier and provide for retirement. Brown's wealth would therefore start small and maybe even become negative for a while, then grow larger at an increasing rate up to retirement age, and finally shrink during retirement to whatever she planned to leave to her heirs.

For many families the years of low income will not all be during retirement. Layoffs, unemployment, and recessions will each generate temporary periods of low income that must be provided for somehow. Brown would plan on accumulating extra wealth for such emergencies as well.

Factors affecting saving behavior

Brown's demand for wealth is just the cumulative result of her past and current decisions to save out of income, so her demand for wealth depends on the same factors as her decision to save; anything that increases savings automatically increases demand for wealth, and vice versa. Brown's savings decision depends on (1) her marginal rate of time preference, *MRTP* (her tastes or needs for present versus future consumption), (2) the income pattern that makes up her income constraint, and (3) the interest rate available.

MRTP

Brown's tastes for present versus future consumption will depend most of all on her family situation. If she is in the middle of raising three children, her current needs will be relatively large and so will her MRTP. If she is single, her current needs will be more or less the same as for future years, so her MRTP will be smaller and might even be zero.

Income

Brown's income pattern will be strongly influenced by her age. If she is just starting out after graduation, her salary will be low relative to that expected in future years. If she is nearing retirement, her current salary will be large relative to that expected in the future (after retirement).

If Brown's current income rises and she does not expect the increase to last, the incease is known as transitory income.[4] Brown will attempt to spread its benefits over the remaining years as well, by consuming little of it in the current year. Her saving and demand for wealth will rise by almost the full amount of the transitory income increase. The extra wealth may be in the form of financial assets, or real assets such as housing or consumer durables.

If the increase in current income is expected to last a lifetime, it is known as *permanent income*. Brown does not need to spread it, because

Permanent income

[4]This is the central part of Milton Friedman's permanent income hypothesis of consumption behavior, first presented in *A Theory of the Consumption Function* (New York: National Bureau of Economic Research, 1955). Friedman added an expectations hypothesis: that households expect income changes to be permanent only after they have persisted for several years. His addition is not necessary to the central part of the theory.

future years are as well looked after by this income increase as the current year, so she spends it. Savings do not rise.

Finally, it is possible to imagine an increase in expected future income, without any change in current income at all. A deferred profit-sharing bonus received from your employer is one example. Brown would attempt to spread such an income increase forward in time, to enjoy some of its benefits now. With her future consumption better looked after out of future income, Brown would do less saving for it now, consuming instead. Demand for wealth would fall.[5]

Interest-rate changes
A change in the rate of interest available will have some effect, but even the direction of effect will differ between individuals in otherwise identical circumstances. "Target savers" with a specific future expense in mind will respond to higher interest rates by cutting down on their saving: if higher interest earnings allow them to buy their dream cottage at the lake with smaller savings flows now, they seize the chance and cut their current savings level; their savings and demand for wealth fall. Those with easily expandable tastes for future consumption will respond the opposite way. For them, a higher interest rate means that a dollar of savings now buys more future consumption. The price of future consumption (the discount factor D in Brown's spending constraint) has fallen. They take advantage of the lower price by diverting more current income to the future. Their savings and demand for wealth rise.

To summarize, the determinants of Brown's savings and demand for wealth are her income pattern now and in the future, her tastes for current versus future consumption (her MRTP), and the interest rate available. Her remaining future income pattern will depend particularly on her age, while her tastes for present versus future consumption will depend particularly on her age and family status.

Demand for wealth for the whole economy will also depend on the number of households like the Brown family and on the distribution of those families among age and family size groups.

SECTION 2 A graphical explanation of saving behavior

Brown's saving behavior can be explained graphically as well as with the algebra of the preceding section. In order to keep the diagrams simple, we will switch from Brown's multi-period problem to one of merely two periods: the case of Stan Jones.

[5]Professor Martin Feldstein has argued, for instance, that the prospect of greater future Social Security benefits in the United States has reduced by 30 to 50 percent the need for households to save out of current disposable income. "Social Security, Induced Retirement, and Aggregate Capital Accumulation," *Journal of Political Economy*, Sept.–Oct. 1974, 905–26.

Jones is a hockey star who thinks of his life as having two periods: his professional career and "afterwards" — his retirement. These two periods are large; their midpoints are twenty years apart. Jones has a fantastic income now, thanks to his talents and those of his agent, but in retirement he would be lucky to earn the average industrial wage. His total income Y_1 during his brief professional career is \$2 000 000. His total income Y_2 during the rest of his life is only \$200 000. Jones' utility depends only on current consumption C_1 and consumption in retirement C_2. Both streams of consumption have positive but declining marginal utility. Jones is well advised by assorted financial representatives and accountants and earns an impressive real after-tax yield of 5 percent per year on his accumulated savings. Over the average twenty-year span between the middle of his professional career and the middle of his retirement period, that 5 percent per year cumulates to a total return of 170 percent, in effect more than doubling his savings contributions between date of savings and date of use. A dollar saved at the midpoint of his professional career thus permits \$2.70 of extra consumption at the midpoint of his retirement period (\$1.70 of compound interest, and the \$1.00 of principal returned).

Figure 6–2 shows Jones' situation for these two periods on a diagram associated with Irving Fisher, a famous American economist of the early twentieth century.[6] Current consumption is measured along the horizontal axis, and future consumption along the vertical axis. The point P_0 is where Jones would be if he saved nothing, consuming all of his hockey income now, and had only his retirement income in retirement. P_0 is called his *endowment point* because it reflects the pattern of income with which he is endowed.

Endowment point

The other points of possible consumption patterns for Jones lie along a line through P_0 with slope of $-(1 + 1.70)$. This is $-(1 + r)$, where the interest rate for the twenty-year period is 170 percent. Jones can give up any amount of current consumption below P_0 and will get an extra \$2.70 of future consumption for each dollar saved. Jones could also borrow against future income, but he would have to give up \$2.70 of future consumption for every \$1 of extra current consumption. The present discounted value of his consumption stream must equal the present discounted value of his income stream, which is \$2 000 000 + \$200 000/(1 + 1.70) =\$2 074 000.

Figure 6–2 also shows a few of Jones' indifference curves. These indifference curves reflect Jones' tastes for current relative to future consumption. Each single indifference curve joins together all of the combinations of current and future consumption that Jones regards as equally desirable (that is, between which he is indifferent). Indifference curves closer to the top right reflect higher levels of satisfaction than those closer to the origin.

---

[6]Irving Fisher, *The Role of Interest* (New York: Macmillan, 1907). A modern rediscovery of Fisher's work is Jack Hirshleifer, "On the Theory of Optimal Investment," *Journal of Political Economy*, Aug. 1958.

FIGURE 6–2 Two-period consumption choice of a hockey star

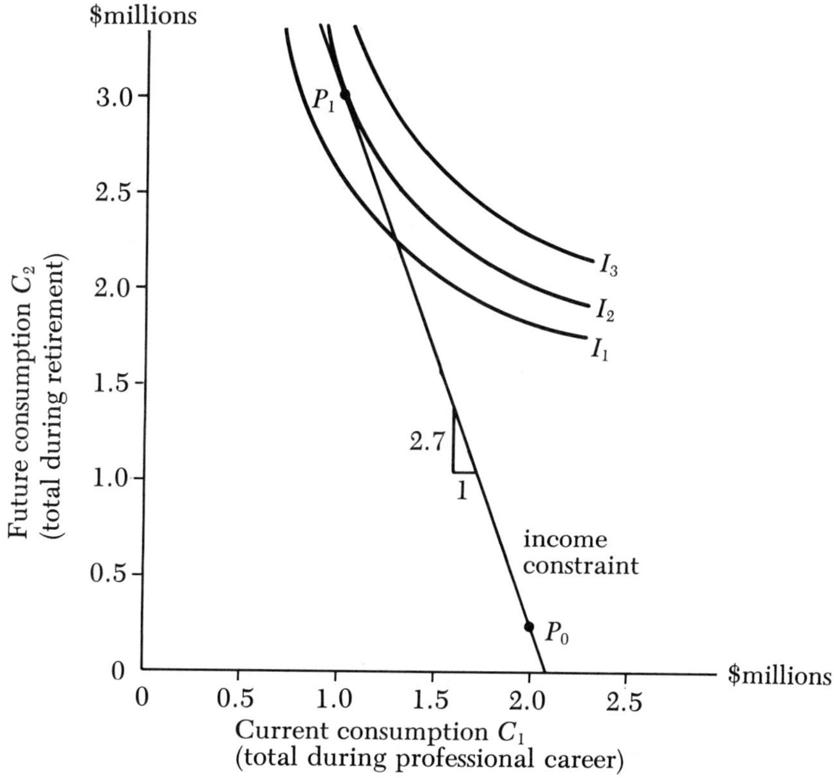

P_0 is Jones' endowment point; P_1 is his optimal point. The line through P_0 and P_1 is his income-constraint line, with slope of $-(1 + r)$. The interest rate r is 1.70, or 170 percent over the period between the midpoint of his hockey career and the midpoint of his retirement.

The optimal consumption choice

With the help of his agent, Jones chooses the point on his income-constraint line with the highest utility; that is, lying on his highest indifference curve. That point, P_1, is at a total current consumption of \$1 000 000 and a total future consumption of \$2 900 000. Since the optimal point P_1 is the point of tangency of indifference curve and constraint line, their slopes must be equal. The slope of Jones' indifference curve is the ratio $-MU_1/MU_2$. The ratio MU_1/MU_2 is Jones' marginal rate of substitution between current and future consumption, or $1 + MRTP$. At Jones' optimal point, $MRTP$ must equal r at 1.70, and MU_1/MU_2 must be 2.70. For Jones to want to spend any

FIGURE 6–3 Effect of transitory income

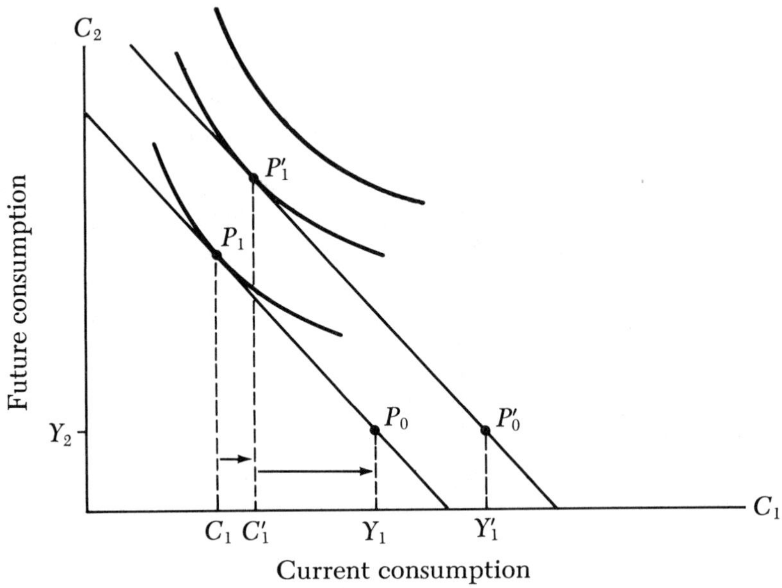

The endowment point P_0 is moved to the right. Consumption increases now and in the future. Current saving rises to provide the extra future consumption.

more of his income now, it must yield at least 2.7 times as much satisfaction as it would yield in retirement. Otherwise Jones would be better off postponing the extra dollar of current consumption and getting an extra \$2.70 of retirement consumption.[7]

With current income of \$2 000 000 and current consumption of only \$1 000 000, Jones' current demand for wealth is \$1 000 000. By retirement his wealth will grow to \$2 700 000, at which point he will spend it; his demand for wealth will then fall to zero again (Jones is a childless orphan who leaves no estate).

[7]If present and future consumption are close substitutes for Jones, he will choose a much larger total future consumption, enough to provide an annual income greater than during his professional hockey years. How much larger future consumption would be in an optimal consumption pattern depends on the elasticity of substitution of current and future consumption, how much rearrangement of the two it takes to push Jones' marginal rate of time preference up to the twenty-year yield of 170 percent. It does not follow from this model that next year's consumption will automatically be $(1 + r)$ times this year's consumption. Jones' tastes are not that mechanical.

Factors affecting Jones' saving

Figure 6–2 can be used to illustrate the effects of changes in income, tastes, and interest rates on savings and the demand for wealth. Figure 6–3 shows that higher income in the first period only (an increase in transitory income) will move the endowment point P_0 horizontally to the right. Desired current consumption will increase, but only by a small fraction of the income increase. Savings will increase by the difference between income increase and consumption increase. An increase in permanent income would move the endowment point P_0 both to the right and upward, with quite different results for saving. Figuring out those results is left as an exercise for the reader.

Figure 6–4 shows the effect of a higher marginal rate of time preference. Greater impatience or more urgent current needs will steepen indifference curves. Desired current consumption will increase, so current savings and demand for wealth will fall.

One of the stranger conclusions of our analysis in this section has been that changes in the interest rate do not have any obvious effect on total saving. Some people save more, others save less; the total amount of savings may change in either direction or not change at all. Figure 6–5 shows two possible effects of the same increase in interest rates. In panel (a) the indifference curves are sharply curved, implying that the *MRTP* changes

FIGURE 6–4 Effect of higher marginal rate of time preference

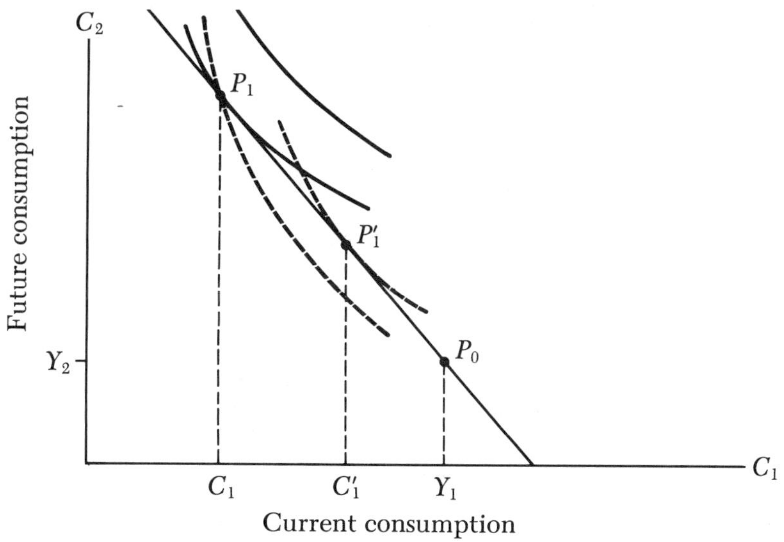

Higher *MRTP* means steeper indifference curves at any point such as P_1. The solid indifference curves are replaced by the dotted indifference curves. Optimal current consumption C_1 increases to C_1', and saving falls by the same amount, as the individual moves to a new optimal point P_1'. The endowment point P_0 is unchanged, and so is the spending-constraint line.

FIGURE 6–5 Effect of higher interest rate on current saving

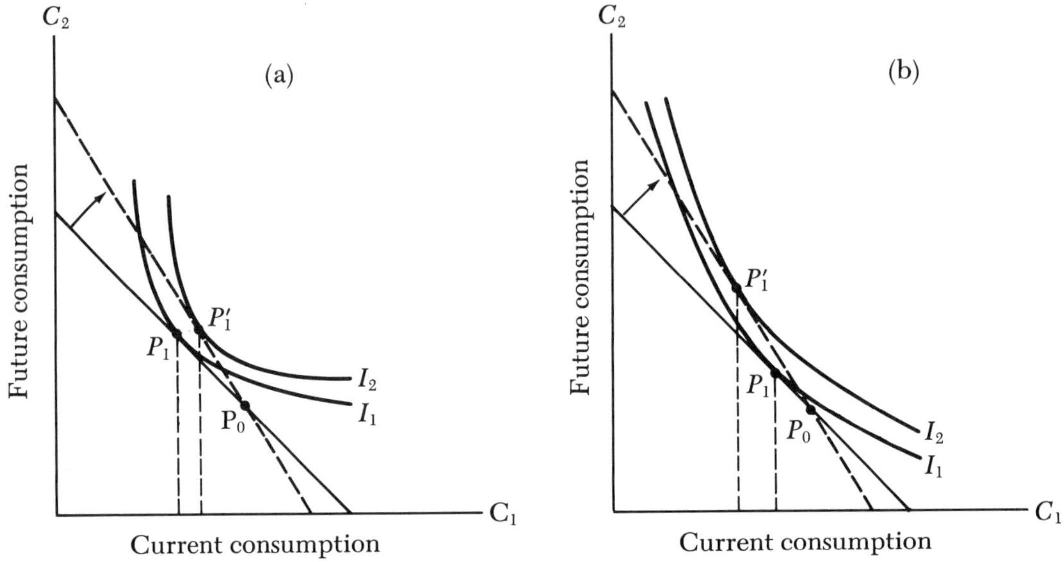

The endowment point P_0 and the two income-constraint lines are the same in both panels. Higher interest rates cause the constraint line to pivot clockwise around P_0. In panel (a) the saver's tastes are such that the new equilibrium P_1' has more current consumption and less saving. In panel (b), different but still plausible tastes lead to less current consumption and more saving.

quickly as levels of current and future consumption change (technically, a low elasticity of substitution of current for future consumption). The response to a higher interest rate is to consume more now, to cut down on current saving, and to demand less wealth.

In panel (b), indifference curves are less sharply curved. *MRTP* is less sensitive to consumption levels. Current and future consumption are more easily substitutable. In panel (b), higher interest rates cause less current consumption, more current saving, and greater demand for wealth. For a nation with some individuals having each type of taste, the net effect of an interest-rate increase on total savings and demand for wealth cannot be predicted from theory alone; the net effect is an empirical question.[8]

Income and substitution effects

An increase in the interest rate changes the price of current relative to future consumption. The effect of price changes on demand is typically broken down in economics into a *substitution effect* and an *income effect*.

[8]Most studies of consumption behavior have not found the effect of interest rates to be significant either way.

FIGURE 6–6 Income and substitution effects of interest rates

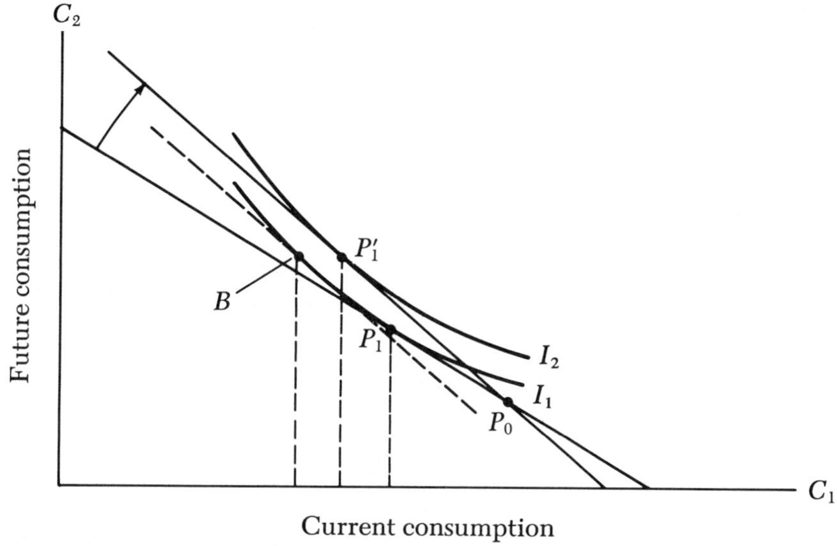

A higher interest rate pivots the constraint line clockwise around the endowment point P_0. The substitution effect is a shift from P_1 to the point B, along the same indifference curve. Current consumption is lowered, current saving raised. The income effect is a shift from B to the new optimal point P_1'. Current saving is lowered, and current consumption raised. The total effect is a move from P_1 to P_1', the sum of income and substitution effects.

Substitution effect

This is done in figure 6–6. The substitution effect always leads to a drop in current consumption and a rise in savings and the demand for wealth, since current consumption has become relatively more expensive. How large the substitution effect is depends on the curvature of indifference curves, which varies between individuals. The income effect leads in the opposite direction, to increase current consumption and reduce demand for wealth. How large the income effect is depends on how much the individual had planned to save (or had already saved).

Income effect

SECTION 3

Household wealth and saving patterns

We have seen what Brown and Jones would save, but Brown and Jones are models, rational by assumption. Is there any sign that actual households come close enough to Brown's behavior for Brown to be a useful predictor of actual demand for wealth? This section briefly reviews some evidence.

We expect wealth to rise with age up to retirement, and then to fall. Wealth will rise both because of age, since savings in early years will have had more time to cumulate and compound, and because income typically rises with experience and seniority. Table 6–1 shows that pattern for typical Canadians. Income rises up to age 55, then tails off and drops

TABLE 6–1 Income and wealth patterns by age, 1977 (dollars)

Age of household head	Income	Wealth
Under 25	9 444	5 466
25–34	16 643	23 664
35–44	20 395	57 257
45–54	21 056	74 405
55–64	16 818	70 300
65 and over	8 604	47 074

Notes: Data are averages for all families and unattached individuals in the sample of the fifth Survey of Consumer Finances, carried out in spring 1977. Families make up 72 percent of the survey. Wealth is total marketable assets less debt. Total marketable assets does not include claims against employer-sponsored pension plans, claims against social security, and human capital.

Source: Statistics Canada, *The Distribution of Income and Wealth in Canada,* Cat. 13–570, 1977, 34.

steeply at 65, when most people retire. Wealth rises to age 55 and is drawn down thereafter.

From the model describing Brown's behavior, we might well expect wealth to be negative for those under 25. Where Brown realizes that her starting salary is only half or less (in real terms) of what it will be twenty years later, it makes little sense for her to do any significant amount of saving out of her starting salary. She should be borrowing to supplement that starting salary. If she did so, her wealth would be negative, like that of students who live off Canada Student Loans during university years. There is no sign in table 6–1 of such behavior. Instead, there is a surprisingly large amount of wealth accumulated by those under 25.

Part of the explanation is that consumption needs are lower before families have children. Most of the explanation is that actual households are not as free to borrow as we assumed for Sarah Brown. Lenders just will not lend money for long periods for consumption; they insist on rapid repayment, which keeps debts down and savings up.

Since families have lifetime income patterns in which incomes rise to retirement and then fall off abruptly, their asset holdings should reflect a desire to build up assets for retirement. There should be a large stock of long-term assets. (It is possible to hold a long series of short-term assets for long periods, but the transactions costs are large over twenty-year periods.) If the other motivation for saving is to build a nest egg for emergencies (low-income or high-need periods, which might occur anytime), families' asset holdings should include a significant stock of liquid assets.

Both effects are clearly reflected in household asset holdings. Table 6–2 gives a breakdown of household financial assets, a more detailed breakdown of the first column of the National Capital Account in table 5–2.

TABLE 6–2 Financial assets and debts of persons and unincorporated business, December 1981 (billions of dollars)

Asset category	Asset holdings	Debts
Currency and bank deposits	96	—
Deposits in other institutions	77	—
Foreign currency and deposits	8	—
Consumer credit	1	45
Trade credit	—	8
Bank loans	—	23
Other loans	—	8
Treasury Bills and short-term paper	5	—
Mortgages	15	112
Government of Canada bonds	25	—
Provincial, municipal, and corporate bonds	14	—
Life insurance and pensions	95	—
Stocks	118	—
Foreign investments	3	—
Other financial assets	18	—
TOTAL	475	196

Source: Statistics Canada, *Financial Flow Accounts*, Cat. 13–002, Fourth Quarter 1981.

The major asset for most households (well over half of total assets) is the house, a very long-term asset indeed. The next most important, though much less common, is equity in a family business, which is likely to be long-term as well. Of the financial assets, life insurance and pension assets (literally, entitlements to future pension benefits in a pension plan) are intended mostly for use much later on. Many households also have large holdings of other, more liquid assets in Registered Retirement Savings Plans (RRSPs). These are a tax-sheltered savings vehicle discussed more fully in chapter 15. Many of the assets in RRSPs are intended only for use in retirement. The longest-term asset of all is common stocks of corporations, which some households own either directly or through owning shares in mutual funds. Some of these are intended to be traded; others are held for much longer periods.

By 1981, households had also accumulated a large nest egg of liquid assets. Deposits of various sorts dominate their holdings of financial assets, and almost all of the deposits are either notice deposits or fixed-term deposits for short terms from ninety days to three years. Most of the deposits are in chartered banks, in either Canadian or foreign currency, but there are significant amounts held in trust companies, mortgage loan companies, insurance companies, credit unions and caisses populaires, and brokerage firms. Holdings of Canada Savings Bonds (CSBs) also fall into the liquid-asset category, since Canada Savings Bonds are redeemable on demand at face value plus accrued interest. CSBs are medium-term bonds at date of issue, but their instant redeemability at face value makes them close substitutes for short-term bank deposits.

Table 6–2 shows the stock of wealth in 1981, produced by saving before and during 1981. A reprinted article from *The Globe and Mail* describes how changes in the level of wealth can cause changes in flows of saving. When wealth falls — whether by loss of assets or just by decreases in asset values — saving must be increased if wealth is to be restored; the article suggests that most Canadians do try to repair such damage to their wealth levels, rather than just accept the prospect of lower future consumption.

Worried over house prices, Canadians keep saving

By Peter Cook

One reason consumers have yet to lead the Canadian economy down the road to recovery is that many families have experienced a decline in their net worth that has made them reluctant to spend.

In the past, even during periods of recession, household net worth in Canada continued to grow, providing a general sense of well-being.

Accustomed to being better off and to seeing their personal wealth grow, consumers in the past 18 months have been shocked into an awareness that some treasured investments are not guaranteed or secure money makers. Most important of all, Canadians have seen the value of their homes go down.

Throughout the 1960s when economic growth was rapid and the 1970s when expansion was hesitant, and largely because of inflation, a great deal of reliance was placed on the property market. The notion was that the price of a house bought today would not only increase in value tomorrow but would stay ahead of inflation.

In the main, this proved to be true. Figures from the Canadian Real Estate Association show that, from 1975 to 1981, the average price of homes covered by multiple listing service sales rose to $78 466 from $45 878. There were increases every year; the gains in the three years, 1979–81, were 10.8 percent, 11.1 percent and 13.1 percent.

Last year, however, the pattern changed. During a year when the inflation rate was running at an average 10.8 percent, house prices tumbled by 6.6 percent to $73 323 — producing for many families a startling fall in the single asset that represents their largest and most crucial investment.

On the surface, a decline in housing prices is of concern only to those who are selling their homes. But most economists think the repercussions of a drop in house prices go much deeper.

Even if, on paper, it does not affect their daily spending habits, people are conscious that their net worth has fallen; as a result, they are often unwilling to commit themselves to making new purchases or increasing levels of household debt. Instead, they concentrate on increasing their savings as a cushion for the future.

"Most households take stock of their wealth," said Percy Thadaney, manager of national forecasting at Toronto-based Data Resources of Canada, "and when you have a fall in the value of people's homes, that is something pretty basic. It's not like the TSE (Toronto Stock Exchange) going up or down, which affects far fewer people directly."

Mr. Thadaney worries that in the current economic climate, house prices will continue to come down. This fall, in turn, would engender more caution among consumers and could serve to postpone an economic recovery.

Nearly all observers agree that a drop in house prices is not as great a blow to consumer morale as some other trends; for example, there is greater concern among people about high unemployment and a lack of job security.

Still, few doubt than an established link exists between falling house prices and consumer pessimism. Nor is the link very surprising. For all but an older generation of Canadians who can recall the 1930s, it is a novel experience for people to be locked into housing investments that are declining in value.

Frank Clayton of Clayton Research Associates of Toronto thinks the poor housing market is a negative factor for the economy, but he said the impact has varied across the country.

"If you bought a house in Vancouver for $160 000 and it is now worth $110 000, then you have a reason to worry," he said. "But in Toronto, where prices have come down by only 4 or 5 percent, it is not likely to be a big factor."

Mr. Clayton makes the same point about any revival in the housing market and in home prices.

Edmonton and Calgary have an oversupply of serviced lots, while in Toronto there is a serious undersupply.

But any revival will take time. There may be signs now of a rebound in lower-priced homes, spurred on by government grant programs to aid house buyers, Mr. Clayton said.

But this is far from creating a robust market and, "looking at the way the world is now, it will probably not be until 1984 that people start moving back into the market in a big way and prices really start to move up."

A long delay before house prices start to rise is what worries economists. Until prices — and not just housing activity — pick up, many argue that consumers will continue to behave conservatively, showing a preference for saving and rebuilding their net worth rather than spending.

Source: *The Globe and Mail*, Toronto, January 31, 1983.

SECTION 4

Supply of financial assets: household borrowing

Financial assets are debts to the issuer, so the supply of financial assets is the stock of debts outstanding (as discussed in chapter 5). Debt outstanding rises only when the flow of borrowing exceeds the flow of repayments; all debts involve some steady flow of repayment, so it takes a significant flow of new borrowing just to keep the stock of debt from shrinking.

Some household debts can be reduced at the discretion of the debtor, by early repayment (for example, demand loans and open mortgages, as opposed to fixed-instalment loans and closed mortgages), but the main reason why outstanding debt changes over time is that the amount of new borrowing changes.

Household borrowing is often classified as one of three types: consumer debt, either unsecured or else secured by a chattel mortgage on consumer durables; home mortgage debt, to buy a house; and investment loans, to buy income-earning assets. The first two categories share the important feature that they are to be repaid out of future wage and salary income. Investment loans may well be repaid out of income generated by the assets bought. This becomes an important distinction when we consider supply under risk in chapter 10. Investment loans by households are relatively small in total. They share most of the features of business borrowing (dealt with in chapter 7), so they will not be discussed separately here.

Consumer borrowing to cover current expenses, such as travel loans or Canada Student Loans, is simply dissaving, letting consumption exceed income. That is an outcome to be expected on occasion from the decision model developed in section 1 for Brown.

A medical-student example

The sort of situation that gives rise to borrowing for current consumption is easily illustrated on a two-period Fisher diagram similar to figure 6–2. Figure 6–7 shows the situation of a medical student, Casey, who has a large future income prospect Y_2 and small current income Y_1. He can borrow against future income at an interest rate r, giving himself an interest-constraint line through his endowment point P_0 with slope $-(1 + r)$. His optimum point P_1 is one with more current consumption C_1 than current income Y_1, and he borrows the difference. His outstanding debt or supply of financial assets is therefore $(C_1 - Y_1)$ by the end of year 1. Next year he repays that debt with interest out of Y_2, consuming only what is left.

The example of Casey is different from that of Jones in two respects. First, Casey borrows while Jones saved in the first year; Casey therefore has negative wealth while Jones had positive wealth. Second, the effect of a higher interest rate is unambiguous for Casey: his borrowing falls. For Casey, both the income effect and the substitution effect of a rise in interest rate will reduce his demand for current consumption and therefore

FIGURE 6–7 Consumer borrowing

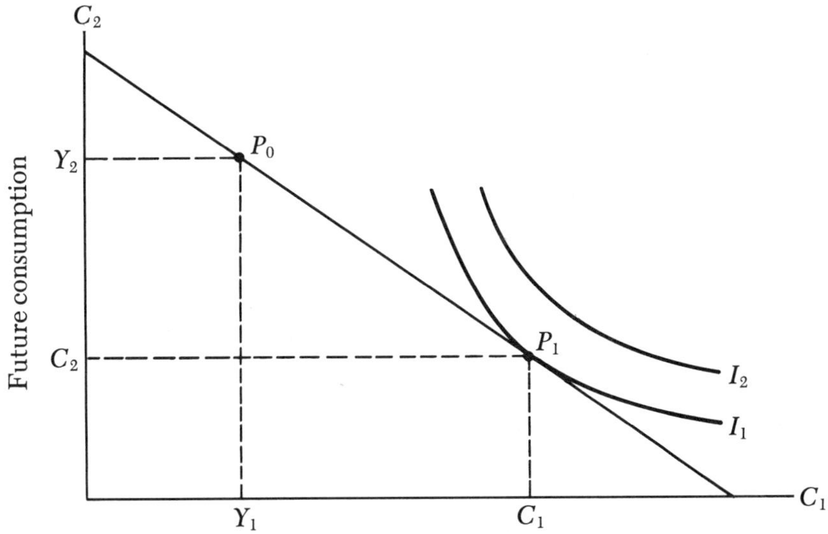

Casey, the medical student, has much larger future income Y_2 than current income Y_1. His optimal consumption pattern is C_1 now and C_2 later, which means borrowing $C_1 - Y_1$ now and repaying it out of Y_2 later (with interest). Casey's demand for wealth is therefore negative, in the amount $(C_1 - Y_1)$. Casey's optimal point is at P_1, where the income-constraint line is tangent to the highest attainable indifference curve.

increase his saving and demand for wealth. Figure 6–8 illustrates the effect of an interest-rate increase on Casey's saving, showing income and substitution effects. Intuitively it is easy to see that pivoting the constraint line clockwise around Casey's endowment point P_0 will result in lower current consumption. This means less borrowing and less debt outstanding — a smaller supply of financial assets from Casey. Future consumption may rise or fall depending on the curvature of Casey's indifference curves, but current consumption cannot help but fall.

Borrowing to finance durable assets

Most household borrowing is not for current expenses like Casey's high living in medical school. Most of it is to finance the purchase of large assets like freezers, cars, or the family home. The borrowing reflects lumpiness of particular kinds of consumption. In North America the services of single-family dwellings, freezers, boats, and many other consumer durables are available only in multi-year packages, by buying title to the durable for its whole life. Cars and especially houses can be rented, but the price is such that most people find outright ownership more attractive.

FIGURE 6–8 Effect of higher interest rates on borrowers

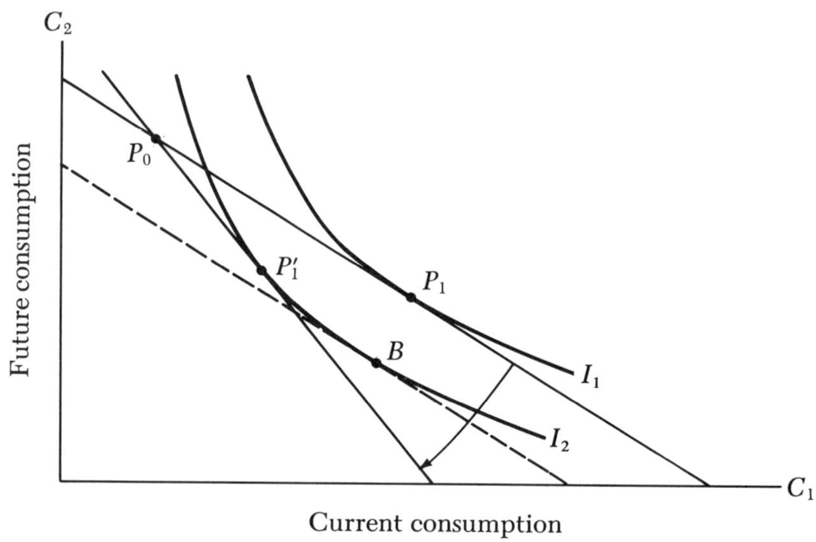

Higher interest rates pivot the constraint line clockwise around the endowment point P_0. The income effect (from a parallel shift of the constraint line inward) is to move the borrower from P_1 to B. The substitution effect is to move the borrower along the same indifference curve from B to P_1'. Both effects reduce current consumption and increase saving (or reduce dissaving).

Even though the services of durable assets must be bought in a large lump in advance, they need not be paid for in advance out of current income. Instead, the asset is bought all at once and paid for slowly over many years. Borrowing to finance asset purchases seldom causes negative wealth, since the extra debt is matched or more than matched by extra assets. The reason is partly that those who supply the funds to finance such purchases often take a lien on the asset bought; to protect themselves in case the asset must be sold in an emergency at fire-sale prices, they usually insist that their loan be no more than 60 to 80 percent of the asset's regular market value. The remaining value of the asset, the down payment, must generally be put up by the buyer. The down payment is an addition to wealth, though only if it has come from current saving.

Supply of financial assets to buy lumpy real assets must reflect (a) demand for real assets, (b) the down payment, and (c) the repayment schedule chosen by the buyer. Only the difference between purchase price and down payment need be borrowed, and the slower the repayment schedule, the more debt is outstanding at any time.

Optimal and actual debt-repayment schedules

Demand for housing and consumer durables is determined by consumer tastes for their services (in turn influenced by the number and age of children), by the relative price or the price to rental ratio of the real asset, and by income levels, as for any other good or service. The amount of down payment and the repayment schedule would rationally be determined as part of allocating the remaining consumption spending over various periods. Optimally, Brown would fix the repayments such that relative marginal utilities of consumption in different periods MU_i/MU_j would be equal to the relative opportunity cost ratio D^{i-j}. This means paying loans back mainly out of high-income years, or before children are born, or after they have left.

Actual households are prevented from arranging such optimal repayment schedules. Lenders usually insist on a significant down payment, so the asset must be paid for partly out of current income. Further, the repayment schedule of a loan is often tied to the depreciation schedule of the asset bought. Lenders will supply funds for long periods only with a lien on the asset for security, and they are careful to see that the remaining value of the asset always exceeds the remaining balance on the loan. Mortgages on homes are therefore available for periods of up to thirty years, whereas loans for cars are available only for periods of up to five years. Unsecured loans such as credit card loans are for still shorter terms.

The mortgage "tilt" problem in an inflationary world

Mortgage debt can be spread over decades. The nominal principal repayments on the typical mortgage are heavily concentrated in the later years, just as in an optimal repayment schedule for most households. In real terms, however, the inflation of the 1970s and the expected inflation of the 1980s have made real repayments of mortgage debt larger in early years and smaller in the final years. This causes households' disposable income and consumption to be more highly tilted to the future and their debt repayment more tilted to the present than most people would choose.

Just why this tilt occurs needs some explanation. With 10 percent inflation, the lender's principal shrinks in real terms at 10 percent per year. The lender insists on adding an extra 10-percent payment, called an *inflation premium*, to the interest payment. (How this occurs is discussed fully in chapter 14.) In receiving the inflation premium, the lender effectively gets almost 10 percent of the principal back in the first year. The early repayment of course comes out of the borrower's first-year income. Later on, the remaining debt is much smaller in real terms and in relation to the borrower's income (which will be higher both because of career advancement and because of inflation). The interest and principal installment payment is therefore a much smaller fraction of income in those later years. This is a perverse pattern of repayments. The perversity may

Inflation premium

disappear if inflation subsides or if mortgage debts come to be indexed, but in the meanwhile it imposes a purely artificial, institutional barrier in the way of young home-buyers.

Actual household debt patterns

Actual patterns of outstanding debt are shown in table 6-3 for the various age levels. Since debt must be issued when durable assets are bought, and the assets are needed first at early stages in the family life cycle, debts are largest in the early years.

Repayment schedules are relatively short, so nonmortgage debt disappears quickly after it is taken out. Mortgage debt lasts longer. Nonmortgage debt could be renewed as household appliances need to be replaced, but households buy more of their replacements outright or with large down payments as they become better-off. Consumer debts therefore dwindle with age.

Table 6–4 shows two breakdowns of debt by type of debt: the first is for the same household sample whose assets are shown in table 6–3, and the second is from the National Capital Account in table 5–2. Mortgage loans clearly dominate. Housing is the largest asset by far, and mortgage borrowing to finance it could be expected to dominate household debt. Other types of debt are available mainly from banks and credit unions, and in two forms: *fixed-instalment debt*, with a fixed interest rate and a level payment and a fixed term; and *floating-rate demand loans*, for which the repayment schedule is constrained only by a deadline for final payment.

Fixed-instalment debt

Floating-rate demand loans

TABLE 6–3 Debt patterns by age

Age of household head	Value of total marketable assets (dollars)	Value of total debt (dollars)	Percentage of households reporting	
			Any debt	Mortgage debt
under 25	9 920	4 474	80	34
25–34	37 384	13 720		
35–44	70 340	13 083	83	52
45–54	83 227	8 822	73	40
55–64	74 156	3 856	55	28
65 and over	47 937	863	22	7

Notes: Total marketable assets does not include claims against employer-sponsored pension plans, social security, and human capital. Data are for all families and unattached individuals in a large sample, as of spring 1977. Families make up 72 percent of the sample.

Source: Statistics Canada, *The Distribution of Income and Wealth in Canada*, Cat. 13–570, 34.

TABLE 6–4 Debt patterns of households

Debt type	1977[a] (percentage of average total debt)	1981[b] (billions of dollars)
Instalment debt or trade credit	2.3	59
Bank consumer or short-term loans	13.1	33
Other consumer or short-term loans	6.9	9
Investment or long-term loans	5.8	—[c]
Mortgage loans	71.9	116

[a]Data are from the 1977 family survey.
[b]Total debts outstanding, persons and unincorporated business.
[c]1981 investment loans are included in bank and other loans.

Sources: Statistics Canada, *The Distribution of Income and Wealth in Canada*, Cat. 13–570, 1977, and *Financial Flow Accounts* , Cat. 13–002, Fourth Quarter 1981.

Not surprisingly, households with level salary income prefer the fixed-instalment debt as a rule, because the level instalment pattern leaves them with level disposable income patterns after instalment payments. Those with variable incomes, such as students and farmers, often prefer the more flexible demand loan, so they can pay large amounts when income is large and little when income is small.

Summary of asset supply behavior of households

To summarize, the supply of financial assets comes from borrowing, which depends on:

1. current relative to future incomes,
2. tastes for present versus future consumption,
3. interest rates available to borrowers,
4. repayment schedules available on loans, and
5. prices and rental rates of houses and consumer durables.

Borrowing will rise as future income rises relative to current income, which in turn changes predictably with age. Borrowing will rise with the level of current versus future needs, which depends predictably on family size and age. Borrowing will fall as interest rates rise, both because of lower asset purchases and because of larger down payments. However, slower repayment schedules may leave larger proportions of debt outstanding. Higher price-to-rental ratios will cause lower demand for ownership of houses and consumer durables. Whether this decrease will reduce the supply of financial assets depends on the elasticity of demand for ownership of the asset. Higher prices themselves increase the need for financing, but lower volumes of asset purchase keep borrowing down.

SECTION 5

Summary

Demand for wealth is a means of storing income for spending in later periods. Households store income in order to arrange a lifetime consumption stream that is more even than the typical stream of labor income. The decision to save or consume can be analysed with a consumer-choice model in which a given lifetime income stream is allocated among consumption in various periods. The model is very similar to the standard, static consumer model in which one period's income is allocated over various goods. It predicts that income will be spent in each period only to the point where relative marginal utilities are equal to relative opportunity costs. The opportunity cost of current consumption is the future consumption it cuts off by reducing current savings. The amount of future consumption actually cut off depends on the interest to be earned on current savings.

Demand for wealth reflects current and past savings decisions. Total savings levels depend on current relative to future income, tastes for current versus future consumption, the interest rate, and the number of households. The age and family size distribution of households are important determinants of relative incomes and tastes. The effect of a change in interest rates on savings is ambiguous.

The actual wealth of Canadian households conforms fairly well to predictions of a rational-choice model. Wealth rises to age fifty-five, then falls off during retirement. The bulk of household assets are long-term assets, many designed to provide for consumption during retirement. There is also a large stock of liquid assets to protect against emergencies — unexpected periods of low income or high need. Wealth held by Canadian households is higher in earlier years than a rational model would predict, however. The reason is that long-term credit is not available for pure consumption, and purchase of durable assets requires significant down payments. Households cannot arrange significant negative wealth even if they wanted to and could afford the interest payments.

The supply of financial assets from household borrowing reflects the same factors as demand for household wealth — current relative to future income, tastes for consumption over time, interest rates, and the number of households. Most household debt is incurred to finance asset purchases, so such debt also reflects price levels, rental rates for houses and consumer durables, and tastes for the services provided by such assets.

Questions for discussion

1. What is the opportunity cost of spending income now rather than ten years from now, if savings yield 3 percent per year over and above inflation?

2. Estimate the present discounted value of your lifetime gross income, measured in dollars of this year.
3. What is your marginal rate of time preference, for extra consumption this year relative to extra consumption five years after graduation?
4. Illustrate on a Fisher diagram the effect of a lottery winning. Is this permanent or transitory income?
5. What effect does a greater marginal rate of time preference (at each income level) have on the indifference map in a Fisher diagram?
6. What difference would it make to a Fisher diagram if borrowing rates were greater than lending rates?
7. If young families have the greatest need to buy new durable assets, why is their wealth not higher than that of older families?

References

Fisher, Irving. *The Role of Interest*. New York: Macmillan, 1907.

Friedman, Milton. *A Theory of the Consumption Function*. New York: National Bureau of Economic Research, 1955.

Hirshleifer, Jack. "On the Theory of Optimal Investment." *Journal of Political Economy*. Aug. 1958.

Modigliani, Franco, and Richard Brumberg. "Utility Analysis and the Consumption Function: An Interpretation of Cross-section Data." In K.K. Kurihara, ed., *Post-Keynesian Economics*. New Brunswick, N.J.: Rutgers University Press, 1954.

Modigliani, Franco, and Donald Lessard, eds. *New Mortgage Designs for Stable Housing in an Inflationary Environment*. Boston: Federal Reserve Bank of Boston, 1975.

Smith, Paul F. *Money and Financial Intermediation*. Englewood Cliffs, N.J.: Prentice-Hall, 1978.

Tobin, James. "A General Equilibrium Approach to Monetary Theory." *Journal of Money, Credit, and Banking* 1 (1969), 15–29.

CHAPTER 7

Nonhousehold Saving and Borrowing Behavior

This chapter extends the analysis of chapter 6 to the asset-purchasing and debt-issuing behavior of firms and governments — entities that are likely to save and borrow at the same time. The new concept introduced for this situation is leverage: buying assets with borrowed funds. Aside from leverage, the analysis is similar to that for households in chapter 6. In this chapter you will therefore learn:

1. to extend the analysis of household behavior to entities that simultaneously save, lend, and borrow,
2. the factors affecting saving and borrowing decisions of nonhousehold lenders and borrowers, and
3. the actual patterns of lending and borrowing carried out by business firms, governments, and financial institutions.

In order to complete the discussion of saving and borrowing behavior in Canadian financial markets, I also include the actual saving and borrowing patterns of the rest-of-the-world sector and the relative sizes of various types of financial institutions — both now and at the start of each decade over the last century.

Explaining total saving and borrowing means explaining total asset demand and total debt issue, and therefore total wealth holdings as well. That is, it means explaining total volume of demands and supplies in financial markets. Chapters 6 and 7 have little to say about the composition of assets, debts, and wealth (that is left to chapters 8 and 10), but it is possible to sketch some of the properties of general financial-market equilibrium, using only the analytical tools developed in chapters 6 and 7. That is done in the last section of this chapter.

SECTION 1

Asset demand and supply with leverage

Nonhousehold sectors save for the same general reason that households do — to provide for the future. The main distinctions between households and nonhouseholds are that (a) most assets bought by business firms, financial institutions, and governments are bought with credit of some sort and (b) most assets bought by nonhouseholds generate a flow of cash income rather than just a flow of housing or other services in kind.

Buying assets on credit means that nonhousehold groups typically decide simultaneously on demand for assets and supply of debts. Buying mainly income-earning assets means that the asset bought will itself generate most or all of the income stream out of which debt interest and principal are to be repaid. Manufacturing firms and financial institutions buy mainly income-earning assets, and many government assets are income-earning also. Nonhousehold groups are therefore nowhere near as dependent as households on a flow of other income to carry debt payments.

The case of Amco

In order to see what nonhousehold groups can do, let us look at a firm called Amco. Amco could be an industrial producer, a corporate farm, or a bank. Which it is makes no difference to our analysis.

We will consider a two-period choice, so we can illustrate it later on a Fisher diagram. The owners of Amco care only about dividend payments in each period, Div_1 and Div_2. The owners are assumed to have agreed on a common utility function for those dividend payments, $U(Div_1,Div_2)$, which the managers are to maximize. Both dividend payments have positive but declining marginal utility.

Assume for simplicity that Amco has a stock of existing assets, but no debt. Amco expects a stream of profits $Prof_1$ and $Prof_2$ to flow from its existing assets. Profits can be used to pay dividends in the year earned. In year 1, profits can also be ploughed back into the firm to buy more assets. The amount ploughed back ($Prof_1 - Div_1$) is retained earnings, or savings (S). The return on savings is the average yield on assets, r_a. The more assets (A) are bought, the lower is the average yield r_a, either because Amco's demand bids up asset prices or because good investments are scarce and with greater demand Amco must settle for less and less satisfactory assets at the margin. That is, $r_a = r_a(A)$, and $dr_a/dA < 0$.

Amco can borrow to finance its asset purchases, or even to supplement dividend payments, at an average borrowing rate r_d. The average borrowing rate r_d rises as Amco issues more debts (D), either because its extra supply of debt lowers the price for new issues or because lenders become more nervous and less willing as Amco's debt totals rise. That is, $r_d = r_d(D)$, and $dr_d/dD > 0$.

A graphical illustration

Amco's investment and borrowing options are illustrated in figure 7–1 on the two-period Fisher diagram used for Jones and Casey in chapter 6. Amco's endowment point P_0 reflects the profits Amco would have if it merely carried over its existing assets from the past. If Amco pays out all of its profits each year in dividends, $Div_1 = Prof_1$, and $Div_2 = Prof_2$; the firm is choosing point P_0. We assume that Amco can invest from P_0 at a higher yield than it can borrow, but the average investment yield falls as Amco demands more assets. Similarly, Amco's borrowing costs r_d increase and its borrowing frontier steepens as Amco's supply of debt grows.

FIGURE 7–1 Investment and borrowing frontiers

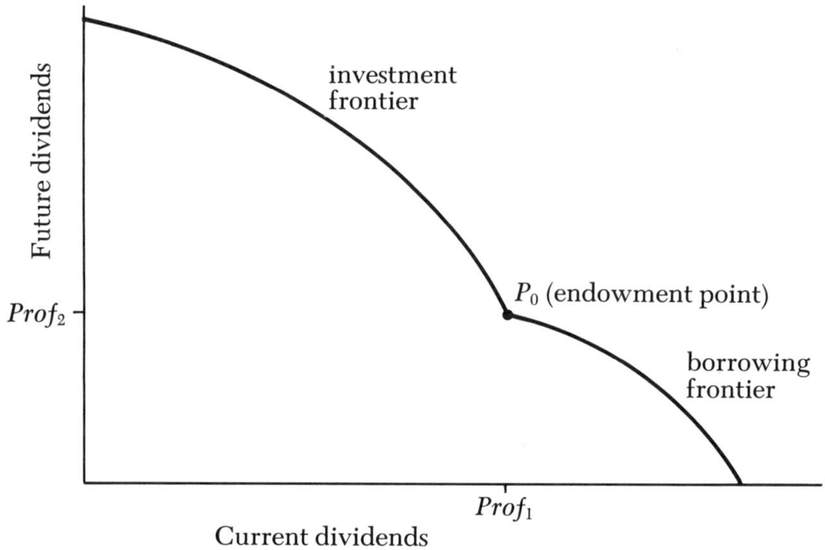

The endowment point reflects current and future profits with no new asset purchases and no new borrowing. The slope of each frontier reflects the marginal yield on investment and the marginal interest cost of debt.

Amco's borrowing frontier starts at P_0 if Amco buys no new assets. If Amco buys assets and borrows at the same time, the borrowing frontier will start instead at the point on the investment frontier that Amco would reach by the investment alone. Figure 7–2 is an illustration. Amco buys new assets in the amount A, equal to half of current profits, and issues new debt D in the same amount (so it is investing entirely with borrowed funds). In figure 7–2, the asset purchase by itself moves Amco from P_0 to point B, along the investment frontier. Taking on the extra debt moves Amco from point B to the right along a borrowing line from B, by the same horizontal distance as from P_0 to B (since $A = D$ in this example). The combination of investment and borrowing leaves Amco at point C, directly above the endowment point P_0. Amco is clearly better off at point C than at P_0.

FIGURE 7–2 Investing entirely with borrowed funds

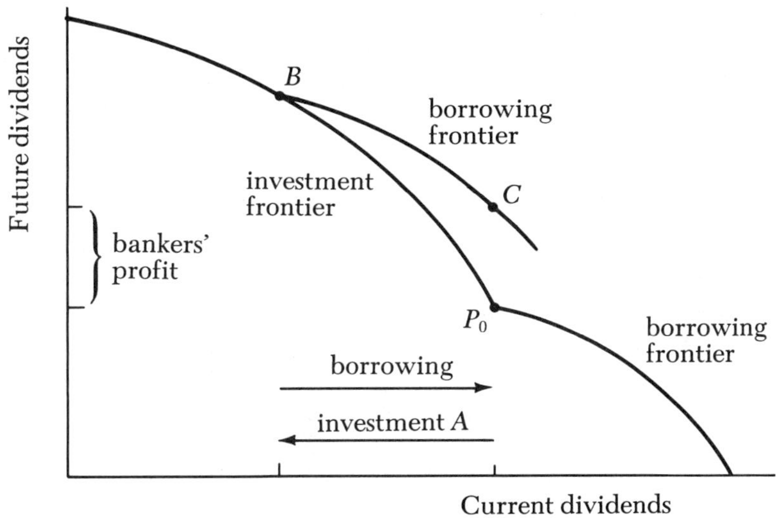

The firm's investment moves it along its investment frontier from P_0 to B. The firm's borrowing moves it along a borrowing frontier starting at B. Since borrowing equals investment, none of current profits is used, and the firm ends up directly above P_0 at C. The extra future dividends all come from bankers' profit, equal to the vertical distance between point C and the endowment point P_0.

The asset purchase by itself gives Amco greater future earnings and dividends of $A(1 + r_a)$. Repayment of the borrowing with interest reduces future dividends by $D(1 + r_d)$. The difference, since $A = D$, is $A(r_a - r_d)$. This is the vertical distance between the original endowment point P_0 and point C. $A(r_a - r_d)$ can be thought of as *bankers' profit,* since it is made entirely from investing with borrowed funds.

Bankers' profit

Amco could invest to point B and borrow a different amount, of course. This would leave it somewhere else along the borrowing frontier BC, depending on the amount of borrowing. An amount of investment other than A would also give a different point B from which to start the borrowing frontier. Which amount of investment and borrowing Amco will want depends on Amco's tastes, decribed by its indifference curves. Amco will want to get onto the highest possible indifference curve.

Figure 7–3 adds indifference curves to Amco's investment and borrowing frontiers. The optimal amount of new asset demand A^* will be the horizontal distance from P_0 to B^*, which moves the borrowing frontier farthest out (that is, reaching the highest indifference curve). The optimal

FIGURE 7–3 Optimal asset demand and debt supply

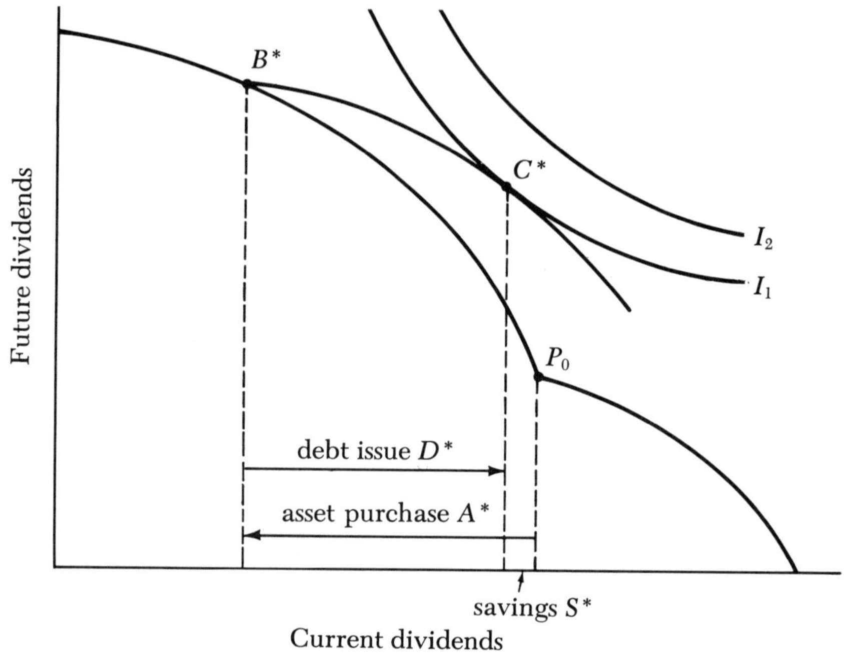

The firm's optimal asset demand is its previous asset holding plus the distance A^* between P_0 and B^* on the horizontal axis. The firm's optimal debt outstanding is its previous debt plus the horizontal distance D^* from B^* to C^*. The slope of the indifference curve at C^* is equal to the slope of the borrowing frontier at C^* and to the slope of the investment frontier at B^*. Part of current profit is used in the investment, so there is positive saving in the current period, equal to $A^* - D^* = S^*$.

amount of new debt D^* will be the horizontal distance from B^* to C^*, which brings Amco to the point of tangency with the highest attainable indifference curve. Amco's optimal saving S^* is then $A^* - D^*$ (the horizontal distance between P_0 and C^*) or, alternatively, the difference between $Prof_1$ and the optimal current dividend payment Div_1^*.

At Amco's optimum, the slope of its indifference curve $-MU_1/MU_2$, or $-(1 + MRTP)$ will equal the slope of its borrowing frontier: $-(1 +$ marginal debt cost). The marginal debt cost is r_d if the borrowing rate is fixed, but a higher amount $r_d + Ddr_d/dD$ if r_d rises with extra borrowing. At Amco's optimum, therefore, Amco's marginal rate of time preference is equal to its marginal borrowing cost, just as for Casey in chapter 6.

Amco's optimal asset purchase will be to the point where the marginal asset yield just equals the marginal borrowing cost.[1] Anything different

[1]Both marginal yield concepts are very similar to the concept of marginal revenue for a producing firm, which is $P + QdP/dQ$.

means foregoing some bankers' profit. Graphically, the marginal asset yield is the slope of the investment frontier at B^*, while the marginal borrowing cost is the slope of the borrowing frontier at C^*. The two slopes must be equal if bankers' profit is to be maximized. Average asset yield r_a will be greater than the marginal asset yield, and the average borrowing cost r_d will be less than marginal borrowing cost, so there will be a positive spread between r_a and r_d.

Recall that Amco could be an industrial producer, a farmer, or a financial institution. The essentials of figure 7–3 apply to all three. If Amco is a financial institution, its investment frontier reflects yields available on financial assets rather than on industrial equipment. The major difference for a financial institution is that financial institutions typically buy assets on a much larger scale relative to their own profits and savings flows than do farmers and industrial producers. Financial institutions can expect their asset purchases A^* to exceed even their total profits, let alone their current savings S^*.

An alternative view: marginal asset yields and marginal debt costs

Amco's optimal asset demand and debt supply choice can be illustrated in a different way. Once the level of savings has been chosen, the level of debt must rise in step with asset purchases, so the marginal cost of debt can be compared with the marginal asset yield as asset purchases increase. This is done in figure 7–4 assuming that savings are fixed at the optimal level S^*. Marginal asset yields fall and marginal debt costs rise with extra asset purchases, so the marginal profit shrinks on both counts. The profit-maximizing, equilibrium asset purchase A^* and debt issue D^* occur at the point of intersection. The shaded area between the marginal asset yield curve and the marginal debt cost curve corresponds to the bankers' profit from investing with borrowed funds. The average asset yield r_a and the average debt cost r_d are shown as well.[2]

An algebraic explanation

Our graphical results for Amco are easily reproduced algebraically, with the simplifying assumption that debt costs r_d are fixed and insensitive to Amco's borrowing.[3] Amco's income constraint is that the present value of its dividends must equal the present value of its profit stream, including any bankers' profit from current asset purchases with borrowed funds. Thus,

$$Div_1 + \frac{Div_2}{(1 + r_d)} = Prof_1 + \frac{Prof_2 + A(r_a - r_d)}{(1 + r_d)}$$

[2] r_a is to $r_a + Adr_a/dA$ as demand is to marginal revenue, and r_d is to $r_d + Ddr_d/dD$ as average cost is to marginal cost.

[3] The borrowing cost is also the discount rate in the income constraint; if the discount rate depends on the level of debt outstanding, the algebra becomes much more complex.

FIGURE 7–4 Optimal asset purchase and debt issue

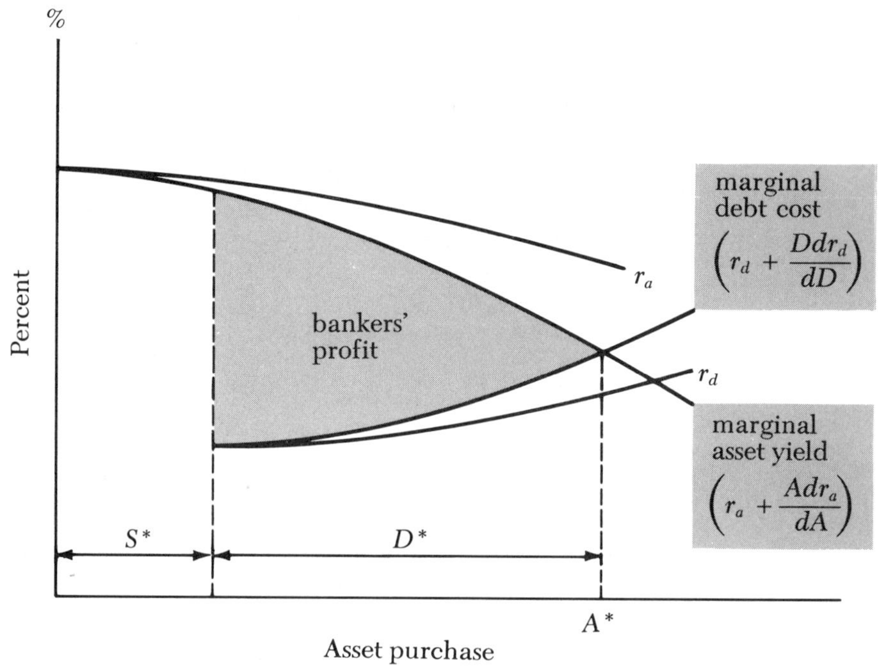

For a given savings level S°, each dollar of asset purchase beyond S° implies a dollar of debt issue D. Optimal asset purchase is at A°, where marginal asset yield equals marginal debt cost. The shaded area between the two marginal curves gives the profit from asset purchases financed with borrowed funds (that is, beyond S°). r_a is the average asset yield, r_d is the average debt cost, D° is the optimal debt issue, and $S^\circ + D^\circ$ equals the optimal asset purchase A°.

The discount rate is r_d because that is the opportunity cost of current dividends; more current dividends means incurring more debt now to finance optimal asset purchases, and the interest cost of debt is r_d.

Amco wants to know the optimal values of Div_1, Div_2, S, D and A but can choose only three of them independently. Two of the five values are determined by the basic identities of the Financial Flow Accounts from chapter 5. Once either Div_1 or S is chosen, the other is determined by the identity that $S = Prof_1 - Div_1$. Once either A or D is chosen, the other is determined by the identity that the savings or change in equity (S) must equal the change in assets (A) less the change in debts (D).

Maximizing $U(Div_1, Div_2)$ with respect to any three of Div_1, Div_2, A, D, and S, subject to the income constraint and the identities above, gives optimal levels of Div_1, Div_2, and therefore D such that:[4]

$$\frac{MU_1}{MU_2} = 1 + r_d$$

or $\quad MRTP = r_d$

and optimal asset purchase A^* such that the marginal asset yield equals the marginal (and average) debt cost:

$$r_a + \frac{Adr_a}{dA} = r_d$$

SECTION 2

Asset demand and supply behavior

The model we have used for Amco has explained purchase of new assets and issue of new debts. Amco's total demand for assets is its previous total assets plus any new purchases. Amco's total supply of debts is its previous total debt plus any new borrowing. The new purchases and new borrowing represent adjustment of previous totals to new desired levels of assets and debts, respectively. If Amco's investment and borrowing frontiers were such in figure 7–3 that the endowment point, P_0, were also the optimal point, we would infer that Amco was content with the level of assets and debts carried over from the previous period.[5]

Amco's purchases of assets and new issues of debts depend on all of the ingredients of figures 7–3 and 7–4: the firm's marginal rate of time preference and its endowment of assets and debts, the yields available on assets, and the costs of borrowing. Amco will demand more assets as marginal asset yields rise and as borrowing costs fall (this can be seen clearly from figure 7–4) and as the firm's *MRTP* falls. Amco will do more new borrowing as borrowing costs fall and as asset yields rise. It is not clear what effect a change in *MRTP* will have on borrowing: higher marginal rates of time preference will cause a larger proportion of any asset purchase to be debt-financed, but total asset purchases will fall.

The firm's endowment of assets and debts from the past will affect current flows of purchases and borrowing just as income levels affected Brown's saving and demand for wealth in chapter 6. It is not clear that the endowment level will affect the total stock demand for assets, however. A

---

[4]Amco's optimal behavior is derived from the first-order conditions for maximizing utility subject to the income constraint. These conditions are that the first derivatives of F with respect to Div_1, Div_2, A, and g be equal to zero, where

$$F = U(Div_1, Div_2) - g\left[Div_1 + \frac{Div_2}{(1 + r_d)} - \left(Prof_1 + \frac{Prof_2 + A(r_a - r_d)}{(1 + r_d)}\right)\right]$$

and $r_a = r_a(A)$.

[5]For a financial institution with mainly short-term assets and debts, few of its assets and debts would carry over from the previous year.

simple example will help. If an electric utility has just built a hydro dam, it will probably not want to buy a new one. However, if an act of God were to destroy both the dam and the debts issued to finance it (changing the firm's endowment), the utility would certainly want to buy a new dam as long as the terms were similar to those for the dam destroyed. Total demand for hydro dams is still one hydro dam in each case, though the amount of hydro dams purchased is zero in the first case and one in the second.

It is noteworthy that, for all nonhousehold groups such as Amco, demand for assets is clearly sensitive to the level of interest rates on both assets and debts. This was not the case for Brown or for the hockey star Jones in chapter 6. If both asset yields and debt costs were to change by the same amount, however, theory would once more be unable to predict the net effect.

The two-period model developed for Amco can be extended to many periods, without any change in the factors affecting demand and supply of assets. Asset yields, debt interest costs, and attitudes toward dividend patterns still determine the firm's decision. Attitudes to dividend patterns vary, but generally firms prefer to keep dividends more stable than profits. This preference for relative stability of dividends leads to more savings in high-profit years and less — maybe even dissaving — in low-profit years. Because low-profit years are not always predictable, firms will keep a significant part of their asset holdings in liquid assets.

Government as a special case

The situation of governments is different in several ways from that of our typical firm Amco. First, the government provides public goods and services instead of dividend payments for its "owners" (the voting public). There is likely to be a strong preference among the voting public for a stable flow of those goods and services over time. Second, the government's income is from tax revenue, which is usually a percentage of the income of all taxpayers (GNP). Total tax revenue will be much more predictable than the profits of any one corporation, but it will still fluctuate over the business cycle. Third, the government is less able to earn income on its assets, at least directly. Wider or smoother roads, better-educated taxpayers, and bigger airports do not generate their own revenue the way a pulp mill does.

Because of fluctuating incomes and stable spending requirements, governments have a cyclical pattern of saving and borrowing, even more than corporations. Lack of cash income from some of the assets they buy throws governments back on their other income, just like households. The difference is that governments can and do borrow extensively against future income, often the income of years decades away; households generally cannot find willing lenders for that sort of credit, except for buying a house.

Governments' supply of debts is affected by interest rates somewhat differently from the supply of debts of business firms. Higher bond yields on new debts would cause governments to postpone some current spending increases and save more. At the same time, the higher bond yields would also lead (eventually) to higher interest costs on the outstanding debt, which would leave less tax revenue for current spending on public goods and services. If governments are not willing to cut other spending to make room for mushrooming interest payments, then current borrowing must be increased. Government debt supply may therefore rise for a time, instead of falling, when interest rates rise.[6]

SECTION 3

Nonhousehold debt and asset patterns

Table 7–1 shows the pattern of financial assets and debts of domestic nonhousehold sectors, from the Financial Flow Accounts. Each column is a more detailed breakdown of the same column in table 5–2, except that assets held and debts issued are shown separately rather than being netted out against each other. The rest-of-the-world sector is excluded, since we do not know total financial-asset figures for that sector; it is treated in section 4 of this chapter.

Table 7–1 does not include real asset holdings. For financial institutions, real asset holdings are typically fairly small, either by law or by convention. For large nonfinancial firms, data for 1981 show inventories to be 19 percent and plant and equipment to be 43 percent of total assets. Only the remaining 38 percent of total assets is in financial assets. If those proportions carry over to all nonfinancial firms, the implied total holding of real assets is about $530 billion. In addition, not all of the financial assets are purely financial. Part of the asset group "stocks and claims on associated firms" is not ownership of shares as a financial investment but simply a roundabout way of buying the real assets of subsidiaries. Consolidation of balance sheets of parent firms and subsidiaries would therefore cancel out some of the financial assets in this category, both as assets of the parents and as debts of the subsidiaries.

Both groups of nonfinancial sectors (corporations and governments) hold significant amounts of liquid assets in currency and deposits and short-term paper, as expected. Beyond that, the pattern of asset holdings generally reflects considerations of risk, which we will not discuss until chapter 8. There is an extra and obvious factor in the asset and debt choices of nonfinancial corporations, and that is the use of *trade credit* for sales

Trade credit

[6]Albert Wojnilower of First Boston Corp. has argued that this apparently perverse borrowing behavior also appears in short-term business borrowing. "The Central Role of Credit Crunches in Recent Financial History," *Brookings Papers on Economic Activity*, 1980, no. 2, 277–326. The perversity will last only until interest costs of existing debt have adjusted to that of new debts, but that could be years.

promotion. Competition for business has forced producers to extend $80 billion of trade credit to business customers — almost as much as the entire sector owes in loans.

TABLE 7–1 Outstanding financial assets and debts of nonhousehold sectors, December 1981 (billions of dollars)

	Nonfinancial corporations		Banks and near-banks		Other financial institutions		Governments[b]	
	Assets	Debts	Assets	Debts	Assets	Debts	Assets	Debts
Currency and bank deposits	23	—	34	308	10	3	17	19
Consumer credit	1	—	40	—	8	—	—	—
Trade credit	80	70	—	—	2	1	1	3
Loans	5	91	129	4	25	11	11	10
Treasury Bills and short-term paper	4	7	13	1	10	11	7	22
Mortgages	5	27	81	—	44	—	4	—
Bonds	2	74	16	5	62	14	55	147
Life insurance and pensions	—	—	—	—	—	108	—	1
Stocks and claims on associated firms	64	258	32	30	50	66	64	7
Foreign investments	1	—	—	—	5	—	—	—
Other[a]	17	39	9	8	6	15	17	12
TOTALS	201	567	353	356	222	230	170	220

[a]Includes official international reserves.
[b]Includes the Bank of Canada.

Source: Statistics Canada, *Financial Flow Accounts*, Cat. 13–002, Fourth Quarter 1981.

Leverage ratio

Debt patterns differ substantially between sectors in table 7–1. The largest difference is not obvious: nonfinancial corporations have debt equal to about 60 percent of their assets, giving them an asset:equity ratio, or *leverage ratio*, of 2.5. Financial institutions have leverage ratios of up to 30. One reason for the difference, which we will analyse fully in chapter 10, is that cash flows from financial assets are generally more stable than cash flows from real assets. Another reason is that financial institutions can match cash inflows from financial assets with the cash outflows needed to service debt. Cash flows of large financial institutions are much more predictable than those of nonfinancial companies.

Generally, short-term debts are used to finance short-term assets, and long-term debts, long-term assets. This pattern will be explained in detail in chapter 10, but you should look for it now in table 7–1. Compare banks and near-banks with other financial institutions, and compare governments with business firms. Bank and near-bank assets are mainly short-term, of less than three years to maturity, and their deposits are of similar term. Other financial institutions (mainly life insurers, mutual funds, and pension funds) have longer-term assets and predominantly longer-term liabilities.

Government assets are typically longer-term than business assets, since governments do not have to finance much inventory or movable equipment — or livestock. Government debts are therefore heavily concentrated in relatively long-term bonds, while corporations have much larger percentages of their debt in shorter-term trade credit and loans.

Gable, June 27, 1981, *The Financial Post*

Governments of course have no stock issues. Furthermore, government bond purchases by the social security funds (the Canada Pension Plan, mainly) take up a significant share of the provincial bond issues, so governments' reliance on bond debt is understated in table 7–1. The government itself does not lend a significant amount of money directly. Instead, government loans are made through one of an arsenal of public lending agencies such as the Farm Credit Corporation.

SECTION 4 International connections: the rest-of-the-world sector

It is obvious that Canadian financial markets are not purely Canadian. Even the nonfinancial press often refers to Swiss francs, the Eurodollar markets, U.S. interest rates, and the like. Canada's international financial connections are revealed in the rest-of-the-world (ROW) sector of the Financial Flow Accounts, as well as in the Capital Account of our Balance of Payments. All Canadian lending abroad generates debts of the rest of the world; all foreign lending to Canadians generates foreign holdings of Canadian debts. Both appear in the ROW sector's column of the Financial Flow Accounts matrix. Only our purchases of real assets abroad and foreign purchases of real assets in Canada are not reflected in that column.

Table 7–2 shows the accumulated totals of Canadian lending abroad and foreign lending to Canada. The rest of the world is a large net lender to Canadians, but it has borrowed half as much as it has loaned.

TABLE 7–2 International connections: foreign assets and debts, 1981 (billions of dollars)

	Held as assets	Outstanding as debts
Official international reserves	—	5
Currency and deposits		
foreign-currency deposits	56	27
domestic deposits	3	—
Loans	11	24
Treasury Bills and other short-term paper	4	—
Mortgages	1	—
Bonds		
provincial	29	—
corporate	20	—
other	10	—
Stocks and claims on associated firms	93	46
Foreign investments	—	9
Other financial assets	5	3
TOTAL	233	114

Note: Lending and borrowing of foreign subsidiaries of Canadian banks are included only where the opposite party is Canadian, including loans to and from the head office.

Source: Statistics Canada, *Financial Flow Accounts*, Cat. 13–002, Fourth Quarter 1981.

The most important part of foreign borrowing in Canada is in-house borrowing of foreign subsidiaries from their Canadian parent firms, by issue of extra stock or loan notes. The other large item is foreign-currency deposits held by Canadians in foreign banks. The Canadians holding foreign-currency deposits issued by the ROW sector are mostly the head offices of Canadian banks investing in deposits of their foreign subsidiaries and other foreign banks. Canadian firms and households hold an equal volume of foreign-currency deposits, but their deposits are issued by Canadian banks and are therefore not a debt of the ROW sector.

Foreign lending in Canada takes a wider variety of forms than foreign borrowing. Foreigners have large investments in Canadian stocks, particularly shares of Canadian subsidiaries. Foreigners have large sums in foreign-currency deposits issued by Canadian banks, mostly in the Eurodollar market. Only those deposits booked with the Canadian bank head offices are included in table 7–2, which means mainly deposits of U.S. residents.[7]

[7]Foreign agencies of Canadian banks in the United States are not allowed to accept deposits in their own name, so their business is recorded as a liability of the head office in Canada. European subsidiaries can and do accept deposits in their own name.

Foreign financial institutions have large holdings of bonds issued by Canadian provinces and Crown corporations, reflecting many fund-raising trips to New York and European bond markets by our provincial finance ministers and corporate treasurers. Foreigners have not made many direct loans as such to Canadians, but they do have a significant holding of money-market assets, relative to the size of the Canadian money market. The extent of their holdings reflects the activity of money-market dealers both in Canada and abroad, who actively solicit international business.[8]

SECTION 5 Growth of financial intermediaries

Data for financial assets and debts give a financial snapshot of the relative sizes of various sectors of the economy, but no sense of history. Which groups were important first? Which are only recently important? Which will decline and disappear?

The fastest-growing groups in table 7–1 are the financial institutions. Debts and assets of nonfinancial corporations have kept more or less even with gross national product, reflecting a more or less stable real capital-to-income ratio for the economy. Debt:income ratios of governments rose sharply in the First and Second World Wars but have been relatively stable since. Debts of financial institutions, however, have risen from only 30 percent of GNP in 1870 to over 170 percent of GNP in 1980.

Within the group of financial institutions, there have been dramatic and sometimes sudden changes. We will discuss the operations of individual types of financial intermediaries more fully in part III of this book, so this section will only sketch the changes in relative shares of each in the financial system. The history of those changes is recorded in compact form in figure 7–5. The figure shows the cumulative distribution of total assets across groups of financial intermediaries, starting from the bottom of the figure and working upward. Private, short-term intermediaries are at the bottom; private, long-term intermediaries are in the middle; government intermediaries are in the shaded portion at the top. Relative shares of total intermediary assets for each group correspond to the relative thicknesses of the bands for each group in figure 7–5. Those groups whose assets are growing faster than the average have bands that grow thicker over time; those whose bands get thinner are growing more slowly than the average.

The most striking relative decline in figure 7–5 is that of the banks from 1870 to 1970. The more recent portion of that long downward trend was caused by aggressive expansion of credit unions and trust companies into the banks' chequing-account and savings-deposit business. Ceilings on banks' loan rates prevented much response by the banks until the 1967 revision of the Bank Act removed the loan rate ceilings. Since then the

[8]Money-market dealers depend on turnover for their revenue, so they have a powerful incentive to keep thinking up better uses for clients' money.

FIGURE 7–5 Shares of total financial-intermediary assets, 1870–198

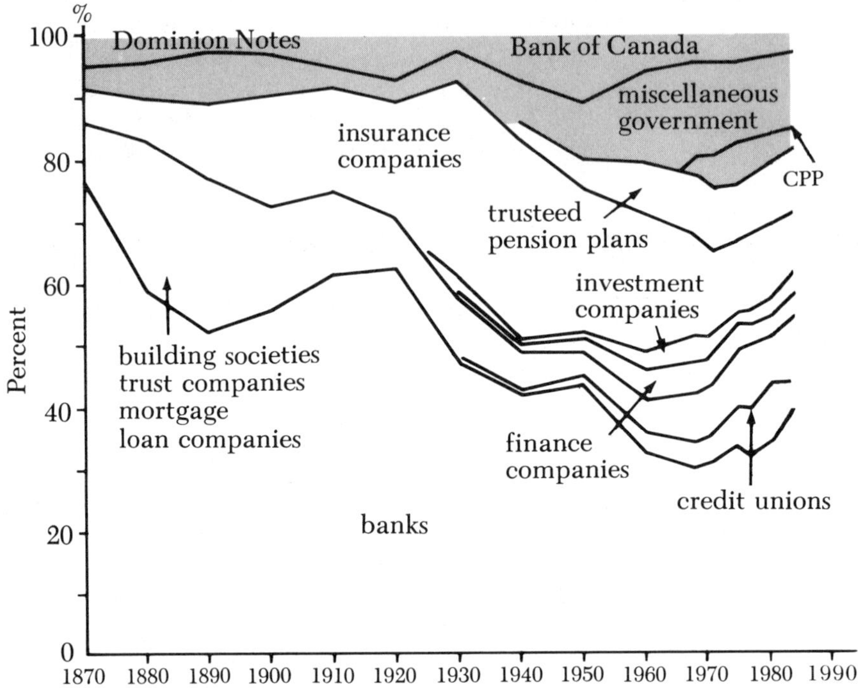

Vertical distances indicate the proportion of the total assets of all financial intermediaries held by each type of institution, so a band that becomes wider over time (the band for trusteed pension plans, for instance) reflects a growing share of total financial intermediation. Dominion Notes were replaced by Bank of Canada notes after 1935. CPP refers to the Canada and Quebec Pension Plans. Investment companies include mutual funds. Examples of miscellaneous government institutions are the Canada Mortgage and Housing Corporation and the Federal Business Development Bank.

Sources: Statistics Canada, *Financial Institutions; Bank of Canada Review*; E.P. Neufeld, *The Financial System of Canada* (Toronto: Macmillan, 1972), statistical appendix.

banks have increased their share of total domestic assets of financial intermediaries. An even more rapid growth of the banks' foreign- currency business with foreigners is not reflected in figure 7–5, which records only shares of domestic business.

The groups most squeezed in the 1970s were the finance, investment, and insurance companies. The category of finance companies includes those extending credit directly to consumers (consumer loan companies) and those who merely take over customer credit first extended by merchants and appliance dealers (sales finance companies). Investment companies are mainly mutual funds — pools of assets owned jointly by those who contribute the funds. Insurance companies include all companies offering insurance, whether life or accident or health or boiler insurance, but life insurance accounts for the vast majority of insurance-company assets.

The most rapidly growing sector in figure 7–5 is the pension sector. Private-sector pension plans, sponsored by employers, have been growing rapidly for the last three decades. The Canada and Quebec Pension Plans have grown enormously since they started in 1965. Group annuity contracts with life insurers are a type of pension plan, and they too have grown rapidly. Finally, private savings in the form of Registered Retirement Savings Plans have mushroomed since 1965, to the point where more than one family in five has some funds accumulated in RRSPs.

Canada Pension Plan
Quebec Pension Plan

The public-sector share of the financial system (the shaded portion of figure 7–5) grew rapidly from 1930 to about 1950, then levelled off, and has shrunk since 1970. The major public-sector financial institutions are the Bank of Canada, which issues currency and its own deposits; the Canada and Quebec Pension Plans, which receive pension-plan contributions and pay out pension benefits; the Canada Mortgage and Housing Corporation (CMHC), which finances public and some private housing construction; and the civil-service pension funds of provincial and federal governments. The CMHC has restricted its activity since 1975. However, there is talk of expanding the coverage and therefore the size of the Canada and Quebec Pension Plans, and such an expansion would further increase the share of the public sector in the financial system.

SECTION 6 General Equilibrium

I have explained demand and supply in financial markets, though still without consideration of risk, and you have at least a general impression of how each sector lends and borrows and why. In this section we consider how a financial market responds to excess demand or supply, and also the interaction of all financial markets together. The subject of general equilibrium in financial markets is dealt with much more thoroughly in chapter 14; this is just a preliminary sketch.

In financial markets, demand usually adjusts to equal supply even over very short periods. Financial asset and debt totals can be adjusted (especially upward) much more easily than real asset holdings. The adjustment mechanism that balances demand and supply is changes in yields, either via changes in coupon yields (for new assets and for old assets with adjustable coupons such as floating-rate demand loans and savings deposits) or via changes in market price (for already-issued assets with fixed coupons such as bonds, stocks, and negotiable term deposits). Market price changes will occur only for those assets that have secondary markets. For fixed-coupon assets without secondary markets, no adjustment at all will take place until the asset matures; only then will the fixed coupon be changed.

Adjustment of relative yields on different assets will quickly remove excess demand or supply. Increases in the yield on the asset in excess supply will cause investors to shift demand into it, and issuers to shift supply out of it, into some other, cheaper source of credit. Demand for assets in total may not be very sensitive to the average level of yields, but demand for any individual asset is usually very sensitive to relative yields. Adjustment of the average level of yields will also bring total asset demand and total debt supply into balance. Increases in yields will discourage borrowing and investment and may also encourage saving.

Where financial yields are adjusted by changing asset prices, the adjustment affects wealth levels of the holders of those assets; changes in wealth levels will also influence saving and demand for assets. Adjustment of yields will also have effects on real income levels by changing demand for investment goods and by affecting the exchange rate of domestic for foreign currency, but effects on real income are likely to be much slower to appear than most financial-market adjustments.

Changes in the yield in any one market not only bring supply and demand into balance in that market, but also have powerful effects on demand and supply in other markets. Many investors and borrowers, especially financial institutions, frequent many different markets at once. It is easy for such participants to switch their demand and supply between markets in response to small changes in yield differentials. Such movements between financial markets, known as *arbitrage*, will always increase demand for assets with relatively high yields, driving their yields down, and increase supply of debts with relatively low yields, driving their yields up. Arbitrage keeps relative yields more or less in line.

Arbitrage

If there is enough arbitrage, we can expect a pattern of yields in which differentials reflect only the relative costs of managing different assets and debts (and risk factors for each).[9] If there is not as much arbitrage as that, relative yields will also reflect the different marginal rates of time preference of particular groups of borrowers and lenders, and relative supplies and demands in each market. The particular yield structures to be expected when there is a lot of arbitrage are discussed more fully in chapter 15.

SECTION 7 Summary

Nonhouseholds typically buy assets at least partly with borrowed funds and rely on cash inflow from the asset to look after most of the cash outflows required for debt payments. We therefore use a two-period model of a

[9]For instance, Professors Wynant, Hatch, and Grant of the University of Western Ontario conclude in a study of chartered-bank lending to small business that the banks charge higher rates for small-business loans than for loans to large firms because of higher administrative costs per dollar of loan (but not higher by the full margin of extra administrative costs). L. Wynant, J. Hatch, and M.J. Grant, *Bank Financing of Small Business in Canada* (London, Ont.: University of Western Ontario, School of Business Administration, 1982).

typical firm to analyse both demand for assets and supply of debts at the same time. The model explains why asset demand will depend on asset yields, debt costs, and marginal rates of time preference. Past savings and current income may be further constraints on asset purchases for some investors.

There is a preference for stable spending (either on dividends, for firms, or on public goods and services, for governments), and there is a fluctuating pattern of incomes over the business cycle, so a fluctuating pattern of savings and wealth is to be expected over the business cycle. Demand for liquid assets is also to be expected, to protect against unexpected swings in incomes.

Actual nonhousehold debt patterns do reflect a demand for liquid assets. Beyond that, the major observable features are matching of maturities of assets and debts — for reasons to do with risk — and huge differences in the degree of leverage of financial and nonfinancial firms. Thanks in part to their great leverage, financial institutions have grown rapidly in the Canadian economy, far faster than their equity base. The banks are still the largest group of financial institutions, but their share has been greatly eroded over the last century.

The international connections of nonhousehold groups are mainly (a) foreigners buying and selling Canadian money-market assets, (b) Canadians buying and selling foreign money-market assets (mainly through Canadian banks), (c) parent firms on either side of the border lending to and buying stock of subsidiaries, and (d) foreign financial institutions buying up the bonds sold abroad by provincial governments and Canadian corporations.

The whole financial system adjusts to equilibrium by changes in yields in each market. Yields change either because the coupon rate changes or because the price changes. Only fixed-yield assets without a secondary market are immune to both adjustments. A change in yield affects both demand and supply to restore market equilibrium, especially if not all yields change together. Changes in yields have longer-range effects on financial markets through changing the value of wealth (when market prices of assets change) and through changing the level of income and output in the real sector of the economy. Arbitrage between different financial markets, if there is enough of it, can be expected to keep relative yields in a more or less stable structure. Financial intermediaries are an important source of such arbitrage.

Questions for discussion

1. What is the difference between an industrial corporation's balance sheet and that of a financial institution?
2. On a Fisher diagram, illustrate the situation of a financial institution that buys assets in a larger amount than its current profits and still pays dividends to shareholders in the current year.
3. Why is marginal asset yield less than average asset yield for the typical firm?
4. If a firm were to find its endowment point optimal, would that imply zero demand for assets? zero supply of debts?
5. What would the government's balance sheet look like?
6. In 1982 Canada had a net outflow of funds to the rest of the world. How can that be reconciled with the data in table 7-2 showing that Canada has twice as much debt as credit with the rest of the world?
7. Why are relative yields in different financial markets generally to be found in relatively fixed relationship to each other?

References

Donner, Arthur. *Financing the Future: Canada's Capital Markets in the Eighties*. Toronto: Lorimer, 1982.

Fisher, Irving. *The Role of Interest*. New York: Macmillan, 1907.

Hirshleifer, Jack. "On the Theory of Optimal Investment." *Journal of Political Economy*. Aug. 1958.

Neave, G. *Canada's Financial System*. Toronto: Wiley, 1981.

Neufeld, E.P. *The Financial System of Canada*. Toronto: Macmillan, 1972.

Sarpkaya, S. *The Money Market in Canada*. Toronto: Butterworths, 1980.

Tobin, James. "A General Equilibrium Approach to Monetary Theory." *Journal of Money, Credit, and Banking* 1 (1969), 15–29.

PART TWO

Asset Demand and Supply under Uncertainty

CHAPTER 8

Asset Demand under Uncertainty

Previous chapters have explained why wealth is accumulated, why saving occurs. The explanation took little account of the central fact of financial markets — uncertainty. Neither did it reveal how individuals choose the mix of different assets in which to hold any accumulated wealth. In this chapter we deal with both of those matters.

By the end of the chapter you should know:

1. the sources of uncertainty facing wealthholders,
2. the relationship between the degree of uncertainty and a particular measure of yield volatility called the *variance*,
3. how wealthholders can reduce the variance of yields on their asset portfolio by diversification,
4. what the logic of portfolio choice implies about demand for individual assets,
5. how hedging markets operate in Canada to counter particular types of uncertainty, and
6. how transactions costs and indivisibilities affect actual and predicted asset choices.

Since there is more than this to the analysis of uncertainty, two further aspects are treated in appendixes to the chapter.

The main part of the chapter requires that you master two statistical concepts, the variance and covariance of probability distributions. Both are defined and illustrated in the chapter, but if you have any prior memories of them, it will help to dust them off.

SECTION 1 Sources and measurement of uncertainty

To some economists, the very notion of describing uncertainty is a contradiction. To them, uncertainty is by definition indescribable, because we know nothing about it. A situation about which we do know something, even though the outcome of the situation is still not certain, is described by these economists as merely risky.[1] This definition of uncertainty as complete ignorance is not a useful one for us, and I do not use it in this book. In the situations facing savers and borrowers in financial markets, there is almost always some information about future prospects, and often a great deal of it. There are no commitments of funds that are absolutely blind. Therefore, when we use the term *uncertainty* it is synonymous with the term *risk*.

Our concern in this chapter is with the risk or uncertainty involved in asset yields for collections of assets accumulated by households and firms.

Asset portfolio

These collections are known as *asset portfolios*. The rate of return or yield on the whole portfolio is simply an average of the yields on each individual asset in the portfolio. The yield on any individual asset comes from whatever explicit cash payments are made to the holder of the asset, such as interest or dividends, and from any gain between the purchase price and the selling or final redemption price.

Riskiness of yields (r) is also riskiness of future values (FV), since the two are related by the identity[2]

$$FV = P(1 + r),$$

where P is the present value of the asset portfolio. It makes no substantive difference which we analyse, riskiness of r or of FV, so we choose the one that is more convenient.

The separate sources of uncertainty about asset yields can be classified as inflation risk, market risk, default or credit risk, and income risk.

Inflation risk

All assets are subject to inflation risk.[3] *Inflation risk* is uncertainty of future purchasing power, where the future nominal value itself is known. Federal government bonds and bank term deposits, for instance, provide known interest payments and nominal values upon redemption in the future, but

---

[1]The distinction can be traced to Frank Knight in *Uncertainty and Profit* (Boston: Houghton Mifflin, 1921), 19–20. For a discussion of its relevance, see Jan Mossin, *Theory of Financial Markets* (Englewood Cliffs, N.J.: Prentice-Hall, 1973), chap. 2.

[2]This formula applies to a simple asset yielding all future value at one point. The general formula is more complicated, for assets providing future values at several points of time, but still each pattern of future values implies one and only one average yield. The average yield is the value of r such that current price equals the present discounted sum of all future values, discounted at the rate r per period:

$$P = \frac{FV_1}{(1 + r)} + \frac{FV_2}{1 + r)^2} + \dots + \frac{FV_n}{(1 + r)^n}$$

[3]Fully indexed pensions are subject to inflation risk, but only to the extent that the recipient's cost of living is not accurately measured by the nationwide price index used to adjust nominal pension payments.

one cannot know in advance what those values will buy, because the inflation rate is not known for certain.

Over long periods, inflation risk is one of the larger sources of uncertainty. A $1000 pension starting at age sixty-five, for example, will still buy $1000 worth of goods in today's prices at age seventy-five if there is no inflation, but only $508 worth of goods if inflation averages 7 percent per year over the ten-year period, and only $386 worth of goods if inflation averages 10 percent per year. Those are large differences for someone planning to live on a fixed pension income.

Market risk

Market risk arises because of uncertainty about the market price of assets at the point in the future when they will be resold. Market risk does not affect assets that will for certain be held until maturity (when they will be redeemed at face value), but assets like stocks and houses and land have no such maturity date. Many assets that do have a certain maturity date are also held for much shorter periods than the full term to maturity, so they too are subject to market risk.

Default risk

Default risk is fairly straightforward. Even if inflation is known and nominal payments are fixed for the future, there is still the possibility that the borrower will in fact make the payments late or not at all. The borrower may be unwilling to repay, or unable because of unforeseeable circumstances such as worldwide recession.

Income risk

Many assets do not promise fixed nominal payments. Stocks, mutual funds, pension funds, most insurance policies, notice deposits at banks, all deposits at credit unions, renegotiable mortgages, and renewable money-market assets all offer a stream of nominal payments that varies unpredictably over time. Let us call this variability *income risk*. The flow of payments may fluctuate with the profits of the company, with the level of prevailing yields on bonds, or with the mortality of groups of insured customers. Many fixed-rate bonds and bank deposits held in Canada are denominated in foreign currency, so their nominal values in Canadian dollars fluctuate with the exchange rate. This specific form of income risk is known as *foreign-exchange risk*.

Foreign exchange risk

Most asset portfolios are exposed to a combination of all four types of risk. Some of the risks are offsetting, some are independent, some are cumulative. For instance, nominal interest rates on short-term deposits tend to move together with expected future inflation rates (we will discuss this in chapter 14). Therefore, where faster inflation is expected to decrease the real value of deposits, higher nominal interest rates can be expected to restore that real value. The net risk to the real value of deposits is clearly smaller than either inflation or income risk separately would suggest. Default risks, by contrast, are mostly independent of the other kinds of risk.

Household risk exposure

By choosing different mixes of assets in our portfolios, we expose ourselves to different amounts of each type of risk. Half of the typical family's total asset portfolio consists of the family home. Since homes last longer than most families wish to live in them, the family home provides two kinds of return. The first is a real return in the form of housing services (shelter, status, and recreation) while the family lives in it. The second is a capital gain or loss, realized when the family sells the home and moves out. The home's resale value depends on future housing markets and is expressed in dollars of some future year, so the capital gain from a house is subject to both market risk and inflation risk. On the other hand, the flow of housing services made available each year is subject to only a tiny amount of income risk, and that only if there is a chance the house will be damaged by lightning or flood.

Household deposits in banks and credit unions, by contrast, are subject only to some nominal income risk, since their interest rates fluctuate, and to inflation risk, which largely offsets the income risk. There is almost no default risk, because almost all of the deposits are federally or provincially insured.

One-third of all families have large holdings in work-related pension plans, discussed in chapter 13. These plans constitute the main financial-asset holding for most of these families, though they do not hold the pension plans' assets directly. The worth of a pension-fund holding to any one household is subject to a large degree of market risk, because of the way in which pension benefits are often calculated. Most retiring workers' pensions are arranged at retirement by using the worker's share of the pension fund to buy a life annuity (a stream of regular income payments to continue for life) from an insurance company. To value the pension fund's assets for that purpose, the market prices as of the worker's retirement date are used.[4] If those market prices happen to be unusually high or low, the worker gets a larger or smaller pension for life.

Measurement of risk

It is not enough just to list four sources of uncertainty and say vaguely that they are reinforcing or cumulative when joined together in an asset

[4]Pension funds' bonds, however, are valued not at market prices, but at an amortized value that is a moving average of the current price and the redemption value.

portfolio. For analysis of risk behavior we need a more detailed definition of risk that allows us to measure it. Such a working definition has been common in economics since the 1950s, publicized as part of the Tobin-Markowitz approach to financial-market analysis.[5]

To use the Tobin-Markowitz approach, we need to make two assumptions. Not all cases will satisfy these assumptions; our analysis will therefore be less general than so far in the book but still general enough to fit almost all financial-market behavior.

Probability distribution

The first assumption of the Tobin-Markowitz approach is that financial-market participants will behave as though they had some idea of the *probability distribution* of yields available on different asset portfolios. A probability distribution is a schedule or graph showing the various possible yields that might occur and the relative probabilities of each one's occurring. Figure 8–1 shows an example of a probability distribution, for course grades of a typical student in my university.

FIGURE 8–1 Probability distribution of course grades

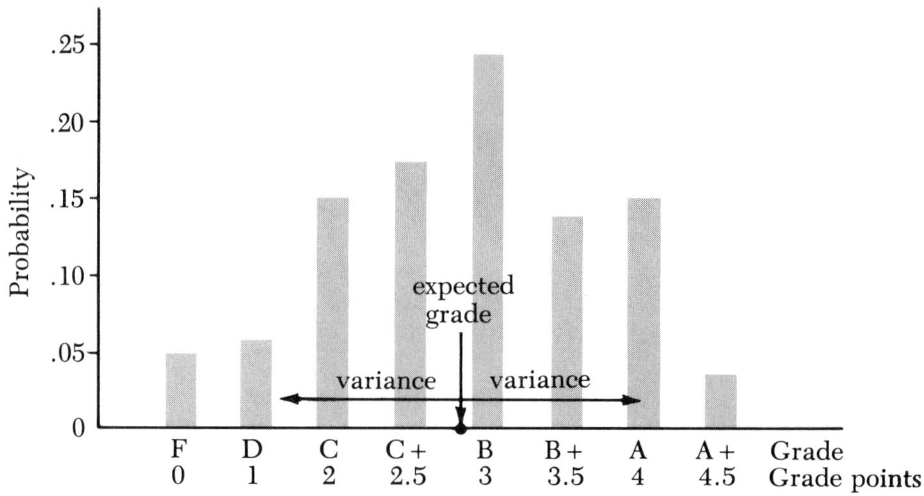

This distribution shows all possible grades and the probability of occurrence of each grade. The probabilities add up to exactly 1.0. In this distribution the midpoint or mean is a grade equivalent to 2.87 points, and the variance (a measure of width) is 1.14.

This assumption means that participants in financial markets will behave as though they had some idea not only of the range of possible

[5]James Tobin, "Liquidity Preference as Behavior Towards Risk," *Review of Economic Studies*, 1958, 65–86; Harry Markowitz, *Portfolio Selection: Efficient Diversification of Investments* (New Haven, Conn.: Yale University Press, for the Cowles Foundation, 1959).

yields but also of the relative probabilities of each possible yield for a particular portfolio. It may seem that that is attributing too much knowledge to financial-market participants, but if you were given a record of past yields on stock portfolios, most of you could probably come up with a plausible probability distribution of future yields on similar portfolios. Financial-market participants have at least that much information about any lending project that really interests them.

Normal distribution

The second assumption is that financial-market participants will generally have to choose only among portfolios whose future yields have a particular but common shape of probability distribution: this is the *normal distribution*, which has a bell shape such that probabilities are largest at the centre and smallest at either end. Such a distribution is unlikely for many individual assets, but for entire asset portfolios it is much more likely.[6]

Expected yield

Variance

With these two assumptions, it can be shown that assetholders will choose among different asset portfolios solely on the basis of two aspects of the probability distributions of their future yields: (a) the mean, or *expected yield*, or midpoint of the distribution and (b) the *variance*, an index of the width of the distribution.

The variance is our measurable index of the riskiness or uncertainty of asset portfolios. Using the width of a probability distribution as an index of riskiness corresponds to our intuitive understanding of risk. For instance, most of us would not hesitate to describe a course as "less risky" if its probability distribution of course grades ranged only from C+ to B+, rather than from F to A+. The less risky probability distribution is narrower (and also taller, since all probabilities must add up to 1 in every distribution, regardless of range) and therefore has a smaller variance.

Analysing responses to uncertainty is thus equivalent to analysing responses to variance. Note before we proceed, however, that uncertainty and variance are equivalent only under the two assumptions we have made.

Definition of variance

The variance is, in full English, "variance of possible yields around the expected yield." Algebraically, it is the weighted average of squared deviations of possible yields from the expected yield, with relative probabilities serving as weights.[7] Where V is variance, E is expected yield, r_i is

[6]There is an alternative to this assumption, which is that financial-market participants have utility functions that are approximately quadratic in shape with respect to future yields. Appendix 1 following this chapter shows that, when this is true, assetholders also care only about the mean and variance of their portfolio yield in making choices between portfolios, regardless of the shape of the probability distribution.

[7]In the formula for variance, the squaring is performed only so that positive deviations from the expected value will not all be cancelled out by negative deviations. Taking the expected or probability-weighted deviation would always give a value of exactly zero. The average absolute deviation (ignoring the sign) is sometimes used instead as a measure of risk, but its statistical properties are not as convenient.

the ith possible yield, and $prob_i$ is its probability of occurring in the future, the formula for calculating a variance is

$$V = \Sigma\, prob_i\, (r_i - E)^2.$$

In this equation, the sum of all probabilities must add up to exactly 1.0, by definition of a probability distribution. In the example in figure 8–1 the variance of grade points can be calculated with this formula to be 1.1 when the expected yield has been found to be 2.9.

The expected yield E that appears in the variance formula is a weighted average of possible yields, with relative probabilities serving as weights.

$$E = \Sigma\, prob_i\, r_i.$$

The formula for E is the same as for a weighted grade-point average, except that in calculating E future probabilities are used instead of past relative frequencies.

SECTION 2 Mean-variance analysis: choosing among portfolios

If wealthholders choose among asset portfolios solely on the basis of the means and variances they offer, their choice can be illustrated quite simply with an indifference-curve diagram.

The portfolio-choice diagram

Each possible asset combination makes up a separate asset portfolio, and each portfolio has its own pair of mean and variance in the wealthholder's mind. Each such pair can be plotted as a point in figure 8–2. The set of such points makes up the feasible set. For all wealthholders who prefer to avoid risk, other things remaining equal (in other words, for all who are risk-averse), only the upper left edge of the feasible set, known as the

Efficient frontier

efficient frontier, is relevant. Risk averters will always want to minimize V for any given level of E and to maximize E for any given level of V. The points satisfying these two requirements must lie on the upper left edge of the feasible set rather than inside it. Risk averters will therefore never choose a point not on the efficient set. Which point on the efficient set will be chosen depends on the tastes of wealthholders, as described in the set of indifference curves relating expected yields and variances.

Risk aversion

We assume in this chapter that assetholders are risk-averse. This does not

Risk averter

imply that they never take risks. Far from it. *Risk averters* are always taking risks, but they take those risks only in the expectation (possibly a mistaken one) of greater expected yield.[8]

FIGURE 8–2 Optimal portfolio choice

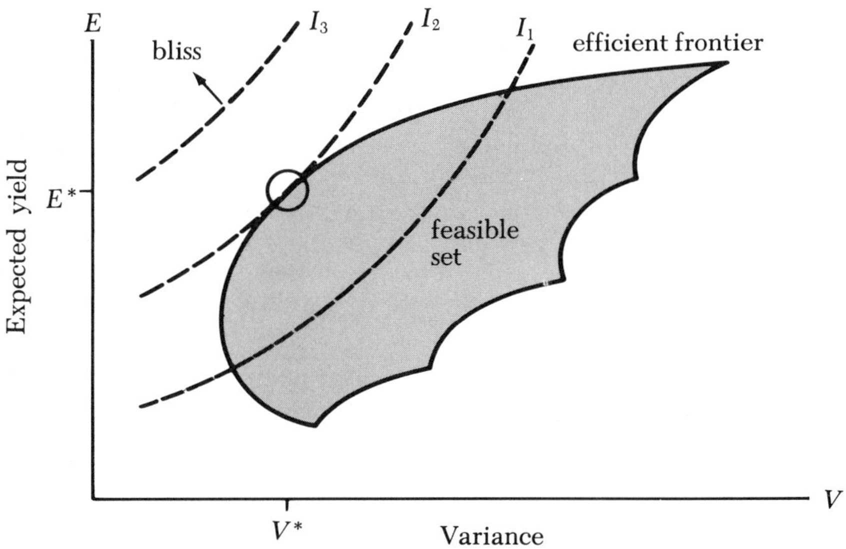

Faced with the range of options making up the feasible set, the assetholder chooses point (E°, V°), which lies on the highest attainable indifference curve I_2. (E°, V°) is one point on the efficient frontier.

Risk seeker

It is possible to derive the property of risk aversion from fairly simple and plausible assumptions about human behavior (as is done in appendix 1 following this chapter), but the property is easiest to establish for financial decisions just by looking around us and recognizing that we know of very few risk seekers. First, accept as a definition of risk aversion the property of choosing a portfolio with more V only if it also promises more expected yield E. A *risk seeker*, the opposite of a risk averter, is someone who actively desires more variance V and will even give up some expected yield in order to get it.

One sure way of increasing variance in financial matters is to put all of your eggs in one basket. If you are a risk seeker, then not only will you bet on a horse race, but you will gamble your entire wealth (and mortgage your

[8]Note that it is quite possible, and even likely, that risk averters will prefer some uncertainty to a life of complete predictability. Surprise spices up life a bit. We merely assume that whatever desire people have for uncertainty is already satisfied by some other aspect of their lives, such as an unpredictable boss, so that they do not want any extra risk when they come to choose among asset portfolios.

future income to gamble that, too) on a single ticket. And, of course, you will bet only to win. Now, how many people do you know who behave that way? Very few. The only reason for not gambling this way is to avoid risk, so it follows that almost all the people you know are risk averters.

Indifference curves on an E,V diagram such as figure 8–2 will therefore slope upward to the right: more E will be required to compensate for more V. Marginal utility of E (MU_E) is positive, but marginal utility of V (MU_V) is negative. If the marginal disutility of risk increases with more exposure to it, as is plausible, then indifference curves are also convex from below; that is, they rise ever more steeply.

Marginal rate of substitution of variance for expected yield

Wealthholders' degree of risk aversion will vary, both between wealthholders and between different points on figure 8–2. The degree of risk aversion can be thought of as measured by the slope of the indifference curve at any point. This slope is the *marginal rate of substitution of variance for expected yield*, $MRS_{V,E}$, which is the absolute value of the ratio MU_V/MU_E. Those strongly averse to risk will have steep indifference curves and relatively large ratios of MU_V to MU_E. Those almost indifferent to risk will have almost flat indifference curves and small ratios of MU_V to MU_E. Figure 8–3 gives examples.

FIGURE 8–3 Risk aversion and portfolio choice

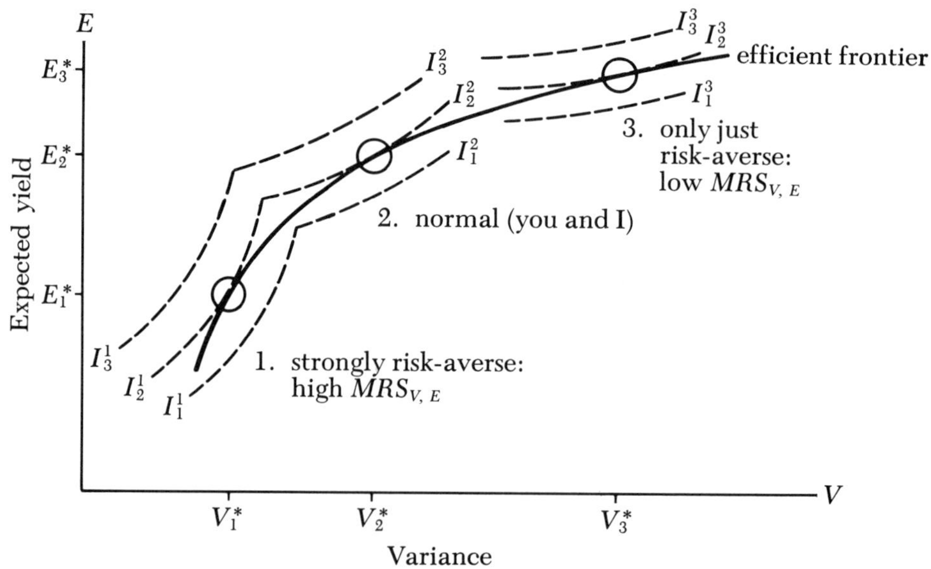

Faced with the same efficient frontier of possible choices, wealthholders with different attitudes toward risk will make different choices. Individual 1 will choose the portfolio offering E_1°, V_1°, whereas those only just risk-averse will insist on E_3° even at the expense of being exposed to the extra risk of V_3°.

The optimal portfolio choice

The optimal portfolio is the one whose combination of expected yield and variance lies on the highest indifference curve. This occurs at the point of tangency of an indifference curve and the efficient frontier in figures 8–2 and 8–3, generating expected portfolio yield E^* and variance V^*.

Two properties of the optimal portfolio choice in figures 8–2 and 8–3 are worth bringing out here. First, the slope of the efficient set at that optimal point gives the price of extra risk for this wealthholder, in terms of extra expected yield. E must be increased along with V at the rate given by the indifference curve just to keep the wealthholder satisfied, and at the optimal point the slope of the indifference curve is the same as that of the efficient set. Indifference curves are unobservable, but on occasion the slope of the efficient set may be known within a limited range.

Second, the choice of optimal portfolio implies demand for individual assets: only those assets that are a large share of wealthholders' optimal portfolios will have large demand, while those that do not form part of optimal portfolios will not be demanded at all. Analysing demand for individual assets is therefore equivalent to analysing total demand for wealth and then analysing the shares of individual assets in optimal portfolios. This analysis is deferred to the next section, after we deal with the special case of portfolio choice with a riskless asset.

The case of the riskless asset

There is a situation in which the efficient set can be drawn as a straight line rather than as the curve shown in figure 8–2. The situation occurs with only a trivial redefinition of risk, in the case where there exists an asset with no risk at all.[9] Tobin introduced portfolio-choice theory to economics by focussing on this situation, where the riskless asset was called money.[10] His analysis is presented more fully in chapter 9, but the central argument is given here as well.

If money is riskless, then all portfolio risk in a portfolio containing money must come from the other assets. For simplicity, let's call these other assets bonds. It is easy to show, with the algebra we will develop in the next section, that total portfolio risk depends on how risky the bonds are and how large their share of the portfolio is. In fact, if we measure risk as the square root of the variance, a measure known as the *standard deviation* (S), risk for the portfolio will rise at a constant rate as the share of bonds in the portfolio rises. This redefinition of risk is trivial, since whatever

[9] This riskless asset could be the result of combining two or more separate assets chosen so that their risks exactly offset each other to produce a constant average yield.

[10] James Tobin, "Liquidity Preference as Behavior Towards Risk," *Review of Economic Studies*, 1958, 65–86.

changes the variance must also change its square root in the same direction and by a comparable amount.

Since portfolio expected yield also rises at a constant rate as the share of bonds rises, starting from the expected yield on money when the share of bonds is zero, it follows that a series of portfolios with ever larger shares of bonds will generate combinations of expected yield and standard deviation that lie along a straight line, as in figure 8–4.

FIGURE 8–4 The efficient frontier with a riskless asset

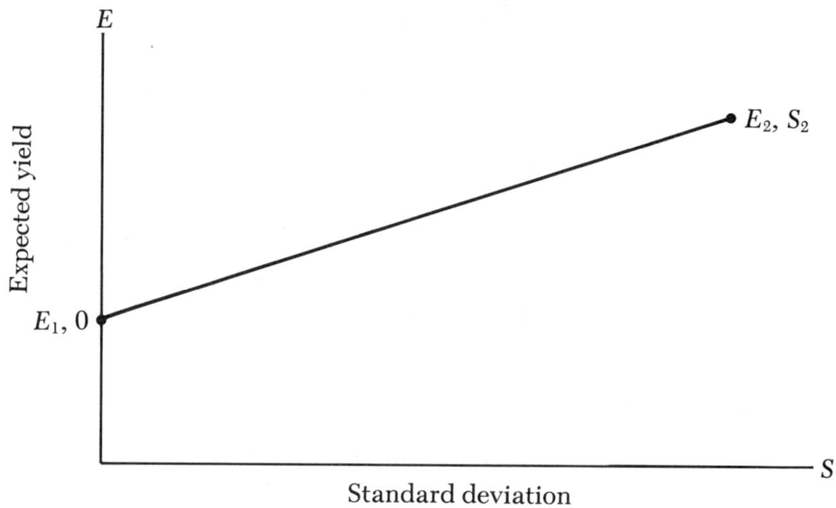

In Tobin's original example, asset 1 is money and asset 2 is bonds. Money is riskless, and a portfolio with just money provides $E = E_1$, $S = 0$. A portfolio with just bonds provides $E = E_2$, $S = S_2$. Combinations provide E, S values lying along the straight line between those two.

SECTION 3 Mean-variance analysis: portfolio choice and demand for assets

Demand for individual assets is derived from their relative contributions to portfolio expected yield (E) and variance (V), since it is portfolio E and V that wealthholders use to rank portfolios. Not surprisingly, the collection of assets that add the most to portfolio E, per unit added to portfolio V, will make up the best portfolio and will be chosen. What we need to do in this section is establish how individual assets contribute to expected yield and variance of a portfolio.

Portfolio expected yield

Expected yield is the easier of the two concepts to explain. It is a weighted average of the expected yields of all assets in the portfolio, with weights equal to portfolio shares. Where X_i is the share of the ith asset in the portfolio, and E_i is the expected yield of the ith asset, the expected portfolio yield E on a portfolio with n different assets is

$$E = \Sigma X_i E_i,$$

where the sum of portfolio shares, ΣX_i, is 1.0.

Because portfolio expected yield is derived from individual assets' expected yields in the same way that a grade-point average is derived from individual course grades, it is easy to see how assets contribute to portfolio expected yield. Those with relatively high expected yield will raise E for the portfolio; those with relatively low expected yield will lower E. Further, the rate of improvement of portfolio expected yield, as more of an asset is added to the portfolio, will be proportional to the difference between the asset's expected yield and that on the rest of the portfolio. Relative contributions of various assets to portfolio expected yields are therefore proportional to the assets' own relative expected yields.[11]

Portfolio variance

Portfolio variance is more complex. It is not a weighted average of variances of individual assets, but generally much less. Portfolio variance depends not only on variances of yields of individual assets but also on their covariances with each other. A *covariance* is a measure of the joint variation that two yields are expected to have around their expected values.

Covariance

Covariance of asset yields reflects two things: the variance of each yield by itself, and the degree of correlation of the two yields — the extent to which they move together or independently or in opposite directions. The degree of correlation of any two asset yields r_i and r_j is measured by a correlation coefficient (RHO_{ij}), whose value must lie somewhere between -1 and $+1$: the correlation coefficient will be $+1$ if the two yields move together linearly (that is, with changes in constant proportion), 0 if the yield changes are independent, -1 if they move in opposite directions linearly, and in between $+1$ and -1 if the relationship is generally positive or negative but not exact and linear. Figure 8–5 provides some examples.

[11]This is not quite true as it is written, but it is very close for most assets. Contributions to portfolio expected yield are measured by differences between assets' own expected yields and the expected yield on the rest of the portfolio. Expected yield on the rest of the portfolio will be defined differently for each asset because as each asset is considered it is excluded from "the rest of the portfolio." Where asset shares are small, exclusion of one asset makes little difference to the average of yields on "the rest of the portfolio," but where the asset share is as big as the share of a house in most household portfolios, clearly it will make a difference.

FIGURE 8–5 Some examples of correlation

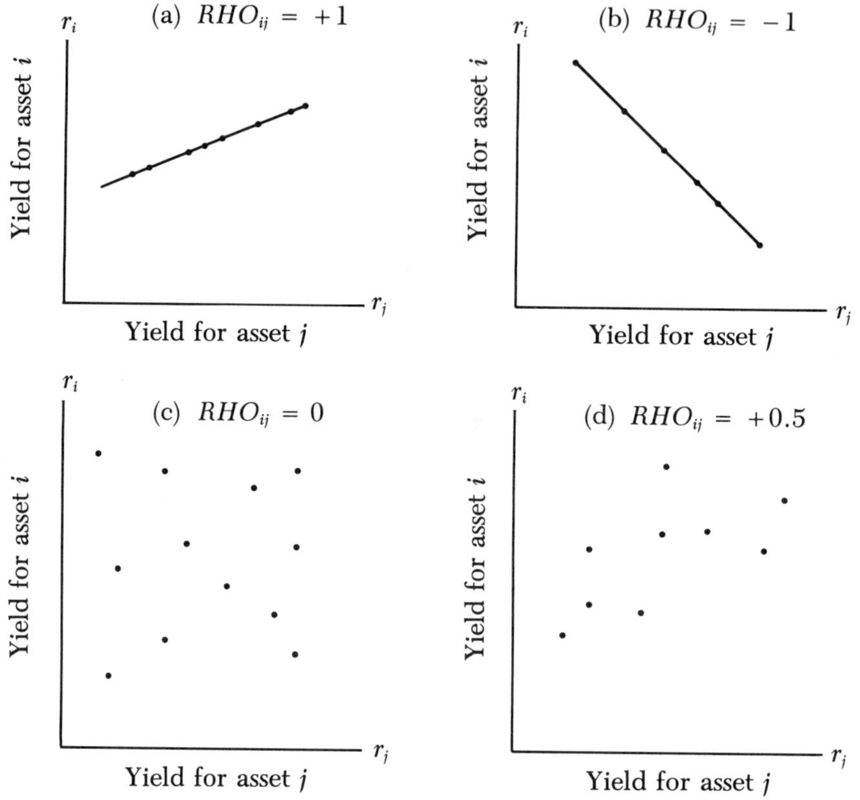

Where observed values of two events always lie along a positively sloped line, there is perfect positive correlation. Where they always lie along a negatively sloped line, there is perfect negative correlation. Where they do not seem to lie along or near any line at all, there is no correlation. Other cases lie somewhere in between, as in panel (d).

Algebraically the covariance COV_{ij} of any two assets i and j is defined as[12]

$$COV_{ij} = \sqrt{V_i}\sqrt{V_j}\, RHO_{ij}$$

[12]The algebraic definition of the correlation coefficient RHO_{ij} for any two assets i and j is

$$RHO_{ij} = \Sigma\, prob_k \frac{(r_{ik} - E_i)}{\sqrt{V_i}} \frac{(r_{jk} - E_j)}{\sqrt{V_j}}$$

where r_{ik} is the kth possible yield of the ith asset, and $prob_k$ is the probability of occurrence of the kth outcome. The correlation coefficient can be interpreted in words as a probability-weighted average of deviation products, each deviation being "standardized" by being expressed in units of its own standard deviation. Substituting this expression in the equation for the covariance gives an alternative formula for the covariance:

$$COV_{ij} = \Sigma prob_k (r_{ik} - E_i)(r_{jk} - E_j).$$

Now that we have defined covariance, we can use it in the definition of portfolio variance. For a two-asset portfolio the portfolio variance is

$$V = X_1^2V_1 + X_2^2V_2 + 2X_1X_2COV_{12}.$$

Since $X_2 = (1 - X_1)$ by definition, V can also be defined as

$$V = X_1^2V_1 + (1 - X_1)^2V_2 + 2X_1(1 - X_1)COV_{12}.$$

It is clear already from the equation for V that it will be lower (that is, the portfolio more desirable, and the assets in it more likely to be demanded) if each asset has low variance, but also if they have low covariances. What is not as obvious is that, for assets making up only a small share of the portfolio, the covariance makes much more difference than the variance. Consider for instance the value of V when $X_1 = 0.01$ and $X_2 = 1 - X_1 = 0.99$:

$$\begin{aligned} V &= (.01)^2V_1 + (.99)^2V_2 + 2(.01)(.99)COV_{12} \\ &= .0001V_1 + .98V_2 + .0198COV_{12}. \end{aligned}$$

The coefficient on the covariance term is 198 times as large as that on the variance term for asset 1 (.0198 versus .0001). As the portfolio share of asset 1 rises, of course, that situation changes. At the limit, where an asset dominates the portfolio the way asset 2 does in this example, the coefficient on the variance term dwarfs that on the covariance term (.98 versus .0198).

Diversification

Another conclusion follows besides the relative importance of covariance. That conclusion is the importance of diversification, among assets with uncorrelated yields. There are two ways of showing the effect of diversification.

First, consider a collection of assets having positive variance but zero covariance with all other asset yields. The asset portfolio can contain either a few of these assets or a lot of them. If there are only a few, their average portfolio share must be large (0.5 for 2, 0.25 for 4, and so on), so their contribution to portfolio risk V will reflect mainly their positive variances rather than their zero covariances; the individual variance terms will have large coefficients. If there are many such assets in the portfolio, their average portfolio shares must be small, so their contributions to portfolio risk hardly reflect their positive variances at all — only their zero covariances. It follows that portfolio variance will be much lower if the portfolio is widely diversified than if it is not.

The second way of showing the effect of diversification is algebraically. Consider a portfolio with n different assets, all having identical variances V_i, identical portfolio shares $X_i = 1/n$, and zero covariances. We will look at the portfolio variance for such a portfolio and then see the effect of simply increasing the number of assets, n. The formula for portfolio variance in this (streamlined) case is

$$V = \Sigma X_i^2 V_i$$
$$= n\left(\frac{1}{n}\right)^2 V_i$$
$$= \left(\frac{1}{n}\right) V_i$$

Clearly, the larger is n the smaller is V. Somewhat less clearly, the gains from diversification fall off quite quickly. For instance, table 8–1 shows how V falls for various portfolio sizes from 1 to 100 if $V_i = 10$ for each individual asset.

TABLE 8–1 Effect of diversification

Number of assets	Porfolio variance
1	10.0
2	5.0
3	3.3
4	2.5
5	2.0
10	1.0
20	0.5
50	0.2
100	0.1

Note: All assets have identical shares in the portfolio, equal to 1/number of assets. All assets have variances of 10, and zero covariance with other assets.

Example: bank loan diversification

In very few cases is diversification as large and effective as it is in the loan portfolios of Canada's large banks. There are over ten million loan notes held by Canadian banks, of which half a million are business loans. The borrowers come from all areas and industries inside and outside the Canadian economy. No one producing sector, for instance, accounts for a larger fraction than 7.5 percent of total business loans.

Each individual loan note has some default risk. Although there is only a small chance of even partial default on the vast majority of loans, complete default means an enormous loss on that loan of −100 percent. The average default rate over the period 1969–79 for Canadian banks appears to have been roughly one complete default or the equivalent for every 350 loans, with the rest of the loans being paid in full and on time. If this rate of loan default is what bankers expect, then their expected yield on an individual loan note whose stated interest rate is 10 percent is

$$\frac{1}{350}(-100) + \frac{349}{350}(10) = 9.7 \text{ percent.}$$

The variance of yields on a typical loan note is therefore

$$\frac{1}{350}(-100 - 9.7)^2 + \frac{349}{350}(10 - 9.7)^2 = 34.8.$$

If diversification did not reduce risk, variance V of the loan portfolio as a whole would be 34.8 as well. As measured for all Canadian banks together over the period 1969–80, the typical loan-portfolio variance due to default risk is only 0.02 instead of 34.8. For individual banks, the loan-portfolio variance may be up to five times larger, but even 0.10 as a variance for the total loan portfolio is still tiny compared to 34.8, the variance of an individual loan note.

This is a good point at which to introduce a concept useful in financial analysis, that of breaking the risk of individual assets down into systematic and nonsystematic parts.

Systematic and nonsystematic risk

We have seen that diversification pays: it reduces variance. This holds, however, only if covariance is low. Where asset yields tend to move together (for example, yields on short-term deposits and short-term bonds), their covariance will be close to the average value of their variances — the maximum value of a covariance — so it will make little difference whether it is their variances or their covariances that are important in the formula for calculating portfolio variance.[13]

This observation leads to a distinction, for any asset, between those of its yield fluctuations that are correlated with fluctuations in yields elsewhere in the financial system, and those that are not. The first type of yield fluctuation has been labelled *systematic risk*; the second type, *nonsystematic* (or *unsystematic*) *risk*. Our discussion suggests that nonsystematic risk need not be much of a drawback to an asset, in that it does not affect portfolio variance much as long as the asset is a small share of the portfolio. Clearly a large variance does prevent wealthholders from demanding so much of an asset that it becomes a large share of their portfolio, but that is unlikely anyway. Systematic risk, on the other hand, is a serious drawback because it cannot be made unimportant by diversification. No matter how small the portfolio share, an asset with large systematic risk will add significantly to portfolio risk.

Systematic risk

Nonsystematic or unsystematic risk

These concepts can be made much more precise with a few extra but restrictive assumptions about the financial system. Such assumptions are

[13]If $COV_{ab} = (V_a V_b)^{1/2}$, then portfolio variance is

$$\begin{aligned} V &= X_a^2 V_a + (1 - X_a)^2 V_b + 2X_a(1 - X_a)(V_a V_b)^{1/2} \\ &= X_a^2 S_a^2 + (1 - X_a)^2 S_b^2 + 2X_a(1 - X_a) S_a S_b \\ &= (X_a S_a + X_b S_b)^2 \end{aligned}$$

so portfolio variance is the square of the weighted average standard deviation. This is not quite an average, but close.

not useful for our main purpose, so this extension is treated separately in the second appendix to this chapter, on Sharpe's systematic-risk model.

Offsetting risks: negative correlation

The preceding section pointed out that adding even a risky asset to an undiversified portfolio can cause portfolio risk to fall rather than rise, if the covariance is near zero. Marginal contributions of an asset to portfolio risk can therefore be negative. Such effects are much stronger if the covariance is not only small, but negative. Recall the formula for the variance of a two-asset portfolio,

$$V = X_1^2 V_1 + (1 - X_1)^2 V_2 + 2X_1(1 - X_1)COV_{12}.$$

If X_1 is a small fraction, so X_1^2 is tiny, and if COV_{12} is negative, then the net contribution of asset 1 to portfolio variance can be to reduce V even if V_1 is large.

The obvious example is the addition of an insurance policy to any asset portfolio, to insure against theft or fire damage to the other assets in the portfolio. Such a policy by itself is as risky as a lottery ticket: it may pay off handsomely relative to its cost if there is a claim, but the chances are slim. If there is no claim, the policy will be a total loss, yielding –100 percent. However, the policy's big payoff would occur precisely in the case in which the other assets would have abysmal yields (–100 percent for theft, possibly only –50 percent for fire damage), so it has strong negative covariance with other yields.

To illustrate that case, we might insert numbers as follows: the policy would cost only 1 percent of the asset portfolio. Its variance might be 1000, that of the rest of the portfolio only 10. Covariance might be –75, which is three-quarters of the minimum possible value of –100. Inserting those values in the formula above gives us the portfolio variance. Without the insurance, portfolio variance is 10. With the insurance policy making up 1 percent of the portfolio, variance is

$$\begin{aligned} V &= (.01)^2(1000) + .99^2(10) + 2(.01)(.99)(-75) \\ &= .1 + 9.8 - 1.95 \\ &= 8.4. \end{aligned}$$

Hedging

The example of an insurance policy is only one of several similar strategies known collectively as *hedging*. Hedging is offsetting one risk by taking on another, exactly opposite, risk, by purchasing an asset or arranging a contract whose yields have close to perfect negative correlation with the yields on other assets held. Section 4 provides some other examples.

Summary of asset demand

The relative desirability of various assets to wealthholders depends on their relative contributions to the expected yield and variance of the portfolio.

Relative contributions to expected portfolio yield depend in straightforward fashion on the assets' own expected yields, so high-yield assets are more desired than low-yield assets. Contributions to portfolio variance are not so simple, but we can reach these conclusions:

1. The logic of portfolio diversification suggests all rational wealthholders will hold well-diversified portfolios if they can, so the typical asset will constitute only a small share of the portfolio.
2. For a given portfolio share, what matters most in relative riskiness of different assets is the relative covariance of their yields with those of other assets. This covariance is a measure of assets' systematic risk — a permanent diasadvantage in the competition for a larger place in wealthholders' portfolios. Nonsystematic risk matters as well, but less and less as the portfolio becomes more and more diversified.
3. Individual assets can subtract from portfolio risk, even though their own variances are high, if either (a) their addition to the portfolio leaves them still a small share of the portfolio or (b) their covariance with other yields in the portfolio is negative, as it is for insurance policies and other hedges.

Because each asset has to compete with other assets for a place in wealthholders' portfolios, it is to be expected that each asset with important disadvantages such as large covariance will have to come up with compensating advantages, such as higher expected yield. In general equilibrium we would expect a pattern of relative yields whose differences compensated exactly for differences in relative contributions to portfolio risk (that is, mainly for differences in relative covariance with other asset yields). Where that is not the case, we expect a shift of asset demand until there is either a change in price or a change in portfolio share that does produce such a compensating yield difference. Just how large the yield difference must be to compensate for differences in relative covariances and variances depends on the degree of risk aversion of wealthholders and their degree of diversification.

The relationship between expected yield and volume of assets held (the slope of a demand curve for each asset) follows from the preceding paragraph. For a given level of wealth, extra holdings of any individual asset imply a larger portfolio share of that asset, which implies a greater portfolio risk because the asset's own variance matters more than before. In order to offset the greater riskiness of extra amounts of this asset, wealthholders will insist on a greater expected yield. So, in equilibrium, greater expected yield will be needed to generate more demand for an individual asset.

This relationship between expected yield and demand for an asset can be illustrated conveniently on a loanable-funds diagram, where demand for an individual asset such as Acme stock is thought of as supply of loanable funds to Acme in exchange for its stock certificates. Figure 8–6 shows such a schedule. The slope of the schedule depends on how much extra risk wealthholders feel they are adding as they increase their holdings of Acme stock, and how risk-averse they are. The position of the schedule reflects expected yields on other assets, relative covariances and variances, and the total wealth of potential Acme shareholders.

FIGURE 8–6 Demand for stock (Supply of loanable funds)

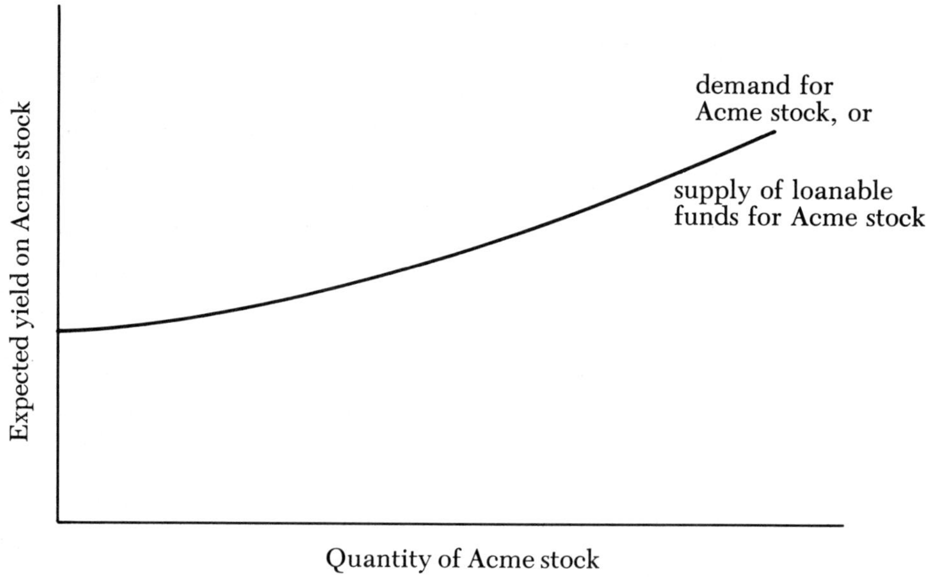

Risk premium

The supply curve in this diagram slopes upward because assetholders require larger and larger *risk premiums* in the expected yield to compensate them for the extra risk of having a larger share of Acme stock in their asset portfolios.

SECTION 4

Hedging markets

We have seen that portfolio variance can be reduced substantially if assets can be found whose yields are negatively correlated with yields on assets already held. Such assets are widely demanded by risk-averse wealthholders. Over time, innovators have created several financial instruments specifically to satisfy this demand. Collectively, these are known as *hedges*. The largest, most pervasive, and best-known hedge is an insurance policy. We have already given an example of that asset and its effect on portfolio risk, and we will be discussing the operation of life insurance companies in chapter 13. Two other, less familiar hedges are futures contracts and options contracts. I will describe and discuss these contracts briefly in this section.

Futures contracts

Most firms must buy their inputs well before they know the price of their outputs. This exposes them to substantial risks on their inventory portfolio. Some producers can reduce or eliminate this risk by adding one or more futures contracts to their portfolio. Futures contracts have substantial risk as well, but their yields move almost exactly opposite to those on the inventory portfolio, so the two risks cancel each other out. Inventory risks can be reduced in this way for any item for which futures contracts are traded on any futures exchange. This includes most grains and oilseeds, cattle and pork bellies, lumber and plywood, propane, several industrial metals, gold and silver in several forms, long and short-term government bonds and mortgages, many foreign currencies, and now even a basket of common stocks.

Here is a detailed example of how a futures contract works. Tastee Bacon Company Ltd. buys pork bellies, smokes them, and slices them up into bacon: a simple operation. TBC's only significant asset is its inventory of pork bellies, which it must hold on average for six months. TBC cannot know when it buys pork bellies what the resale price will be in the bacon market six months later, so its yields on pork-belly inventories are uncertain.

In order to get rid of that risk for each shipment of pork bellies it buys, TBC arranges at the time of purchase to sell an equal volume of pork bellies six months later in futures contracts. (This is done on the Chicago Mercantile Exchange at a tiny commission of $50 per two-way transaction, on contracts of 36 000 lbs. each.) TBC puts down a *margin deposit* of only 1 percent of the contract value, which is the firm's only financial commitment to this investment. Its investment in futures-contract deposits is therefore 1 percent of its investment in pork-belly inventories, or 1/101th of the total asset portfolio. No pork bellies change hands yet, since the futures contract calls for delivery six months in the future.

Margin deposit

Toward the end of the six months, TBC starts to sell its finished bacon in the *spot market* (the ordinary sort of market where delivery is immediate rather than at some future date). At this point TBC also "cancels" its futures contracts, by arranging to buy exactly the same quantity of pork bellies it had previously arranged to sell on the futures market, for the same delivery date. All futures contracts are entered into with the Exchange itself, rather than with an opposite party, so when TBC has arranged both to buy and to sell the same quantity on the same date, the Exchange regards both obligations as cancelled and pays whatever gain there is between buying price and selling price. That gain is the only source of yield on TBC's 1 percent deposit put down against these contracts.

Spot market

TBC will make a loss on its bacon business if bacon prices fall during the six-month period. If bacon prices fall, however, pork-belly prices are sure to fall as well on the *futures market*, and by roughly the same amount per pound. TBC will have to cancel out of its futures contracts by buying at a

Futures market

lower price than it had previously arranged to sell for. The gain on its futures contracts will cancel out the loss on its bacon business, leaving it unaffected by changes in bacon prices. Exactly the opposite pattern of losses and gains will occur if the bacon price rises instead; the net effect will still be nil.

Gains and losses will generally match each other dollar for dollar on futures contracts and pork-belly inventories, but the percentage yields will differ wildly because of the different amounts invested. TBC's investment in pork-belly inventories is 100 times its (deposit) investment in the futures contracts. What causes yields on its inventory to rise by 2 percent will therefore cause yields on its futures contracts to fall by 200 percent (that's right: there is no floor of −100 percent to potential losses on futures contracts; investors can lose much more than their investment).

The probability distribution of possible yields on futures contracts will therefore be 100 times as wide as the probability distribution of yields on pork-belly inventories, so the variance of futures-contract yields will be 10 000 times as large as that of inventory yields. Let the variance of inventory yields (V_1) be 1 (any number will do; only relative risks are of interest here). The variance of futures-contract yields (V_2) will then be 10 000.

If the two yields always move in opposite directions in the same proportion of 100 to 1, they are perfectly negatively correlated. Their covariance is then $\sqrt{V_1}\sqrt{V_2}\,(-1)$, which is $(1)(100)(-1) = -100$. Portfolio variance with a 1/101th share in futures contracts and 100/101th share in pork-belly inventories is then

$$V = \left(\frac{100}{101}\right)^2(1) + \left(\frac{1}{101}\right)^2(10\ 000) + 2\left(\frac{1}{101}\right)\left(\frac{100}{101}\right)(-100)$$

$$= 0.98 + 0.98 - 1.96 = 0.$$

In words: portfolio risk is eliminated by the small extra investment in futures contracts, even though the futures contract by itself is a wildly risky asset.

Stock options

Options are generally options to buy or sell common stocks of widely held, well-known companies, though some gold options are available as well. Options are like rights to first-round draft picks in professional sports leagues. They are valuable only on or before an expiry date, they are salable in advance, and they need not be exercised.

Call option
Strike price

Call options are contracts, sold by the options exchange, that entitle the holder to buy the optioned or "underlying" stock at a set *strike price* up to the expiry date. Here, as in futures markets, all contracts are directly with the exchange (as one of the principals in each contract) rather than with

Put option

other customers. *Put options* are contracts that entitle the holder to sell the underlying stock to the put-option seller, at the strike price, on or before the expiry date. Both types are issued for units of 100 shares of the underlying stock, for only a few expiry dates in each year. Even the strike prices are held to round numbers; this concentrates demand in order to ensure that there is a ready secondary market, which makes options much more liquid.

FIGURE 8–7 Effect of options on probability distributions

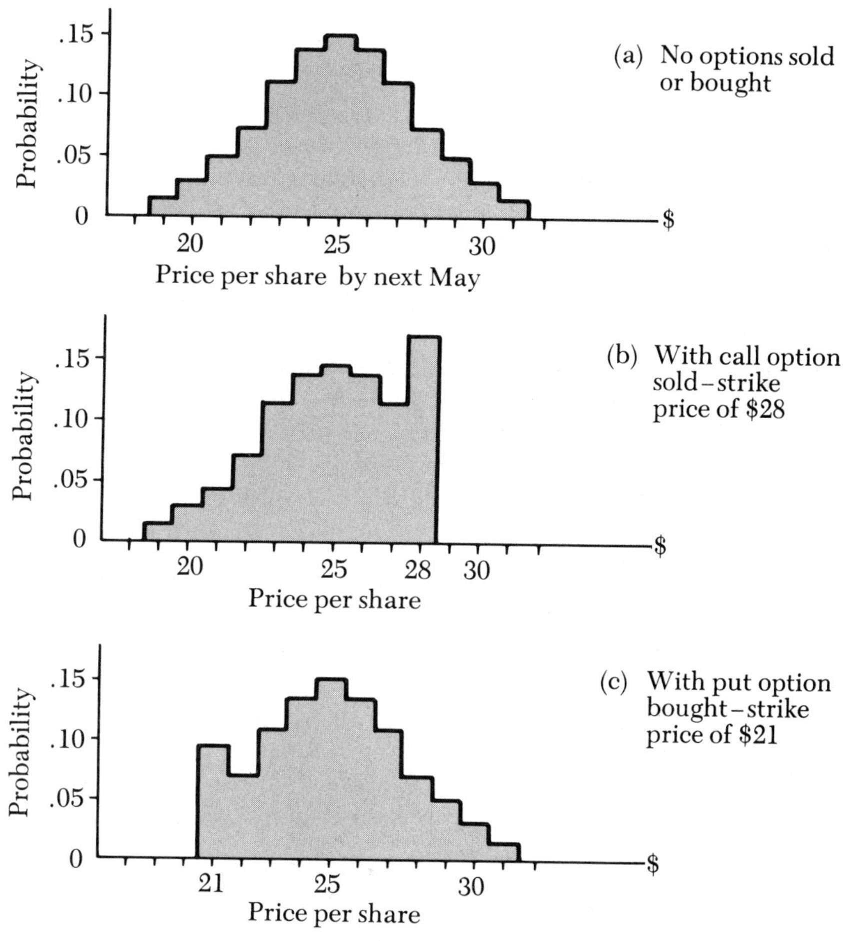

The probability distribution of the stock price is given in panel (a). With a call option outstanding for a strike price of $28 — panel (b) — the stockholder will not receive any extra capital gain above $28: that will go to the option holder, who will exercise the option at $28. With a put option in hand with a strike price of $21 — panel (c) — the stockholder need not realize any price below $21: any extra capital loss will be passed on to the put-option seller through exercise of the put option when the price falls to $21.

The logic of an options market can be seen easily with a probability distribution. Figure 8–7(a) shows an assumed probability distribution for Royal Bank stock on or before the end of May of next year. Assume that you hold 100 shares of this stock now and that its current market price is $25. Suppose you "write" a call option on those shares for a strike price of $28 to expire next May. Should the stock price move above $28 by then, the option buyer would exercise the option, and you would have to hand over the stock for $28 per share. Your total proceeds would be $28 per share plus the call-option price per share. The call-option price per share would be approximately the profit the call-option buyer expected to make from buying the stock at $28. This would be found as

$$\text{Expected profit} = \Sigma\, prob_i(P_i - \$28),$$

for all possible prices P_i greater than $28, where $prob_i$ is the probability of occurrence of the *i*th price level.

Your probability distribution looks different after selling the call option, since you will now receive only $28 from the option holder instead of the higher prices should they occur. Your probability distribution now looks like that shown in figure 8–7(b). All the probability attached previously to prices above $28 now attaches instead to $28. You have sold off the top end of your probability distribution, essentially, in exchange for the certain sale price of the option contract.

In buying a put option for the same stock, say for a strike price of $21, you would be paying to truncate the bottom end of your probability distribution. With a put option for $21, you would not fear your stock value's falling below $21, because if the market price did fall below $21 you could unload your stock on the put-option seller for $21. Your probability distribution would look like that in figure 8–7(c), with all the probabilities previously attached to the low prices now attached instead to a price of $21.

It is possible to sell a call option and buy a put option on the same stock for the same strike price. This truncates both the top end and the bottom end of the probability distribution. There is no uncertainty left. The probability distribution is a straight line above the strike price. Normally this will not be profitable, because of transactions costs, but for alert market professionals such deals do occur occasionally.[14]

Options and futures contracts for speculators

Speculator (in options and futures markets)

Underlying market

Many people use the options and futures markets to hedge, but the same markets are also used by *speculators*. The price fluctuations in both markets are about as large in dollar terms as in the *underlying markets* for the

[14]For this strategy to be profitable, the difference between the call-option price and the cost of the put option (the net receipt from option trading) would have to exceed the gap between the stock's purchase and strike prices (the net cost of stock trading) by more than the commissions on both stock and options transactions.

commodity and stock. For example, stock-option prices for Royal Bank stock move around in the option market by almost as much in dollars as does the price of Royal Bank stock in the stock market itself, and the futures-contract price for barley or for gold fluctuates by as much as the spot-market price for barley or gold.

However, the purchaser of futures contracts or options has much less money tied up in the asset than would be tied up in a purchase of the underlying asset (Royal Bank stock or inventories of barley or gold), since the purchaser has only a margin deposit put down for the futures contract and only the price of the option itself for the stock option. Therefore the percentage gains and losses that the dollar fluctuations represent are much larger than in the stock and commodity markets themselves. Gains and losses of 100 percent, especially the latter, are common. Some wealthholders are attracted by the prospects of extra gain, despite the risk. Note that very few of them have any significant part of their wealth in these markets, however; even speculators in commodity markets believe in diversification of their total wealth portfolio. The article by A.C. Dunbar reports that adding futures contracts to a diversified portfolio could well reduce risk rather than raise it, in addition to increasing expected yield on the total portfolio.

"Futures could help performance"

By A. Carlyle Dunbar

Is there a future for futures investing by prudently-managed investment portfolios? Investment analysts at this week's Financial Analysts Federation conference in Toronto were given the answer: yes.

This response to the question was provided by John Lintner, professor of economics and business administration at Harvard Business School, speaking in a workshop session on financial and stock market futures.

Lintner was reporting on his study of the performance of futures account managers and commodity funds in the U.S. in 1979–82.

"As would have been expected, the managed futures accounts ... are investments with high risks but also high returns," he said. "It turns out that the return/risk ratios of a substantial fraction of the futures-managers and funds are higher than those on diversified stock (or stock and bond) portfolios."

By augmenting conventional stock or stock-and-bond portfolios with selected sub-portfolios of managed futures accounts, overall returns can be improved by "very considerable margins," Lintner said.

Such combined portfolios "show substantially less risk at every possible level of expected return than portfolios of stocks (or stocks and bonds) alone," he said.

An executive of one such futures account manager, Vice-President William E. Burt of Friedberg Mercantile Group, Toronto, described some of his firm's successes (such as a 228% profit in 18 months on the Mexican peso) and failures in commodities trading.

"When we think we are onto something, we take a large position, keep our stops conservative, and try to be patient," Burt said.

"The key to success in futures is to think creatively and audaciously, to imagine major profits, and then have the courage and patience to see it through."

Burt listed some of Friedberg's current positions: going short on the price of oil (the firm expects it to drop to US$10 a barrel), working a spread on U.S. Treasury Bills and Eurodollar futures (in expectation of a default on Third World debt), and potential bull markets in copper, cocoa and cotton.

Source: *The Financial Post*, May 21, 1983.

The futures and options markets are happy to see speculators, provided they are well-informed and fairly well-heeled. The extra activity not only adds to the sales revenue of the brokerage houses, but it also makes the assets traded more liquid and therefore attractive to hedgers.

SECTION 5 Transactions costs and indivisibilities

We have ignored transactions costs so far and assumed that all assets are available in whatever sizes are needed to make up the desired proportion of each investor's asset portfolio. With those assumptions, there is no reason for anyone not to hold exactly the desired portfolio share of each asset. Once transactions costs are introduced, adjustment of actual to desired portfolio shares may take place with a lag.[15] Once indivisibility or lumpiness of assets is taken into account, it may cause assetholders to hold permanently either more or less than they would otherwise hold.

Transactions costs and indivisibilities affect the nature of a new equilibrium portfolio allocation as well as the speed of adjustment toward it. It is worthwhile to look at the actual composition of household asset portfolios, shown in table 8–2, to see the impact of these costs and indivisibilities.

Households have over half of their asset portfolio tied up in a single asset, the family home. This reflects the indivisibility of houses: it is not

[15]Benjamin Friedman notes that adjustment to desired portfolio shares is likely to take place with no lag for that part of total wealth generated out of current savings. Such funds must be invested somewhere, so transactions costs must be incurred anyway and there is no saving from delay. "How Important Is Disaggregation in Structural Models of the Rate of Interest?" *Review of Economics and Statistics*, May 1980.

TABLE 8–2 Asset portfolio composition of family units, 1977

Assets	Percentage Composition	Percentage of family units having any at all
Cash and deposits	10.1	87.7
Canada Savings Bonds	2.4	23.5
Other liquid assets	0.4	
Total liquid assets	12.9	96.2
Stocks (including affiliates)	1.7	8.5
Registered savings plans	1.8	16.8
Other financial assets	3.7	
Total financial assets	20.1	96.3
Homes	49.9	59.6
Business plant and equipment	19.3	13.0
Other assets	10.7	
TOTAL	100	

Average per family unit: $54 556

Notes: Family units include unattached individuals. Holdings in work-related pension plans are not shown.

Source: Statistics Canada, *Incomes, Assets and Indebtedness of Families in Canada*, Cat. 13–572, 1980.

possible to buy them one room at a time. Most home-owners (which includes three out of five families in Canada) therefore have to accept much less diversification of their asset portfolio. Because the family home is such a large share in household portfolios, volatility of residential real estate prices dominates household financial risk. It is understandable that families are very concerned about developments that affect the value of their particular property.

Besides the family home, most households have remarkably few other assets. They are not at all widely diversified. Many households have only savings deposits; some have Canada Savings Bonds, which are the equivalent of savings deposits. About one household in three has savings built up in life insurance policies, and the same proportion belong to work-related pension plans. Most families have no significant holding of risky assets other than the home they live in.

This lack of diversification and the absence of risky assets is partly due to transactions costs and partly a response to the high risk forced on most families by having so much of their wealth tied up in housing. In a world of zero transactions costs, households could be very risk-averse and still hold stocks, by diversifying broadly over different companies and different countries the way banks diversify their loans. With small portfolio shares for each stock, the marginal contributions of each stock to portfolio risk would be small. But so many different stock purchases imply that each purchase would be very small. After all, the total family holding of financial assets of all types was only $11 389 in 1977. Transactions costs can be high for such small transactions. The normal stockbroker's commission for a trade is 2 percent, but for small trades of $100 or so it can be very much larger. This lowers expected yield enough to make wide diversification in stocks not worthwhile. But without broad diversification, each stock adds too much risk to the portfolio, so stocks are avoided.

Transactions costs include not only explicit brokerage commissions but also the cost of monitoring investments. Different assets require different amounts of regular attention. Bank deposits can be forgotten about for years without much danger, but futures contracts and options and many stocks require that the investor keep up-to-date. The consequences of not doing so can be swift and painful. The cost of keeping informed is usually a fixed cost, so the cost per dollar invested is much larger for small investments. Adding in the implicit costs of portfolio diversification gives households one more reason for not splitting up their limited financial wealth into many different assets.

Households could still spread their financial assets fairly easily among many deposits in different institutions. Yields on those deposits tend to change together, however, so their risk is systematic and there is little risk reduction to be gained from diversification.

SECTION 6 Summary

Investors cannot be certain of the future values of the assets they hold, and therefore they face a whole set of possible future yields instead of just one. Uncertainty is due to one or more of inflation risk, market risk, default or credit risk, and income risk. Various assets are subject to various combinations of these types of risk. Some of the risks offset each other, some are independent, and some are reinforcing.

Risk can be visualized as a probability distribution with a set of possible yields and a set of probabilities of each yield's actually occurring in the future. Under two extra assumptions, rational wealthholders will choose asset portfolios on the basis of only two aspects of such probability distributions: the expected yield and the variance of the probability distribution. Expected yield is the midpoint of a probability distribution; variance is an index of its width. Variance corresponds to what we mean in ordinary language by *risk*. Rational investors choose the portfolio with the best mix of expected yield and variance, at the point of tangency of the efficient frontier and the highest attainable indifference curve. For almost all investors variance or risk is undesirable, so extra variance is chosen only if accompanied by extra expected yield.

Individual assets are desired for their contributions to portfolio expected yield and risk. Relative contributions to portfolio yield reflect relative expected yields of individual assets.

Relative contributions to portfolio variance depend particularly on relative covariances of each asset with the rest of the portfolio (their relative systematic risks) as well as on relative variances and portfolio shares. Assets that have negative covariance with the rest of the portfolio are particularly effective in reducing portfolio variance, as is diversification of the asset portfolio into many different, independent assets.

Demand for individual assets therefore depends on relative expected yields, relative covariances, relative variances, and assetholders' degree of risk aversion.

Indivisibility of housing forces many households to tie up half or more of their asset portfolio in a single, relatively risky asset: the family home. This lack of diversification makes household portfolios much riskier than many families would want. The families respond partly by being more conservative in their other wealth holdings than might otherwise be the case, holding mainly deposits rather than stock. Transactions costs also explain lack of diversification, in portfolios small enough that transactions costs bulk large per dollar invested. Transactions costs are high enough to keep many households out of even blue-chip stocks.

Questions for discussion

1. Draw what you think is the probability distribution of future real values of $100 in today's money.
2. What is the probable shape of the probability distribution of default losses on a typical loan?
3. What does the probability distribution look like for future yields on a "sure thing" investment offering 10 percent?
4. What is the expected average deviation of possible yields from the expected yield on a risky asset? Why does it always have this value?
5. What would a risk seeker's indifference curves look like on a portfolio-choice diagram such as figure 8–2?
6. Why is the efficient set the only relevant part of the feasible set?
7. Give two examples of negative correlation from your own family experience.
8. If bank loans had individual yield variances of 34.8 and were completely uncorrelated, what would the approximate variance of the whole business-loan portfolio be for all banks together? (There are half a million individual business loans outstanding.)
9. Is demand for lottery tickets consistent with the theory of rational asset choice by risk-averse individuals?

References

Baumol, William J. *Portfolio Theory: The Selection of Asset Combinations*. Morristown, N.J.: General Learning Press, 1970.

Hieronymus, Thomas A. *Economics of Futures Trading for Commercial and Personal Profit*. New York: Commodity Research Bureau, 1971.

Jean, William H. *The Analytical Theory of Finance*. New York: Holt, Rinehart and Winston, 1970.

Markowitz, Harry. *Portfolio Selection: Efficient Diversification of Investments*. New Haven, Conn.: Yale University Press, for the Cowles Foundation, 1959.

Mossin, Jan. *The Theory of Financial Markets*. Englewood Cliffs, N.J.: Prentice-Hall, 1973.

Sharpe, William F. *Portfolio Theory and Capital Markets*. New York: McGraw-Hill, 1970.

Tobin, James. "Liquidity Preference as Behavior Towards Risk." *Review of Economic Studies*. Feb. 1958, 65–86. Widely reprinted.

Most major brokerage houses also have brochures on the operation and use of options and futures markets, free for the asking.

Appendix 1

Expected utility and attitudes toward risk

In chapter 8, risk aversion was simply assumed. In this appendix it is derived from more basic assumptions.

Under certainty, rational individuals are defined as those who act so as to maximize utility. Under uncertainty, rationality is usually defined as acting so as to maximize expected utility, a probability-weighted average of the possible utilities that might result from any one action. If U_i is the level of utility attached to a possible outcome i, $prob_i$ is its probability of occurring, and there are n possible outcomes, the expected utility $Exp(U)$ is

$$Exp(U) = \Sigma prob_i U_i.$$

Now consider a simple pair of choices. The first alternative provides a certain future value of \$100. The second is a fifty-fifty gamble, a raffle ticket worth \$200 if it wins and nothing if it loses, with one chance in two of winning. The expected value of the raffle ticket $Exp(V)$ is $0.5(200) + 0.5(0) = \$100$, as for the first alternative. Which alternative will be preferred?

The only difference between them is the greater degree of uncertainty associated with the second alternative, so preference for the first alternative amounts to risk aversion. The answer turns out to depend only on whether marginal utility of wealth (or yield; either can be used) rises or falls as wealth levels rise.

FIGURE 8A–1 Risk aversion

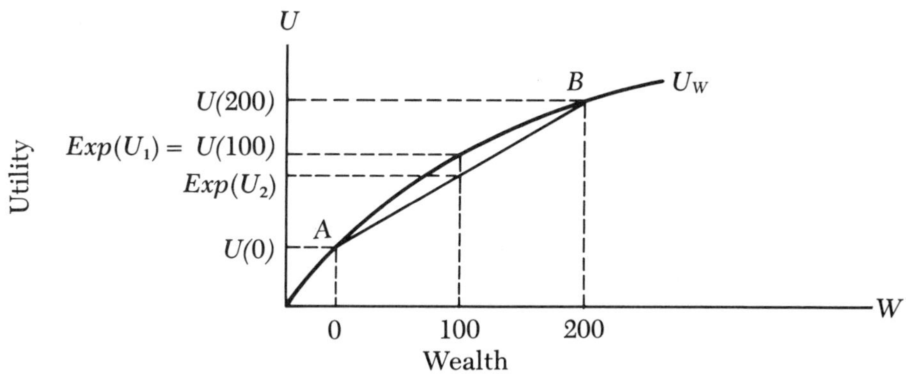

The wealthholder measures the expected utility *Exp(U)* of two alternatives (one promising a sure $100 and the other promising a fifty-fifty chance of $200 or nothing) on the vertical axis. Both alternatives have the expected value of $100 on the horizontal axis. When the marginal utility of wealth MU_W declines, as it does here, the riskier second alternative is avoided.

Figure 8A–1 shows the utility function of an individual whose marginal utility declines over all relevant wealth levels. The possible outcomes for each alternative are given on the horizontal axis, their associated possible utility levels on the vertical axis. The expected utility of the second alternative is the point midway between $U(200)$ and $U(0)$ on the vertical axis. This level of expected utility is also opposite the point on the chord *AB* directly above *Exp(V)*, which gives an easy way of finding expected utilities in simple gambles like this. For this investor, the expected utility of the raffle ticket is less than that of the certain $100, so the investor must be risk-averse.

In figure 8A–2 the same exercise is carried out for an individual whose marginal utility increases with extra wealth. The same two alternatives are plotted, and here the expected utility of the raffle ticket is greater than that of the certain $100. This individual is a risk seeker.

Many other situations can be illustrated on this diagram, but the most important conclusion is the one we have already reached: to be risk-averse, it is sufficient (a) to follow an expected-utility rule in making choices under uncertainty and (b) to have declining marginal utility of yield or wealth.

FIGURE 8A–2 Risk seeking

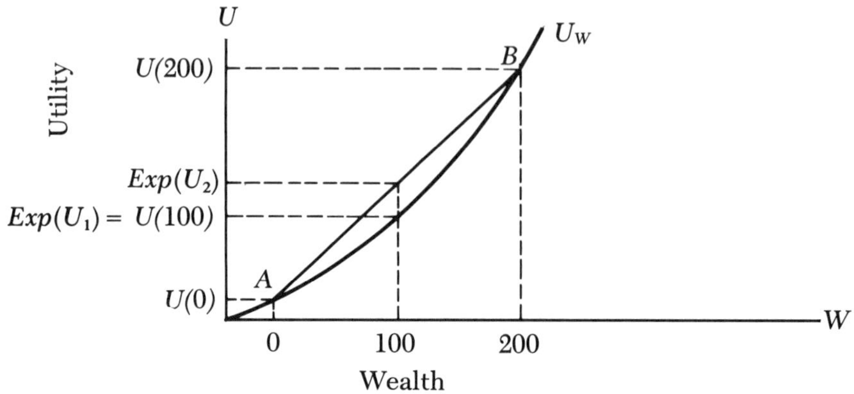

As in figure 8A–1, the wealthholder measures expected utility *Exp(U)* of the alternatives on the vertical axis. Again, both alternatives have the expected value of $100 on the horizontal axis. But here the marginal utility of wealth increases; therefore, the riskier second alternative is preferred.

The rate of decline of marginal utility of wealth is a useful index of degree of risk aversion. The lower the second derivative U'' of the utility function relative to its first derivative U', the more risk averse the investor is, and the steeper the indifference curves in the portfolio-choice diagrams used in chapter 8. A commonly used measure of risk aversion is the ratio $-U''/U'$.

It also follows from the theory of expected utility that, for particular shapes of utility function, maximizing expected utility is exactly equivalent to maximizing a utility function dependent only on expected yield and variance. All other aspects of the portfolio's probability distribution become irrelevant. The particular shape of utility function is quadratic, as in $U = a + br + cr^2$. If this function is substituted in the expression for expected utility, we get

$$\begin{aligned} Exp(U) &= \Sigma\, prob_i\, (a + br_i + cr_i^2) \\ &= a + b\, \Sigma\, prob_i r_i + c\, \Sigma\, prob_i r_i^2. \end{aligned}$$

Let $\Sigma\, prob_i\, r_i = E$, as in the chapter. Then

$$\begin{aligned} Exp(U) &= a + bE + c\Sigma prob_i[(r_i - E) + E]^2 \\ &= a + bE + c\Sigma\, prob_i(r_i - E)^2 + cE^2, \end{aligned}$$

since $\Sigma\, prob_i\, [(r_i - E)\, E] = 0$.

Now $\Sigma\, prob_i(r_i - E)^2 = V$, so

$$Exp(U) = a + bE + cV + cE^2$$

This expression clearly involves only the expected yield and variance of the probability distribution. Nothing else matters.

Appendix 2

Sharpe's systematic-risk model

William F. Sharpe developed the first index model of demand for financial assets in 1963. In an index model, all asset yields are correlated in unison with one or more market indexes but otherwise vary independently of each other.

Index models make some extra assumptions that are fairly restrictive, so the models are not as widely applicable as the general asset demand model used in chapter 8. On the other hand, the problem of estimating relative marginal risks of different assets is reduced in practice to something that can easily be done on a calculator.

Suppose there is an index yield r_I that reflects the average of all market yields, including all deposits, bonds, and stocks. Suppose also that the actual yield on any asset j in the financial system r_j is related to the index yield r_I as follows:

$$r_j = \alpha_j + \beta_j r_I + u_j,$$

where α_j and β_j are constant coefficients that can be estimated for each asset j, and u_j is a random component of r_j that is also peculiar to asset j. This equation is called the *characteristic equation* of asset j. Finally, suppose that u_j varies independently of r_I and the similarly defined random component u_k of any other asset yield r_k; that is, covariances of u_j and r_I and all u_k are zero.

Figure 8A–3 illustrates the characteristic equation. Pairs of yields r_j and r_I for past periods are plotted, and a line is drawn through the middle of the scatter of points. α_j is the vertical intercept, β_j is the slope, and u_j is the vertical distance between actual plotted points and the line.

Another way of looking at the equation is to think of the first two terms $(\alpha_j + \beta_j r_I)$ as the part of r_j that reflects the influence of the financial system as a whole. Call this part the *systematic part* of r_j. This influence is common to all assets in the economy to some extent. The remaining part of r_j (the term u_j) is peculiar to asset j and does not reflect influence of the financial system as a whole. Call it the *unsystematic* (or *nonsystematic*) *part*.

FIGURE 8A–3 The characteristic equation

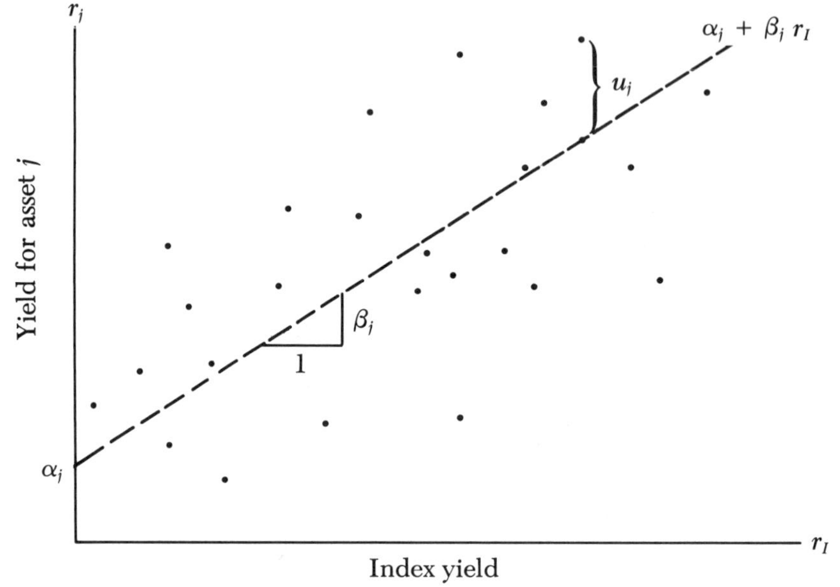

Each point represents an observed past pair of values for r_j and r_I (observed on the same date).

Expected yield for each asset j is $\alpha_j + \beta_j E_I$, where E_I is the expected yield for the market index. The unsystematic part of r_j does not appear at all, because the expected value of the random element u_j is zero. Expected portfolio yield is then

$$E = \Sigma X_j E_j$$
$$= \Sigma X_j \alpha_j + \Sigma X_j \beta_j E_I.$$

The risk of asset j can also be broken down into a systematic risk and an unsystematic risk. Let the variance of the index yield (r_I) be called V_I, and let the variance of the unsystematic part of r_j (u_j) be V_u. It can be shown that the variance of r_j simplifies to

$$V_j = \beta_j^2 V_I + V_u$$

The systematic risk is the part that is contributed by the dependence of the asset yield r_j on the index yield r_I; that is, $\beta_j^2 V_I$ in the equation above. Unsystematic risk is what is left — V_u above. Systematic risk $\beta_j^2 V_I$ reflects the overall "system" or market index risk V_I, moderated (or amplified) by the way in which this individual yield r_j fluctuates with the market index yield. If β_j is 1.0, then the systematic risk of r_j is the same as that of the "system" — that is, V_I.

The importance of dividing asset j's variance into two parts in this way is in what it implies for covariance with other yields in the portfolio. The systematic part of asset j's yield has maximum covariance with all of the other systematic parts of the yields of all other assets, since they are all linearly related to the same index yield r_I. The unsystematic part has (by assumption) zero covariance with anything else.

Diversification cannot reduce portfolio yield volatility when all yields move together linearly; such risks are just averaged and not offset at all. Completely uncorrelated yield fluctuations are another matter. When many independent risks are combined in a portfolio, most of them cancel out, and portfolio risk is only a small fraction of the average of the independent risks. If this diversification is taken to the limit (in a world with no transactions costs and infinitely divisible assets), all of the independent or unsystematic risk is offset — diversified away. For this reason unsystematic risk is often called *diversifiable risk*, and systematic risk is called *nondiversifiable risk*.

Assume for the moment that diversifiable risk is all diversified away. Nondiversifiable risk alone is left, so that all relevant yield fluctuations of assets in the portfolio are effectively in unison. In that case, portfolio variance depends only on the systematic, nondiversifiable variances of individual assets. To be precise,

$$V = V_I(\Sigma X_j \beta_j)^2.$$

The marginal contribution of asset j to portfolio variance must be through the effect of higher X_j on the term $\Sigma X_j \beta_j$. The term $\Sigma X_j \beta_j$ is a weighted average of the beta coefficients of all assets in the portfolio, just as the portfolio expected yield is a similarly weighted average of the expected yields of all assets in the portfolio. $\Sigma X_j \beta_j$ will increase or decrease as X_j rises, in proportion as β_j is greater than or less than the average beta coefficient for the whole portfolio. For any two assets j and k, therefore, the difference between their marginal contributions to portfolio variance is proportional to the difference between their two beta coefficients β_j and β_k. The necessary risk premium in the yield on asset j is therefore also proportional to the difference $\beta_j - \beta_k$.

The convenience of this index model of portfolio choice is that it provides a single, marketwide measure of the relative marginal contribution to risk for each asset, a measure that does not depend on which other assets are held in the portfolio. The model thus greatly simplifies modelling of portfolio selection. Further, the beta coefficient can be found quite easily from a historical scatter diagram such as figure 8A–3. Of course, the relationships of the past may not hold in the future, but that is true of all other estimating methods that make use of past experience. Studies that have compared beta coefficients over time suggest that the relative beta coefficients for various assets have been fairly stable so far.

The drawback of Sharpe's index model is that its assumptions of zero covariance of unsystematic yield components and zero transactions costs do not hold in practice. Diversifiable risk is therefore not as diversifiable as the index model assumes, and costs of diversification lower expected yields. Unsystematic risk therefore remains. The index model does point up the great importance of covariance as opposed to variance of individual asset yields in determining portfolio risk.

Reference

Sharpe, William F. "A Simplified Model for Portfolio Analysis." *Management Science*. 1963, 277–93.

CHAPTER 9

The Demand for Money

This book is not just about money, but it is no accident that money appears at the front of the title. You have already read two chapters (3 and 4) on money in Canada's present and past, and chapters 17 to 24 will be aimed mainly at explaining the impact of money-supply changes on the rest of the economy. In this chapter I tie together the institutional considerations of chapter 3 with the general asset demand theory of chapter 8, to explain the demand for money in particular. The topic turns out to be central to much of macroeconomic policy making in advanced industrial economies, and research on it has produced a range of theories with very specific predictions about money-demand behavior.

In this chapter you will therefore learn:

1. how money is defined in Canada,
2. how economists have explained the demand for money,
3. the specific explanations of money demand, including transactions demand, precautionary demand, and speculative demand for money, and
4. the evidence for and against these explanations.

In addition, I include at the end a brief section on the adjustment mechanism in the market for money, to explain how demand adjusts to supply despite money's having no yield or interest rate to bring about such equality. You will learn why it is that when the demand for money differs from the supply of money, it is the rest of the economy that adjusts to restore equilibrium in the market for money.

SECTION 1 The definition of money in Canada

You have already learned, in section 3 of chapter 3, the four different measures of money in Canada, so this section will be short. The narrow definition of money includes the major assets commonly accepted as means of payment. In Canada, that includes at least currency in circulation in the hands of the public (that is, outside banks) and demand deposits in chartered banks excluding deposits of the federal government. Demand deposits are more commonly known outside economics as chequing accounts, but their key legal feature is that they are payable on demand. All other deposits (both notice deposits, such as personal savings deposits, and fixed-term deposits) are known generically as *time deposits*.

The narrowest definition of money, M1, ignores several other assets also used as money in Canada: chequing accounts in credit unions and trust companies and other intermediaries (see table 3–1), chequable saving deposits in banks and elsewhere (including brokerage houses), some notice deposits that are automatically transferred to chequing accounts whenever a cheque is presented for payment, and even some U.S. currency that circulates in Canada near the border. The Bank of Canada publishes an alternate measure of narrow money, M1A, which includes daily interest and nonpersonal notice deposits of chartered banks, but the other assets listed above that also serve as money are not included in any of the money measures used. Both M1 and M1A measures of money are given in table 9–1. Of the demand deposits included in M1 and M1A, one-fifth are held by households, the rest by business firms and other organizations.

Broad-money definitions include several other types of chartered-bank deposits that are very liquid but that are not means of payment. The liquid assets most easily convertible into currency or demand deposits are the remaining Canadian-dollar notice deposits and personal fixed-term deposits, which are added to M1A to make up M2.[1] Only deposits in chartered banks are included, even though there is a large block of such deposits in trust companies and credit unions, and even though Canada Savings Bonds, for instance, are more liquid than many fixed-term deposits in banks. Nonpersonal fixed-term deposits and all foreign-currency deposits of residents recorded on banks' books in Canada (that is, not deposits with the banks' European subsidiaries) are added to M2 to make up the broadest money measure in Canada, M3. Again, only chartered-bank deposits are included. Table 9–1 shows the relative sizes of these monetary aggregates.[2] Note that narrow money is a small fraction of broad money and that the bulk of broad money consists of financial assets for which holders have fairly close substitutes in credit-union and trust-company liabilities and in Canada Savings Bonds. It will be important in discussing monetary-policy rules in chapter 24 that there are important substitutes for many of the assets included in our broad-money measures.

---

[1]All bank personal term deposits are redeemable before maturity, though the interest rate paid will be several percent below the promised yield to maturity.

[2]The accounts of the banks' ten mortgage loan subsidiaries are consolidated with the parent banks in reporting deposit totals to the Bank of Canada under the Bank Act, so M2 and M3 totals do contain a significant volume of term deposits of mortgage loan companies.

TABLE 9–1 Monetary aggregates

	Value, April 1983		Required cash reserve ratio (percent)
	Billions of dollars	Percentage of 1982 GNP	
(1) Currency outside banks	11.1	—	—
(2) Demand deposits[a]	16.6	—	10
(3) Narrow money, M1 (= 1+ 2)	27.6	7.9	—
(4) Daily-interest chequable and nonpersonal notice deposits	7.0	—	2,3[b]
(5) Narrow money, M1A (= 3 + 4)	34.6	9.9	—
(6) Other notice deposits (personal savings deposits)	54.6	—	2,3[b]
(7) Personal fixed-term deposits	44.5	—	2,3,0[c]
(8) Broad money, M2 (= 5 + 6 + 7)	133.7	38.3	—
(9) Nonpersonal term deposits	40.6	—	2,3,0[c]
(10) Foreign-currency deposits of residents recorded in Canada	10.6	—	2,3[b]
Broad money M3 (= 8 + 9 + 10)	184.9	53.0	—
Some totals of excluded assets:			
Canada Savings Bonds	32.6	—	—
Credit union and caisse populaire deposits	28.9	—	—
Trust and mortgage loan company deposits[d]			
chequable	2.5	—	—
nonchequable notice	8.4	—	—
term deposits, < 1 year	2.6	—	—
other term deposits	30.6	—	—

[a]Adjusted to remove estimated float.
[b]The cash reserve ratio is 2 percent for the first half billion of such deposits for each bank, and 3 percent thereafter.
[c]The cash reserve ratio is nil for all term deposits having an original term to maturity of over one year, and 2 or 3 percent for the rest (see note b).
[d]These totals exclude deposits of the ten mortgage loan companies owned by chartered banks.

Sources: Bank of Canada Review and Bank of Canada, *Weekly Financial Statistics*.

SECTION 2 Major approaches to the demand for money

If money were just a normal financial asset, we would expect after reading chapter 8 that the demand for money in any year would be a stable fraction of total wealth, the fraction depending on relative expected yields on money and on substitute assets (that is, on money's own yield and on the

Opportunity yields

opportunity yields), on relative risks (mainly reflecting covariances with other asset yields), and on wealthholders' degree of risk aversion. In this chapter we see that the demand for money does and does not behave that way.[3]

Demand for money does depend on the return from holding money, on yields available on substitute assets, on relative risks, and on the degree of risk aversion. However, the return from holding money is mainly in the form of medium-of-exchange services, which we identified in chapter 3 as allowing a better stream of consumption spending than would otherwise be possible. The return from holding money depends heavily on the level of prices (P) and the level of real income (Y), in that the marginal utility of extra medium-of-exchange services rises and falls with the level of prices and real incomes. Demand for money therefore depends on prices and real incomes as well as on the other factors.

Further, demand for money may not be a particularly stable fraction of total wealth. The marginal utility of extra money holding comes from rescheduling consumption spending (from the date the money is accumulated to the date when it is spent). The marginal utility of such rescheduling is likely to fall fairly rapidly for most households if their total spending is unchanged. The appeal of nonmoney assets, however, rests solely in their yield of extra income in the form of interest, dividends, or capital gains. The marginal utility of extra income is not likely to fall quickly. It follows that extra wealth that is not accompanied by higher nominal income (such as an inheritance) is likely to be held increasingly in nonmoney assets rather than in money. The desired share of money in total wealth will therefore fall as the ratio of wealth to nominal income (PY) rises.

Theories developed to explain the demand for money in particular have not only pointed out the importance of price and income and interest rates on money substitutes; they have also produced very specific predictions about the sensitivity of money demand to those other variables. We will start with the earliest of these theories, the quantity theory of money.

The Quantity Theory

The Quantity Theory of the demand for money goes back centuries, but it was best explained by Irving Fisher at the turn of this century.[4] Fisher and others of the time started with the idea that money (M) must change hands whenever there is a transaction in the economy. If money changes hands with a constant frequency (known as the *velocity of circulation*, V) then one can simply calculate what stock of money is required if a given volume of transactions (T) is to take place at a given average price level (P). Algebraically, this produces the Quantity Equation: $MV = PT$.

Velocity of circulation

Quantity Equation

---

[3]This section is based on an excellent summary in D.E.W. Laidler, *The Demand for Money: Theories and Evidence*, 2d ed. (New York: Dun-Donnelley, 1977), chap. 4.

[4]Irving Fisher, *The Purchasing Power of Money* (New York: Macmillan, 1911).

Fisher believed that velocity was indeed relatively constant over short periods of time, reflecting payments technology and habits. He was left with the Quantity Theory of the demand for money, which states that desired money balances must be proportional to the total volume of transactions and to the average price level for those transactions.[5]

Subsequently, an income version of the Quantity Theory was developed, which replaced the volume of transactions T with the level of final real output, Y. There are several differences between T and Y. Y ignores all asset transfers such as stock-market sales, which are included in T; Y includes some flows of income not involving cash, such as the imputed rent received by home-owners from living in their own home, which are not included in T. There are other, smaller differences as well, but as long as variations in the total T are also reflected in similar variations in the total Y, differences in levels of the two measures do not matter. In most countries measures of Y are readily available from national statistical agencies, while measures of T are not, so Y is normally used in applications of the Quantity Theory. The Quantity Equation then becomes $MV = PY$, where V is called the income velocity of circulation, P is an output price index, and Y is real national income.

Income velocity of circulation

The Cambridge equation

Fisher's Quantity Theory was a macroeconomic theory, using macroeconomic variables such as total transactions, total money stock, and the average price level. Neoclassical economists at Cambridge University, led by Alfred Marshall and A.C. Pigou, produced a similar result from a quite different, explicitly microeconomic starting point.[6] They asked how much of an individual's wealth that person would want to hold as money. Their answer was that desired money holdings would tend to be a fairly constant proportion (k) of nominal income. They recognized that the proportion k would itself change over time both with payments technology and habits, and also with the level of interest rates on alternative assets. They played down the role of interest rates, however, and because the other factors influencing the proportion k change only gradually, they tended to regard k as fairly stable in the short run. In that same short run, therefore, money demand (M_d) is a stable function (k) of nominal income (PY). The idea is expressed in the *Cambridge equation*:

Cambridge equation

$$M_d = kPY.$$

[5]Quantity theory is more than just a theory of money demand. Quantity theorists went on to assert that (in the long run) T is also constant at full employment, so that changes in M must produce only equi-proportional changes in P. This macroeconomic theory of output and price behavior was replaced by Keynes in 1936 but is irrelevant to our discussion of money-demand theory. One can believe the Quantity Theory of money demand without believing the rest.

[6]See, for instance, A.C. Pigou, "The Value of Money," *Quarterly Journal of Economics*, 1917, 38–65.

This looks much like the income version of the Quantity Equation. The coefficient k in the Cambridge equation is the same (empirically) as $1/V$ in the income version of the Quantity Theory.

Keynesian and post-Keynesian explanations

Precautionary demand

Speculative motive

Liquidity-preference theory

John Maynard Keynes basically accepted the Cambridge logic of a *transactions* demand for money, but he split it into a regular, transactions part and an irregular, *precautionary* part.[7] Keynes also added a separate class of *speculative* demand for money by investors who shift their demand from bonds to money (that is, who prefer liquidity) whenever they think interest rates are low enough that interest rates are about to rise and bond prices about to fall. Keynes emphasized with his new *liquidity-preference* argument that demand for money in total (including speculative demand) is sensitive to interest rates on substitute assets — playing up a relationship that Marshall and Pigou had acknowledged but played down.

Post-Keynesian economists have accepted Keynes' emphasis on money demand's sensitivity to interest-rate levels, though they have mostly replaced his explanation of why interest rates matter. Three alternative explanations have been put forward, all of which can hold at once. First, William Baumol (and later James Tobin) refined the Cambridge notion that transactions demand itself will be sensitive to the net opportunity yield foregone by holding money.[8] Second, James Tobin used portfolio theory to explain interest sensitivity of money demand as quite possibly just a normal response by investors to changes in the terms upon which expected yield and portfolio risk are available.[9] This is the special case of portfolio-choice theory mentioned briefly at the end of section 2 of chapter 8. Third, later refinement of Keynes' concept of precautionary demand has established that it too implies sensitivity of demand for money to relative expected yields on money and its substitutes.

Transactions-demand theory is presented in more detail in section 4. The modern precautionary-demand theory and Keynes' original speculative-demand theory are presented in section 5. Tobin's portfolio-theory explanation is presented here.

---

[7]J.M. Keynes, *The General Theory of Employment, Interest, and Money* (London: Macmillan, 1936).

[8]W.J. Baumol, "The Transactions Demand for Cash: An Inventory Theoretic Approach," *Quarterly Journal of Economics*, Nov. 1952, 545–56 (widely reprinted); James Tobin, "The Interest Elasticity of the Transactions Demand for Cash," *Review of Economics and Statistics*, Aug. 1956, 241–47.

[9]"Liquidity Preference as Behavior Towards Risk," *Review of Economic Studies*, Feb. 1958, 65–86. Widely reprinted.

Tobin's liquidity-preference theory

Tobin presented a very simple version of a mean-variance portfolio-choice problem in which (a) portfolios consist only of various combinations of money and bonds, (b) bonds and money have expected yields E_b and E_m respectively, and (c) money's yield is certain and bond yields are variable. The variability of bond yields is measured by the standard deviation S_b (the square root of the variance) of possible yields around the expected yield. Wealthholders wish to find the optimal mix of expected yield and risk (S) on the portfolio, by choosing the right mix of money and bonds. With money being riskless, asset portfolio risk (S) can be expressed simply as

$$S = X_m 0 + (1 - X_m)Sb$$
$$= (1 - X_m)Sb,$$

where X_m is the share of money and $(1 - X_m)$ is the share of bonds in the portfolio. Portfolio risk is a linear function of X_m. Since portfolio expected yield (E) is also a linear function of X_m,

$$E = X_m E_m + (1 - X_m)\ Eb$$

the efficient frontier of risk-yield choices is itself linear on a risk-yield diagram, with risk measured by S instead of V (as in chapter 8). This is shown in the top panel of figure 9–1.

As the investor moves to the right along the frontier, the money share X_m falls and the bond share $1 - X_m$ rises. At either extreme, wealth is held entirely in money ($X_m = 1.0$) or entirely in bonds ($1 - X_m = 1.0$). For a normal individual with increasing risk aversion — and therefore with convex indifference curves — the optimal combination at the point of tangency of indifference curves and efficient frontier will include both money and bonds. Such an optimum is shown as the point providing E^* and S^* as yield and risk levels for the portfolio.

Demand for money in dollars is easy to derive graphically from the top panel of figure 9–1. First we derive the demand for bonds. We know that the share of bonds in total wealth rises proportionally with portfolio risk S, so bond demand is 0 when S is 0 and rises with S at a constant rate until, when $S = S_b$, demand for bonds equals total wealth W. If we measure bond demand downward from the origin in figure 9–1, the downward-sloping line in the bottom panel of the figure shows the demand for bonds at each level of portfolio risk S.

Now we can derive demand for money. Demand for money is simply total wealth less demand for bonds. Demand for money can therefore be measured in the bottom half of figure 9–1 as the vertical distance of the same downward-sloping line in the bottom panel from the level of wealth W on the vertical axis. Where $S = S_b$, money demand is zero; where $S = 0$, money demand is equal to total wealth. If the chosen portfolio risk level is S^*, then the chosen money demand is the vertical distance from W to M^* in the figure.

FIGURE 9–1 Tobin's liquidity-preference theory

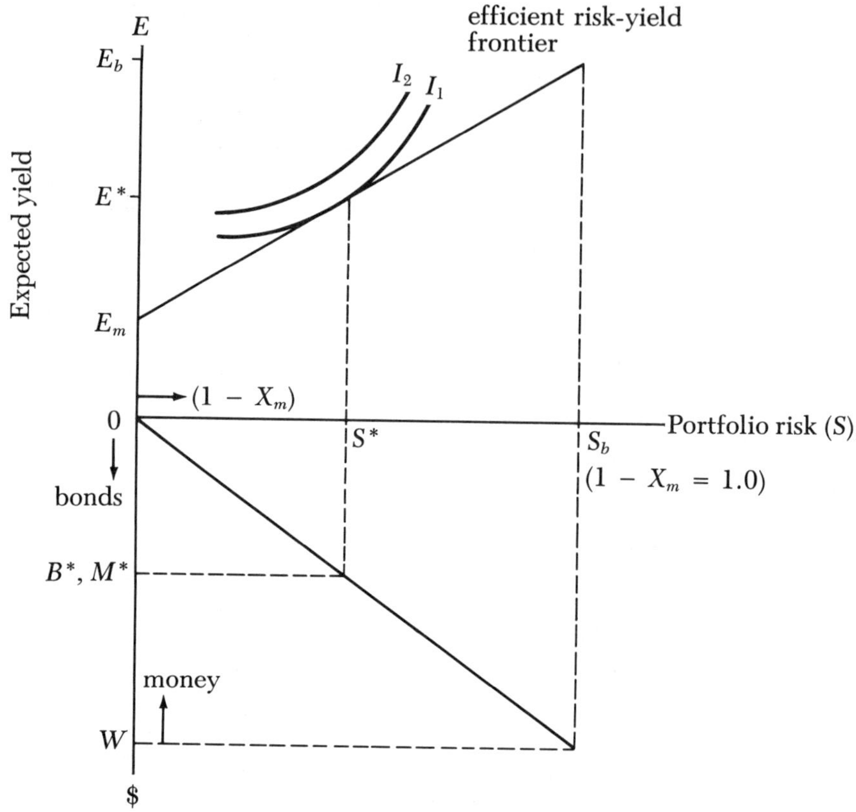

The rational, risk-averse wealthholder chooses the portfolio that offers expected yield E^* and risk level S^*. The choice implies a portfolio mix with OB^* of total wealth OW in bonds, and the remainder M^*W in money. The choice depends on all the ingredients of the diagram: tastes, the expected yield on bonds (E_b) and on money (E_m), the risk of bonds (S_b), and total wealth W.

Money demand in Tobin's simple portfolio model depends on all of the ingredients of figure 9–1: degree of risk aversion, relative expected yields on money and bonds, the risk of bonds, and the level of wealth. An increase in wealth increases the scale of the vertical axis in the bottom half of figure 9–1: the point W then refers to a larger level of wealth than before. Both M^* and B^* are increased proportionally with wealth W. A greater degree of risk aversion would steepen indifference curves and shift the optimum point on the frontier to the left. Any change in relative yields or risks would shift the frontier itself. We will look at the effect of a change in bond yields, since that is the change most frequently encountered.

Higher bond yields E_b cause the endpoint of the frontier to be higher, as in panel (a) of figure 9–2. The frontier becomes steeper but still starts at $S = 0$ and $E = E_m$ when all of the portfolio is held in money. If the original equilibrium was at A, with portfolio risk of S^* and money demand of M^* in panel (b), the extra incentive to take on the riskier bonds is likely to cause a shift from money to bonds.[10] This is shown for the investor in panel (a) as a shift from point A to a new optimal point B. Point B implies a higher level of risk $S^{*\prime}$ and a lower level of money holdings $M^{*\prime}$.

Panel (c) of figure 9–2 puts together the money holdings and the level of bond yields. M is still measured vertically, starting at point W. Bond yields are measured horizontally to the left from the vertical axis. A change in bond yield from E_b to E_b' causes a change in money demand from M^* to $M^{*\prime}$. Plotting those two points and others for other bond yields in panel (c) shows the relationship between money demand and the yield on nonmoney assets (the opportunity cost of money). The downward-sloping curve is a version of the Keynesian liquidity-preference curve. It is often referred to as a demand curve for money, though in fact it is a cross-demand curve — relating money demand to the price and yield of other assets. Note as we leave it that the position of that curve is still affected by the level of wealth, tastes, the yield on money, and the level of risk on bonds.

For parts of total wealth that will be held for long periods, such as a year or so, Tobin's choice between money and bonds should be interpreted as a choice between short-term liquid assets and long-term bonds. Long-term bonds have large market risk that short-term assets do not. Investors can avoid market risk of long-term bonds by shifting into Treasury Bills or term deposits without foregoing as much interest as they would by holding chequing deposits, so narrow money would be an inferior and irrelevant alternative. For parts of total wealth that can be held only for short periods, however, the transactions costs of getting into and out of Treasury Bills and term deposits reduce their expected yields significantly. For sufficiently short holding periods, even chequing deposits become preferable to interest-earning liquid assets; there is not enough time to earn enough interest to offset transactions costs, so they are better avoided entirely by holding money instead. Tobin's theory therefore does explain the demand for money as well as demand for other liquid assets.

The modern quantity theory

The other major strand in the modern theory of the demand for money came from Milton Friedman in 1956, just two years before Tobin put forth

[10]It is not inevitable that higher bond yields will lead to greater risk-taking. The substitution effect will cause more risk-taking when the reward for it (bond interest) is increased, but there is also an income effect working in the opposite direction. Investors earning higher yields on their original bond holdings may decide they can now afford greater security than before, and lower rather than increase their risk exposure.

FIGURE 9–2 Effect of higher bond yield on money demand

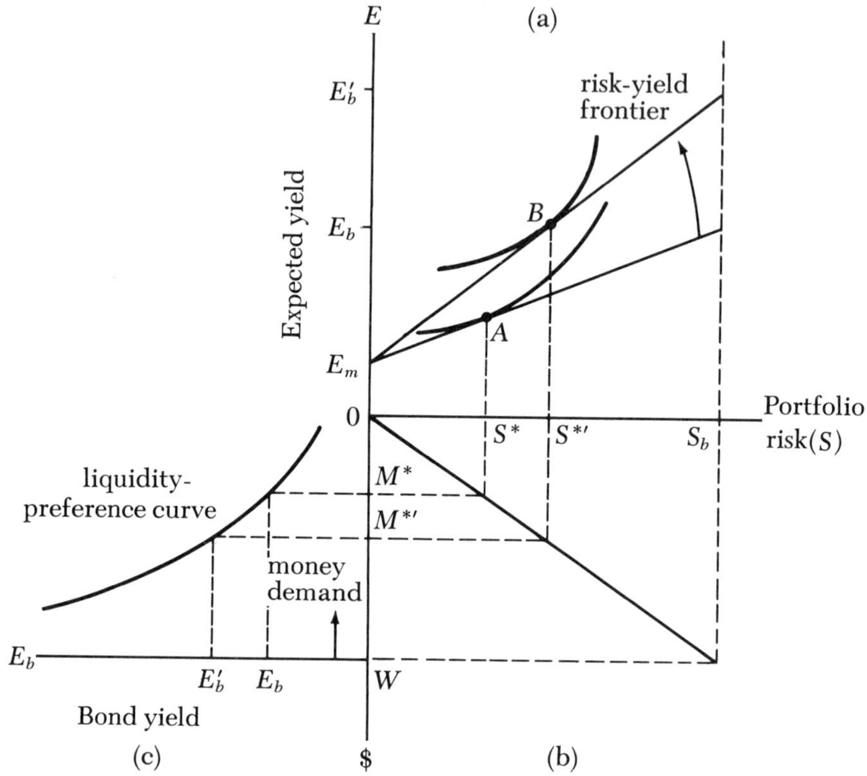

A rise in bond yield from E_b to E_b' steepens the risk-yield frontier in panel (a), causing the optimal portfolio choice to move from A to B. The shift implies a larger portfolio share in bonds and less in money. Demand for money falls in panels (b) and (c), from M^*W to $M^{*\prime}W$. Plotting other combinations of bond yield and money demand in panel (c) gives the liquidity-preference curve for this individual. The liquidity-preference curve is a cross-demand curve for money (one of the few cross-demand curves ever used in economics).

his explanation of Keynesian liquidity preference. Friedman called his work a restatement of the Quantity Theory, and the name stuck.[11] Actually it was an important extension of Marshall's approach to the demand for money, an extension that gave much greater prominence to wealth levels (but, like Marshall's theory, downplayed the role of interest rates).

Friedman was more explicit than Marshall and Pigou had been in arguing that the demand for money is demand for a financial asset and

[11]"The Quantity Theory of Money, A Restatement," in M. Friedman, ed., *Studies in the Quantity Theory of Money* (Chicago: University of Chicago Press, 1956).

therefore that money competes with other financial assets for a place in people's portfolios. Friedman argued that demand for money as a financial asset naturally depends on the level of wealth, the expected yield on money assets, expected opportunity yields on other substitute assets such as equities and bonds and even human capital, and the overall degree of liquidity of the asset portfolio. Demand for money was cast in real terms, so demand for nominal money balances was predicted to vary proportionally with the price level. In 1956 Tobin had not yet introduced economists to an explicit treatment of risk in asset choices, so it is not surprising that Friedman did not mention relative risks of bonds and money.

In Friedman's explanation, real income does not appear explicitly. Instead, it appears as an ingredient in total wealth. Friedman defined total wealth to include *human wealth*, which is the capitalized present value of expected future labor income. Higher expected real incomes increase human wealth, and that increases demand for money, so real income does affect the demand for money. However, an increase in current real income has only a small effect if it is transitory, because higher current real income has little effect on human wealth if it is not expected to persist for long. We discussed Friedman's concepts of transitory and permanent income in chapter 6 in explaining responses of household saving to changes in real income. Only if higher real income is viewed as permanent will human wealth and the demand for money be much affected.

Human wealth

Friedman further asserted that changes in current income affect permanent income only gradually, over many years. It follows that changes in current income will affect money demand only gradually as well.

Friedman's definition of wealth has not been widely copied in subsequent theory. Many economists do use his concept of permanent income rather than current income to explain demand for money, however, and permanent income was conceived of as simply the constant annual flow of income that the stock of human wealth would make possible over a lifetime; as such it is merely the flow counterpart of the stock of human wealth.

SECTION 3 Transactions demand for money

The basic rationale for holding such low-interest assets as currency and chequing accounts is that they make possible a better or cheaper stream of transactions, as explained in chapter 3. These services will be valued in any economy that has differences in timing of receipts and expenditures plus either (a) positive transactions costs in time and money of switching into and out of nonmoney assets or (b) uncertainty about the financial status of other individuals to whom goods and services are sold. If there were no uncertainty about anyone's financial status, we would all be able to pay for purchases (up to our income level) by just running up debts. With no uncertainty, these debts would be riskless and liquid, indistinguishable from money. There would be no point in accumulating government-currency balances, since doing so involves postponement of spending.[12]

The inventory-theory model

Transactions demand

Professor William Baumol of Princeton University has provided the simplest analysis of how *transactions demand* — that is, demand for money for transactions purposes — would behave. Baumol focusses on the situation in which income is received in a series of regular lumps while spending occurs in a steady stream; this situation fits most households. Baumol's analysis also applies without significant change to the opposite situation, in which income is received in a steady stream and spending occurs in a series of regular lumps; this situation fits most firms, whose payrolls and interest payments tend to be regular lumps but whose sales revenue comes in more evenly. Baumol's theory therefore fits the situation of most of those holding narrow money (M1) in Canada.

We will explain the logic of Baumol's model with a particular case, the Smiths. Let the Smith household receive $\$PY$ of nominal income every two weeks, all of which Mrs. Smith spends on their behalf at an even rate over the two weeks. P is the price level; Y is real income. If the whole PY were held as money until spent, then the Smiths' average money holding over each two-week period would be $PY/2$. (This is shown in a *sawtooth diagram* in figure 9–3.) However, the Smiths can put some of the money into a daily-interest savings account and withdraw the money later when it is needed. Assume the interest rate per two-week period is r and that there is a fixed nominal charge of Pb dollars for every savings-account deposit or withdrawal transaction regardless of size (the cost of a trip to the nearest branch); b is the real transactions cost in time and commissions, and P is the price level as before.

As long as the interest to be earned exceeds the fixed nominal transactions cost, Mrs. Smith will be better off parking some of the income temporarily in a savings account. For instance, if she holds half of the income ($PY/2$) in a savings deposit for the first week and then withdraws it to spend over the second week, she will incur $2P_b$ of transactions costs (Pb on the way in and Pb on the way out) and earn $(r/2)$ $(PY/2)$ of extra interest from her economizing on money balances. As long as $2Pb < (r/2)$ $(PY/2)$, the Smiths are ahead by their investment. Figure 9–4 shows what their pattern of money balances and savings account would look like over the two weeks. Money holdings slide from $PY/2$ to zero every week, with an

[12] This is the central point made by K. Brunner and A.H. Meltzer in their influential article "The Uses of Money: Money in the Theory of an Exchange Economy," *American Economic Review*, Dec. 1971, 784–805. One could object that under certainty anyone's debts would be so acceptable in transactions as to be money. Rather than removing the need for money, certainty would merely widen the range of possible issuers.

FIGURE 9–3 Time pattern of money holding (with no holdings of nonmoney assets)

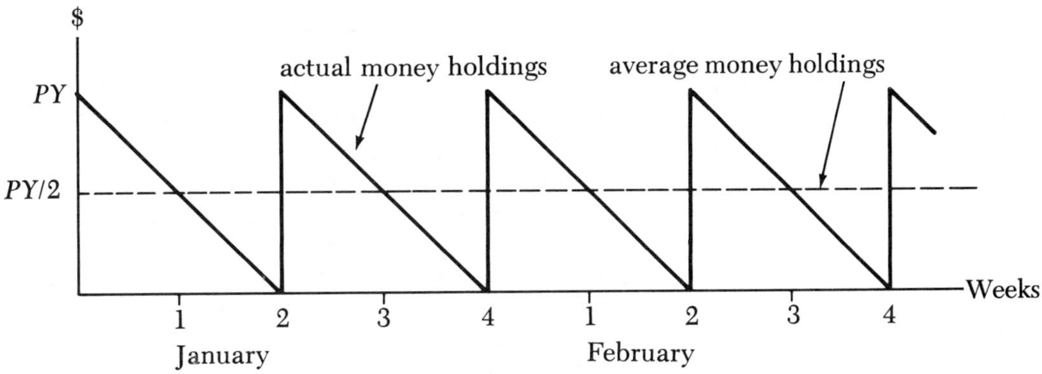

Nominal income *PY* is all put into a chequing account each pay period (every two weeks) and is drawn down steadily until the next payday. The average cash balance is *PY*/2 in this case.

FIGURE 9–4 Time pattern of money holding (with purchase of nonmoney assets)

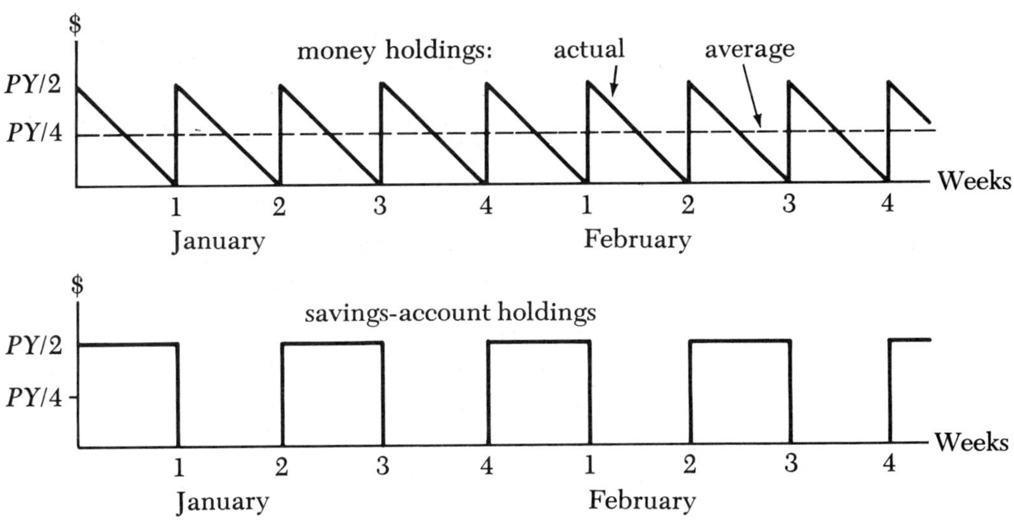

Half of biweekly income *PY* is put into a savings account; the rest (*PY*/2) is held as money in the form of currency and chequing accounts. Money balances are drawn down and replenished each week either from income (on even weeks) or by withdrawals from the savings account (on odd weeks). The average money holding is *PY*/4. The average amount held in nonmoney assets is also *PY*/4 in this case.

average of only $PY/4$. The savings account is filled and emptied alternately each week.

The Smiths are not restricted to the choice in figure 9–4. They can add to their savings deposit and withdraw from it as many times as they wish. They will increase the amount of their savings deposit and their frequency of withdrawal until the marginal interest gain is just offset by marginal transactions costs.

In order to see what level of optimal money holding is implied, let the Smiths put $(PY - C)$ into a savings deposit at the start of each pay period, so they keep back $\$C$ as cash balance and withdraw a further $\$C$ every time their cash balance falls to zero. With that size of withdrawal there are $(PY/C) - 1$ withdrawal transactions (the first $\$C$ is received as cash income, not withdrawn from an investment, so there are one less than PY/C withdrawals). There is one deposit transaction to deposit $\$(PY - C)$ in the

FIGURE 9–5 Time pattern of money and other asset holdings

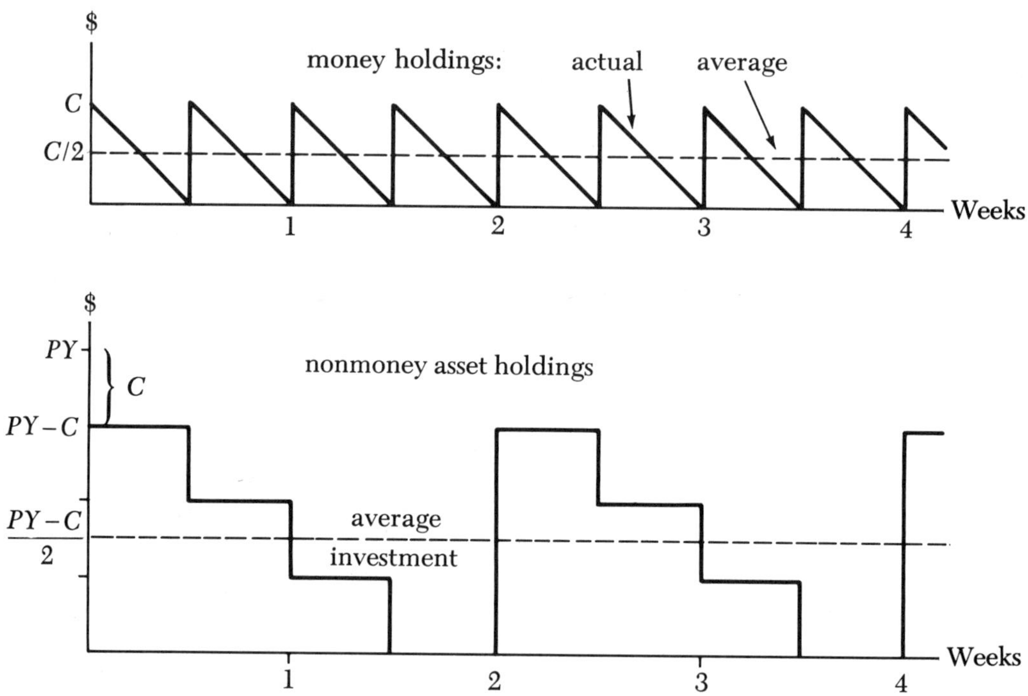

Nominal income is PY every two weeks. C is taken immediately in cash. The remainder, $PY - C$, is put into other assets. An extra C is withdrawn from the other asset holdings at regular intervals to replenish cash balances, so the average amount held in nonmoney assets is only $(PY - C)/2$. Average cash balances are $C/2$.

savings account. Figure 9–5 illustrates what this might look like if \$$C$ were one-quarter of \$$PY$. Total transactions costs are Pb per transaction for PY/C transactions, or $Pb(PY/C)$. The average money holding is $C/2$, and the average investment is $(PY - C)/2$.

The Smiths' total interest earnings equal the interest rate r per period multiplied by the average amount invested per period. The bottom part of figure 9–5 shows the average amount invested to be $(PY - C)/2$, so total interest earnings are $r(PY - C)/2$.

The Smiths' profits from investment (F) are the difference between interest earnings and transactions costs:

$$F = \frac{r(PY - C)}{2} - Pb\left(\frac{PY}{C}\right).$$

Mrs. Smith wants the level of C that will maximize those profits. This is the amount such that (using calculus)

$$\frac{dF}{dC} = -\frac{r}{2} + \frac{PbPY}{C^2} = 0.$$

By rearranging this equation, the optimal level of C that maximizes profits (and therefore satisfies the equation above) is

$$C^* = P\left(\frac{2bY}{r}\right)^{1/2},$$

and the average money holding $= \dfrac{C^*}{2} = P\left(\dfrac{bY}{2r}\right)^{1/2}.$

In the equation for money demand, the exponents on each variable are the elasticities of money demand with respect to that variable. We can rewrite the equation to make those exponents more obvious, as:

$$\frac{C^*}{2} = P^1 b^{1/2} Y^{1/2} 2^{-1/2} r^{-1/2}.$$

The interest-rate elasticity of money demand is $-\frac{1}{2}$, so increases in interest rates reduce money demand at a decreasing rate. Figure 9–6 illustrates that result for a fixed level of the other variables P, b, and Y.

In Baumol's approach the interest rate r is the net opportunity cost of holding money; it should therefore be interpreted as the difference between the expected yield on nonmoney assets and that on money. For narrow money, the normal assumption has been of a zero interest payment on money, though that is less true in the 1980s. For broad money, the interest rate on money is well above zero, and the net opportunity cost may often be negative.

Real income increases transactions demand, but at a decreasing rate. There are economies of scale in money holding just as in the holding of other inventories. The price level, however, affects money demand proportionally, just as the Cambridge equation asserted.

Baumol and the Cambridge equation

Baumol's transactions-demand model is the direct descendant of the earlier quantity-theory models, which focussed mainly on money as a medium of exchange rather than merely as a liquid asset. It is useful to compare the two directly to see what new implications Baumol's approach adds.

The Cambridge equation of money demand for an individual is $M_d = kPY$. Baumol has amended the Cambridge equation in two ways. First, the Y term has an exponent (that is, an elasticity) of $\frac{1}{2}$ rather than 1. Second, the fraction k now varies explicitly with the opportunity cost of money, so in general terms $k = k(r)$. With these changes, the Cambridge equation becomes:

$$M_d = k(r)PY^{1/2}.$$

To be specific, Baumol predicts the relationship of k to r as:

$$k = \left(\frac{b}{2r}\right)^{1/2}.$$

FIGURE 9–6 Demand curve for money

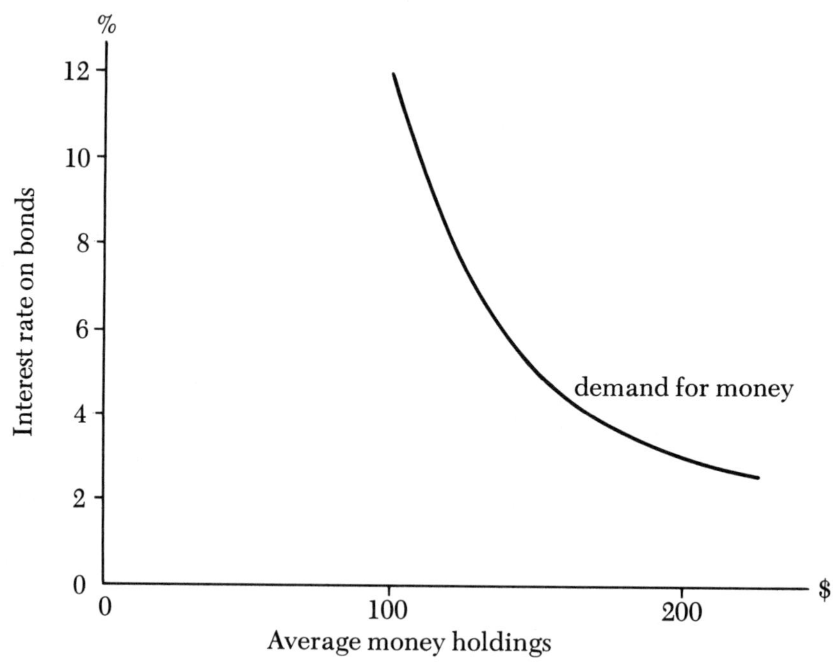

This cross-demand curve relates money demand to the opportunity cost of holding money, the yield on bonds. The curve is drawn for an interest-elasticity of money demand of exactly $-1/2$.

Substituting for k in the modified Cambridge equation produces a rearranged version of Baumol's equation:

$$M_d = \left(\frac{b}{2r}\right)^{1/2} PY^{1/2}$$

$$= P\left(\frac{bY}{2r}\right)^{1/2}$$

Extensions of Baumol's model

Baumol's model can be extended in many ways.[13] In all of the extensions, money demand depends positively on price and real income and transactions costs, and negatively on the net opportunity cost of money. In almost all of the extensions, money demand varies proportionally with the price level and less than proportionally with real income and has an interest elasticity of $-\frac{1}{2}$.

One of the more important extensions of Baumol's model is to allow transactions costs to vary with real wage levels as well as with price levels.[14] Since much of Mrs. Smith's cost of shifting wealth into and out of nonmoney assets is the use of her own scarce time (making telephone calls, filling out transfer forms, travelling to branch offices, standing in lines), the full cost of each transaction will increase whenever the opportunity cost of Mrs. Smith's time increases. Her real income level will be a reasonable index of that opportunity cost. When the transactions cost b varies also with the real income level Y, the real income elasticity of money increases from $\frac{1}{2}$ toward

---

[13]Tobin, for instance, independently considered a version of Baumol's problem with a variable transactions cost instead of just a lump-sum cost. "The Interest Elasticity of the Transactions Demand for Cash," *Review of Economics and Statistics*, Aug. 1956, 241–47. Edgar L. Feige and Michael Parkin extend Baumol's model to allow for real capital and commodity holdings as well as bonds and money in "The Optimal Quantity of Money, Bonds, Commodity Inventories, and Capital," *American Economic Review*, June 1971, 335–49. Robert Clower and Peter Howitt used a sort of mathematics different from Baumol's to see how transactions demand would behave if the pattern of receipts and expenditures varied, in "The Transactions Theory of the Demand for Money: A Reconsideration," *Journal of Political Economy*, 1978, 449–66. Merton Miller and Dale Orr considered the case of random changes in cash flows, in "The Transactions Demand for Money by Firms," *Quarterly Journal of Economics*, 1966, 413–35. Jurg Niehans has extended Baumol's analysis to allow formal choice of receipt and expenditure pattern as part of the decision problem in *The Theory of Money* (Baltimore: Johns Hopkins Press, 1978), chap. 2.

[14]D.S. Dutton and W.P. Gramm, "Transactions Costs, the Wage Rate, and the Demand for Money," *American Economic Review*, Sept. 1973, 652–65, and also Thomas R. Saving, "The Value of Time and Economies of Scale in the Demand for Cash Balances: A Comment," *Journal of Money, Credit, and Banking*, Feb. 1974, 122–24.

1. If b varies proportionally with Y, the real income elasticity will be exactly 1.0, just as in the Cambridge equation.[15]

Moving from the individual to the economy

Baumol's optimal model refers to an individual household or firm. In order to talk about money demand for the economy, we must add up the money demands of all households and firms. When we do so, we find that the aggregate demand for money also depends on the distribution of income and the number of separate bank accounts being used. The number of separate accounts depends on the number of households and firms and also on the degree of consolidation of cash management within firms and households. Both variables matter because real income or the volume of transactions affects money demand only with an elasticity of $\frac{1}{2}$. Someone with four times our income is predicted by Baumol's approach to have an average money balance only $\sqrt{4}$, or 2, times as large as ours. Redistribution of income from the poor to the rich would therefore reduce the money holdings of the poor by more than it would increase the money holdings of the rich. Total money demand in the economy would fall.

Similarly, consolidating four of a firm's bank accounts into one, so that the remaining account handled four times the volume of receipts and payments, would lower the firm's total money holding; the one remaining account would be $\sqrt{4} = 2$ times as large as the average bank account before consolidation, but the number of accounts would be smaller by a factor of four. Consolidation of firms' bank accounts has been the major innovation in corporate cash management in the last ten years, brought on by the high opportunity cost of money and computerization of bank accounting.

Some applications of transactions-demand theory: four financial innovations

We will find in parts V and VI of this book that the demand for money plays a crucial role in the choice of stabilization policies. It is important for policy makers to know how it behaves and to know whether that behavior is stable over time. Recent financial innovations, and some in the foreseeable future, are such that we can expect dramatic changes in the behavior of money demand — both in its sensitivity to income and interest rates and in

---

[15]If transactions cost b is proportional to Y, as in $b = xY$ where x is a constant fraction, then Baumol's equation for money demand can be written as:

$$\frac{C^\circ}{2} = P\left[(xY)\,\frac{Y}{2r}\right]^{1/2}$$

$$= PY\left(\frac{x}{2r}\right)^{1/2}$$

so M_d varies proportionally with both P and Y.

its level. I will use the Smith family to illustrate these changes, even though most money demand is by firms rather than by households.

Interest on daily versus minimum monthly balances
Suppose that Mrs. Smith is moved backward in time to a year before 1979, when there were no daily-interest savings accounts available. Savings accounts paid interest only on the minimum monthly (or quarterly, or even annual) balance. Her interest rate for a two-week period would have been zero. She would have kept the entire paycheque in money just to avoid the transactions costs. Her average balance would have been insensitive to changes in reported interest rates, and it would have risen proportionally with her real income. The introduction of daily-interest savings accounts in 1979 therefore had exactly the opposite effects: it increased interest sensitivity and reduced income sensitivity of demand for money.

Cash-management accounts
Move Mrs. Smith back to the present again and allow her the privilege of using one of the special *cash-management accounts* first made available to business customers in 1976 and 1977. With this account, or rather, combination of accounts, funds are automatically moved from her savings account to her chequing account whenever the chequing account is short of funds.

Effectively, the cost to Mrs. Smith of making a withdrawal from her savings account to make payments by cheque is reduced to nil. The bank does it for her without charge. Mrs. Smith will respond by putting all of the family income in the savings account, none in the chequing account. Her money balance will therefore be zero at all times except the instant before the cheque is cancelled by the bank. Her average demand for chequing-account money will be nearly zero. She will hold only currency, and that only for her liquor purchases and race track bets, for which personal cheques and VISA are not accepted.

Interest on chequing deposits
Suppose Mrs. Smith's chequing account itself pays interest. In that case the net opportunity cost of holding money rather than nonmoney assets is reduced. Mrs. Smith will not be so keen to keep her funds invested, and she will increase her average money balance.

This innovation is not particularly troublesome so far.[16] Suppose, however, that the yield payable on Mrs. Smith's chequing account moves together with the yield on her daily-interest savings account, as is the case with marginal yields on some of the new interest-bearing chequing accounts introduced by the banks in July 1980. In this case nothing happens to the net opportunity cost of holding money as yields rise on savings accounts. If nothing happens to the net opportunity cost of holding

[16]The only complication is that the predicted interest elasticity of $-\frac{1}{2}$ refers to the net opportunity cost and not to the gross expected yield on nonmoney assets.

money, nothing happens to the demand for money. The response of money demand to yields on money substitutes is then nil, as in the Cambridge and quantity-theory approach. The significance of this change in chequing-account practices is that it applies to both small households and large firms.

Use of VISA and MasterCard to schedule payments

Canadians lead the world in per capita ownership of bank credit cards, so let us allow Mrs. Smith to use her VISA card. She still consumes steadily during the pay period but pays almost all of her bills for that consumption on payday. Mortgage interest and property tax payments, utility bills, and all bills rung up on the family's bank credit card are payable once a month rather than in a steady stream. Only grocery bills and movie tickets have to be paid for on the spot. Now most of Mrs. Smith's spending occurs at the same time as her income is received. She has an asset-allocation problem only with the remainder of her income, which must be much less. Suppose it is only \$200, as in figure 9–7. If Mrs. Smith were to put half of that away in her savings account for the first week of the pay period, at 10 percent per year, she would earn only 19 cents. This is much less than the transactions cost. Instead, Mrs. Smith will hold the whole \$200 in money. Her average balance will be \$200/2 = \$100, and it will be insensitive to interest-rate levels over a wide range.

FIGURE 9–7 Average money balances with coincidence of income and bill payments

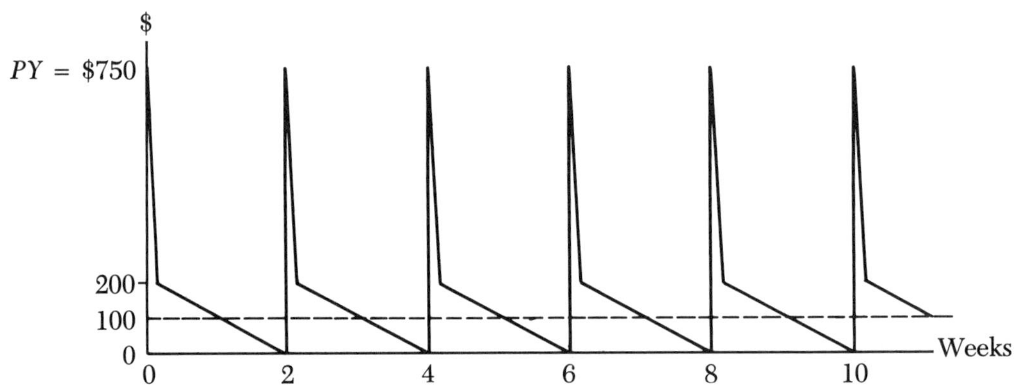

Biweekly income of \$750 is mostly used to pay month-end bills, leaving only \$200 to be used for spending during the pay period. If none of it is put into other assets, the average cash balance will be just over \$100.

The last result suggests that Y in Baumol's model should be interpreted not as real income but rather as real income left over after payment of regular month-end bills — something like "discretionary real take-home pay." The latter is much smaller than the former and will vary substantially with such payments innovations as the credit card and automatic payroll deductions.

SECTION 4

Precautionary demand (relatively advanced material)

Baumol's approach and its many extensions fit situations where individuals' income and expenditure streams are certain but different. Now allow the stream of income and expenditure to be uncertain. In any month the Smiths might get an extra cheque in the mail or they might not; they might find a special deal on new furniture or they might not. Whenever special spending opportunities come up, or expected income is not received on time, the Smiths must make some special financial arrangements or pass up some spending they would like to do. The arrangements may be to cash in part of a term deposit early or to sell off some stock or mutual fund shares, or just to borrow on their bank credit card. All of these arrangements involve extra transactions costs. Alternatively, the Smiths may only run down a money balance accumulated as a precaution against just such needs. Running down a money balance avoids the extra transactions costs, but holding money until that point involves foregoing interest that could have been earned on other assets. Mrs. Smith, a rational person, balances off these two considerations to arrive at an optimal *precautionary demand* for money — the demand for money as a precaution against unexpected needs.[17]

In order to see the expected gain and the expected opportunity cost of holding wealth in the form of precautionary money balances, assume

1. that Figure 9–8 gives the probability distribution of possible gaps between income and spending during a typical period,
2. that all shortfalls of income below spending must be met — that the spending or income flow itself is not adjusted instead,
3. that, if nonmoney assets must be sold off or withdrawn early to meet shortfalls, the transactions cost is c per dollar, and
4. that the net extra interest to be earned on nonmoney assets is r per period.

Starting with any amount M of precautionary balances, consider adding one more dollar. The probability of that dollar's being used to meet a

[17]Precautionary-demand theory has developed, after Keynes, from the approach of Don Patinkin in *Money, Interest and Prices*, 2d ed. (New York: Harper and Row, 1965), chap. 5. Laidler provides a concise summary of the theory in The *Demand for Money*, 81–88.

FIGURE 9–8 Probability distribution of possible shortfalls of income below spending needs

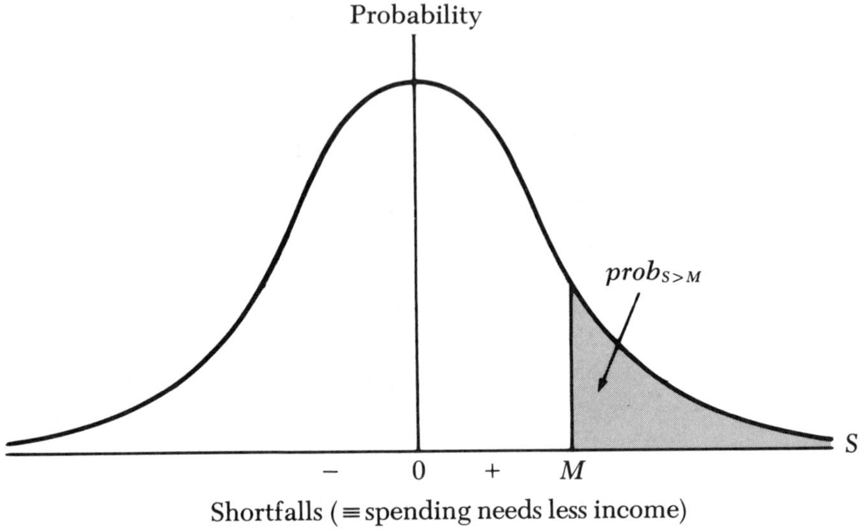

M is the amount of money available to meet positive shortfalls (negative shortfalls imply surpluses and are not a problem). The probability of shortfalls greater than M — labelled $prob$(shortfall>M) — is the area under the curve to the right of M, as a proportion of the total area. As M is increased, the area under the curve to the right of it shrinks.

shortfall (S) is the cumulative probability of all shortfalls larger than M. This is the area under the probability distribution to the right of M in figure 9–8. Call this $prob_{S>M}$. If the extra dollar is needed to meet a shortfall, transactions costs of c are avoided by having that dollar in the chequing account to use. If the dollar is not needed, there is zero gain from having it. The marginal expected gain from having the extra dollar is therefore

$$E = prob_{S>M}c + (1 - prob_{S>M})0$$
$$= prob_{S>M}c.$$

Because the probability of shortfalls' being large enough to exceed the money balance must drop as the money balance itself grows (that is, as M moves to the right along the horizontal axis of figure 9–8), the marginal expected gain from extra dollars of precautionary balances must drop as well. The marginal expected gain is shown in figure 9–9 for various levels of money holding.

The marginal opportunity cost of keeping each extra dollar of wealth in money is r if the money is not needed. If the money is needed — that is, if a

FIGURE 9–9 Marginal gain and marginal opportunity cost from precautionary money balances

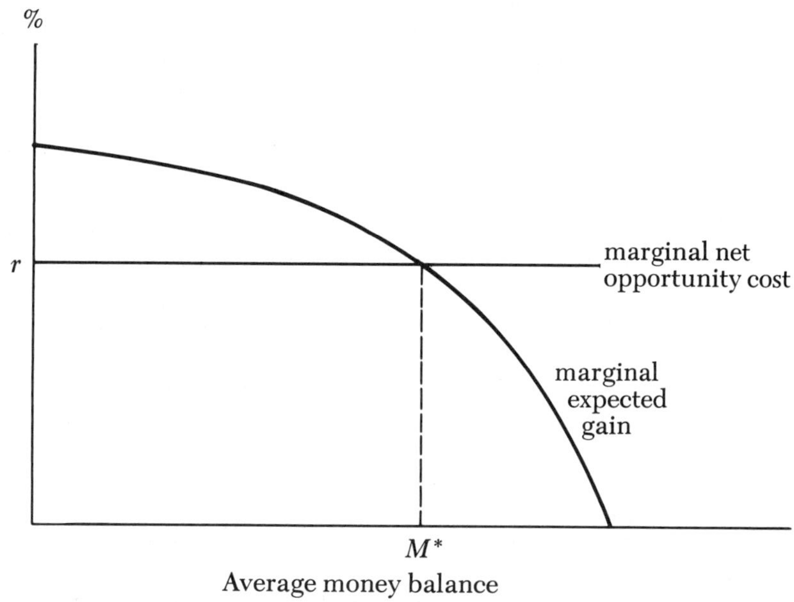

Marginal expected gain from money balances falls because the probability of the marginal dollar's being used must fall as M is increased. Marginal expected opportunity cost is constant, or nearly so, at the net opportunity yield. The optimal precautionary balance is M^*, at the intersection of the two curves. The optimal amount depends on the net opportunity yield r and on the probability distribution of possible income shortfalls.

shortfall occurs that is large enough to call for use of the dollar — then it will have earned interest only up to the point where it is needed to cover the shortfall. Assume this point is close enough to the end of the pay period to make little difference, so the expected marginal opportunity cost of extra precautionary balances is just r, as is shown in figure 9–9.

Mrs. Smith's optimal precautionary balance is at the intersection of expected gain and expected opportunity cost lines, at M^*. Her precautionary demand depends on all ingredients of figure 9–9: net opportunity cost of holding money, transactions cost, and dispersion of possible shortfalls. Higher net opportunity costs decrease desired precautionary balances. Higher transactions costs raise the expected gain from holding money (since holding money allows us to avoid those transactions costs); precautionary demand is increased. Greater probability of large shortfalls would make the expected gain line flatter in figure 9–9 and probably increase precautionary demand.[18] It is not at all clear whether an increase in real income would increase the dispersion of possible shortfalls, though it seems plausible that higher price levels would do so.

In summary, precautionary-demand theory essentially adds uncertainty to Baumol's transactions-demand theory. Interest rates and transactions costs are shown to be important again, as well as the level of uncertainty about future transactions. Not much extra light is shed on the role of prices and incomes.

An extension

The logic of transactions and precautionary demand for money can easily be extended from the situation of the Smith family, buying and selling in the Canadian economy, to that of Canada as a whole, buying and selling in the world economy. Canada as a whole requires transactions and precautionary balances of the money used in international trade; that is, foreign exchange. Canada's demand for foreign-exchange reserves should reflect most of the same considerations as the Smiths' demand for money.[19]

SECTION 5 Keynes' speculative demand

When Keynes reformulated monetary theory in *The General Theory of Employment, Interest, and Money* in 1936, he identified three motives for holding money: a transactions motive, a precautionary motive, and a *speculative motive*. The first two have been developed further by Keynes' successors. The third motive has been almost ignored. Tobin's portfolio-theory explanation of money demand as a response to risk aversion largely replaced it. Keynes relied on speculative demand to argue that interest is an important factor in the demand for money, but we now recognize that interest is important even without speculative demand. Nevertheless, speculative demand can be important at times for the demand for broad money. In order to understand it we must first understand the yield that bond-market speculators expect from bonds.

Speculative motive

---

[18]Laidler, for instance, notes that greater probability of larger shortfalls must be accompanied by smaller probability of smaller shortfalls because total probability must add up to 1.0. Marginal expected gain may increase for larger money-demand balances, but it must also fall for smaller balances. *The Demand for Money*, 87.

[19]Application of transactions-demand theory to demand for international reserves is discussed in N. Saidi, "The Square-root Law, Uncertainty, and International Reserves under Alternative Regimes: Canadian Experience, 1950–76," *Journal of Monetary Economics*, May 1981, 271–90.

Short-holding-period yields on long-term bonds

Keynes argued that many investors would be choosing between (a) money and (b) long-term bonds held for short periods. The short-period yield r_s on long-term bonds consists of a coupon yield from the interest coupon and a capital gain g from the change in price over that holding period:

$$r_s = \text{coupon yield} + \text{capital gain}.$$

The coupon yield is C/P, where C is the coupon payment per year (in dollars) and P is the bond price. The coupon yield C/P clearly falls as the bond price P rises. The bond price in turn rises as the current yield available on other long-term investments falls. This is easiest to demonstrate for a perpetual bond (one whose interest payments stretch on in perpetuity, with no redemption), so for this section we will assume all long-term bonds are perpetuals. Pressure of excess demand or excess supply will always keep the price of a perpetual bond such that its coupon yield equals the other long-term yields (r) available. Thus,

$$\frac{C}{P} = r.$$

So $P = \dfrac{C}{r}$.

Because the coupon amount is fixed (eternally, for a perpetual bond), the price of the bond and the long-term interest rate must move in opposite directions in the same proportion. The capital gain expected on the perpetual bond is $(P^e - P)/P$, where P^e is the expected future price. If $P = C/r$, then $P^e = C/r^e$, and we can substitute for both P and P^e in the expression for total short-period yield r_s:

$$\begin{aligned} r_s &= \text{coupon yield} + \text{capital gain} \\ &= r + \frac{(P^e - P)}{P} \\ &= r + \frac{(C/r^e) - (C/r)}{(C/r)} \\ &= r - \frac{(r^e - r)}{r^e} \end{aligned}$$

The second term $(r^e - r)/r^e$ is the proportional expected rise in long-term yields. The larger it is, the larger the capital loss and the smaller the short-period yield r_s.

When wealthholders expect r to rise substantially, therefore, they will avoid long-term bonds and hold short-term liquid assets instead. When they expect r to fall, they will shift out of liquid asets into bonds. The argument is unassailable to this point, but wealthholders' expectations are unobservable. Keynes asserted that wealthholders have a conception of a "normal" range of long-term yields and that they expect actual long-term yields r to return to that normal range. Different wealthholders have different conceptions of normal, but as actual yields rise, more and more wealthholders will perceive actual yields as above normal and expect a reversal. Higher long-term yields on bonds are therefore associated with expected future declines, lower yields with expected future increases. What goes up must come down, and vice versa. Higher long-term yields on bonds therefore mean large expected capital gains on bonds — an expectation that shifts speculators' asset demand from money to bonds. Low yields do the opposite.

There are two important defects in Keynes' explanation. The first is that expectations will not always work the way he assumed. An increase in interest rates does not always cause bond-market participants to expect a fall in interest rates. James Pesando of the University of Toronto, for instance, suggests that rational investors do not change their expectations at all when interest rates rise.[20]

The second defect is that investors have more than just money and bonds to choose from. If long-term bonds are unattractive because of expected bear markets, then short-term assets such as Treasury Bills are preferable to money balances for most large financial investors. Keynes' theory explains the demand for liquid assets better than it does the demand for media of exchange. His theory is more useful in understanding the demand for broad money than the demand for narrow money.

SECTION 6 Evidence on the demand for money

There have been dozens of attempts to test money-demand relationships against historical data, for just about every economy that has an economist. The money-demand function is a key relationship for macroeconomic stabilization policy, and much of the data are conveniently produced by national statistical agencies. This section is not a survey of these tests, since that requires a book in itself (already written by Professor Laidler of the University of Western Ontario).[21] This section contains only a summary of the results.

The predictions

Table 9–2 summarizes the predicted money-demand relationships from sections 2 through 5 of this chapter. In general, money demand will depend

[20]James E. Pesando, "On the Random Walk Characteristics of Short- and Long-Term Interest Rates in an Efficient Market," *Journal of Money, Credit, and Banking*, Nov. 1980, 457–66.

[21]*The Demand for Money: Theories and Evidence*, 2d ed. (New York: Dun-Donnelley, 1977).

TABLE 9–2 Predicted money-demand relationships

Explanatory variable	Predicted effect	Size of effect
Financial wealth	+	elasticity < 1, near zero (Tobin)
Expected yield variables		
Yield on money	+	elasticity of net opportunity cost between $-\frac{1}{2}$ and 0 (Baumol)
Opportunity yields	−	
Expected inflation	−	same as opportunity yields (Friedman)
Transactions variables		
Real income	+	elasticity between $\frac{1}{2}$ and 1.0, with long lag (Baumol and Friedman)
Price level	+	elasticity of 1.0 (all)
Transactions costs	+	elasticity of $\frac{1}{2}$ for lump-sum costs (Baumol)
Risk variables		
Variance of yield on money	−	
Covariances with other yields	−	
Variance of other yields	+	
Covariances of other yields	+	
Degree of risk aversion	+	
Uncertainty of income	+	

Note: A positive sign indicates that an increase in the explanatory variable increases the demand for money; a negative sign, that demand for money is decreased. Demand for money is predicted to depend on all of the variables above, though for simplicity some theories leave out some of the variables.

on wealth levels, relative expected yields, and relative risks. Wealth as a constraint on money demand is best reflected in financial wealth, though its predicted impact on money demand is small. Expected yields include any explicit interest rate paid on money (especially the interest on time deposits, where broad-money measures like M2 or M3 are being used) and opportunity yields on substitutes. There are many possible opportunity yields, all of which are relevant in principle but most of which move together so closely that their respective effects cannot be separated. The list of substitute assets includes real assets such as inventories of goods. Their nominal yield is the expected rate of price inflation, which is sometimes included specifically in tests. Note that, in estimates of demand for the narrow-money measures M1 and M1A, the interest yield on time deposits is an opportunity yield and not a yield on money.

Table 9–2 includes the relative-risk variables — the variances and covariances of money yields and of opportunity yields — as well as investors' degree of risk aversion. Since income determines the need for transactions services from money, uncertainty of income has been added to that otherwise normal list of risk variables in the table.

In practice, most researchers have followed Tobin's lead in treating money as a riskless asset. In that case money yields have zero variance and covariance. Yields on substitute assets have positive variances, but zero covariance with money yields. The list of relative-risk variables is made much shorter.

Tests of the predictions

There have been very few tests of the importance of relative-risk variables for the demand for money. Most researchers have probably felt there was little evidence of change in relative risks, or that it was impossible to measure, or both. Professors Alan Gregory and James Mackinnon have provided an exception in testing explicitly for the effect of postal strikes on demand for money in Canada. Postal strikes cause sudden and sharp increases in uncertainty about future income receipts. Gregory and Mackinnon found that the demand for money rose sharply during the postal strikes in 1976 and 1979.[22]

There have been many tests of the impacts of wealth, price, income, and relative-yield variables on the demand for money. Impacts are measured generally as elasticities, ratios of percentage change in money demand to percentage changes in wealth and in yield levels.[23] The elasticities estimated have been generally in line with the predictions of table 9–2. To be specific, and starting from the top of table 9–2:

1. Financial-wealth measures are important in explaining the demand for money if real income is left out, but when real income is left in, financial wealth tends to have a relatively insignificant impact on the demand for money.
2. Explicit interest paid on time deposits is important as a yield on money in explaining demand for broad money and as an opportunity yield with the opposite sign in explaining demand for narrow money. For narrow money there have been attempts to devise measures of an implicit own-yield by calculating the extent of bank subsidies of cheque transfer costs, but with mixed results.

---

[22]"Where's My Cheque? A Note on Postal Strikes and the Demand for Money in Canada," *Canadian Journal of Economics*, Nov. 1980, 683–88.

[23]Consider money demand M and any explanatory variable X. The X elasticity of M is defined as the ratio $(dM/M)/(dX/X) = (dM/dX)(X/M)$. If M is regressed against X directly, the coefficient of X in the regression is the value (dM/dX); multiplying the coefficient by the average level of (X/M) gives the elasticity. If both M and X are transformed logarithmically so that LnM is regressed against LnX, the observed coefficient of LnX is itself an elasticity, since $dLnM/dLnX = (dM/M)/(dX/X)$.

3. Opportunity yields are always important in money-demand studies. It is not possible to identify which particular opportunity yield is most important, but neither is it necessary. All of the yields on substitute short-term assets move together as a rule and presumably all of them have some impact. Using any one or two of the many available short-term yields therefore picks up or reflects the combined impact of all of them.

   Interest elasticities for short-term opportunity yields have been in the range of −0.1 to −0.2 percent in narrow-money demand studies. Elasticities for less volatile long-term yields are higher, in the range of −0.5 percent, as predicted in Baumol's model. For broad-money demand studies the elasticities have varied widely depending on which own-yield was used and the functional forms used. In tests that put own-yield and opportunity yield in separately, rather than putting in just the difference between them, the elasticities were usually of the same size but with opposite sign, indicating that it is only the difference — the net opportunity costs — that matters.
4. There have been few tests of the impact of expected inflation on the demand for money, except indirect ones. Where it is included specifically (however it is estimated, since expectations are unobservable), it has the expected negative elasticity as befits an opportunity yield. Even where expected inflation is not introduced explicitly, it appears implicitly by affecting the level of nominal opportunity yields on substitute assets. Higher expected inflation tends to cause higher nominal interest rates, as we will see in chapter 14, so it affects money demand indirectly as well — again with negative elasticity as predicted.
5. Real income is always important to the demand for money, though usually with long enough lags to support Friedman's idea that it is permanent income that matters. For narrow-demand studies, the real income elasticity is generally below but close to 1.0, while for broad money the elasticity is 1.0 or slightly over. Baumol's theory, which explains demand for narrow money rather than broad money, is therefore supported here as well.
6. The price elasticity of the demand for money has been exactly 1.0 in almost all studies, but by assumption rather than because the data suggest it. William White of the Bank of Canada has concluded from a thorough investigation that price and income levels have moved too closely together over time to allow us to separate out the amount of impact that is from price changes and the amount that is from income changes.[24] Since all of the theory predicts that prices should have

[24]William White of the Bank of Canada conducted especially elaborate tests of ability to pinpoint the price elasticity and concluded it was not possible. *The Demand for Money in Canada and the Control of Monetary Aggregates: Evidence from the Monthly Data* (Ottawa: Bank of Canada, 1976).

proportional effects, researchers typically assume that and then use that assumption to help estimate the real income elasticity.

7. Transactions costs are like the relative-risk variables: they have seldom changed enough over short periods to have had observable effects. Two changes in the late 1970s offer exceptions. In 1976 and 1977, the banks made available to firms some cash-management facilities that drastically lowered the transactions costs of investing funds overnight. In 1979, daily-interest savings deposits were introduced. We have already explained that such an innovation makes a large difference to the opportunity cost of holding money for short periods. The results of both innovations appear to have been significant decreases in money demand, as predicted.

Lags and stability

All the evidence supports Friedman's idea that real income affects the demand for money only gradually, as if it were permanent income that mattered rather than current income. For that matter, all the other variables affect money demand gradually as well, over periods as long as five years. Economists have not been very successful at extracting from past data exactly how long it takes for most economic causes to have effects on economic activity, so we cannot be very confident about assertions that a gradual effect is spread over three years rather than five, for instance, or vice versa. In most estimates, however, the bulk of the impact of a change in any determining variable will have occurred by the end of one year.

In Canada, evidence up to the mid-1970s suggested that demand for narrow money M1 had been a fairly stable function of real income, price levels, opportunity yields, own-yields on money, and variables reflecting seasonal factors. That is, the elasticities of money demand have not seemed to change much over time, almost all of the variation in money demand is accounted for by these variables, and in Canada there have been few large and persistent forecasting errors. Money-demand behavior in both the U.S. and Canada since 1975 has been less predictable, however. Now the Bank of Canada in particular is not satisfied it can accurately predict even the demand for narrow money.[25]

Demand for broad money (M2 and M3) has generally been found to be less stable over time, by the same tests. The reason would seem to be that Treasury Bills, Canada Savings Bonds, and trust company Guaranteed Investment Certificates or credit-union term deposits are very close substitutes for bank term deposits, so small movements in their relative yields or in their other attributes suffice to cause large changes in demand for term

---

[25]This lack of predictability was the central message of Governor Bouey's address to the International Monetary Fund in September 1982. "Monetary Policy: Finding a Place to Stand," *Bank of Canada Review*, Sept. 1982. The position is confirmed by the Bank's abandonment of its M1 growth targets in November 1982.

deposits. Not all of those relative-yield movements are reflected in the few opportunity-yield series used in estimates of broad-money demand, so the estimates are subject to large errors.

In the United States, researchers have found even the demand for narrow money (M1) to be unstable in the 1970s. The reason seems to be distortions in financial flows caused originally by a set of interest-rate ceilings on bank and other intermediary savings deposits. As these ceilings have been reached, or breached in some way by innovative bankers, there have been large shifts of households' and firms' funds from one type of account to another, causing large gaps between predicted and actual money demands.

SECTION 7

Adjustment patterns in the market for money

Adjustments of demand and supply of money

All the evidence suggests long lags in adjustment of money demand to changes in expected yields, income, and price levels. The lags in adjustment to real income levels are particularly long — lasting up to sixteen quarters in tests using quarterly data and longer than four years using annual data. The lag in adjustment to real income changes is consistent with Milton Friedman's claim that all that matters is permanent income (or its capitalized value, human wealth). Lags in adjustment to interest rates and price levels require a different explanation: the delays are probably due to some combination of perception lags, transaction costs, and waiting for other assets to mature (for example, where an individual wishing to shift into money from a trust-company GIC has to wait six months or more for the GIC to mature).

Adjustment of the supply of deposits by banks is much faster than adjustment of demand, in some ways. Banks have highly paid staffs to forecast future yield trends and adjust the banks' borrowing strategies to minimize costs and risks. Banks shift their borrowing pattern by changing the relative rates they offer on different kinds of deposits, and those interest-rate changes are listed each week on the banks' interest-rate quote sheets. The only supply lag comes from the banks' not being able to reduce quantity of deposits outstanding before maturity. If there are too many five-year term deposits outstanding (at rates that are too high from the banks' point of view), the banks cannot simply cancel a few; they must wait for passage of time to persuade holders to shift into shorter-term deposits.

Further, it takes some time for banks to adjust their asset portfolios following an increase in cash reserves. Initially, any excess cash reserves not needed against deposits will be held in liquid assets such as Treasury Bills, to be sold off later when the funds can be used for business and consumer lending.[26] Banks do not delay, however, in issuing the maximum amount of deposits that cash reserves can support. As you will see in chapter 11, Canadian banks never hold any significant amount of excess cash reserves, not even for periods as short as two weeks.

Adjustment to excess demand or supply

Because demand for money adjusts so slowly, adjustment to excess demand or supply of money occurs gradually. Most of the adjustment seems to be complete after one year, though estimates vary. The most peculiar part of the adjustment process, however, is that the adjustment does not take place in the yield on money.[27] Instead, the adjustment is in all other yields in the economy. The reason is that the yield on money (cash and demand deposits; that is, narrow money) is more or less fixed at zero in the Canadian economy, as in almost all others. Excess demand in the market for money is mirrored by equal excess supply in markets for nonmoney assets, so it is the yields in these other markets that are called on to do all the adjusting.

Money is different from other assets in one other respect that is critical to the process of adjustment: unlike the usual market, where excess supply remains on the seller's shelves, the banks have no trouble issuing more demand deposits than holders wish. Banks pay for any asset they purchase by just adding to the seller's demand deposit. The seller may well spend that deposit balance immediately, but it still exists; spending it merely transfers it to somebody else's bank account. Once created, demand deposits must be held by somebody.

Thus, instead of the banks' having to decide how to sell their excess supply of demand deposits, it is the holders who have to decide how to get rid of them. Holders of unwanted demand deposits try to buy other assets instead. In the process, they bid up the prices and lower the yields of the other assets. As these opportunity yields fall, the demand for money increases until eventually all the demand deposits in existence are willingly held. The market for money is then in equilibrium, but not because of adjustment of the yield on money.

When lower opportunity rates start to have an effect on the level of real incomes and prices, demand for money will increase further, so there will be excess demand for money. Again, the adjustment mechanism is for all opportunity rates to adjust (back upward again) instead of for the yield on money to fall. Those wanting to hold more money balances try to sell off some of the other assets now in excess supply by lowering their prices and raising their expected yields. As opportunity yields for money rise, the

---

[26]The process of chartered-bank asset-portfolio adjustment is well described in William R. White, *Management by the Canadian Banks of Their Domestic Portfolios, 1956–71* (Ottawa: Bank of Canada Staff Research Study 11, 1975).

[27]James Tobin made this point very clearly in "Commercial Banks as Creators of Money," in Deane Carson, ed., *Banking and Monetary Studies* (Homewood, Ill.: Irwin, 1963).

demand for money falls until once again the amount in existence is willingly held. Throughout this adjustment process the yield on money itself does not change; instead, all other yields adjust.

Adjustment patterns of nonmoney yields: overshooting and J curves

Finally, we can put together the ideas that money demand adjusts slowly and that adjustment takes place initially through changes in opportunity yields. Consider a sudden increase in available cash reserves. Banks can expand their assets and liabilities, which they do by buying more liquid assets in the money market and handing out demand deposits in exchange.

FIGURE 9–10 Dynamic response of interest rates to a sudden increase in money supply

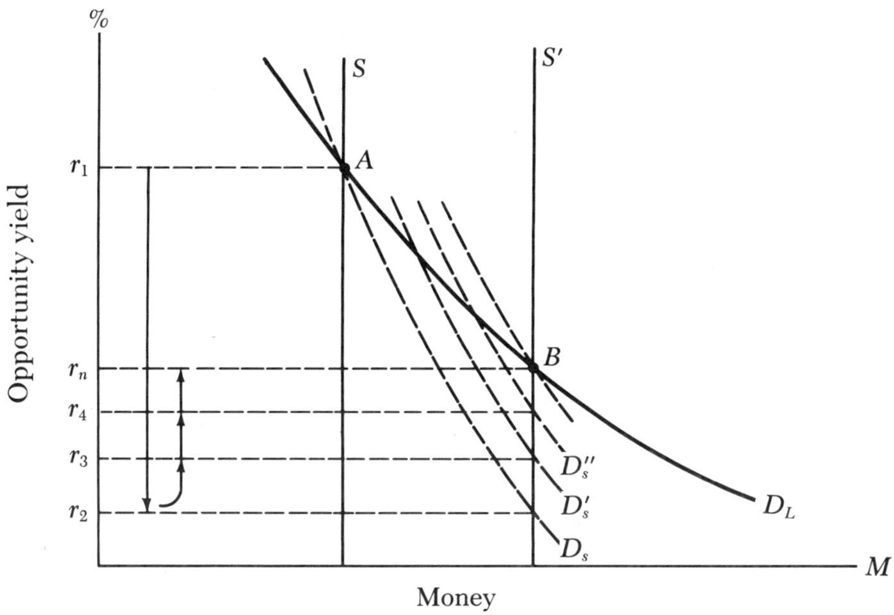

When the money supply is increased from S to S', the initial demand response is a movement along the short-run demand curve D_s, so the interest rate falls to r_2. As time passes, more demand response occurs (shifting the short-run demand curve to D_s', D_s'' and so on), and the interest rate rises back from r_2 toward the long-run equilibrium at r_n, where the new supply curve S intersects the long-run demand curve.

Holders of these extra money balances bid down yields on money substitutes until someone is persuaded to hold onto the extra money. If money demand adjusts slowly to changes in opportunity yields, however, a large change in yields will be needed initially to generate the required extra demand for money. Opportunity yields will initially fall by more than would be needed after full demand adjustment. As demand adjusts more fully, opportunity yields will rise again, following a sort of reverse J pattern on a time-series chart.

Figure 9–10 illustrates the pattern on a diagram with an assumed vertical supply of money and a downward-sloping cross-demand curve for money (relating money demand to expected yields on other assets). There are two demand curves, one long-run and one short-run, intersecting at the initial equilibrium point A. The supply curve shifts quickly from S to S', lowering the short-run equilibrium yield along D_s to r_2. Over the next few quarters, as more of the adjustment of money demand to lower opportunity yields occurs, D_s shifts outward to D_s', D_s'', and so on, generating even higher yields r_3, r_4, and so on. Eventually a new equilibrium is reached at B, by which time the interest rate has followed what is known as a *J-curve path*.

SECTION 8 Summary

This chapter has explained demand for money. The currency and bank deposits that make up the money supply are in principle financial assets like any other, and their demand is subject to many of the same market forces as other financial assets. Money demand differs mainly in that money provides medium-of-exchange services, and narrow money at least pays little or no explicit interest.

Demand for money is based mainly upon the transactions services that money provides. The need for transactions services rises with the level of nominal income, a proposition recognized long ago in monetary theory and enshrined in the Quantity Theory.

Keynes emphasized that the demand for money was also sensitive to the level of opportunity yields; Baumol, Tobin, and others provided sound theoretical explanations to back up Keynes' contention. Holders of money value the transactions services provided by money, but they recognize that holding money means foregoing interest on alternative assets. Holders of money as a store of value recognize the liquidity and certainty that money provides, but they also take into account that other assets provide higher expected yield. For both reasons the amount of money demanded is sensitive to the level of opportunity cost as well as to the necessary volume of transactions.

Milton Friedman has emphasized that demand for money, like that for any other financial asset, must depend on wealth levels. However,

Friedman's definition of wealth reflects mainly the level of real income, whose capitalized value is human wealth; demand for money may not be very sensitive to the other, nonhuman part of total wealth. Friedman also has emphasized that responses of money demand to observed income levels will be slow.

The many tests of money-demand relationships in Canada and elsewhere support the main contentions of modern money-demand theory. Broad money is not so well explained, in that there is evidence of substantial change over time in the relationship of money demand to its explanatory variables. For both narrow and broad money, the major explanatory variables are real income, the price level, any explicit own-yield payable on money, and one or more opportunity yields on money substitutes. There is much less evidence that is conclusive on the length of lags in adjustment of demand to change in the important variables.

There are long lags in adjustment of the demand for money, especially to changes in real income. Money supply often adjusts much more quickly. Since adjustment of the market for money is by changes in yields on other assets rather than by changes in the yield on money, long lags in adjustment of demand imply large initial changes in those other yields when there is any large change in money supply.

Questions for discussion

1. How is money different from other financial assets?
2. If you suddenly won a lottery and had your financial wealth rise abruptly, what proportion of it would you choose to hold in narrow-money assets, on average over the next year? Is this greater or less than the proportion of money in your existing financial wealth?
3. How much money do you hold, on average in a typical week, as a fraction of your weekly expenditures?
4. What demand-for-money curve would Tobin's mean-variance model imply for a risk-seeking individual, or for one with decreasing risk aversion?
5. What is your human wealth in today's dollars?
6. How would the Smiths' optimal-withdrawal problem have to be reworded to fit the situation of a typical firm with relatively smooth inflow of sales revenue and relatively lumpy payment of bills?
7. How does your own money-demand behavior differ from that of the Smiths, in our analysis of the Baumol model of transactions demand for money?
8. If you never left home without your American Express card, why would you need to carry money balances?
9. What is the likely effect of higher real income levels on the probability distribution of possible shortfalls, as shown in figure 9–8?

10. If coupon yields on perpetual bonds are 10 percent, and they are expected to rise within a year to 12 percent, what is the one-year holding-period yield on those bonds?

References

Binhammer, H.H. *Money, Banking and the Canadian Financial System*. 4th ed. Toronto: Methuen, 1982, chap. 22.

Goodhart, C.A.E. *Money, Information and Uncertainty*. London: Macmillan, 1975.

Laidler, David E. W. *The Demand for Money: Theories and Evidence*. 2d ed. New York: Dun-Donnelley, 1977.

Niehans, Jurg. *The Theory of Money*. Baltimore: Johns Hopkins Press, 1975.

Wilton, D.A., and D.M. Prescott. *Macroeconomics: Theory and Policy in Canada*. Don Mills, Ont.: Addison-Wesley, 1982, chap. 18.

CHAPTER 10

Supply of Assets under Uncertainty

Chapter 8 explained the demand for assets under uncertainty with the aid of mean-variance analysis. This chapter extends that explanation to the debt side of the balance sheet. Using the same analytical approach that was used in chapter 8 — the mean-variance approach — this chapter comes to quite different conclusions about debts from those chapter 8 reached about assets. In particular, what is important about debts is that they match assets, rather than that borrowing be done in many different forms for diversification.

The analysis in this chapter is applied first to household borrowing and then to business borrowing. The analysis of business borrowing is very general, in that it applies both to financial institutions and manufacturing firms. The situations of various types of financial institution are discussed in more detail in chapters 11 to 13.

In this chapter you will learn:

1. how quickly stocks of debts in existence can be changed by their issuers, and how much debt supply is fixed by past borrowing decisions,
2. the nature of uncertainty facing borrowers, and measures that approximate that uncertainty,
3. how debt supply behaves when the debt is used to finance non-income-earning assets, which means mainly household borrowing,
4. how actual households in Canada do their borrowing,
5. how debt supply behaves where the debt is used to finance income-earning assets, and
6. some of the borrowing strategies commonly used by producing firms and financial institutions to reduce their risks.

In the appendix you will see an important proposition first put forward by Modigliani and Miller in 1958: that the average cost of funds to a firm will not vary at all, in equilibrium, with the ratio of bond to share financing used. Their conclusion was later modified (because of taxation), but the analytical approach is important in itself.

SECTION 1 Supply adjustment

Debt supply

Debt supply available in the current year is made up of last year's debt carry-over plus net new issues, where net new issues is the difference between this year's new borrowings and this year's debt retirements. Last year's debt carry-over cannot be changed in this year, so debt supply can change in this year only as net new issues change. Thus we need to explain only net new issues.

Net new issues can be adjusted of course by changing new borrowing but also by changing retirements. We generally think of retirements as mechanical, fixed by a repayment schedule agreed on at time of issue. In fact, for many debts the retirement schedule is quite flexible.

Fixed retirement schedules

Examples of fixed retirement schedules are easy to find. Nonredeemable fixed-term deposits in trust and mortgage loan companies are redeemed only at the end of the fixed term (for instance, ninety days, one year, or three years). Bonds also have fixed retirement schedules, since most bonds have sinking fund arrangements specified in the bond indenture agreement; these provide for funds to be set aside in a sinking fund to retire the bond issue gradually at a set rate over the period to final maturity. Term preferred shares are likewise redeemed automatically on a schedule, just like bonds.

Flexible retirement schedules

There are also many examples of flexible, discretionary debt-retirement arrangements. Ordinary preferred shares are usually redeemable at the discretion of the issuing firm rather than on a fixed schedule. Bond issues may have a purchase fund arrangement rather than a sinking fund arrangement. Purchase fund arrangements allow the issuer more flexibility in deciding how much of the debt to retire each year. Demand loans, *open mortgages*, call and short loans from banks to brokers are all repayable in advance by the borrower, though repayment cannot be deferred as easily.

Open mortgage

Many debts can be retired early at the discretion of the holder or lender rather than the issuer.[1] Notice deposits, fixed-term deposits in banks (which are almost all redeemable before maturity), and day loans from banks to money-market dealers can all be redeemed or called whenever the lender wishes. Convertible or retractable preferred shares and bonds can also be removed from the market (by conversion or early redemption) at the holder's discretion.

---

[1]Where redemption is at the holder's discretion, any reduction in demand by the holder will automatically be matched by an equal reduction in supply (even if undesired by the issuer) as the demander turns in the asset for redemption.

Common shares are not usually retired at all, but in some cases they may be purchased and cancelled by the issuing company. In the 1950s, for instance, five large life insurance companies bought up all of their outstanding shares and retired them, in order to convert themselves into mutual companies owned only by their policyholders.

Speed of adjustment

The relative importance of debt supply carry-over from the past year and of net new issues in the current year will vary widely between types of debt. For instance, net new issues of common shares are both infrequent and relatively small for most companies. The total of common shares outstanding in any year is determined mainly by issues of previous years. At the other end of the spectrum, the day loan notes issued by money-market dealers to banks (in order to finance the dealers' inventories of money-market assets) are all retired very quickly; for dealers, supply carry-over from last year plays no significant part in determining this year's outstanding supply.

FIGURE 10–1 Net new issues as a percentage of outstanding debt of nonfinancial corporations, 1975–82

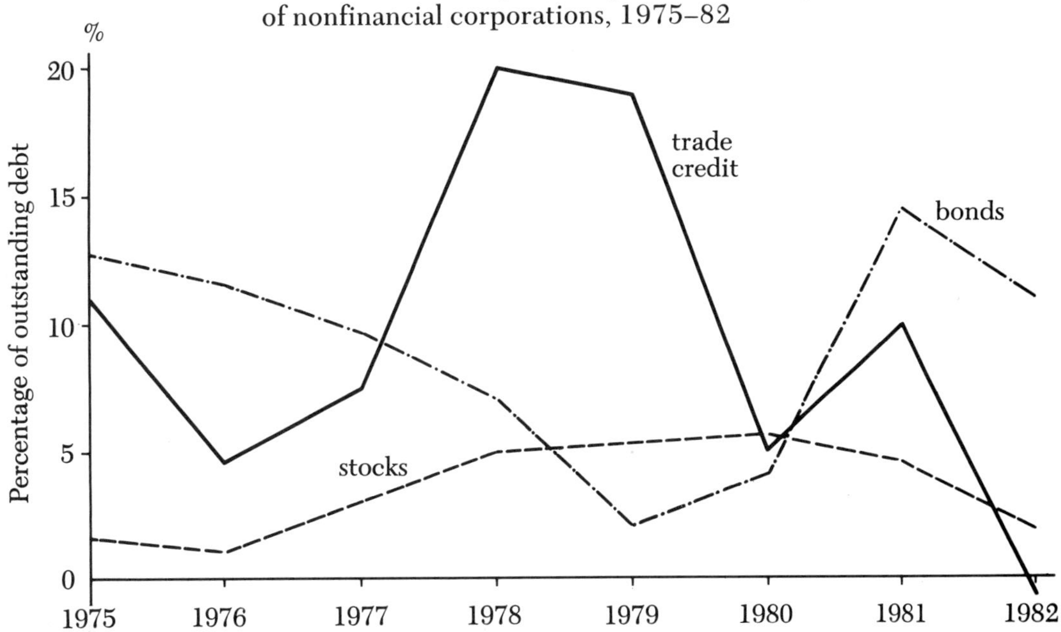

Note that stocks include only those issued to the public, not those issued to parent firms or affiliates.

Other assets fall in between the two extremes of stocks and day loans. For almost all financial assets, however, two statements will hold. First, the supply outstanding generally adjusts more slowly than demand, particularly downward. Even for increases in supply, new stock and bond issues take weeks of preparation. Second, there is significant flexibility of supply of almost all types of debt over periods as long as a year. For such periods it is dangerous to assume supply is fixed and unresponsive to current market risks and yields.

Figure 10–1 shows net new issues of various types of debt since 1975, as percentages of the outstanding stock. The flows obviously change dramatically from year to year, and they make a significant difference to the total outstanding supply within a year. Supply must therefore be explained rather than just assumed to be fixed.

SECTION 2 Sources and measures of uncertainty

Debts outstanding may be subject to inflation risk, income risk, and market risk. There is no default risk for borrowers, but there is liquidity risk instead. The first three types of risk were defined in chapter 8 and need not take up much time here.

Inflation risk

The future real value of interest payments and principal repayments will vary inversely with the inflation rate, for any given schedule of nominal debt payments. Where r is the nominal yield to maturity and i is the expected inflation rate over the same period, the real interest rate on a debt can be calculated as $(1 + r)/(1 + i) - 1 = (r - i)/(1 + i)$. Where the inflation rate i is uncertain, so is the real interest rate, and borrowers are exposed to inflation risk. Note, of course, that a risk of inflation's going up means a risk of the real interest rate's going down.

Income risk

Future nominal payments may not be fixed. For instance, the nominal interest rate payable may float with the bank prime rate from month to month. Such arrangements subject borrowers to income risk just like that faced by lenders.

Market risk

In a very few types of borrowing, the debt principal repayable is tied to market prices of assets. For instance, mutual funds must redeem their shares at a price determined by the average value of the mutual fund's assets when the redemption is requested. The obligation of some pension funds to their members (repayable at retirement of each member) is determined the same way, as an accumulated share of the market value of the pension fund's assets. However, mutual funds and pension funds are not really separate legal entities, distinct from their members. Some life insurance policies also have death-benefit liabilities that vary with the market value of assets held in special *segregated funds* by the insurance company. All such debts are subject to uncertainty because of variations in market prices of assets. These are definitely the exceptions rather than the rule, however. Market risk is just not very important for borrowers.

Liquidity risk

Liquidity risk

Income risk shades off at the margin into a separate kind of uncertainty known as *liquidity risk*, or sometimes as *bankers' risk*. This is uncertainty not over the rates of interest at which debt refinancing can be arranged, but over whether refinancing is available at all.[2] Where the borrower has a callable loan, the uncertainty is over whether the lender will in fact call it. If refinancing is not available, the rejected borrower's assets may need to be sold off prematurely and at some loss. Liquidity risk therefore affects possible yields on the assets concerned rather than the costs of debt. Where the loss due to forced sale of assets would wipe out the borrower's equity, liquidity risk threatens bankruptcy.

Measures of risk for debtors

In measuring risk for assetholders, we started with a probability distribution of possible yields on their asset portfolio; then we concentrated on the expected yield and the variance of that probability distribution, as summary measures of yield and risk. We could start in this chapter with a probability distribution of yields on debts and repeat the same analysis, but that would not be useful. It is better to remember that debtors are usually buying assets as well as issuing debts: they merely use borrowed funds as well as their own funds to finance their asset portfolios.

Debtors are therefore concerned about what is left over out of asset yields or other income after debt service costs are paid. It is this residual that finances debtors' consumption. It is volatility of this residual, not volatility of debt costs by themselves, that constitutes risk. Figure 10–2 illustrates the difference with three different patterns of debt financing for the same asset. The debt with the most stable costs is not the one that provides the most stable spread between asset yields and debt costs. It

[2]For example, Chrysler Credit Canada Ltd. was a frequent and creditworthy borrower in Canadian bond markets in the early 1970s. When the parent company ran into financial trouble in the late 1970s, demand for Chrysler Credit Canada's bonds fell by enough to raise their yield to fully 9 percent above prevailing corporate bond yields. This is not a feasible yield, and a new issue by Chrysler Credit Canada Ltd. would require a still larger yield.

FIGURE 10–2 Patterns of asset yields and debt costs

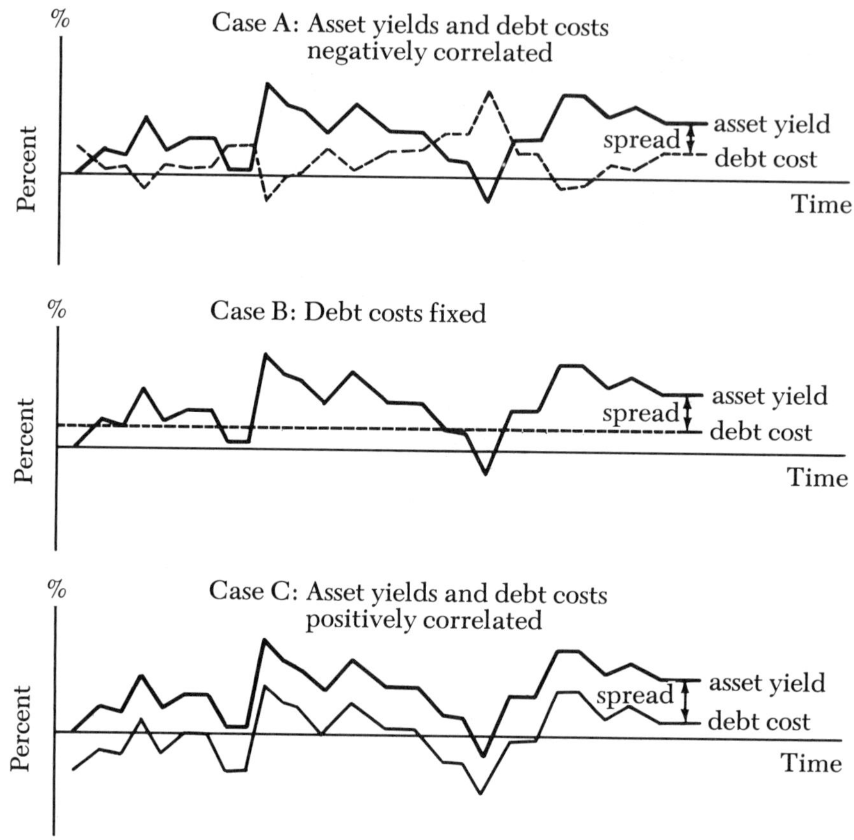

In each case the asset yield fluctuations are the same. In case A, the debt costs move exactly opposite to the asset yield. In case B, the debt cost is fixed. In case C, the debt costs move together with the asset yield. The spread between asset yield and debt cost, from which equity yield is earned, is least stable in case A and most stable in case C.

follows, incidentally, that diversification of debts is not necessarily desirable; where volatility of debt costs can be an advantage, it will not pay to reduce it. Debt costs should be perfectly correlated with, and just as volatile as, the flow of income out of which they must be paid.

The kinds of debt that will leave the smoothest consumption or dividend pattern will vary with each investor, depending on the investor's sources of income. We divide those sources into two groups. Some borrowers, especially households, will repay debts and interest out of labor income that is not directly connected with the purpose of the debts incurred. Other borrowers, expecially financial institutions, will repay debt service costs out of investment income, from the very investments that the debts helped to finance. The two groups are treated separately in the sections to follow.

SECTION 3

Debt supply behavior of households

We considered the supply of debts to finance consumer spending when we looked at the problem of Casey, the medical student, in chapter 6. Here we consider debts used to finance consumption or housing or any asset that does not generate its own flow of cash income. For all of these debts there is a fixed income constraint, in that the borrower is giving up some future consumption to repay the debts incurred, just as Casey did. All we need do here is add some uncertainty to Casey's future.

Assume Casey is uncertain about his actual future income (Y_2) and the actual debt service payments he will have to make (both interest and principal repayments) on any loan. His debt service payments are determined by his total debt (D) and the size of debt service payments per dollar of debt (R). Total debt is known for certain, so only R is uncertain. Uncertainty of R reflects mostly uncertainty about future interest rates (on floating-rate loans), but in some cases it could also reflect uncertainty about the size of principal repayments. Let Casey's future income have variance V_y, and let total debt service payments have variance V_R.

Uncertainty of future consumption

Casey's future consumption C_2 is the difference between future income Y_2 and debt service costs RD:

$$C_2 = Y_2 - RD.$$

C_2 is uncertain both because of uncertain Y_2 and because of uncertain RD. Casey faces a probability distribution of possible levels of C_2 for any one decision on current saving, choice of debt level, and choice of debt type. Casey is risk-averse and generally responds to uncertain situations like most investors: he looks at the expected value and the variance. The expected value $E(C_2)$ is the difference between the expected value of future income $E(Y_2)$ and the expected debt cost. Since the total debt D is certain, the expected debt cost is $E(R)D$.

$$E(C_2) = E(Y_2) - E(R)D.$$

Expected future consumption clearly rises, the lower is $E(R)$ and the lower the amount borrowed.

Variance V of future consumption is the expected squared deviation of possible C_2 levels around $E(C_2)$, which is

$$V = V_y + V_R - 2COV_{yR},$$

where COV_{yR} is the covariance of Y_2 and RD. COV_{yR} reflects both the variances of income and debt service costs and their degree of correlation with each other.

Note the contrast between the formula for V here and the formula for variance of asset yield in a two-asset portfolio in chapter 8 (where $V = X_1^2V_1 + X_2^2V_2 + 2X_1X_2COV_{12}$). In chapter 8, the covariance term was added to the sum of variances of individual assets, so extra covariance meant extra risk. Here, the covariance term is subtracted from the sum of variances, so extra covariance means less risk. The reason is illustrated in figure 10–2, which puts together a given pattern of income variation with different patterns of debt cost variation.

Matching debt to income

If future income is certain (so $V_y = 0$), then minimizing uncertainty of future consumption implies only minimizing uncertainty of debt service costs, V_R. Fixed-interest, long-term, regular-instalment loans will be the answer. If future income is variable, there may be benefit in having variable loan payments, as long as the pattern of loan payment variations is correlated with the pattern of income variations. Casey will want large debt payments in years of fat income, low debt payments in years of lean income.

As in our discussion of asset portfolios in chapter 8, a change in variance of either income or debt costs generally causes a change in their covariance as well, since

$$COV_{yR} = \sqrt{V_y}\,\sqrt{V_R}\,RHO_{yR},$$

where RHO_{yR} is the correlation coefficient. We can divide the variability of debt costs into that which is not correlated with future income, called *unsystematic risk*, and that which is correlated with future income, called *systematic risk*. The former is still undesirable, since more of it means higher V_R but without higher COV_{yR} to compensate.[3]

A graphical illustration

Casey now has a three-dimensional choice. His utility function depends on current consumption C_1, expected future consumption $E(C_2)$, and the variance of future consumption V. However, for any level of debt incurred, the level of current consumption C_1 is fixed also; any change in debt outstanding could only come about through a change in current saving and therefore through a change in current consumption, so C_1 must be fixed if debt D is fixed. For any level of debt, Casey is choosing only between the

[3]Lower variance of debt costs means a lower standard deviation of debt costs as well. That lowers COV_{yR} all by itself, but the effect is offset by a higher correlation coefficient RHO_{yR}. A larger proportion of the remaining variability of debt costs is of the type that matches variability of future income, and that is essentially what RHO_{yR} measures.

various pairs of $E(C_2)$ and V that different types of borrowing would produce. Figure 10–3 shows four pairs of $E(C_2)$ and V for four different types of debt — all for the same level of total debt. With the tastes for present and future consumption shown by the indifference curves in figure 10–3, Casey prefers the pair at point A, the pair on the highest indifference curve. A different four pairs of $E(C_2)$ and V could be plotted on figure 10–3 if Casey considered a different level of current saving and therefore borrowed a different amount. For each level of borrowing, the debt type Casey would use depends on its expected service cost, $E(R)$, on Casey's degree of risk aversion, and on the variances and correlation of future income and debt payments.

FIGURE 10–3 Choice of debt type

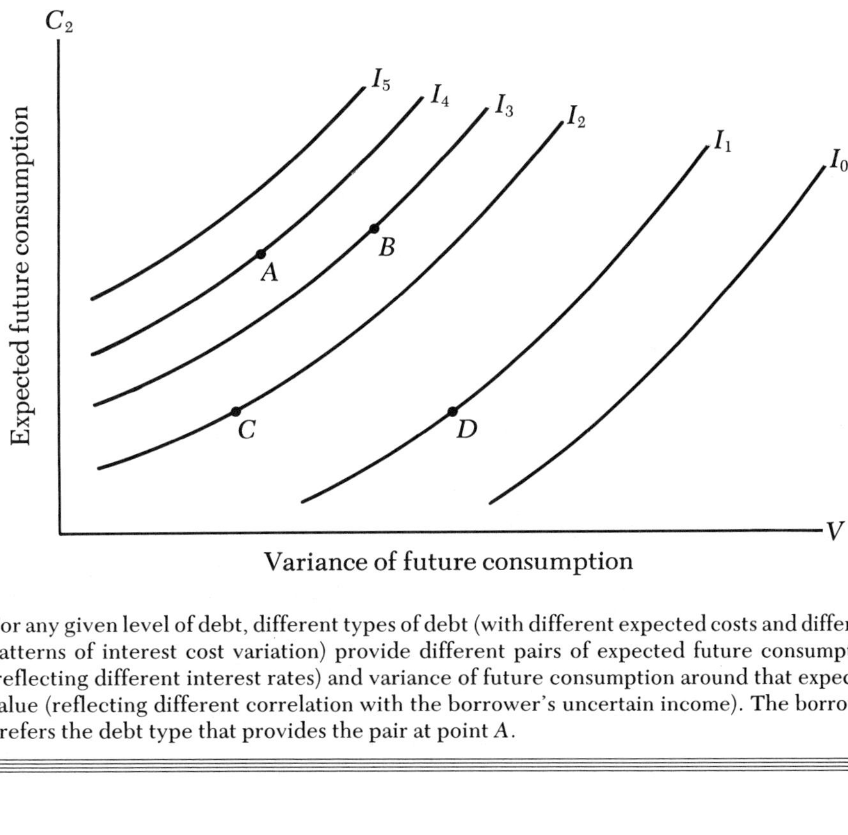

For any given level of debt, different types of debt (with different expected costs and different patterns of interest cost variation) provide different pairs of expected future consumption (reflecting different interest rates) and variance of future consumption around that expected value (reflecting different correlation with the borrower's uncertain income). The borrower prefers the debt type that provides the pair at point A.

Household debt supply

The actual debt level chosen essentially reflects Casey's decision to consume now rather than later. Even if he has a fixed asset to buy (a summer cottage on Eagle Lake), he still has a choice of how much to finance by debt and how much by saving. The more that is borrowed, the more current income is available for current consumption. We discussed in chapter 6 Casey's choice of consumption now versus later. The choice depends on debt cost, marginal rates of time preference, and the time pattern of expected income.

Total supply of each type of debt reflects the level of borrowing in total (both current and past) and the choice of debt type to use for that borrowing. The important variables explaining supply of a particular debt are therefore:

1. expected debt costs for each type of debt,
2. marginal rates of time preference and degrees of risk aversion of borrowers,
3. the time pattern of borrowers' incomes, which determines borrowers' ability to save and replace debt with equity,
4. the variance of future incomes, and
5. relative variances of different types of debt, and their relative correlation with future income.

A debt will be more desirable as its expected cost falls, as the unsystematic part of its variance falls, and as its correlation with the pattern of future income rises.

Now let us see how these factors are reflected in actual household borrowing patterns.

SECTION 4 Household debt patterns

The striking fact about household labor income is its stability in real terms. There is some fluctuation (particularly in construction) with overtime hours, unemployment, and layoffs, but generally labor income is very stable. One of the surprises in macroeconomics has been how unresponsive wage rates are to unemployment levels and how little unemployment in turn responds to slackness in demand.[4] Employers tend to keep their staff on even when demand levels are not enough to keep them busy full time, and most employers do not lower wage increases of employed workers just because the number of unemployed workers in the labor force increases. Even if it would be more desirable socially (so that inflation would slow down more quickly), it does not seem to happen unless the recession is severe.

[4]For instance, this is the core result of Arthur Okun's *Prices and Quantities: A Macroeconomic Analysis* (Washington, D.C.: Brookings, 1981).

Short-term debts

If the variance of future nominal income is small, then a debt will be more attractive (less repulsive) with relatively stable service payments as well. Over short periods such as one year or less, nominal incomes are typically fixed. The most desirable type of debt for such short periods will therefore be one with fixed payments, such as an instalment loan.[5] Casey would therefore be willing to pay more in order to borrow with instalment debt (rather than with a more variable bank demand loan whose interest rate fluctuates with the level of the banks' prime rate). Casey might agree as a borrower to pay what could be called a *security premium* — the opposite of a risk premium — in the interest rate on instalment loans.

Financial intermediaries in the consumer loan market oblige by providing mainly instalment debt for short-period loans. These loans spread the principal repayments over time at increasing rates so that together with declining interest payments (on a shrinking principal) each required payment is the same. Such a service payment pattern leaves an even amount for the rest of the borrower's budget. Table 10–1, which shows the actual

TABLE 10–1 Assets, equity, and debt composition of households, 1977

Total assets	$55 502
Total debts	$12 706
Equity or net wealth	$46 273
Debt : equity ratio	0.27 : 1
Debt composition	
Instalment debt	2.3%
Bank consumer and short-term loans	13.1%
Other consumer and short-term loans	6.9%
Investment loans	5.8%
Mortgage loans	71.9%

Source: Statistics Canada, *Incomes, Assets and Indebtedness of Families in Canada*, Cat. 13–572, 1980.

breakdown of household debts, contains many instalment debts. In addition to the category labelled explicitly *Instalment debt*, almost all of the bank consumer loans and many of the other consumer loans are instalment loans.

[5]If consumption patterns have a pronounced cyclical pattern (for example, heating, vacation, and Christmas spending), then the optimal type of debt might be a variable-payment loan to be repaid when other spending needs are low. To counter that, utility companies usually arrange the billing for heating expenses to be even over the year, regardless of the cyclical nature of fuel consumption.

Long-term debts

Over longer periods, the price level is not stable at all, and neither is nominal income. The variance of nominal income is at least significant, if not high. The most attractive debt for a longer period is therefore one having a large covariance with nominal income. One form of debt with high covariance would be an indexed debt, whose principal and interest payments are indexed to the price level. For such a debt, nominal service payments would fluctuate with the general price level, but real service payments would stay constant. As long as real income were stable and the expected debt cost were not higher, this would be a risk averter's preferred choice.

Demand loans

Borrowers whose real income is not stable will prefer to have debt payments fluctuate in the same pattern as their real income. Strange as it may seem, this can be arranged on a customized, individual basis. Few lenders are willing to receive interest payments only at the borrower's discretion, but all bank demand loans provide for principal repayments as and when the borrower's cash flow permits. Credit-card debts are of this sort as well. Gamblers and university students can be expected to prefer these more flexible debts, as can jockeys and novelists (and textbook authors).

Debt service payments on demand loans also vary because the interest rate payable floats with the prime rate, even on already outstanding loans. Such variations in debt payments do not match variations in the borrowers' incomes, as a rule. They add to the unsystematic part of the variance of debt payments, the part nobody likes. In the 1980s the prime rate has been exceptionally volatile, so the extra perceived unsystematic risk of demand loans is likely to be unusually large. Casey would use demand loans for his financing only if he were offered a substantial carrot, in the form of lower expected debt cost relative to fixed-payment instalment loans. Most demand loans are in fact made to finance the purchase of income-earning assets, whose income pattern is not as stable as that of labor income.

Mortgages

The bulk of household debt in table 10–1 is long-term mortgage debt, incurred for long terms at rates that are renegotiated (adjusted to whatever the market level is) every few years. I explained in chapter 6 that the expected time pattern of payments on a mortgage is perverse — that relatively more is taken from lean years than from fat years. The risk pattern is not so perverse, in that the interest rate payable is at least adjustable relatively frequently in response to changes in nominal yields, which in turn tend to reflect changes in expected inflation. Inflation of nominal incomes because of price and wage inflation is therefore likely to be accompanied also by some inflation of mortgage payments at the next renegotiation date for the mortgage.

The risk problem for a mortgage, dramatized in the editorial cartoon that appeared at the peak of one interest-rate swing in 1981, is that the changes in mortgage payments are likely to be proportionally much larger than the changes in nominal incomes, leaving less real income for spending on current consumption.

Reprinted with permission – the *Winnipeg Free Press*

For instance, if an increase in expected inflation from 0 to 10 percent were fully reflected in higher nominal yields, raising them from 5 percent to 15 percent, the blended principal and interest payment on a $50 000 mortgage would change from $296 per month to $645 per month — a breathtaking 118 percent increase. Even if the change occurred over a three-year period, it would leave much less real income for regular consumption.

The other problem with renegotiable mortgage debts is the same as that with demand loans: the interest rate varies partly independently of, and partly even counter to, the level of borrowers' real incomes. Mortgage interest rates consist of a real interest rate plus an inflation premium, and the real rate is far from constant. Figure 10–4 shows the path of one-year

FIGURE 10–4 Real and nominal interest rates, 1960–83

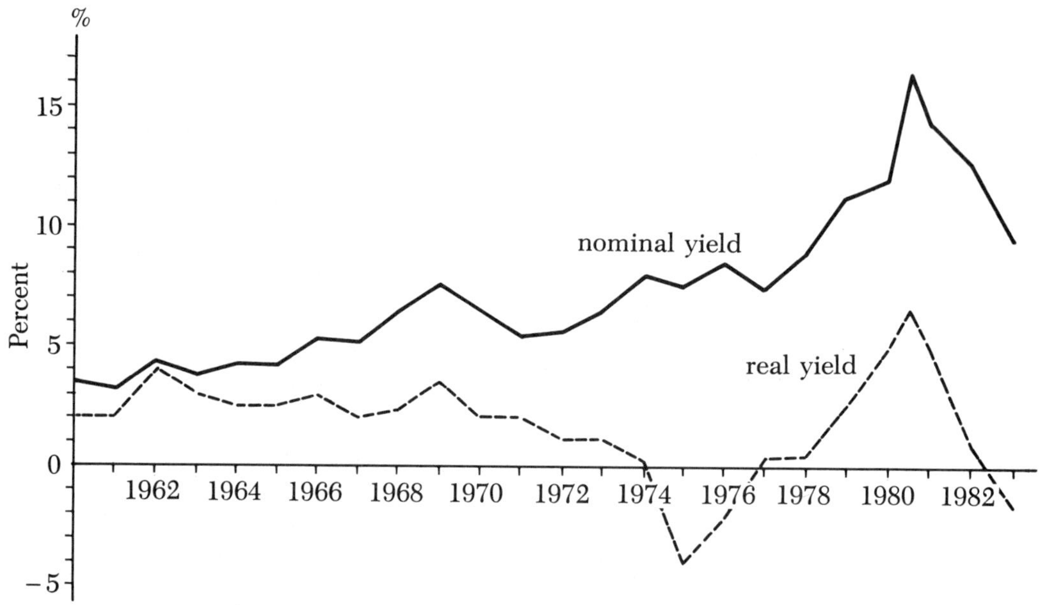

Nominal yield is on one-year federal government bonds. Real yield is nominal yield less expected inflation, divided by one plus expected inflation. Expected inflation is estimated as two-thirds of inflation in the previous year and one-third of inflation in the year before.

government bond yields from 1960 to 1983, which is similar to that of mortgage rates. An estimate of the real yield is shown as well. Note the level of both yields in 1981, when the editorial cartoonist was at work. The real yields on that chart clearly became more volatile in the 1970–82 period. For most households, that variation in real interest rates was just unsystematic risk, not correlated with their nominal incomes and not making their residual consumption more stable. For others, the years of high real interest rates coincided with years of unemployment and low real income; for them, the variation in real interest rates was perverse, worse than merely unsystematic.

Because of the pattern of risks on current mortgages, we can expect some support from households for a mortgage instrument that (a) responds less clumsily to expected changes in price levels and (b) does not respond to changes in real yields in the short run. An example is an indexed mortgage made for a long term at a fixed real interest rate. Such mortgages are not currently available, though the federal budget of June 1982 suggested that they be introduced.[6]

The reprinted article from *The Financial Post* describes many of the factors that mortgage borrowers take into account and the range of responses of borrowers in various situations.

Many mixes in mortgage market

By Carolyn Green

Business is booming for most mortgage-lenders in Canada and chances are the house-hungry consumer will continue buoying up activity for the remainder of 1983.

At the same time, today's purchaser is less willing to take a risk than before. As a result, says Peter Carter, head of retail lending and mortgage services for the Royal Bank of Canada, a "tremendous" number of people are putting in 30%–40% downpayments on a house purchase vs a measly 10% a few years ago.

There's a lot of guesswork, though, when it comes to choosing the life of the mortgage, and that's reflected in the wide mix of terms being taken out. People, it seems, are doing their own forecasts of where mortgage rates (recently about $10\frac{1}{4}$%–11% for a one-year term, $12\frac{1}{2}$%–$12\frac{3}{4}$% for a three-year term and 13%–$13\frac{1}{4}$% for five years) are headed over the next few years and picking the style of mortgage that suits their own family needs, and income prospects.

While the figures vary from institution to institution, lenders say the majority of business (60%–70%), involves new loans for house purchases rather than refinancing of loans from other companies or conversions from short-term vendor takebacks (the mortgages that people who were trying to sell their houses were often forced into providing in order to make the sale when markets were weak and rates were high).

Mortgage terms are all over the place. What suits one borrower may prove too risky for another. In selecting mortgage life, it's a question of the consumer's perception of interest rate stability. The one-year gamblers

---

[6]In June 1982 Finance Minister Allan MacEachen proposed changing the tax laws to allow indexed loans to selected groups including new home-buyers, along with indexed term deposits. The advisory committee appointed to study it rejected the proposal only because the arrangement was restricted to selected groups. The committee approved the idea of "real-terms" borrowing instruments. See *Report of the Ministerial Advisory Committee on Inflation and the Taxation of Personal Investment Income* (Ottawa, 1982). The idea is also discussed in Economic Council of Canada, *Intervention and Efficiency* (Ottawa: Supply and Services, 1982), chap. 4.

(recently accounting for about 20%–30% of mortgages, most lenders say) obviously think rates will decline further whereas the middle-of-the-road types (about 30%–40%) — those choosing a three-year term — want some security but don't want to be locked in forever when rates, in fact, could be significantly lower three years down the road.

Those opting for the five-year mortgage, which started seeping back into the marketplace last autumn, are diehard conservatives, wanting fixed and affordable rates as long as possible.

Lenders suggest today's purchaser is a lot more wary and aware than at any other time. "I'm more and more impressed by how people have become more sophisticated on the matter of interest rates, what's best for them and what's happening in the economy," says Garth Smith, general manager, CIBC (Canadian Imperial Bank of Commerce) Mortgage Corp.

Source: *The Financial Post*, July 9, 1983.

SECTION 5

Debt supply behavior of producing firms and financial institutions

Producing firms and especially financial institutions typically issue debts to finance assets that themselves earn income. Thus future income for repayment of debts also changes with the amount borrowed, and increasing the outstanding debt does not necessarily imply less future consumption at the point where the debt is paid off. If debt is incurred to buy assets yielding more income than the debt service costs, the net effect is greater future consumption rather than less. Changes in debt outstanding therefore imply nothing about the allocation of consumption or dividends over time.

Separation of borrowing decisions from consumption decisions makes a significant difference to analysis of borrowers' risk. In particular, it allows us to separate the problem of spending allocation over time from the problem of balancing expected yields and risks in investment choices. In chapter 7 we explained the logic of allocation of spending over time for a firm called Amco, and uncertainty does not affect that logic at all. This section explains Amco's balancing of yields versus risks in choosing among various debt types and amounts. Amco's current saving is taken as given, so changes in its debt imply equal changes in its total asset holdings.

As either a nonfinancial firm or a financial institution, Amco's concern is for the level and stability of its net profit from investment and borrowing combined. Profit is the product of Amco's equity and the yield on equity. In the short run, equity is fixed (it can be adjusted only by saving), so the only source of uncertainty is the yield on equity. Equity yield has a probability distribution, and a rational firm like Amco would prefer a probability distribution with high expected yield E_e and low variance V_e. What we have to do is explain E_e and V_e for a firm whose equity yield comes from investing with borrowed funds.

Expected yield on equity

First we will explain equity yield r_e. Amco's income statement for each year can be seen as consisting of a revenue stream from operating the firm's assets, less expense streams that are basically the costs of operating the assets and the interest cost of debts. For our purposes, it is convenient to deduct operating costs from gross asset revenues to get net asset revenues, so that profit for shareholders is just net asset revenues less debt costs. Net asset revenues are in turn the product of total assets A and the average net yield on assets r_a. Debt costs are the product of total debt D and the average debt cost per dollar, r_d.

If we let EQ stand for equity outstanding, accounting definitions tell us that Amco's profit must be $r_e EQ$ and that it must also be the total dollar return on assets (net of operating costs) less the total dollar interest cost of servicing debts. That is,

$$r_e EQ = r_a A - r_d D.$$

If we divide both sides by total equity EQ,

$$r_e = r_a\left(\frac{A}{EQ}\right) - r_d\left(\frac{D}{EQ}\right)$$

Because $A = D + EQ$ from the basic balance-sheet identity, we can substitute for A in this equation and rearrange slightly to get:

$$r_e = r_a\left(\frac{D}{EQ} + \frac{EQ}{EQ}\right) - r_d\left(\frac{D}{EQ}\right)$$

$$= r_a + \frac{D}{EQ}(r_a - r_d)$$

Thus, the firm will earn on its equity what it earns on its assets plus a bankers' profit on any assets purchased with borrowed funds.

Now we can explain the expected yield and variance that Amco cares about. Let E_a and E_d be the expected yields on assets and debts. Expected yield on equity (E_e) is

$$E_e = E_a + \frac{D}{EQ}(E_a - E_d).$$

Variance of equity yield

Deviations of actual yield r_e from expected yield E_e can be written as

$$r_e - E_e = \left(\frac{A}{EQ}\right)r_a - \left(\frac{D}{EQ}\right)r_d - \left[\left(\frac{A}{EQ}\right)E_a - \left(\frac{D}{EQ}\right)E_d\right]$$

$$= \left(\frac{A}{EQ}\right)(r_a - E_a) - \left(\frac{D}{EQ}\right)(r_d - E_d).$$

Where V_a and V_d are the variances of r_a and r_d respectively, and COV_{ad} is their covariance, the variance of r_e around E_e is

$$V_e = \left(\frac{A}{EQ}\right)^2 V_a + \left(\frac{D}{EQ}\right)^2 V_d - 2\left(\frac{A}{EQ}\right)\left(\frac{D}{EQ}\right)COV_{ad}.$$

Substituting $(D/EQ + EQ/EQ) = (D/EQ + 1)$ for A/EQ gives

$$V_e = \left(\frac{D}{EQ} + 1\right)^2 V_a + \left(\frac{D}{EQ}\right)^2 V_d - 2\left(\frac{D}{EQ} + 1\right)\left(\frac{D}{EQ}\right)COV_{ad}.$$

Covariance of asset and debt yields can be written as the product of the square roots of two variances (V_a and V_d) and a correlation coefficient (RHO_{ad}):

$$COV_{ad} = \sqrt{V_a}\sqrt{V_d}RHO_{ad}.$$

These formulas are essentially the same as for the two-asset portfolios in chapter 8, and similar to that for Casey's net consumption in section 3 of this chapter.[7] Positive covariance and correlation is a "good" rather than a "bad" for risk averters, whereas extra variance without extra correlation is still a bad.

Mean-variance frontiers with debt financing

Amco's attitude toward debt — how much of it is desired, and of what type — can be extracted from Amco's degree of risk aversion and the properties of E_e and V_e. As Amco's debt rises relative to equity, D/EQ rises in the formulas for both E_e and V_e. Expected equity yield rises with the debt-to-equity ratio at a constant rate equal to the expected spread $(E_a - E_d)$. The variance of equity yield rises at an ever-increasing rate, unless $V_a = V_d = COV_{ad}$ (which is rarely if ever the case).

Higher levels of a particular type of debt therefore produce levels of E_e and V_e that trace out a rising but flattening path on a mean-variance diagram such as figure 10–5. Each type of debt will produce its own curve, because each type of debt will affect variance differently. The rate of

---

[7]If outstanding debt is regarded as simply a negative asset holding, then the formula for variance of equity yield can be transformed to be identical to the formula for variance of yield on a two-asset portfolio. The asset:equity ratio A/EQ $(=D/EQ + 1)$ is the share of total assets in wealth or equity, and the share of debts is $-D/EQ$. Note that the two shares add up to exactly 1.0, as required for portfolio shares. Let the asset share be called X_a and the debt share X_d. Replacing $D/EQ + 1$ and $-D/EQ$ with X_a and X_d in the formula for variance of equity yield gives

$$V_e = X_a^2 V_a + X_d^2 V_d + 2X_a X_d COV_{ad},$$

which is exactly the formula for variance of asset yield in a portfolio with two assets a and d.

FIGURE 10–5 Elements of debt choice

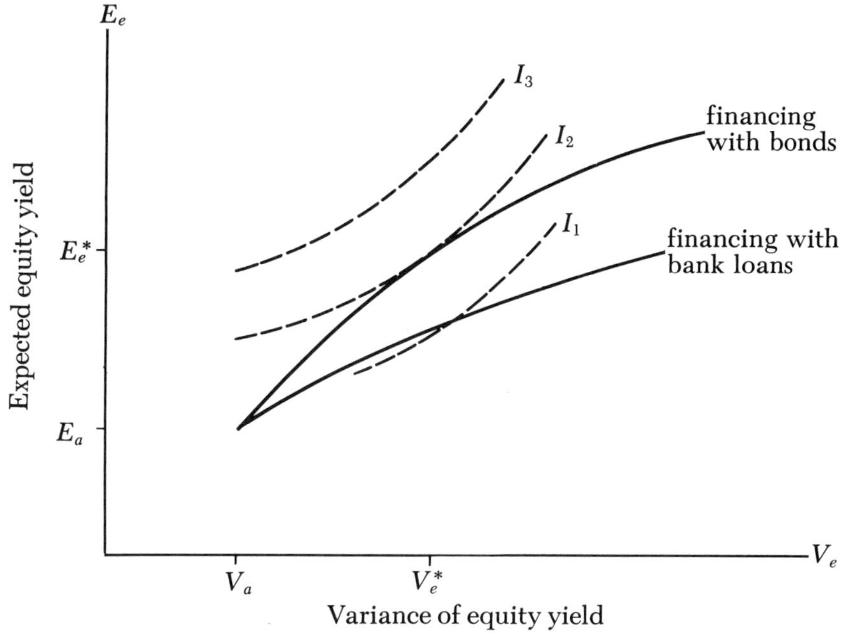

V_a is the variance of the asset yield. Higher debt:equity ratios with a particular type of debt produce combinations of E_e and V_e along a choice set for that debt. All choice sets must start where $E_e = E_a$ and $V_e = V_a$ when there is no debt whatsoever outstanding. Equity yield rises with the debt:equity ratio at a constant rate equal to the expected interest spread between asset yields and debt costs. Variance rises with the debt:equity ratio at an increasing rate.

Different types of debt produce different choice sets, two of which are shown here. If the choice set using bonds is the best (that is, lies farthest to the top left of the graph), then the borrower will want bonds outstanding in an amount to produce E_e° and V_e° at the tangency of the choice set and the highest attainable indifference curve.

change of variance with respect to changes in debt:equity ratio is

$$\frac{dV^e}{d(D/EQ)} = V_a\left[2\left(\frac{D}{EQ}\right) + 2\right] + V_d\left[2\left(\frac{D}{EQ}\right)\right] - COV_{ad}\left[4\left(\frac{D}{EQ}\right) + 2\right].$$

Extra debt adds less extra risk as V_a and V_d are smaller, and as COV_{ad} is larger. Higher levels of V_a and V_d by themselves (without any change in their covariance with each other) correspond to more of what we have previously called unsystematic risk. Higher levels of COV_{ad} with no change in V_a or V_d mean higher degrees of correlation — risk that is more systematic. Unsystematic risk is undesirable; systematic risk is desirable.

Mean-variance frontiers on figure 10–5 will therefore be steeper (have less variance per unit of expected yield) for debts that have lower expected interest costs, lower nonsystematic risk, and higher covariance with asset yields. All such curves must start at the point where $E_e = E_a$ and $V_e = V_a$, since total equity equals total assets when the debt-to-equity ratio is zero; equity yield is the same as average asset yield. Two possible mean-variance frontiers are shown in figure 10–5, for financing a given asset portfolio with either bonds or bank loans.

Optimal debt supply

The best type of debt for Amco will be the type that generates the steepest tradeoff curve in figure 10–5. Once the optimal type of debt is chosen, Amco will choose the amount of debt by trading off expected yield for risk to the point where its marginal rate of substitution of risk for yield ($MRS_{V,E}$) just equals the slope of the tradeoff curve. The point of tangency gives the optimal debt-to-equity ratio.

The amount of debt desired by Amco is derived explicitly in figure 10–6. Panel (b) of this figure is the same as figure 10–5.

Because

$$E_e = E_a + \frac{D}{EQ}(E_a - E_d),$$

$$\frac{D}{EQ} = \frac{E_e - E_a}{E_a - E_d}; \frac{D}{EQ} > 0$$

and

$$D = EQ\left(\frac{E_e - E_a}{E_a - E_d}\right).$$

Equity and expected asset and debt yields are given in the short run, so total debt D is a linear function of expected equity yield E_e. Rearranging the equation for D gives

$$D = E_e\left(\frac{EQ}{E_a - E_d}\right) - \frac{E_a EQ}{E_a - E_d}; D > 0.$$

Total debt rises as E_e rises, at a rate that depends only on the firm's equity base EQ and its expected interest spread $E_a - E_d$. This linear function is shown in panel (a) of figure 10–6, relating E_e on the vertical axis to total debt on the horizontal axis.

Optimal debt:equity ratio

If the optimal debt-to-equity ratio is such as to provide expected equity yield E_e^* in panel (b), then the desired debt level is D^* in panel (a). If Amco has less debt than that already outstanding, Amco will borrow more. If Amco has more than that already outstanding, Amco will pay off some of its debt as soon as possible.

Amco's desired debt D^* depends on all the ingredients of figure 10–6: Amco's equity base, its degree of risk aversion, expected yields on assets

FIGURE 10–6 Choice of desired debt level

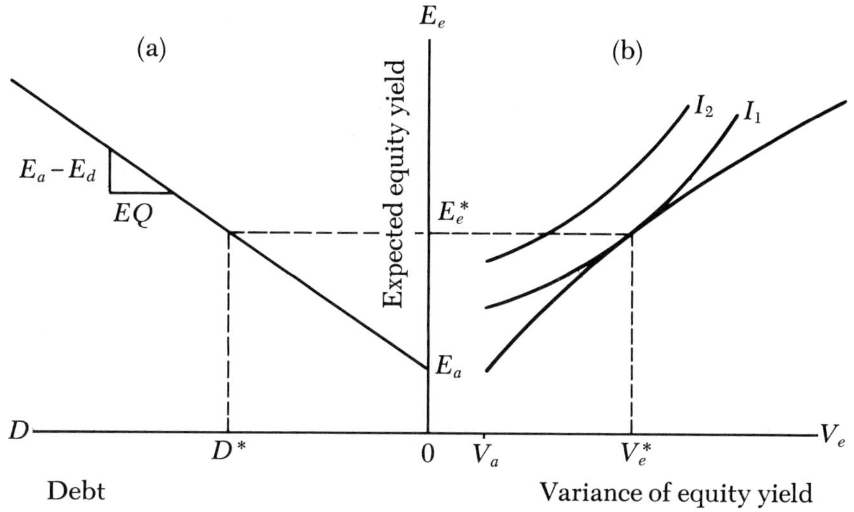

For the best type of debt (see figure 10–5), different debt levels change the debt:equity level and therefore the expected equity yield. Particular debt levels are associated with each level of E_e as shown by the line in panel (a). Every time outstanding debt is increased by the amount of the firm's equity, E_e rises by exactly the expected interest spread ($E_a - E_d$). If the optimal pair of E_e and V_e is E_e° and V_e°, then the optimal debt level for the firm is D° in panel (a).

and debts, the variance of assets, relative variances of different debts, and the relative degrees of correlation of debt yields with those on the asset portfolio. In the short run, when wealth is fixed, the supply of a particular type of debt such as bonds, S_b, is determined by the choice of debt-to-equity ratio and can be written algebraically as

$$S_b = \frac{D}{EQ}\,(MRS_{V,E}\;,\;\{E_i\}\;,\;\{V_i\}\;,\;\{COV_{ij}\})\;EQ,$$

where $MRS_{V,E}$ is the degree of risk aversion, $\{E_i\}$ and $\{V_i\}$ are the set of expected yields and variances on the different debts available and on the asset to be financed, and $\{COV_{ij}\}$ is the set of covariances of different debts with the assets.

In the longer run where equity is not fixed, that too must be explained. In chapter 7 equity was explained by the firm's marginal rate of time preference ($MRTP$), by expected yields on assets and debts, and by the time pattern of expected profits $\{Y\}$ from assets already held. In the longer run there are therefore two new variables $MRTP$ and $\{Y\}$ to be added to our algebraic list of variables explaining supply of bonds:

$$S_b = S_b\,(MRS_{V,E},\, MRTP,\, \{E_i\},\, \{V_i\},\, \{COV_{ij}\},\, \{Y\}).$$

Implications for debt supply

Our explanation of supply of different debts has the following implications:

1. The optimal type of debt, determined from the list of factors above, is optimal only for the specific type of asset to be financed. Yields of different assets vary in different patterns, so in general each asset yield will be best matched by a different type of debt. This is nothing more than recognition that what is appropriate to finance a pipeline is not so good for financing finished-goods inventory. Changes in the economy's pattern of real asset purchases therefore imply changes in relative supplies of different types of debt.
2. Raising the debt:equity ratio by issuing more of a debt will raise not only V_e but also its rate of increase. This second derivative of equity risk is $2(V_a + V_d) - 4COV_{ad}$, which is positive as long as $RHO_{ad} < 1.0$.[8] The mean-variance frontier gets flatter as more debt is issued. Further debt issues are thereby made less desirable. The response of borrowers is not to switch to other types of debt, however, in the way that lenders diversify into other types of assets. Instead, borrowers just give up on further asset purchases so they will not need more debt finance of any kind. The extra risk associated with the extra debt is what sets an upper limit on total asset purchases when high leverage is possible. For trust companies and foreign bank subsidiaries, there are even legal limits on the leverage ratio, which we will discuss further in chapters 11, 12, and 16.
3. A type of debt whose yield has lower correlation with asset yields will be avoided by borrowers unless and until it offers sufficiently lower expected yield to compensate. Debts with higher correlation will command higher expected yields, since they imply less residual risk to the owners of equity.
4. A type of debt whose yield has high variance without high correlation (that is, high unsystematic risk) will be avoided by borrowers unless it offers sufficiently lower expected yield to compensate.

SECTION 6

Actual debt strategies of producing firms and financial institutions

We have already looked in broad terms at the pattern of borrowing by nonfinancial corporations and financial institutions in chapter 7. We will look at the pattern of assets and debts of financial institutions in more detail

[8] If $RHO_{ad} = 1$, and $V_a = V_d$, then $COV_{ad} = V_a$, and the second derivative is $2(V_a + V_a) - 4V_aa = 0$. In this extreme case the slope of the frontier itself is vertical, so $V_e = V_a$ regardless of the level of debt. The optimal debt is infinite as long as $E_a > E_d$. This seems like a ridiculous case, but the chartered banks have come close to it. Their debt is not infinite, but it is 30 times their equity. Chapter 11 elaborates on the banks' situation.

in chapters 11 through 13. Table 10–2 provides the only extra information not given elsewhere — the debt:equity ratios of various groups of borrowers. We saw in table 10–1 that household borrowing is small relative to equity. Nonfinancial firms average a level of debt that is greater than their equity, but not by much even in 1981, a year of great financial strain and unprecedented debt levels.[9] Financial institutions have debts much larger than equity, from 7.0 times as great for finance companies to 30 times as great for banks. It is part of the purpose of chapters 11 through 13 to explain what difference such enormous leverage makes to management of financial institutions. For now, I will merely sketch some of the financing strategies used by nonhousehold borrowers, which illustrate the preceding theory in action.

TABLE 10–2 Debt : equity ratios, 1981

Households[a]	0.27 : 1
Large nonfinancial firms	1.42 : 1
Banks	30 : 1
Trust companies	22 : 1
Mortgage loan companies	12 : 1
Finance companies	6 : 1
Life insurance companies (stock companies only)	12 : 1

[a] 1977 data.

Sources: Bank of Canada Review; Statistics Canada, *Financial Institutions, Corporation Financial Statistics*, and *Incomes, Assets and Indebtedness of Families in Canada*.

Matching

There are many ways of arranging financing to reduce the variance of possible equity yields. These arrangements all involve choosing debts whose yields match the volatility of yields on the assets to be financed. For instance, entrepreneurs setting up mining exploration companies have highly uncertain revenue streams; they finance almost all of their exploration with stock issues, whose yields are highly correlated with the company's revenue flows. Power companies with hydroelectric generating stations have assured, stable, long-term demand, so they can easily finance most of their total assets with fixed-rate, long-term bonds. A forestry company like MacMillan Bloedel, which sells much of its output in the United States for U.S.-dollar revenue, can also reduce its equity risk by financing partly with debt denominated in U.S. dollars: then if revenues fall

[9]See discussion by H.-P. Rousseau, "The Dome Syndrome: The Debt Overhanging Canadian Government and Business," *Canadian Public Policy*, March 1983, 37–52.

because of depreciation of the U.S. dollar in which those revenues are earned, the firm's U.S.-dollar interest bill also shrinks, and its profits are less squeezed than they would otherwise be.

All firms and intermediaries can reduce equity risk by matching the terms to maturity of their assets and debts. Consider first the financing of a single asset with an expected life of ten years. Assume that its revenue flow can be forecast over ten years with some degree of accuracy. If Amco finances the asset partly by issue of a five-year term loan note to a financial institution, the firm is left uncertain about what rate it will have to pay for financing after the first five years have passed. Variance of possible debt yields V_d is higher with mismatched borrowing than it need be, and without any gain in covariance to show for it. By issuing a ten-year debt instead, the firm can eliminate the extra uncertainty of its future interest costs over the second five-year period.

Firms producing a diversified collection of consumer goods could even match their debts to their revenue stream by issuing bonds whose principal value was tied to the Consumer Price Index level. Asset yields and debt costs would not be highly correlated, but more so than with fixed nominal debt charges.

Matched Floating

Banks have found an even more convenient way of arranging high covariance of asset and debt yields. They have managed to tie debt costs to asset yields even when the two have different terms to maturity: costs and yields float together.

Banks arrange very high covariance of asset yields and debt costs by (a) having most of their deposit interest costs fluctuate in close sympathy with money-market yields (for example, with the yield on ninety-day Treasury Bills), (b) tying all their business loan rates (their asset yields) to a single benchmark yield, the bank prime rate, so that yields on all business loans (new and outstanding) adjust immediately to changes in the prime rate, and (c) adjusting their prime rate more or less in line with the Bank of Canada's Bank Rate, which in turn is tied explicitly to the ninety-day Treasury Bill rate.

The connection of average demand loan rates to average term deposit rates is not cast in bronze. There is some slippage in that all loan rates move immediately while term deposit rates change only as fast as term deposits mature and are replaced. Nevertheless, banks managed over the years 1975–80, for instance, to keep the correlation of their asset and debt yields at 0.997, within 0.3 percent of the maximum possible. As a result, the variance of banks' equity yield has been comparable to or better than that of other intermediaries, despite much greater leverage. Table 10–3 shows the basic results, to be discussed further in chapter 11. Had the banks' correlation coefficient been only 0.99, instead of 0.997, their equity risk would have been three times as large.

TABLE 10–3 Bank equity yield and variance, 1976–80 (percent)

	Average yield	Variance
Assets	10.8	4.0
Debts	8.0	5.2
Equity	20.3	25.8

Correlation of asset and debt yields: 0.997
Average debt : equity ratio: 24 : 1

Note: These figures represent an average for the years 1976–80, for an average Canadian bank. Average yield is not quite the same as expected yield. Variance is calculated around the average yield rather than the expected yield. Asset yield is gross, before deducting any operating costs.

Sources: Financial Post Record Service, chartered-bank annual reports, and *The Canada Gazette*.

Bridge financing

Occasionally firms and intermediaries will mismatch maturities of assets and debts, to save on expected interest cost. One occasion is when long-term rates are expected to fall in the near future. In that situation, corporate treasurers will often arrange temporary short-term *bridge* financing for long-term assets, expecting to arrange the proper long-term financing more cheaply six months to a year later. In the opposite situation, where long-term rates are expected to rise in the near future, some firms will do their long-term borrowing early. Some will even finance short-term assets with longer-term debt.

SECTION 7 Summary

Supply of financial assets is the same thing as issue and maintenance of outstanding debts. Some outstanding debts are fixed in existence and cannot be redeemed early, but there is usually significant room to decrease supply over medium-run periods such as a year or two.

Debt costs are uncertain because of inflation risk, income risk, market risk, and liquidity or bankers' risk (the risk that a loan will no longer be available, either because it has been called or because it cannot be renewed). The uncertainty borrowers care about is volatility of debt costs relative to the income out of which debt service payments are to be made; the two should vary together. Consumer and house mortgage borrowers therefore prefer debts to have payments patterns that match labor income flows. Industrial firms and financial intermediaries prefer debts whose costs fluctuate together with yields on the assets those debts help finance.

Households typically have relatively stable nominal incomes in the short run and relatively stable real incomes in the long run. Household borrowers therefore prefer stable debt payments in nominal terms in the short run, and stable payments in real terms in the long run. Fixed-instalment loans are common and popular for short-term debt, but the main type of mortgage loan used now is not particularly suitable for long-term debt; the mortgage payments adjust excessively to changes in expected inflation, as these expectations are reflected in changes in nominal interest rates. More volatile real yields in the 1970–82 period have also made real mortgage payments too variable.

Borrowers financing income-earning assets prefer debts with low expected yields and a pattern of yield changes that matches that of asset yields; this leaves a larger spread and less residual risk for equity shareholders. Positive covariance or correlation of debt yields with asset yields is therefore a virtue, even though correlation of asset yields with one another is a vice. Issue of extra debt increases both expected equity yield and variance. Since variance increases at an increasing rate, risk-averse borrowers will never borrow without limit. Total supply of each type of debt then depends on asset yields available, relative expected yields on debts, and relative variances and covariances. Because covariances with possible asset yields will change abruptly as the type of desired asset changes, so will the relative attractiveness of various debt instruments.

The main borrowing strategies that reflect our theory of debt supply behavior are matching of asset and debt maturities, developed by banks into matched floating, and bridge financing to take advantage of expected yield changes.

Questions for discussion

1. Why do most bonds have sinking fund or purchase fund provisions?
2. Why is it that supply of debts can usually adjust less quickly than demand to desired levels?
3. Would you prefer to borrow with an instalment loan or a demand loan? Why?
4. How would an indexed mortgage reduce borrowers' risk?
5. What must the debt cost be per dollar for a bank to generate an equity yield of 15 percent, if its asset yield is 10 percent and its leverage ratio is 25? if its leverage ratio is only 10?
6. What must the asset yield be for an industrial firm to generate an equity yield of 15 percent, if its debt cost is 12 percent and its leverage ratio is 1.5?
7. What does the mean-variance frontier look like for issues of a type of debt that is perfectly correlated with asset yields and has the same variance?

8. Why must all mean-variance frontiers, for all kinds of debt, start at the same level of equity yield and risk when leverage is zero?
9. What is the optimal leverage ratio for a risk seeker?
10. What, if any, is the relationship between matching maturities of debts and assets, and covariance of asset and debt yields?

References

Donner, Arthur W. *Financing the Future: Canada's Capital Markets in the Eighties*. Toronto: Canadian Institute for Economic Policy, 1982.

Economic Council of Canada. *Intervention and Efficiency*. Ottawa: Supply and Services, 1982, chap. 4.

Lusztig, Peter, and Bernhard Schwab. *Managerial Finance in a Canadian Setting*. 3d ed. Toronto: Butterworths, 1983, parts 3 and 4.

Modigliani, Franco, and Merton H. Miller. "The Cost of Capital, Corporation Finance, and the Theory of Investment." *American Economic Review*. June 1958, 261–77.

———. "Corporate Income Taxes and the Cost of Capital: A Correction." *American Economic Review*. June 1963, 433–42.

Report of the Ministerial Advisory Committee on Inflation and the Taxation of Personal Investment Income. Ottawa, 1982.

Rousseau, H.-P. "The Dome Syndrome: The Debt Overhanging Canadian Government and Business." *Canadian Public Policy*. March 1983, 37–52.

Smith, Adam. *Paper Money*. New York: Dell Publishing, 1981, chap. 5.

Van Horne, James C., Cecil R. Dipchand, and J. Robert Hanrahan. *Financial Management and Policy*. 4th ed. Scarborough, Ont.: Prentice-Hall of Canada, 1977, parts 5 and 6.

Appendix

The Modigliani-Miller propositions

No discussion of corporate financing is complete without reference to the two propositions put forward by Modigliani and Miller in 1958 and 1963. Suppose a firm has a certain total of assets to finance. Assume for simplicity that there are only two types of borrowing instruments — bonds and common stock. What is the (expected) cheapest mix of bond and stock financing for those assets? Which mix will have the lowest average (expected) cost of capital? The average cost of capital is a weighted average of the expected interest cost per dollar of bond debt and the expected equity yield required by new shareholders; the weights are the relative shares of bonds and common stock in the total amount to be financed. Modigliani and Miller first demonstrated that there is no optimal mix of bonds and equity — that all mixes will have the same average cost of capital.

They reasoned that, whatever the mix of bonds and stock, if total assets are the same for all debt:equity mixes, then so is the flow of revenue from those assets (net of operating costs). They assumed that an investor could secure the same flow of net revenue by either of two routes: directly, by buying up the assets themselves; or indirectly, by buying up all of the bonds and stocks issued to finance those assets. If the two routes produce the same flow of net revenue, then arbitrage in financial markets will force the two purchases to have the same total price. The argument holds for any mix of bonds and common stock used to finance the assets; all mixes must have the same total value as the assets they finance. Therefore all mixes must have the same total value. If all mixes have the same total value and offer the same expected revenue flow in total, then the average revenue flow per dollar must be identical. The average revenue flow per dollar is the average cost of capital, so the average cost of capital must be identical.

Normally, because of the extra guarantees provided to bondholders, the expected cost per dollar of debt for bonds is less than the cost per dollar for funds raised through issue of common or preferred stock. Other things being equal, this difference would lead the expected cost of capital to fall as bonds were substituted for stock, at least over some range of debt levels. The Modigliani-Miller theorem implies that other things are not equal, and in a very specific way. The higher debt:equity ratio generated by the bond issue drives up equity risk, as we have seen in chapter 10; this must have the effect of driving up the required yield on the stock by just enough to offset any saving from greater reliance on lower-yield bonds.

Modigliani and Miller's first version of this theorem was derived for a world without any difference in tax rates for stocks and bonds. Where there are tax differentials, the mix of bonds and equity will make a difference to total after-tax net revenue, simply because of the different tax treatment of bond interest and stock dividends: bond interest shelters corporate revenue from corporation income tax, while stock dividends do not. The result is a difference in the after-tax flow of net revenue to lenders from the same bundle of assets for different mixes of bond and stock financing. Other chinks in Modigliani and Miller's first result are caused by the risk of bankruptcy, by barriers to arbitrage such as transactions costs, and by extra risk aversion on the part of managers whose entire salaries are tied to the stability as well as the expected level of profits. Modigliani and Miller's basic result stands as a reminder nonetheless that what can be paid out in total to bondholders and stockholders is limited to what the assets earn: the total value that can be put on the bonds and stocks together is therefore limited to the present value of the asset earnings of the firm or intermediary.

References

Modigliani, Franco, and Merton H. Miller. "The Cost of Capital, Corporation Finance, and the Theory of Investment." *American Economic Review*. June 1958, 261–77.

——. "Corporate Income Taxes and the Cost of Capital: A Correction." *American Economic Review*. June 1963, 433–42.

PART THREE

Financial Intermediation

CHAPTER 11

Chartered Banking

Financial intermediaries were discussed in chapter 7 (where we considered the borrowing of Amco, which could be a financial institution), in chapter 8 (where we considered the asset choices of all assetholders, including banks), and in chapter 10 (where we considered the asset supply decisions of both financial and nonfinancial firms under risk). In the next three chapters we will apply the principles outlined in those chapters, in a detailed treatment of the major financial institutions that dominate the Canadian financial system.

We have two concerns in this chapter, one micro and one macro. First, what sort of risk problem do these financial institutions face, and how does it constrain their choice of assets to buy and debts to issue? Financial institutions collectively absorb two-thirds of the flow of primary lending. Limits on their choice of investment therefore affect real investment and the economy's capital stock; limits on the kind of debts they can issue affect savers' ability to realize long-term financial plans.

The second, macro concern is how these financial institutions respond when the financial system is disturbed from equilibrium — for instance, by a change in money-market interest rates. Do financial institutions respond sensitively, so the change in money-market rates is mirrored by changes in all other rates in the financial system, thereby affecting the full range of savings and investment decisions? Or are only some rates affected? These questions are important when we analyse the use of monetary policy to stabilize the economy. Keep them in mind as we take a detailed look at the major financial institutions in Canada.

There is not space in this text to discuss a third concern, how Canada's banking system came to look as it does now. A few of the major events were mentioned at the end of chapter 4, but that may merely have whetted your appetite. Readers are referred to other works for more about banking history — in particular, E.P. Neufeld's *The Financial System of Canada.*

Your task in this chapter is to learn:

1. the source of positive interest spreads in financial institutions generally,
2. the legal background of banking in Canada,
3. the types of assets banks handle,
4. the types of liability with which those assets are financed, and the joint results of asset and liability management on shareholders' risk and yield, and
5. the place of the banks in the financial system, and their response to a change in monetary policy.

SECTION 1 Financial Intermediation: the source of positive spreads

Most financial intermediaries exist to provide large and stable equity yields for their owners. You saw in chapter 10 that equity yields depend upon the spread between debt costs and asset yields, as well as upon the debt:equity ratio, but you have not learned why the spread should be positive. Why is it that financial institutions manage, reliably, to borrow at lower rates than they lend?

There are several answers, some or all of which may hold at once for a particular intermediary. Positive spreads can come from differences in risk between assets and debts, from differences in maturity of assets and debts, from customizing in retail financial markets, and from market power and economies of scale.

Risk differences

Debts issued by many financial institutions have much less default risk, less income risk, and less market risk than the debts they buy. Compare, for instance, a fixed-yield bank term deposit with a floating-rate demand loan

Reprinted with permission: Tribune Company Syndicate, Inc.

note held by a bank. The term deposit offers a certain nominal yield to maturity, is virtually free of default risk, and is redeemable at any time at par plus a known amount of accrued interest. The term deposit is subject only to inflation risk. The demand loan is subject to the vagaries of the prime rate to which its yield is tied, is subject to default risk, is repayable only when borrowers wish, and is really not marketable at all. The demand loan note as an asset is subject to generous amounts of all four kinds of risk identified at the start of chapter 8.

If assetholders perceive term deposits as so much less risky than loans to business firms, they will be willing to hold term deposits at an expected yield much lower than they would insist upon for holding a demand loan note. With low interest costs on its term deposits, the bank may have a positive spread even after incurring operating costs to service its deposits and monitor and collect its loans.

The logic of portfolio theory suggests that rational individuals would not be dismayed by the volatility of yields on loans to business, as long as they were not closely correlated with other yields. To keep portfolio risk low, individuals would merely have to diversify widely. In other words, a demand loan note would involve very little extra risk exposure when added to a well-diversified portfolio. However, demand loan notes don't come in tiny bites, so wide diversification is not possible in household or firm portfolios, and loan notes with high variances therefore add a lot to portfolio risks, regardless of how their yields are correlated with other yields.

For financial institutions, which pool the funds of many depositors, there is room to diversify broadly despite the size of individual loans. As we saw in the example of bank loan portfolios at the end of chapter 8, the extra risk that one more demand loan note adds to a broadly diversified portfolio is close to zero (unless all borrowers are affected by the same factors, such as world recession). Therefore the revenue stream from banks' asset portfolios is fairly stable. Banks' revenue stream is the source of debt payments and profits, so debt payments can be kept stable as well. The conversion of risky assets to less-risky debts is known as the *transmutation of assets*. The process is accounted for almost entirely by pooling of independent risks in large portfolios; that is, by diversification.

Transmutation of assets

Risk absorption by shareholders

In total, the pattern of yield to debt and equity owners combined must mirror the pattern of yield on assets, since that is the only source of revenue to provide debt and equity yields. The Modigliani-Miller theorem, presented in the appendix to chapter 10, is built on this fundamental fact. The risk of debts can be less, however, if owners of equity are willing to absorb more risk themselves. Thus banks may guarantee redemption of term deposits, even though the values of their assets are not guaranteed. If asset values fall, bank shareholders — and not bank depositors — absorb the loss. Absorbing this risk will be to the benefit of banks' shareholders only if they are less risk-averse than depositors. Only in that case will the reduction in deposit yields (which depositors accept in exchange for lower risk or greater liquidity of deposits) more than compensate bank shareholders for the extra risk they bear.

Borrowing short to lend long

In general, long-term assets have higher expected yields than shorter-term assets. We will see the reasons for this in chapter 14, but essentially it is because many investors find long-term debts riskier. The greater price volatility (market risk) of long- than of short-term debts is sufficient excuse by itself. A financial institution can achieve a positive spread, therefore, if it buys long-term assets with funds raised by issuing an otherwise identical short-term debt. Some financial institutions do this in part, though differences in maturity of assets and debts are often small. Finance companies, for instance, finance one- to three-year instalment loans with issues of three- to six-month finance paper. In recent years shorter-term rates have often been higher than longer-term rates, however, so this intermediation strategy can lead to negative spreads instead.

Customizing for convenience and risk reduction

The interest rate paid on debts reflects not only their relative marginal risk to assetholders but also their relative convenience. Relative convenience can be thought of as the time and effort saved by holding them rather than the nearest substitute. For example, money is held even at zero interest because of the extra convenience of its medium-of-exchange services relative to those of notice deposits. Convenience is provided in many ways, but the most important is customizing to suit the creditor's requirements. Demand deposits, notice deposits, and redeemable term deposits are prime examples. In all of them creditors can redeem their assets at whatever time suits them. Creditors compensate the issuing institution for this convenience by accepting a lower interest rate.

The larger banks have an extra advantage: large branch networks located close to creditors. Big banks are able to rely much more heavily than small banks on demand and notice deposits, which are cheaper than term deposits.

As an example from the other side of the balance sheet, demand loans from banks can be repaid by debtors at whatever time suits their convenience. Debtors compensate banks by accepting a slightly higher loan rate than they otherwise would. (Demand loans can also be called by the bank at its convenience, but both bank and customer know that this provision will be used only if the borrower is already headed for bankruptcy.)

A similar sort of customizing explains demand for insurance policies. Here the benefit to policyholders is enormous risk reduction rather than mere convenience. Because each insurance policy pays off only when the individual policyholder suffers a loss on other assets (or life or health), an insurance policy greatly reduces overall portfolio risk (as we saw in chapter 8). Policyholders respond by accepting very low or even negative expected yields on their investment in insurance policies. The marginal risk is negative only because the payoff of each insurance policy is customized to fit the circumstances of each individual policyholder.

Such customizing of deposits and insurance is worthwhile only if the extra interest margin provided compensates for the extra risk borne. The extra risk is mainly liquidity risk — the risk that creditors will all want their money back at once. With pooling of many different creditors, however, the probability of large net withdrawals or of a rash of insurance drains all at once is very small (as long as creditors' needs or losses are not positively correlated, as in a regionwide disaster such as drought or flooding of a major river). Customizing is therefore fairly cheap as long as risks can be pooled.

Market power: economies of scale and scope

In some cases extra size of operation allows financial institutions to reap economies of scale denied to small-scale investors, or allows them to develop market power that can be used to lower debt costs or push up asset yields. Where loan or debt processing costs are fixed, larger-scale loans or debts will have lower percentage processing costs; a demand loan for \$100 million would therefore be much more profitable than 1000 loans for \$100 000. If the risk associated with large demand loans is to be kept to an acceptable level, the individual loans must comprise only a small part of a diversified portfolio. It follows that only large financial institutions, with billions of dollars of total assets, can afford to take advantage of the lower administrative costs of very large loans.

Size may also benefit financial intermediaries by augmenting their ability to get special terms from borrowers. Insurance companies large enough to buy up whole issues of new bonds in *private placements* are able to get better terms than if they bought the bonds in the open market.

The wider the range of assets and liabilities in which a firm deals, and the wider the range of services it offers, the greater the convenience for its customers. The intermediary may also be able to use the extra types of business to spread its overhead costs more widely. The extra types of business will contribute to wider profit margins, and the extra diversification will help to reduce volatility of profits.

Different financial institutions make varying use of these different sources of positive spread, as we will see. We turn now to banks in particular.

SECTION 2

The legal structure of banking in Canada

Chartered banks

In Canada, the term *bank* is almost always used to refer to a *chartered bank* — an institution chartered under the federal Bank Act.[1] There are now twelve in Schedule A (widely held and domestically owned) and fifty-nine in Schedule B (closely held banks, almost all foreign-owned). Banking is entirely under federal jurisdiction by an explicit provision of the Constitution, so there are no provincially chartered banks.

Letters patent

Formal entry into banking has been much easier since the latest revision of the Bank Act (in 1980), which allows charter by *letters patent* (a legal form not requiring a special Act of Parliament for each bank). Table 11–1 shows how the numbers have mushroomed since 1967 and especially since 1980. Almost all the new banks are subsidiaries of foreign banks, but Morguard Bank was set up in 1983 to allow conversion of Morguard Trust Company to a bank, and Western and Pacific Bank is a brand-new, Canadian-owned bank.

TABLE 11–1 Banks in Canada, 1792–1982

	1792–1866	1867–1929	1930–1967	1968–1980	1981–1982
Banks chartered	80	76	3	5	59
charters not used	22	38	1	0	0
commenced business	58	38	2	5	59
merged with other banks	2	34	4	3	0
failed or wound up	21	28	0	0	0
Active at end of period	35	11	9	11	70

Sources: For data to 1978, S. Sarpkaya, *Canadian Banker & ICB Review*, October and December 1978, where all the banks are given by name; since 1978, *The Canada Gazette*.

Informal entry into banking is even easier, as the experience of the 1970s shows. By 1975, over one hundred foreign bank agencies had set up shop in Canada without any special licence, as ordinary companies under

[1]There are three other banks, each chartered under its own Act of Parliament, that we do not consider in this section: the Bank of Canada, the Federal Business Development Bank, and the Montreal City and District Savings Bank. Other than these, no financial institution is allowed to call itself a bank without a charter under the Bank Act. Unfortunately, financial jargon in Canada still includes loose terms such as *investment bankers, merchant banks*, and, worst of all, *country banks* to generate confusion about the definition of a bank.

provincial company legislation. They borrowed funds in the commercial-paper market and made business loans formerly reserved to Canadian domestic banks. Except for not issuing deposits, not using the word *bank* in their names, and not being subject to all the restrictions and reporting requirements of the Bank Act, these firms were banks. Their competition referred to them as "suitcase banks" (because some of them were alleged to be operated out of suitcases in hotel rooms).

The Bank Act contains significant limits on chartered banks' activities. Banks cannot engage in any trust business, sell insurance, manage mutual funds, underwrite corporate securities, or even provide computer services that are not "banking-related." For all those activities there are powerful groups of domestic producers who greatly fear the banks' competition and have so far managed to keep these restrictions in the Bank Act. As this is written, the investment dealers have just lost a hard fight before the Ontario Securities Commission to keep the Toronto Dominion Bank from developing its discount brokerage arm, Green Line Investment Services.

Schedule B banks are limited in two ways. Individually, their total assets may not exceed twenty times their authorized capital. Collectively, their authorized capital is limited by the Minister of Finance such that their total assets do not exceed 8 percent of the domestic assets of the banking system.[2]

Bank holdings of shares in other companies are limited, except in subsidiaries formed to do factoring, leasing, mortgage lending, and venture-capital lending business. There is no limit on foreign subsidiaries of Canadian banks, however, which carry out a full range of banking and trust services in Europe and other international banking centres.

Banks are subject to inspection by the Office of the Inspector General of Banks, a branch of the federal Department of Finance, and they are subject to some moral suasion. In an example of moral suasion, banks agreed to a limit on individual loans of 50 percent of bank equity, at the "suggestion" of the Inspector General in the summer of 1982. Banks are subject to cash reserve and secondary reserve requirements, which we will discuss in the next section.

Banks used to be subject to many more restrictions on the type of assets they could hold. The restrictions were designed to keep them mainly in the business of commercial loans and to keep them out of term loans, personal loans, and mortgages. The theory was that banks should lend only on security of goods in process or in transport, whose sale would automatically provide funds for loan repayment. There were many reasons for these restrictions, but the most relevant now is the short-term nature of deposits. All such restrictions have been removed, but still the core of chartered-bank activity is commercial lending.

[2]As of late 1983, this ceiling seems likely to be raised. The foreign banks are close to the limit already, after only two years of existence as chartered banks.

SECTION 3

Asset management

Table 11–2 gives a breakdown of total chartered-bank assets by currency and by type of asset. A 1960 breakdown is included for comparison. The major changes since 1960 are an increased share of foreign-curency business, and much lower shares of reserves and liquid assets. A few of the asset categories require a brief explanation.

TABLE 11–2 Chartered-bank assets, 1982 and 1960

	September 1982		December 1960
	Billions of dollars	Percent	Percent
Canadian-dollar assets			
Cash reserve assets	6.1	1.7	5.9
Secondary reserve assets	8.8	2.4	6.7
Other liquid assets			
government of Canada bonds	1.3	0.4	12.3
special call loans	1.2	0.3	0.0
other call and short loans	0.2	0.0	0.7
Total liquid assets	17.7	4.8	25.6
Loans			
general	123.4	33.6	28.6[a]
other	2.2	0.6	9.2
Mortgage loans			
residential	28.7	7.8	5.7
nonresidential	2.7	0.7	0.0
Leasing receivables	2.5	0.7	0.0
Bonds (excluding government of Canada)	10.1	2.7	5.9
Other assets	11.2	3.0	7.1
TOTAL CANADIAN-DOLLAR ASSETS	198.4	53.9	82.4
Customers' liability under acceptances	13.4	3.6	1.5[b]
Foreign-currency assets			
Call and other loans	103.4	28.1	9.6
Bonds	6.8	1.8	3.3
Deposits with other banks	37.9	10.3	3.1
Other foreign-currency assets	8.0	2.2	0.1
TOTAL FOREIGN-CURRENCY ASSETS	156.0	42.4	16.1
TOTAL ASSETS	367.8	100.0	100.0

[a]Loan totals for 1960 have already been adjusted downward by the amount of accumulated appropriations for losses, an item that now appears separately with shareholders' equity.
[b]In 1960 this item refers to customers' liability under letters of credit and guarantees as well as under acceptances.

Sources: Bank of Canada Review; Bank of Canada, *Statistical Summary*.

Definitions of asset categories

Cash reserve assets
Vault cash

Cash reserve assets consist of coin and Bank of Canada notes (known collectively as *vault cash*) and deposits in the Bank of Canada. Cash reserve assets must be equal to at least 10 percent of demand deposits, plus either 2 or 3 percent of notice deposits and term deposits with an original term to maturity of one year or less (known as *reservable* term deposits), and 3 percent of foreign-currency deposits of Canadian residents held with banks in Canada.[3] The 2 percent rate on notice and term deposits applies to the first $500 million of notice and reservable term deposits, and the 3 percent rate to all amounts above $500 million.

Secondary reserve assets
Excess cash reserves

Secondary reserve assets are Treasury Bills, day loans to money-market dealers, and any *excess cash reserves* over and above the cash reserve requirement. The vast bulk of secondary reserve assets are Treasury Bills. Secondary reserve assets plus any excess cash reserves over and above the cash reserve requirement must equal at least 4.5 percent of total Canadian-dollar deposit liabilities. The secondary reserve requirement can be changed by the Bank of Canada but has purposely been kept at nonrestrictive levels since the mid-1970s.

Special call loans

Special call loans are call loans to stockbrokers that really are callable; that is, redeemable at the banks' discretion. There is an understanding that banks will never call ordinary call loans except in emergencies, despite their name, so ordinary call loans are not as liquid from the banks' point of view.

Income debentures

Bonds include a significant volume of corporate *income debentures*, whose interest payments are conditional on the issuer's income level's being satisfactory. Income debentures have special tax status in that the interest income is not treated as taxable revenue to the banks as long as it is passed through directly to bank shareholders. Income debentures are very popular with banks, although the government has moved to prevent new issues for terms of less than ten years; these bonds have had a large impact on banks' exposure to corporate income tax.[4]

Chartered banks' *other Canadian-dollar assets* include items in transit, such as cheques not yet collected from other banks. Items in transit are not a likely source of extra liquidity for any one bank, since for each bank there

---

[3]The cash reserve requirements were lowered in the 1980 Bank Act, with the change being phased in over the years 1981–84. The previous required ratios were 12 percent for Canadian-dollar demand deposits and 4 percent for Canadian-dollar term notice deposits, and 0 percent for all foreign-currency deposits.

[4]Income to banks from income debentures is not counted as part of taxable revenue in calculating taxable profits. Even a small percentage drop in taxable revenue makes a huge difference in taxable profits for institutions as highly levered as banks, so taxable profit has been lowered by more than half. The result of bank purchases of income debentures and term preferred shares (whose tax status is the same) was to lower the ratio of tax paid to total profits (including revenue from those instruments) from 41 percent in 1977 to 21 percent in 1981 and 6 percent in 1982.

will also be cheques drawn against it being held as items in transit by other banks.

Customers' liability under acceptances is a contingent asset: such assets are collectible only if firms whose debts the bank has marked as "accepted" are unable to pay the sums the bank's mark has guaranteed. Very seldom is the bank's guarantee called upon. However, there must be some acknowledgment on the liability side of the bank's balance sheet that the banks have to pay up should the customers default, even if the chance of customer default is small. This item on the asset side merely offsets that contingent liability in order to leave the banks' equity unaffected. For most purposes the total of bank assets excludes this item.[5]

Foreign-currency call loans are mainly loans to stockbrokers and investment dealers in New York. The Canadian banks have been making such loans throughout this century. Other foreign-currency loans are mostly wholesale loans made in the Eurocurrency markets in London, Luxemburg, Singapore, Hong Kong, and Nassau. These markets were discussed briefly in chapter 5 and will be treated more fully in chapter 25 at the end of the book.

Foreign-currency deposits with banks are almost all short-term, large-scale deposits loaned to the Eurodollar-market agencies of Canadian, American, Japanese, and European banks. Most of these deposits are in U.S. dollars, the rest in Deutsche Marks or Swiss francs.

Asset-risk management

A bank's management of its assets involves keeping the expected yield up and keeping the risk either down or matched by an equal and offsetting risk on the deposit side. Keeping expected yields up, in any lending business, means negotiating a high interest rate when a loan is made and then seeing that the borrower does not default. Banks have several kinds of asset risk to manage, each in a different way.

Default risk

Default risk is serious for chartered banks, as figure 11–1 shows. It has become much more serious since 1970. The increase in default loss from the 1969 level to the 1982 level has meant a drop in equity yield of 450 basis points (4.5 percentage points).

Default risk is dealt with partly by diversification, which stabilizes actual average default losses in each year so that they will be close to an

---

[5]Until 1981, the Bank Act required banks to report as a liability the full amount of contingent liabilities for acceptances, guarantees, and letters of credit — a much larger total than just for acceptances.

FIGURE 11–1 Loan loss rates of chartered banks, 1970–82

Source: Derived from data in *The Canada Gazette*, on the assumption that actual loan losses in each of the years 1965–69 were identical.

expected default loss, and partly by steps to reduce the default risk for each asset. Diversification has been very successful until recently, as the example in chapter 8 demonstrated. Diversification of loans can do little, however, when all borrowers are hit with the same worldwide recession and the same high interest rates, as in 1980–82. The soaring line of actual loan loss rates in figure 11–1 tells the story eloquently. Even diversifying abroad, by taking small shares of the many large, syndicated international loans made in the Eurodollar market, has been of little help in reducing default risk. Most of the international borrowers, especially Third World governments, have been hit just as hard as or even harder than domestic borrowers by high interest rates and world recession.

Steps taken to reduce default risk on individual assets include (a) taking out life insurance on consumer borrowers in the amount of their loan, (b) using fixed-instalment loans for those with stable incomes, (c) insisting on collateral whose value exceeds the remaining loan balance, (d) taking personal guarantees of owners for small business loans, (e) using government or private insurers for mortgages, export loans, student loans, farm loans, and several other types of loans, (f) trying to monitor loan customers' affairs before the customers get into trouble, and (g) "rescheduling" principal repayments and even interest payments (as a last resort, and mainly to avoid default by Third World governments).

One step the banker seldom takes is to cut off a customer's access to credit. In the long run doing so is very bad for repeat business; the firm cut off might survive, but it would never bring its business back to such an unreliable bank. In the short run the banker just increases the amount of collateral and the personal guarantees required, as in the risky years 1982–83.

In the short run, bankers are generally unable to cut off a customer's access to credit. This is because almost all business loans and many personal loans are made under a line-of-credit arrangement, which works just like the borrowing privilege on a VISA or MasterCard. The bank approves the line of credit in advance, reviewing it only once each year, and thereafter it is entirely up to the customer whether or not to borrow; the bank has already committed itself to lending. Since there are usually from two to three dollars of approved line of credit for every dollar of business loan outstanding, customers have substantial leeway to increase bank credit when they need it. The banker controls only the lending rate in the short run, and even there the banker can raise the rate for one loan only by raising the prime rate and with it the whole set of loan rates.

Market risk

Market risk is not much of a problem for domestic-currency assets, because banks hold few long-term assets that are negotiable and therefore valued on an organized secondary market. Bonds are the only exception.[6] Foreign-currency assets are more of a problem, since we live in a world of floating and volatile exchange rates. Banks offset exchange risk by matching foreign-currency assets with foreign-currency liabilities in each currency. Thus any increase in asset value is offset by an equal increase in liability value. The only effect on profits is from the revaluation of the net foreign-currency profit stream, which is far smaller.

---

[6]Market risk for the assets held by banks can be measured approximately by the total adjustment of posted values of corporate bonds, gold, and other non-foreign-exchange items banks hold. This total is recorded each year as an extraordinary item on the banks' income statements. The total is small. From 1976 to 1980, for instance, it averaged only 0.25 percent of just the income from securities, which is only a small part of total revenue.

Income risk

The risk of fluctuating nominal payments on assets held is large but does not worry bankers much. The source of the fluctuation is under the bank's control in almost all cases. Business loan and some consumer loan rates float with the bank's prime rate; other yields change as each asset matures and is replaced at prevailing yields. Neither source of income risk is reduced by diversification, since all yields move together. The income risk therefore remains to be either offset by liability management or just borne by shareholders. The particular form of liability management practised by chartered banks we described in section 6 of chapter 10, under the heading "Matched Floating." That liability management is the banks' major means of reducing their income risk.

Inflation risk

Inflation risk is large because almost all bank assets have a fixed nominal par value. Because bank liabilities are equally fixed in nominal terms, there is almost no inflation risk left for bank shareholders.

Liquidity risk

The major risk banks must deal with is liquidity risk — the possibility that they will have insufficient funds to finance their assets. This might happen because of a run of deposit withdrawals, or a surge of loan customers drawing on their lines of credit, or both at once.

However it is generated, a bank liquidity crisis would be felt first in the form of large net clearing losses with other banks at the end of each day's cheque clearings (see section 4 of chapter 3 for a description of the clearing process) and a drop in the bank's cash reserve holding below the level required by the Bank Act. Required reserves are calculated as a fraction of the previous month's deposit liabilities and required only as a daily average over each half of the month (known as a *reserve averaging period*);[7] each bank therefore knows before each month begins exactly what its cash reserve holdings have to be. Nevertheless, a series of large reserve losses still constitute a liquidity problem.

Reserve averaging period

Bankers have several lines of defence against reserve losses that are important both to bankers and to the functioning of monetary policy:

1. Bankers diversify across borrowers to stabilize the average use of lines of credit. Banks' lines of credit are as diversified as their loans. However, common influences such as the inventory buildup that heralds a recession will cause all of those credit needs to be positively correlated; diversification is not effective when risks are not independent.
2. Bankers could hold significant excess cash reserves, so that a series of large clearing losses would still not lower actual reserves below

[7]The actual statutory liability definition is the average of the four Wednesdays preceding the last Wednesday of the preceding month.

required levels. This line of defence is not used in Canada, though it is used in the U.S. A typical excess cash reserve holding in Canada is one percent or so of total reserves, and in the middle of a reserve averaging period, many banks are below the required level. By contrast, many banks in the U.S. will hold 10 to 20 percent more reserves than they need.

Bank Rate

3. Bankers can borrow extra reserves from the Bank of Canada, at the *Bank Rate*. This borrowing is expensive, since the Bank Rate is set $\frac{1}{4}$ percent above the Treasury Bill yield, but it will replenish reserves the same day and is sometimes used when cash reserve holdings are short on the last two days or so of a reserve averaging period. Otherwise domestic banks have shied away from Bank of Canada advances, so most of the time there is no debt outstanding from any bank to the Bank of Canada. Again, this is in direct contrast to the actions of U.S. banks, which make liberal and almost continual use of borrowing from their central bank.
4. Bankers can sell off liquid assets. If the liquidity crisis is in only one bank, there will generally be one or more other banks with matching excess cash reserves to buy up the first bank's liquid assets. Neither total demand for assets nor yields will be disturbed. If the liquidity crisis is general for all banks, each bank's liquid assets must be sold to nonbanks; the assets' prices will have to drop and their yields to rise for that sale to happen. Banks hold significant amounts of "free" liquid assets (over and above all reserve requirements), so this is a feasible line of defence. Figure 11–2 shows that banks have made extensive use of their free liquid assets in the past. However, free liquid assets are now a much smaller share of total assets than in 1970.

   Banks could sell off Treasury Bills and short-term government bonds, or they could call in day loans or special call loans. All four actions would replenish reserves the next day.[8] Selling off assets would raise money-market yields directly; calling in day or call loans would raise yields indirectly by forcing money-market dealers and stockbrokers to borrow elsewhere in the money market.
5. Bankers can raise their term-deposit yields to attract wholesale domestic or foreign-currency term deposits or even interbank deposits in the money market. By this route a banker can borrow back funds to replace those lost by deposit withdrawals.[9] This stratagem works fairly well if

[8]If the day loan were called before 10:00 A.M. it would be settled the same day, just like an advance from the Bank of Canada. For the timing of reserve settlements for various types of bank transactions, see W. R. White, *Management by the Canadian Banks of Their Domestic Portfolios* (Ottawa: Bank of Canada, 1975), 169n.

[9]In the U.S. and the U.K. there are well-developed overnight lending facilities for unneeded central-bank reserves, which solve the liquidity-risk problem for many banks. This is the federal-funds market in the U.S. Settlement is the same day in the federal-funds market, whereas it is only the next day for Canadian interbank deposits.

FIGURE 11-2 Free-liquid-asset ratio of chartered banks, 1968–83

The ratio is the share of liquid assets over and above the cash and secondary reserve requirements, in total Canadian-dollar major assets.

Source: Bank of Canada Review.

one bank does it alone, but if all banks do it together the effect is mainly to raise term-deposit yields. The extra term deposits of course further increase required reserves, but only starting the next month, and by not nearly so much as the extra deposit increases the individual bank's reserves.

6. Finally, bankers can send more of their Bank of Canada notes to the Bank of Canada for deposit. This peculiar action would actually increase measured reserves temporarily. The vault-cash total that is counted toward each month's actual reserves for statutory purposes is in fact the preceding month's vault cash.[10] A transfer of vault cash to the Bank of Canada this month therefore lowers next month's vault cash for statutory purposes but raises this month's Bank of Canada deposits.

Bank asset portolios show evidence of liquidity risk in the excess secondary reserve assets and in the other liquid-asset holdings. Both are

[10]Actually, the statutory vault-cash total for any one month is the average of vault-cash totals for the four Wednesdays immediately preceding the last Wednesday of the previous month — the same dates that are used for measuring statutory deposits.

sharply lower now than in 1960 however, with no lessening of liquidity risks to explain the drop. Liquid assets yield less than loans and mortgages, so it would appear that banks have simply been taking on greater liquidity risk in exchange for greater asset yield.

SECTION 4

Liability management

The liability portfolio of the chartered banks is shown in table 11–3 for 1960 and 1982. There have been several major changes in bank liability portfolios over the last two decades. The share of foreign-currency liabilities has grown even faster than the share of foreign-currency assets. Growth of shareholders' equity has not kept up with growth of liabilities, so the ratio of debt to equity for the domestically owned banks has risen from at most 17 in 1960 to 33 in 1982.[11] Within the total of Canadian-dollar liabilities, demand deposits have shrunk in importance, and nonpersonal term deposits have taken their place. Personal savings deposits were important in 1960 and remain important in 1982 but now consist mostly of term deposits rather than lower-paying and less interest-sensitive notice deposits. Only some of the individual bank liabilities shown in table 11–3 need further explanation.

Definitions of liability categories

The federal government's *demand deposits* have received interest for many years, reflecting the market power of such a big customer. The federal deposits are not used for writing cheques but are transferred to and from the federal account in the Bank of Canada for the purposes of monetary policy. We will return to these deposits in chapters 23 and 24.

Other demand deposits include deposits of provincial governments (which also receive interest) and deposits of other banks. Deposits of other banks are partly correspondent deposits of foreign banks and partly interbank deposits of Canadian banks. The former are used by foreign banks to help their customers make payments in Canada, while the latter are a means of borrowing and lending domestic cash reserves.[12]

---

[11]The ratio of debt to equity cannot be calculated accurately for 1960 because Accumulated Appropriations for Losses (a part of equity) was deducted from loan values instead of being shown separately. If Accumulated Appropriations for Losses were the same share of equity as in 1981, the debt:equity ratio in 1960 would have been only 13. Jack Mintz estimated the ratio at 14.6 in 1963. *The Measure of Rates of Return in Canadian Banking* (Ottawa: Economic Council of Canada, 1979), 39.

[12]Correspondent deposits held in the Royal Bank by the Westdeutsche Landesbank, for instance, are held so that the German bank's customers can buy bank drafts in Canadian dollars on that account to make payments to their Canadian suppliers. Similar correspondent accounts are held in German banks by Canadian banks.

TABLE 11–3 Chartered-bank liabilities and equity, 1982 and 1960

	September 1982		December 1960
	Billions of dollars	Percent	Percent
Canadian-dollar liabilities			
Government of Canada deposits	1.7	0.5	3.0
Other demand deposits			
personal	3.7	1.0	25.4
other	13.4	3.6	
Personal savings deposits			
chequable notice	6.8	1.8	42.6
nonchequable notice	47.5	12.9	0
fixed-term	46.2	12.6	0
Nonpersonal deposits			
notice	4.6	1.3	3.4
other	46.7	12.7	0
Bank of Canada advances	0.1	0	0
Debentures	2.6	0.7	0
Other Canadian-dollar liabilities	7.3	2.0	0.5
TOTAL CANADIAN-DOLLAR LIABILITIES	180.5	49.1	76.9
Liability under acceptances	13.4	3.6	1.5[a]
Foreign-currency liabilities			
Deposits held by other banks	85.1	23.1	3.8
Deposits held by others	64.1	17.4	4.0
Other liabilities	11.5	3.1	7.8
TOTAL FOREIGN-CURRENCY LIABILITIES	160.8	43.7	15.7
Appropriations for contingencies	0.7	0.2	0[b]
Shareholder's equity	12.5	3.4	5.9
TOTAL LIABILITIES AND EQUITY	367.8	100.0	100.0

[a]This item for 1960 includes liability for letters of credit and guarantees as well as for acceptances.
[b]Before 1967, appropriations for contingencies were deducted from loan values.

Sources: Bank of Canada Review; Bank of Canada, *Statistical Summary*.

Banks have been allowed to issue *debentures* (a type of bond) only since 1967. The Bank Act requires that debentures have an original term to maturity of at least five years, that they be nonredeemable during the first five years, and that no bank have debentures outstanding that amount in total to more than half the shareholders' equity. Debentures were initially issued for twenty-year terms, but more recent issues have been for much shorter terms or have been retractable.

Foreign-currency deposits held by other banks are Eurodollar term deposits. Many of these deposits are held by U.S. banks, whose business is attracted by U.S. agencies of Canadian banks and booked with the Canadian head office.

Of the *foreign-currency deposits held by others*, those held by residents are ordinary term-deposit business denominated in foreign currency. The others are mainly Eurodollar term deposits.[13]

Appropriations for contingencies are essentially a specially-marked part of shareholders' equity. Banks deduct specific provisions for losses on each doubtful loan before reporting loan values, but they are also allowed to set up a special loss reserve called "Appropriations for Contingencies" and plough part of each year's profits into it. Then if there are loan losses greater than provided for in provision for loan losses, they can be deducted from "Appropriations for Contingencies" instead of from the category called "Equity." The equity account is made to appear more stable, which reassures both depositors and shareholders. Since banks do not expect such losses, appropriations for contingencies are expected to be left at year-end as part of the residual value we call shareholders' equity. We therefore treat this extra reserve fund as just a specially marked part of shareholders' equity.

Liability-risk management

Our analysis of liability risks in chapter 10 revealed that, in order to keep equity risks down for a given asset portfolio whose yields fluctuate, banks must offset variations in asset yields with equal variations in debt yields. It is not to banks' advantage to have stable debt costs when asset yields are volatile.

In addition, banks must avoid liquidity risk if they wish to hold onto their asset portfolio; otherwise they might be forced to sell off parts of their asset portfolio in a hurry if a significant volume of depositors were to withdraw their funds at the same time. Liquidity risk was dealt with in the preceding section. Managing liquidity risk is mainly but not wholly a matter of asset management.

On the liability side of the balance sheet, banks have Bank of Canada advances when they do borrow reserves from the central bank, but this loan of last resort is rarely used. The main defence against liquidity risk is diversification of sources of funds across millions of depositors in various regions and industries. The only big individual depositor in Canada is the federal government, and it is not a fickle customer. Federal deposits are spread among banks in stable proportions.[14] Further, federal deposits are changed to offset major swings in public deposits due to tax payments or

[13]The banks still do some retail foreign-currency deposit business in branches in the Caribbean.

[14]For an analysis of how the proportions are determined, see K. Acheson, "The Allocation of Government Deposits among Private Banks," *Journal of Money, Credit, and Banking*, 1977, 447–59.

Canada Savings Bonds campaigns, so that federal-deposit changes substantially reduce volatility of total deposits.

Diversification is not a complete defence against liquidity risk in the foreign-currency deposit business, because a large block of funds is held by individual OPEC countries. In fact, diversification is not a good defence in one sense for the whole block of term-deposit funds, since all are sensitive in common to changes in relative yields. However, losses due to changes in yields on competing assets are easily countered by changes in yields on term deposits.

Matching asset risks

The remaining liability-management problem is the need to arrange the bank's debts so that debt yields vary in step with asset yields. Bank asset yields generally tend to move with prevailing yields in financial markets, but with different lags. Yields on business loans and some personal loans float immediately with the prime rate. Short-term liquid-asset yields move quickly with money-market yields. However, government and corporate bonds, term loans, mortgages, and instalment loans may have several years to maturity before the yield can be adjusted, so their yields respond with a longer lag.

The story of banks' liability management over the last two decades shows banks moving more and more into deposits with yields as volatile as asset yields, and out of deposits with stable yields. For instance, demand and chequable personal savings deposits have virtually fixed yields. These deposits accounted for 68 percent of total deposits in 1960, but only 6.6 percent in 1981. This change has also meant movement from low-cost to high-cost sources of funds for banks, so interest spreads have narrowed in the process.[15] More stable spreads have allowed banks to double their leverage ratios since 1960, so that the narrower spreads have not meant lower equity yields.

Now that banks have types of deposits with yield variations of almost exactly the same size and timing as assets, keeping equity risk down is merely a question of matching the quantities of each asset and deposit type. How well this matching is done can be seen in table 11–4, which groups the assets and liabilities of tables 11–2 and 11–3 into rough categories of yield volatility.

---

[15]The shift from low-cost to high-cost funds accelerated in the late 1970s. The Annual Report of the Toronto Dominion Bank for 1980, for instance, showed that since 1976 the share of low-cost domestic funds (chequing deposits) had fallen from 30 to 19 percent, the share of medium-cost domestic funds (notice deposits) had stayed about constant at 25.6 and 24 percent, and the share of high-cost domestic funds (term deposits, government deposits, and debentures) had risen from 44 to 57 percent. Toronto Dominion Bank, *Annual Report*, 1980, 23. Foreign-currency funds are all relatively high-cost funds, and they, too, have grown in importance.

TABLE 11–4 Matching of assets and debts by chartered banks

Class of asset or debt, by variability of interest rate	Percentage of total assets
Constant interest rates	
assets: cash reserves	1.7
liabilities: demand deposits, chequable personal savings deposits	6.4
Floating interest rates	
assets: business loans, liquid assets excluding government bonds and Treasury Bills	25.5
liabilities: Bank of Canada advances, government of Canada deposits, notice deposits	15.9
Interest rates fixed for short to medium terms	
assets: personal loans, mortgages, government bonds of less than 3 years to maturity	19.5
liabilities: term deposits	25.3
Interest rates fixed for longer terms	
assets: government bonds of 3 years or more to maturity, other bonds	2.9
liabilities: debentures	0.7
Interest payments denominated in foreign currency	
assets	42.4
liabilities	43.7

There is broad matching of assets and liabilities in each category. The mismatches in the floating-yield category and the short-term category are misleading because they are due mainly to the crudity of the asset and deposit categories. Many nonpersonal term deposits are for short periods like one to three months, which makes them almost floating-rate deposits. Also, although personal notice deposits have floating yields, their adjustment lags behind the rest of the floating yields. With those adjustments to the floating-rate and short-term categories, the mismatch of assets and liabilities all but disappears. By contrast, consider how table 11–4 would have looked in 1960 with 68 percent of yields fixed.

The significance of banks' liability management can be seen in announcements in early 1981, for instance, that some banks had stopped buying mortgages for five-year terms, because the banks were not getting any five-year term deposits at their posted rates. Likewise, banks' willingness to extend term loans at fixed rates to customers varies with their ability to attract funds to similar term deposits at fixed rates.

Further, banks actively shifted their mortgage lending business to their ten subsidiary mortgage loan companies in 1980–81 precisely because of the better matching the move made possible: bank term deposits are generally withdrawable before maturity, although with some interest penalty, so the banks could not be sure that five-year term-deposit funds would not have to be re-attracted in year three or four if prevailing yields were to rise a lot. Such deposits are a risky means of financing five-year mortgages, relative to using the nonwithdrawable deposits issued by their mortgage loan company subsidiaries. Mortgage loan company deposit costs are a bit higher than those of banks, so the interest spread is less, but the banks find the reduced risk exposure more than sufficient compensation.[16]

There still remains some degree of mismatching, visible when yields rise and fall. When prevailing interest rates rise, all business and personal demand loan rates rise immediately. Notice-deposit yields rise, but not all the term-deposit yields. Term-deposit yields rise only as each deposit reaches maturity. For a while, therefore, the banks' yield spread widens. On a downturn, exactly the opposite happens, and bank yield spreads are squeezed. The squeeze is prolonged by the public's speculative shifts out of long-term deposits when they expect yields to rise, and into long-term deposits when they expect yields to fall. Figure 11–3 illustrates the effect of interest-rate changes on bank margins.

Aside from these differences in timing, banks have eliminated or reduced other sources of independent variations in debt costs; independent variations in debt costs represent unsystematic risks that cannot serve to offset asset risks and merely increase equity risks. To avoid unsystematic debt risks, all business and personal demand-loan yields are changed together, not independently, since they are all pegged to the one prime rate. Short-term foreign-currency loans similarly have their interest rates pegged to the current level of the London Inter-Bank Offer Rate (*LIBOR*), rather than determined independently of each other. The remaining sources of independent variation in asset yields and debt costs are (a) default losses, which cannot be matched on the liability side, and (b) costs of servicing demand and notice deposits — the cost of the branch network.

LIBOR (London Inter-Bank Offer Rate)

Results of banks' liability management can be seen in the pattern of average yields to assets, debts, and equity over time. Table 11–5 gives the variance of the average yield, of average debt costs, and of equity yields for ten Schedule A chartered banks over the period 1976–80. For contrast, the level and variance of equity yield for ten randomly chosen industrial firms are also included for the same period. The banks' average debt:equity ratio was 25 over this period, and interest rates were volatile, so it is remarkable that banks' yield on equity was so stable. As mentioned in one of the

[16]As another step to improve the matching of mortgage yields and term-deposit costs, many of the banks have recently made their mortgage loans closed — not repayable even with an interest penalty — for a larger portion of the loan period (such as four years for a five-year mortgage). This move prevents early repayment of mortgage loans when market yields fall, leaving banks still locked into higher-cost deposits issued when the original mortgage was taken out.

FIGURE 11–3 Asset yields and debt costs of the Royal Bank, 1980–81

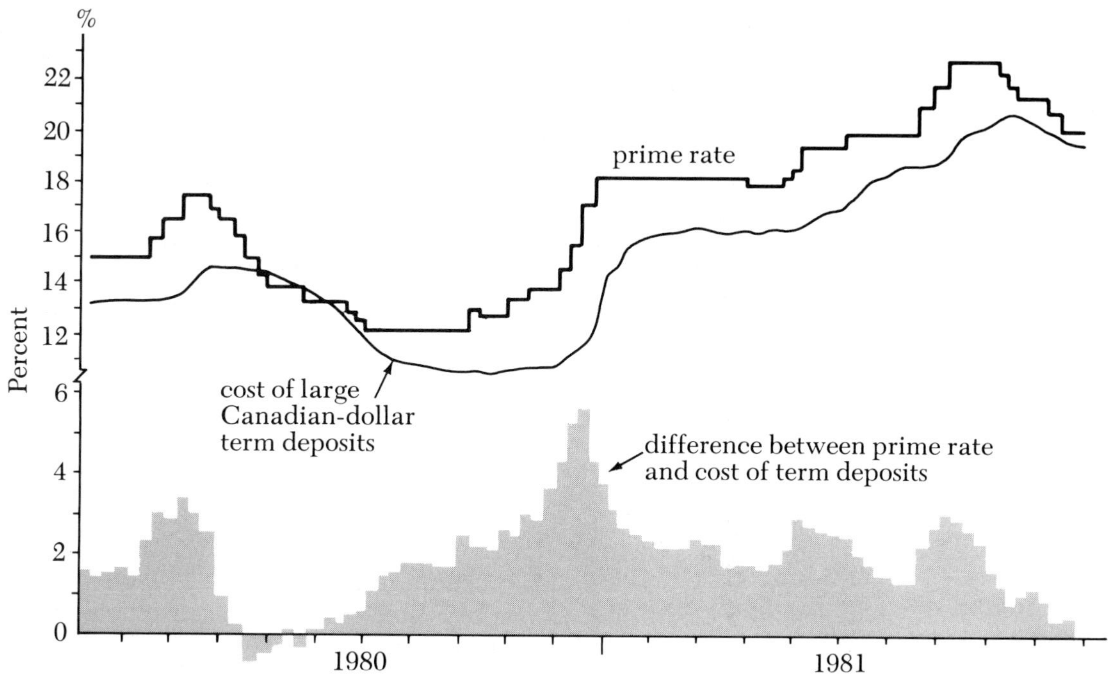

Source: Royal Bank Annual Report, 1981.

TABLE 11–5 Asset, debt, and equity yields of chartered banks and industrial firms (percent)

	Average yield	Variance[a]
Ten domestic banks		
assets	10.8	4.0
debts	8.0	5.2
equity	15.1[b]	14.8
Ten industrial firms		
equity	14.5[b]	19.8

[a]The average of variances for each firm over the period 1976–80.
[b]After-tax yield.

Source: Financial Post Record Service.

examples at the end of chapter 10, the banks collectively have managed a degree of correlation of 0.997 between asset and debt yields — about as high as they can get.

SECTION 5

Banks and the financial system

We have seen and explained banks' demand for assets and supply of debts. Both are simply special cases of the general theoretical explanations of asset demand and supply presented in chapters 8 and 10. In this section we will extract the implications of banks' behavior for the rest of the financial system, and in particular for monetary policy. We have not yet discussed the details of how the Bank of Canada conducts monetary policy, but we are well armed to look at the chartered banks' role in diffusing the impact of monetary policy throughout the financial system.

Banks and financial-market behavior

First, banks participate in a very broad range of asset and debt markets, even if only with a small portion of their assets or debts. The scale of banks is so large that what is a small portion of banks' balance sheets (such as chequing deposits or money-market assets) is often a large and important part of the market itself. Participation in a broad range of markets implies that a wide range of relative yields and risks (those on all bank assets) influences banks' demand for any one type of asset — that banks would shift demand into and out of Treasury Bills, for instance, in response to changes in yields on a wide range of other assets, from corporate bonds to prime loan yields. Such sensitivity tends to hold yields in a fairly constant structure over time, as long as banks' assessments of relative risks do not change.

Second, some of the banks' demand and supply behavior is fairly mechanical. Banks' demand for cash reserves, for instance, is basically the required cash reserve formula. In the U.S., banks hold large excess cash reserves whose total varies sensitively with money-market yields and the central-bank discount rate (the equivalent of the Bank Rate in Canada). Not so in Canada. Similarly, chartered banks' demand for funds from the Bank of Canada through advances is most usefully thought of as zero. Banks' supplies of demand deposits and chequable savings deposits also simply adapt mechanically to demand, at unchanged interest rates of 0 and 3 percent respectively.[17]

[17]The yield on demand and chequable notice deposits may be adjusted in part in the indirect form of subsidized chequing costs, or even (since 1980 and for corporate deposits) by explicit payment of interest at rates that (for large deposits) adjust with money-market yields. Instances of the latter kind of deposit are still insignificant in number, but growing rapidly.

Third, banks have enough market power to set their own loan rates and term- and notice-deposit yields. Those rates reach equilibrium not by an auction market process as in the money market but by intelligent guesswork at each bank. The rates do reach equilibrium, though, in the sense that banks supply all term deposits and make all loans requested, at the rate at which (a) the marginal asset yield from loans just matches marginal debt cost from term deposits and (b) the level of term-deposit rates is such as to attract just the demand for bank term deposits that banks can support with the cash reserves left over after supporting demand deposits. Banks don't stop short of that point, because of competition (especially in wholesale financial markets, with the entry of foreign banks), and they don't go beyond it, because of a normal desire to avoid losses.

Fourth, banks' leverage is so high that bankers avoid mismatching for each category of assets. That means each change in their asset demand is matched by a predictable change in their supply of deposits. To look at it a different way, for each type of debt, the yields that matter most are those of the debt itself and of the assets whose yield pattern (fixed, floating, adjustable within three months, or whatever) matches that of the debt. A large shift in relative debt yields will not cause banks to shift from one type of borrowing to another on a large scale, without at the same time causing them to shift their demand for assets in the same direction. If floating-rate yields fall because of extra demand for notice deposits, while fixed-term yields rise because of smaller demand for term deposits, banks will try to expand their demand-loan business and contract mortgage lending to match by lowering demand-loan rates and raising mortgage-loan rates. The same logic holds for banks' response to a large change in relative yields on assets.

The banks and monetary policy

The implications of bank behavior for monetary policy are easiest to see if we assume banks to be in equilibrium and then imagine a disturbance of the sort caused by monetary policy. Assume that monetary policy has increased the available cash reserves of the banks, by one of the means to be described in chapter 23. The following sequence of bank and public responses is likely to spread the impact of this action around the financial system.

1. Banks use excess cash reserves to buy liquid assets in the short run, because demand and consumer loans and mortgages cannot be turned on like water from a tap. This buying drives down short-term liquid-asset yields. At the same time, banks' purchases create extra demand deposits. The holders of these deposits are likely to convert them to term deposits or buy other wholesale financial assets, just for the extra yield. After all, there has been no change in wealth or nominal income yet to cause extra demand for chequing deposits. The extra

demand for term deposits leads to a fall in equilibrium yields on term deposits. Banks don't need to pay as much to attract term deposits, so they don't.

2. A widening margin between yields on term deposits and yields on the loans that term deposits finance causes banks to expand; they do so by lowering loan rates to attract new business. If short-term deposit yields have fallen, banks lower demand-loan and consumer-loan rates. If longer-term deposit yields have fallen, banks lower term-loan and five-year mortgage-loan rates.
3. Lower yields in the money market will cause some reduction in demand for bank credit (which can also be seen as a reduction in the supply of bank loan notes) as larger firms shift their borrowing from bank loans to the issue of commercial paper and acceptances. The reduction in demand for funds in the bank-loan market is a further reason for interest rates on bank loans to fall.

As the banks lower interest rates on term deposits, they cause part of the public's demand to shift to other assets such as near-bank deposits, bonds, stocks, and real assets.

SECTION 6 Summary

Financial intermediaries require a positive spread between asset yields and debt costs. This positive spread comes mainly from transmutation of assets — the process of taking in assets that would seem relatively risky to other lenders, and issuing debts that would seem relatively safe and secure to the same individuals. Assets that would seem risky are loans with high default or income or market risk, or very large assets that would not leave room in smaller portfolios for any diversification. Debts that would seem safe are those with low default or income or market risk, those small enough to permit diversification, and especially those whose redemption date has been customized to suit each investor or whose payoff has been customized to offset other asset yields for investors (such as insurance). The risks that customized debts imply for financial intermediaries are reduced to manageable size by pooling.

Canadian banks earn positive spreads in several of these ways. Banks are a broadly diversified group of federally chartered firms with relatively few remaining restrictions on their business activities. Their main activity is still business lending, but that part of their operations is not as dominant as before. Banks are engaged to some degree in almost all other types of financing, especially consumer lending. Their main source of funds is term and notice deposits, not the traditional demand deposits associated with commercial banks.

Bank assets reflect the banks' range of lending but also a significant liquidity-risk problem that arises from having very short-term debts and from guaranteeing credit in advance to loan customers, via lines of credit. Banks have several lines of defence against liquidity risk, resting mainly on diversification of deposits and holding of a stock of liquid assets readily resalable in the money market.

Bank liabilities have changed dramatically since the 1960s. Competition for funds has forced banks beyond just demand and chequable notice deposits into higher-cost term and nonchequable notice deposits. Because of banks' high leverage, banks' liability portfolios are now matched fairly closely to their asset portfolios in the timing of interest-rate adjustability, so interest spreads are kept stable. This stability is reflected in a relatively high equity yield and in an equity risk that is very low considering the banks' leverage.

Banks are large relative to most of the markets in which they participate, so they tend to be price (that is, interest rate) setters rather than price takers. Banks use that power to end up with close to a profit-maximizing quantity of assets and deposits of each type. One result of banks' interest adjustment power is that when monetary policy increases the level of cash reserves, banks are likely to expand quickly, and their expansion in turn is likely to force down at least several of a broad range of interest rates in financial markets; the impact of monetary policy is widely diffused across financial markets by the banks' responses.

Questions for discussion

1. Which of the sources of positive interest spread do the banks rely on in their banking business?
2. What are secondary reserve assets?
3. Why has diversification of bank lending business across millions of borrowers (some in other countries) not succeeded in completely stabilizing loan loss rates?
4. What is the significance of lines of credit for bank asset management?
5. Why can banks not manage to change their average asset yield at the same rate as their average deposit cost? Does this lag serve to increase bank profits when interest rates are rising, or when they are falling?
6. What is the significance of tying foreign-currency loan rates to LIBOR?
7. Will an increase in cash reserves (caused by monetary policy) always lead to the same pattern of changes in bank loan rates and deposit rates? Explain.

References

Binhammer, H.H., and Jane Williams. *Deposit-taking Institutions: Innovation and the Process of Change.* Ottawa: Economic Council of Canada, 1976.

Clendenning, Wayne G. *The Eurocurrency Markets and the International Activities of Canadian Banks.* Ottawa: Economic Council of Canada, 1978.

Department of Finance. *Canadian Banking Legislation.* Ottawa, 1976.

Economic Council of Canada. *Efficiency and Regulation.* Ottawa: Economic Council of Canada, 1976.

Galbraith, John A. *Canadian Banking.* Toronto: Ryerson Press, 1970.

House of Commons, Standing Committee on Trade, Finance, and Economic Affairs. *Bank Profits.* Ottawa: Supply and Services, 1982.

Mintz, Jack M. *The Measure of Rates of Return in Canadian Banking.* Ottawa: Economic Council of Canada, 1979.

Neave, Edwin. *Canadian Financial Markets.* Toronto: Wiley, 1981.

Neufeld, E.P. *The Financial System of Canada.* Toronto: Macmillan, 1972.

CHAPTER 12

Near-Banking

Chapter 11 explained how one type of financial intermediary — chartered banks — chooses its assets and liabilities to achieve satisfactory levels of equity yields and equity risks. Banks are important because they issue most of our money supply and are therefore the vehicle of monetary policy as well as the major lenders and suppliers of savings instruments.

This chapter explains the asset and liability choices of near-banks. Like banks, these institutions are engaged in issuing short- to medium-term deposits, or in short- to medium-term lending, or (usually) in both. Some Canadian near-banks would be known as savings banks in other countries. The main distinction between banks and near-banks as a group is that near-banks do not normally issue a large volume of chequing deposits.

The group of near-banks includes credit unions and their francophone counterparts, the caisses populaires; trust companies; mortgage loan companies; finance companies; mortgage investment companies; the sole remaining Quebec Savings Bank; two provincial government savings institutions; and real estate investment companies. Until 1981 the list also included foreign bank agencies operating a bank lending business with funds borrowed in the commercial-paper market; now all of the significant foreign agencies have federal bank charters as Schedule B banks and borrow funds by issuing term deposits. The group of near-banks excludes long-term lenders such as insurance companies, pension funds, mutual funds, term lenders, financial leasing companies, and venture-capital lenders.

Collectively, the Canadian-dollar assets of near-banks are almost 80 percent as large as those of the chartered banks, so the near-bank group is clearly large and important even if its business is spread over many different types of firms.

The focus of this chapter is the same as the focus in chapter 11, so your tasks for this chapter are similar: in general you will learn what sort of financial-intermediary business near-banks do, how they manage the risks involved, and how they are affected by changes in yields in the rest of the financial system.

More specifically, you will learn:

1. the legal background of each type of near-bank, including the extent to which each is forced by law to be unique,
2. how near-bank asset portfolios and asset-risk management problems are different from those of banks,
3. how near-bank liability management differs from that of banks, and
4. the role of near-banks in financial markets and their probable impact on the diffusion of monetary policy in the financial system.

SECTION 1 The legal structure of near-banking

Near-banks are generally subject to a mixture of federal and provincial jusrisdiction. Many provincially chartered deposit-taking institutions, for instance, have their deposits insured by the Canada Deposit Insurance Corporation (*CDIC*) and are therefore inspected by the CDIC or its provincial delegate.

Both provincial and federal financial legislation has become more permissive over the last two decades; more emphasis has been placed on disclosure and inspection and less emphasis on enforcing guidelines for asset and liability proportions. In the distant past there was a notion of a niche for every type of financial institution and every institution in its niche, but that is no longer true. Most financial institutions can now engage in most types of financial intermediation despite differences in their names and legislation.

Credit unions and caisses populaires

Credit unions and caisses populaires are provincial, co-operative savings and lending associations, owned by their member depositors and borrowers. They were started in 1900 in Quebec by Alphonse Desjardins, whose name is still given to the Quebec movement. They are still strongest by far in Quebec, where the number of caisse populaire offices outnumbers the total for banks and trust companies combined. The scale of the credit union movement in Canada is best shown by the ratio of total membership to population. In 1970 the ratio was 24.7 percent, but by 1980 it had grown to 40.1 percent. Two out of five Canadians belonged to a credit union or caisse populaire. Quebec has the highest ratio, at 78.7 percent, but Saskatchewan is not far behind at 57.5 percent. Average assets per local credit union have grown from just under $1 million in 1970 to $8.3 million in 1980, a growth rate of almost 25 percent per year over the decade.

The basic unit is the local credit union or caisse (known as a *local*), which may have a few branches. Provincial or regional centrals have been formed by the local credit unions or caisses to perform cheque-clearing and inspection and some central banking services for the member locals. Most provinces have one provincial central (or one for credit unions and one for caisses populaires), but Quebec has several. There are two "national" centrals: the Canadian Co-operative Credit Society is a central for the provincial credit union centrals, and La Caisse Centrale Desjardins du Québec was set up in 1979 to be the central organ for the caisses populaires. Cheques written on credit union and caisse populaire accounts are cleared through these two national centrals, which are clearing members of the new Canadian Payments Association.

The credit unions are limited to one province by their legislation. They are limited in size by the type of organization they are, and by their objective: they are co-operatives owned by their members, and their aim is to have the members manage their own financial affairs. In recent years there has been a shift toward more professional management, and many mergers of weak locals with stronger ones, but credit unions and caisses are still small-scale. In 1980 the average credit union membership was only 2685 members, less than the average number of customers for a single bank branch. The only really big credit union, the Vancouver City Savings Credit Union, with assets of $1.1 billion in 1982, is over three times as big as the next biggest credit union.

We will discuss credit unions and caisses populaires as though they were the same institution, but there are some substantive differences. Principally, the emphasis of the Desjardins movement was on savings, and prudent investment of those savings, while the western credit union movement in particular has put much more emphasis on generating credit for members.

Credit unions in Ontario were restricted in their growth until 1978 because the Ontario credit union legislation required a common bond of association among members (the same employer, the same town, the same church, or whatever). This restriction has since been removed, and credit unions can now be regarded simply as co-operative banks. There are few legal restrictions on the activities of credit unions and caisses. As evidence, some Quebec caisses have established true financial supermarkets, selling trust services and through their subsidiary trust and insurance companies.

Trust companies

There are about sixty federally and provincially chartered trust companies. Most trust companies are federally chartered now that federal charters are available by letters patent. The alternative method of securing a charter is to have a private member's bill passed by Parliament, which is much more expensive and time-consuming. Of the provincially chartered companies, most are chartered in Ontario.

Provincial trust company regulations are generally similar. Alberta's rules are currently the most permissive. Ontario's laws give the government greater powers of investigation and intervention, in the wake of the failure of Astra Trust and Re-Mor Mortgage Corporation in 1980 and the political uproar over the lending practices of three Ontario trust companies in the fall of 1982 (discussed further in chapter 16). The Quebec government also has given its Inspector General of Financial Institutions broad and sweeping powers to inspect and intervene.

Trust companies started in the 1880s as corporate trustees to manage others' money. This estate, trust, and agency business (known as ETA business) is still what distinguishes trust companies from other financial intermediaries. Trust companies became financial intermediaries in the 1920s by starting to borrow in their own name, and as a group they now have $1 of their own debts and assets for every $2 of ETA funds. Trust companies were originally forbidden to issue deposits or debentures, as these were the exclusive preserve of banks and mortgage loan companies, but the restriction has long since been abandoned.[1] Trust companies are still forbidden to have debt outstanding greater than twenty times their equity, but firms are finding a way around that restriction as well.[2]

Trust companies are permitted to have branches, and also subsidiaries of many kinds other than banks. They are forbidden to sell insurance. As of 1982, trust companies were still forbidden to hold a significant quantity of commercial loans, real estate, unsecured personal loans, and stocks of companies without a stable earnings record over the previous five years.[3] On the other hand, trust companies generally must hold liquid assets at least equal to 20 percent of their deposits.

There are few barriers to entry in the trust business, though only trust companies can engage in estate, trust, and agency business as trustees. The ETA business is highly concentrated, however: two-thirds of the ETA business is handled by the four largest trust companies (Royal Trustco, Canada Trust Co., National Trust, and Montreal Trustco). Some trust companies do no ETA business at all.

One important difference between banks and trust companies is that there is no limit on ownership of a trust company; no one may own more than 10 percent of a Schedule A bank, and banks may not own shares of a trust company, but any individual may own the entire stock of a trust

---

[1]The trust companies got around this restriction by calling their deposits Guaranteed Investment Certificates, which means the same thing to all intents and purposes. The fiction is carried over to trust company accounting, where the balance sheet is divided into "company funds" and "guaranteed funds."

[2]Owners of trust companies have set up holding companies. By financing the holding companies partly with debt, the owners can increase their leverage to equity in the holding company to whatever level they wish.

[3]Literally, trust companies are forbidden by the Trust Companies Act to accept "movable wares" as collateral (except for the "basket clause" lending of up to 7 percent in otherwise forbidden forms). The provision effectively rules out commercial lending secured by other than real estate or fixed equipment. Federal draft legislation brought out for discussion in 1983 proposes to allow commercial lending by trust companies, but only up to 15 percent of assets.

company.[4] The danger of unlimited ownership is that the owners will be tempted to divert trust company funds to benefit other of their enterprises, to the possible disadvantage of depositors. This threat was raised when Campeau Corporation attempted to take over Royal Trust in 1980, and confirmed when Leonard Rosenberg took over Crown Trust in the fall of 1982; within four months, Crown Trust had been taken over by the Ontario government to protect depositors' money. Despite this recent problem, almost all major trust companies are controlled by a single shareholder or group of shareholders.

Mortgage loan companies

Mortgage loan companies originated as terminating (that is, self-liquidating) co-operative building societies, in which members pooled their savings so that each member (in turn) could borrow to build a house. These building societies flourished in the nineteenth century, in a time when there were few other sources of long-term funds. Now building societies are permanent and not co-operative, and they are called mortgage loan companies.[5] They raise funds with their own deposits and invest mainly in mortgages. There are about thirty mortgage loan companies, mostly chartered under federal legislation. Their charters are not restrictive now: not much is forbidden them except selling insurance, serving as a corporate trustee, and making unsecured loans. There is no type of intermediation business restricted solely to mortgage loan companies, though there was in the past.[6]

Ten of the large mortgage loan companies are wholly owned subsidiaries of chartered banks, an arrangement that banks use to get around the Bank Act ceiling on banks' holdings of residential mortgages. Many others are owned or controlled by other financial institutions such as trust companies, the Montreal City and District Savings Bank, the Ontario Credit Union League, and groups of pension funds.[7]

There are also two different mutant forms of mortgage loan companies. The first is the *investment contract company*. Such a company issues long-term savings contracts instead of deposits. A long-term savings contract commits the individual lender to contribute funds on a regular basis out of savings. The steady inflow of savings accumulates, becoming a

Investment contract company

[4]This is a slight exaggeration. The Ontario government intervened directly to prevent control of Northern Trust from passing to a twenty-year-old would-be purchaser in December 1982.

[5]The name *building society* is still used in the United Kingdom, the birthplace of this type of financial institution.

[6]The right to issue debentures was important before 1914, because it gave the mortgage loan companies access to the important London capital market — access that other intermediaries did not have.

[7]For a complete listing of trust and mortgage loan companies operating in Ontario, together with their principal ownership, see *The Financial Post*, Jan. 15, 1983, p. 4.

substantial asset by the end of the contract. Savings contracts are similar to savings plans sold by insurance companies. Principal Group Ltd. of Edmonton is the best-known of the investment contract companies.

Mortgage investment company

The second mutant form of mortgage loan company is the *mortgage investment company*, or MIC. In 1973 the Federal Residential Mortgage Financing Act amended the Loan Companies Act and the Income Tax Act to allow dividends of a special type of mortgage loan company to pass through to shareholders free of corporate income tax. These MICs were to hold at least half and preferably two-thirds of their assets in residential mortgages and cash, they were to hold less than 25 percent in real estate equity, and they were to pay out all of their net income and half of their realized capital gains to shareholders each year. MICs are also prohibited from issuing deposits, and their debenture issue is restricted to five times their capital. A number of these special firms have been set up since 1973, generally as subsidiaries of trust companies.

Quebec Savings Banks

There is only the one Quebec Savings Bank left, the Montreal City and District Savings Bank. The other one converted to a chartered bank (La Banque Populaire) in 1969 and merged with the Provincial Bank in 1970. The original form of these banks was the trustee savings bank, a partly charitable institution set up to enable the poor to save. Only two of these savings banks survived even to the twentieth century, mostly because the largely volunteer management of the others was insufficiently motivated to do a good job.

Until 1980 the Montreal City and District Savings Bank was restricted to Quebec, and its lending restricted to mortgages and personal loans, but now both limits have been removed. The bank now has commercial lending powers for loans of $100 000 or less and can hold stock of nonfinancial firms. Its largest investment is ownership of Crédit Foncier, a medium-size trust company with offices all across Canada. The Quebec Savings Bank Act imposes a 5 percent cash reserve requirement and an additional 15 percent secondary reserve requirement.

Alberta Treasury Branches and the Province of Ontario Savings Offices

Alberta Treasury Branches, set up in 1938, are a division of the Alberta government. The division acts like a bank in every respect except that it does no foreign borrowing or lending and is not required to keep cash reserves in the form of deposits in the Bank of Canada (it may do so as a member of the Canadian Payments Association, however, if it chooses to have its cheques cleared in its own name rather than through some other clearing member of the association). The Alberta Treasury Branches issue deposits and make loans just like banks but of course are restricted to the province of Alberta. The Alberta Treasury Branches had assets of $2.9 billion as of September 1982, making the division just under three times the size of the Vancouver City Savings Credit Union and a major financial competitor in the Alberta financial system.

Province of Ontario Savings Offices were opened in 1920 to help finance a farm loan program in that province. All of the funds attracted in deposits are put straight into the province's general revenue fund rather than being used to acquire specific financial assets. Province of Ontario Savings Offices had only $672 million in assets as of September 1982.

Finance companies

Finance companies are an outgrowth of private moneylenders. Most of the finance companies are provincially incorporated. Those in the small-loan business have been regulated by the federal government in the past through the Small Loans Act, which until 1980 set limits on small-loan interest rates and provided for an inspection of each licensed lender.[8]

There are several types of finance company business. First, there are four federally incorporated consumer loan companies (Household Finance, Beneficial Finance, Canadian Acceptance, and Laurentide Finance) and two dozen provincial moneylending firms like Avco Financial Services Ltd., which make direct cash loans to household customers. At the end of World War II, direct lending by these firms took over from the customer credit commonly provided by merchants until then. Since 1950, direct personal lending by finance companies has gradually been replaced by personal loans from chartered banks and credit unions.

Acceptance company

A second type of finance company business is that of the sales finance and *acceptance companies*, which buy accounts receivable or credits from an originating firm such as a car dealership or equipment supplier. Such sales finance and acceptance companies buy short-term personal or business loan notes, usually secured by movable property such as a car or trailer. Some of these companies are the captive financing arm of large retailers (Ford Credit Canada, General Motors Acceptance Corp. of Canada, International Harvester Credit Corp. of Canada, Chrysler Credit Canada). Some, such as Canadian Acceptance Company and Traders Group Ltd., are independent firms financing many different types of goods purchase.

A third type of finance company business is in second mortgage loans to households. Second mortgages use the family home as collateral, but the first mortgagee has prior claim on the property value in event of default.

---

[8]The Small Loans Act was repealed with little fanfare in 1980, as the rising level of nominal interest rates had made the legislated ceiling on small loans far too low. Almost every credit union would have had to register under the Act if it had been left in place, and the administrative burden was not one the federal Department of Finance wanted to take on.

Second mortgages are a relatively risky form of collateral loan, so they usually have shorter amortization periods and higher interest rates than first mortgages.

The fourth type of finance company business is financial leasing of equipment. Finance companies have about one-quarter of the financial leasing business. Specialized financial leasing companies (many of which are chartered-bank subsidiaries) have most of the rest. Financial leases have terms almost as long as the lifetime of the equipment being financed, so this is the longest-term business of most finance companies.

There are few restrictions on finance companies. They are not prohibited from issuing deposits, for instance, though none of them do. They have diversified across various types of lending because their consumer lending business has fallen off since the 1950s. Consumer lending accounted for half of total assets in 1968 but is now only one-fifth of total assets. Their other financing is of commercial, industrial, and wholesale accounts receivable, and equipment leasing. The ceilings on small-loan rates (removed in 1980) caused massive exit from the small-loan sector. The amount of small-loan balances outstanding in 1979 was 75 percent below that of 1965, the peak year.

SECTION 2 Asset management

Table 12–1 shows the distribution of assets for each major group of near-banks. The asset categories need only a little comment before we turn to asset-risk management.

Demand deposits are almost all held in chartered banks or credit union centrals, for cheque-clearing purposes. Similarly, almost all of the term deposits of other than credit unions and caisses populaires are held at banks. Credit union locals and caisses populaires generally keep liquid balances in term deposits with their centrals, which in turn keep their liquid balances in banks, in trust companies, and in money-market assets. The large personal and business loan totals shown for finance companies were mostly acquired by secondary purchases of retail and wholesale credits from retailers and other suppliers, rather than by direct lending to consumers and businesses.

Very little foreign-currency business is done by near-banks. This is partly because the federal government levies a 15 percent withholding tax on all interest paid on foreign-currency deposits, except those issued by chartered banks.

Table 12–1 shows the extent to which near-banks specialize in particular types of lending. There is not much evidence of specialization left, especially since mortgages are no longer long-term assets. Since 1969 almost all residential mortgages have been renegotiable after at most five

TABLE 12–1 Asset distribution of near-banks, December 1981 (percentage of total assets)

Asset type	Credit unions: Locals	Credit unions: Centrals	Trust companies	Mortgage loan companies	Finance companies
Cash and demand deposits	10.4	5.9	1.4	0.6	0.4
Term deposits	7.4	21.5	4.9	2.0	0.3
Other short-term liquid assets	0	9.4	4.8	0.7	0.3
Federal government bonds	0.3	9.5	2.4	1.0	0.1
Total liquid assets	18.2	46.3	13.5	4.3	1.0
Other bonds	2.7	19.2	7.1	2.8	0
Stocks	1.1	2.1	4.6	1.9	0.4
Investments in subsidiaries and other Canadian securities	0.2	6.3	1.0	2.9	3.2
Foreign securities	0	0	0.1	0.2	1.2
Loans					
personal	18.3	0	4.1	0.4	31.3
business	6.3[a]	18.5	1.9	1.2	42.7
Mortgages					
residential	39.2	0.9	54.3	74.6	7.0
nonresidential	11.2	3.0	9.6	9.0	2.5
Financial lease contracts	0	0	0.7	0.2	8.8
Other assets	2.8	3.8	3.2	2.4	1.9
TOTAL ASSETS (MILLIONS OF DOLLARS)	$32 550	$7313	$43 641	$20 691	$14 818

[a]Includes farm loans of 2.1 percent.

Source: Statistics Canada, *Financial Institutions*, Cat. 61–006, Fourth Quarter 1981.

years.[9] This change has moved residential mortgages from the long-term to a medium-term category of assets. Whenever interest rates rise, as in 1980–81, most new mortgages have even shorter terms than five years, so there is less and less distinction between mortgage lending on the one hand and business and consumer lending on the other. Furthermore, demographic changes suggest that demand for new mortgage funds will not grow

[9]It has been part of Canadian interest legislation since 1888 that after five years individuals should be able to repay residential mortgage loans before maturity with only a three-months' interest penalty. Only after 1969 did financial intermediaries start to make available mortgages that were automatically renegotiable without penalty after five years. This change was brought about by a decision of the Canada Mortgage and Housing Corporation to insure such mortgages against default risk under the National Housing Act. The new household debt instrument was very popular with lenders.

as fast in the future as it did in the 1970s. As a result, near-banks are more likely to expand into several types of lending business rather than stick to just the one. This diversification is in stark contrast to the situation in the United States, where the thrifts (savings and loan associations and mutual savings banks) have been restricted mainly to mortgage lending by law.[10]

Some specialization will remain, however. Mortgage loan companies that are subsidiaries of banks will probably remain as specialized mortgage lenders, just because they will not be allowed to compete with their parent banks in other fields. Similarly, credit union centrals will remain specialized because of their role in servicing the needs of member locals. The other near-banks can be expected to spread their business even more. IAC Limited, the largest finance company, even went so far as to convert itself into the Continental Bank, and Morguard Trust Co. is being converted into Morguard Bank.

The asset risks faced by near-banks are the same as those faced by banks: default risk, income risk, market risk, inflation risk, and the liquidity risk posed by deposits.

Inflation risk

Inflation risk is not a serious problem for near-bank shareholders. Almost all near-bank assets have fixed nominal value and are therefore subject to inflation risk, but near-bank shareholders do not bear the brunt because near-bank liabilities also have fixed nominal value. The result is that higher price levels reduce the real value of both assets and liabilities, with little effect on the real value of near-bank equity.

Default risk

Near-banks take the same sort of steps as banks to reduce chances of default on individual loans. They arrange life insurance on loans, a practice introduced into loan markets by the credit unions. They rely on fixed-instalment loans for consumers, in order to match repayment schedules more closely with income and to make repayment easier. They insist upon high collateral values for mortgages, at least one-third greater than the loan amount. They arrange mortgage default insurance with either the Canada Mortgage and Housing Corporation (a federal Crown corporation) or with the privately-owned Mortgage Insurance Corporation of Canada. Finally, their loan officers and credit committees screen loan requests.

Trust companies and mortgage loan companies avoid unsecured lending; they are permitted to make unsecured loans under a "basket clause" in their legislation that allows limited amounts of otherwise forbidden investments, but the companies do not take full advantage of even that limited

---

[10]For a discussion of the problems of the "thrifts" in the United States, see Andrew S. Carron, *The Plight of the Thrift Institutions* (Washington, D.C.: Brookings, 1982).

power. They insist on having their loans secured by real estate or by securities (that is, they make only mortgage or collateral loans). Even that kind of security is not always enough: in mid-1983 the federal Superintendent of Insurance had to arrange the takeover or management of Fidelity Trust's business by First City Trust, because of difficulties that Fidelity Trust was having with large real estate loans to its owner's company, Patrician Land Corp. Credit union centrals have also been making a significant volume of loans in recent years, but mainly to municipal governments and co-operative organizations.

Credit union locals and finance companies both do a large volume of personal lending, and both have a special default-risk problem. Local credit unions cannot diversify because they are small: they have only 2685 members on average, all in the same locality and often therefore in the same sort of occupation as well. (Credit unions in British Columbia are typically twice as big as those in other provinces, but they are still tied to specific towns.) Business and personal loans in any one town are bound to have highly correlated default risks, which even the tightest screening by credit committees cannot remove. Most credit union locals therefore avoid the larger volume business credit entirely, since they can hardly diversify it at all. Instead, they stick to small personal loans and mortgages.

The caisses d'entraide (a type of caisse populaire in southern Quebec) ignored this logic. They concentrated on business loans to members and suffered almost terminal losses in 1980–81 because of a series of defaults on business loans. Those defaults would not have been serious wounds for a medium-size bank, but they were mortal for small caisses d'entraide.

The credit union movement can still handle large loans to business, but only by having the loan granted through the central. This is equivalent to having all the member locals syndicate the loan, with the central acting as lead manager; the locals own the central and are almost its only source of funds, so liabilities of the central are essentially liabilities of the collective group of locals. To some extent the national credit union association, the Canadian Co-operative Credit Society, will be able to syndicate loans too large to be handled by any one central. Within Quebec, the Caisse Centrale Desjardins du Québec can play that role for the caisses populaires and for the other Quebec centrales.

The finance companies' special default problem is not lack of diversification but rather lack of opportunity to screen at the outset those loans extended originally by automobile and appliance dealers. Original lenders who are more interested in selling cars and appliances naturally tend not to screen credit risks as well as would a financial intermediary. The results show in the 1980 loss provisions in table 12–2.

The loan loss provisions in table 12–2 include those for mortgage loans, but the second column of table 12–2 shows that mortgage loans have much less default risk than other loans. Those intermediaries with the largest proportions of mortgage loans in their loan portfolios also had by far the lowest loan loss provisions. Even so, the finance companies' loss experience

TABLE 12–2 Loan loss provisions, 1981

Institution	Loss provision°	Loans°
Finance companies	0.97	88.6
Chartered banks	0.43	85.0
Credit unions		
locals	0.27	32.8
centrals	0.10	82.7
Mortgage loan companies	0.02	1.9
Trust companies	0.04	8.6

°as a percentage of total loans plus mortgages

Sources: The Canada Gazette; Statistics Canada, *Financial Institutions*, Cat. 61–006, Fourth Quarter 1981.

is over twice as bad as that of the banks. Finance companies clearly have a special default-risk problem.

The high default risks of consumer loans relative to business loans also show up in the reported default rates for loans under various government loan guarantee schemes. Under the Farm Improvement Loans Act (since 1945) and the Fisheries Improvements Loans Act (since 1955) the government has paid out claims of private lenders for loan defaults amounting to 0.15 and 0.19 percent, respectively, of the total amount loaned since the start of each program. Under the Small Business Loans Act (since 1961) the government has paid out default-loss claims amounting to 0.42 percent of amounts loaned. Under the Small Loans Act, where the government does not guarantee the loans but merely receives reports, the registered lenders reported a bad-debt loss in 1979 of 3.3 percent on small loans (under $1500) and 3.8 percent on other loans. These percentage loss rates are higher than in earlier years, but even in 1969 they were 1.8 percent and 1.0 percent respectively. As extra evidence of the probability of default, almost one-quarter of all small loans outstanding were reported to be in arrears in each year.

Market risk

Trust companies and credit union centrals both have significant holdings of marketable long-term securities (bonds and stocks), whose prices fluctuate. Market risk on bonds is not much of a problem, because bonds are typically held to maturity, redeemed at par value, and recorded at acquisition cost or par value on the company's books. Unrealized capital gains on bonds held are therefore not recorded on either the balance sheet or the income statement.

Stock holdings by near-banks do present a significant market risk. Even though trust companies diversify their stock holdings, there is nevertheless a significant systematic risk in stocks; because stocks are recorded at market value on trust companies' books, fluctuations in stock values cause fluctuations in the asset and equity values in trust companies' annual reports. Realized capital gains and losses on both stocks and bonds are reported in the income statements of credit union centrals and of trust companies in the year they are realized. For credit union centrals, realized capital gains and losses were not a significant share of income until 1979, when they amounted to 19 percent of net income. Realized capital gains and losses are roughly similar shares of income for trust companies.

Income risk

For almost all loans held by near-banks, the interest rate is fixed either until maturity or until a specified maturity date. There are few floating-rate loans. Income risk is therefore not a problem. Stock dividends do fluctuate, but that is a tiny part of total income. Near-banks have no significant holdings of foreign-currency assets, so exchange risk is not a problem.

Liquidity risk

The dramatic differences in asset proportions in table 12-1 are in shares of liquid assets. Credit union centrals are awash in liquid assets, while finance companies have virtually none.

None of the near-banks have line-of-credit loans like those extended by banks, so they are not subject to unpredictable and unrefusable loan requests for that reason. Near-banks need liquid assets for other reasons. First, trust companies and especially credit unions have significant volumes of notice deposits that can be withdrawn unpredictably. Credit unions' depositors in particular are not widely diversified, so they are more likely to have common payments patterns that could draw down all of their deposits at once (for example, withdrawal of funds at the end of the pay period by the workers in a town's main industrial plant).

The second reason for near-banks' holdings of liquid assets is that mortgage lending does involve the lender in the same sort of advance commitment that banks give to their line-of-credit borrowers. Mortgage borrowers planning to buy a house will normally seek a commitment from the lender six months or more before actually borrowing money on a mortgage loan, and the lender must come through once that commitment has been made. Large trust companies also make an implicit commitment once they have posted their term-deposit and mortgage-loan rates for all to see: that they will accept whatever creditworthy business comes through their door. Where mortgage lending business is referred to them by their subsidiary real estate sales divisions, the commitment is even stronger. It is not good long-term business strategy to turn away creditworthy customers.

Mortgage loan companies need fewer preparations for unexpected credit demands. Many of them buy their mortgages in blocks on the secondary market or from a parent bank, so they can just delay such purchases if they are short of cash. Such companies have no liquidity problem at all from their mortgage business.

Finance companies also do the bulk of their business by taking over blocks of debts of other, "originating" lenders, such as appliance dealers and wholesalers, and can vary the timing of their lending without much cost. Finance companies' deposits are all fixed-term and nonredeemable in advance, so their debts do not cause a liquidity problem either.

The near-banks' lines of defence against liquidity risk are roughly similar to those of the banks, but each is used to a greater or lesser extent:

1. All cash reserves held are usable, since there are no cash reserve requirements for any of the near-banks in table 12–1. Cash reserve holdings are very large for credit unions and trust companies, and even for mortgage loan companies, given that their entire holding is usable. Cash reserves are far larger, for instance, than the 0.04 percent of assets typically held by banks as excess cash reserves. Because all credit union locals hold reserves with their central, the central's deposit totals are likely to be volatile. The central therefore has a special need for large cash reserves.
2. Credit union locals and caisses populaires can and do borrow from their central. Other near-banks can and do borrow from chartered banks.
3. Near-banks hold large stocks of liquid assets. Term deposits held by credit union centrals in banks are redeemable or resalable in money markets, so these deposits plus short-term bills and notes constitute a liquid-asset reserve equal to almost one-third of the typical central's total assets. Local credit unions' term deposits in their central are less liquid, which explains the locals' huge cash reserves. Trust companies have both huge cash reserves and large liquid-asset holdings. For trust companies incorporated in Ontario, much of the liquid-asset holding reflects the legal requirement that liquid assets total at least 20 percent of deposits. Credit union locals too have liquid-asset requirements in various provinces.
4. Finance companies maintain ready access to money markets, in order to be able to borrow back liquidity lost through sudden loan demand. This is the main liquidity strategy of finance companies, most of whose funds come from regular issues of sales finance paper to money markets. This strategy accounts for the tiny cash reserves held by finance companies.

SECTION 3 Liability management

The liability-management problem is one of arranging low debt costs and of matching the volatility of asset yield and debt costs. Both mortgage loan yields and consumer credit yields are relatively stable; they change less, and more slowly, than money-market yields. Only the credit union centrals have a significant volume of short-term assets with volatile yields. We expect near-banks, in order to minimize risk to shareholders, to have debt portfolios whose yields have the same flexibility as their asset yields. If that is not available, we expect near-banks to have a much lower leverage ratio than banks, or much higher expected yield on equity to compensate (or both). If neither is available, we expect near-banks to leave the industry and become banks instead.

Table 12–3 shows how near-banks actually finance their assets. The debt types used by near-banks are also used to some extent by chartered banks and were explained in chapter 11.

Each near-bank group differs significantly from the others in its strategy for choosing types of debt to issue. Near-banks generally borrow for intermediate terms roughly coincident with the term of their assets, but the coincidence or matching is not as close as banks'. Table 12–4 crudely

TABLE 12–3 Liability proportions of near-banks, December 1981 (percentage of total assets)

Liability type	Credit unions: Locals	Credit unions: Centrals	Trust companies	Mortgage loan companies	Finance companies
Demand deposits					
chequable	12.2	38.1	4.1	0.3	0
nonchequable	28.2	0	16.3	2.2	0
Term deposits					
less than 1 year		24.7	14.0	5.9	0
1 to 5 years		15.8	40.4	50.6	0
more than 5 years		0	0.5	4.0	0
tax shelter deposits		0	14.0	0.2	0
Total term deposits	43.1	40.5	68.8	60.6	0
Notes payable					
less than 1 year	—	6.3 (both)	0	4.2	25.0
other	—		0	10.3	31.6
Loans					
from banks	0.2	0.9	0.2	3.9	9.8
from affiliates	2.1	0	0	0	15.6
from others	0.6	1.9	0.3	0	0
Other liabilities					
short-term	2.9	2.1	4.5	3.6	1.7
long-term	0	2.9	1.2	7.3	0.1
TOTAL LIABILITIES	89.2	92.8	95.5	92.3	83.9
Equity and reserves	8.3	7.2	4.6	7.7	16.1
Debt:equity ratio	8:1	13:1	21:1	12:1	5:1

Source: Statistics Canada, *Financial Institutions*, Cat. 61–006, Fourth Quarter 1981.

classifies assets and debts by how long their yields are fixed, as we did in chapter 11 for banks. Cash and demand deposits have constant yields as a rule (except for the interest-bearing demand deposits of credit unions and credit union centrals). Short-term liquid assets have yields that change quickly enough to be considered floating. Term deposits, loans, and mortgages have yields fixed for terms varying from a few months to a few years. Long-term bonds, nonresidential mortgages, and financial leases all have yields fixed for long terms. Stocks and investments in subsidiaries have yields that are not fixed but that also do not move in unison with financial-market interest rates, so they have been dumped into the constant-yield category.

The category of assets and debts with yields fixed for "short and medium terms" is particularly crude. There is room for significant mismatching of interest patterns within this category even if totals for assets and debts are identical for the group as a whole. We will look at the matching (or mismatching) patterns of each group of near-banks separately.

Credit union locals

Credit union locals have a large mismatch in floating-rate notice deposits. Notice-deposit rates in credit union locals do not vary as sensitively with money-market yields as do notice-deposit rates in chartered banks, but still

TABLE 12–4 Matching of yield volatilities by near-banks (percentage of assets or debts)

Yield pattern	Credit unions		Trust companies	Mortgage loan companies	Finance companies
	Locals	Centrals			
Constant or independently varying yields					
assets	4	18	10	8	6
debts	12	4	4	0.3	0
Floating yields					
assets	10	9	5	1	0
debts	28	34	16	2	25
Yields fixed for short to medium terms					
assets	71	41	65	78	81
debts	49	52	74	78	58
Yields fixed for long terms					
assets	14	32	20	13	13
debts	0	3	2	11	0

Source: Statistics Canada, *Financial Institutions*, Cat. 61–006, Fourth Quarter 1981.

they change faster than the bulk of credit union locals' asset yields. What saves the credit unions from the consequences of their mismatching is their co-operative nature. Since a credit union's creditors and debtors are also its owners, it is not possible for "owners" to bear risk separately from its creditors and debtors. Each year the credit union sets its loan rates and deposit rates to produce a surplus and then rebates the surplus pro rata to depositors and loan customers at the end of the year. The prospect of a year-end bonus keeps depositors content even when competing yields rise elsewhere, so the credit unions can adjust their notice-deposit rates more slowly.

There is an asymmetry in credit unions, in that debtors and creditors are not assessed in event of a deficit, while the system of floating deposit costs and pegged asset yields makes deficits inevitable when interest rates vary as much as they did in the late 1970s and early 1980s. Better-managed credit unions have arranged for their mortgage and loan rates to float, to get around that risk. Other credit unions merely try to build up large surplus as a cushion to draw on when deficits occur. Nevertheless, a number of credit unions fail each year.

Credit union centrals

Credit union centrals have a large mismatch of assets and liabilities in the long-term part of their portfolio. There is very little long-term debt to match long-term bond holdings. Table 12–4 also shows a large excess of floating-rate debt not financing floating-rate assets. The floating-rate debt is demand deposits held by member locals, however. The centrals can adjust the interest rate paid on those demand deposits to match what is earned on their other assets, without any danger of losing large volumes of business from their member locals.

Trust companies

Trust companies have some of the same mismatches as credit union centrals, in long-term assets and debts. Trust companies have a large block of floating-rate debts invested in fixed-yield assets with long maturities. This position left trust companies with badly squeezed profits when interest rates rose in 1979–81. Despite the mismatch, trust company leverage ratios are high.[11]

---

[11]Trust companies have been subject to ceilings on their leverage ratio throughout their existence. The maximum leverage ratio has been steadily raised over time: from 5 in 1914 to 7 in 1931, 10 in 1947, 12.5 in 1958, 15 in 1965, 20 in 1970. Mintz reported actual leverage ratios of 10.5 in 1963 and 18.8 in 1973. *The Measure of Rates of Return in Canadian Banking* (Ottawa: Economic Council of Canada, 1979), 39. The maximum limit is likely to be eliminated or raised further in future revisions of federal trust company legislation.

Mortgage loan companies

Mortgage loan companies' assets and liabilities are less mismatched than those of trust companies, because mortgage loan companies do not rely on savings deposits as much for their borrowing. They also have only a small amount of medium-term assets financed by long-term debt. Despite this matching, mortgage loan companies' leverage is still relatively low. Part of the reason is that, although their term deposits are nonredeemable, their mortgages can often be repaid early. Sometimes there is a penalty of three months' interest, but often the mortgagor can partially repay the loan without incurring any penalty charge. If mortgage rates fall, a mortgage loan company can expect a rash of repayments of long-term mortgages and will find itself reinvesting at lower asset yields. With unchanged debt cost on its nonredeemable deposits, its yield spread will be badly squeezed.

Finance companies

Aside from problems of default risk on consumer debts, finance companies also have a mismatch of long-term assets financed by shorter-term debts. This mismatch subjects them to losses when interest rates rise, and gains when interest rates fall, as soon as their short-term debt costs are affected.

A more serious problem for finance companies is that their debt costs are sensitive to money-market yields while their asset yields are relatively insensitive. Their debts are wholesale, liquid, money-market instruments sold in public auction markets, while their assets are retail, illiquid, negotiated in private markets. Yields on the former adjust much more quickly than yields on the latter. For the finance companies' business, merely matching maturities is not enough to keep spreads stable. As a result, finance company debt-to-equity ratios are kept down to only 5:1.

A comparison of expected debt costs

Debt costs of near-banks vary widely with their different financing strategies. Some trust companies and all credit unions have tapped retail savings markets with a network of local offices. As a result, these intermediaries have high operating costs but low interest rates. Mortgage loan companies tap the more competitive and higher-cost term-deposit market, but they do so without extensive branch networks. Finance companies tap their parent firms, the banks, and the money market for funds.

The relative interest costs of these different financing strategies are shown in table 12–5. In 1981, the credit unions were raising funds over 2 percent more cheaply than the finance companies, and 1 percent more cheaply than banks. (A comparison with the retail deposit and lending business of the banks would certainly reveal much lower retail deposit rates for banks, but it is not possible to get such a breakdown of bank figures.) The extra margin on the cost of funds gives the credit unions substantial

TABLE 12–5 Debt costs of banks and near-banks, 1981

Institution	Interest costs as percentage of total debt	Salary costs as percentage of total assets
Credit unions and caisses populaires		
locals	11.0	1.7
centrals	11.4	1.2
Trust companies	11.6	1.8
Mortgage loan companies	10.5	0.4
Finance companies	13.2	1.4
Chartered banks	12.0	1.2

Note: The interest costs are quoted at annual rates and calculated as the ratio of total interest payments divided by end-of-period interest-bearing liabilities. Extra year-end bonus payments made on credit union deposits are excluded, but they represent only 0.3 percent of total interest paid by credit unions.

Source: Statistics Canada, *Financial Institutions*, Cat. 61–006, Fourth Quarter 1981.

leeway in lending and in management efficiency. Mortgage loan companies typically have longer-term debts than the other near-banks, so their average debt cost is relatively low during periods of rising interest rates; mortgage loan companies have more "old money" at "old money rates" than do the other near-banks. Of course, just the opposite happens during periods of falling interest rates. In periods of stable interest rates, mortgage loan company debt costs are usually higher than those of credit unions and banks.

In addition to explicit interest costs, there are implicit costs of providing records, branches, tellers, and so on, which are reflected in salary costs per dollar of liabilities. These costs are also shown in table 12–5 for 1981. Those near-banks that have extensive branch networks have much higher salary costs than the others. Trust companies and credit unions need the branches to collect deposit funds and to make retail personal and mortgage loans. Finance companies need the branches only to make (and collect) retail personal loans. Mortgage loan companies are in neither the retail deposit nor the retail lending business, so they have the lowest salary costs of all.

Near-bank performance

The result of different degrees of mismatching of assets and liabilities, different costs of funds, and different asset mixes is quite different performance of equity risk over time. The standard deviations of asset yields, debt costs, and equity yields are shown in table 12–6 for a sample of firms from each group over the second half of the 1970s. Credit union locals are excluded from table 12–6 because of the problem of distinguishing between equity and debt in a credit union.

The mortgage loan companies and trust companies had relatively stable asset yields, reflecting generally longer-term assets. They also had more stable debt costs. The big difference, however, is in the extent to which asset yields and debt costs moved together. Banks, as we saw in chapter 11, had very close correlation of asset yields and debt costs. Trust companies were close behind. Credit union centrals lagged far behind trust companies, and mortgage loan companies were behind them. Bringing up the rear were the finance companies, which had almost independent variations in asset and debt yields. The effect of correlation on equity risk is multiplied by the leverage ratio, as we discovered in chapter 10. The last two columns of table 12–6 show the final results for equity risk, both before tax and after tax.

Credit union centrals would have had very large risk except that they had low leverage. Banks, with high leverage, had a risk level only slightly above that of trust companies, despite the much more stable yield pattern of trust companies. Mortgage loan companies, with lower leverage than trust companies but similar lending business, had twice the equity risk because of their mismatching. Finance companies had the highest equity risk of all despite the smallest leverage of all.

Equity risks in table 12–6 are paired with the average equity yields reported for those firms over the late 1970s and plotted as points in a portfolio-choice diagram in figure 12–1.

Finance companies fared worst and mortgage loan companies next worst. Banks and a sample of industrial corporations were about equal

TABLE 12–6 Analysis of near-bank equity risk

	Asset risk	Debt risk	Correlation coefficient	Leverage ratio	Equity risk Before tax	Equity risk After tax
Eight trust companies 1975–80	0.5	0.6	0.94	19.7	3.3	1.9
Nine mortgage loan companies 1975–79	0.6	0.5	0.64	16.3	7.1	4.2
Nine finance companies 1975–79	1.8	1.4	0.39	5.7	7.1	5.3
Six credit union centrals 1975–79	1.4	1.6	0.77	7.6	2.8	2.8
Ten chartered banks	2.0	2.3	0.997	24.9	5.1	3.9

Sources: Bank of Canada Review; Ontario Registrar of Trust and Loan Companies, *Report*; *Financial Post Record Service*; company annual reports.

despite huge differences in leverage. Trust company shareholders received one-third less yield than bank shareholders, and trust company shareholders had only half the yield volatility from their shares.

The picture in figure 12–1 suggests that, if these trends were to continue over time, finance companies would leave their sector of the financial industry, while more banks and trust companies would be formed. Alternatively, finance companies would shed their skin and become either trust companies or banks. All these predictions have been realized. I have already described the influx of new chartered banks. On the other side, the finance company IAC Ltd. converted itself into Continental Bank. The next-largest finance company is in the process of converting itself essentially into a trust company: Traders Group has closed half of its three hundred branches and has shifted the bulk of its business to its trust company subsidiary, Guaranty Trust. Household Finance and Avco Financial Services have both set up their own trust company subsidiaries. All the large finance companies have shifted aggressively into financial leasing.

Figure 12–2 supports this anecdotal evidence with the longer-term growth paths of various types of institutions since 1953.

FIGURE 12–1 Risk and yield for near-bank shareholders, 1975–80

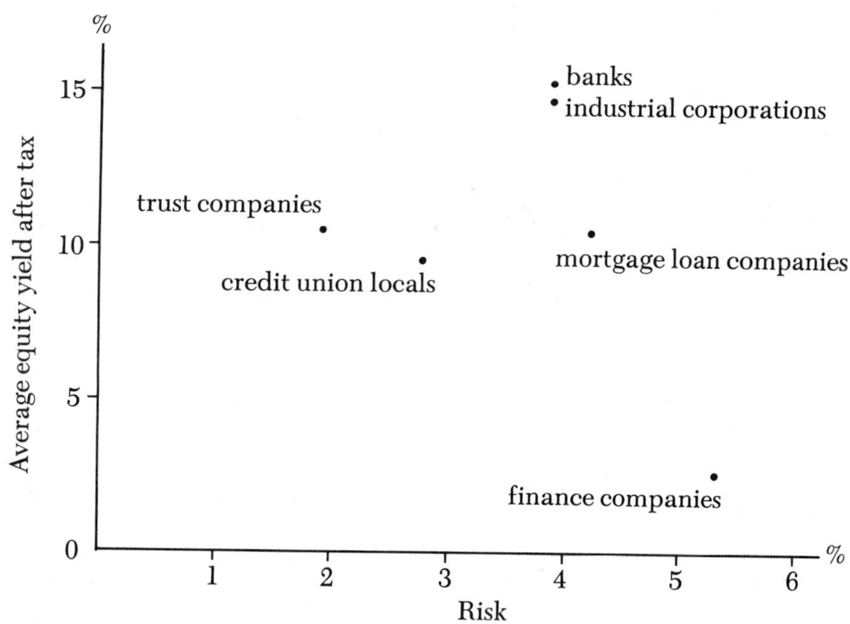

Risk is the standard deviation of after-tax yield on equity over the sample period, averaged over all companies in the group sample. The points represent the combinations of risk and average equity yield experienced by owners of selected near-banks over the period 1975–80.

FIGURE 12–2 Growth of financial intermediaries, 1954–82

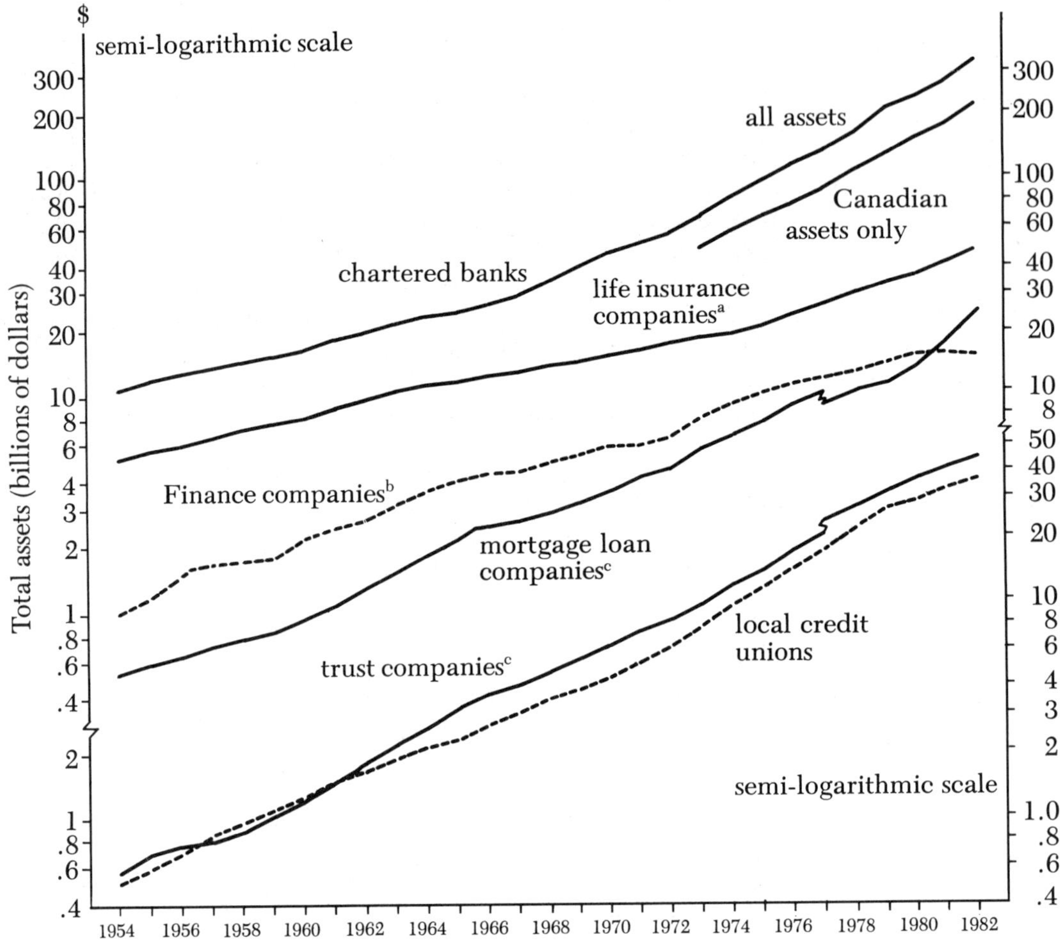

[a]Canadian business only; excludes segregated-funds business.
[b]Includes wholly owned acceptance subsidiaries of merchandisers and manufacturers as of third quarter 1972.
[c]Large change in first quarter 1977 due to a consolidation.

On a semi-logarithmic graph such as this, a faster rate of growth implies a steeper line, regardless of the size of total assets.

Source: Statistics Canada, *Financial Institutions*, Cat. 61–006, Fourth Quarter 1981.

The relative success of banks in the late 1970s is a recent phenomenon, prevented before 1968 by the 6 percent interest ceiling on bank loans and therefore on bank deposits. As soon as that ceiling was removed, banks surged ahead. Profits on bank lending precipitated an invasion of a hundred or so foreign bank subsidiaries. The subsidiaries operated in Canada under provincial company legislation instead of the Bank Act and made large business loans with money raised in the Canadian money market. If foreign bank subsidiaries' business were added to the chartered banks' growth path, it would be even steeper than in figure 12–2.

From the late 1950s to 1967, when banks were held down by the legal interest ceiling, all near-banks had a field day. Growth of both finance companies and mortgage loan companies was stopped in 1965 by the failure of Atlantic Acceptance and British Mortgage and Trust Co., and both groups suffered after banks were free to compete in 1967. Trust companies and credit unions have maintained their growth into the 1980s, spreading more and more into the banks' retail deposit business and coming closer to being banks.

The rapid growth of mortgage loan companies after 1979 is mainly the result of the chartered banks' setting up mortgage loan company subsidiaries and funnelling the banks' mortgage lending business into them, as we discussed in chapter 11.

SECTION 4 Near-banks and the financial system

Near-banks as a group are as important as banks in tying different financial markets together by the force of arbitrage (shifting their demand from one market to another in response to changes in relative yields). Individual types of near-bank are much more specialized in their investments than chartered banks, but each type bridges one or more pairs of markets. For instance, credit union centrals, trust companies, and mortgage loan companies have significant holdings of money-market assets and bonds, as well as mortgages. Credit union locals have large holdings of short- and long-term retail loans in their consumer and mortgage loan business. Finance companies have a mix of second mortgages and financial leases, of consumer debts and business accounts receivable. All these firms span two or more markets, so their shifting of demand from one to the other keeps relative yields more in line than they would otherwise be.

Near-banks also have much larger and more flexible cushions of liquid assets than do the chartered banks. An increased inflow of funds into near-bank deposits of a particular type would therefore be more likely to cause an increase in the near-banks' liquid-asset holdings. Later on, the near-banks would lower their lending rates on the matching type of loan (matching the type of deposit receiving the inflow) in order to adjust their lending to their deposit intake. Many near-banks are small enough that they take lending rates as given, but their activity puts more pressure on the price-setting firms to change their rates.

Near-bank debts are not as tied to particular assets as are banks' debts — though near-banks have suffered from this mismatch recently, and some are revising their matching strategy. With looser matching of assets and debts, greater demand for one type of debt will cause greater demand and lower yields for a wider range of assets than otherwise. The same logic means that near-banks are more likely to shift their sources of funds around between types of debt, without any change in the assets to be financed. Finance companies may shift between money-market paper and bank loans, mortgage loan companies between two- and five-year term deposits, and so on. All this shifting helps to keep relative yields in line (although it does not guarantee that result) and makes financial markets less segmented into insulated compartments.

Near-banks and the transmission of monetary-policy effects

Near-banks are not vehicles of monetary policy, because they are not required to hold a minimum amount of cash reserves with the Bank of Canada. They generally hold only demand deposits, in chartered banks or credit union centrals. Only near-banks that are members of the Canadian Payments Association and that want their cheques cleared directly rather than through another member will need to keep clearing balances in a deposit with the Bank of Canada; some of the larger trust companies and the two national credit union centrals fall into this camp.

Near-banks are part of the monetary-policy transmission process, though. It is useful to sketch the likely impact on and response of near-banks to the monetary-policy action introduced at the end of chapter 11, an increase in chartered banks' cash reserves. The immediate effects are an increase in demand for money-market assets by banks (which lowers yields in the money market) and an increase in the amount of demand deposits held by other money-market participants (either because the other participants have sold off assets to banks or because they are issuing more money-market debts).

Near-banks are likely to be affected in two ways. They may be sellers of some of the money-market assets that banks are buying, and therefore find themselves with more cash and demand deposits. Even if they are not the sellers referred to above, lower money-market yields and extra demand deposits held by other investors will cause greater demand for near-banks' term deposits. Either the flow of funds into term deposits of credit unions, trust companies, and mortgage loan companies will increase, or else their cost of funds will fall. The choice depends only on whether near-banks' term-deposit interest rates stay fixed or not. For finance companies borrowing in the money market, with its sensitively adjusting yields, the cost of funds will certainly fall. Either way, near-banks will expand their intermediation business by advertising more, by lowering interest rates on mortgage and other loans, and by screening loan applications less stringently. Some of the retail loan rates are fairly sticky — especially those on consumer credit — so consumer lending business will be expanded more by advertising or by offers of longer repayment terms than by lower loan charges.

Where trust companies and mortgage loan companies in particular cannot drum up extra mortgage business by lowering yields, which is often the case, they will use the extra funds to buy marketable bonds and stocks, driving yields down in those markets.

Figure 12–3 is a causal-chain diagram summarizing the impact of monetary policy, working through near-banks, on relative expected yields in the financial system. In summary, the actions of near-banks spread the impact of monetary policy more widely than banks alone would spread it, especially to mortgage markets and therefore to demand for housing. Near-banks also provide competition for banks in the term-deposit business, forcing those yields to change more quickly when demand for them shifts.

A theory popular in the early 1960s was that the growing presence of near-banks would undermine monetary policy because near-banks' debts would be too easily substitutable for bank demand deposits. The effect of greater demand-deposit issue by banks would be to shift demand to near-bank term deposits, but it was argued that little drop in term-deposit

FIGURE 12–3 Effects of monetary policy on and through near-banks

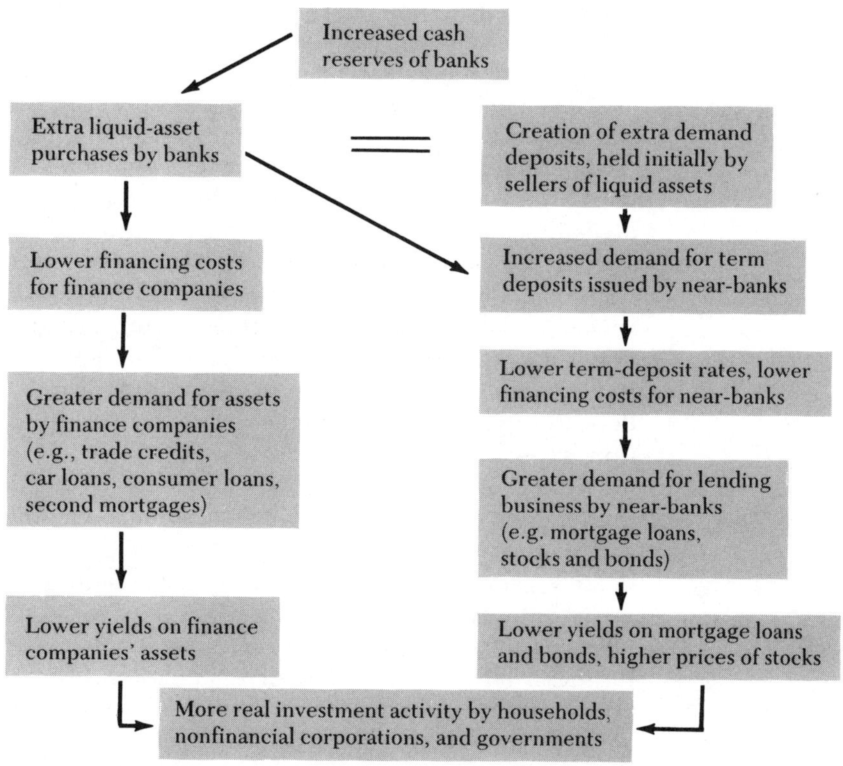

yields would be needed to persuade the public to hold onto the extra demand deposits instead. With little drop in their term-deposit yields, near-banks would lower their mortgage interest rates very little, if at all. The impact of monetary policy on housing markets would be small.

In fact, near-bank deposits are almost all close substitutes for bank term deposits, but not for bank demand deposits. The growth of near-banks has not (so far) prevented the central bank from pushing interest rates sharply in either direction. The concern of the early 1960s seems to have been misplaced.

SECTION 5 Summary

Near-banks are generally engaged in slightly longer-term intermediation than banks. Credit unions do a retail banking business, with emphasis on consumer loans and mortgages rather than business loans. Trust companies and mortgage loan companies emphasize residential mortgage lending. Finance companies specialize in unsecured consumer loans, second mortgage loans, and consumer and trade credit taken over from merchants and producers. Some finance companies have been spreading into longer-term business also, with financial leasing. Near-banks finance their lending partly with retail notice and chequing deposits but mainly with term deposits. Finance companies are the exception, relying instead on money-market paper, bank loans, and long-term credit from parent firms.

Near-banks are specialized partly because of law (which keeps trust companies and mortgage loan companies out of any significant volume of commercial lending, and all but trust companies out of trustee business), partly because of scale (credit unions must be local, and therefore can't diversify commercial loans), and partly because of ownership (many mortgage loan companies are owned by banks and therefore do not compete with banks in demand-deposit business). Near-banks are becoming less specialized over time, and existing barriers are gradually being removed. For instance, federally chartered trust companies are likely to have both the prohibition on commercial lending and the ceiling on their debt-to-equity ratio removed in the next revision of trust company legislation, expected in 1984.

Risk problems vary widely across near-banks. Trust companies and mortgage loan companies do little unsecured lending, while credit unions and finance companies do a lot. Mortgage loans can be insured against default risk, but consumer loans cannot. Liquidity risk is less serious for near-banks as a rule, because repayments are more scheduled, there are fewer demand and notice deposits, and there is little line-of-credit lending business. There is much less diversification across customers, however, so credit unions and trust companies both keep large liquid-asset balances.

Relative to banks, near-banks do much less matching of assets and debt types, with the result that their equity risk is much larger for a given degree of leverage. This risk is compensated for by lower leverage levels, but even with less than one-quarter the leverage, finance companies have more volatile equity yields than banks.

The major near-banks are relatively specialized individually, but collectively they connect several different credit markets, and their shifting from one to the other when relative yields change helps to keep yields in line and to spread yield changes from one market to the others. Near-banks therefore contribute to monetary policy by spreading yield changes from the money market to the rest of the financial system — especially to mortgage lending and term-deposit markets.

Questions for discussion

1. What legal barriers are there to prevent trust companies from competing with banks?
2. How different is the consolidated asset portfolio of all near-banks (together) from that of the chartered banks? the liability portfolio?
3. If near-banks compete with banks, can the banks be described as an oligopoly?
4. What is the point of a near-bank's arranging for life insurance on all personal loans?
5. What sort of liquidity problems do near-banks have? Do banks have the same liquidity problems?
6. Why does a mortgage loan company have a matching problem even when it finances a five-year mortgage with issue of five-year term deposits?
7. Why do finance companies have such high risk, with such low leverage?
8. Do the actions of near-banks cause interest rates in different markets to be held in a more stable structure, or do they cause greater volatility of relative yields? Explain.
9. If the purpose of monetary-policy actions is to influence the level of demand for real goods and services by bringing about changes in interest rates, is the presence of near-banks a help or a hindrance?

References

Binhammer, H.H., and Jane Williams. *Deposit-taking Institutions: Innovation and the Process of Change.* Ottawa: Economic Council of Canada, 1976.

Economic Council of Canada. *Efficiency and Regulation: A Study of Deposit-taking Institutions.* Ottawa: Supply and Services, 1976.

——. *Intervention and Efficiency.* Ottawa: Supply and Services, 1982.

Neufeld, E.P. *The Financial System of Canada.* Toronto: Macmillan, 1972.

Statistical Sources

Bank of Canada Review. Monthly.

Canada, Superintendent of Insurance. *Report on Co-operative Credit Associations.* Annual.

———. *Report on Trust and Loan Companies.* Annual.

Ontario, Minister of Consumer and Commercial Relations, Registrar of Loan and Trust Companies. *Report.* Annual.

Statistics Canada. *Credit Unions.* Quarterly.

———. *Financial Institutions.* Quarterly.

CHAPTER 13

Long-Term Intermediaries

This is the third of three chapters on asset and debt choices of groups of financial intermediaries. Chapter 11 discussed the choices of chartered banks; chapter 12, the choices of near-banks. Both banks and near-banks have short-term liabilities. In this chapter we look at two groups of institutions with long-term debts — life insurance companies and pension funds. Life insurance companies have been important in the Canadian financial system throughout the last century, whereas the pension funds have become important only since 1960. Life insurers and pension funds are the major long-term lenders in the Canadian financial system, so they are important to all who want to finance long-term assets.

Two major features distinguish life insurers and pension funds from banks and near-banks. The first is the long-term nature of the former's liabilities. The second is the lack, in many insurance companies and all pension funds, of shareholders on whose behalf management must be concerned about equity risk. These firms are essentially co-operatives, owned by their creditors and therefore managed for the benefit of their creditors. We will see that this second feature has a marked effect on asset-choice behavior.

The organization of this chapter is similar to that of chapter 12. You will learn about the following features of life insurers and pension funds:

1. their legal structure and the exact nature of their intermediation between primary borrowers and primary lenders,
2. how they manage their asset portfolios,
3. the constraints imposed by their liabilities, and
4. their place in financial markets and in the transmission of monetary policy.

SECTION 1

Legal structure

Increasingly, the life insurance and pension sectors overlap. In the past, life insurers sold mainly insurance policies paying a lump sum on death of the insured. Now over half of the insurance companies' revenues each year come from the sale of *annuities* (contracts providing for a regular stream of payments in the future, usually during retirement). Group annuities sold by life insurers are one of two main forms of employee pension-funding arrangement. However, the life insurance and pension sectors are still separate sectors, operating under different laws and supervised by different government agencies.

Annuities

Life insurance

There are two dozen large firms and a large fringe of smaller companies selling life insurance products in Canada. Even giant Sun Life has only a small share of the Canadian market. There have been few legal entry barriers since federal charters were made available by letters patent in 1970. There are many types of life insurance companies: domestic and foreign; stock (stockholder-owned) and mutual (policyholder-owned) and fraternal benefit societies (for members of a fraternal order); federally and provincially registered. The bulk of the insurance business done in Canada is done by federally registered, domestic companies. Over half of the total business of federally registered companies is done by *mutual insurance companies*.

Mutual insurance companies

Life insurance companies are subject to some restrictions, most of them minor. Companies can hold only 30 percent of the voting stock of an unrelated company. Total stocks held by a life insurance company cannot exceed 25 percent of its total assets.[1] Companies are inspected annually by the Superintendent of Insurance of the government (federal or provincial) with which they are registered. They pay a 2 percent tax on all *premiums* collected in most provinces (in lieu of sales tax, it is argued). All the companies, whether federally or provincially registered, are subject to provincial regulations on contract provisions (what the contract must specify) and agent licensing (what training and backing each agent must have). Companies can and do set up subsidiaries to provide many services, including real estate and mutual-fund management. Foreign insurance companies are required to keep assets in Canada equal to their liabilities, but otherwise they are as free as Canadian firms.

Premiums

[1]This restriction was added only after Sun Life found itself in difficulties in the 1930s (the company held 58 percent of its assets in common stock on the eve of the Depression). Since then, no company has had even close to 25 percent of its assets in stocks, so this restriction does not constrain insurers much.

The two main products issued by life insurance companies are life annuities and life insurance policies.

Annuities

Figure 13–1 shows a typical timepath of financial flows for an annuity policy: the flows consist of contributions by the policyholder, benefit payments by the insurance company, and asset accumulation in the policyholder's account. The amounts shown are in current dollars, unadjusted for any inflation. The policy is taken out when the policyholder is forty-five; monthly annuity payments to the policyholder start at age sixty-five and continue as long as either the policyholder or the spouse lives. Figure 13–1 is based on the assumption that at least one of them lives until the policyholder's eighty-second year.

FIGURE 13–1 Financial pattern of an annuity policy

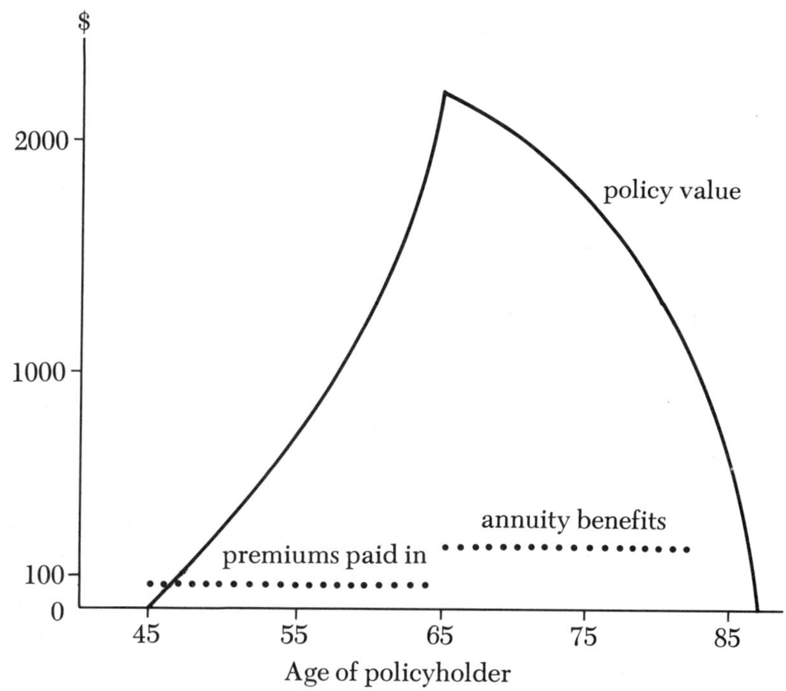

Premiums or annuity considerations are paid into this policy starting at age 45. The annuity benefits start at age 65 and continue for life (expected to last to age 82). The policy value increases to age 65 with compounding of premiums and any dividends (on participating policies) and thereafter declines at an increasing rate.

The annuity policy's accumulated value rises as annuity policy premiums are paid in, from age forty-five to age sixty-five. Compound interest on accumulated contributions causes the value to rise more rapidly in the later years. When the policyholder turns sixty-five and the annuity benefit payments start, the policy's asset value starts to fall. The annuity benefit payments are a constant amount but are made up of a changing mix of interest earnings and principal repayment. Initially, while the accumulated asset value is still large, most of the annuity payment consists of interest; the policy value is eaten into very little. As the principal continues to shrink in future years, so do the interest earnings; the amount of principal repayment in each annuity payment rises, and the principal shrinks faster. For the average annuity policy, the asset value of the policy will be exactly zero at the end.

Lump sum, immediate annuity

There are many variations of annuity policy. The *lump sum, immediate annuity* is probably the most common. This policy involves the purchase of a stream of annuity payments for life, starting immediately and paid for with a single payment. This policy is very common because many savers use it to convert Registered Retirement Savings Plan (RRSP) funds into a stream of retirement income. The tax laws that govern RRSPs allow continued tax deferral after age seventy-one only if the funds are put into either a life annuity or another, roughly similar instrument issued by trust companies.[2]

Life insurance policies

Permanent insurance

Life insurance is usually provided by either permanent or term insurance policies. *Permanent insurance* policies are designed to provide insurance coverage at a fixed level for life, with a pattern of premium payments usually set at a fixed level either for life or for some shorter period such as to age sixty-five. Permanent insurance policies give rise to important savings accumulation and thus involve the insurance companies in financial intermediation.

Term insurance

Term insurance policies, by contrast, are designed to provide insurance coverage only for one to five years at a time; for each successive period, the premium rises to reflect the increasing mortality risk of those in the next older age group. All of the term insurance premium is used to provide current insurance protection and company profit, so there is no savings accumulation by the policyholder in term insurance policies. Term insurance business therefore does not involve significant financial intermediation by the insurance company — merely redistribution of income from survivors to the estates of those deceased during the term insured.

---

[2]Between the sixtieth and seventy-first birthdays of contributors to an RRSP, the proceeds must be put in one or more of (a) a life annuity, (b) an increasing life annuity (whose payments increase each year either at 4 percent or in line with some price index), (c) a straight annuity payable for thirty years to the policyholder or the policyholder's estate, or (d) a registered retirement income fund (RRIF), which provides an increasing stream of income to age ninety. Proceeds not put in one of these instruments become taxable as regular personal income, in the year they are withdrawn from the RRSP.

FIGURE 13–2 Financial patterns of a whole life insurance policy

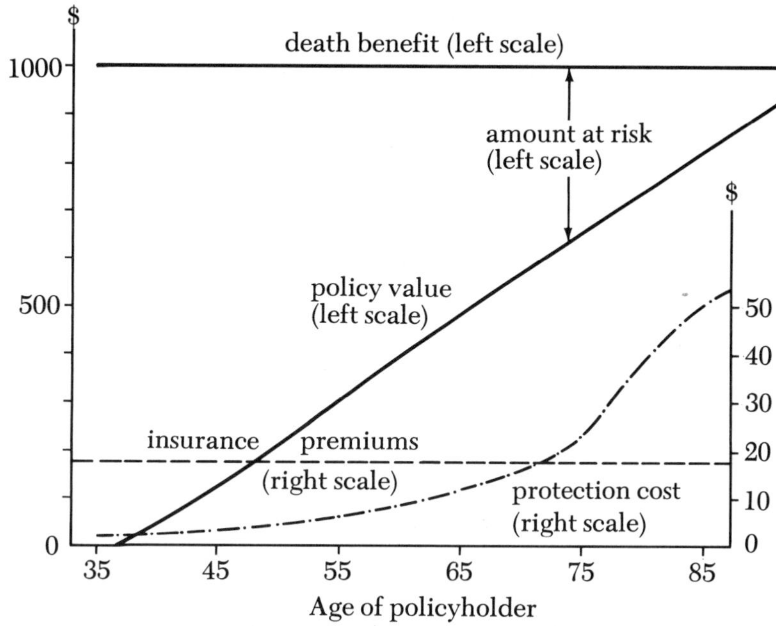

The policy is for $1000 of insurance protection. Premiums are payable for life. Each year any surplus of premium over cost of protection (net of investment earnings on policy value) is added to the policy value, or policy reserve. The amount at risk, which must be paid out of current premiums of all policyholders, is the difference between the death benefit and the deceased policyholder's policy value. Cost of protection rises, but its rate of increase is slowed by the decrease, with age, in amount at risk. Figures are approximate.

Recently many companies have mixed features of both permanent and term insurance in a type of policy known as universal life insurance, whose popularity is growing rapidly.

Figure 13–2 shows the pattern of financial flows for a typical permanent life insurance policy that is sold to Sarah Brown when she is thirty-five. The policy calls for premium payments to be made for life, so this is a *whole life* policy. Brown holds it until death, which she feels will be at age eighty-two. In each year until then, part of her insurance premium is used to cover operating costs and the cost of insurance protection to the whole group of policyholders. The rest is added to the policy's asset value (called the *policy reserve* by the insurance company).

Policy reserve

Cost of insurance protection

The *cost of insurance protection* in any year comes from the risk-pooling feature that underlies all insurance: all policyholders pay a little toward the large death benefits received by (the estates of) the few policyholders who die in each year. The total amount to be paid by the surviving policyholders is the total of death benefits paid less the amount of policy reserve accumulated by those who died. The cost of protection for Brown is pulled two ways as she and her cohort of policyholders grows older: on the one hand, an increasing proportion of the remaining policyholders dies each year, so there are more death benefits to be paid; on the other hand, each of those who die has a larger accumulated policy value, so there is less of each death benefit to be made up by surviving policyholders.[3]

In the early years of Brown's policy, her premiums are large enough to leave a surplus after operating costs and protection costs. Later on, those premiums need to be supplemented by earnings on Brown's accumulated policy reserve.

Almost 90 percent of life insurance policies (but none of the individual annuity policies) have the added feature of being participating policies.

Participating policies

Participating policies are eligible to receive a rebate of part of the premium paid if the actual cost of protection or the investment earnings or the operating costs are better than was anticipated when the premiums were set.

Policy dividend

The rebate is known as a *policy dividend* and can be received as an offset against future premiums, in cash, as credit to a deposit with the insurance company, or in the form of extra insurance coverage. The participating feature has a big impact on the risk exposure of life insurance company shareholders, a point we will return to in section 3.

Pension Funds

The formal legal structure of pension funds is fairly simple. A pension fund is not a financial intermediary itself because it is not an independent legal entity. It is just a trust fund, with trustees and managers, containing the contributions of employees or employer or government (depending on the fund), which are used to buy a life annuity for beneficiaries at retirement. Unless the pension fund manager is the federal government or an insurance company, pension funds are supervised by provincial pension commissions. Only a 1951 constitutional amendment allowed the federal government into the pension field, but now the federal government has a powerful influence over the sector with its Pension Benefits Standards Act.

The provinces regulate employer-sponsored pension funds. The regulations generally restrict asset holdings to those that trust companies and insurance companies are permitted to hold. This means deposits, secured loans, mortgage loans, bonds, and stocks of companies with established earnings records. Pension funds are allowed to hold limited amounts of other assets (to between 7 and 10 percent of total assets, depending on the province) under so-called basket clauses in their legislation. Provincial regulations contain solvency, or *funding*, provisions to ensure that accumu-

[3]When the policyholder reaches age ninety-six, the accumulated asset value of a whole life policy is exactly equal to the death benefit, so there is no remaining amount to be paid by surviving, ninety-six-year-old policyholders, regardless of their mortality rate. There are not many who survive to ninety-seven, so that is just as well.

lated assets plus future contributions will be sufficient to meet future commitments of the pension plan sponsor to the pension fund's beneficiaries. Pension funds take several distinct forms.

Canada Pension Plan and Quebec Pension Plan

Enrolment in these is mandatory for all full-time paid workers. The plans receive contributions by employee and employer in the amount of 3.6 percent of earnings, up to a maximum contribution of $529 in 1981. The plans promise a pension at sixty-five of up to 25 percent of the average industrial wage being paid at the time.

The plans are not just financial intermediaries, since the contributors do not get out just what they put in, even with accrued interest. The contribution rate is such that the inflow and accrued interest will not be enough to provide for all of the outflow of pension payments after about 1995, so the accumulated fund will be run down. After the fund is exhausted, the shortfall will have to be met out of extra taxes on working Canadians; the Canada Pension Plan and the Quebec Pension Plan therefore include a substantial measure of intergenerational transfer that is not present in the other financial intermediaries we discuss.

Canada Pension Plan
Quebec Pension Plan

Government consolidated-revenue funds

Employees in the public service, the Armed Forces, and some Crown corporations contribute to these funds, but their contributions are put

TABLE 13–1 Size of pension plans in Canada, March 1982 (billions of dollars)

Government consolidated revenue funds	
federal public service pensions	14.8
Armed Forces, RCMP, and MPs' pensions	13.3
Canada Pension Plan	21.6
Quebec Pension Plan	8.0
Insured plans[a]	23.7
Trusteed plans	
federal	5.2
provincial	10.0
municipal	15.3
corporate	31.5
Registered Retirement Savings Plan funds[b]	20.2

[a]Contains some Registered Retirement Savings Plan funds.
[b]Excludes the retirement savings plan funds included in the pension assets of the general life insurance business.

Source: Statistics Canada, *Financial Institutions*, Cat. 61–006, First Quarter 1982, table 129.

straight into the government's consolidated revenue and spent for general government purposes, rather than managed as a separate fund. This treatment of their contributions is similar to that given to deposits in the Province of Ontario Savings Offices, discussed in chapter 12.

Insured plans, trusteed plans, and combinations
Insured pension plans are group annuity plans offered or managed by insurance companies. Trusteed pension plans are managed by trust companies or by individual trustees. The individual trustees usually rely heavily on a specialized pension fund management company of some sort; many of these are subsidiaries of trust companies.

Table 13–1 shows the relative importance of various pension funds and other retirement savings vehicles as of March 1982, by volume of assets held. The trusteed plans generate the largest block of funds and tend to be larger than the insured plans.

Alternative sources of retirement income

Pension funds are only one source of retirement income. Because adequacy of retirement income is an important issue for this sector, the other sources are worth mentioning. The first is the set of universal state pensions paid out of tax revenues as a form of transfer payment, on a "pay as you go" basis. This includes old-age pensions under the Old Age Security (OAS) system (available since 1951); the Guaranteed Income Supplement (GIS) to old-age pensions for those below a given income level (available since 1966); and provincial supplements to the GIS that have been added in six provinces.[4]

The second alternative source of retirement income is individual retirement annuities. These are set up mainly as Registered Retirement Savings Plans (RRSPs), because of such plans' favorable tax status (to be discussed in chapter 15). RRSPs can be managed either by the individual or by some financial institution, though the funds must in all cases be administered by a trustee. RRSPs were first allowed in 1957 for the self-employed, to take the place of employer-sponsored plans. In the 1960s, employees were allowed to set up RRSPs, and the plans are now very popular. Federal government taxation statistics record that $15.1 billion was contributed to RRSPs between 1970 and 1979 — almost as much as total contributions to employee-sponsored pension plans and one and a half times as much as employee contributions to the Canada and Quebec Pension Plans over the same period.

The third alternative source of retirement income is other assets accumulated for retirement. These may include the family home, a family business, stocks, and savings deposits.

---

[4]The provinces are Nova Scotia and all others west of Quebec.

SECTION 2 Asset management

The Canada and Quebec Pension Plans need not detain us long in this section. The Canada Pension Plan (CPP) contributions are all invested in special nonmarketable provincial bonds that are distributed among the provinces according to a fixed formula. The bonds pay an interest rate that floats slightly above the Treasury Bill rate. This unusual arrangement is the result of Prime Minister Lester Pearson's negotiations with the provinces in the early 1960s, in order to allow federal intrusion into what is constitutionally a provincial area. The Quebec Pension Plan's funds are invested much more broadly by the Caisse de Dépôt et Placement, which holds significant quantities of corporate shares and corporate bonds as well as government bonds.

Segregated funds

Table 13–2 gives a breakdown of the assets held by life insurance companies and trusteed pension funds. Assets of life insurance companies are divided into regular assets and segregated-fund assets. The *segregated-funds* business of life insurance companies will be discussed more in

TABLE 13–2 Asset composition of life insurance companies and trusteed pension funds (percentage of total assets)

	Life insurance companies		
	Regular business	Segregated funds	Trusteed pension plans
Cash and demand deposits	0.5	3.8	3.5
Short-term bills and notes	2.3	13.6	4.8
Term deposits	0.9	0.7	0.6
Government of Canada bonds	6.4	10.9	9.2
Total liquid assets	10.1	29.0	18.2
Mortgages			
residential	21.4	7.3	9.9
nonresidential	17.3	12.0	
Bonds (excluding government of Canada)	28.6	16.0	33.7
Shares	6.0	31.9	27.9
Policy loans	6.2		
Income-producing real estate	5.4	2.0	1.1
Other assets	5.1	1.8	9.2
TOTAL ASSETS (MILLIONS OF DOLLARS)	$42 455	$7041	$53 958

Note: The data for life insurance companies and segregated funds are for 1981; the data for trusteed pension funds are for 1980.

Sources: Statistics Canada, *Financial Institutions*, Cat. 61–006, Fourth Quarter 1981; *Trusteed Pension Plans, Financial Statistics*, Cat. 74–201, 1980.

the section on liability management. Segregated-fund assets are those held against segregated-funds liabilities, which are specific kinds of life insurance and annuity policies with flexible benefits that do not involve the insurance company in fixed nominal commitments. Because of the lower risk to the insurance company, there are far fewer restrictions on the assets in which segregated funds can be invested, but the insurance company must keep the two kinds of business segregated in its accounts.

The major investment objective of both life insurance companies and pension funds is to prepare for claims a long time in the future, so it is not surprising that both portfolios have a large share of long-term assets. Many of the assets in table 13–2 are even longer-term than they look. Many of the government of Canada bonds in the liquid-asset category are long-term assets as well as liquid assets. Nonresidential mortgages often have interest rates fixed for long terms, unlike house mortgages, whose interest rates are renegotiable every five years or less. Income-producing real estate is often held under lease-back arrangements with long leases. Many of the corporate bonds bought by insurers and pension funds in private placements have the feature of being noncallable — that is, not repayable by the issuer before the stated maturity date.

The long-term asset portfolios of life insurance companies and pension funds present different risks from those of banks and near-banks. Partly this is because of the assets held, but partly it is because of the long holding period that life insurers and pension funds can count on.

Default risk

Neither life insurance companies nor pension funds need concern themselves much with default risk. Mortgages can be insured, policy loans are all secured by excellent collateral (the policy's own cash value), and the shares of stock these intermediaries hold are almost all in firms with five-year earnings records at least sufficient to pay a 4 percent dividend.[5]

Market risk

Market risk is not a serious risk for life insurance companies and pension funds. This is despite the high share of long-term assets in their portfolios and despite the fact that prices of long-term assets are generally more volatile than prices of short-term assets.[6] Each of these financial intermediaries has a relatively predictable holding period for its assets, since redemptions of its liabilities are much more predictable than for notice

---

[5]Under federal law, both pension funds and insurance companies may hold stocks not meeting that criterion only as part of basket-clause assets, whose total is limited to 7 percent of total assets.

[6]Short-term yields are about twice as volatile as long-term yields, but changes in short-term yields have much less effect on short-term bond prices than long-term yield changes do on long-term bond prices, so long-term bond prices are still much more volatile.

deposits of banks and near-banks. In addition, for growing insurance companies and pension funds the inflow of new premiums or pension contributions exceeds the outflow of insurance, annuity, and pension benefit payments, so there is a net cash inflow in all periods. Early sales of assets are therefore not needed to pay claims to beneficiaries. Fluctuating stock and bond values do create a problem for insurers and pension funds, though, and generate volatility of reported asset yields. In order to counteract market risk for assets that will generally be held to maturity and redeemed at par rather than sold off before then at an uncertain market price, insurance companies have special valuation rules that take account of market price changes only with a substantial lag, if at all.[7]

Income risk

Income risk is significant for stocks, for real estate properties, and for holdings of short-term assets that are rolled over into new short-term assets at maturity. For long-term bonds and mortgages, nominal yields are relatively fixed. Insurance companies are therefore not greatly concerned about income risk on their regular business. On their segregated-funds business and for the trusteed pension funds, the share of stocks is large enough that income risk is much larger; however, in both of those cases the income risk on the asset side of the balance sheet is well matched by similar fluctuations on the debt side of the balance sheet. We will return to this point in the next section.

Inflation risk

Inflation risk is high for fixed, long-term nominal yields, but lower for short-term yields, to the extent that expected inflation is reflected in nominal yields. In any case, neither life insurers nor pension funds have liabilities fixed in real terms; they need be concerned about inflation risk only if there is some other set of assets that promise better protection against inflation risk. In this respect the life insurers and pension funds are in the same boat as the banks and near-banks. The issue of protection against inflation risk is addressed more thoroughly in chapter 14.

---

[7]Life insurers have some choice in the matter, but they are required to include only the following in reporting their assets on the balance sheet: 10 percent of changes in market values of bonds and mortgages, and that only when the gap between book and market values is over $1\frac{1}{2}$ percent; less than one-third of current changes in market values of shares, plus the same proportion of changes over the previous two years; and all of the change in market value of real estate holdings. However, 7 percent of any difference between book and market value of shares is taken into income each year, to reflect the fact that shares need not, like bonds and mortgages, return to par at maturity. By contrast, realized losses on bonds actually sold can be taken into income gradually over twenty years. For further details, see Department of Insurance, *Report of the Superintendent of Insurance for Canada,* 1978, I, 39A–43A.

Liquidity risk

Life insurers and pension funds are exposed to liquidity risk because of the possibility of sudden large claims or redemptions. Such risk affects the assets of life insurance companies but is not serious for trusteed pension funds. Both generally have inflows of premiums or pension plan contributions each year greater than outflows of benefit payments, so they have a net cash inflow rather than outflow. Further, the contributions and payouts of pension funds are relatively predictable.

Pension funds have a small risk of unexpected outflows from two types of event. First, most pension funds will refund the total of a member's contributions if the member dies before retirement; such deaths are not very predictable even on average for the small groups involved in most pension plans. Second, an increasing number of pension plans will transfer a member's contributions to another pension plan if the member changes jobs; such "portability" is not common yet and is still not available until the member has accumulated a minimum number of years of service or a minimum age level, but where there is portability the pension fund is more uncertain about its cash outflows. Pension funds do not usually need to worry about members' withdrawing their funds in cash before retirement, since such withdrawals are fully taxable as income in the year of withdrawal unless the funds are promptly rolled over into another pension savings instrument of some sort.

Life insurance companies have a greater liquidity-risk problem than trusteed pension plans, for several reasons. First, they are liable to pay death benefits on insurance policies whenever the policyholder dies, and that is not closely predictable even for large companies. Second, insurers are liable to have policies surrendered for their cash value, and on a large scale. Table 13–3 shows that payments of surrender values were the largest type of payments made in 1979.

TABLE 13–3 Payments by life insurers (millions of dollars)

	Insurance business	Annuity business	Row total	Percentage of total payments
Death claims	1022	35	1057	32.9
Disability claims	53	1	54	1.7
Annuity payments	—	639	639	19.9
Maturity payments	84	—	84	2.6
Cash surrender values	546	837	1383	43.0
TOTAL	1705	1512	3217	100.0

Source: Department of Insurance, *Report of the Superintendent of Insurance for Canada* 1, 1979.

Third, life insurance companies try to prevent surrenders by offering policy loans. Policy loans are essentially collateral loans that use the accumulated savings value of the policy as collateral. They are offered at relatively low interest rates and are available automatically, as on a line of credit. Not surprisingly, there is likely to be a surge of borrowing by policy loans whenever debt costs rise on alternative sources of credit.[8] This borrowing adds to insurers' liquidity-risk problem just as borrowing against lines of credit does to banks'. Fourth, and finally, life insurers introduced a new type of insurance policy, universal life, in the 1970s. This kind of policy has a very flexible premium schedule, which means convenience for the policyholder but uncertainty about cash inflows for the insurer.

Life insurance companies take two main steps to reduce liquidity risk. One is to diversify their life insurance business across individuals and regions and occupations. Mortality risks are by and large independent, so diversification yields a big gain in predictability of death benefit payments. There is still significant variability left, though, especially for smaller companies. To diversify more broadly, insurance companies can sell off blocks of policies to reinsurance companies and buy different insurance from them — for a fee.

The second step taken by insurance companies to reduce liquidity risk is to reduce surrenders by (a) offering policy loans at the low rates appropriate for a fully secured loan (as mentioned two paragraphs ago) and (b) levying a penalty on early surrenders, like the partial interest penalty on early surrender of fixed-term deposits at a bank. Some insurance companies also try to screen new business as agents bring it in, in order to reduce business likely to be surrendered, and they offer special "persistency" bonuses to agents for business not surrendered after the first few years.

The third step to counter liquidity risk is to hold liquid assets that can be sold off quickly and without loss if need be. Both segregated funds and trusteed pension funds have larger shares of cash and liquid assets than can be explained as a precaution against their liquidity risk. Part of the explanation is that with net cash inflow each month there is a problem of where to put it all, so the inflow is temporarily held as cash. Part of the explanation is just Keynesian liquidity preference as described in chapter 9: these assetholders are holding cash and Treasury Bills because they expect a large fall in bond prices. Finally, the excess in liquid-asset holdings may well be a response to extra inflation risk of fixed-yield long bonds, a preference for a series of short yields more likely to be correlated with inflation (see chapter 14).

---

[8]Policy loans are not a large part of life insurers' asset portfolio, but they can absorb a large part of the flow of funds when alternative borrowing costs rise. In the last quarter of 1979 and the first quarter of 1980, as bank prime rates climbed to 15 and then to $17\frac{1}{2}$ percent, the net increase in policy loans absorbed first 10 and then 16 percent of the net Canadian investment of the sixteen largest life insurance companies.

SECTION 3

Liability management

Given the risks of an asset portfolio, the logic of liability management for a privately owned insurance company implies raising funds at low cost and matching asset risks where possible. Low-cost borrowing is less important for pension funds and mutual insurance companies than for stockholder-owned insurance companies. Minimizing risk to pension plan sponsors and to mutual policyholders' surplus is nevertheless an important objective.

To appreciate how risks are minimized, it is important to know a little more about the risks involved in pension and insurance liabilities.

Pension plan liabilities

For each pension plan one can calculate the present value of the expected future pension entitlements of beneficiaries and then subtract the present value of members' and employer's contributions still to be paid in. The net result is an actuarial valuation of the plan's liability. However, the fund itself and its trustees and managers are not responsible for that liability. It is the plan sponsor who is liable — an employer or the government, depending on the pension plan.

The pension plan sponsor's extra liability can be large. For the consolidated-revenue funds shown in table 13–1, there are no assets held by the plans; all of those pension fund liabilities are unfunded in a formal sense, though because the government may have invested the pension contributions in new roads or other capital infrastructure for the economy it could plausibly list those assets against the liability. For the Canada Pension Plan, the federal Department of Insurance calculated the net liability (over and above assets held) as $81.3 billion back in 1977, increasing at $7 billion per year. At that rate of increase, the net liability in 1983 is $123 billion, more than the combined assets of all the life insurers and trusteed pension plans in table 13–2.

By 1990 all private pension plan sponsors in Ontario are required to build up their pension fund assets to match the actuarial liability. This should prevent the buildup of large unfunded pension liabilities in the private sector.

Not all private pension plans generate fixed actuarial liabilities even for the plan sponsor. Defined-benefit plans do, but money-purchase plans do not, and most pension plans are money-purchase plans.

Defined-benefit pension plans

Defined-benefit pension plan

Under these plans, the size of pension benefits is specified in advance — usually as a percentage of each member's highest or final income during the years of membership. Such benefits vary with members' years of service and with their income levels, but not with the level of earnings on assets held by the pension fund. It is quite possible for the actuarial value of defined-benefit plans to vary independently of the asset value of the pension fund and therefore to cause changes in the net unfunded liability for the pension plan sponsor.

Money-purchase pension plans

Money-purchase pension plan

These do not specify pension benefits in advance of retirement. Instead, they promise only whatever life annuity stream can be purchased at retirement with the assets held in each member's account at that time. The value of each member's account is determined by multiplying the member's share of the total pension fund by the market value of the fund's total assets at the member's retirement date. We have already noted (in chapter 8) that this procedure for determining pensions leaves pension plan members exposed to substantial market risk. The other side of the coin is that it leaves pension plan sponsors completely unexposed. The pension plan liability is defined to be exactly the same as the pension plan's assets.

Mixed plans

There are many pension plans with both money-purchase and defined-benefit features. Many university pension plans, for instance, pay money-purchase pensions but have a defined-benefit floor tied to each member's years of service and final income level, below which money-purchase pensions are not allowed to go.

In table 13–1 pension plans are classified into insured and trusteed plans, according to whether they were managed by insurance companies or trustees. Both groups of pension plans contain defined-benefit and money-purchase pension plans. The money-purchase pension plans handled by insurance companies are usually called *deposit-administration plans*, or *segregated-funds plans*. Neither type exposes the insurance company to risk of unfunded liability should the asset values shrink unexpectedly. Such money-purchase pension plans account for about two-thirds of insurance companies' pension plan assets. The remaining third of the insured plans are group annuity contracts in which the insurance company itself promises specific annuities at retirement. Group annuity contracts are defined-benefit plans, which do expose the insurance company shareholders to risk: the actuarial liability to beneficiaries of group annuity contracts is determined independently of the accumulated value of plan members' contributions. If there is any shortfall when annuities must be paid, it is made up from shareholders' equity of the life insurance company (or from the company's surplus, for mutual companies).

Insurance company liabilities

Insurance company liabilities include liabilities for both their pension plan or life annuity business and their life insurance business. Table 13–4 gives a

TABLE 13–4 Liabilities and equity of life insurance companies in Canada, 1981

	Millions of dollars	Percentage of total
Liabilities		
actuarial reserve and outstanding claims	31 234	60.0
deposits	2 067	4.2
bank loans	404	0.8
staff benefit plan liability	594	1.1
long-term debt	204	0.4
owing parent and affiliated firms	35	0.1
other liabilities	2 164	4.2
TOTAL LIABILITIES	36 815	70.7
Equity and reserves		
capital and retained earnings	4 950	9.5
investment, contingency, and general reserves	3 080	5.9
TOTAL EQUITY AND RESERVES	8 030	15.4
Segregated-funds liabilities	7 253	13.9
TOTAL LIABILITIES AND EQUITY	52 098	100.0

Notes: The accident and sickness business of federally registered companies is excluded, as is the foreign business of all companies. Fraternal benefit societies and provincial companies are also excluded.

Source: Statistics Canada, *Financial Institutions*, Cat. 61–006, Fourth Quarter 1981.

breakdown of those liabilities and of the companies' equity, for their Canadian business.

Only three categories of table 13–4 need further explanation. First, the segregated-funds business of insurers (introduced in 1961) mixes regular insurance and annuity business with the properties of a mutual fund. The policyholders or annuitants are entitled to benefits, on death or retirement, whose value is determined by the holders' accumulated share of the segregated fund and by its market value at the time.[9] The value of segregated-funds liabilities is therefore by definition equal to the value of segregated-funds assets. The insurance company is not subject to risk on segregated-fund business.

Second, deposits are policy proceeds and policy dividends left with the company by policyholders. These deposits accumulate interest and are withdrawable on notice. No funds are solicited for such deposits except

[9]Each member's account is denominated in units, whose value is changed as the market value of the fund changes. Each member's share of the fund is calculated as simply the share of units in the total held by all members of the fund.

from the proceeds of policies (dividends or death benefits or annuity payments due from the company to the policyholders). Insurance companies do not try to sell their deposits to the general public the way that banks and near-banks do. They could, legally, but the extra liquidity risk would outweigh the benefits.

Actuarial reserve

Third, the *actuarial reserve* is the present value of expected future benefits to be paid out under existing insurance and annuity policies, less the present value of the expected future stream of contributions still to come from policyholders, net of operating costs to be paid out of those contributions. Both future benefits and future premiums are discounted to the present at the rate of return expected on invested funds. The actuarial reserve is the basis for calculating each policy's *cash surrender value* — the amount to be paid out to the policyholder if the policy is terminated and given back to the company.

Cash surrender value

Keeping liability costs down

Like borrowers in general, insurance companies can reduce the cost of borrowed funds by providing guarantees, flexibility, or liquidity to the lender. Nonparticipating insurance policies and annuities have fixed nominal benefits and fixed nominal premiums, both guaranteed over very long periods into the future. These two types of policy also include guaranteed borrowing privileges, at attractive interest rates, for up to 95 percent of the asset value of the policy; this is the policy loan provision. For policyholders who want out, the policies have a cash surrender privilege as well, more or less on demand.

Participating insurance policies have the same automatic borrowing privilege and cash surrender option as nonparticipating policies, but they have less of their future benefits guaranteed; more of the expected future benefits are provided instead by unguaranteed policy dividends.

In periods of rising interest rates, the value of the automatic borrowing privilege can be substantial whenever the borrowing rate is specified in the policy rather than (as is now the rule) adjusted periodically by the insurance company. Policyholders can borrow against their policy at the low interest rate, put the money even in short-term deposits at higher rates, and pocket the difference. The borrowing privilege thus allows the same outside investment possibilities as surrendering the policy completely, but the insurance protection is not cancelled and the policy value continues to grow within the company. It is not surprising that the number of policy loans outstanding grows rapidly whenever interest rates rise.

Still more flexibility is provided by the new universal life policies introduced in the late 1970s. For these policies, the amount and timing of premium payments is fully adjustable to suit the cash flow situation of the policyholder, and the amount of insurance can be changed as well.

Life insurers can suffer high costs if policies are cancelled early. The company incurs substantial costs for each policy right at the start — to set up its records and to pay sales commissions — and it stands to lose part of these "front-end" costs if premiums are not accumulated over more than two years. Of the policies surrendered, the vast majority are surrendered in the first two years, so policy lapses are a serious threat to life insurers' profitability. The companies have many techniques for controlling early lapse rates, but they all involve getting agents to screen new business more carefully and to restrain their well-developed selling drives. None of the techniques for preventing policy lapses are fully successful: table 13–3 showed that payments of surrender values to policyholders are still larger than total death benefits paid.

Matching liability and asset risks

The vast bulk of pension funds and most insurance policy liabilities are very well matched to asset yield fluctuations. Money-purchase pensions provide at retirement whatever funds have accumulated in the member's account, at current market value. Therefore, the yield to a member from his or her contributions (which is the debt cost to the pension plan) is identical to the pension fund's yield on assets, net of management costs.

Participating insurance policies match asset yields and debt costs in the same way, and they account for 87 percent of individual life insurance in effect. The yield to a policyholder's savings (the debt cost to the insurance company) has a minimum guarantee, but above that it is determined by dividends accruing to the policy.[10] The dividend payments to policyholders reflect (with some lag and imprecision) the difference between actual and expected mortality rates, operating-cost margins, lapse rates, and asset yields. Debt costs on these policies can therefore be perfectly correlated with all other risks of an insurance company, if the dividend rate is adjusted flexibly enough. Typically, however, dividend rates are not adjusted that frequently.[11]

Segregated-funds policies are very much like money-purchase pension plans. The yield to policyholders from their contributions is exactly equal to the yield on assets less operating costs.

Annuity policies, which account for 60 percent of the actuarial reserve of insurance companies, have less flexible yields. There are no participating retirement annuities for individuals, so the yield to individual annuitants depends on how long they live to collect benefits and not on the insurance company's asset yields or on its operating costs. Group annuities sometimes have an experience refund, which is essentially the same as policy dividends on participating insurance policies.

---

[10]Dividends accruing to holders of life insurance policies are really partial refunds of premiums and as such are not subject to the usual taxes on dividend income.

[11]Insurance companies set up dividend reserves to hold or account for dividends earned but not yet paid out to policyholders. Understandably, insurance companies are loath to adjust dividends downward, so they raise dividends only when they are fairly sure the increase can be permanent.

Nonparticipating insurance policies and regular individual annuities involve a substantial unmatched volume of debt costs. In chapters 10, 11, and 12 I explained matching of assets and liabilities in terms of matching variations in debt costs with variations in asset yields — or vice versa. In life insurance, policy liabilities and payments are not usually discussed and presented in such a way that debt costs can be calculated without a computer.[12] Even when they are calculated with a computer, debt costs vary in response to factors quite different from those to which asset yields respond. It is not possible to find assets whose yield fluctuations will match those of debt costs.

In particular, debt costs of insurance policies to the insurance company will vary with actual policyholder mortality experience and with the company's operating costs. In order to reduce variability of mortality experience, companies diversify widely across policyholders, but the variability is still large. Most important, it is completely uncorrelated with asset yields.

To compensate for the volatility of debt costs, insurance firms have significant equity and try to accumulate surplus beyond that. Table 13–5 shows that, for stockholder-owned companies, the debt:equity ratio is lower than for trust companies (see chapter 12). Surprisingly, the mutual companies have even larger surplus than the combined capital and surplus of stock companies, despite their large size, their diversification, and the fact that policyholders bear all the risk.[13]

It is not possible to measure the extent of correlation of debt costs and asset yields for insurance companies, because debt costs are never given explicitly in company reports. For mutuals, the measure is no more relevant than for credit union locals, since the creditors are also the owners of the company.

Performance

Some indication of the relative performance of the insurance and pension sector is given in table 13–6. Table 13–6 compares revenues and noninterest expense margins as a percentage of assets for the major financial intermediaries we have looked at in this chapter and in chapters 11 and 12.

---

[12]For any policyholder, the yield on savings put into the policy is the discount rate r such that the present value of benefits to be received just equals the present value of payments still to be made, when both are discounted at the same rate r.

[13]The relative size of this surplus could reflect greater risk aversion on the part of the directors elected by participating shareholders, but in stock companies, too, a large proportion of the directors are elected by participating shareholders. In a study comparing the performance of stock and mutual life insurers, I found supportive but not conclusive evidence that mutuals are more risk-averse than stock companies. "The Effect of Mutual Status on Life Insurer Behaviour," *Canadian Journal of Economics*, Feb. 1981.

TABLE 13–5 Leverage ratios for large stock and mutual companies in Canada, 1978

	Assets (millions of dollars)	Leverage (1)	(2)
Stock companies			
Great-West Life	3362	11.6	11.6
London Life	3121	13.1	11.9
Crown Life	1603	18.3	10.1
Imperial Life	913	15.9	15.4
Excelsior Life	693	22.9	22.9
Dominion Life	675	8.4	7.4
National Life	565	18.7	15.2
Monarch Life	356	11.2	8.5
AVERAGE LEVERAGE RATIOS		15.0	12.9
Mutual companies			
Sun Life	6190	8.7	5.2
Manufacturers Life	4192	15.6	8.6
Canada Life	2558	28.7	9.7
Mutual Life	2443	17.0	10.2
Confederation Life	2190	30.9	17.2
North American Life	1426	18.7	13.6
Assurance-Vie Desjardins	304	38.6	19.0
AVERAGE LEVERAGE RATIOS		22.6	11.9

Notes: Leverage (1) is the ratio of total assets (including those held against foreign business and segregated-fund assets) to unappropriated surplus and capital (if any). Leverage (2) is the ratio of total assets to the sum of unappropriated surplus, capital, and any appropriated surplus or reserves in excess of those required by the Department of Insurance.

Source: Department of Insurance, *Report of the Superintendent of Insurance for Canada* 1, 1978, 47C.

Yields on assets are lower for insurance companies and pension funds than for shorter-term intermediaries because more of the assets of life insurers and pension funds are in bonds bought before 1975, when coupon rates were much lower. Holding longer-term assets is an advantage when yields fall but a disadvantage when they rise. The yields of both life insurers and pension funds exclude unrealized capital gains and losses. Unrealized capital gains and losses are more important for institutions holding larger proportions of stocks and long-term bonds, which means insurance companies and pension funds rather than near-banks and banks.

Pension funds and the segregated funds of life insurers have minimal expenses to deduct from asset yield, but the regular insurance and annuity business of life insurance companies has very large expense margins. The

TABLE 13–6 Revenues and operating expenses per $100 of assets, 1981

Intermediary	Interest and dividend income[a]	Salaries and commissions	Other	TOTAL
Banks	15.43	1.22	1.07	2.29
Trust companies	12.95	1.82	1.14	2.96
Mortgage loan companies	12.45	0.35	0.79	1.13
Finance companies	17.03	1.39	3.00	4.39
Credit union locals	13.41	1.69	1.41	3.10
Credit union centrals	12.15	1.20	1.15	2.35
Life insurance companies[b]	6.97	2.46	1.15	3.94
Trusteed pension funds[c]	9.41	—	—	0.25
Segregated funds	8.23	0.33	0.07	0.41

[a]Includes realized capital gains and losses.
[b]Excluding segregated-funds business and accident and health insurance business.
[c]Figures are for 1980.

Source: Statistics Canada, *Financial Institutions*, Cat. 61–006, Fourth Quarter 1981.

implied yield on savings in normal, unsegregated policies of life insurance companies is therefore very low: drawing from table 13–6, we can see that it averaged only 6.97 − 3.94 = 3.03 percent in 1981. The comparable figure for 1980 was 6.4 percent.

The high costs of life insurance reflect mainly a very expensive distribution system for life insurance products. Most sales are made by agents urging customers to take out more insurance, rather than by customers seeking policies. This kind of sale requires an endless round of personal contacts by agents. Their rewards are commissions that absorb most or all of the first year's insurance premiums and parts of later premiums. Although the agent system is an effective way of generating new business, it is also expensive — so much so that it constitutes a barrier to entry for new firms: a full sales force is too expensive to create from scratch, and there is no other way to join the big league. Heavy commission costs depress yields to savers and partly explain the slow growth of life insurance companies relative to the other intermediaries shown in figure 13–3.

Growth

Domestic life insurance company assets other than in segregated funds have grown at only 8 percent per year. Total premiums and annuity contributions have grown more rapidly, at $10\frac{1}{2}$ percent, but an increasing proportion of them have been for term insurance; this kind of insurance

FIGURE 13–3 Growth of pension funds and life insurance, 1966–81

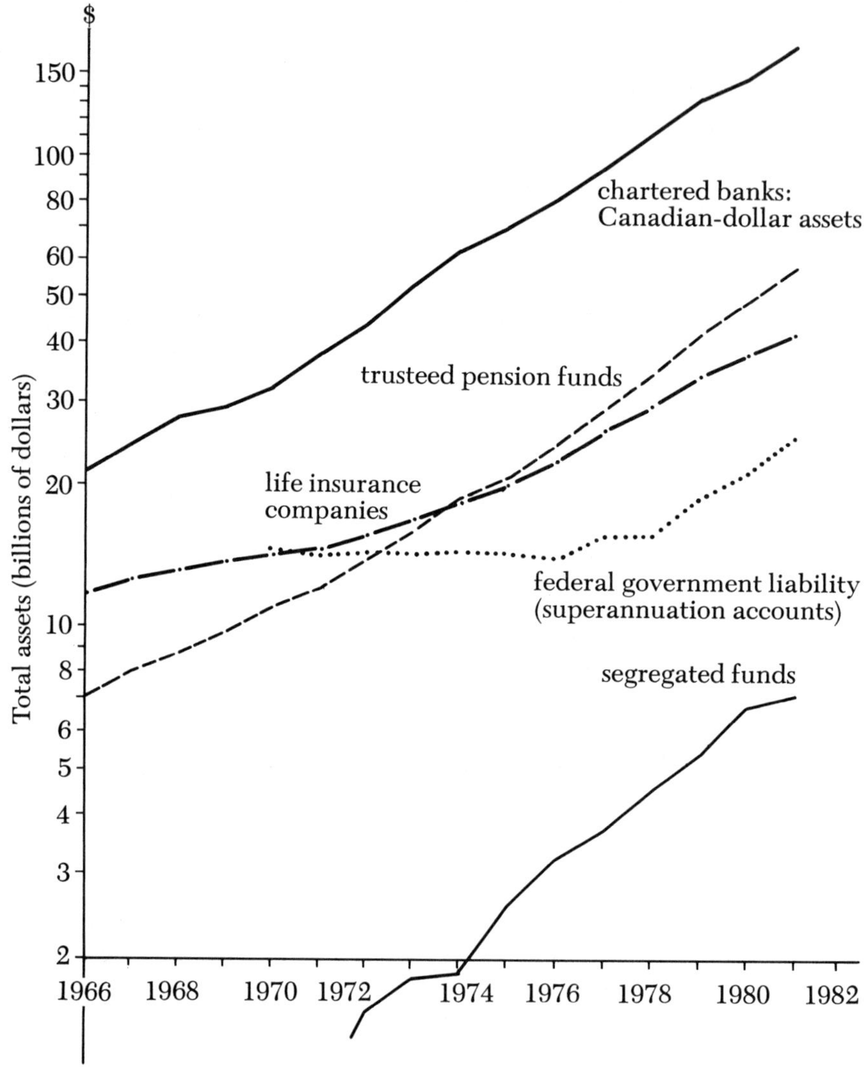

The figures for life insurance companies represent Canadian business only, excluding segregated-funds business.

Source: Statistics Canada, *Financial Institutions*, Cat. 61-006, Fourth Quarter 1981.

generates little if any savings accumulation by policyholders. Canadian life insurance asset growth has therefore been even slower than that of finance companies (8 versus 9 percent per year).

Gross assets of individual insurance companies have grown more quickly because of rapid growth of foreign business and because of expansion into segregated-funds business, but the core domestic insurance market for the traditional products has not kept up with the growth of substitutes. Within the core market, annuities have grown most rapidly, and life insurance assets have grown more slowly than the average of 8 percent per year. This slow growth is despite the skilful and aggressive efforts of over 17 000 full-time insurance sales agents — two for every bank branch in the country.

The reasons for slow growth of the insurance market are not hard to find. The operating results in table 13–6 reveal an indifferent earnings record for life insurance asset portfolios, as is inevitable for long-term portfolios in a period of rising interest rates. Table 13–6 also reveals a large operating-cost margin, especially for sales commissions.

The following demographic trends have also worked against sales of permanent life insurance (the kind that accumulates assets and cash values):

1. Pension arrangements have reduced the need for insurance after age sixty-five. The main argument for permanent insurance is precisely that it is the only way to arrange for insurance after age sixty-five since term insurance is either prohibitively expensive or unavailable at that age.
2. Two-income families are becoming more prevalent. These families face much less risk of their income's being cut off than single-income families, and less provision need be made for the surviving spouse in event of premature death.
3. Families are smaller, and small families need less insurance.
4. Greater asset accumulation of households since 1945 has gradually provided a bigger cushion of financial security for many families. So has the spread of health, dental, and now even legal insurance. The number of contingencies for which one might find an insurance policy convenient are gradually being reduced. Life is much safer financially.
5. The spread of life insurance for personal loans and mortgage loans has further reduced the number of contingencies in which whole life policies would be helpful. An extra blow is the change in income tax legislation in 1983 (introduced in the November 1981 budget) that taxes savings income on precisely those policies that generate high savings totals per dollar of insurance.
6. Finally, aggressive competition by insurance companies for group business (a form of term insurance) has made group insurance so much cheaper that many individuals have responded to relative prices and bought into group plans.

Pension fund growth responds with long lags to changes in the number of people demanding pensions. A pension fund will continue to grow even if the number of members is constant, just because of the continued inflow of savings and the ploughing back of income from accumulated assets. As the members of a pension plan grow older, however, the rate of contribution will slow down and the flow of pension payments increase, so the pension fund's assets will stop growing and may even start to decline. The federal government employees' pension plan, whose value is shown in figure 13–3, is an example of the aging process at work.

Pension funds' growth is also spurred by favorable tax treatment (the yield on pension funds is not taxable) and by the convenience of the payment pattern. Unlike a level-payment life insurance policy, where the fixed nominal payment absorbs a larger percentage of income in the early years, pension contributions are a constant percentage of income. Also, half of the pension fund contributions are paid by the employer, and the other half are deducted from employees' pay at the source. For most of us this is a convenient and almost painless method of saving.

SECTION 4 Long-term intermediaries and the financial system

Both life insurance companies and pension funds intermediate by providing a liability that is customized to offset variations in customers' other income. The companies and funds offset the risk to themselves by diversifying and by tying the size of their payments to their asset yields, their operating costs, and their mortality risk. Insurance and pension products are unique. There are no close substitutes except within each group (for example, term insurance for permanent insurance, one type of annuity for another). Demand for each product is relatively insensitive to yields elsewhere. Pensions are especially insensitive to other yields, because they are contractual for all employees. Insurance policy premiums are contractual as well, but there are more ways to get out of an insurance policy than to get out of a pension plan. Both insurance policies and pension plans are sensitive to changes in demographic variables and to expected future income.

Life insurance companies and pension funds invest whatever flow of funds they receive, either in short-term or in long-term assets. It is insurance companies and pension funds whose asset demands really bridge the long- and short-term markets. Despite the long-term nature of their debts, their debt costs are sufficiently tied to asset yields that these intermediaries can afford to shift asset demand from long to short maturities without much extra equity risk, in their search for the largest expected yield. For the fast-growing segregated-funds insurance business and for money-purchase pension plans, there are almost no significant restrictions on asset choice, and no particular difference in equity risk between asset maturities held. In the next chapter, the issue will arise whether there is sufficient arbitrage between long- and short-term bonds. Life insurance companies and pension funds should be kept in mind as the institutions most free to shift their supply of loanable funds between the two markets without much extra risk exposure.

Both life insurers and pension funds are fairly remote from the workings of monetary policy, but nevertheless they are affected. Neither group's liabilities are close substitutes for money-market assets or term deposits of near-banks, so we do not expect much change in demand for debts of life insurance companies and trusteed pension funds when monetary policy changes money-market yields. The main impact of monetary policy on life insurers and pension funds is to change the desired proportions of the various assets in their portfolios, rather than to change the total amount of their assets. Both life insurers and pension funds demand money-market assets, long-term government and corporate bonds, and stocks; all of these demands are sensitive to relative expected yields. Lower short-term yields will therefore cause these firms to reallocate new cash inflows to longer-term assets, especially new isues of bonds and stocks. The effect is to lower yields on long-term bonds and on stocks; that is, to transmit the impact of monetary policy to long-term markets. It is here that most economists look for the major impacts of changing interest rates on the real sector.

In stark contrast, the Canada Pension Plan is the largest single long-term financial intermediary in Canada, yet it plays virtually no role in the transmission of monetary policy. Contributions are mandatory, and insensitive to anything but inflation and real income growth. The CPP invests in special provincial bonds only, so its demand is not sensitive at all to relative yields and does not play any part at all in transmitting yield changes from one market to another.

SECTION 5 Summary

Life insurance companies and pension funds are the major long-term financial intermediaries in the Canadian economy, the major collectors and redistributors of the long-term savings of the household sector. Life insurance companies are mainly federally registered and federally supervised. Many of the insurance companies are mutual companies — owned by their policyholders. The pension sector is dominated by government plans — the Old Age Security system and the Canada and Quebec Pension Plans — and is strongly influenced by the government's tax treatment of individual retirement arrangements via RRSPs. Trusteed, insured, and government service pension plans fit in the middle of this retirement income system and will be affected by coming changes in other parts.

Pension funds face a risk situation different from that of other intermediaries, in that the fund and its managers are not responsible for meeting pension annuity obligations. That risk is borne by the plan sponsor, who is usually the beneficiaries' employer.

Inflation risk, default risk, and income risk are not very important for these long-term intermediaries. Market risk on their holdings of stocks is more significant, despite their efforts at diversification. Liquidity risk is not serious for pension funds, which nevertheless hold a significant quantity of short-term, liquid assets. Liquidity risk is significant for life insurance companies, though, because of automatic policy loans, uncertain death benefits, and uncertain surrenders of policies.

Most insurance policies and most pension plans have payouts whose value is explicitly tied (perhaps above some minimum guarantee) to the accumulated market value of assets held. Many participating insurance policies, all of the segregated-fund insurance policies, segregated-fund annuities, and money-purchase pension plans are of this type. Others involve fixed commitments over uncertain lifetimes — commitments that are desirable for those insured but that leave substantial risk for the insurance companies.

Life insurance companies' leverage is relatively low and their reserves are large, so equity risk is kept within bounds. Nevertheless, life insurance growth has been relatively slow in the last two decades compared to that of other financial intermediaries. Yields to savers on life insurance have been relatively low, and demographic changes have been unfavorable to the sale of ordinary, permanent insurance products. Pension funds have mushroomed, by contrast, even though their future depends heavily on what the federal and Quebec governments do with the Canada and Quebec Pension Plans.

The nature of pension funds and insurance companies' liabilities is such that demand for their liabilities is almost contractual, insensitive to relative yields in the short run, at least, but sensitive to expected income, demographic changes, other retirement income provisions, and the level of uncertainty of future income or needs. Life insurers' and pension funds' demand for assets, however, is not particularly constrained to match the maturity of their debts, so they are able to switch easily between long- and short-term assets. Further, they are big investors in all types of long-term assets, including real estate, so insurance companies and pension funds are important arbitrageurs between these markets. Lower yields in short-term markets are therefore likely to be spread to the long-term markets by the portfolio-management decisions of pension funds and life insurers.

Questions for discussion

1. What would be roughly the average period for which savings would be left in an insurance company or a pension fund?
2. What is participating insurance, and how does it affect yield and risk for life insurance company policyholders?

3. Who are the primary lenders and primary borrowers whose lending and borrowing are intermediated by the Canada Pension Plan? by the Quebec Pension Plan?
4. Why are there much looser restrictions on holdings of assets in segregated funds than on the rest of life insurance companies' asset portfolio?
5. Why do life insurers need liquid-asset balances? Are they all held essentially for the reasons given by Keynes (see chapter 9) for speculative demand for money?
6. How is the liability of a life insurance company calculated for a specific group of insurance policies?
7. Is extra risk incurred by life insurance companies and pension funds if they shift from holding long-term to holding short-term assets, given that their liabilities are generally long-term? Why or why not?
8. If demand for deferred pension benefits and life insurance is insensitive to relative yields on financial assets, does it follow that pension funds and life insurance companies' demand for assets will also be insensitive to relative yields? Explain.
9. How do life insurance companies and pension funds contribute to the transmission of monetary-policy effects across financial markets?

References

Canadian Life Insurance Association. *Canadian Life Insurance Facts*. Annual.

———. *This Business of Life*.

Department of Insurance. *Report of the Superintendent of Insurance for Canada*. Annual.

Neufeld, E.P. *The Financial System of Canada*. Toronto: Macmillan, 1972, chaps. 8 and 13.

Pedoe, A., and C.E. Jack. *Life Insurance, Annuities and Pensions*. Toronto: University of Toronto Press, 1978.

Statistics Canada. *Financial Institutions*. Cat. 61–006. Quarterly.

———. *Pension Plans in Canada 1978*. Cat. 74–401. Occasional.

———. *Trusteed Pension Plans, Financial Statistics*. Cat. 74–201. Annual.

"The Life Insurance Industry in Canada, 1961 to 1979." In Statistics Canada, *Financial Flow Accounts*. Third Quarter 1980.

U.S. Federal Trade Commission. *Life Insurance Cost Disclosure*. Washington, D.C.: U.S. Government Printing Office, 1979.

PART FOUR

General Equilibrium in Financial Markets

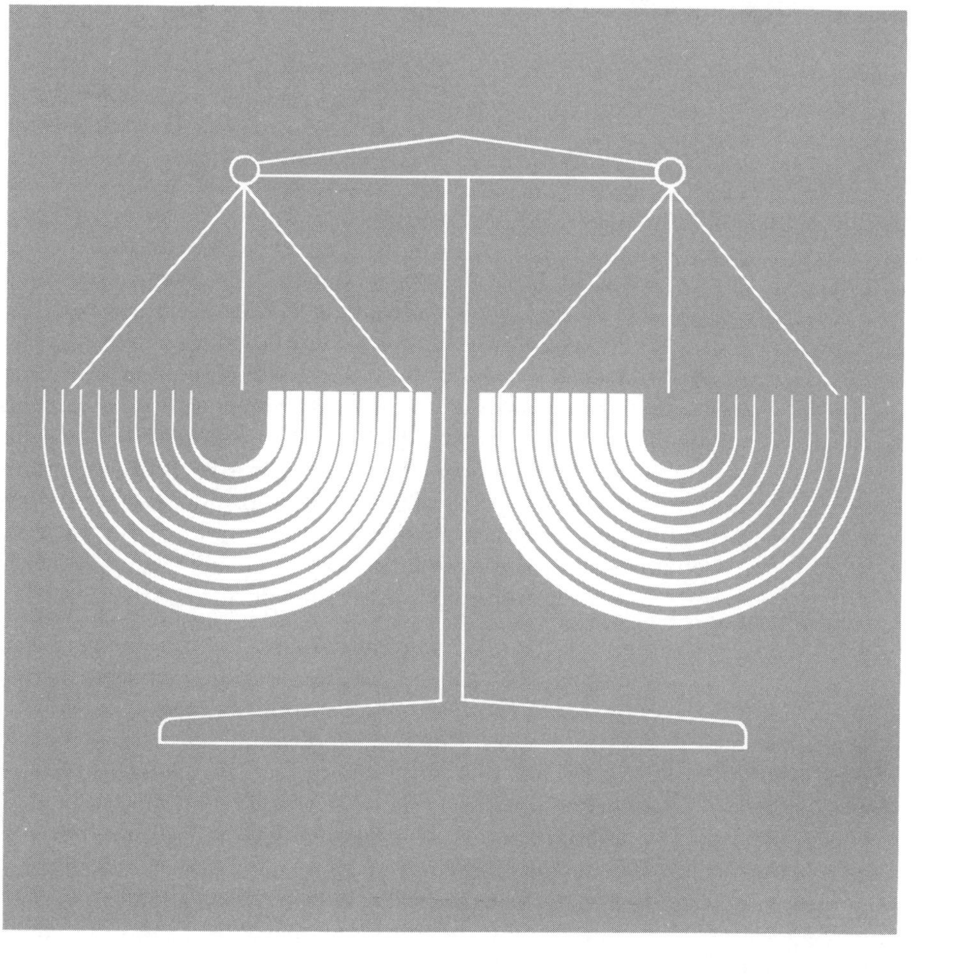

CHAPTER 14

Financial-Market Equilibrium

This chapter and chapter 15 tie together the first half of the book. Chapters 8 to 10 described the factors affecting demand for assets and supply of assets in a world of uncertainty, and chapters 11 through 13 described in detail the demand for and supply of assets by major financial institutions. In this chapter we will put together all the various demands and supplies, to look at the complete financial system.

The complete financial system is a set of financial markets, each with demand and supply by individual sectors of the economy as in the National Capital Account shown in chapter 5. These demands and supplies are subject to all the constraints that we identified in section 1 of chapter 5. In particular, each sector's total assets less its total debt must equal its equity.

Putting separate markets together into a whole system is only a start. From what we know about the individual demand and supply of each sector we can make several predictions about patterns of relative yields that will emerge in a general equilibrium — predictions about relative financial flows to various sectors and about the effects of exogenous factors (such as changes in taxes, changes in risk, and monetary policy) on those relative yields and flows. In particular we should be able to predict the effect of changes in expected inflation on financial markets.

Your task in this chapter is therefore to understand:

1. a general equilibrium model of the financial system, collecting all demands and supplies of the economy in what is a general model of behavior of the National Capital Account,
2. the patterns of adjustment of financial markets to equilibrium — both the mechanism of adjustment and the probable time path,
3. the efficient-markets hypothesis, an important theorem about the speed of response of large, continuous auction markets to new information, and
4. the impact of expected inflation on the pattern of nominal yields. Other aspects of general equilibrium are deferred until chapter 15.

SECTION 1

General equilibrium in financial markets

The financial system as a set of equations

The financial system is a set of markets for all financial assets in the system; each market has its own demand and supply. The financial system is a subset of the complete set of asset markets in the economy, as we saw in the National Capital Account in chapter 5. In order to consider general equilibrium in financial markets, we must also take into account the markets for real assets such as land, housing, and capital equipment. A model of the whole set of asset markets consists of a set of demand and supply equations, which Tobin has cast in the following general form, using the structure of the National Capital Account:

	Sector										
Asset	Households		Business		Financial insts.		Gov't.		Rest of the world		TOTAL
1. Money	D_{1h}	+	D_{1b}	−	S_{1f}	−	S_{1g}	−	D_{1r}	=	0
2. Deposits	D_{2h}	+	D_{2b}	−	S_{2f}	−	D_{2g}	+	D_{2r}	=	0
.											
.											
.											
7. Housing	D_{7h}	+	D_{7b}	−	D_{7f}	+	D_{7g}	+	D_{7r}	=	H
8. Plant and equipment	D_{8h}	+	D_{8b}	+	D_{8f}	+	D_{8g}	+	D_{8r}	=	K

where each D_{ij} or S_{ij} refers to the net demand or net supply of asset i (i=1, 2, ..., 8) by sector j ($j = h, b, f, g,$ and r), and H and K are the existing stocks of housing and plant and equipment in the economy.[1] In the short run, while each sector's wealth W is fixed, the demand function for each asset explains the desired portfolio share X^d_{ij}, as in the general form given at the end of chapter 8: for each asset i and for each sector j,

$$D_{ij} = X^d_{ij} (\{E\}, \{V\}, \{COV\}, MRS_{E,V})\, W_j,$$

where $\{E\}$, $\{V\}$, and $\{COV\}$ are the set of expected yields, variances, and covariances of different assets; $MRS_{E,V}$ is the degree of risk aversion; and W_j is the equity or net wealth of sector j.

[1] James Tobin, "A General Equilibrium Approach to Monetary Theory," *Journal of Money, Credit, and Banking* 1 (1969), 15–29.

Similarly, supply of asset i by sector j is explained in the short run as a desired fraction or multiple X^s_{ij} of equity W_j:

$$S_{ij} = X^s_{ij}\,(\{E\}, \{V\}, \{COV\}, MRS_{E,V})\; W_j,$$

where symbols stand for the same list of variables as in the demand equation. The list of variables in the supply and demand equations is the same, but response of supply is quite different from response of demand. In particular, the expected yields and covariances that matter most to demand will be different from those that matter most to the supply of any asset. For instance, the supply of deposits by mortgage loan companies (part of the item S_{2f} in the equation system above) is very sensitive to expected yields on mortgages. The demand for deposits either by households (D_{2h}) or by businesses (D_{2b}) is hardly sensitive at all to mortgage interest rates; instead, those demands are sensitive to Canada Savings Bond yields and money-market interest rates.

We need to allow for the fact, introduced in chapter 9, that demand for money also rises with real income and price levels. More demand for money must mean less demand for other assets or greater supply of debts: the other asset demands and supplies in total must therefore fall, and in equal total amount, as real income and prices rise. Close substitutes for money will be most affected, while other assets like life insurance policies will hardly be affected at all. In general, however, supply of each asset will depend on real income and prices as well as on the list of variables shown above. The desired fraction of equity to be held in each asset (X^d_{ij}) or to be left outstanding in each debt (X^s_{ij}) will depend on the ratio of real income and prices to the sector's equity. That is, where P is the price level and Y_j is real income of the jth sector,

$$D_{ij} = X^d_{ij}\left(\{E\}, \{V\}, \{COV\}, MRS_{E,V}, \frac{P}{W_j}, \frac{Y_j}{W_j}\right)W_j,$$

and $$S_{ij} = X^s_{ij}\left(\{E\}, \{V\}, \{COV\}, MRS_{E,V}, \frac{P}{W_j}, \frac{Y_j}{W_j}\right)W_j.$$

Constraints

Because portfolio sizes are constrained by wealth levels and by leverage ratios for each investor, several relationships among the various demand and supply functions must always hold. First, for each sector j the sum of demand proportions X^d_{ij} less the sum of supply proportions X^s_{ij} must equal exactly 1.0. In an unlevered portfolio where there are no debts, the sum of the asset demand proportions alone must add up to 1.0.

Second, the total impact of a change in any one variable on all asset demands and supplies together must add up to exactly zero for each sector.

For instance, a higher expected yield on term deposits will cause households to demand a larger share in term deposits, but their extra equity share in term deposits must be exactly offset by some combination of lower demand for other assets and extra borrowing. Where wealth is constant, then total asset demand less total debt supply must by definition be constant as well.

If we have done enough applied research to know the structural form of each of the general demand equations $X^d_{ij}(\dots)W_j$ and of each of the supply equations $X^s_{ij}(\dots)W_j$ (for example, whether they are linear or not), and if we know the levels of real incomes, prices, wealth levels, and the variance and covariance terms, we can think of the set of equations for all n assets as n equations in n unknown expected asset yields $E_1, E_2, \dots, E_n$. However, it is not quite that simple even at this heroic level of abstraction.

Because of the wealth constraint, the full set of financial-market equilibrium equations are not independent. When the stock of wealth is fixed, then knowing the equilibrium demand and supply levels in all but one market is sufficient to determine the demand and supply level in the one remaining market; each sector's demand or supply of the one remaining asset must be the sector's wealth less all other asset demands and plus all other debt supplies. That is, for n assets there are only $n - 1$ independent equations.

In algebraic terms, this means there are not enough equations to determine n different expected yields, but only $n - 1$. If the nth yield is that on money, for instance, we can find the solution for each of the other $n - 1$ assets only relative to the expected yield on money; we can find $n - 1$ yield differentials, not $n - 1$ yields. What has saved monetary and financial-market theory so far is that the yield on money has been arbitrarily fixed at zero. In that case, knowing the yield differential relative to money is the same as knowing the yield itself. This point is worth stressing, since computer technology is making it easier for banks to pay interest on demand deposits. Chartered banks started to pay interest on chequing accounts of large business customers in 1980. As this institutional change spreads in the 1980s, we may find that our monetary theory really can explain only interest differentials, not interest levels.

General equilibrium results

The set of $n - 1$ independent financial-market equilibrium equations, plus the wealth constraint, produces general equilibrium values of demand and supply in each market, and an equilibrium set of yields relative to a zero yield on money. Our analysis in chapters 7, 8, and 10 leads us to predict that the following conditions will hold in this general equilibrium:

1. Demand will equal supply, and total wealth will be invested.
2. Each investor will be holding assets in proportions such that differences between assets in expected yields just compensate for differences in

what each asset adds, at the margin, to portfolio risk; marginal portfolio risks in turn will mainly reflect relative covariances, as long as asset portfolios are well diversified.

3. Each investor will be exposed to just the risk at which the marginal gain in expected yield from taking on extra risk is equal to or less than the investor's degree of risk aversion (as measured by the investor's marginal rate of substitution of risk for expected yield).
4. Marginal borrowers will feel that any differential in expected interest cost of any two debts they use will just compensate for differences in the debt costs' relative covariances with yields on the assets to be financed.[2]
5. Borrowers such as intermediaries, whose asset portfolios are finely adjustable rather than lumpy or discrete, will have borrowed to the point where expected asset yield just equals expected debt cost on marginal business, plus an allowance for any extra equity risk brought on by higher leverage.
6. In the long run, the volume of demands and supplies by intermediaries will adjust until expected yields on equity of intermediaries are just equal to those earned elsewhere in ventures of similar risk.

Partial equilibrium diagrams

So far in this section I have laid out the formal structure of general equilibrium in financial markets and described its properties. We can illustrate it piecemeal with partial-equilibrium demand and supply diagrams. One such is figure 14–1, a *loanable-funds diagram*. For the purposes of this illustration we will call the supply of bonds the demand for loanable funds in the bond market (just because the slope of the curve corresponds to what we expect from a demand curve rather than from a supply curve). Sensitivity of the supply of bonds to the expected bond yield is then illustrated by the demand curve for loanable funds in figure 14–1. The quantity of loanable funds demanded rises and falls along the demand curve as expected long-term bond yields fall and rise respectively; the whole demand curve shifts with any other change.

Demand for bonds by investors is the supply of loanable funds in the bond market. Its response to long-term bond yields traces out the supply curve for loanable funds in figure 14–1. Quantity of loanable funds supplied in the bond market rises along the supply curve with expected yields on bonds, and the whole supply curve shifts with everything else. The equilibrium expected yield E^* is at the intersection of demand and supply.

---

[2]Many, perhaps most, borrowers will be intramarginal, which means that they would do the same type and amount of borrowing even at slightly higher expected debt costs.

FIGURE 14–1 Supply and demand for loanable funds in the long-term bond market

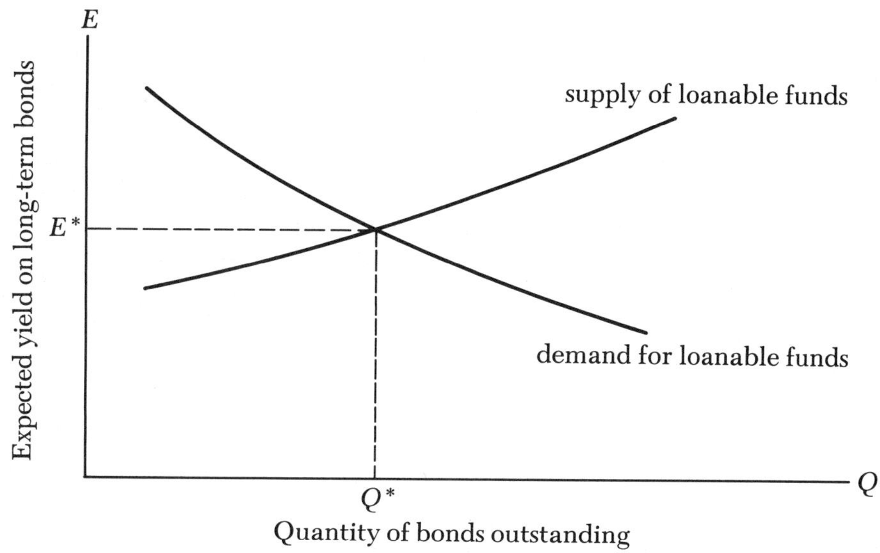

The supply curve for loanable funds shown here is simply the demand for long-term bonds by assetholders. The quantity of bonds demanded rises as their expected yield rises, as is shown by a movement to the right along the supply-of-loanable-funds schedule. All other factors affecting demand for bonds cause the supply-of-loanable-funds schedule to shift.

The demand for loanable funds is the supply of long-term bonds outstanding at each interest rate.

Partial-equilibrium market diagrams such as figure 14–1 are useful for illustrating the impact effects of financial-market disturbances, although the diagrams quickly become too messy if there are many market interconnections to be handled.

It is possible to use a different partial equilibrium diagram for each financial market — a diagram that will relate demand and supply of the asset not to the asset's own expected yield, but to expected yields on other assets. The one financial market for which this is usually done is the market for money (currency and demand deposits). The staple diagram of intermediate macroeconomics courses is the diagram relating demand for and supply of money to the expected yield on other financial assets such as bonds, as in figure 14–2. Supply is assumed fixed, as a rule, and the demand curve has a negative slope for all of the reasons given in chapters 8 and 9. The demand curve will shift with changes in all relevant variables other than the expected yield on bonds.

FIGURE 14–2 Partial-equilibrium diagram for the money market

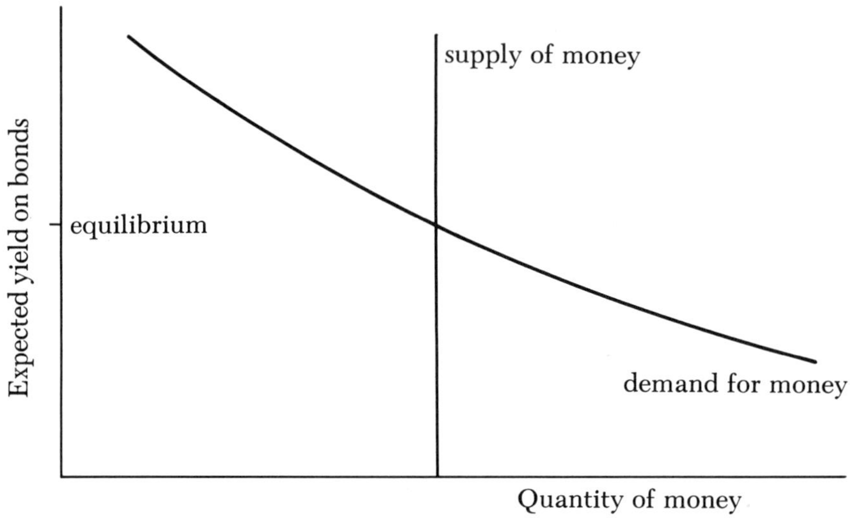

The supply of money is fixed by the level of cash reserve assets created by the Bank of Canada. The demand for money is sensitive to yields on bonds and other assets, as well as to its own yield, income, and wealth. Changes in bond yields cause movements along the demand curve, while all other changes cause shifts of the curve.

SECTION 2

Adjustment patterns and speeds of response

Adjustment mechanism: prices and coupons

In general, financial markets adjust to equilibrium even in the short run, in the sense that yields change until supply equals demand. Adjustments of yields may be through changes in interest coupons payable, or through changes in price, or both. For nonredeemable assets traded on secondary markets (such as marketable stocks and bonds), adjustment is by change in price. For redeemable assets such as notice deposits or chartered-bank term deposits, adjustment is by change in interest coupons as old deposits are turned in to be replaced by new deposits. For fixed-term, nonredeemable assets such as mortgages, term loans, consumer loans, and many near-bank term deposits, there is no market price to change, and the coupon is fixed. Only when these assets have matured and are being replaced will the investor and borrower have to adjust to a new yield.

Adjustment of yields on real capital assets is by change in price. The equivalent of the interest coupon on a real capital asset is the amount of extra revenue generated by the asset, which is its marginal revenue product. The marginal revenue product of capital equipment (MRP_k) does not vary reliably with levels of interest rates in financial markets, though it will be sensitive to changes in prices and real incomes. The price of a real capital asset is the discounted present value of its lifetime stream of expected marginal revenue products. This present discounted value approaches $P_k = MRP_k/r_k$ as the asset's useful lifetime approaches infinity, where r_k is the yield on capital assets that in equilibrium balances supply and demand. When this price is divided by the marginal cost of production of new real capital assets, we get the ratio known as *Tobin's q*, or sometimes as the supply price of capital. Tobin's q ratio is an important theoretical link between financial and real sectors. We will be using this ratio in the second half of the book.

Tobin's q

Wealth effects

Where adjustment is by price, the adjustment process itself affects recorded wealth levels, so the adjustment process has wealth feedback effects. These feedback effects are fairly obvious for stocks and real capital assets (such as houses and land) but not so obvious for bonds and other debts. At first glance it seems that a rise in bond prices leaves the bond issuer worse off by just as much as the bondholder is better off, so total wealth is not affected. There is an asymmetry here, though. The bondholder may well feel better off when bond prices rise, but the bond issuer is unlikely to care at all. The bond issuer after all owes only the par value of the bond, not the market value. Thus there will be a net positive effect on perceived and recorded wealth when bond prices rise as well as when stock and real-asset prices rise.

We therefore need to acknowledge that the wealth constraint is partly endogenous, that wealth levels themselves are affected by yield levels. Let the value of an investor's holding of asset i be the product of its price P_i and its quantity Q_i. Assume all debts are recorded at fixed par values. The wealth constraint for an investor holding n assets is therefore

$$W = \Sigma P_i Q_i - \text{Debt}.$$

The prices P_i of the marketable assets fall as current yields r_i rise. In the simplest but extreme case of a perpetual bond, $P_i = \text{coupon}/r_i$, so the price falls always by the same proportion as the increase in expected yield.[3] This relationship of price and yield is shown in figure 14–3 as a rectangular hyperbola. For all assets with shorter lives, the price response to changes in yields is less than equi-proportional, but in the same direction as in figure 14–3. In order to recognize the general effect of price and yield on wealth we can rewrite the wealth constraint as

$$W = \Sigma P_i(r_i)Q_i - \text{Debt}; \frac{dP_i}{dr_i} < 0.$$

The effect of wealth changes induced by yield changes reinforces the effect of yield changes by themselves. For instance, imagine an investor such as Brown faced with a rise in bond yields and a drop in the market value of her existing bond holdings. The higher expected yield causes greater demand for bonds and less demand for other assets. Lower wealth causes lower desired holdings of all assets at market value, just to keep their shares of wealth constant. For all assets other than bonds, that means fewer are demanded. For bonds, it means more are demanded. The market value of bonds is reduced by the fall in price of bonds, and in a larger proportion than wealth is reduced: for instance, if bond prices fall by 50 percent and bonds make up only one-fifth of Brown's asset portfolio, then her wealth falls only by 50 x 0.2 = 10 percent. In order to get back to the same desired fraction of wealth in bonds, Brown must buy more bonds. The feedback effects of wealth changes induced by yield changes therefore cause more of the reactions that are caused by relative yield changes directly.

In some ways, Brown is a poor example. Many of the bonds and stocks in Canada are held by financial institutions, and financial institutions do not always record their assets at market value. If changes in market value caused by yield changes do not affect recorded wealth, one cannot expect

---

[3]The price P is the present value of an infinite stream of coupon payments of $\$C$ per year. That is,

$$P = \frac{\$C}{(1+r)} + \frac{\$C}{(1+r)^2} + \ldots + \frac{\$C}{(1+r)^\infty}.$$

Multiplying P by $(1 + r)$ gives

$$P(1+r) = \$C + \frac{\$C}{(1+r)} + \ldots + \frac{\$C}{(1+r)^{\infty-1}}.$$

Subtracting P from $P(1 + \text{r})$ and rearranging gives

$$P + rP - P = \$C - \frac{\$C}{(1+r)^\infty},$$

so $$P = \frac{\$C - (\$C/(1+r)^\infty)}{r}.$$

Since $1 + r > 1$, $(1 + r)^\infty = \infty$ and $\frac{\$C}{(1+r)^\infty}$ is zero. That leaves

$$P = \frac{\$C}{r}.$$

FIGURE 14–3 Price-yield relationship for bonds

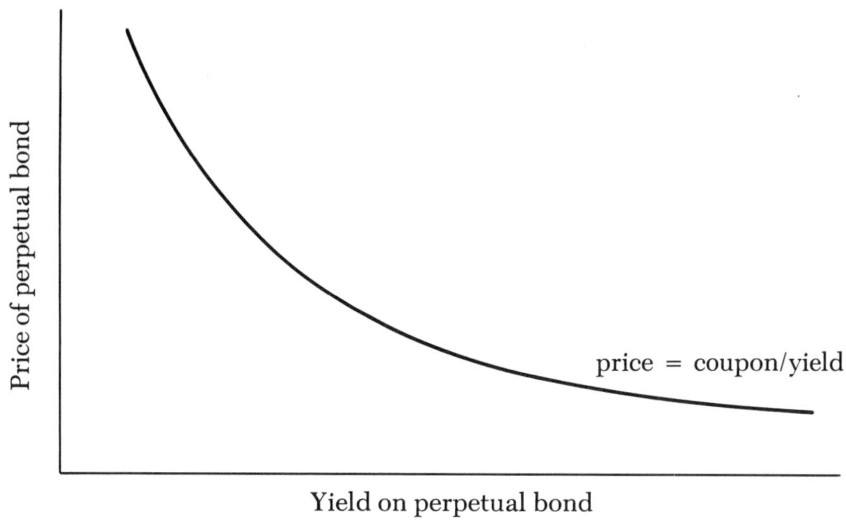

The relationship illustrated here is for a perpetual bond, one that pays a fixed-interest coupon forever and is never repaid. Its price is equal to the coupon divided by yield, so the price-yield relationship is a rectangular hyperbola. For small changes, the percentage change in yield is exactly equal to the percentage change in price but with the opposite sign.

For bonds with terms shorter than infinity, the price is less sensitive to changes in yield, so on a diagram the curve will be flatter. The relationship is still negative, though, for all bonds and for all other assets that offer a fixed payment such as an interest coupon.

much wealth feedback effect. Bonds and mortgages are commonly recorded at *amortized value*, which is a mixture of purchase price and redemption value; amortized value is not sensitive at all to current market value. Stocks and real estate holdings of financial institutions are usually recorded at market value, but they are not as reliably sensitive to changes in interest rates as are bonds, so wealth feedback effects from yield changes in financial markets are less certain.

Amortized value

Adjustment lags

Investors are unlikely to adjust assets and debts to desired levels immediately, regardless of how the adjustment of debt and asset portfolios takes place. Some investors may take substantial time even to change their desired portfolio composition, let alone their actual asset holdings. Many small-scale household investors devote very litle time, over the course of a year, to managing their assets, except for initial investment of savings not done under contractual arrangements such as debt repayment, a pension contribution, or an insurance policy premium. Many large investors with professional asset management, such as pension funds, life insurance companies, and mutual funds, have large enough holdings of particular assets that they can change their holdings quickly only at the risk of drastically depressing or inflating the price of those particular assets. Most investors also need much more than a month to make significant changes in the mix of outstanding debt; many debts cannot be retired until maturity, and often maturity is far more than just weeks away.

Adjustment lags can create many different types of yield pattern over time, as demand and supply shift. One such pattern, frequently encountered in economics, is the *reverse J* pattern already illustrated in figure 9–10. It is caused by relative inelasticity of either supply or demand in the short run: a sudden increase in supply, for instance, requires a large fall in relative yield to generate a matching increase in demand in the short run, but as demanders and other suppliers have more time to adjust, demand grows more and supply shrinks, so that the market-clearing yield rises much closer to the initial level again. Negligible long-run changes in relative yields can therefore be consistent with violent short-run yield fluctuations.

Goodhart has suggested that adjustment may take place in two or more separate steps.[4] For instance, if investors come to perceive mortgage loans as adding relatively more to portfolio risk, they will first shift out of mortgage loan notes and into some liquid asset such as short-term deposits (known by large-scale investors as cash). Then they will set about reallocating the extra cash holdings into other assets that may be closer substitutes for mortgage loan notes.

Goodhart's suggestion implies oscillating cycles of demand and supply volumes in various markets together with lags in adjustment of relative yields. To use the example of reduced supply of funds to the mortgage market, only yields on mortgage loans and on short-term deposits are affected initially: mortgage yields rise as demand for them falls, while equlibrium yields on short-term deposits fall as their demand rises. Subsequently, in stage two, yields on mortgage substitutes (bonds, term loans, preferred shares) will fall and some of the downward pressure on deposit rates will ease off as investors shift out of short-term deposits and into bonds, term loans, or preferred shares. In stage three, falling yields on mortgage substitutes cause further changes in demand for mortgage loan notes. Figure 14–4 illustrates the three stages of impact. The example shows that adjustment to a new equilibrium need not be smooth or immediate.

---

[4]C.A.E. Goodhart, *Money, Information, and Uncertainty* (London: Macmillan, 1975), 126.

FIGURE 14–4 A possible sequence of equilibrium yield adjustments

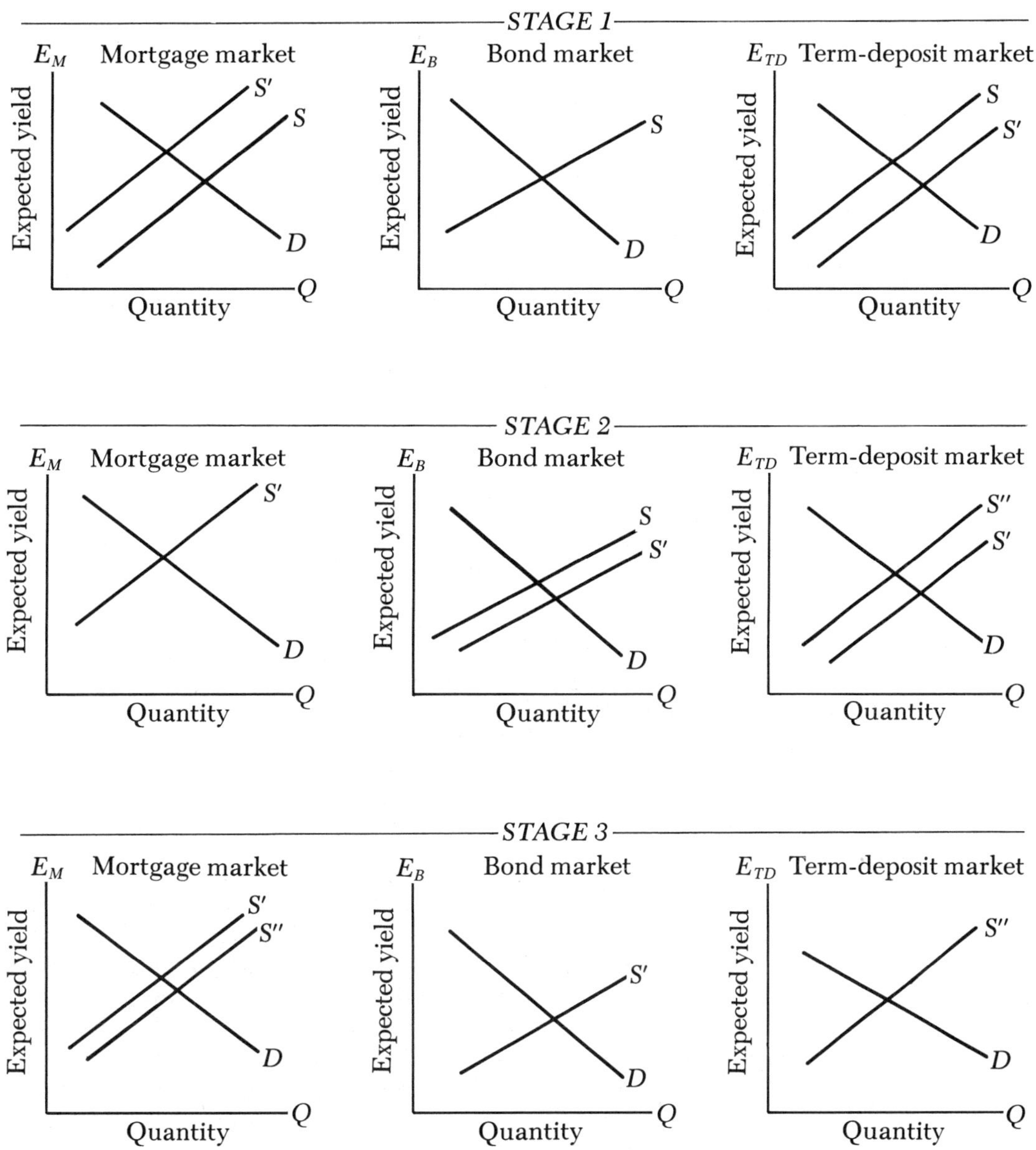

In stage 1 assetholders shift out of mortgages and supply loanable funds in the term-deposit market instead. In stage 2 they reallocate the extra term-deposit holdings into "mortgage substitutes" such as bonds. In stage 3 the lower bond yields cause some shift back into mortgages.

FIGURE 14–5 Response of borrowing to interest differentials, 1980–82

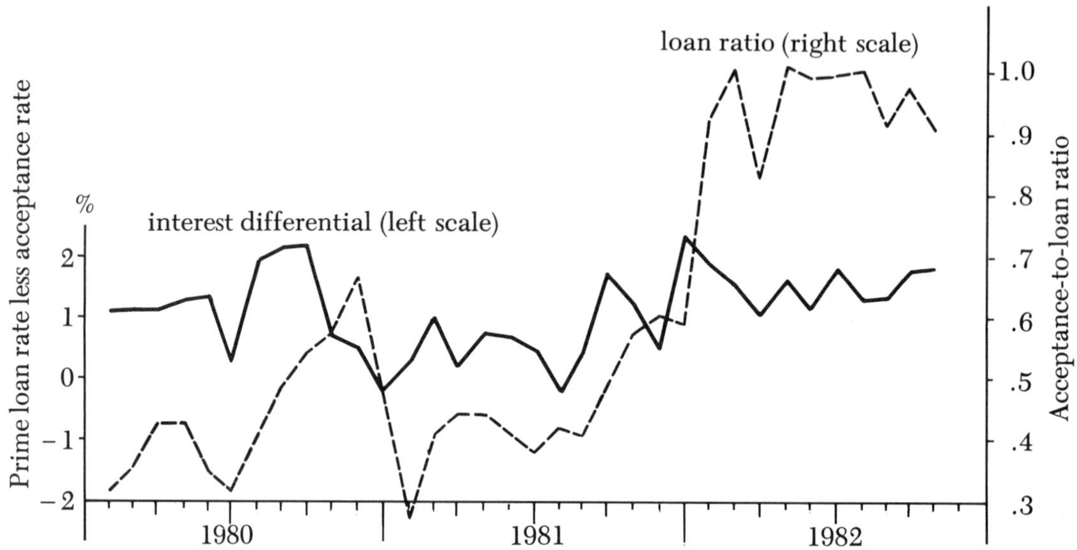

The acceptance rate is the month-end yield on thirty-day bankers' acceptances, used by medium-size corporations as an alternative or supplement to bank loans. The acceptance-to-loan ratio is the ratio of acceptances outstanding to bank loans made under lines of credit of between one and five million dollars (at month-end). That group of loans approximates use of bank credit by medium-size businesses. From 1980–82, the acceptance-to-loan ratio rose as bank loans became relatively more expensive, and fell, or rose more slowly, as bank loans became relatively cheaper.

Timing of yield changes

The pattern of adjustment of yields in Canada also reflects differences in pricing mechanisms. Some yields are set by continuous trading of price takers in competitive markets. Yields in the money market, the stock market, and the bond market are determined in this way. In other markets, yields are posted by the major market participants and are changed less frequently than in the money market. Banks and trust companies post term-deposit rates, banks post commercial loan rates, trust companies post mortgage interest rates, and major suppliers of manufactured goods post interest rates on trade credit to customers.

Some posted rates (such as those for consumer loans and trade credit) are changed only very infrequently, so large differentials can open up temporarily between market-determined yields and the posted yields. Large yield differentials can be expected to lead to large financial flows as borrowers shift to the cheaper source of funds and investors shift to higher yields. Figure 14–5 shows an example of such borrower behavior from 1980–82. The interest rates on bankers' acceptances are determined in the money market, but demand-loan rates are posted by chartered banks. For medium-size companies, bankers' acceptances and demand loans are substitute forms of debt, and arbitrage can be expected when their relative costs change. As the interest rate on bankers' acceptances rises above the demand-loan rate (as in early 1981), these firms increase their reliance on bank loans and pay off more of their bankers' acceptances coming due. When the gap widens the other way (as in late 1981), they do the opposite.

Where posted rates are changed more slowly than market-determined rates, adjustment of demand and supply in the posted markets will take place with a lag after that in the unposted markets. The posted rates that adjust most slowly are the rates on personal notice deposits and on consumer loans, so it is the household sector whose portfolio adjustment will be delayed.

SECTION 3 The efficient-markets hypothesis

There is an hypothesis and a powerful body of evidence to suggest that the adjustment process in organized, large-scale auction markets is almost immediate. This is the core implication of the *efficient-markets hypothesis*.[5]

Efficient-markets hypothesis

The efficient-markets hypothesis assumes first that participants in financial markets are efficient in processing information. In forming expectations about future yields (that is, about future dividends and future price changes) investors such as Brown take into account all available information. Having formed that expectation, Brown acts on it immediately, buying more stock if the expected yield has risen and selling off holdings if the expected yield has fallen. These changes in demand for stocks will change the market price until once again Brown and the rest of the stock market are in equilibrium. Because Brown has taken account of all relevant information, it follows that the stock market price also reflects all relevant information.

The second assumption of the efficient-markets hypothesis is that, in organized, large-scale, continuous secondary markets such as the stock and bond markets, the market professionals have available all the information they think relevant (given the cost of each type of information). There are no barriers to acting on that information, and market prices adjust within

[5]For an early survey of this literature, see Eugene Fama, "Efficient Capital Markets: A Review of Theory and Empirical Work," *Journal of Finance*, May 1970; or, more recent, Burton Malkiel, *A Random Walk Down Wall Street*, 2d ed. (New York: Norton, 1981), chap. 7. The first person to extract the implications of efficient-markets theory for expectations theory was William Poole, in "Rational Expectations in the Macro Model," *Brookings Papers on Economic Activity*, 1976:2, 463–505.

minutes to any surge of buying or selling. Therefore in these markets the adjustment period is a few hours. At the end of each trading day the price should come close to reflecting all available information.

The most direct implication of the efficient-markets hypothesis is that changes in prices during any trading day are caused only by new information — not by lagged adjustment to old information. If there were lagged adjustment to old information, market professionals would realize it and revise their investment strategy to take advantage of it. They would buy early when lagged adjustment would later cause prices to rise, and sell early in the opposite situation. Their actions would cause prices to rise in full immediately, thereby removing the lag.

Random-walk hypothesis

New information is random and unpredictable — predictable news is not really news, after all — so changes in stock prices caused by new information must be random as well. Because of this implication, the efficient-markets hypothesis is also known as the *random-walk* hypothesis.

FIGURE 14–6 Daily changes in the TSE 300 composite index, 1980 (adjusted for dividends)

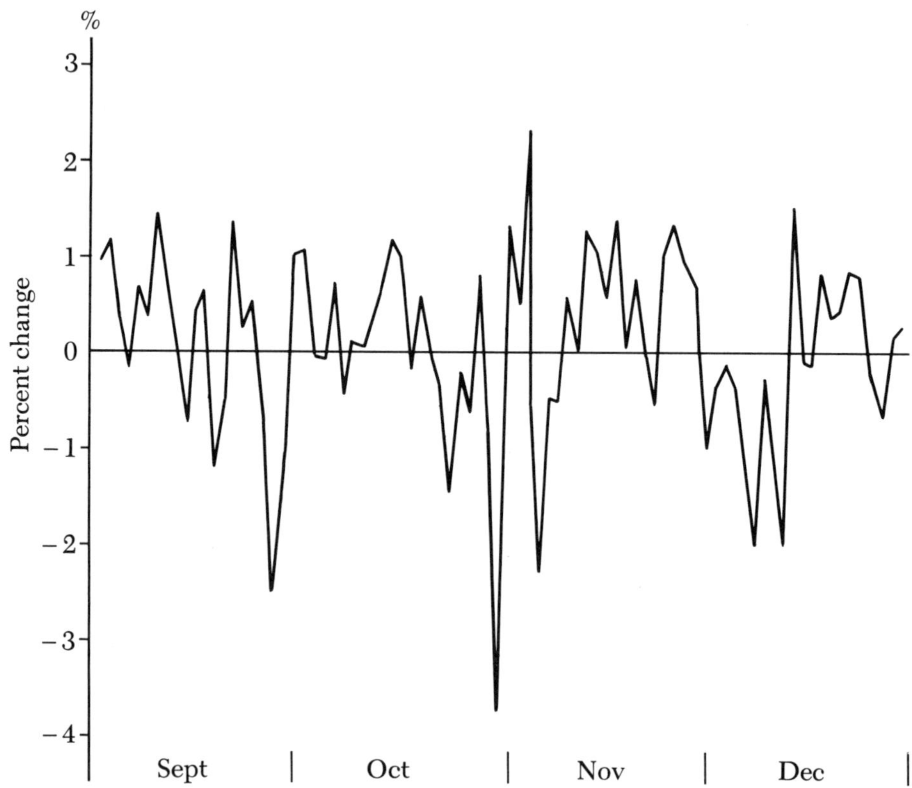

It says that tomorrow's price P_{t+1} of any stock is equal to today's price P_t plus a random component U_t. Rearranging this statement gives

$$P_{t+1} - P_t = U_t.$$

The test of whether prices do follow a random walk is to see whether there is any correlation of the price changes U_t over time. Figure 14–6 shows the daily price changes of the Toronto Stock Exchange 300 index over a four-month period in 1980, as an example of the sort of behavior the random-walk theory attempts to describe. There have been many tests of the randomness of price changes over time, and most of them have shown that the price changes are not correlated. Stock prices follow a random walk. Adjustment to new information is immediate.

It follows from these results that on average investors use a correct model of the economy to generate stock price forecasts on the basis of new information. All individuals may be wrong individually, but their average is not. If it were, systematically, then price changes would reflect that error by systematically over- or undershooting in response to particular kinds of new information. Speculators would recognize the phenomenon and take advantage of it. Their actions would affect the average and also would cause other investors to revise the way they formed expectations, until once again the average was accurate.

A second implication of stock prices' following a random walk is that buy-and-hold strategies for common-stock investment are superior to trading strategies. The reason is that, if price changes are random, then the expected price change is zero and there is no expected capital gain to be made or capital loss to be avoided by trading one asset for another. This rule will be wrong most of the time, but half on one side and half on the other. No other rule will do better. However, all other rules must involve more trading of assets and therefore greater trading commissions and lower net yield.

It does not quite follow that investors should choose stocks by throwing darts at the financial pages, because there is a risk element to be considered as well. It is possible to forecast relative future price volatilities. Prices of blue-chip stocks have been less volatile in the past than prices of penny mining stocks (stocks of mineral exploration companies), and that relative performance is likely to continue. However, within a group of stocks whose past risk (that is, their own yield volatility and their correlation with the average yield on the rest of the portfolio) has been similar, one might just as well choose stocks by throwing darts. The only important decisions that the efficient-markets hypothesis leaves to the investor are how much to save and how much risk exposure to take on.

A final implication of this section is for the way that people form expectations — an important factor in macroeconomic demand behavior. Evidence from stock markets suggests that once information is received, professional investors take very little time indeed to adjust their expectations of the future. The lags that obviously exist in actual responses in other sectors therefore should not be blamed on lags in adjustment of expectations unless the mental processes of people in other sectors are demonstrably different from the mental processes of stock-market professionals. One must instead explain response lags in other sectors of the economy in terms of slower receipt of information, or slower action once expectations have been changed, or some combination of the two.

SECTION 4 Inflation and financial markets

The Fisher effect

In 1896 Irving Fisher suggested that expected inflation might be neutral in its effects on financial markets; that is, an increase in expected inflation by x percent, expected for one year, might increase the nominal yield on a one-year debt by exactly x percent.[6,7] The real yield would be unaffected, and so would all financial flows (assuming, as Fisher did, that financial flows respond only to relative real yields and not to nominal yields). This hypothesized effect of expected inflation is known as the *Fisher effect*.

Fisher effect

Much work has been done since then on Fisher's proposition, especially since the outbreak of rapid inflation in the 1970s. The issue is a burning one for several reasons. If inflation is really neutral in the financial system, then the costs of inflation are reduced, and anti-inflationary policy is less desirable. If inflation distorts the pattern of real yields by penalizing financial as opposed to real yields, then anti-inflation policy is more urgent.[8]

Fisher's argument can be couched in terms of the simple two-period model of intertemporal choice used in chapter 6. In this model, savers save out of current income to provide future real consumption. Savers are

---

[6]"Appreciation and Interest," *Proceedings of the American Economics Association* (New York: Macmillan, 1896), 331–442.

[7]To be exact, extra inflation of x percent will lower the real interest rate on a one-year debt (with interest payable annually) by $(x + rx)/(1 + x)$ percent, where r is the nominal interest rate. The nominal inflation premium needed to offset the effect of x percent extra inflation is therefore $x + rx$ percent rather than just x percent. For small values of r and x, the difference is not significant: $x + rx$ is approximately equal to just x.

[8]Several Canadian economists have noted also that the flow of interest income caused by inflation premiums in nominal interest rates is not really income: it is merely an offset to real capital loss on fixed-nominal-value assets. Inflation, by this accounting, causes spurious increases in our measures of nominal and real income. If we are to remove these spurious increases, we must know how large the inflation premium is. For a fuller version of this argument, see C.L. Barber, "Inflation Distortion and the Balanced Budget," *Challenge*, Sept.–Oct. 1979, 44–47, or Greg Jump, "Interest Rates, Inflation Expectations, and Spurious Elements in Measured Real Income and Saving" (Economic Council of Canada Discussion Paper 150, Feb. 1980).

concerned only about real yields on their savings rather than with nominal yields in currency of uncertain purchasing power. If expected inflation increases, but at the same time the nominal yield increases by the same number of percentage points, the real yield will be unaffected. Savers will therefore leave their savings level unchanged and continue to demand the same quantity of savings instruments.

The same analysis applies to borrowers. Assume that borrowers use their borrowed funds to buy real assets whose marginal products and prices are expected to rise with inflation, so that extra expected inflation does not affect the real yields on the assets. However, inflation lowers the real value of debts and debt interest, since both are expressed in nominal values. Real borrowing costs fall by the amount of extra expected inflation. If the amount of extra expected inflation is added to borrowers' nominal interest payments, their real borrowing cost is not affected, and then neither is their borrowing decision. Borrowers will continue to supply the same quantity of debts in financial markets.

Adding to nominal interest rates an inflation premium that exactly equals expected inflation will therefore leave both demand and supply unchanged in financial markets. If the market was at an equilibrium level of demand and supply before, it must still be after this change, so the equilibrium yield must be increased by exactly the inflation premium. Figure 14–7 illustrates on a loanable-funds diagram the case of an increase in expected inflation of 2 percent. Both demand and supply of loanable funds shift upward by 2 percentage points (an increase in demand, and a decrease in supply at the old equilibrium interest rate). The equilibrium yield rises by 2 percent, while the equilibrium quantity of debt is unchanged.

Adjustments to the Fisher effect

From observing actual interest-rate behavior, Fisher himself did not actually believe the Fisher effect would occur even approximately.[9] Since then more economists have come to believe in it, but research since Fisher's time has uncovered many reasons for not expecting Fisher's result to hold exactly. Economists do not now expect even fully anticipated inflation to be completely neutral in its effects on the financial system. Both financial flows and relative real yields will be affected. When all is said, however, Fisher's hypothesis remains a good first approximation of the effect of expected inflation on nominal yields. I will sketch eight amendments that need to be made to Fisher's theory to make it fit a modern financial system, and then summarize results of tests of Fisher's hypothesis.

[9] *The Theory of Interest* (New York: Macmillan, 1930), 43.

FIGURE 14–7 The Fisher effect

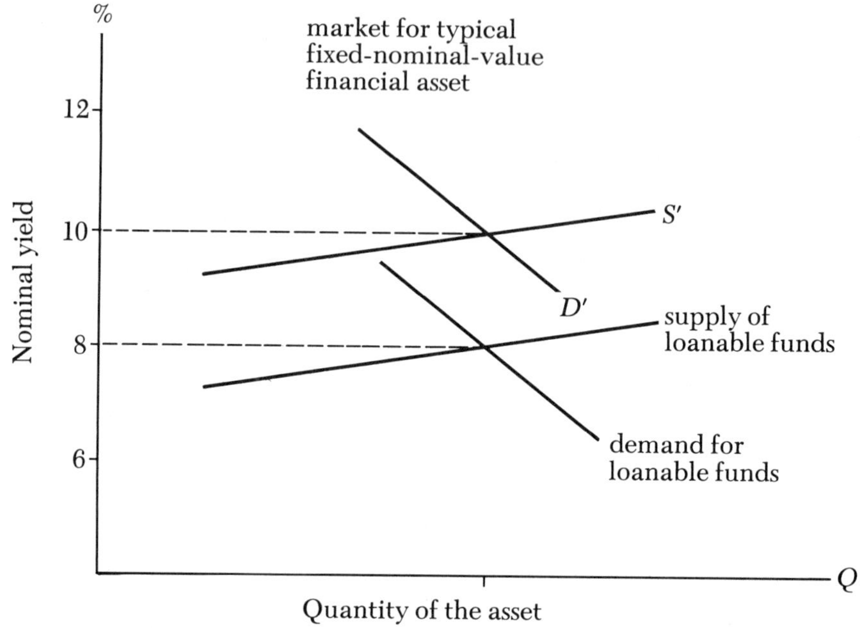

When expected inflation increases by 2 percent, lenders interpret each nominal yield as meaning a 2 percent lower real yield. Lenders reduce their supply of loanable funds at each nominal yield to what they previously supplied at a nominal yield 2 percent lower: the supply curve of loanable funds shifts to the left to S'. Borrowers reinterpret nominal yields in the same way and increase their demand for loanable funds at each nominal yield to what they previously demanded at a nominal yield 2 percent lower: the demand for loanable funds shifts to the right, to D'. The equilibrium yield increases by exactly 2 percent, and the equilibrium quantity is unchanged.

Tax effects

Michael Darby of the University of California at Los Angeles introduced taxes into Fisher's model.[10] Income taxes are levied on the inflation premium in nominal interest rates for many investors (though not for pension

[10]"The Financial and Tax Effects of Monetary Policy on Interest Rates," *Economic Inquiry*, June 1975. Martin Feldstein of Harvard University has noted in a series of papers that inflation also raises real corporate income tax by (a) lowering the real tax shelter provided by fixed nominal depreciation allowances and (b) taxing nominal gains on inventory that are not sheltered from tax by extra interest costs. See, for instance, "Inflation, Tax Rules, and the Stock Market," *Journal of Monetary Economics*, July 1980, 309–32. The net effect of Darby's and Feldstein's arguments is to limit nominal interest-rate increases to about the amount of any increase in expected inflation and no more. Lenders therefore suffer a loss in real yield when expected inflation increases. See James Pesando, "Inflation and the Rates of Return on Bonds and Equities" (Economic Council of Canada Discussion Paper 148, Jan. 1980).

funds and small household investors). Investors do not get any allowance, however, for losses in real value of their principal due to inflation. Investors' after-tax yield therefore does not rise as fast as expected inflation if the inflation premium merely equals the extra expected inflation. For instance, a 2 percent before-tax inflation premium would incur tax of $2t$ percent at a tax rate of t, leaving only $2(1 - t)$ percent after tax. The inflation premium would have to be bigger than expected inflation by the multiple $1/(1 - t)$ to leave real after-tax yields the same as before the expected inflation.

The same arguments apply in reverse to borrowers. An extra inflation premium in nominal interest rates lowers borrowers' taxable profit, so the net, after-tax cost of their borrowing rises by less than the inflation premium. In order for real borrowing costs to be constant, the inflation premium would again have to be larger than the expected inflation by the multiple $1/(1 - t)$. In figure 14–7, both the supply and demand schedules for loanable funds would have to shift upward by $2/(1 - t)$ percent to leave real yields constant when expected inflation rose by 2 percent. For other investors who do not pay tax on investment income — such as pension funds — an increase in nominal yields by $2/(1 - t)$ percent would increase their real yields by the fraction t times the change in nominal interest rates. Pension funds would find it desirable to shift into fixed-nominal-value assets, and out of stocks. If the nominal interest rates rise only by enough to keep real yields on fixed-nominal-value assets constant for pension funds, then taxable investors would suffer a fall in real after-tax yields and would shift out of those assets. Either way, expected inflation is not neutral in its effects.

Fixed-yield assets

Some assets have fixed yields that cannot be changed. Currency and existing long-term bonds are examples. Their real yields relative to other assets must be changed as a result of extra expected inflation, so the impact of expected inflation cannot be completely neutral.

Holders of such assets suffer a prospective real capital loss from extra expected inflation, while issuers enjoy a prospective capital gain.[11] Those suffering capital losses might be expected to increase savings to repair their wealth position, while the debtors might take advantage of their greater wealth to reduce savings. It is unlikely that the two groups' responses would cancel each other out exactly, so there would be some net shift of supply or demand for loanable funds in figure 14–7 and some change in the equilibrium nominal yield from that in the figure. Financial flows would not be constant. Both Fisher himself and James Tobin have argued that the

[11] Government debt is a special case, since only holders are likely to feel their wealth position affected by depreciation of nominal bond values. Taxpayers are the debtors, and in their personal decisions they are unlikely to take much account of the real value of the government debt. This issue is an empirical one, however, and the evidence so far is not conclusive either way.

debtors' response to their capital gain is likely to outweigh bondholders' response: there will be a net upward shift of the demand for loanable funds and an increase in the equilibrium nominal yield.[12]

Uncertainty of future income
Extra expected inflation is likely to be accompanied by extra uncertainty about the future, including future employment income. Such extra uncertainty will stimulate risk-averse households to save more now, since the chance of larger future income shortfalls is increased. Extra saving now increases the supply of loanable funds and depresses nominal yields below those expected from figure 14–7.

Relative price effects
Robert Clower and Peter Howitt have argued that higher expected inflation increases the relative price of consumption next year, especially for purchases of durables.[13] Consumers will shift some of their spending on durables to the present, and in the process they will reduce their net lending in financial markets. Supply of loanable funds will fall. Equilibrium nominal yields will be increased. If households go into debt at all to buy durable goods, then demand for loanable funds will increase, and nominal yields will be driven further upward.

Relative risks
Any extra uncertainty caused by extra expected inflation is not likely to be equally distributed across all assets. Uncertainty of real yield on houses, for instance, will be less affected simply because much of the yield from owning a house is received in kind as shelter. Real assets are not a perfect hedge against inflation, but they are likely to be a better hedge than financial assets with fixed nominal interest coupons. Extra uncertainty about future inflation will therefore make long-term, fixed-nominal-yield assets less desirable than either real assets or short-term assets with flexible yields. Fixed-term deposits will be less in demand than notice deposits, for instance. Long-term bonds will be less in demand than short-term bonds. Financial assets will be less in demand than real assets. Each of these changes will change relative real yields and cause changes in financial flows.

Speeding up loan repayment
Extra expected inflation has no effect on the final redemption date for financial assets, but it has a dramatic effect on the average term to repayment of the loan in real terms. When inflation speeds up, the real value of

---

[12]James Tobin, *Asset Accumulation and Economic Activity* (Yrrho Jahnsson Lectures; Chicago: University of Chicago Press, 1980), 9, 10.

[13]"The Transactions Theory of the Demand for Money: A Reconsideration," *Journal of Political Economy*, June 1978, 449–66.

FIGURE 14–8 Real principal repayments with inflation

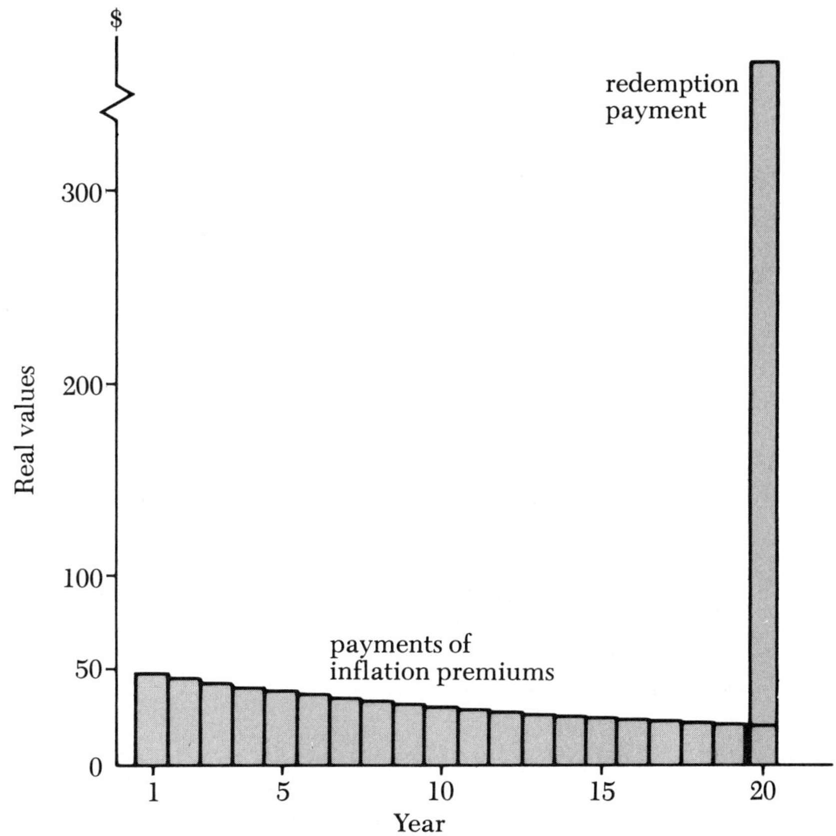

Inflation proceeds at 5 percent per year. The inflation premium built into nominal interest rates is 5 percent as well, or \$50 per year in nominal terms for a bond with \$1000 face value. The real values of those coupon payments shrink at 5 percent per year just like the final redemption payment. The total of all real repayments is \$1000.

the principal repayment at final redemption date becomes much smaller. With 5 percent inflation per year, for instance, the \$1000 principal of a twenty-year bond is worth only \$376 in today's dollars by the redemption date. Lenders are compensated for the loss of purchasing power by receiving inflation premiums in nominal interest rates, and those inflation premiums effectively repay the remaining \$1000 – \$376 = \$624 of real purchasing power. The inflation-premium "repayments" are made along with real interest payments, continually throughout the life of the bond, so the average term to repayment of the real value of a bond becomes much shorter at higher rates of expected inflation.

Figure 14–8 illustrates the repayment schedule with 5 percent inflation for a twenty-year bond. The inflation premium is assumed to be exactly 5 percent, or $50 in nominal dollars each year. Real interest payments over and above the the inflation premiums are ignored. The schedule of repayments of the real principal consists of the inflation-premium payments for the first nineteen years, and then an inflation premium and the redemption payment in the twentieth year. The inflation premiums have steadily decreasing real value because of inflation, starting with

$$\$50/(1 + .05) = \$47.62$$

in year 1 and falling at 5 percent per year to only

$$\$50/(1.05)20 = \$18.84$$

in year 20. The real value of the redemption payment in year 20 is $1000/(1.05)20 = $376.

The total real repayment from all sources comes to exactly $1000, as in a situation with no inflation and no payment of inflation premiums. In figure 14–8, however, $47.62, or 4.762 percent of the $1000, is effectively repaid at the end of year 1. Over 20 percent has been repaid by the end of year 5. Almost two-thirds of the real repayment is made before year 20; only one-third is repaid by the final redemption payment in year 20. In a world of no inflation, the entire real repayment would be made in year 20. An average of repayment dates, weighted by the amount repaid at each date, gives an average term to repayment of only 12.7 years in figure 14–8, instead of 20 years.

A shortening of the average term to repayment makes a big difference to the matching of cash flows of assets with cash flows of debts, and therefore to the risks borne by levered investors. Investors with long-term assets to finance will find themselves with a worse match of asset yields and debt costs, and as a result some long-term assets will not be built and financed. Assets with shorter-term payoffs, on the other hand, will be in greater demand. The impact is clearly not neutral.

Lack of alternatives

James Pesando of the University of Toronto has noted that not all assetholders can shift their demand from financial to real assets when expected inflation rises.[14] To the extent that this is true, the supply of loanable funds in financial markets as a whole will not fall by as much as otherwise, and the equilibrium nominal yield will not rise as much as Irving Fisher expected.

---

[14] *The Impact of Inflation on Financial Markets* (Montreal: C.D. Howe Research Institute, 1977), 23.

Extra income
Increased demand for real assets, whether by savers or by borrowers, will raise income levels in the short to medium term. Higher income levels imply higher demand for money balances for transactions purposes. Extra demand for money requires reduced demand for other assets, so demand for other assets must fall. Equilibrium yields on those other assets must rise, increasing the inflation premium in figure 14–7.

Evidence on the Fisher effect

Research since Fisher's time suggests that extra expected inflation is unlikely to generate higher nominal interest rates in exactly the same amount. However, many of the additions to Fisher's hypothesis have offsetting effects; some push nominal yields higher, some lower. Theory alone does not tell us which to expect as a net result. Since so many of the effects are offsetting, it does seem likely that Fisher's hypothesis can serve as a rough rule of thumb, a first approximation, even if the impact is obviously not neutral in detail.

There has been considerable testing of Fisher's hypothesis, but all the tests are subject to the same fundamental problem: the researcher must first come up with a way to measure expected inflation. There is no perfect way to do this, since expectations are unobservable, so the test results could all be due to errors in measurement of expectations rather than to anything suggested by Fisher's theory.

Nevertheless, the results from many different specifications of expected inflation have not been all that different from one another. The general result is support for Fisher's basic idea of an extra inflation premium in nominal yields, though not of an inflation premium that exactly equals extra expected inflation. James Pesando notes that results suggest at most a one-for-one response of nominal yields before tax to expected inflation.[15] He reports some evidence of lower responses in more recent years. Some of the estimated response rates are as low as 0.46, and the highest in his survey is only 1.04. It follows that nominal yields do not rise by enough to prevent real after-tax yields from falling significantly for taxable investors. The effect of expected inflation is to make investment in financial assets less desirable for savers, to make borrowing more desirable, and to increase demand for nonfinancial assets such as gold and houses.

In a recent study using United States inflation and interest-rate data from 1860 on, Lawrence Summers of Harvard University found virtually no relationship between inflation and nominal interest rates; what relationship there is exists only for the postwar years. He argues that price levels had been stable enough before 1939 (rising and falling, but with no upward

[15]For a convenient summary of this research, see Pesando, *The Impact of Inflation on Financial Markets in Canada*, 22, or his more recent study for the Economic Council of Canada, "Inflation and the Rates of Return on Bonds and Equities" (ECC Discussion Paper 148, Jan. 1980).

FIGURE 14–9 Inflation and real yields, 1937–82

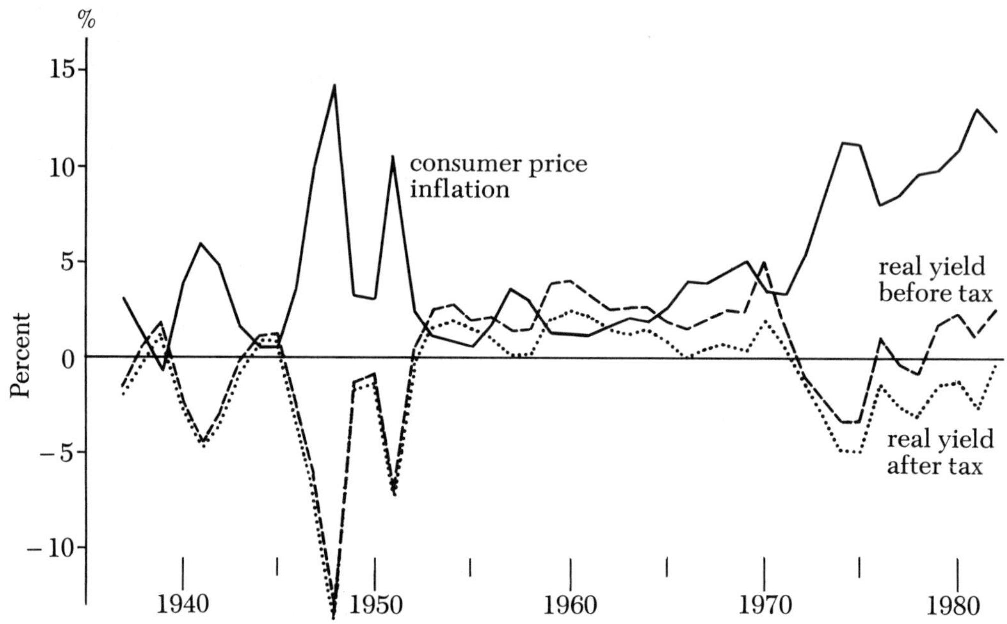

The real yields are on short-term bonds of the government of Canada, rolled over at the start of each year shown. After-tax yields assume a one-third tax rate on all nominal interest income.

Sources: M.C. Urquhart and K.H. Buckley, *Historical Statistics of Canada* (Toronto: Macmillan, 1965), 274, and CANSIM Databank.

trend) that lenders and borrowers expected inflation of about zero in the long run, regardless of the current rate of inflation.[16]

As an illustration of the relationship between actual inflation and nominal interest rates in more recent years in Canada, figure 14–9 shows the time path of consumer price inflation and of real yields on short-term government of Canada bonds since 1937. The bonds are assumed to be bought at the end of the previous year, held during the year shown, and then rolled over into a new bond at the end of the year. After-tax yields are calculated assuming a marginal tax rate of one-third on all nominal interest income. The effect of taxes is clearly greater at the recent end of figure 14–9, where inflation and nominal interest payments are both high. As suggested by the research Professor Pesando surveyed, real after-tax yields have fallen as inflation has speeded up, even though little of the inflation is now unexpected.

[16] "The Non-adjustment of Nominal Interest Rates: A Study of the Fisher Effect," in James Tobin, ed., *Macroeconomics: Prices and Quantities* (Washington, D.C.: Brookings, 1983), 201–46.

SECTION 5

Summary

General equilibrium in financial markets produces a set of relative yields that balance supply and demand for each type of asset, with both demanders and suppliers at their optimal portfolio allocation and leverage ratios. Since it is only relative yields that are determined in asset markets, only $n - 1$ of n possible yields can be found. The yield on money is still mostly fixed at zero in the Canadian financial system, so the other $n - 1$ yields are all determined relative to the yield on money. Each individual market equilibrium can be illustrated with a partial equilibrium diagram of supply and demand for loanable funds in that market.

Adjustment in financial markets is normally swift, in the sense that yields will change until demand equals supply. Adjustment of demand and supply to changes in yields and in wealth is slower, so there is a set of equilibrium responses to changes in yields, as in Marshallian economics — market period, short-term, and long-term responses. The adjustment process involves some changes in wealth whenever the adjustment is in the market value of long-term assets rather than in the coupon rate. Different adjustment speeds in different asset markets can lead to fairly substantial swings in flows of funds as investors and borrowers take advantage of changes in interest differentials.

The efficient-markets hypothesis has been developed for large, professional, continuous auction markets. It predicts that investors will use all available information to predict future yields of stocks and that stock prices at any time will reflect all available information. It implies that stock price changes are caused by new information only, not by lagged adjustment to old information. Tests of this implication (the random walk of stock prices) have supported efficient-markets theory. It is not implied that all other markets adjust equally fast to new information, but it is likely that at least expectations are adjusted quickly when new information is received.

Our theory of market demand and supply is mostly couched in terms of relative real yields, but actual financial markets report nominal yields. Irving Fisher suggested that nominal yields might differ from real yields only by an inflation premium equal to expected future inflation. Subsequent work on the Fisher effect has found that his prediction holds only approximately and only partially. In particular, real after-tax yields on financial assets fall as expected inflation rises.

Questions for discussion

1. What must be the effect of higher real income levels on demand for nonmoney assets if wealth is unchanged? Why?
2. What will relative yields between any two assets depend on, in equilibrium?

3. Which important assets in household wealth portfolios are likely to have their values affected significantly when interest rates rise in financial markets?
4. For a market to be efficient in the sense discussed in this chapter, is it necessary for all participants to be fully informed and up to date? Explain.
5. Does the random-walk hypothesis imply that stocks should be picked solely by throwing darts? That participants in the stock market are always right?
6. Why might some borrowers care about the nominal interest rate on their debt, as well as the real interest rate?
7. If the marginal tax rate is 40 percent, how much extra nominal yield is required to leave after-tax real yields constant when expected inflation rises by 1 percentage point?
8. What sort of factors would you expect to shift the demand for loanable funds in the stock market? the supply of loanable funds? What one factor will cause movement along those curves?

References

Goodhart, C.A.E. *Money, Information, and Uncertainty.* London: Macmillan, 1975, chaps. 4–7.

Malkiel, Burton G. *A Random Walk Down Wall Street.* 2d ed. New York: Norton, 1981.

Okun, Arthur. *Prices and Quantities.* Washington, D.C.: Brookings, 1981, chap. 4.

Pesando, James. *The Impact of Inflation on Financial Markets.* Montreal: C.D. Howe Research Institute, 1977.

Tobin, James. "A General Equilibrium Approach to Monetary Theory." *Journal of Money, Credit, and Banking* 1 (1969), 15–29.

CHAPTER 15

Equilibrium Yield Structures

In chapter 14 we pulled together what we knew about the behavior of typical borrowers, lenders, and financial intermediaries to explain general equilibrium in financial markets. You should understand by now how that equilibrium comes about and how fast it is likely to be reached in various asset markets.

In this chapter we will exploit some of the properties of general equilibrium to see what the pattern of relative expected yields will generally look like. The basic hypothesis is that there are a few stable structures of relative yields that persist over time because of yield-sensitive arbitrage between certain sets of financial markets, by lenders or borrowers or both. If such stable structures do exist, then knowing the behavior of any one yield in any structure is sufficient to explain and predict the behavior of all the others in that structure — a great simplification.

Your task in this chapter is to learn why these structures should exist, what they look like in Canada, and whether in fact they have been stable. The structures are for relative yields on assets differing only with respect to:

1. the term to maturity of the asset,
2. the level of default or liquidity risk,
3. the tax status of income from the asset, and
4. the currency in which the asset is denominated.

SECTION 1 The term structure of interest rates

Term structure of interest rates

The best-known part of the complete structure of equilibrium yields in the financial system is the *term structure of interest rates* — the structure of yields by term to maturity on assets of otherwise similar characteristics. The set of assets for which the term structure has been investigated has almost always been marketable federal government bonds; they are available in the full range of maturities, they are widely traded, and yields to maturity are widely reported. Yields on short-term and long-term government bonds are also good indicators of other short-term and long-term yields in the financial system, so explaining the term structure of federal government bond yields is essentially the same as explaining the relationship between long- and short-term yields for the financial system as a whole.

In general equilibrium, we expect assetholders to hold government bonds of various maturities such that differences in expected yields just compensate for differences in the risk that each bond adds to the portfolio. Unfortunately, the expected yields that bondholders take into consideration are often not the reported yields to maturity but rather expected yields over each holder's planned holding period.

That leaves us with two questions to be answered: (a) what differences are there between expected yields on bonds of different maturities for the same holding period, to reflect differences in risk, and (b) what does any given pattern of holding-period yields imply about the observed term structure of yields?

The answers to the first question make up a large chapter in the history of monetary theory, starting in the 1930s and continuing today. We will look at four theories in historical order, then review the evidence provided by empirical tests, and finally see what is implied by these theories for the term structure of observed yields to maturity.

Pure expectations theory

As the theory of the term structure of interest rates was first advanced by Irving Fisher, and later by Friedrich Lutz, it was argued that arbitrage between long-term and short-term bond markets would cause holding-period yields to be equal, with no differences due to risk.[1] Assetholders with a three-year holding period would require no less an average annual yield on a series of one-year bonds than is available on a single three-year bond, or else they would shift their asset demand to three-year bonds. Sufficient demand pressure of this sort would in turn keep the two yields equal. Where $r^e_{1,t}$ is the expected yield on a one-year bond held during year t, and r_3 is the yield currently available on a three-year bond, the Fisher-Lutz theory can be expressed algebraically as:

$$1 + r_3 = [(1 + r_{1,1})\ (1 + r^e_{1,2})\ (1 + r^e_{1,3})]^{1/3}.$$

In this simplest theory of the term structure of interest rates, known as the *pure expectations theory*, the yield to maturity on a three-year bond is equal to the (geometric) average of current and expected future one-year

Pure expectations theory

[1]Irving Fisher, *The Theory of Interest* (New York: Macmillan, 1930); F.A. Lutz, "The Structure of Interest Rates," *Quarterly Journal of Economics*, Nov. 1940, 36–63.

yields over the next three years. In general, the yield to maturity on an n-year bond is an average of the current and $n - 1$ expected future one-year bond yields.

Capital gains income

Bondholders can also consider holding bonds of a term longer than their holding period, with the intention of selling them in the secondary bond market before maturity and reaping *capital gains income* equal to the margin of any increase in the bonds' market price over their holding period. As before, the Fisher-Lutz theory suggests that expected yields will be the same from holding and reselling a long-term bond as from holding a bond that matures precisely at the end of the holding period. This implies a slightly different equilibrium result algebraically. For instance, the expected one-year yield on a twenty-year bond ($r^e_{20,1}$) is the coupon yield $C_{20}/P_{20,1}$ plus the expected rate of price increase $dP^e = (P^e_{20,2} - P_{20,1})/P_{20,1}$. In equilibrium, this yield will equal the yield to maturity on a one-year bond, because of arbitrage by bondholders with one-year holding periods. That is,

$$r_{1,1} = r_{20,1} = \frac{(C_{20} + P^e_{20,2} - P_{20,1})}{P_{20,1}}.$$

The arbitrage would have effect by raising or lowering $P_{20,1}$, thereby changing the capital gain or loss expected on twenty-year bonds over a one-year period.

Liquidity-preference theory

Liquidity-preference theory

J. R. Hicks added to the pure expectations theory the idea, borrowed from Keynes, that assetholders value the greater liquidity (that is, lower market risk, greater resalability) of shorter-term assets and will therefore insist on a slightly higher expected yield from holding longer-term bonds before they will switch from shorter-term to longer-term bonds.[2] In this *liquidity-preference* version of term-structure theory, the equilibrium condition for one-year and three-year bond yields, for instance, is

$$1 + r_3 = [(1 + r_{1,1})\ (1 + r^e_{1,2})\ (1 + r^e_{1,3})]^{1/3} + prem_3,$$

where $prem_3$ is the liquidity premium required on three-year bonds. Hicks suggested that, because market risk rises with the term to maturity of the bond, the required liquidity premiums should rise as well. In other respects, Hicks' theory is the same as the pure expectations theory.

Segmented-markets theory

J.M. Culbertson backed off from the assumption that assetholders are very sensitive to relative holding-period yields on long- and short-term bonds

[2]J.M. Keynes, *A Treatise on Money* (New York: Harcourt Press, 1930); J.R. Hicks, *Value and Capital*, 2d ed. (London: Oxford University Press, 1946).

(whether or not they insist on a liquidity premium).[3] Instead, Culbertson argued that assetholders have distinct preferences about which maturity of bond they will hold: long- and short-term bonds are not close substitutes, and their cross-elasticities of demand are not large. This is the *segmented-markets* hypothesis. If markets are segmented in this way, rather than linked together by sufficient arbitrage, yields will vary between different maturities of bond depending on demands and supplies of bonds of each term to maturity. Also, expected future short-term rates will not play any role in determining long-term yields if there is no arbitrage between the two market segments.

Segmented-markets hypothesis

Preferred-habitat theory

Modigliani and Sutch have proposed a theory that combines all three of the theories outlined, called the *preferred-habitat theory*.[4] They argue that for reasons of risk aversion each group of assetholders has a preferred habitat in a specific maturity segment of the bond market, but that each group will shift its demand into bonds of other, less preferred segments if expected yields in those segments contain a large enough premium to compensate for the extra risk exposure. Generally, extra risk exposure rises for each group of assetholders with the difference between actual and preferred terms to maturity, and therefore so does the necessary compensating liquidity premium. This relationship is illustrated in figure 15–1 for three groups of bondholders (with short-, medium-, and long-term preferred habitats).

Preferred-habitat theory

Since there is arbitrage between segments of the bond market under the preferred-habitat hypothesis, expectations of future short-term bond yields do influence long-term bond yields. If future short-term yields are expected to rise, some bondholders will be persuaded to shift from longer-term to shorter-term bonds, so prices of longer-term bonds will fall and their yields will rise. The quantity of bonds supplied in each term segment will also be important in determining relative yields; as the supply of long-term bonds rises, first medium-term and then short-term bondholders must be enticed from their preferred habitats to hold long-term bonds. Larger and larger liquidity premiums must be added to long-term bond yields to do that enticing.

Of these four versions of term-structure theory, all but the segmented-markets hypothesis predict expected future short-term rates to be an important factor in determining long-term yields. Demand for each

[3]John M. Culbertson, "The Term Structure of Interest Rates," *Quarterly Journal of Economics*, Nov. 1957, 485–517.

[4]Franco Modigliani and Richard Sutch, "Innovations in Interest Rate Policy," *American Economic Review*, May 1966, 178–97; also "Debt Management and the Term Structure of Interest Rates: An Empirical Analysis of Recent Experience," *Journal of Political Economy*, Aug. 1967, 568–89.

maturity of bond is elastic with respect to the yields on other maturities of bond. The pure expectations hypothesis stops there. The liquidity-preference theory adds a rising liquidity premium for longer-term bonds. The preferred-habitat theory asserts that the structure of liquidity premiums is not constant but depends on relative supplies of long- and short-term bonds.

FIGURE 15–1 Liquidity premiums under the preferred-habitat hypothesis

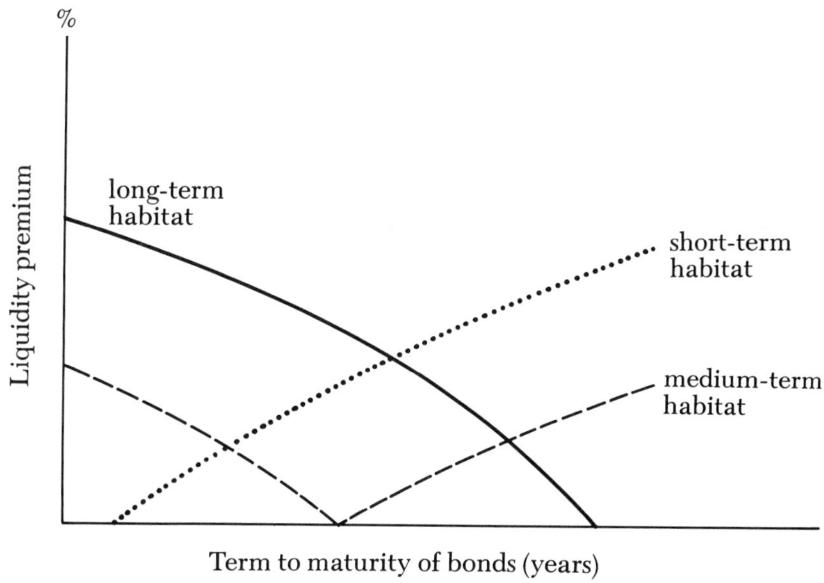

Holders whose preferred habitat is the short-term segment of the bond market will insist on extra liquidity premiums from all bonds with longer terms to maturity. Holders whose preferred habitat is the long-term segment will insist on extra liquidity premiums for all bonds with shorter terms. Holders whose preferred habitat is the medium-term segment will insist on extra liquidity premiums for both shorter- and longer-term bonds.

Preferred habitats in Canada

It will help us to apply term-structure theories in the Canadian context if we review who holds federal government bonds and what their likely preferred habitats are, if any. Modigliani and Sutch assumed (like Hicks before them) that most bondholders prefer to hold short-term bonds, other things being equal. This assumption is worth reviewing for the financial system of the 1980s.

Table 15–1 shows the distribution of federal government marketable bond holdings, both by holder and by term to maturity. Chartered banks hold large quantities of government bonds (including Treasury Bills held to satisfy the secondary reserve requirement); concerned with matching the interest sensitivities of their assets and debts, banks will have preferred habitats in the short-term segment of the bond market. Table 15–1 also shows large, discretionary government bond holdings by life insurance companies, and the huge "Other" category is made up largely of holdings by pension funds and by estate, trust, and agency accounts managed by trust companies. We saw in chapter 13 that life insurers and pension funds do not have to match maturities of assets to maturities of liabilities for most of their business. Their liabilities, unlike bank deposits, are for the most part not in fixed nominal terms; they have some leeway to vary the return on their liabilities to match whatever yield they earn on assets. These bondholders are likely to be a major source of interest-sensitive arbitrage in bond markets.

TABLE 15–1 Holdings of marketable federal government bonds

Demand by type of holder (September 1981)	Millions of dollars
Bank of Canada	15 996
Other government bodies (federal)	1 064
Private financial institutions	
chartered banks	11 755
life insurers	4 196
trust companies	1 529
investment dealers	920
Other institutions and residents	25 055
Nonresidents	8 599

Holdings by remaining term to maturity (general public only)	Percentages December 1975	December 1979	December 1981
Treasury Bills	9.8	15.1	18.7
Bonds			
3 years and under	27.2	13.5	26.3
3–5 years	16.5	21.5	16.2
5–10 years	23.9	7.0	3.6
10 years and over	22.2	38.6	32.7
Other securities	0.4	4.3	2.4
TOTAL	100.0	100.0	100.0
Average term to maturity (years/months)	6/5	10/1	7/10

Note: "General public" excludes Bank of Canada, chartered banks, and federal government.

Source: Bank of Canada Review.

If life insurers and pension funds have a preference for a particular segment of the bond market, that preference will be based on lower volatility of yield rather than on possible covariance with some specific liability cost. So will holdings of ETA funds in trust companies, which generally have no offsetting liability to be concerned about.

It is not obvious which type of bond will have lower volatility for life insurers and pension funds. In nominal terms, the yield from holding a long-term bond to maturity is more certain, in advance, than the yield from holding a series of short-term bonds, and both life insurers and pension funds can hold bonds to maturity without worrying much about liquidity in the interim. In periods of stable price levels, it is therefore reasonable to expect these bondholders to prefer longer-term bonds, other things being equal.

However, in a period of substantial uncertainty about future inflation, locking funds into a fixed nominal rate for a long term maximizes uncertainty of real return. Putting funds into a series of shorter-term assets, whose yields can vary in part at least with expected inflation, provides greater expected stability of real yields. Many pension funds in the 1970s stated as their investment goal the achievement of a small positive real yield, so this logic is clearly important for the recent past and the near future at least. It suggests that large groups of bondholders besides banks have short-term preferred habitats.

Evidence on liquidity premiums

There is a vast amount of evidence from tests of the four theories of the term structure of interest rates — too much to go over in a book such as this.[5] None of the evidence is conclusive, because all of the tests suffer from a common weakness: in order to calculate yields for either long or short holding periods for different maturities of bonds, the researcher must find some way of approximating bondholders' expectations of future short-term or long-term interest rates. There is no perfect way of doing this.[6]

The bulk of the test evidence points the same way, however, which makes up for some imperfection in individual test results. The evidence

---

[5]A convenient source for evidence on the term structure of interest rates is C.A.E. Goodhart, *Money, Information, and Uncertainty* (London: Macmillan, 1975), chap. 4, or James C. Van Horne, *Financial Market Rates and Flows* (Englewood Cliffs, N.J.: Prentice-Hall, 1978).

[6]The existing methods are (a) assuming perfect foresight, so that investors in 1965 are assumed to expect for 1966 exactly what happened in 1966, (b) assuming that expectations, whatever their level, change only in response to past errors in expectations, (c) assuming that expectations of future short-term rates reflect extrapolation of recent trends but also regression toward more distant past levels regarded as normal, (d) assuming that changes in future expectations are caused only by new information received in this period, and not by old information already available from past periods, (e) borrowing implied expectations from financial-futures markets, the earliest of which started up in Chicago in 1976, and (f) using expectations provided explicitly by questionnaire surveys of financial-market professionals.

supports the following propositions about relative holding-period yields on different maturities of government debt:[7]

1. Short- and long-term yields are not independent. Long-term yields do move sensitively in response to higher current or expected future short-term yields, so there is significant arbitrage between short-term and long-term segments of the bond market.
2. There generally are liquidity premiums in holding-period yields on longer-term bonds, though it is not clear whether these premiums rise steadily with the length of term to maturity. In some studies, the liquidity premiums seem to level off and stop rising after eight years or so.
3. Relative supplies may make some but not very much difference to relative yields. Even for the period from 1958 to 1960, when the Canadian government conducted a massive conversion of short-term to long-term debt, the evidence concerning supply effects is mixed.[8] Any supply effects that were detected were very small for such a huge change in relative supply.[9]

These three conclusions imply that government bonds of different maturities are fairly close substitutes in the asset demand functions of some investors — most likely life insurance companies, pension funds, and trust accounts managed by trust companies.

Implications for observed yields to maturity

If there is significant arbitrage between segments of the bond market in response to differences in expected yield, and if the liquidity premiums are constant, then changes in the structure of yields to maturity (the yield curve) are predictable from changes in expected future short-term yields. The reverse is also true: changes in expected future short-term yields can be inferred from observed changes in the yield curve, as in figure 15–2.

---

[7]For the most recent Canadian evidence, see Maureen E. Howe and John S. McCallum, "The Term Structure of Interest Rates in Canada: The Empirical Evidence," *Journal of Business Administration*, Fall 1980, 137–146.

[8]C.L. Barber and John S. McCallum, 'The Term Structure of Interest Rates and the Maturity Composition of the Government Debt: The Canadian Case," *Canadian Journal of Economics*, Nov. 1975, 606–9; Steven W. Dobson, "The Term Structure of Interest Rates and the Maturity Composition of the Government Debt: The Canadian Case," *Canadian Journal of Economics*, May 1973, 319–31; and L.N. Christofides, "Supply Variables in Term Structure Equations," *Canadian Journal of Economics*, May 1975, 276–81.

[9]In 1964 the U.S. government attempted to take advantage of the influence of supply on the term structure of interest rates to push short-term rates up and long-term rates down (to stimulate capital inflows with short-term rates and to stimulate the economy with long-term rates, both at the same time). Their action was to replace long-term debt with short-term debt. The effect was negligible. See Modigliani and Sutch, "Debt Management and the Term Structure of Interest Rates: An Empirical Analysis of Recent Experience," *Journal of Political Economy*, Aug. 1967, 568–89.

FIGURE 15-2 Yield curves in Canada, 1970–81

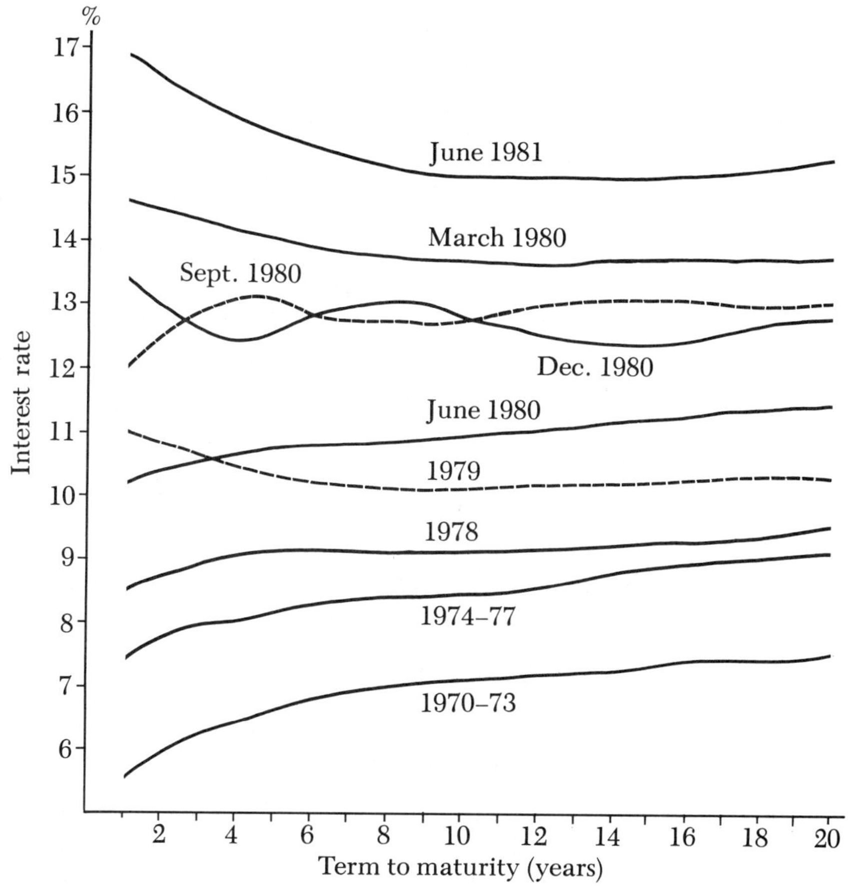

Each curve joins together yields to maturity on federal government marketable bonds (that is, excluding Canada Savings Bonds) for different terms to maturity. Where months are not indicated, data are averages of month-end figures.

Source: Department of Finance, *Economic Review*, April 1980, 1981, and 1982.

In order to see this, consider the liquidity-preference equation for a long-term yield. The evidence suggests that in equilibrium, longer-term bond yields to maturity will be equal to an average of current and expected future short-term yields over the same period, plus an extra liquidity premium. For an n-period bond, the yield to maturity (r_n) can be found from the equation

$$1 + r_n = [(1 + r_1)\ (1 + r^e_{1,2})\ (1 + r^e_{1,3})\ \ldots\ (1 + r^e_{1,n})]^{1/n} + L_n,$$

where L_n is the liquidity premium and $r^e_{1,n}$ is the expected one-year rate for year n. This equation can produce many different types of yield curve, depending on the pattern of future expected short-term yields:

1. If all of the expected future short-term yields equal the current short-term yield r_1, then the yield curve will look more or less as in figure 15–2 for the year 1978. The yields excluding liquidity premiums will be flat across the whole range of terms to maturity.
2. If future short-term yields are expected to be higher than current short-term yields, then current long-term yields will be above current short-term yields by more than is explained by liquidity premiums. The yield curve will slope upward more steeply, as in figure 15–2 for 1970–73.
3. If future short-term yields are expected to be lower than current short-term yields, then current long-term yields will fall, relative to current short-term yields, by an amount that increases with the term to maturity. The yield curve will be flatter or may even slope downward if the drop in future short-term yields is large enough. Examples in figure 15–2 are the yield curves for June 1981, March 1980, and 1979.
4. If bondholders expect the Bank of Canada to produce a period of monetary tightness leading after a few years to a recession, then expected future short-term rates will first rise, then fall. The yield curve will reflect this expectation by first rising, then falling again but more slowly, as in September 1980.

Two properties of the yield curves have not yet been mentioned. First, the currently observed long-term rates already contain the effects of predicted future changes in short rates. Analysts sometimes express this by saying that long-term rates "lead" short-term rates.

Second, current long-term rates will change in the same direction as future short-term rates, but by less. This differential occurs because a long-term yield is like an average of short-term yields, and averages always change by less than the changes in individual items in the average. For this reason, long-term yields are normally much less volatile than short-term yields. The two will move by equal amounts only if current and all expected future short-term rates change by the same amount, such as when inflation is expected to be higher by 5 percent for all future years.

SECTION 2 Other yield differentials due to risk

We have looked at differences between long- and short-term bonds in holding-period yields. These differences, called liquidity premiums, are due partly to differences in marketability and seem to rise with length of term to maturity, at least for short and medium-length terms. There are some other yield differentials in financial markets that can also be accounted for by differences in risk.

Market-risk differentials

Concern of bondholders about market risk is reflected in extra liquidity premiums, because primary lenders and financial institutions will not commit loanable funds to new bonds with greater market risk unless they are compensated by the prospect of extra expected yield. There are many different parts of bond markets, each of a different size and daily volume of trading, so market risk varies widely.

Greater liquidity premiums are required on provincial bonds, still greater on municipal bonds, and greater still on industrial bonds, the differentials due largely to differences in market risk. The premiums are between 0.5 and 1.3 percentage points over federal government bond yields of similar maturity, as a rule. Within each category there is a further differentiation by rating, which is a grouping of bond issues by the Canadian Bond Rating Service and the Dominion Bond Rating Service (in Canada) or by Standard and Poor's and by Moody's (for issues sold in the United States). To some extent these ratings reflect risk of default, which we will discuss shortly, but they also reflect differences in market risk because markets are thinner for lower-grade bonds. For provincial bonds, a change in rating from A+ to A will typically call for an extra liquidity premium of about 0.25 percentage points.

TABLE 15–2 Average interest rates on term deposits, January 8, 1983

Term to maturity	Chartered banks	Bank-affiliated mortgage loan companies
One year	9.30	9.90
Three years	9.425	10.31
Five years	9.47[a]	10.46[b]

[a]Using one less chartered bank than in the other averages.
[b]Using two fewer mortgage loan companies than in the other averages.
Note: All deposits have semi-annual compounding of interest. All require a minimum deposit of $1000, and in a few cases $5000.

Source: Fiscal agent's survey for *The Globe and Mail*, January 8, 1983, p. B2.

We can expect similar liquidity premiums in yields on term deposits that are not redeemable before maturity. Such deposits represent the ultimate in illiquidity, as they can be neither sold nor redeemed. Table 15–2 gives some examples of term-deposit yields that illustrate the point. Term deposits of mortgage loan companies are typically not redeemable before maturity, while those issued by chartered banks typically are redeemable. Both types of deposit are insured against risk of default by the Canada Deposit Insurance Corporation, so there is no default-risk difference between them. Households and firms do bear extra liquidity risk in the short term by putting their funds in a nonredeemable deposit, since they will be forced to borrow rather than just run down their term-deposit balance if they have a sudden need for cash. As a result, households will not lend to mortgage loan companies unless they are offered a liquidity premium that ranges from 0.6 percent for one-year deposits to about a full percentage point for five-year deposits.[10]

Default-risk differentials

We have already noted that industrial bonds with different bond ratings have different expected yields and that some of the difference in yields reflects differences in market risk. The rest of it reflects differences in default risk. Lower-grade bonds have a greater expected default loss, which is defined as size of loss (per dollar of par value) in event of default, multiplied by the probability of default. A default-risk premium in the promised or quoted yield that is just equal to the expected default loss does not convey any extra advantage to the lender. The lender's expected yield is the promised yield less the expected default loss rate. As compensation for the extra variability that extra default risk implies, the lender would have to insist on a default-risk premium greater than the expected default loss rate. There is evidence from a long-term study conducted some time ago in the United States that default-risk premiums are only just equal to differences in expected default loss rates for different rating classes of bonds, leaving no margin at all to compensate for extra risk or for differences in marketability.[11]

SECTION 3 The tax structure

We generally expect greater demand for assets whose income is taxed at lower rates. That greater demand will force up prices of the favored assets and force down the prices of other assets, so the relative before-tax yield of favored assets will be depressed. The total effect of the tax advantage will be to depress the relative before-tax yield of the favored assets by a margin equal to the value of the tax advantage, so that after-tax yields will be equal on otherwise similar assets. There are several examples of pairs of assets in financial markets for which such tax-induced differentials are particularly clear. We will look at two of them.

---

[10]The extra liquidity premium on mortgage loan company deposits can be analysed with the precautionary-demand theory we used in chapter 9 to explain the demand for money. In equilibrium the extra liquidity premium should be equal to (a) the extra expected cost of meeting sudden needs for cash, caused by having to use sources other than the term deposit, plus (b) a risk premium to compensate the assetholder for any extra uncertainty about whether future cash needs will be met at all. The expected extra cost is a product of the extra cost of the next-best source of funds, and the probability of the funds' being needed.

[11]Harold G. Fraine and Robert H. Mills, "Effects of Defaults and Credit Deterioration on Yields of Corporate Bonds," *Journal of Finance*, Sept. 1961, 423–24.

Bonds and preferred stocks

Shares of preferred stock provide a relatively fixed coupon yield where the issuing company has a stable revenue flow (for example, a utility company). There is little chance of capital gain except as a result of a drop in the discount rate used to value the share's expected future dividends. In short, such a preferred share is similar to a bond in many respects. However, dividends on preferred shares are eligible for the dividend tax credit, while bond interest is not. The dividend tax credit effectively reduces the tax rate on dividend income by about 33 percentage points.

As a result, demand for preferred shares is strong enough that preferred-share coupon yields (the coupon divided by the market price) are generally much less than the yield on bonds despite the greater income risk of preferred shares. Table 15–3 gives some examples. The tax-induced margin for preferred shares is also present for common stocks, but it is much more difficult to detect because of the many other differences between common stocks and bonds.

TABLE 15–3 Yield differentials between preferred shares and bonds

Issuer	Debt	Yield (%)
Bell Canada	bond, due 2004	12.47
	preferred share	10.29
Canadian Utilities	bond, due 1997	14.41
	preferred share	10.67
NOVA Corporation	bond, due 1997	14.95
	preferred share	12.50

Source: The Globe and Mail, December 29, 1982, pp. B6, B8.

Deep-discount versus shallow-discount bonds

The second easily observable before-tax yield differential is between bonds selling at a large discount from par value and bonds selling at close to par value. The former are bonds whose original coupon rates are well below current yields; their prices have dropped to compensate. Since the bond will be redeemed at full par value at maturity, the holder will realize a capital gain equal to the full discount on the bond at time of purchase. Such bonds therefore provide the holder with a mixture of interest income and capital gains income, rather than just with interest income.

Capital gains income is taxed at only half of the personal income tax rate, and the tax is deferred until the asset is sold or otherwise transferred. Because of the lower tax rate on the capital gain portion of the yield, purchasers require a smaller combination yield of interest and capital gains income before tax from deeply discounted bonds than they do from bonds providing income only in the form of interest. Table 15–4 gives some examples from the market for government bonds.

TABLE 15–4 Yield differentials between deep- and shallow-discount bonds, November 26, 1982

Coupon and date	Asking price ($)	Yield to maturity (%)	Yield differential
3% September 1996	44.00	10.96	
10% October 1995	88.50	11.75	0.79
$8\frac{1}{4}$% July 1987	92.75	10.26	
$14\frac{3}{4}$% June 1987	111.25	11.49	1.23
$5\frac{3}{4}$% September 1992	68.38	11.14	
$13\frac{1}{2}$% October 1992	107.00	12.25	1.11
$8\frac{3}{4}$% February 2002	76.88	11.82	
$15\frac{1}{2}$% March 2002	120.00	12.69	0.87

Source: Richardson Greenshields of Canada Ltd., *Bond and Money Markets*, November 26, 1982.

SECTION 4

International yield differentials

In general equilibrium, differentials in assets' yields should reflect only differentials in the risk that each asset adds to the portfolio. The principle applies even to assets denominated in different currencies. If there is sufficient arbitrage between different national financial markets, there will be a stable structure of yields for assets whose only difference is in currency of denomination. That structure will provide equal expected yields.

International arbitrage

The expected yield for a Canadian buyer of a U.S.-dollar deposit is the stated U.S. interest rate plus the expected percentage change in the Canadian-dollar price of the U.S. dollar (at annual rates, if the interest rate is quoted at annual rates). For a U.S. lender, the expected yield on a Canadian-dollar deposit is the stated Canadian interest rate plus the expected percentage change in the U.S.-dollar price of the Canadian dollar.

Lenders on both sides of the border (chiefly cash managers for large corporations) will switch loanable funds between Canadian- and U.S.-dollar deposits until the difference in expected yields just compensates for any extra risk. For Canadian investors the U.S.-dollar deposit has extra exchange risk. For foreign investors the Canadian-dollar deposit has extra exchange risk. The risk premium on Canadian-dollar deposits could be positive or negative, depending on which way the lending had to be persuaded to move across the border.

Aside from the risk premium, and if there are no barriers to the flow of lending and borrowing between national financial markets, equilibrium differences between stated nominal yields in different currencies should equal expected appreciation in currency values. In a world of fixed exchange rates, this view implies a single world interest rate — that is, a situation in which no one nation can determine its interest rate independently of other countries. We will return to this implication in chapter 25.

In a world of floating exchange rates, where currency appreciation can be substantial, national interest rates can and do differ substantially. Table 15–5 shows what the structure of international short-term interest rates looked like, for instance, on December 14, 1982. Japan has effective controls on the amount of international lending and borrowing in its financial system, but lenders and borrowers in the other countries are relatively free to go abroad if better yields beckon. If there is sufficient arbitrage and absence of risk aversion to equalize expected yields on money-market assets in different currencies, then lenders in table 15–5 must have expected rates of currency appreciation or depreciation that will exactly offset the nominal yield differentials shown in the table.

TABLE 15–5 International short-term nominal interest differentials, December 14, 1982

Country	Three-month money-market yields (%)	Differential relative to the United States
United States	8.75	—
United Kingdom	10.56	1.79
Belgium	12.35	3.60
France	12.88	4.13
West Germany	6.60	−2.15
Holland	6.13	−2.62
Italy	19.63	10.88
Switzerland	3.94	−4.81
Japan	5.63	−3.12
Canada	10.20	1.45

Note: The money-market rates refer to prime commercial paper for the U.S., Canada, and France; to interbank deposit rates in the U.K., West Germany, Holland, Italy, and Switzerland; to four-month Fonds des Rentes certificates in Belgium; and to two-month Treasury Bills in Japan.

Source: The Economist, December 18–24, 1982, p. 85; for Canada, *Bank of Canada Review*.

Forward cover

It is possible to avoid exchange risk entirely, by using futures or forward-exchange contracts to cover against it. These contracts work like any futures contract (see chapter 8, section 4); effectively the investor arranges, for a tiny commission, a return to domestic currency at an exchange rate fixed in advance. The only significant cost is the *cost of forward cover*, which comes from the premium of the forward exchange rate over the spot exchange rate (the forward premium).

Cost of forward cover

With forward cover, the expected yield for a Canadian from a 90-day U.S.-dollar deposit is as follows, where r_{US} is the nominal U.S. deposit rate (in percent), and *fwd* and *spot* are the forward and spot U.S.-dollar prices of the Canadian dollar:

$$\begin{aligned} E_{US} &= r_{US} - \text{cost of cover} \\ &= r_{US} - 100\left(\frac{fwd - spot}{spot}\right)\left(\frac{360}{90}\right). \end{aligned}$$

The forward premium ($fwd - spot$) must be divided by the spot price to put it in fractional form, multiplied by 100 to convert it to percentage units, and then multiplied by 360/90 to convert to annual rates (since r_{US} is always expressed at annual rates).

The equilibrium condition, with exchange risk removed, is simply that the expected yield in Canada equal that in the United States:

$$E_C = E_{US},$$

where E_C is the Canadian nominal interest rate. This equilibrium condition will hold if there is anough arbitrage across the border. For that point, remember from chapters 5 and 10 that Canadian investment dealers do a lot of business precisely by bringing to people's attention any gains to be made from shifting funds across the border; as a result of their efforts, we can safely assume a lot of arbitrage.

We can therefore predict a large shift of demand into U.S.-dollar assets whenever the U.S. interest rate, less the cost of forward cover, is greater than the Canadian interest rate. The opposite will occur if the Canadian interest rate is higher, until the two expected yields have been brought back into equality. Such shifts of demand between U.S.-dollar and Canadian-dollar assets will affect both U.S. and Canadian interest rates and the cost of forward cover. The largest impact by far is on the cost of cover, so it is fair to say that the equilibrium condition should really be written as

Cost of forward cover = U.S. interest rate − Canadian interest rate.

Table 15–6 illustrates this proposition by showing the national interest-rate differentials from table 15–5 and also the cost of forward cover for a lender in each of those countries considering instead a covered purchase of three-month, U.S.-dollar money-market assets. What is left over after deducting the cost of forward cover from the simple or uncovered interest

TABLE 15–6 Covered interest differentials, December 14, 1982

Country	Uncovered differential on 90-day money-market assets	Cost of 90-day forward cover against the US$ (annual rates)	Covered interest differential
United States	0	0	0
United Kingdom	1.79	0.95	0.84
Belgium	3.60	5.22	–1.62
France	4.13	12.30	–8.17
West Germany	–2.15	–3.04	0.89
Holland	–2.62	–3.40	0.78
Italy	10.88	15.16	–4.28
Switzerland	–4.81	–5.52	0.71
Japan	–3.12	–2.37	–0.75
Canada	1.45	1.07	0.38

Note: See note, table 15–5.

Sources: The Economist, December 18–24, 1982, p. 85; for Canada, *Bank of Canada Review*.

FIGURE 15–3 Interest differentials in favor of Canada, 1970–82

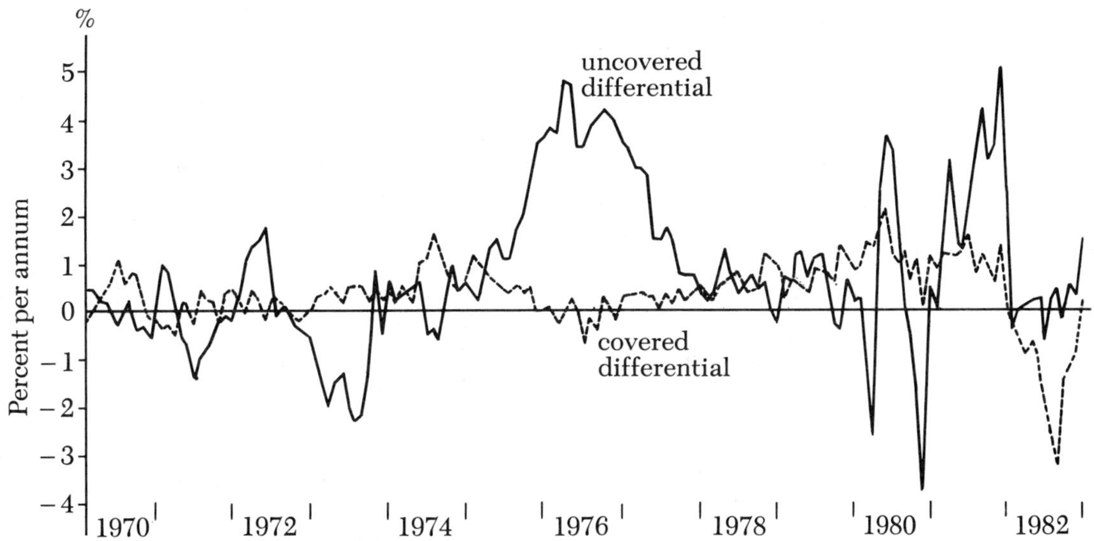

The uncovered differential is the difference between the ninety-day Canadian finance-paper rate and the ninety-day U.S. finance-company-paper rate (the commercial-paper rate after August 1972). The covered differential is the uncovered differential less the percentage forward premium of the U.S. dollar at an annual rate.

Covered interest differential

differential is the *covered interest differential* in favor of the U.S. That covered interest differential is very small in all but two cases (France and Italy, both with very unsettled foreign exchange markets at the time); the cost of forward cover has adjusted to reflect interest differentials.

A further set of Canadian evidence is provided in figure 15–3, which shows the uncovered and covered differentials for short-term Canadian and United States money-market assets from 1970 to 1982. The cost of forward cover eliminated enough of the uncovered interest differential that what remained often did not justify the extra transactions costs of investing abroad. Since 1980, the covered interest differentials have been much wider. The power of the cost of forward cover to offset simple interest differentials is most obvious in the 1975–77 period; a huge simple interest differential opened up between Canada and the United States, but the covered interest differential actually moved the other way.

The forward premium as a predictor of exchange-rate changes

If the cost of forward cover against U.S.-dollar exchange risk equals the differential between Canadian and U.S. interest rates, and if uncovered lenders (those not using forward cover) shift between Canadian- and U.S.-dollar deposits until any differential between the two interest rates just matches the expected appreciation of the Canadian dollar, it follows that in equilibrium the cost of forward cover (the percentage forward premium on the Canadian dollar) will also equal the expected appreciation of the Canadian dollar.

There is a separate reason for believing that the forward premium on a currency will be a good predictor of its expected future appreciation. The forward-exchange market is a vehicle for currency speculation as well as for hedging. If Brown is a speculator in forward-exchange contracts for Canadian dollars, her gain is from selling forward Canadian dollars at a higher price than she expects to pay to buy them (in the spot market in the future, in order to deliver against or to cancel her forward-exchange contract). If she expects the Canadian dollar to appreciate 5 percent over a three-month period, she will buy forward Canadian dollars as long as the forward premium is less than 5 percent. The selling pressure of Brown and many other speculators like her will help the forward premium to reach 5 percent.

The power of the forward premium as a predictor of exchange-rate changes has been tested several times, against the alternatives of econometric forecasting models estimated from past data.[12] The forward-exchange-rate premiums have usually given the most accurate predictions of actual exchange rate changes, though even those forecasts have been far from a runaway success.

[12]See "Judgement Day for the Forecasters," *Euromoney*, Sept. 1980, 65–66; for a fuller discussion of the behavior of interest differentials that discriminates between nominal and real differentials, see Jeffrey A. Frankel, "On the Mark: A Theory of Floating Exchange Rates Based on Real Interest Differentials," *American Economic Review*, Sept. 1979, 610–22.

SECTION 5 Summary

There is a pattern to the general equilibrium structure of yields by term to maturity. Yields to maturity for bonds of different terms are generally such that a lender can expect to earn the same yield over any one holding period from bonds of any term. Longer-term bonds typically command a liquidity premium as well, one that is only mildly sensitive to changes in relative supplies of different bonds. The implication is that bonds of different maturities are close substitutes for each other and therefore that long-term rates are an estimate (though an upward-biased one) of the average of expected future short-term rates.

Similarly, liquidity premiums explain differentials among federal, provincial, municipal, and industrial bonds, and among different qualities of bonds in each category, since their marketability differs and lenders wish to be compensated for any loss of liquidity. There are differences in quoted yields due to default risks as indicated by different bond ratings, but the limited evidence on the subject suggests those differences are equal only to differences in expected default loss rates; that leaves expected yields the same on bonds of all ratings, with no extra margin as compensation for risk.

There is a pattern of differences in before-tax yields due to differences in tax treatment of different sources of income. Dividend income and capital gains income are taxed more lightly than regular interest income, so there is extra demand for assets generating income in the first two forms. The extra demand pushes up the market price and depresses the yield relative to other assets.

There is a predictable pattern of relative yields across nations as well, producing in equilibrium a set of relative nominal yield differentials that provide equal expected yields after allowance for expected exchange-rate changes. Differences in nominal yields therefore reflect expected currency appreciation, plus an uncertain risk premium for foreign exchange risk. It is possible to avoid exchange risk by forward cover, but in equilibrium the cost of forward cover will also equal the expected change in the exchange rate; the cost of forward cover can therefore be expected to change so as to eliminate any expected yield differential between assets in different currencies.

Questions for discussion

1. If the yield on any one asset always bears a fixed relationship to the yield on some other asset, what does that imply for the slopes of demand or supply curves in the loanable-funds diagram for that market?
2. If either the demand or the supply of an asset must be very interest-elastic to allow stable yield structures, which is more likely to have that property, and why?

3. Why would banks typically find short-term bonds preferable to long-term bonds, while life insurers might well feel just the opposite?
4. What pattern of expected future short-term yields would produce a U-shaped yield curve?
5. What pattern of expected future short-term rates is implied by a perfectly flat yield curve?
6. Does the extra yield promised on lower-grade corporate bonds really compensate for extra default risk by raising the expected yield relative to that on higher-grade corporate bonds? Explain.
7. What explains the size of margin between yields on redeemable versus nonredeemable term deposits, of 0.6 to 1.0 percent?
8. Why would the forward-exchange premium on the Candian dollar serve as a reasonable predictor of future appreciation of the Canadian dollar?

References

Aliber, Robert Z. *Exchange Risk and Corporate International Finance*. New York: Halsted Press, 1978.

Goodhart, C.A.E. *Money, Information, and Uncertainty*. London: Macmillan, 1975, chap. 4.

Officer, Lawrence H. "Effective Exchange Rates and Price Ratios over the Long Run: A Test of the Purchasing Power Parity Theory." *Canadian Journal of Economics*. May 1980, 206–31.

Van Horne, James C. *Function and Analysis of Capital Market Rates*. Englewood Cliffs, N.J.: Prentice-Hall, 1970.

CHAPTER 16

Government and the Financial System

Previous chapters have explored how demand and supply of assets behave in the financial system. Chapters 14 and 15 described and analysed patterns of relative yields in general equilibrium. It is appropriate in this last chapter of the microeconomics half of the book to consider what impact the government has had on the structure and performance of the financial system, what trends there are in government involvement, and what future changes are likely. The financial system we know today, far from being a pure outgrowth of unchecked private-sector initiative, is very much the product of past government decisions to allow, prohibit, tax, or induce various types of lending and borrowing.

Your task in this chapter is therefore to learn:

1. the various ways in which governments shape the financial system,
2. the main types of government regulation affecting the financial system,
3. the major government financial intermediaries and their functions, and
4. how governments can and do intervene to manipulate prices and yields in particular financial markets.

SECTION 1 Types of government influence

There are four ways in which federal and provincial governments influence the financial system:

1. Governments regulate financial practices: they regulate accounting rules and standards, financial trading procedures, the rights of borrowers and lenders, and methods of enforcing contracts. Perhaps most important in a financial system where two-thirds of primary lending passes through financial intermediaries, governments regulate the range of intermediary activities permitted to each type of financial institution, through such legislation as the Bank Act.

2. Governments use the financial system in their roles as lenders and borrowers. The federal government in particular borrows on such a large scale that the federal government bond market is the centre of the financial system. Government bonds (especially Treasury Bills) serve as an important liquid asset for the rest of the economy.
3. Governments have established a host of specialized financial intermediaries to supplement, compete with, or replace private intermediaries. Some of the government intermediaries lend and borrow funds directly, like other lending institutions; others merely guarantee private debts against default loss.
4. Governments manipulate financial markets in order to stabilize either the financial markets or the real sector of the economy, in order to redirect private flows of funds within the financial system, and in order to redress disparities or provide extra opportunities for particular groups in the economy.

Of the four kinds of government involvement, borrowing and lending has been dealt with already in our chapter 7 survey. It raises no issues for the proper functioning of the financial system, so it is ignored here. The others we will deal with in turn.

SECTION 2 Government as regulator

Types of regulation

There are basically two groups of regulations in the financial system. The first group is contained in the enabling legislation for each type of financial intermediary — the Bank Act, the Trust Companies Act, the Loan Companies Act, the insurance company acts, and the federal Pension Benefits Standards Act. The most important of these is the Bank Act, dealt with separately in the next subsection. These enabling acts all specify limits on asset holdings, on liabilities, on other business, and on ownership, and they all outline reporting procedures. We covered the major provisions of these acts in chapters 11 through 13, so in this chapter we will deal specifically only with the Bank Act, which is typical in many respects as well as important in its own right.

All of the financial-institution acts provide for some form of reporting, or inspection, or both, so that regulators can easily check whether the required practices are being followed. If they are not, the company's licence can be cancelled, or it can be renewed for periods as short as two weeks until the company has corrected the situation. Fidelity Trust, for instance, was put on a series of two-week licences from March 1983 until its management was handed over to First City Trust to be wound down in mid-1983.

The federal and provincial Superintendents of Insurance receive reports and make inspections of insurance companies, trust companies, small loan companies, and even provincial credit union centrals in most provinces. These reports are summarized and published for the general public to see. The Inspector General for Banks, the provincial Pension Commissions, and the various provincial Securities Commissions do the same for banks, pension funds, and securities dealers respectively. The Canada Deposit Insurance Corporation (CDIC) inspects all deposit-taking institutions whose deposits it insures, and which are not already inspected by some other official deemed acceptable by the CDIC. The Ontario Securities Commission in particular must approve the prospectus of any firm issuing new shares, and it has very strict requirements on the information that must be contained in the prospectus. Even the Bank of Canada receives some reports, such as the weekly reports of chartered banks on their asset and deposit composition.

The second major group of regulations are those that set limits on financial transactions in general, regardless of whether a financial institution is involved. The following are examples:

1. Under a 1980 amendment to the Criminal Code, no loan can be made that provides for an annual interest rate over 60 percent.
2. Minors cannot enter into financial contracts on their own behalf without a parent or guardian's approval.
3. Only licensed salespeople can trade securities on behalf of customers in either the stock or the bond market.

One purpose of specific regulation in the financial system is to prohibit certain transactions known to be improper or unsafe, such as loan sharking or putting trust funds heavily into venture-capital loans. Another is to ensure as far as possible that financial transactions represent informed choices of people competent to choose. The best example of regulations serving the latter purpose are the not infrequent orders of the Toronto Stock Exchange and the Ontario Securities Commission to cease trading in particular stocks, on occasions where information about the company's affairs seems to be either absent or misleading in some way. Investors are to be allowed to take whatever risks they wish and then to suffer the consequences, but only if they have access to the relevant facts beforehand. Emphasis has shifted over the last two decades toward improving the information flow and away from prohibiting particular types of transactions. Disclosure and reporting requirements are much stricter, and investment restrictions much looser, than in 1960.

The Bank Act

The Bank Act has always been the centrepiece of financial regulation because banks have always been the major type of financial institution. Establishment of other types of financial institutions has gradually eroded the banks' share of financial markets since 1870, but banks still dominate most short-term markets in Canada.

Objectives of the Bank Act

There are several objectives behind the Bank Act. One is protection of bank depositors' funds, achieved by restricting the range of permissible bank assets. Another is preservation of the banks' role in the transmission of monetary policy, achieved by requiring certain minimum levels of cash reserves. A third is assurance of efficiency in the financial system, in the sense of getting the least-cost intermediation, achieved by allowing banks to compete with other financial institutions. A fourth is preservation of a range of different, separate financial institutions, achieved by keeping banks out of competition with some other financial institutions.

The third and fourth objectives are contradictory, but the explanation is fairly simple. The federal government recognizes that allowing more open competition in financial markets will initially lead to better terms for customers, smaller profit margins, leaner operations, more innovation. In the longer run, however, uncontrolled competition would lead to a shake-out, with the weaker institutions going bankrupt or merging or retreating from the market. It is feared that the banks would always be the stronger because of their size, market power, and depth of management talent and that flows of credit in Canada would thus come to be dominated by the banks to a much greater extent even than now.

Provisions of the Bank Act

The following is a complete list of the major provisions of the Bank Act, many of which were mentioned in chapter 11.

1. The Bank Act serves as the charter for all banks listed in the schedules at the end of the Act. Schedule A is for widely held, domestically owned banks, Schedule B for the others. The charters extend for ten years because the Bank Act itself runs for only ten years. This time limit is designed to force legislators to keep bank regulations in step with a changing financial system and has been a feature of banking law since the first Bank Act, right after Confederation. The feature is not built into the Trust Companies Act or the Loan Companies Act, but those groups have come to expect their legislation to be revised whenever there is major a change in banking legislation.
2. The Bank Act specifies conditions for entry into banking, including minimum size ($2 million of capital) and composition of ownership and of boards of directors. Since the last revision took effect in December 1980, entry into banking has been possible by letters patent, a relatively easy route. Ownership of domestic banks is generally limited to 10 percent for any group of associated shareholders, though foreign bank subsidiaries can remain wholly owned. Domestic banks starting with more concentrated ownership are first put in the Schedule B list, rather than in Schedule A, and have up to ten years to reduce the controlling interest of each shareholder to less than 10 percent. This

requirement reflects a continuing concern by Canadian governments that the enormous financial power of Canadian banks never be concentrated in a few hands.

Boards of directors are constrained mainly in that no director of a trust company may also be a director of a chartered bank, and at least half of the board must be Canadian. The provision against interlocking directorships was put in in 1967 to force more competition between banks and trust companies, since there were tight pairings of banks and trust companies to that point.

3. The Bank Act sets growth limits on foreign bank subsidiaries: each is limited in its total assets to no more than twenty times its deemed authorized capital, which in turn is specified by the Minister of Finance. Collectively, the total of deemed authorized capital is doled out by the Minister so that total assets of foreign bank susbsidiaries will not exceed 8 percent of the total domestic assets of all banks. This provision is designed to allow competition from foreign banks, but within limits.
4. The Bank Act imposes cash reserve requirements and also secondary reserve requirements. The latter are variable at the discretion of the Governor of the Bank of Canada.
5. There are some limits on asset holdings and therefore on the types of business that banks can get into by investing in subsidiaries. Some of these limits are for prudence, such as limiting mortgages to 10 percent of Canadian-dollar deposits and debentures, limiting the amount loaned on an individual mortgage to 75 percent of the value of the property pledged (unless the mortgage is insured against default risk), and prohibiting ownership of real estate except for bank premises.

   Some of the asset restrictions are to limit banks to banking, in order to keep them out of other institutions' markets: banks are limited to no more than 10 percent ownership of Canadian companies in non-banking-related fields. The definition of banking-related does include mortgage lending, factoring, leasing, and venture-capital lending, and there is absolutely no restriction on ownership of foreign subsidiaries.
6. The Bank Act sets limits on other activities of banks. They cannot sell trustee services, mutual funds, life insurance, or even computer services that are not related to banking. Banks cannot participate in the underwriting of corporate securities, nor can they solicit brokerage business. They can participate as members of a selling group for corporate securities, and they can pass on securities trading business to a broker on behalf of their customers, but those functions are more passive. Factoring and leasing are allowed, but only since 1980 and only through wholly owned subsidiaries. Foreign bank subsidiaries are limited to no more than 10 percent ownership of any foreign corporation of any sort, to enable the Inspector General of Banks to keep a close eye on their activities.
7. The Bank Act specifies the reporting requirements to the Inspector General of Banks and to the Bank of Canada.

8. The Bank Act sets limits on liabilities to be issued. The main limit is on debentures, which must be originally for a term of at least five years and may not exceed half of the bank's equity.

Recent trends and concerns in financial regulation

The trend in government regulation of intermediaries has been to remove the barriers to competition among them while restricting the extent of cross-ownership. Chartered banks have been allowed into almost all types of financial intermediation except trustee activity, insurance, and underwriting of corporate securities.[1] Trust companies may shortly be allowed into commercial lending. The effects of removing legal barriers have been more vigorous competition among banks, narrower expense margins, and a much greater variety of deposits used to attract the public's savings.

Financial regulators in Canada have avoided two dangerous pitfalls, at least so far. The first is specific regulation of interest rates — the imposition of floors and ceilings. The 6 percent interest-rate ceiling on bank loans was removed in 1967, and the interest-rate ceiling on small loans was removed in July 1980. Removal of these ceilings has enabled Canadians to avoid the continuing liquidity crisis that has plagued the U.S. thrift institutions for much of the last quarter-century.

The second pitfall that has been avoided is the creation of a patchwork quilt of financial regulations differing from province to province and between federal and provincial levels. We do have a patchwork quilt of responsibilities; for instance, the federal government regulates solvency of federally chartered insurance companies, while the provinces regulate the firms' policy provisions. Nevertheless, the eleven governments have co-ordinated their actions in the past well enough that Canada still has a close approximation to uniform financial legislation.

Six areas of concern remain, despite what is regarded as a successful set of financial controls.

The first concern is over the timeliness of regulatory supervision. The Ontario and federal governments were seriously embarrassed when Re-Mor Investment Co. and its parent, the federally regulated Astra Trust Co., failed in 1980 only shortly after Re-Mor had its licence renewed by the Ontario Registrar of Trust and Loan Companies. The Quebec government was equally embarrassed at the troubles of the Caisses d'Entraide movement. Since these incidents, both Quebec and Ontario governments have

---

[1]Banks are allowed to trade securities (through licensed dealers) on behalf of clients. Until deregulation of stock exchange commission schedules in April 1983, banks' trading on behalf of clients made no difference. Now, however, the banks can use their buying power to negotiate much lower commission rates than their clients would ever be able to get on their own, so the stockbrokers are very upset. The Toronto Dominion Bank has set up a separate division, Green Line Investors Services, to handle this type of "discount" brokerage business for clients, so the threat is real. The Ontario Securities Commission has ruled that Green Line can operate, but there is still controversy over the decision.

given themselves much wider powers to act when they scent trouble in a financial institution.

The second concern is over concentrated ownership of financial institutions, especially trust companies. The major trust companies are almost all closely held companies, in great contrast to domestic banks, credit unions and caisses populaires, and mutual life insurance companies. The government moved in the 1960s to limit foreign ownership of financial firms, but recently the problem has come from concentrated ownership by domestic citizens. The problem lies in the temptation to use a trust company's funds to benefit other activities of the owner, at the expense of the trust company's depositors and trust beneficiaries.

This issue arose when Campeau Corporation bid for control of Royal Trust Company, the largest trust company in Canada, in 1980. Campeau Corporation is a large real estate developer, and it was feared that Royal Trust would become a captive lender to Campeau. Campeau's bid failed, and the issue submerged for a while. The issue arose again when Leonard Rosenberg, a real estate speculator, bought control of Crown Trust, the eleventh largest trust company in Canada. Crown Trust and Greymac Trust (also owned by Rosenberg) then took on some very controversial third mortgage loans that were key parts of a huge real estate deal masterminded by Rosenberg and associates. The episode (details of which are included in an appendix to this chapter) is likely to have a long-lasting impact on financial regulation in Canada. The government's reaction was to take over control of all the financial institutions involved (three trust companies and three affiliated mortgage loan companies) and to arrange for their business to be taken over permanently by other companies — effectively removing the companies from their owners and winding them up.

The lesson learned by many is that concentrated ownership of a financial institution can lead to lending practices that endanger the security of deposits, and that fast regulatory response is vital.

A third area of concern is that there are still important barriers to competition and efficiency in the trust business, in underwriting, and in insurance. Entry to each of these sectors is easy in one sense: any group of individuals with the necessary capital can set up shop and get a charter. However, the firms that already have the necessary capital and financial skills, and that could operate with the lowest costs because of shared overheads, are exactly the firms excluded by legislation. Banks are prevented from doing trust business, from underwriting, and from selling insurance.

The reason for concern about banks' engaging in trust and underwriting business is mostly that the banks would be "too efficient," driving existing firms out of the business entirely. An argument is made about conflict of interest between trust activities and financial intermediation, but the same conflict does not seem to cause much of a problem in other countries, where the union of banking and trustee functions is common. Further, the argument about conflict of interest is not made for the intermediary activities of the trust companies themselves; one can only infer that the real concern is not with conflict of interest but rather with preserving a market for relatively inefficient firms.

A fourth area of concern is lack of innovation in indexed savings and lending instruments. With a matched set of indexed loans and deposits, intermediaries could remove much of the artificial "front-end loading" of debt service costs now imposed by building inflation premiums into nominal interest rates rather than into the principal amount. The federal government tested intermediary opinion on this topic in the summer of 1982 but has not pushed the matter.[2]

A fifth source of concern is the high level of expense margins incurred by life insurance companies. The degree of competition in selling life insurance (as opposed to annuities) has not increased much over thirty years, and the agency distribution system is still very expensive. The nature of the distribution system — in-home, personalized sales — raises other efficiency questions about satisfying demand. If the products do satisfy consumer demand, then why is such a large selling expense needed? If they do not satisfy demand (and large surrender values each year suggest that many life insurance policies do not), then how is the selling expense justified? Selling life insurance through the present system of agents is a built-in feature of the life insurance market; although that distribution system is no longer imposed by provincial laws forcing each agent to represent just one company, the agents and companies are not about to abandon it.[3]

A sixth area of concern, in which governments have played a major part, is the greater level of inflation risk in the financial system since 1965. Inflation risk was not a serious concern in the 1950s, but now it dominates all retirement planning.

Since 1970, as interest rates and inflationary expectations have become more volatile, Canadian investors have become less certain about the distant future and less willing to commit themselves to any nominal return over long periods. The form of financial assets has therefore changed increasingly to either short-term assets or else long-term assets with frequent renegotiability of the interest rate. Intermediaries have had to make this adjustment in their liability pattern in order to raise funds. They have had to force the same pattern on borrowers in order to match asset yields to changing liability costs.

---

[2]The Minister of Finance set up a consultative committee in June 1982 to advise him on establishing indexed loans for specific types of borrowers. The committee (consisting mainly of executives of financial intermediaries) approved the general idea of indexing savings instruments but rejected the government's specific limitations on use of the funds. See Report of the *Ministerial Advisory Committee on Inflation and the Taxation of Personal Investment Income* (Ottawa: Dept. of Finance, 1982).

[3]Until recently, each agent had to be sponsored by a life insurance company and could represent only one company in the normal line of business. This prevented the rise of a general agency system to supplement field forces of single-company agents.

If the extra volatility of nominal yields since 1970 reflected only volatility of inflation, so that real yields were still relatively stable, one could argue that in an important sense savers and borrowers were not being subjected to extra risk. However, real interest rates have not been at all stable. They have swung from 2 to 3 percent over most of the 1960s to below zero in 1975–76 to over 8 percent in 1980–81. Because of this instability, savers and borrowers are now subjected to much more risk in their financial decisions than they were twenty years ago. In this sense our financial system is worse off now than it was in 1960.

SECTION 3 Government as intermediary

Both the federal and provincial governments have established many different types of intermediaries. There are over one hundred different government loan schemes in existence now, and more are born each year.[4] Federal financial institutions accounted for almost 11 percent of total financial assets in 1980, and provincial agencies for over 7 percent.[5]

In part, proliferation of loan schemes reflects gaps that need to be filled in the network of private intermediation. In part it reflects government replacement of private intermediation. In part it reflects the ease with which a loan scheme can be started up in order to mollify particular interest groups in society or to meet some other policy goal. Loan schemes are much cheaper for the government budget than subsidies or tax credits.

Government intermediation takes two forms. The first is straight borrowing and relending, usually through a specialized government intermediary. This amounted to $19 billion in 1980. The second is by guarantee schemes to supplement private intermediation. This amounted to $29 billion in 1980.[6] In guarantee schemes the government makes good all or part of default losses on loans, but the borrowers actually borrow from a private financial intermediary such as a chartered bank or credit union. Most of this financing goes into housing, with almost all of the rest spread equally over the business sector, export financing, and farming.[7]

Government intermediaries

The following is a short list of major financial intermediaries set up by the federal and provincial governments. In almost all cases the government

[4]Neufeld reports that from 1867 to 1971 about 168 government financial intermediaries (including loan schemes) were established, of which about two-thirds remained in 1971. *The Financial System of Canada* (Toronto: Macmillan, 1972), 441.

[5]Economic Council of Canada, *Intervention and Efficiency* (Ottawa: Supply and Services, 1982), 2.

[6]This issue is discussed at length by the Economic Council of Canada in *Intervention and Efficiency*.

[7]*Intervention and Efficiency*, 6.

intermediaries can borrow on their own or in the name of their parent government to raise funds.[8]

1. The Bank of Canada exists to issue currency and deposits and thereby to control chartered-bank cash reserves. Its lending function is unimportant: it lends almost entirely in federal government bonds. We will be looking at this intermediary in great detail in chapter 23.
2. The Canada Deposit Insurance Corporation and the Quebec Deposit Insurance Board guarantee deposit liabilities of private intermediaries (up to a ceiling of $60 000 per depositor in any one institution, as of 1983) and also inspect the insured institutions.
3. The Canada and Quebec Pension Plans receive and lend out all of the individual and employer contributions to each pension plan, as we discussed in chapter 13. The Quebec investment body, the Caisse de Dépôt et Placement, has wide discretion in lending its funds and is an important lender in Quebec financial markets. CPP funds are put entirely in special nonmarketable provincial bonds.
4. The Province of Alberta Heritage Savings Trust Fund is an intermediary set up to receive and to lend out or invest a share of the province's oil and natural gas royalties.
5. The Export Development Corporation extends long- and medium-term credit to foreign customers to spur Canadian export sales and insures short-term loans made by banks to export customers.
6. The Federal Business Development Bank lends start-up and expansion money to new ventures that cannot find financing elsewhere. It also provides extensive management assistance.
7. The Farm Credit Corporation provides almost all of the long-term credit used by farmers.
8. The Canada Development Corporation provides funds to new ventures and buys existing companies on the same basis as any other development lender, but with an eye to national ownership and economic growth rather than just private profit.
9. The Alberta Treasury Branches operate as Alberta banks in all but name. We discussed these in chapter 12.
10. The Province of Ontario Savings Office only issues deposits; the funds contributed flow directly into the provincial treasury and are not thereafter distinguishable from tax revenues. (See chapter 12 for this intermediary also.)
11. The federal and provincial superannuation accounts are branches of government set up to handle contributions to and payment of public service pensions. The federal government also issued annuities to the general public until 1975.

---

[8]This borrowing has accounted for 25 percent of federal long-term debt, 57 percent of that of Alberta, and 42 percent of that of British Columbia.

12. The Canada Mortgage and Housing Corporation lends its borrowed funds for specific types of housing construction, such as low-income townhouse development projects, and insures private mortgage loans on new houses for up to 90 percent of default losses.
13. The federal Department of Regional Industrial Expansion lends funds at attractive rates to firms that locate or expand in relatively depressed areas. These loans are often supplemented by other government grants.

The list goes on much further, covering lending to almost every sector of the economy. The role of the Canada and Quebec Pension Plans may well be sharply increased in the near future. One of the larger current issues in the financial system is the coverage and size of pensions in Canada — both considered inadequate — and one of the obvious alternative solutions is to expand the scope and size of these universal pension plans.

Government loan guarantees

The second form of government intermediation, government guarantee schemes, insures in part or in full against default risk. The two largest guarantee schemes are deposit insurance, carried by the Canada Deposit Insurance Corporation, and mortgage insurance, carried by the Canada Mortgage and Housing Corporation (CMHC) for specific types of residential first mortgages under the National Housing Act. CMHC's guarantees have had a large influence on Canadian flows of funds.[9] In 1969, when the CMHC approved insurance of residential mortgages with only a five-year term (renewable, but at whatever the market rate had become), the trust and morgage loan companies gained a new lease on life: the term to maturity of their main asset could be matched much more closely to that of their main liability. Mortgage insurance has been expensive for the CMHC, however: the loan loss rates ranged from 1.5 percent to 1.9 percent from 1979 to 1981 — six to nine times the loan loss rate of the only private mortgage insurer.[10]

The federal government has loan guarantee schemes for student loans, farm improvement loans, fisheries improvement loans, home improvement loans, and medium and small business loans. In the 1970s all of the loan amounts were relatively small, as were the loan losses.[11] More recently the loan losses increased sharply as the 1981–82 recession took hold.

[9]The CDIC may also have affected the flow of funds, less desirably. It has been alleged that by not allowing any depositor losses, even above the insured limit, the CDIC has made depositors careless about the quality of management of the firms handling their funds.

[10]*Intervention and Efficiency*, 74.

[11]The student loans are an exception. While the small business loans from 1961 to 1976 caused a total default loss of only 0.42 percent, the student loans from 1964 to 1977 caused loss claims (less recoveries) of 5.55 percent. Secretary of State, *Canada Student Loans Program Annual Report*, 1976–77.

Government intermediation and guarantee programs have greatly reduced creditor risks. The low loan losses reported for most of the guarantee programs suggest that the risk insured against was really quite small and that the loan guarantees may not have been necessary once the lending institutions became used to those types of lending. The loss experience of the student loan program, however, is the exception; the large losses of this program that are covered by government guarantees can be justified only by a policy of subsidizing post-secondary education as a public good.

SECTION 4 Government as manipulator

Governments manipulate individual financial markets, the structure of relative yields, and flows of funds in the financial system. They do this by direct participation in some markets and by special taxes and subsidies in others. In some cases the manipulation is intended to help with stabilization policy for the economy as a whole, and microeconomic credit-allocation effects are secondary. Such cases include government buying and selling of foreign exchange, the Bank of Canada's supply of cash reserve assets for chartered banks, and (on the other side of its balance sheet) the Bank of Canada's purchase and sales of government securities.

Taxes and subsidies

Most microeconomic manipulation in the financial system is by taxes and subsidies. The important classes of income singled out for favored treatment are capital gains and dividend income, and income from principal residences. We have discussed the first two; income from principal residences is entirely tax free.

There are special tax incentives for particular kinds of intermediation. The most important is the requirement that all household funds put into Registered Retirement Savings Plans be rolled over at maturity into one of a restricted list of annuities (or else face a substantial tax penalty). Another is the 15 percent withholding tax on interest paid on foreign-currency deposits in near-banks, which keeps near-banks out of all but the retail foreign-currency deposit business. Income from regular whole life insurance policies is untaxed until maturity. Chartered banks are effectively taxed by being forced to hold non-interest-bearing cash reserves. The average cash reserve requirement is being reduced significantly as part of the Bank Act revision of December 1980, so this "tax" is not too serious (see chapters 11 and 23 for details of bank cash reserve requirements).

Life insurance policies are still subject to a 2 percent premium tax by provincial governments — a front-end load, effectively. Some of the premium tax is a form of sales tax on the service of current insurance protection. The rest is a capital tax on policyholders' contributions to the accumulated savings element in their life insurance policies; as such it is exactly the opposite of the special subsidy provided to investors in Registered Home Ownership Savings Plans, Small Business Development Corporations, and the other tax shelters.

Government manipulation of relative after-tax yields through the tax system is both extensive and complicated. With the escalation of before-tax nominal yields due to escalating inflationary expectations, differences in relative tax rates have come to matter much more than before. The net impact on flows of funds and allocative efficiency is hard to unscramble, because many of the tax advantages offset each other; the premium tax on life insurance sales, for instance, is offset by the tax incentive on RRSPs, which must eventually be converted to annuities and will probably be placed in a life insurance company. Perhaps the main effect of government manipulation of after-tax yields is on the total flow of savings rather than on the composition of the total.

A form of government manipulation that has only recently become prominent is the interest subsidy for particular groups of borrowers. Provinces and municipalities had used low-interest loans to entice new industrial development before, but in the early 1980s several provincial governments set up interest-rebate schemes. These were to help home-owners with mortgage loans and to help small businesses with bank loans. The provincial governments undertook to pay to the borrower the difference between the regular interest cost of the loan and some benchmark rate. In June 1982 even the federal government launched such a scheme, but falling interest rates shortly thereafter made the scheme unnecessary. These interest-rebate schemes were very popular, so they can be expected to reappear whenever monetary policy again raises interest rates to high nominal levels.

Manipulation and risk

In November 1981 the federal government introduced a budget with drastic and unexpected revisions to many tax provisions that had been in place for many years — on the grounds that the beneficiaries of existing tax provisions were mainly high-income groups that had no claim to such special treatment. The suddenness of the federal tax changes introduced a great deal of uncertainty into investment planning in Canada. The risk attached to after-tax yields on long-term portfolios has increased substantially, wherever the yield depends in any way on special tax provisions. Tax rates themselves have now become uncertain variables, with their own probability distribution.

Government manipulation has also added to risk in another way. Governments have played a significant role in causing the high levels of inflation risk of the early 1980s. Their major policy goal of the 1980s is to lower that level of inflation risk without sacrificing excessive amounts of output and employment in the process. Inflation was slowed down dramatically by the recession of 1981–82, but at a very high cost to the economy in lost skills and lost capital investment.

SECTION 5 Summary

The government is a regulator, a user, an intermediary, and a manipulator in the financial system.

The government regulates to set limits of financial prudence on those dealing with others' money, and to ensure provision of accurate, timely information to investors.

Both federal and provincial governments are important users of the financial system as borrowers and lenders, both for their own current and capital spending and on behalf of some of their Crown corporations.

Both levels of government have set up dozens of financial intermediaries and loan schemes to handle specialized types of lending. Some of these types of lending have always been too risky for private intermediaries, some have been taken over from private intermediaries, and some were created mainly to provide a subsidy for particular private groups or regions.

The federal government and some provincial governments manipulate the financial system for their own ends — both for stabilization of the real sector and to redirect financial flows to needy areas, sectors, and regions. Some of the manipulations may also be purely the result of a political desire to give a tax break to particular groups of savers. Some of the manipulation is by direct intervention in financial markets, but most is by special tax treatment of certain kinds of investment income and of particular kinds of savings flow.

There is still room for improvement in the Canadian financial system, but some major pitfalls have been avoided so far. In particular, we have not made use of interest ceilings to any significant extent, and the patchwork of federal and provincial regulation in financial markets has produced a surprisingly uniform network of legislation. Concerns remain about efficiency (especially in life insurance) and about risk (from concentrated ownership of trust companies and from sudden shifts in government policy itself).

Questions for discussion

1. What are the objectives of government intervention in the financial system, and how are these objectives different from those for government intervention elswhere in the economy?
2. How have you been the beneficiary of government intervention in the financial system?
3. How have you been hurt by government intervention in the financial system?
4. Outline some of the consequences for financial markets if the CMHC were no longer to insure residential mortgages against default risk.

References

Boadway, Robin W., and Harry M. Kitchen. *Canadian Tax Policy*. Toronto: Canadian Tax Foundation, May 1980.

Economic Council of Canada. *Intervention and Efficiency*. Ottawa: Supply and Services, 1982.

Neufeld, E.P. *The Financial System of Canada.* Toronto: Macmillan, 1972, chap. 13.

Zimmer, Henry B. *The New Canadian Tax and Investment Guide*. Edmonton: Hurtig Publishers, 1980.

Appendix

The Crown-Greymac affair: a case study of regulatory action

The Crown-Greymac affair is easily the most dramatic financial crisis of the last twenty years, and also one with far-reaching implications for the limits we may wish to set on ownership of our financial system or on the powers of government regulators. The details of the affair are therefore set out in this appendix, even though final reports of inquiries into the affair are not yet completed.

In November 1982 a huge real estate deal started the whole affair. A large real estate company (Cadillac-Fairview) sold twenty-six apartment buildings in Toronto to Leonard Rosenberg's holding company, Greymac Credit Corp., for $270 million. Rosenberg had already arranged to resell the buildings to William Player's holding company, Kilderkin Investments Ltd., for $312 million. Mr. Player in turn resold them without delay to a group of numbered companies incorporated in Ontario (but rumored to be owned by Saudi Arabians) for $500 million, undertaking to manage the apartments and guarantee the mortgage payments for the first ten years.

The increase in value was startling and not entirely credible. What made it of concern to financial regulators was the fact that each resale accumulated more mortgage liabilities, and three Ontario trust companies ended up holding an extra $152 million in third mortgages on the properties. Furthermore, payment of interest on those mortgages was guaranteed for the first ten years by Kilderkin Investments, the seller.

A further complication was added at this point, as the Ontario government promptly moved to tighten rent controls on those buildings in order to limit as much as possible the pass-through of extra financing costs. This action must have lowered the value of the buildings to the new purchasers, and unexpectedly so.

The extra mortgage debt raised two questions. One concerns the imprudence shown by the trust companies in taking on such a large third mortgage, and whether imprudence on this and other loans was such as to endanger the safety of the trust companies' deposits. The second question is whether the mortgages were sufficiently secured under the Ontario trust company legislation.

Crown Trust, controlled by Rosenberg at this point, held $62 million, a large enough share of its total assets of $700 million, but Greymac Trust and Seaway Trust were much smaller; their holdings of $11 and $76 million respectively were much larger shares of total assets. Clearly they were not diversifying their default risks as much as other companies, and the transaction was not at arm's length, since the firms' principals were directly involved.

On the matter of security, Ontario trust company legislation specifies that mortgage loans must not exceed 75 percent of the value of the real estate security provided. The total mortgage debt amounted to $375 million (including first, second, and third mortgages), which is 75 percent of the final resale price of $500 million. However, it appeared that the final resale was not really a sale, since the buyers did not have any of their own money at risk, so the $500 million price tag was not really a market price; appraisals of the properties' value had put it considerably below $500 million, which implied that the mortgages were not properly secured.

Whether the final sale was or was not a sale hinged on whether the buyers had or had not put up a $125 million deposit, which Kilderkin could then have used to back up its guarantee of interest payments on the mortgages for the first ten years. In effect, they had not, though Mr. Player had arranged a transaction with a Cayman Islands bank clearly designed to give the impression that they had. The principals of the numbered companies had a deposit, but it was given only to their representative rather than to Kilderkin Investments, so they retained control of it for at least the first ten years.

As this is written, the companies involved have been more or less wound up, with undisclosed loan losses to be made up by the CDIC (protecting depositors). The companies' financially sound business has been taken over by other companies. The principals have lost all of their equity in all of the companies. Leonard Rosenberg is attempting to sue for damages, in a court wrangle that may go on for years. Reports are still due from several government bodies, and no criminal charges have yet been laid.

PART FIVE

Macroeconomics and Financial Markets

CHAPTER 17

Elements of Stabilization Policy

In previous chapters I have described and analysed how the financial system channels funds from savers to investors, how it provides a payments mechanism, and how it allows households to make long-term financial plans for transferring income from early years to retirement. In this chapter we will start to analyse the financial system's contribution to the government's goal of stabilizing capacity use, employment, price levels, and output growth.

The explanation will make use of an aggregate model of the entire economy. Such models are fascinating but complex. There are so many trees to attract our attention in these models that it is easy to lose sight of the forest. Therefore this chapter will provide a simple overview of the forest. The overview will do more than just provide a map with which to keep track of the individual parts later: it will also bring out some fundamental aspects of stabilization policy that are not easily seen in complex models.

Your task in this short chapter is:

1. to make or renew an acquaintance with the aggregate supply and demand model of output markets — a model that is presented only briefly here and more formally derived in chapters 18 to 22, and
2. to understand the basic logic of stabilization policy and some of its implications.

SECTION 1 A simple view of output and prices

The title of this section is too modest. We will look not only at output and prices but also at real growth, inflation, unemployment, and capacity use — in fact, at all the major economic issues of today.

FIGURE 17–1 Inflation and growth in the sugar-beet market

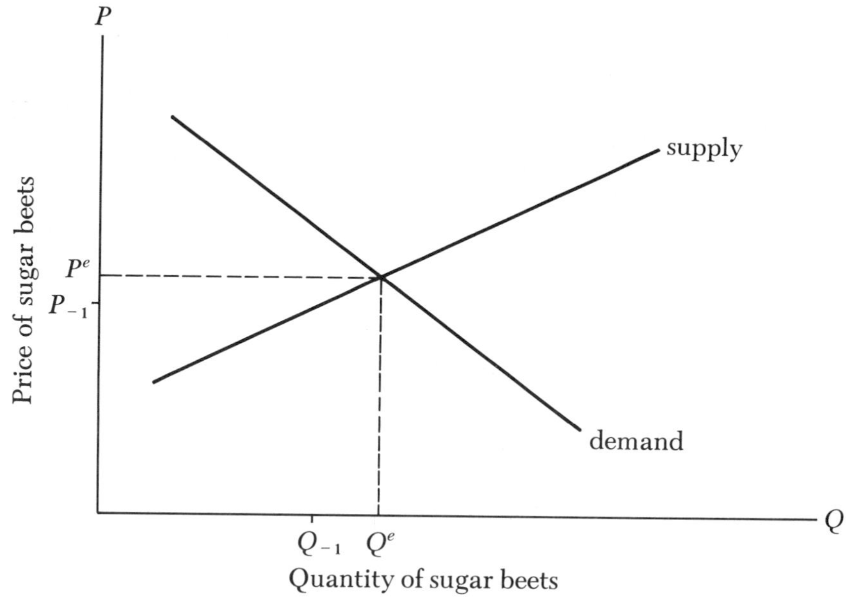

In the current period, P^e and Q^e are the equilibrium price and quantity that occur in the sugar-beet market. The previous year's price and quantity are given as P_{-1} and Q_{-1}. Inflation of sugar-beet prices in the current period relative to all other prices can be calculated as $100(P^e - P_{-1})/P_{-1}$, and real output growth as $100(Q^e - Q_{-1})/Q_{-1}$.

In individual markets such as that for sugar beets, quantity and price are explained by the behavior of demand and supply in each market. The market price and quantity are generally such as to cause demand to equal supply. The rate of price change and the rate of quantity change in the market (that is, the market's real growth) can be found from such equilibrium results by comparing the current price and quantity with those of the preceding period. Figure 17–1 gives an illustration using the market for sugar beets. The behavior of price and quantity in each individual market is explained by the factors that lie behind demand and supply curves: tastes, the price of the item itself relative to prices of substitutes, income levels, technology, and costs of necessary inputs.

The equilibrium approach can be used for aggregate demand and supply of goods and services per year, with only a few major differences.[1]

[1]For a fuller derivation of aggregate demand and supply curves than is given in this chapter, see either chapters 18 to 21 or an introductory or intermediate macroeconomics text such as R. Dornbusch, S. Fischer, and G. Sparks, *Macroeconomics*, First Canadian Edition (Toronto: McGraw-Hill, 1981).

Figure 17–2 shows aggregate demand and supply curves with normal-looking slopes, leading to equilibrium levels of aggregate output and the aggregate price level at which aggregate demand equals aggregate supply. Real output growth and inflation are found by comparing the current equilibrium to that of last year. If capacity can be measured, then the degree of *capacity use* is the ratio of equilibrium output to capacity output. If levels of aggregate output imply also levels of employment (which they do in the short run with relatively stable technology), then the unemployment rate can also be found by comparing the level of employment to the size of the labor force. Real growth, capacity use, inflation, and unemployment depend, like output and the price level, on all the factors that explain aggregate demand and supply.

Capacity use

FIGURE 17–2 Inflation and growth in the real sector

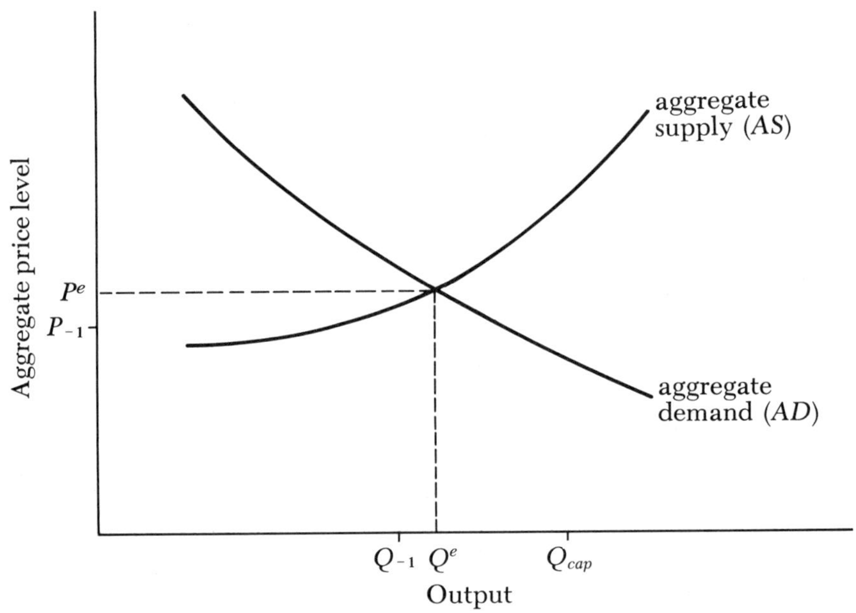

Q^e and P^e are the current period's output and price level. The previous year's price and quantity are given as P_{-1} and Q_{-1}, and full capacity output is estimated as Q_{cap}. Current inflation can be calculated as $100(P^e - P_{-1})/P_{-1}$, real output growth as $100(Q^e - Q_{-1})/Q_{-1}$, and capacity use as $100Q^e/Q_{cap}$.

Aggregate demand and supply curves have the normal slopes, but they do not behave in quite the same way that demand and supply curves for an individual market do. The demand and supply of sugar beets, for instance, vary with the price of sugar beets relative to all other prices and incomes.

Aggregate demand and supply vary with the aggregate price level, which involves changing all prices together. It follows that responses of aggregate demand or aggregate supply to the price level in figure 17–2 cannot be responses to relative price changes, which are the main sort of response encountered in microeconomic theory. This difference in the meaning of "a change in the price level" is the major difference between, and the major source of confusion about, aggregate and individual market models.

When the price level that changes and the output level that changes are the aggregate price and output levels for the whole economy, we need to take into account in our model some effects of price and output changes that are normally small enough to ignore safely in microeconomic theory. In macroeconomic analysis we include the effect of price changes on the real value of money and other nominal wealth; we also include the effect of output changes on national income levels and aggregate demand.

Aggregate demand

Because of the differences between aggregate and individual market models, the downward slope of the aggregate demand curve in figure 17–2 is not explained as buyers' response to better deals. Instead, it is explained by a quite different logic whose essence is as follows: lower aggregate price levels raise the real value of the money supply and financial wealth — an increase that stimulates demand for financial assets and even consumer spending on durables. Extra demand for financial assets pushes up prices of financial assets and lowers financial-asset yields throughout the financial system. The lower yields on financial assets make real assets seem a better buy and borrowing to finance them a more reasonable proposition, so investment in real capital assets is increased. The two stimuli to aggregate demand (extra consumption demand and extra investment demand) in turn raise income levels as producers fill their new orders; higher income levels cause consumption demand to rise some more, and so on.

The aggregate demand curve, it should be noted, shows the levels of aggregate demand that would occur at each possible price level, assuming in each case that sufficient aggregate supply is produced to satisfy aggregate demand. This extra assumption about aggregate supply is not needed in microeconomic analysis, because demand and supply are independent, but in macroeconomic analysis the level of aggregate supply (measured as national income) is an important determinant of aggregate demand behavior. The extra assumption about aggregate supply may be unrealistic for most levels of aggregate demand (that is something we find out only when we derive an aggregate supply curve), but it is a necessary starting point in deriving an aggregate demand curve. Because we assume in deriving the aggregate demand curve that supply is available, increases in aggregate demand imply increases in supply and therefore in incomes and therefore in aggregate demand again (in other words, the standard spending multiplier process).

The slope of the aggregate demand curve depends on how sensitively investment demand, consumption demand, and net foreign demand (exports less imports) respond to interest rates and to changes in income levels. The position of the aggregate demand curve is determined by the level of all the factors that affect aggregate demand at any given price level. The list of these factors is long and will be explained in chapters 18 and 19, but the influential factors are those we would learn from any introductory treatment of macroeconomics: government spending, tax levels, the money supply, the exchange rate, foreign export demand, tariff barriers, and the like. A change in any one of these factors shifts the aggregate demand curve.

Aggregate supply

Just as the aggregate demand curve is more than a sum of microeconomic demand curves from individual markets, so the aggregate supply curve is more than a sum of microeconomic supply curves from individual markets. The individual market supply curve for sugar beets, for instance, has a positive slope because when sugar beet prices rise, producers can always find more inputs with which to increase output. If necessary, producers can raise the wages or other input prices they are paying in order to attract more of whatever factor input is needed to increase supply. In doing so, producers are raising their offer price relative to the going market price for those desired inputs. Since input suppliers are sensitive to relative prices, they go where the rewards are greatest, and beet sugar producers are able to increase their supply when relative prices of sugar beets rise.

For aggregate supply, this story contains a fallacy of composition. Increasing the aggregate price or wage level does not affect relative wages, for a start. To continue, an increase in aggregate supply implies a need for more inputs for the economy as a whole. Unless there are idle stocks of inputs available at current price levels that can be coaxed into production by a general price increase (such as the time of youths and women not fully in the labor force), then the economy as a whole cannot get more inputs by raising price levels. If extra inputs are not available, then aggregate supply will not be sensitive to price, and the aggregate supply curve will be close to vertical.

In the short run, supply of factor inputs and aggregate supply of output do respond to increases in the general wage and price level, for two reasons. First, when suppliers bid up wages in an attempt to get more labor, workers at first interpret the extra wages as higher relative wages — relative to other wages whose increases they have not yet heard about, and relative to price levels that have not increased yet. Second, in most goods markets price levels are posted by major suppliers rather than left to fluctuate as in an auction market. In these posted-price, or *price-tag*, markets (to use Arthur Okun's term),[2] suppliers generally respond to extra demand by increasing output first and then increasing prices only as costs increase; in this way they can retain customer goodwill by always having cost increases on which to blame price increases.

FIGURE 17–3 Output and the inflation rate

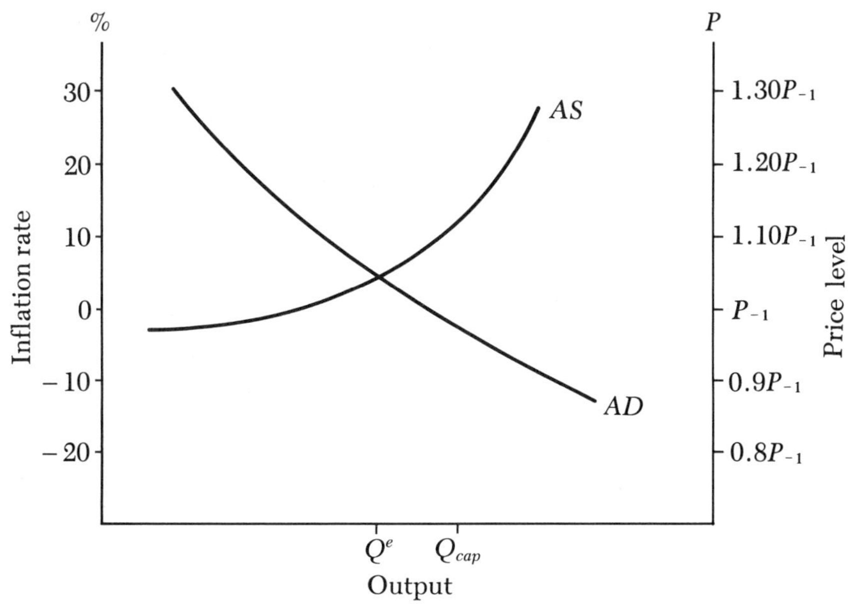

The vertical (price) axis of figure 17–2 appears on the right, scaled into fractions of the previous year's actual price level. The vertical axis on the left expresses that same scale as rates of inflation associated with each possible price level in the current period. Otherwise figure 17–3 is identical with figure 17–2.

In the long run, workers realize that their wage increases are part of a general wage-price inflation and do not represent a rise in relative wages, and producers pass on wage increases in price increases. In the long run, therefore, there is no reason to expect an increased supply of factor inputs: aggregate supply will be insensitive to the general price level, and the aggregate supply curve will be close to vertical.

The position of the agregate supply curve is determined by all the factors behind aggregate supply at any given price level: technology, supplies of available inputs, taxes, and any other barriers or incentives to the supply of inputs.

---

[2]Arthur Okun, *Prices and Quantities* (Washington, D.C.: Brookings Institution, 1981), chap. 4.

An alternative way of illustrating aggregate demand and aggregate supply is with the rate of inflation, rather than the level of prices, on the vertical axis. Figure 17–3 is an example. Given the price level in the previous period, each possible current price level must imply a particular rate of current price inflation, since current inflation is simply $(P_t - P_{t-1})/P_{t-1}$. The logic of aggregate demand and supply is not changed a bit by what amounts to a simple rescaling of the vertical axis to put a zero where the previous period's price used to be. Higher current inflation, for instance, reduces aggregate demand just the way that higher current price levels do in figure 17–2. In the short run extra aggregate supply is available with only a moderate increase in inflation, because posted prices are sluggish and because wage increases are treated as relative wage increases rather than as part of a general wage and price inflation. In the long run, input suppliers recognize general inflation for what it is and are not moved to supply more, so aggregate supply is insensitive to inflation in figure 17–3 just as it is to price levels in figure 17–2.

A third and even more useful way of depicting aggregate demand and supply is by rescaling the horizontal axis as well, as in figure 17–4. Let total demand be divided by the capacity or potential output level, so that each demand level now corresponds to demand for a specific proportion of total

FIGURE 17–4 Inflation and capacity use

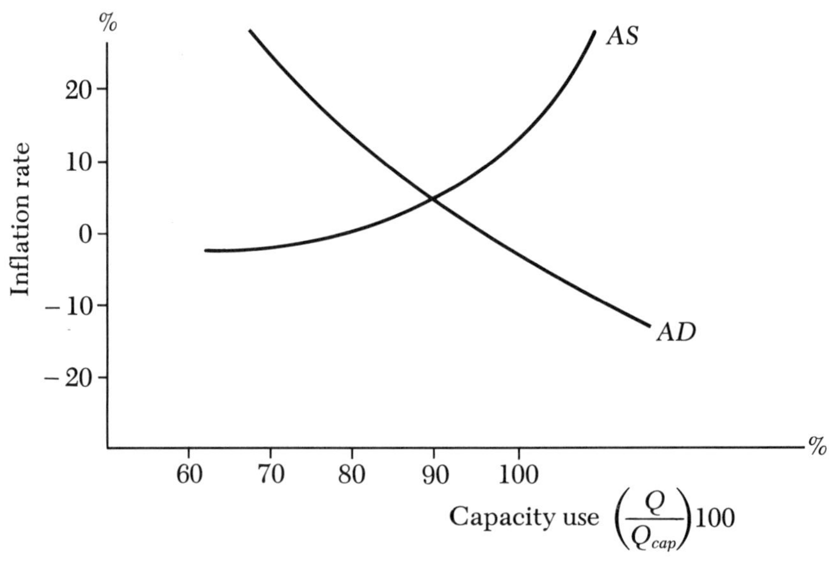

This diagram is the same as figure 17–3, with the horizontal axis scaled in percentage units of estimated capacity output (Q_{cap} in figure 17–3).

output capacity. Likewise, each level of aggregate supply implies a specific rate of capacity use. Rates of capacity use in turn imply rates of use of both capital and labor, and therefore unemployment rates.

SECTION 2

The logic of stabilization policy

The purpose of stabilization policy can be seen as pushing aggregate demand and aggregate supply into positions in figures 17–2 to 17–4 that produce an output level near capacity and a price level unchanged from that of the previous year. Output levels must therefore be increased in line with capacity growth, and prices prevented from rising or falling.

When aggregate demand and supply are subject to random shocks that cause them to shift up and down over time, it is the job of stabilization policy to counter those shocks. Stabilization policy must have available separate tools with which to influence both aggregate demand and aggregate supply if it is to achieve both full capacity output and price stability. Figure 17–5 illustrates a situation in which both demand and supply have shifted out of a position that originally provided both full capacity use and zero inflation. An adverse supply shock has moved aggregate supply temporarily to the left, and a positive demand shock has moved aggregate demand to the right. Government stabilization policy cannot move the economy back to both full capacity and zero inflation by moving just one of the two curves back to its original position. Both curves must be moved. Two policies are needed.

Demand management and supply management

Demand-management policy

Supply-management policy

Figure 17–5 immediately suggests a useful distinction between stabilization policies: some policies influence aggregate demand, and some influence aggregate supply. We can think of the former as *demand management policies* and of the latter as *supply management policies*. In figure 17–5, any number of demand management policies will not restore both full employment and price stability, since they will shift only the aggregate demand curve and move the economy along the aggregate supply curve. At least one supply management tool is needed as well. If the government does not have a supply management tool at its disposal, or cannot use with sufficient strength the ones it has, the two goals of full employment and price stability may not be achievable simultaneously.

The need for both demand management and supply management tools is not affected by one of the major disputes in macroeconomics in the 1970s: whether the aggregate supply curve is or is not vertical. Classical macroeconomics, both as asserted by classical quantity theorists and as reintroduced by modern "rational expectations" theorists, suggests that aggregate supply curves will be vertical even in the short run. Even so, both a demand management policy and a supply management policy are necessary to push both capacity use and inflation back to desired levels when there have been unexpected shocks in both *AS* and *AD* curves. The main difference that a vertical *AS* curve makes is that only supply management tools have the power to influence output levels, and demand management tools influence only price levels.

FIGURE 17–5 The job of stabilization policy

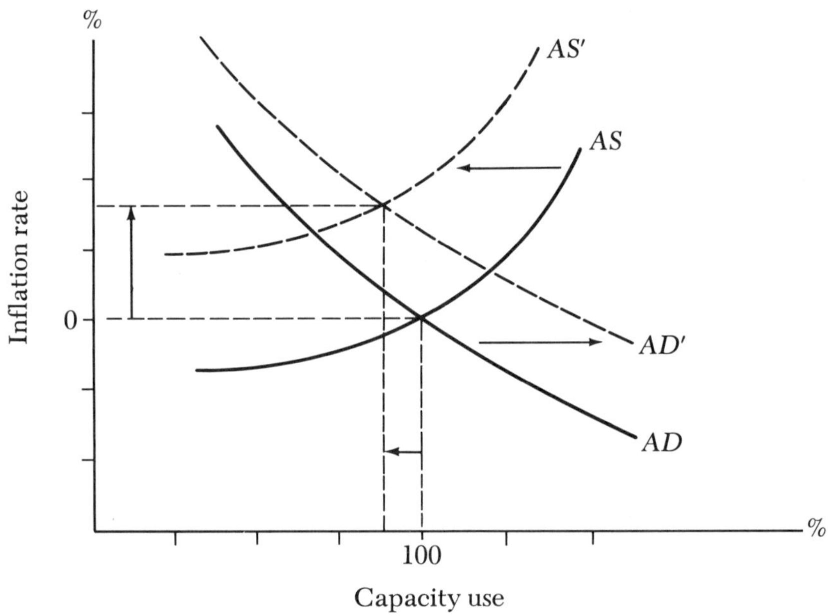

An adverse supply shock has moved *AS* to the left, and a positive demand shock has moved *AD* to the right, so neither full capacity use nor price stability will be achieved without use of stabilization policy. To restore both full capacity use and zero inflation, the government must have policy tools to influence both *AS* (supply-management policies) and *AD* (demand-management policies).

Multiple objectives

If the government also has a third objective, such as maintaining the domestic interest rate at a particular level, then it will need at least three policy tools. The general rule is that, for *n* independent targets, the government will need *n* different, independent policy tools. A simple analogy is to archery: even a Robin Hood would need sixteen arrows to hit sixteen different targets. The explanation of this general rule comes from multidimensional versions of diagrams like figure 17–5, and from algebra.

The algebraic explanation is as follows. Behavior of the economy can be described in the short run or in the long run by a set of simultaneous equations, each of which is satisfied in equilibrium. If there are n different equations to be satisfied, the set of equations provides a unique solution for n unknown variables, known collectively as endogenous variables (the prefix *endo-* signifies that they are determined inside the model). All other variables are exogenous — that is, determined outside the model somehow, such as by the government or in the outside world. Any change in the exogenous variables will change the solution for the set of endogenous variables.

An example will help to illustrate the algebra and to explain the relationship between exogenous and endogenous variables. Suppose that our economy can be described by just two equations. The first says that aggregate demand (AD) depends on the price level (P) and the nominal money supply (Ms) and the level of government spending (G):

$$AD = -aP + bMs + cG.$$

The second equation says that the price level (P) depends on aggregate demand (AD) and taxes (T):

$$P = dAD + eT.$$

The two equations produce a unique solution for AD and P, the endogenous variables, given the values of the exogenous variables Ms, G, and T. Different values of Ms, G, and T produce different solutions for AD and P.

If the government controls G, it can change the solutions for AD and P by changing G; there is some level of G that will cause the solution value of AD to equal the government's desired level. In such an exercise the variable G is the policy tool, or *instrument*, and AD is the *target* variable. The value of P will also be affected by using G to achieve the optimal value of AD, but the setting of G's level that achieves the optimal level of AD will not usually achieve the optimal level of P at the same time.

By changing the value of a second instrument such as T, and adjusting its first policy instrument G appropriately, the government can vary the solution value of P while holding AD constant. That allows the government to select a second endogenous variable as a target variable, and to cause that second variable to reach a desired level as well. If the government has three different policy instruments, then it can fix the solution values of three different targets. And so on.

To work this way, the government's policy variables must be independent of one another. If two policy variables both affect targets the same way (for example, if the level of Ms and the level of G both affect AD the same way and do not affect P directly at all), then the government cannot use those two policy tools to change the level of one target variable while holding the other target variable constant: any change in the pair of policy tools that changes P will also change AD. If two policy tools are not independent in their effects, they are effectively just two versions of one policy tool.

The assignment problem

Not only must stabilization policy have as many policy tools as targets, but it must match up policy tools to targets in certain ways if the policy is to counter demand and supply shocks without destabilizing the economy.[3]

Assignment rule

The assignment rule is that the policy tool that has a comparative advantage in affecting a particular target variable should be used to keep that target variable near desired levels. "Having a comparative advantage" is defined as being relatively more efficient, just as in the theory of international trade.

For example, suppose that the government is interested in both high employment levels and stable interest rates, and the government controls both its own spending and the flow of credit in the economy. Government spending has a comparative advantage in affecting employment, and the supply of credit has a comparative advantage in stabilizing interest rates, though each tool also affects the other target variable. Government spending should be adjusted to keep employment on target, even if this action has spillover effects on interest rates; supply of credit should then be adjusted to offset any such spillover effects and keep interest rates near target.

The opposite strategy would destabilize the economy. A change in spending to affect interest rates would cause large spillover effects on employment. A change in the supply of credit sufficient to control those spillover effects on employment would have enormous spillover effects on the level of interest rates — probably larger than a change in government spending could counter.

Uncertainty

It is easy to add uncertainty to this discussion of stabilization policy. We will do this more formally in chapter 24, but the topic can be introduced here. The aggregate demand level and the aggregate supply level in figure 17–2 can be seen as expected levels, with possible levels of actual demand and supply distributed around those expected values according to a probability distribution with known or estimated width. The actual outcome of output and price level in any year would then depend on the random components in demand and supply and on their degree of correlation. For instance, if positive demand shocks were typically accompanied by positive (propitious) supply shocks, and negative demand shocks by negative (adverse) supply shocks, then fluctuations of price levels would be relatively small and fluctuations of output levels relatively large. If demand and supply shifts are negatively correlated, then output levels will be stable but

[3]Assignment theory was introduced by Robert Mundell. See "The Appropriate Use of Monetary and Fiscal Policy for Internal and External Stability," *International Monetary Fund Staff Papers*, 1962, 70–79, or Mundell, *International Economics* (New York: Macmillan, 1968).

price levels will be highly unstable. Figure 17–6 illustrates these two possibilities.

FIGURE 17–6 Correlation of demand and supply shocks

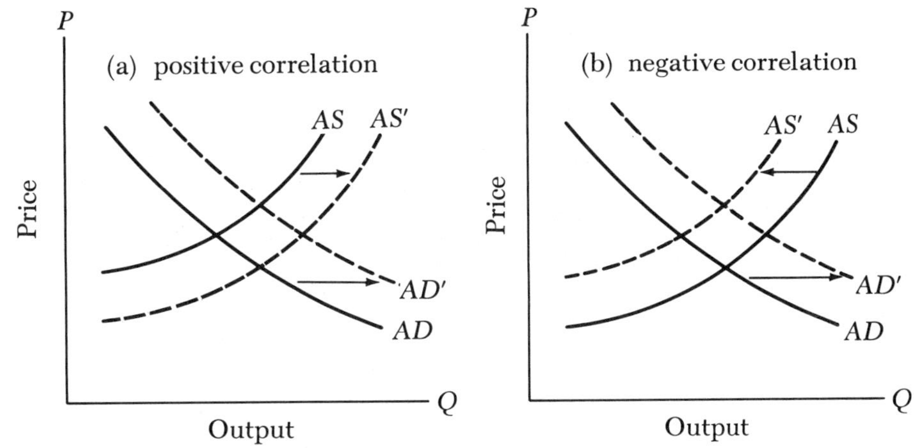

In panel (a), a positive shock to *AD* (shifting it to *AD′*) is accompanied by a positive shock to AS (shifting it to *AS′*). The result is a large change in output level and a small change in price level. In panel (b), a positive demand shock to *AD* is accompanied by a negative supply shock to *AS*. The result is a large change in price level and only a small change in output level.

The algebra behind the results in figure 17–6 is fairly straightforward. We will use linear forms of demand and supply curves. Let Q be output and P be price, and let a, b, c, and d be constant coefficients. The aggregate demand curve is

$$Q_d = a + bP + u_d, \tag{1}$$

and the supply curve is

$$Q_s = c + dP + u_s, \tag{2}$$

where u_d and u_s are random elements. The equilibrium condition in this aggregate goods market is that $Q_d = Q_s$. By substitution for Q_d and Q_s from (1) and (2) we can solve for the price level P as

$$P = \left(\frac{a - c}{b + d}\right) + \left(\frac{1}{b + d}\right)(u_d - u_s). \tag{3}$$

Equation (3) shows that the price level depends on $(u_d - u_s)$, which is the difference between shifts of demand and shifts of supply. The higher the positive correlation between the two curves, the more u_d and u_s will move together, and the less their difference will change — that is, the more stable prices and inflation will be.

By rearranging equations (1) and (2) we can solve in the same way for the equilibrium quantity level. The aggregate demand equation (1) can be written as

$$P_d = -\frac{a}{b} + \left(\frac{1}{b}\right)Q + u'_d, \tag{4}$$

and the aggregate supply equation (2) can be written as

$$P_s = -\frac{c}{d} + \left(\frac{1}{d}\right)Q - u'_s, \tag{5}$$

where u'_d and u'_s are random deviations of *AD* and *AS* measured vertically instead of horizontally on an aggregate demand–aggregate supply diagram. Equilibrium requires that the two price levels be identical, so the quantity level can be solved for as

$$Q = e + f(u'_s + u'_d), \tag{6}$$

where e and f are expressions consisting only of constant coefficients.[4] In words: output levels depend on the *sum* of random shifts in demand and supply curves. The higher the positive correlation between shifts in demand and supply, the larger the fluctuations in their sum will be, and the more variable output will be. Changes in the correlation of demand and supply behavior will therefore affect output and price variability in opposite directions.

Stabilization policy can attempt to reduce the variability of output and inflation, as well as to improve their expected levels. In an uncertain world with risk-averse constituents, governments are quite likely to have such an objective. The government could reduce risk levels for output and price levels by following rules that automatically moved to offset random fluctuations in both demand and supply schedules. For instance, most OECD (Organization for Economic Cooperation and Development) countries now have taxes and many government spending programs set up so that taxes fall and government transfer payments automatically increase when the economy moves into a slump; the negative demand shock causing the slump is offset in part by a positive demand shock from fiscal policy. Similarly, government agricultural and mineral stockpiling policies may be a source of offsetting supply shocks to counter sudden surges or declines in demand for specific materials or commodities.

Two points should be noted about such stabilizing policy. First, the timing of the policy's effects is very important. Policy might well have a destabilizing effect if the government responded to each positive demand shock by slashing its spending or raising its taxes a year or two later — especially if the government's actions took a year or two to have effect. The result of such policy responses would be a whiplash economy, with large

---

[4] $e = \frac{ad - cb}{d - b}$, and $f = \frac{bd}{(d - b)}$.

positive demand shocks followed by large negative demand shocks. The average outcome would be desirable, but any individual year could well be awful.

Second, arranging a positive demand shock to offset an adverse supply shock will stabilize output levels but worsen the instability of price levels. Alternatively, arranging to match adverse supply shocks with policies of demand restraint (tight monetary or fiscal policies) will stabilize prices but destabilize output. This is the message of figure 17–6. In order to stabilize both output and inflation, policy must reduce simultaneously the random fluctuations of both demand and supply curves. If that is not possible, the best policy may be no reaction at all.

FIGURE 17–7 Price levels, 1800–1981

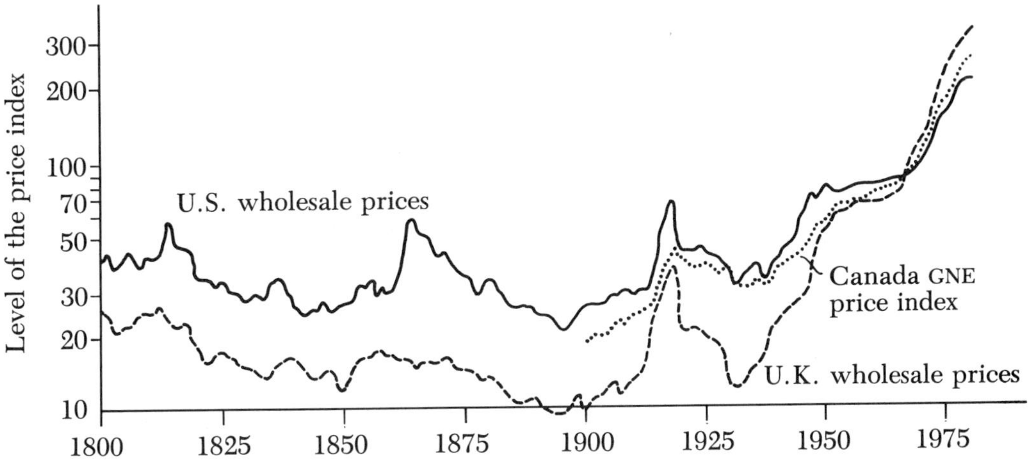

Sources: For U.S. and U.K., Michael D. Bordo, *Federal Reserve Bank of St. Louis Review*, May 1981, 8–9. For Canada, M.C. Urquhart and K.H. Buckley, eds., *Historical Statistics of Canada* (Toronto: Macmillan, 1965); CANSIM Databank; Robert E. Ankli and Jane Foster, "Components of Canadian GNP: 1900–1925" (Discussion paper, University of Guelph Economics Dept., n.d.).

The past record

Optimal policy under uncertainty is the most pressing concern in today's macroeconomics, and we will deal with it more fully in chapter 24. For now, I will only provide the past record of price and output stability to put current policy concerns into perspective. Figure 17–7 shows the time path of wholesale price levels in the United States and the United Kingdom since 1800, and in Canada since 1900. Figures 17–8 and 17–9 show the growth rates of real output in the United States and Canada since 1900. The figures for the early years in all three charts are not very reliable, but we are interested only in the gross differences between early periods and the period since 1945.

FIGURE 17-8 Real GNP growth in Canada, 1900–82

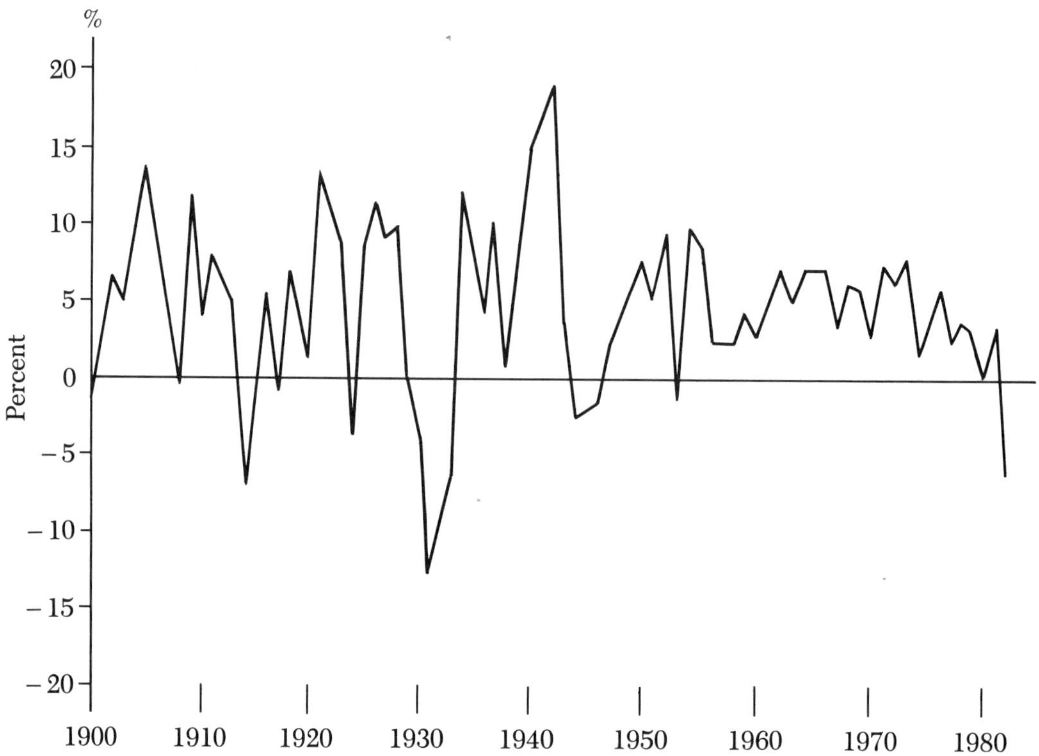

Sources: CANSIM Databank; M.C. Urquhart and K.H. Buckley, eds., *Historical Statistics of Canada* (Toronto: Macmillan, 1965); Robert E. Ankli and Jane Forster, "Components of Canadian GNP: 1900–1925" (Discussion paper, University of Guelph Economics Dept., n.d.).

For the 150 years up to 1945, price levels clearly followed a pattern of rising during wars and declining thereafter. The Napoleonic Wars (1803–15), the American Civil War (1861–65), the Crimean War (1853–56), and the First World War (1914–18) all produced that pattern. After the Second World War (1939–45), however, the price level did not come down. Inflation, it seems, could not be negative after 1945. Coincidentally or not, it was in 1944–45 that western governments acknowledged their responsibility for demand management policy in a series of acts like Canada's Full Employment Act of 1944.

Output levels, on the other hand, have fluctuated over a much narrower range since 1945 than they did before 1945. Some of this change may be due to changes in the nature of western economies, such as less dependence on primary industries and greater diversification, but the volatility of output growth fell by two-thirds after 1945. Some of that huge improvement must be due to the efforts of governments to pump up demand in times of slack.

The long-run performance of prices and output levels in these diagrams should be kept in mind as we look in the succeeding chapters at how the government uses the financial system to influence demand and supply in goods markets.

FIGURE 17–9 Real GNP growth in the United States, 1900–82

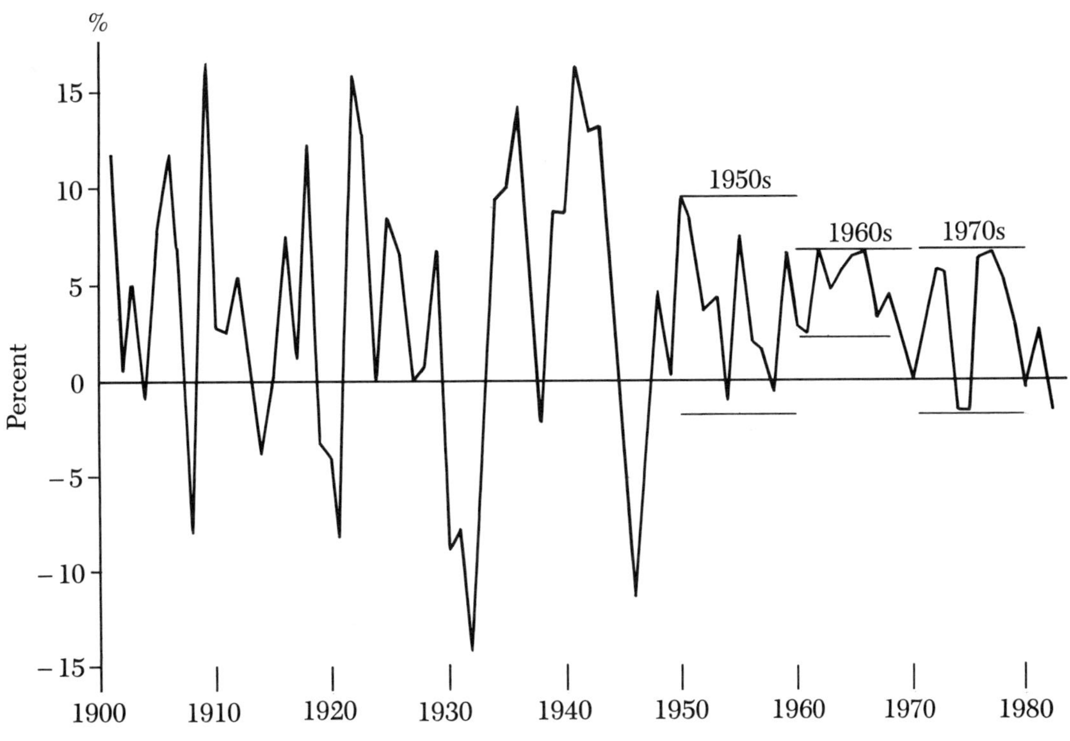

Sources: Martin Neil Baily, "Stabilization Policy and Private Economic Behavior," *Brookings Papers on Economic Activity*, 1978:1, 14. *Economic Report of the President, 1982* (Washington, D.C.: U.S. Government Printing Office, 1983).

SECTION 3

Summary

Stabilization policy is the use of the financial system by government to manipulate levels of price and output in the real sector of the economy and thereby to manipulate the rate of inflation, the rate of growth of real output, and the level of unemployment and capacity use. Real-sector output and price levels are determined by aggregate demand and aggregate supply behavior and can be analysed with demand and supply curves that look much like the demand and supply curves used in microeconomic analysis.

Stabilization policy consists of arranging for stable output growth and price levels by pushing aggregate demand curves and aggregate supply curves into the desired positions. In general, both curves will need to be nudged (possibly continually), and therefore the government must have at its disposal policy tools that will affect both aggregate demand and aggregate supply.

In a world of uncertainty, both demand and supply are subject to unforeseeable disturbances. The interaction of such shocks will produce various combinations of output and price instability, depending on how supply shocks are correlated with demand shocks. Government policy can reduce instability and uncertainty only by offsetting those random shocks, for both demand and supply. If there are any time lags in the effect of policy, then the government must anticipate the random shocks to be offset, or else its policy intervention could be destabilizing instead of stabilizing.

Questions for discussion

1. Why does aggregate demand not necessarily rise when the relative price of some items falls?
2. Why does aggregate supply not slope upward more steeply in the short run than in the long run, as in microeconomics?
3. What would the slope of the aggregate demand curve look like if we assumed, in drawing the aggregate demand curve, that aggregate supply were constant instead of rising in line with aggregate demand?
4. What would be the net effect of using two demand management policy instruments in opposite directions? Of using a demand management tool to expand the economy and a supply management tool to contract it?
5. Is the economy better off or worse off if its aggregate demand and its aggregate supply are positively correlated? Why?

CHAPTER 18

Real-Sector Demand Behavior

Chapter 17 presented a model of the entire economy, in as simple a form as possible. It is the task of chapters 18 to 21 to explain how that aggregate model is derived from more elementary market behavior in parts of the economy. Chapter 22 will then explain how the model predicts the economy will behave, so that later chapters can address the question of how policy might be used to stabilize cyclical fluctuations.

The aggregate model of chapter 17 consists of an aggregate demand curve and an aggregate supply curve. Chapters 18 and 19 explain how the aggregate demand curve is derived and how it behaves. The explanation in this chapter is of spending behavior in markets for real goods and services, whereas chapter 19 will deal with the interaction of real markets and financial markets. The theory presented in this chapter is a mainstream theory mostly derived from or inspired by John Maynard Keynes' *General Theory of Employment, Interest, and Money*.[1] The bare outline of this theory makes up the core of macroeconomic theory in almost every introductory economics text, so this chapter will be broadly familiar.

Your task is to learn:

1. the basic ingredients of aggregate demand in the Keynesian model,
2. what equilibrium demand is, and how it responds to disturbances,
3. the dynamic time path that the economy would be likely to follow after a disturbance, on the way to a new equilibrium, and
4. the impact of the price level in particular on the level of aggregate demand.

---

[1]John Maynard Keynes, *The General Theory of Employment, Interest, and Money* (London: Harcourt Brace, 1936).

SECTION 1

The Keynesian demand model

Aggregate demand (*AD*)

Aggregate demand for real goods and services (*AD*) is the same thing as planned, real gross national expenditure (GNE). Aggregate demand is the total of planned spending on final goods and services produced by Canadian residents in a year, measured in dollars of constant purchasing power. Including the adjective *planned* in the definition excludes unplanned inventory accumulation, which Statistics Canada includes in its measure of real GNE.

The components of aggregate demand are the same as the components of real GNE: real consumption spending by households (*C*), real investment spending on new housing, inventories, and plant and equipment (*I*), real government spending (*G*), real export demand from foreigners (*X*), less the import content of those four categories of demand (*M*). Note that government spending includes only spending on currently produced goods and services and excludes transfer payments such as old-age pensions and unemployment-insurance benefits, which are not given in return for performance of any service. Many newspaper accounts include transfer payments in reports of government spending, but transfer payments do not represent a demand for goods and services.

The behavior of aggregate demand (*AD*) is the behavior of the sum of its components, so we can start with the demand identity familiar from introductory economics:

$$AD = C + I + G + X - M. \tag{1}$$

We can lump the last two terms together and refer to $X - M$ jointly as net exports, which leaves us with only four components to explain: consumption, investment, government spending, and net exports. They will be explained in that order.

Consumption

The decision to consume this year rather than save for consumption later was analysed in chapter 6. Current consumption rises with accumulated household wealth and with current and future after-tax income. The ratio of consumption to income (the average propensity to consume) will rise with the share of the population in the high-spending age groups of under twenty-five and over sixty-five. Household consumption may also be sensitive to the level of real interest available on savings, but the direct effect of real interest rates (separate from the indirect effect of interest rates through their impact on the recorded value of wealth) is generally estimated as too weak to matter. In the short or even medium run of four to five years that a government has to worry about politically, the age distribution of the population does not change significantly, so we can ignore it. That leaves wealth levels and current and future incomes as the main determinants of consumption demand.

We noted in chapter 6 that the effect of an income increase on current consumption depends greatly on whether the income increase is expected to last only for the current year (*transitory income*) or to continue over time (*permanent income*).[2] Actual, observed income increases are usually a mixture of the two. How people classify a particular income increase will depend on how they form their expectations of future income, but generally the proportion of an increase that is seen as permanent will rise as the income increase persists. Friedman argued that the marginal propensity to consume will be high out of permanent income and near zero out of transitory income. Subsequent research on spending behavior of lottery winners has tended to confirm Friedman's theory.[3]

Transitory income

Permanent income

The simplest algebraic form of consumption function using only observable variables and reflecting the ideas above is

$$C = aW + b(Y - T), \tag{2}$$

where W is the level of real wealth, T is real taxes, Y is real income, a is the marginal propensity to consume out of extra wealth, and b is the marginal propensity to consume out of after-tax income. The marginal propensity to consume will depend on how much of any increase in real income is expected to be permanent and how much is seen as transitory. Strictly speaking, the level of personal labor income should be used instead of the level of aggregate income Y, since nonlabor income is already reflected in the level of total wealth W.[4] However, over short periods the two measures of income will not differ substantially enough to concern us.

Investment

Investment demand

Investment demand is demand for newly produced real assets — housing, plant, equipment, and inventories. Newly produced real assets are needed, however, only if the total demand for real assets cannot be satisfied by the stock of existing real assets (last period's capital stock less depreciation). Investment demand is therefore explained by last period's capital stock, by the rate of depreciation, and by the factors explaining total demand for real assets.

The logic of demand for assets was discussed in chapters 6, 7, and 8 and again in chapter 10 when the asset purchase involved borrowing. Demand for real assets is just a particular case of demand for assets. Demand for real assets depends mainly on relative yields on real and financial assets and on

---

[2]The terms are from Milton Friedman, *A Theory of the Consumption Function* (New York: National Bureau of Economic Research, 1955).

[3]Friedman's theory refers to actual consumption, as opposed to consumption spending. Purchase of a new car by a lottery winner would be counted in full as extra consumption only if the lottery winner managed to consume the entire car in one year. Consumer spending could respond significantly to extra lottery winnings without actual consumption's responding much, if the extra spending were all on long-lived consumer durables.

[4]See, for example, William H. Branson and James M. Litvak, *Macroeconomics*, 2d ed. (New York: Harper and Row, 1981), 188.

relative risks. The relative risks are sensitive to investors' level of wealth or equity, since that determines the amount of debt and the degree of leverage required to finance any one level of total assets. For a given degree of leverage, the relative risks depend on relative covariances of asset yields — either with yields of other assets in the portfolio or with debts used to finance the asset portfolio.[5]

For housing demand, which is a large part of total investment demand, the level of current income serves as an additional constraint, since cash

FIGURE 18–1 Relationship between investment and financial yields

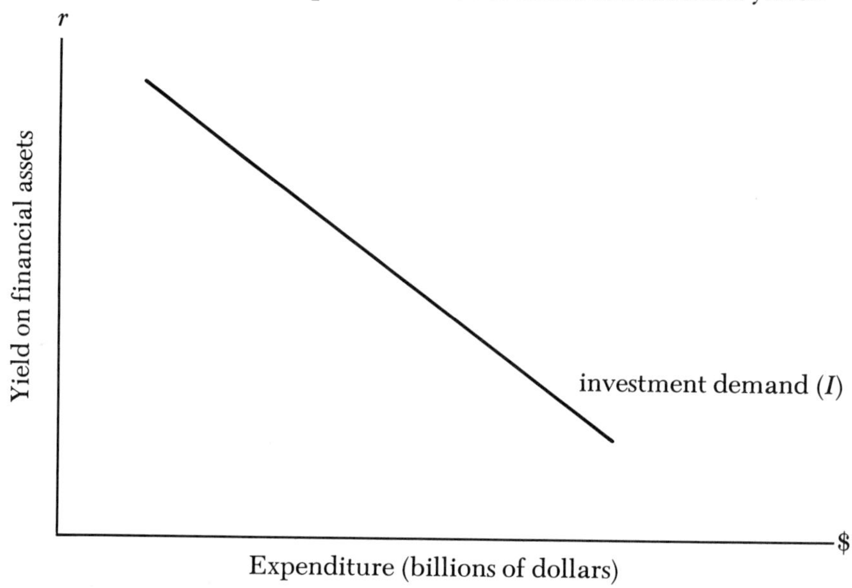

Lower yields on financial assets cause higher demand for other types of investments, including real capital assets. Extra demand for real assets drives up their prices, and these higher prices make newly produced real assets more competitive with existing real assets. As more investors decide to order new real assets, investment demand is increased.

outflows to service a house mortgage must be made out of current income with enough left over to pay for other necessary current consumption. For simplicity, we will ignore the effect of income levels on housing demand in our algebra, since the effect of current income level on aggregate demand is well enough captured in our explanation of consumption demand.

The higher the relative yield on financial assets, the higher the demand for them and the lower the demand for real assets. Lower demand for real assets implies less need for new real assets and therefore lower investment

[5]Relative variances will matter where assetholders cannot achieve broad diversification or cannot match up asset risks with similar debt risks.

demand in *AD*. The effect of financial-asset yields on investment demand is shown in figure 18–1. Lower interest rates raise demand for capital assets; once any assetholder's demand for capital assets exceeds the amount of existing capital assets available, the extra demand will be translated into investment demand for newly produced capital assets. The lower the interest rate relative to the return on real capital assets, the larger that excess demand for capital assets.

Tobin's *q* theory

James Tobin has explained the relationship between interest rates and investment demand more indirectly, in what is known as Tobin's *q* theory.[6] Tobin explains that in the very short run, where capital is fixed at last period's capital stock less depreciation, the equilibrium yield on capital assets will be the level needed to balance demand for capital with the fixed supply available. Panel (a) of figure 18–2 shows the equilibrium price of capital assets (P_k) being determined by the demand curve and a vertical short-run supply curve. Since supply is fixed, the equilibrium expected yield on capital assets depends on the factors that determine the position of the demand curve, which are the level of expected yields on financial assets, relative risks, and the equity base or wealth of investors. Where relative risks and equity levels are constant, only the financial-asset yields matter.

If the expected rental income or the marginal product from existing capital assets (MP_k) is constant in the short run, then higher prices P_k on capital assets imply lower yields r_k. For continually replaced capital assets, the relationship is the same as between yield and price of a perpetual bond:[7]

$$P_k = \frac{MP_k}{r_k}$$

The same statement applied to corporate shares is that, for any given level of expected earnings per share, higher expected yields on shares imply lower share purchase prices.

The second stage in Tobin's argument is to move from capital asset prices to investment in new capital assets. If the market price of existing capital assets (for example, the price at which existing companies can be bought on the stock market by takeover bids) is less than their replacement

---

[6]James Tobin, "A General Equilibrium Approach to Monetary Theory," *Journal of Money, Credit, and Banking* 1 (1969), 15–29.

[7]This equation assumes that the portion of the asset's gross revenue set aside as depreciation allowances is used to repair or replace worn-out parts of the real asset so that the investment lasts indefinitely, like a perpetual bond. The logic is not changed if the real asset does not last that long, but the pricing formula is made much more complex. The marginal product of capital is defined as net of the depreciation allowance.

FIGURE 18–2 Tobin's q and investment demand

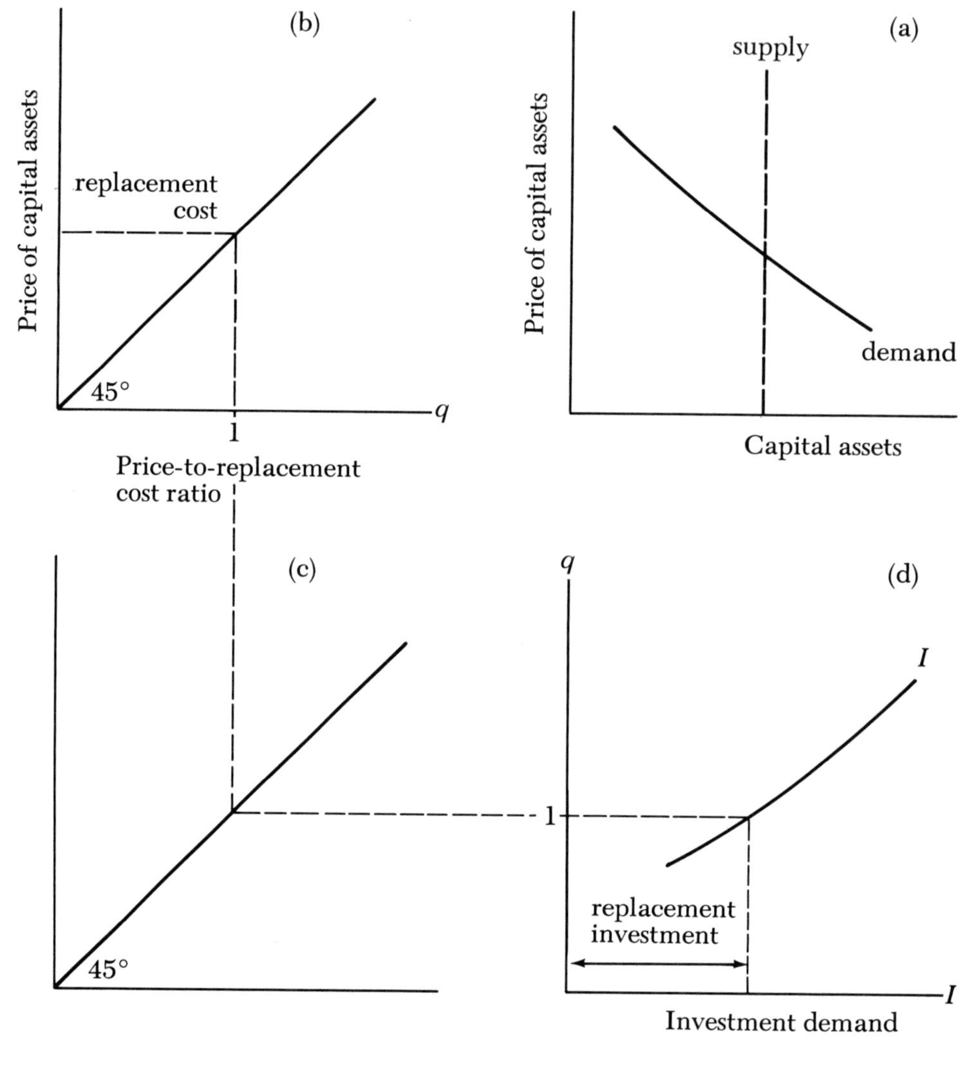

As financial-asset yields fall from 10 percent to 8 percent, the demand curve for real capital assets in panel (a) shifts outward to the right. At the existing level of the stock of real capital, the equilibrium price of real capital rises. In panel (b), the price level is converted into the q ratio (that is, divided by the replacement cost of capital). Panel (c) is just a 45-degree line that allows panel (d) to relate investment demand to q. When $q = 1$, the existing capital stock is maintained by replacement, but not added to.

costs, then investors will buy existing capital assets (or take over existing companies) rather than build new plant and equipment. The ratio of market price to replacement cost will be less than one, and real investment demand will be small. Tobin called the ratio of market price to replacement cost the *q ratio*. If the q ratio of market price to replacement cost is greater than 1, new capital assets will be cheaper than existing capital assets, and investors will build new companies rather than attempt to buy up existing ones. In the housing sector, developers expecting a q ratio greater than 1 will build new houses on speculation to profit from the difference between market price and construction cost. The relationship of market price P_k to q is straightforward and is given in panel (b) of figure 18–2. The relationship of q to investment demand is given in panel (d).

q ratio

To summarize: investment demand depends on the capital stock in the previous period, the rate of depreciation, and Tobin's q. Tobin's q depends in turn on expected yields on financial assets, on relative risks of real and financial assets, on the marginal product of capital assets, and on the equity or wealth of investors.

A simple linear form of investment demand function that reflects the ideas above is

$$I = I_0' + c'q; \quad q = q_0 - dr.$$

$$\text{So} \quad I = I_0' + c'q_0 - c'dr, \tag{3}$$

where c' and d are constant coefficients and r is the level of a representative interest rate reflecting expected yields on financial assets. The constant term (I_0') reflects the influence of the existing capital stock — that is, of the previous period's capital stock and of depreciation. The constant term q_0 reflects the influence of the marginal product of capital, relative risks, and wealth or equity of investors on demand for real capital assets. Higher levels of existing capital stock will depress I_0'; lower marginal products of capital, lower wealth, and lower relative risk on financial assets will depress q_0. In short-run analysis, we normally expect these factors to be relatively constant, so they are summarized by a constant term. It will be more convenient to simplify equation (3) to just

$$I = I_0 - cr, \tag{4}$$

where $I_0 = I_0' + c'q_0$ and $c = c'd$.

Government spending

The level of government spending on real goods and services reflects demand for the public goods and services that government provides. Ultimately those public goods have to be paid for out of taxes — a fact that individuals take into account when deciding to vote for or against high-spending political parties — so the demand for public goods must depend in some loose way on the economy's ability to pay taxes. The obvious measure of a nation's ability to pay taxes is the level of its national income, Y. Using the same logic, we could argue that, because the government has the option of saving or dissaving in any year by spending less than or more than its tax revenue, the amount of public spending in any year will also depend on the real interest rate available on government savings and on extra government borrowing.

In practice, neither the real income level nor the interest rate is usually an important determinant of government spending in the short run. Figure 18–3, for instance, shows the relationship between real income growth and government spending growth since 1953: in general, positive changes in

FIGURE 18–3 Relationship of changes in income to changes in government spending, 1953–80

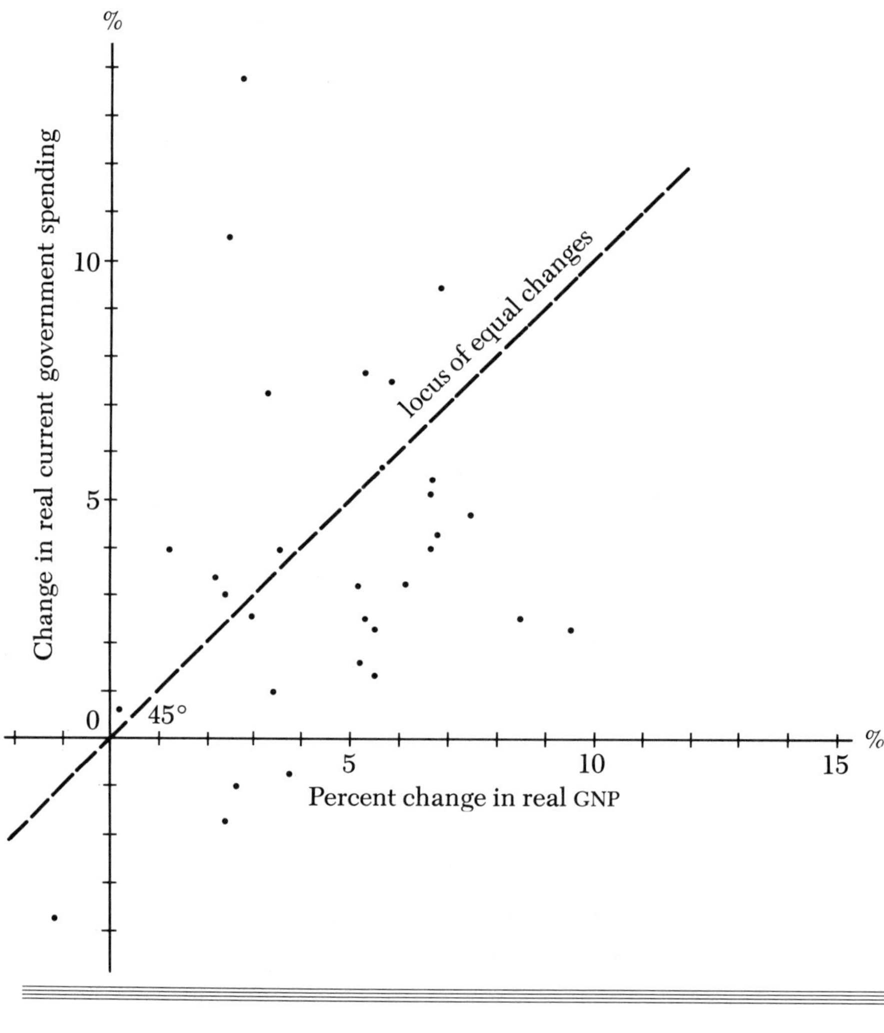

the one have been accompanied by positive changes in the other, but the relationship is extremely loose in the short run. We will therefore not assume any relationship at all between government spending and either income or interest rates. Government spending will be an exogenous lump G that can be changed by the government to suit the needs of stabilization policy.

Net exports

Net exports are total export demand by foreigners for Canadian goods and services, less Canadian demand for foreign goods and services. Canada's export demand by foreigners is simply Canadian producers' share of the total foreign demand for goods and services. Total demand for goods and services in foreign countries depends on the same list of factors abroad that Canadian domestic demand for goods and services depends on at home: income and wealth levels (for consumer goods), relative expected yields and relative risks (for capital goods), and government spending decisions.

Canadian producers' share of this total foreign demand depends on their competitive position, which is roughly measured by foreign price levels relative to Canadian price levels.[8] For this measurement, the foreign price level is multiplied by the foreign exchange rate to convert it into Canadian dollars. The foreign exchange rate is the price of foreign currency in terms of Canadian dollars ($P_{US\$}$), which can be thought of as "Canadian dollars per U.S. dollar." Canada's competitive position is then measured by the ratio

Foreign exchange rate

$$\left(\frac{P_f}{P}\right)P_{US\$}$$

where P_f is the foreign price level in foreign currency and P is the domestic Canadian price level. The higher the foreign price level or the higher the price of foreign currency in Canadian dollars, the higher is the share of Canadian producers in total foreign demand for goods and services — that is, the higher is Canadian export demand.

Import demand is foreign producers' share of total Canadian demand for goods and services, including imports. AD is a good proxy for that total, though AD excludes imports. The share of domestic demand secured by foreign producers will fall as the competitive position of Canadian producers is improved. The higher the foreign price level and the higher the price of foreign currency, the smaller will be foreign producers' share of total Canadian demand, and the smaller will be Canadian imports.

---

[8]Strictly speaking, only the prices of tradable goods and services are relevant. For our level of analysis in this chapter, we will assume that tradables' prices move in unison with the aggregate price level.

A simple version of the arguments above is

$$X - M = X_0 - eAD + f\left[\left(\frac{P_f}{P}\right)P_{US\$}\right] \tag{5}$$

where e and f are constant coefficients, and X_0 is an exogenous component of net exports that reflects the combined effect of foreign income and wealth levels, foreign expected yields, foreign relative risks on capital and financial assets, and foreign government spending. The coefficient e is the marginal propensity to import out of extra domestic demand. The coefficient f reflects the combined effect of higher export demand and lower import demand as Canada's competitive position is improved.

We should note that, because import demand depends on total domestic demand AD, imports are affected by all of the variables that affect C, I, G, and X.

Aggregate demand

Combining the explanations for component parts of aggregate demand gives an explanation of aggregate demand itself. Gathering together the simple linear equations we have used so far gives

$$\begin{aligned} AD &= C + I + G + X - M \qquad (1)\\ &= [aW + b(Y - T)] + (I_0 - cr) + G + \left\{X_0 - eAD + f\left[\left(\frac{P_f}{P}\right)P_{US\$}\right]\right\}, \end{aligned}$$

where a, b, c, e, and f are constant coefficients (propensities to spend, mostly) and the other variables are as defined above. The level of taxes can be explained simply as an exogenous lump and a portion dependent on the level of real income Y:

$$T = T_0 + tY,$$

where T_0 is an exogenous component of taxes and t is the marginal tax rate for the economy as a whole. The exogenous component T_0 will change with tax policies that change the tax structure or the basic tax-exemption limits, and the like. Substituting for T in our equation for aggregate demand gives

$$AD = aW + b(1 - t)Y - bT_0 + I_0 - cr + G + X_0 - eAD + f\left[\left(\frac{P_f}{P}\right)P_{US\$}\right] \tag{6}$$

If we rearrange this equation and group together all of the terms not depending on either Y or AD, we get the simpler expression

$$AD = AD_0 + b(1 - t)Y - eAD, \tag{7}$$

where the term AD_0 gathers together all of the terms not depending on either Y or AD:

$$AD_0 = aW - bT_0 + I_0 - cr + G + X_0 + f\left[\left(\frac{P_f}{P}\right)P_{US\$}\right]. \tag{8}$$

For simplicity in what follows, let us replace the term $b(1 - t)$ in equation (7) with the coefficient b' — the marginal propensity to consume out of extra before-tax income. Equation (7) then becomes

$$AD = AD_0 + b'Y - eAD. \tag{7'}$$

Moving eAD to the left-hand side and dividing both sides by $1 + e$ gives an equation for aggregate demand:

$$AD = \left(\frac{1}{1+e}\right)AD_0 + \left(\frac{b'}{1+e}\right)Y, \tag{9}$$

which is shown in figure 18–4 as the standard Keynesian-cross aggregate spending schedule.[9] The intercept in figure 18–4 at the vertical axis is $AD_0[1/(1 + e)]$, and the slope of the aggregate spending schedule is $b'/(1 + e)$. The slope of the aggregate spending schedule is the marginal propensity of the economy to demand domestic goods and services when real national income increases.

SECTION 2 Equilibrium aggregate demand

In equilibrium in the goods market, demand will equal supply; AD will equal AS. Since the real value of aggregate output AS is also by definition equal to the total value of real income payments Y accruing to factors of production (including profits to capital, the residual item), AD must also equal Y in equilibrium. We can substitute for Y in our aggregate demand equation above, to get an equilibrium demand level AD^e:

$$\begin{aligned} AD^e &= AD_0 + b'AD - eAD \\ &= AD_0\left(\frac{1}{1 - b' + e}\right). \end{aligned} \tag{10}$$

In figure 18–4, imposing the equilibrium requirement is the same as requiring that the level of aggregate demand lie not only on the aggregate spending schedule but also on an equilibrium locus that joins all points for which $AD = Y$. That equilibrium locus is the 45-degree line in figure 18–4, and the equilibrium aggregate demand level is at the intersection of the aggregate spending schedule and the 45-degree line. The equilibrium level of aggregate demand can be read off either the vertical or the horizontal axis, since the values are identical along the 45-degree line.

---

[9]Equation (7) differs from the aggregate demand equation presented in most introductory textbooks in that import demand depends directly on AD instead of on real income. In the formulation in equation (7), any surge in demand will generate extra demand for imports even if there is no response of production and therefore of real income. This change from the standard treatment allows for greater accuracy in describing real economies, with no effect on the static equilibrium analysis in section 2.

FIGURE 18–4 The aggregate spending schedule (the Keynesian cross)

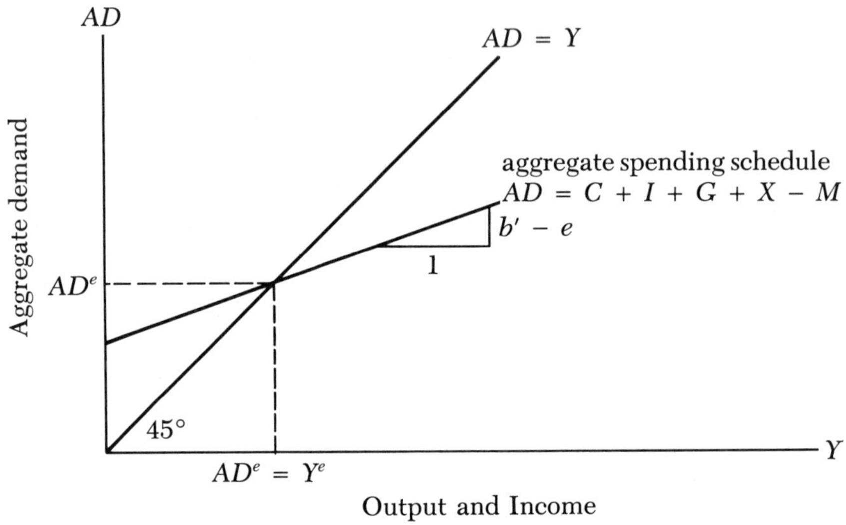

Higher income levels increase aggregate demand at a rate equal to $b' - e$, the marginal propensity to consume domestic goods out of national income. The intercept on the vertical axis reflects all influences on aggregate demand other than real income. The equilibrium level of aggregate demand occurs at the point of intersection of the 45° line (on which $AD = Y$) and the aggregate spending schedule.

Multipliers

Aggregate demand multiplier

The equilibrium level of aggregate demand depends on all of the ingredients in the term AD_0 and on the size of each of the coefficients in the term $1/(1 - b' + e)$. This latter term is known as an *aggregate demand multiplier*, in that any change in AD_0 has an effect on equilibrium aggregate demand that is a multiple equal to $1/(1 - b' + e)$ of the change in AD_0. The denominator of the multiplier is less than one as long as the marginal propensity to consume out of before-tax income is greater than the economy's marginal propensity to import, which is usually the case. The multiplier is therefore greater than 1.0 as a rule.

The expression $1/(1 - b' + e)$ is a multiplier relating changes in the term AD_0 to changes in equilibrium aggregate demand. AD_0 is made up of many ingredients, each of which affects AD_0 differently, and it is of interest to see what multiplier effect some of these ingredients have individually on the equilibrium level of aggregate demand. Substituting for AD_0 from equation (8) into equation (10) gives

$$AD^e = \left\{ aW - bT_0 + I_0 - cr + G + X_0 + f\left[\left(\frac{P_f}{P}\right)P_{US\$}\right]\right\}\left(\frac{1}{1 - b' + e}\right). \quad (11)$$

This equation shows that different components of AD_0 will have different multiplier effects on equilibrium aggregate demand, because different components have different impacts on AD_0. An increase in government spending, exogenous investment, or exogenous export demand by \$1 million will raise AD_0 by \$1 million and will therefore raise equilibrium aggregate demand by $\$1/(1 - b' + e)$ million. An increase in wealth, however, will increase AD_0 only at the rate a, the marginal propensity to consume out of extra wealth; aggregate demand will therefore increase by the factor $a/(1 - b' + e)$. An increase in taxes by \$1 will decrease equilibrium aggregate demand by the amount $\$b/(1 - b' + e)$. Similarly, an increase in the interest rate will lower AD_0 at the rate c and will lower equilibrium aggregate demand by the multiplier $c/(1 - b' + e)$. Each of the other variables in AD_0 also has a multiplier effect on equilibrium aggregate demand equal to the product of its coefficient in AD_0 and the simple multiplier $1/(1 - b' + e)$.

Multiple equilibria: the *IS* curve

The equilibrium in figure 18–4 looks unique, but it is not. That equilibrium occurs only for specific values of the ingredients in the term AD_0—that is,

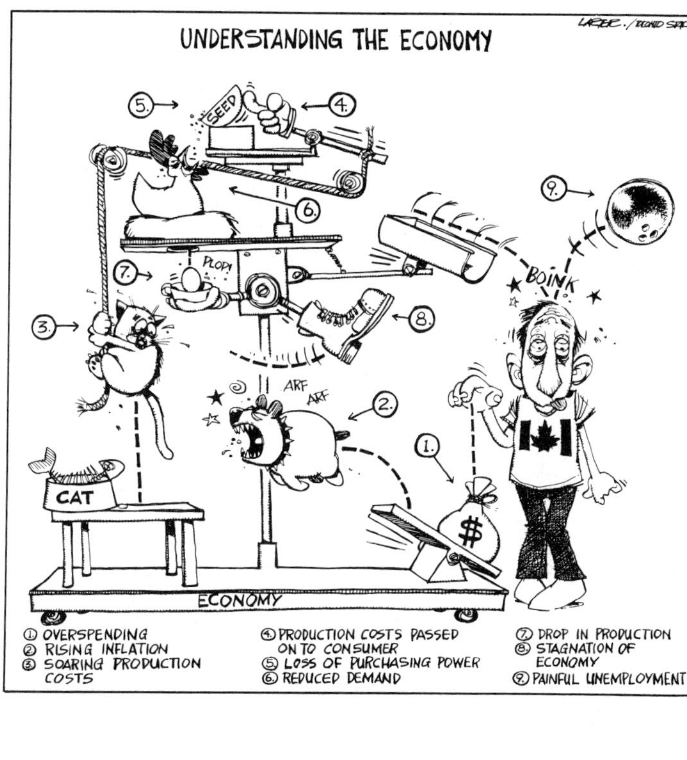

for specific values of interest rates, of exogenous consumption, of Canadian producers' competitive position, and so on. A different value for any one of the ingredients in AD_0 will mean a different position of the aggregate spending schedule as in figure 18–5, and a different equilibrium level of aggregate demand. Figure 18–5 shows, for instance, the different levels of AD^e that are caused by different levels of interest rates (that is, expected yields on financial assets). Higher interest rates cause less investment in new capital assets, since the relative market price of existing capital assets falls as interest rates rise; with lower prices of existing capital assets, it is cheaper for expansion-minded firms to take over existing firms and their assets than it is to build equivalent new productive capacity from scratch.

IS curve

We can summarize the effect of interest rates on equilibrium aggregate demand in an equilibrium locus called the *IS curve*, which is derived in figure 18–6. The *IS* curve joins each level of financial-market yield with the equilibrium *AD* level at that financial yield. Of course, the *IS* curve reflects the effect of r (by way of effects on the capital-asset price ratio q) assuming all other factors stay constant, and also assuming a particular relationship between r and q. If any of those assumptions change, then so does the *IS* curve.

FIGURE 18–5 Interest rates and equilibrium aggregate demand

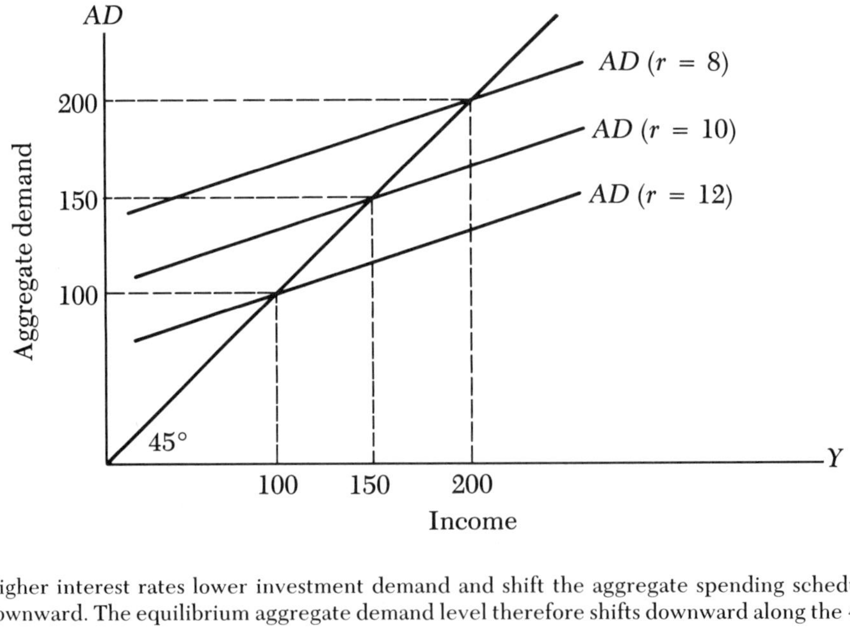

Higher interest rates lower investment demand and shift the aggregate spending schedule downward. The equilibrium aggregate demand level therefore shifts downward along the 45° line.

Algebraically, the *IS* curve in figure 18–6 is found by rearranging the equilibrium aggregate demand equation:

$$AD^e = \left\{ aW - bT_0 + I_0 + G + X_0 + f\left[\left(\frac{P_f}{P}\right)P_{US\$}\right]\right\}\left(\frac{1}{1-b'+e}\right) - \left(\frac{c}{1-b'+e}\right)r. \tag{12}$$

FIGURE 18–6 The *IS* curve

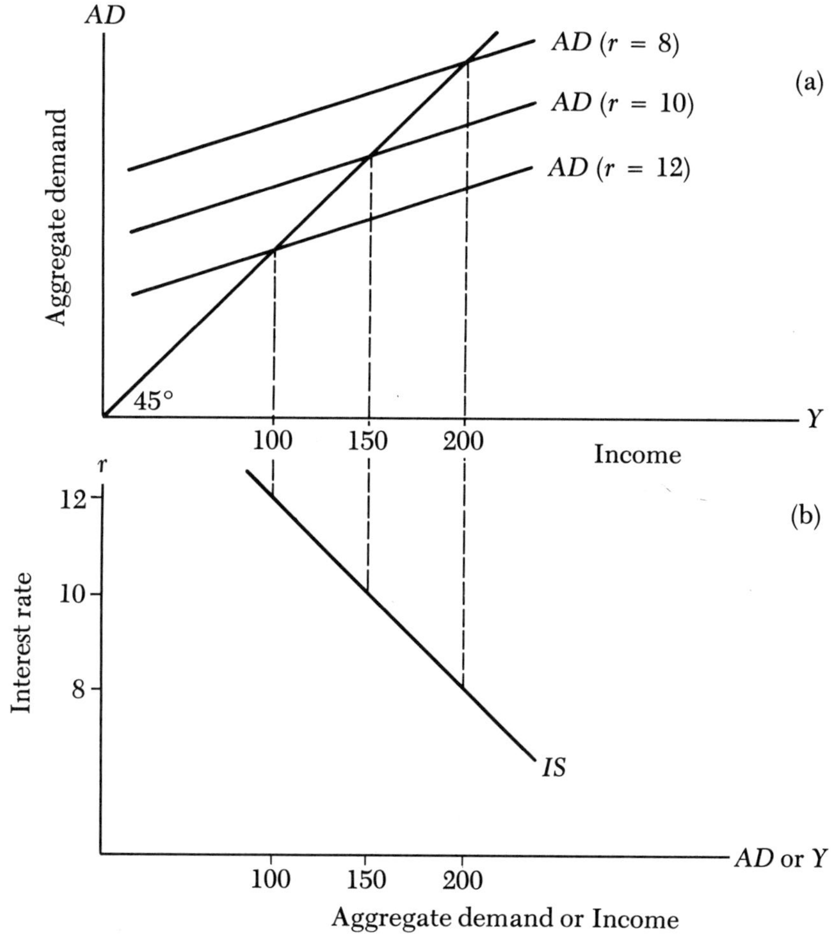

Different levels of the interest rate imply different levels of investment and therefore different levels of equilibrium aggregate demand in panel (a). When the interest rate and equilibrium aggregate demand combinations are plotted together on the same diagram, the result is the *IS* curve.

The first term is the horizontal intercept of the *IS* curve, and the coefficient of r is the inverse of the slope of the *IS* curve, dr/dAD^e. The slope depends on the simple multiplier $1/(1 - b' + e)$ and on the sensitivity of investment demand to changes in r. The position of the *IS* curve will be changed by any change in any factor affecting the horizontal intercept term in equation (12). Any disturbance in the expression in brackets in the numerator of the intercept term (for example, an increase in G) will shift the *IS* curve by a multiple of that disturbance, the multiple being the multiplier $1/(1 - b' + e)$.

Foreign exchange rate effects

In a large open economy such as Canada's, we are also interested in the effect of foreign price levels and of the exchange rate $P_{US\$}$ on aggregate demand. Figure 18–7 derives an equilibrium locus for aggregate demand and the exchange rate in the same way that figure 18–6 does for expected yields on financial assets. The result is analogous to the *IS* curve except that it holds interest rates constant and varies the exchange rate rather than the other way around. Since the exchange rate influences aggregate demand in exactly the same way that foreign price levels do, the equilibrium locus in figure 18–7 could be used as an equilibrium locus for foreign price levels instead of the exchange rate.

If the foreign exchange rate is fixed somehow, such as by exchange controls or by the central bank's buying and selling whatever foreign exchange is needed to keep the exchange rate constant in the foreign exchange market, then figure 18–7 is all we can say about the effect of the foreign exchange rate on domestic demand levels. However, Canada does not have a fixed exchange rate, and we can actually say considerably more.

Under the floating-exchange-rate system Canada has had since 1970, the exchange rate $P_{US\$}$ (the price of foreign currency) is allowed to float up and down to balance supply and demand for foreign exchange in the foreign exchange market. As a result, the exchange rate is strongly influenced by both the level of domestic demand *AD* and the interest differential between foreign and domestic interest rates. In order to explain this result, we need to add an explanation of the foreign exchange market to our model of aggregate demand.

The foreign exchange market

All transactions in the foreign exchange market fit into one of the three accounts in the *Balance of Payments* — the set of accounts that records Canadians' transactions with nonresidents. The first account is the *Current Account*, containing all trade flows of exports and imports (on merchandise

Balance of Payments
Current Account

FIGURE 18–7 Aggregate demand and the exchange rate

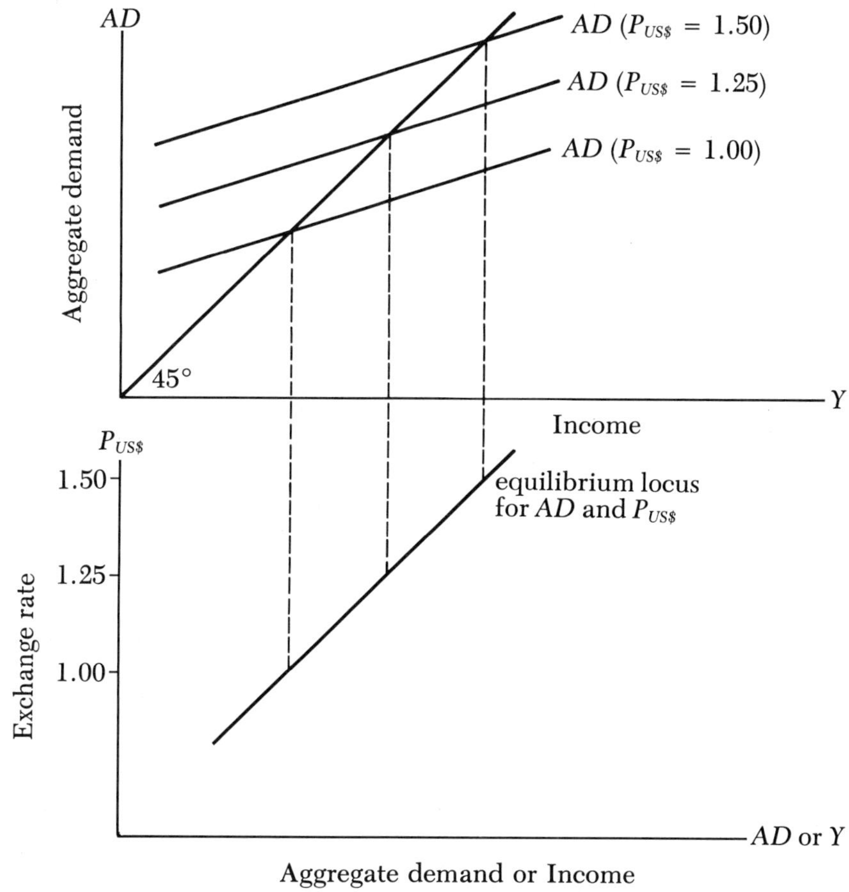

Higher values of the exchange rate $P_{US\$}$ increase net exports and stimulate aggregate demand, producing higher equilibrium levels in the top panel. When the exchange rate and aggregate demand levels are plotted together, the result is an equilibrium locus for aggregate demand and the exchange rate, much like the *IS* curve.

account if in goods, and on services account otherwise). The second account is the *Capital Account*, containing all changes in asset holdings involving foreign exchange transactions. The Capital Account records as capital inflows all purchases of Canadian assets by foreigners with foreign

Capital Account

exchange, and as capital outflows all purchases of foreign assets by Canadians with foreign exchange.[10]

Net Official Monetary Movements

The third account of the Balance of Payments is *Net Official Monetary Movements*, which records any changes in foreign exchange holdings of the monetary authorities (the Bank of Canada, the Exchange Fund Account of the Department of Finance, and the Receiver General for Canada). The

FIGURE 18–8 The foreign exchange market

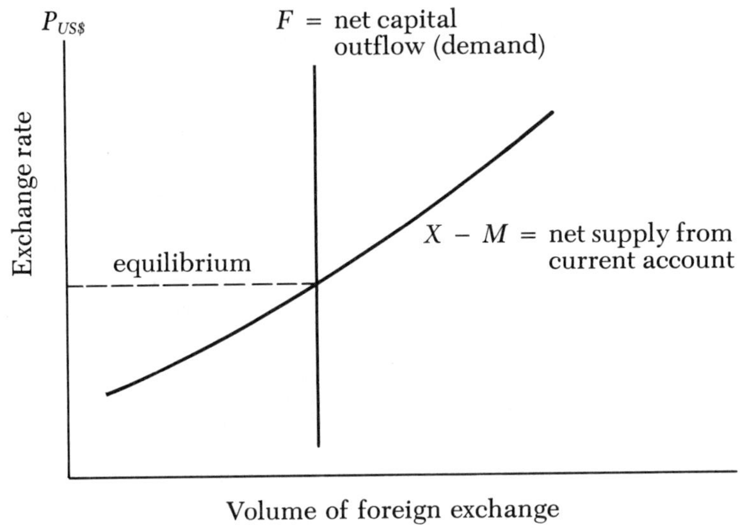

Net capital outflows measure the net demand for foreign currency each year for capital (nontrade) transactions. Net capital outflows are not reliably sensitive to the exchange rate, so the net-capital-outflow schedule is vertical. Net exports measure the net supply of foreign exchange from trade transactions. Higher exchange rates improve the competitive position of domestic producers, so net exports increase as the exchange rate increases. The equilibrium exchange-rate level is at the intersection of the demand and supply schedules.

monetary authorities do intervene in the foreign exchange market from time to time in order to dampen random fluctuations in the exchange rate and to smooth adjustments of the exchange rate from one level to another, but usually this intervention is only temporary and does not affect the

[10]The Balance of Payments does not reflect purchases of Canadian assets by foreigners with Canadian currency earned in Canada (for instance, in domestic subsidiaries). Such purchases affect the degree of foreign ownership and the Balance of International Indebtedness, but not the Balance of Payments and the foreign exchange market. Only later, as greater foreign ownership of Canadian assets starts to generate a larger outflow of investment income abroad, will the Balance of Payments be affected: the Current Account will then record the outflow of investment income as a larger import from foreigners of the services of their assets (in exchange for interest and dividend payments).

equilibrium level of the exchange rate that is eventually reached (it is called a *managed float*, which conveys the idea well). We will therefore ignore Net Official Monetary Movements and explain only the Current and Capital Accounts.

Managed float

The Current Account, or net exports

The Current Account provides Canada with a net supply of foreign exchange equal to net exports, which we have already discussed:

$$X - M = X_0 - eAD + f\left[\left(\frac{P_f}{P}\right)P_{US\$}\right]. \tag{5}$$

The effect of higher prices of foreign exchange is to improve Canada's competitive position and to increase its net export earnings, so the relationship between net exports and the exchange rate is as shown in figure 18–8.

Net capital outflows

The Capital Account gives rise to a net demand for foreign exchange equal to the difference between capital outflows and capital inflows. Call this difference the *net capital outflow* (F). The net capital outflow reflects Canadians' adjustments of their holdings of foreign assets (real or financial), and foreigners' adjustments of their holdings of Canadian assets (also real and financial). We have considered at length in this book what influences demand for assets: wealth levels, relative yields, and relative risks are the main factors. Foreign demand for Canadian assets will therefore depend on foreign wealth, Canadian yields relative to foreign yields, and Canadian risks relative to foreign risks. Some of the relevant yields will be expected yields on real assets, which reflect marginal products of capital, capital goods prices, and the exchange rate that translates foreign prices into Canadian currency. Other relevant yields will be long- and short-term bond and deposit yields, for investors such as pension funds and corporations with surplus cash for short periods. Remember from chapter 5 that money-market dealers in Canada spend much of their time trying to drum up customers for short-term investment packages involving foreign-currency deposits.

Net capital outflow

The relative yields that matter will be after-tax yields, so relative tax rates will matter as much as relative before-tax nominal yields. Investors contemplating foreign asset purchases must also take into account possible fluctuations in the exchange rate. In case the investment is for a period short enough to have protection against exchange rate changes through a forward-exchange contract, the cost of forward cover will matter instead, but we saw in chapter 15 that the cost of forward cover reflects the same three factors: Canadian and foreign interest rates and expected changes in the exchange rate.

Changes in any of the factors we have discussed will change demand for Canadian assets by foreigners or demand for foreign assets by Canadians.

Any change in demand will cause a temporary change in the net capital outflow while actual holdings are being adjusted to desired levels.

Many of the factors we have listed are powerful, but exogenous to our model: foreign wealth, foreign interest rates, foreign tax rates, foreign expected yields on real assets, and foreign risks. Some of the other factors are within Canadian control but are unlikely to change much in the short run except perhaps by explicit government decision: Canadian tax rates, Canadian risk levels, and Canadian marginal products of capital. One other factor, the expected change in the exchange rate, is both powerful and rapidly changing but not reliably connected to anything in our model in the short run. We cannot explain expected exchange rate changes, so we must ignore them for now and acknowledge that they will be one of the sources of random departures of actual events from those predicted by our model.

The process of elimination in the preceding paragraph leaves us with the net capital inflow responding to differences in relative expected yields on financial assets in Canada and abroad. The response is temporary, in that it continues only long enough to adjust actual holdings of Canadian and foreign assets to desired levels, but the "temporary" adjustment may well continue over several quarters and have a large impact on the domestic economy. In the short run, therefore, we can approximate the behavior of the net capital outflow by the linear equation

$$F = F_0 + g(r_{US} - r), \tag{13}$$

where r_{US} is a single measure of foreign interest rates such as the U.S. Treasury Bill rate, r is a single measure of Canadian interest rates such as the Canadian Treasury Bill rate, and F_0 is an exogenous component reflecting all of the other influences we mentioned but did not exclude explicitly from the equation. The coefficient g is positive, so the net capital outflow falls as our domestic interest rates rise.

The explanation of net capital outflows does not depend on the level of the exchange rate at all, except to the extent that at some times a change of level may give rise to expectations of further change in some direction. The net capital outflow is therefore the same at all levels of the exchange rate, and the demand for foreign exchange that the net capital outflow represents is described by a vertical line in figure 18–8 when the exchange rate is on the vertical axis.

Equilibrium exchange rate

Putting net exports and net capital outflows together in figure 18–8 gives us both parts of the foreign exchange market: net supply from the Current Account, and net demand from the Capital Account. The equilibrium exchange rate is the level at which net exports equals net capital outflows — that is, at the intersection of the two schedules. Algebraically,

$$X_0 - eAD + f\left[\left(\frac{P_f}{P}\right)P_{US\$}\right] = F_0 + g(r_{US} - r), \tag{14}$$

so the equilibrium level of $P_{US\$}$ must be

$$P_{US\$} = [F_0 - X_0 + g(r_{US} - r) + eAD]\,\frac{P}{fP_f}. \tag{15}$$

The *IS* curve with induced-exchange-rate effects

From equation (15) it is clear that the exchange rate is influenced by the level of domestic interest rates, and we already know from figure 18–7 that the level of the exchange rate influences aggregate demand levels. We can therefore add a further, indirect effect of domestic interest rates on aggregate demand via the exchange rate, as long as the exchange rate is allowed to float toward equilibrium without more than temporary central-bank interference.

Intuitively, the extra impact of interest rates can be added to an *IS* curve fairly easily, as in figure 18–9. A drop in domestic interest rates in figure 18–9 increases aggregate demand by lowering the equilibrium yield required on existing capital, which raises the price of existing capital and makes many new capital assets profitable to build and to buy. That effect is already built into the *IS* curve we derived in figure 18–6.

FIGURE 18–9 The *IS* curve with a floating exchange rate

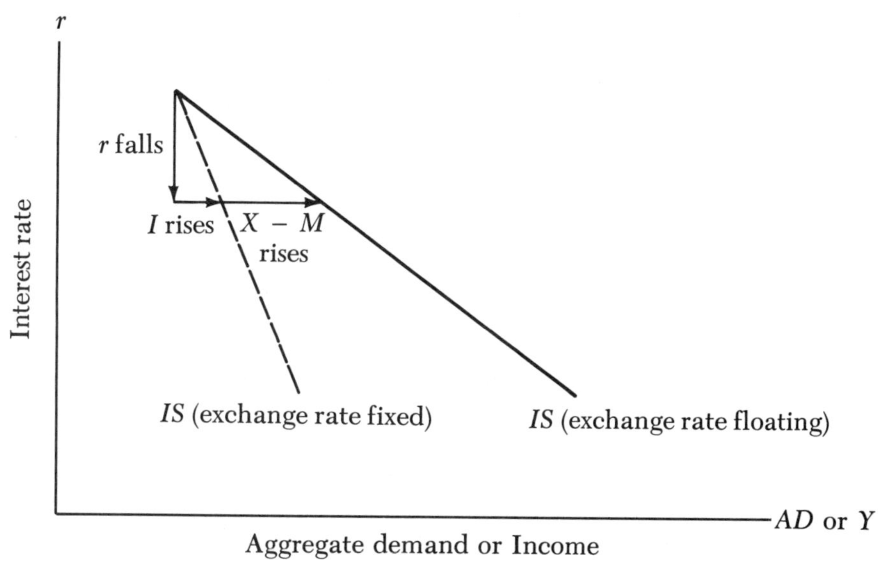

When the exchange rate floats, a lower interest rate stimulates net exports as well as investment. Aggregate demand is therefore more sensitive to interest rates with a floating exchange rate than if the exchange rate were fixed and only investment demand responded to interest-rate changes, and the *IS* curve is flatter.

Lower domestic interest rates also make foreign financial assets relatively attractive and stimulate a larger net capital outflow as Canadian and foreign investors adjust portfolios to higher shares of foreign assets. The higher net capital outflow is extra demand for foreign exchange in the foreign exchange market, which pushes up the exchange rate (the price of foreign exchange in units of Canadian currency). A higher exchange rate improves Canadian producers' competitive position and stimulates Canada's net exports. In figure 18–8, the net-capital-outflow schedule is shifted to the right, and the equilibrium level of $P_{US\$}$ rises until net exports have risen to match the extra net capital outflow. Aggregate demand is increased even further than is implied by the *IS* curve in figure 18–6 — that is, allowing for the indirect effects of interest rates on the exchange rate and on net exports in a floating-exchange-rate system gives a flatter *IS* curve (in figure 18–9) than occurs in an economy with a fixed exchange rate.

Algebraically, the new *IS* curve incorporating induced-exchange-rate impacts is arrived at by substituting for the exchange rate $P_{US\$}$ in the *IS* equation (12). Equation (15) gives the equilibrium value of the exchange rate in terms of interest rates and the level of domestic demand. Substituting that equilibrium expression for $P_{US\$}$ into the *IS* curve equation gives

$$AD^e = \left(aW - bT_0 + I_0 + X_0 + G - cr \right.$$
$$\left. + \left\{ f\left(\frac{P_f}{P}\right)[F_0 - X_0 + g(r_{US} - r) + eAD]\frac{P}{fP_f} \right\} \right) \left(\frac{1}{1 - b' + e}\right). \qquad (16)$$

Equation (16) simplifies considerably to[11]

$$AD^e = \left[aW - bT_0 + I_0 + G + F_0 + gr_{US} - (c + g)r \right] \left(\frac{1}{1 - b'}\right). \qquad (17)$$

---

[11]The simplification of equation (16) involves several steps. Let $Mult = 1/(1 - b' + e)$. Equation (16) can then be rewritten as

$$[aW - bT_0 + I_0 + G + F_0 + gr_{US} - (c + g)r]\, Mult + eADMult$$
$$= [aW - bT_0 + I_0 + G + F_0 + gr_{US} - (c + g)r]\, \frac{Mult}{1 - eMult}.$$

The last term, $Mult/(1 - eMult)$, simplifies on being multiplied out as

$$\frac{1/(1 - b' + e)}{1 - e\,[1/(1 - b' + e)]} = \frac{1/(1 - b' + e)}{[(1 - b' + e) - e]/(1 - b' + e)}$$
$$= \frac{1}{1 - b'}$$

Equation (16) can therefore be written as

$$AD^e = \frac{aW - T_0 + I_0 + G + F_0 + gr_{US} - (c + g)r}{1 - b'}.$$

The slope of this new *IS* equation is the inverse of the coefficient of r:

$$\frac{dAD^e}{dr} = \frac{-c - g}{1 - b'}. \tag{18}$$

This coefficient can be contrasted with the coefficient of r in equation (12), without induced-exchange-rate effects:

$$\frac{dAD^e}{dr} = \frac{-c}{1 - b' + e}. \tag{19}$$

The effect of r on AD^e in equation (18) is larger in absolute terms because it has larger absolute numerator and smaller denominator. If response of equilibrium aggregate demand to domestic interest rates is larger when indirect exchange rate effects are included, then the resulting *IS*-curve locus is flatter in figure 18–9 than in figure 18–6.

Position and shifts of the *IS* curve

It is now time to pause and remember some ignored variables. The position of the *IS* curve in figure 18–9 depends on all of the other variables in the *IS*-curve equation (12) other than the domestic interest rate. The list includes wealth, the exogenous components of investment spending, government spending, taxes, net capital outflows, and foreign interest rates.

Each of those terms in turn reflects the other variables we did not include explicitly in our algebraic version of the model. The exogenous component of consumption, for instance, depends on the age distribution of the population and on expectations about future income. Exogenous investment depends on marginal revenue products of capital, relative risks of real versus financial assets, equity levels of business firms, and degrees of risk aversion by investors. Exogenous net capital outflows depend on foreign and domestic yields on real assets, foreign and domestic risks and tax rates, foreign and domestic wealth levels, and expectations about future exchange rate changes. Government spending and taxes depend on the host of factors that lie behind public-sector decisions — the province of the political scientist more than of the economist.

It will come as no surprise, after the list of extra factors added in the preceding paragraph, that the position of the *IS* curve (that is, the equilibrium level of aggregate demand at any domestic interest rate level) is likely to change significantly from year to year, as in figure 18–10. There are so many different factors affecting the *IS* curve that one might hope many of the disturbances in any one year would cancel each other out and leave the actual *IS* curve relatively stable. However, there is no presumption that the separate influences we have identified are at all independent. We have seen, for instance, that domestic interest rates and the exchange rate are likely to change together in such a way that they reinforce each other's effect on aggregate demand. It is likely that expectations of future real

FIGURE 18–10 Shifts of the *IS* curve

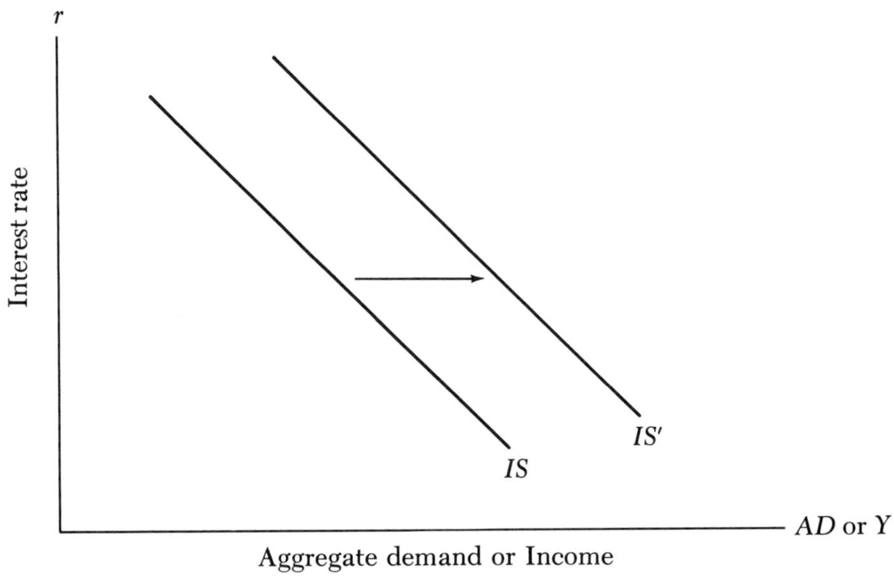

Increasing the level of G or reducing the level of taxes T_0 will shift the *IS* curve to the right: at each level of the interest rate, aggregate demand will be larger.

income and of marginal products of capital are likely to change together too, both of them depressing or stimulating aggregate demand.

One pair of variables we have not shown as affecting aggregate demand in equilibrium are Canadian and foreign price levels. You will see later that changes in price levels are likely to affect demand by changing the real value of household wealth, and therefore consumption demand. Also, relative price levels at home and abroad will influence net export demand whenever the exchange rate does not move to compensate. In the short run of a year or so, the exchange rate may well not move to compensate for changes in relative price levels, even though it does over longer periods. In the short run, therefore, changes in domestic and foreign price levels are likely to be a further source of disturbance in aggregate demand. Figure 18–11 shows, for instance, the ratio of export prices to import prices, both converted into Canadian dollars at the current exchange rate; this ratio, called *the terms of trade*, is a measure of the competitive position of Canadian producers. Figure 18–11 shows that the terms of trade are not held always at 1.00 by changes in the exchange rate. The terms of trade can be different from 1.00 for several quarters at a time.

Terms of trade

FIGURE 18–11 Terms of trade, 1977–82

Source: Bank of Canada Review.

SECTION 3

Dynamic aspects of demand behavior

It is clear that, in an economy such as Canada's, aggregate demand is subject to many outside influences. Those outside influences will probably not all stand still long enough for the economy ever to adjust to full equilibrium AD^e, even if the adjustment process is stable. We therefore need to know roughly how long the adjustment process takes. If the process is slow, the final equilibrium level is less relevant, since the economy is not likely to get close to it before being disturbed again by another demand shock. If the adjustment process is fast, then the economy may well get close to a new equilibrium before being disturbed by another demand shock; in that case static equilibrium models are useful as predictors of actual demand levels.

We also need to know about the speed of the adjustment process in order to estimate whether the adjustment path will be smooth, oscillating, or even explosive. The desirability of stabilization policy is strongly affected by which sort of adjustment path is likely to follow from a change in government spending, for instance. Finally, we need to know about the speed of the adjustment process in order to know which of the variables we have assumed constant in the short run are likely to have changed significantly by the time the economy approaches a new equilibrium. Changes in exogenous variables like I_0 (exogenous investment) can give rise to important cycles in aggregate demand, even if they do not affect the final equilibrium solution in the algebraic model.

Lags

How long does a demand shock take to have all or even most of its effect? How long after the shock can we expect lingering effects still to be occurring? This is an unsettled area of economic research, one in which it is very difficult to get firm answers from the data of past experience. A comparative simulation using four large econometric models of the Canadian economy (built with the same basic demand model we are using in this book, but assuming exchange rates stay fixed) nevertheless gives an idea about lags by showing the cumulative response of real aggregate demand levels to a positive demand shock. The positive demand shock took the form of a sustained increase in government spending levels over three years.[12]

The time paths produced by the simulations show that the multiplier effect of the demand shock reaches its maximum level of approximately 2.0 by the end of three years and is well above 1.0 by the end of the first year. Two of the models show larger multipliers at the end of the first year than at the end of the third year, but for reasons having to do more with supply behavior than with aggregate demand. The implication of the comparative simulation is that demand effects occur fairly quickly in the Canadian economy, with most of the demand effect occurring within the first four quarters after the initial demand shock.

The multiplier process that amplifies demand responses could take time for several reasons. One reason is that the process of spending income, noticing that inventory levels are falling, stepping up production orders, and paying out the extra incomes takes finite amounts of time. The demand multiplier process is a series of rounds, which have to be in sequence to some extent. Spending could respond more quickly if households, for instance, rushed out to spend in anticipation of a future income flow, before the income was actually received, but that is not common behavior. Milton Friedman's permanent-income hypothesis and Ando and Modigliani's life-cycle hypothesis both suggest that expectations are indeed important in household and firm behavior, but the empirical evidence suggests that households adjust their expectations of future income only slowly in response to changes in current income. If anything, the effect of allowing for expectations is to slow down the multiplier process rather than to speed it up.

Another reason for lags in demand response is one that operates in different directions for different demand shocks. The impact of higher

[12] L. de Bever et al., "Dynamic Properties of Four Canadian Macroeconomic Models," *Canadian Journal of Economics*, May 1979, 133–94.

interest rates on investment and net export spending takes time. Investment decisions are usually taken some months before the actual spending occurs on new capital assets, and foreign trade is not adjusted quickly either: new connections must be established, lines of trade credit set up, customs procedures checked, and several other time-consuming processes completed before new trade flows will respond to changes in a nation's competitive position.

When the demand shock is a direct increase in one of the exogenous spending items in equation (17) (such as G or I_0), the lag in response of demand to interest-rate changes means that any offsetting impact of higher interest rates induced by such a demand shock will be slow to appear. When the demand shock is having its initial effect through a change in interest rates, the demand shock itself may be slow to appear.

Other dynamic responses

Over any adjustment path to new equilibrium levels of aggregate demand, some of the exogenous variables are bound to change slightly. The changes may not be predictable enough to include in our model, or they may be only temporary and therefore not affect the final equilibrium state. For dynamic adjustment patterns, however, the changes are important.

First, any demand shock that increases demand levels is likely to affect expectations of future demand levels, which in turn affect firms' expectations of future marginal products of capital. That last change will increase the market price of existing capital relative to its replacement cost (that is, Tobin's q ratio) and stimulate construction of new real assets. The initial demand shock will be amplified — quite possibly by a factor of 10 or more — by a surge of investment demand.

However, the very process of investment over time must change the size of the capital stock. Investment is undertaken only to adjust the capital stock to a new desired level, so that increases in the actual capital stock mean the adjustment process is closer to completion. Eventually the investment boom will peter out. Before that slowdown occurs, business firms will anticipate it and slow down their own estimates of future sales growth. With lower forecasts of future sales growth, firms will need less expansion of capacity, and their own investment demand will be lowered. Amplification of an initial demand shock is followed by just the opposite.

Accelerator mechanism

The dynamic adjustment pattern we have described is the *accelerator mechanism*. The dynamic effects are not permanent, in that they do not affect the final equilibrium value of aggregate demand, but they can be very strong and can produce important cycles of real demand and output in the economy. The cycles generated by the accelerator mechanism may well affect investors' estimates of the relative risks of investing in real versus financial assets, with long-run effects on the demand for new capital assets.

SECTION 4

Price-level impacts

So far we have ignored the domestic price level as an influence on aggregate demand. In this section we will make up for that neglect. The price level has significant effects on aggregate demand through inflationary expectations, through the level of wealth, and indirectly through the financial system. We will discuss the indirect effects through the financial system in the next chapter. The other two price impacts will be dealt with here.

Expected changes in the price level

Expected inflation raises nominal interest rates, as we discussed in chapter 14. Higher expected inflation leads to higher nominal interest rates in approximately the same amount. The net effect is to lower after-tax nominal interest yields on financial assets for investors who pay tax on their entire nominal investment income and for borrowers who can deduct the entire nominal debt cost from their revenue in calculating taxable income. Lower after-tax yields on financial assets encourage borrowers to borrow (to finance purchases of real assets such as housing, which are taxed less heavily). Lower after-tax yields on financial assets also encourage lenders to invest in real assets instead of bonds and deposits. Both responses are likely to increase investment demand.

Higher expected inflation also reduces the tax shelter provided by a fixed nominal schedule of depreciation allowances; this reduction lowers both the after-tax marginal product of capital assets and the market value of existing capital. Perhaps just as important, higher nominal interest rates will seriously impair the cash flow position of some firms even if the real interest costs are not any higher. The reason is that an increase in expected inflation can increase nominal interest costs much more quickly than the firm's revenues. Over time, if the expected inflation materializes, borrowers' revenues will gradually catch up with their high but constant nominal interest payments. To start with, however, borrowers' liquidity may be so constrained that borrowers cannot even finance assets that in the long run are good investments. We considered an extreme case of this cash flow effect in chapter 6, when we looked at the effect of high nominal interest rates and inflation on the demand for housing. The same effect occurs for some firms.

Higher expected inflation reduces the expected future real income from unindexed pension plans — a change that effectively reduces the real pension wealth of households belonging to such plans. The longer the inflation is expected to last, the larger the reduction in households' wealth. According to Friedman's theory of consumption behavior, such households will realize their permanent income has dropped, and they will reduce consumption spending accordingly. In our model, the exogenous consumption component C_0 will fall, and the *IS* curve will shift to the left as in figure

18–12. On the other hand, expected inflation will reduce the real cost of pensions to employers. It is not clear that employers will change their demand levels much, though lower real pension costs to employers must reduce total costs and increase aggregate supply. We will defer discussion of supply effects until chapter 21.

FIGURE 18–12 Effects of higher expected inflation on aggregate demand

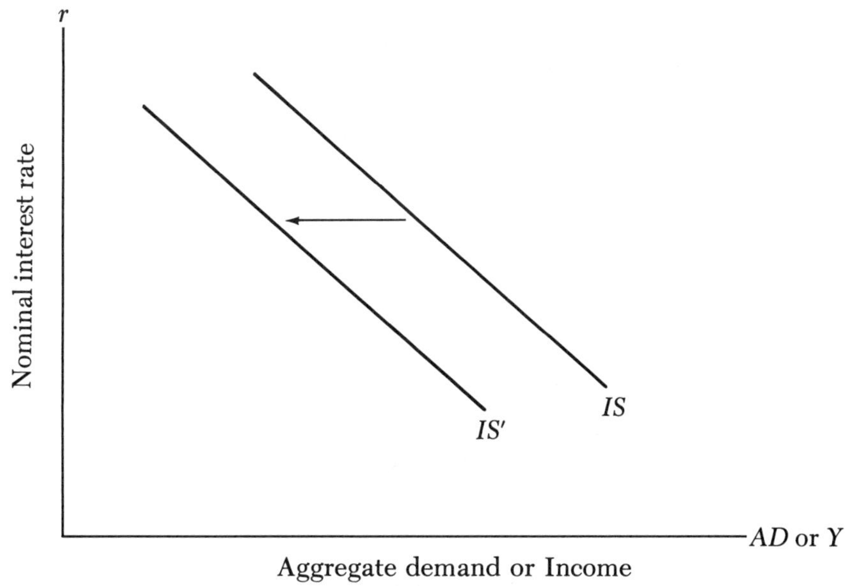

Higher expected inflation will reduce household net wealth and may also reduce permanent income because of fears of restrictive stabilization policies to deal with the inflation. Both changes will reduce the level of aggregate demand at each level of nominal interest rates, shifting the *IS* curve to the left. Other impacts (see text) will tend to shift the *IS* curve in the opposite direction. The net effect cannot be deduced from theory alone.

For holders of existing bonds, especially long-term bonds, any rise in nominal interest rates such as those that would accompany a rise in expected inflation will also cause a large nominal capital loss in the bonds' market value. The existing bonds are part of households' wealth, so a nominal capital loss must also reduce real wealth and therefore consumption spending. We discussed this effect in chapters 6 and 7, however, and concluded the effect would be weak. Households do not have much wealth in the form of bonds that are resalable on a secondary market (Canada Savings Bonds, for instance, are redeemable at par value at any time and are not subject to any risk of nominal capital loss). Debtors with long-term bonds outstanding do not care about market values before maturity, so their wealth is not affected. Many of the financial institutions that hold long-term bonds also do not record their bondholdings at market value and are therefore not affected much either. The net effect of a rise in expected inflation on recorded wealth of those responsible for aggregate demand is therefore small, and so is the effect on aggregate demand.

It should be noted that the effect of higher expected inflation is a one-shot effect, causing a disturbance in aggregate demand at the time the expectations change but not again later as actual inflation unfolds. By contrast, effects of changes in the price level cumulate over time as inflation continues, since steady inflation produces ever-rising price levels. Price-level effects may well be smaller in the short run than the effects of changes in expected inflation, but they are inevitably huge in the long run if inflation is allowed to continue long enough.

Price levels and wealth effects

The price level affects aggregate demand by affecting the real wealth of households and firms and by affecting the competitive position of Canadian producers. The higher the price level, the lower the real wealth of those holding assets with fixed nominal values, and the higher the real wealth of those with such debts outstanding. Households are typically net lenders, holding more debts issued by firms and governments than they have debts of their own outstanding, while business firms are in the opposite situation. Responses by households therefore offset responses by firms to some extent, and the net "real wealth" effect of price-level changes on aggregate demand is not clear.

Furthermore, it is not always the case that an increase in the price level reduces real wealth. If the price-level increase was foreseen, lenders may have been able to secure an increase in their nominal yields that compensates them for the reduced real value of their assets; if so, their wealth will be unaffected. Lenders will even have a more liquid asset portfolio, since the extra money they receive as compensation is much more liquid than the portion of the real value of the long-term bond that has been eroded by inflation. Similarly, the real wealth of the bond issuer will be unaffected, but the issuer will have a less liquid balance sheet: the firm has to give up some liquid assets (cash) to compensate for lower long-term debt. Creditors could respond to the extra liquidity and debtors to the lower liquidity, but both impacts are likely to be small.

Higher nominal interest rates can compensate bondholders for a higher price level if the inflation is anticipated and if the bondholders have time to adjust their nominal coupon rates. Holders of long-term bonds are unlikely to have such time, and they will suffer a loss in real wealth. Further, taxable investors will suffer a loss in real wealth even if the inflation is anticipated, since nominal interest rates do not rise with expected inflation sufficiently to leave after-tax yields constant.

Unanticipated price-level increases provide a simple transfer of wealth from creditors to debtors. Creditors can be expected to decrease consumption and increase saving in order to restore wealth levels. They will show reduced demand for foreign assets as well, which by itself will lower the net capital outflow, lower the exchange rate, and depress net export demand. Debtors will have larger equity and find it less risky to expand their borrowing. Debtors' demand for assets (real and foreign) will be greater; this will stimulate aggregate demand by stimulating greater investment and by offsetting creditors' downward pressure on the exchange rate (thereby keeping net exports from falling).

The net effect on aggregate demand from both creditors and debtors together is usually assumed to be about nil except for two classes of asset for which there are no obvious debtors. These two classes of asset are government bonds and the cash reserve assets issued by the Bank of Canada (currency and deposits in the Bank of Canada). The ultimate debtors who have to repay government bonds are the taxpayers, but most economists do not expect taxpayers to respond directly to the size of the government's debt in real terms. Further, the government may just continue borrowing to refinance its debt, so the taxpayers' burden becomes a perpetual stream of interest payments; it is even less plausible that taxpayers would respond significantly to changes in the real value of such a stream of potential future tax liabilities. The currency and deposits issued by the central bank do not even bear interest; there is no group at all that is liable to repay that class of debts, and therefore no debtor response is to be expected.

Many economists argue that it is only the change in real value of these two "net assets" of the private sector (government bonds and cash reserve assets) that will influence spending. Their argument is that for all the other fixed-nominal-value debts there will be impacts on creditors and on debtors that will cancel each other out. If this argument is valid, price-level impacts on aggregate demand by way of effects on real wealth are fairly small. Government debts were only $220 billion of a total debt of all domestic sectors of $1570 billion in 1981, so the private sector's net financial wealth is only a small share of its total financial assets. Even large changes in that net wealth will not have large effects on total financial assets of the private sector, so the impact on aggregate demand cannot be expected to be large. For instance, an unanticipated 10 percent increase in the aggregate price level would reduce the real value of government debt by $22 billion. If the response of consumer demand to changes in real wealth is of the order of 6 percent, as originally estimated by Ando and Modigliani[13] (that is, about equal to the extra real income to be gained from

[13]A. Ando and F. Modigliani, "The 'Life Cycle' Hypothesis of Saving: Aggregate Implications and Tests," *American Economic Review*, March 1963.

extra real wealth, as though the extra wealth were being used to increase consumption over a whole lifetime), then the effect of a drop in real wealth of $22 billion would be a drop in consumption demand of only $1.3 billion, or 0.3 percent of GNP. The cash reserve assets issued by the central bank are only $19 billion in total, so the effect on aggregate demand of a 10 percent shrinkage in that total would be relatively tiny — probably on the order of $100 million or so.

Not all economists agree that the reactions of creditors holding the rest of the $1570 billion of debts would be offset by the reactions of the debtors. James Tobin, following Irving Fisher, has argued that there may well be a much larger spending response by the debtors than by the creditors.[14] Tobin's argument is as follows. At any point of time, many debtors are up against liquidity constraints; they have a larger demand for capital assets than they can finance, because their bankers will not lend more once a firm's debt:equity ratio passes what the bank considers a prudent ratio (even if the firm does not share the bank's definition of a prudent debt:equity ratio). Any price-level increase that raises the value of a firm's real assets but not its debt will lower its debt:equity ratio and may cause the supply of bank credit to loosen up. The result, for what Tobin calls *liquidity-constrained firms*, is a surge in demand for capital assets, much larger than is likely to be offset by lower consumption of creditors. The net real wealth effect of an unanticipated price-level increase is therefore likely to be an increase rather than a decrease in aggregate demand.[15]

Net export effects

A domestic price-level increase can affect aggregate demand by worsening the competitive position of Canadian producers. This will occur if the exchange rate does not move to offset the change in domestic relative to foreign price levels. Where there is no exchange rate change to offset it, a higher domestic price level will clearly reduce net exports and reduce aggregate demand.

Under a flexible-exchange-rate system, the lower net exports generate a net excess demand for foreign currency in the foreign exchange market. The exchange rate will rise, and sooner or later the price of Canadian funds in foreign currency will return to its old level. When that occurs, net exports can be expected to be more or less at its original level. Aggregate

---

[14]James Tobin, *Asset Accumulation and Economic Activity* (Chicago: University of Chicago Press, 1980).

[15]In the short run, Tobin's argument applies mainly to price increases not accompanied by an increase in expected inflation. Price increases accompanied by higher expected inflation will also be accompanied initially by matching increases in nominal interest rates. Looser liquidity constraints are likely to be more than offset in this case by tighter cash flow constraints. The effect of a change in price is cumulative, though, whereas the effect of higher expected inflation on nominal interest rates occurs only once, when the expectations change.

FIGURE 18–13 Price inflation and exchange rates, 1973–79

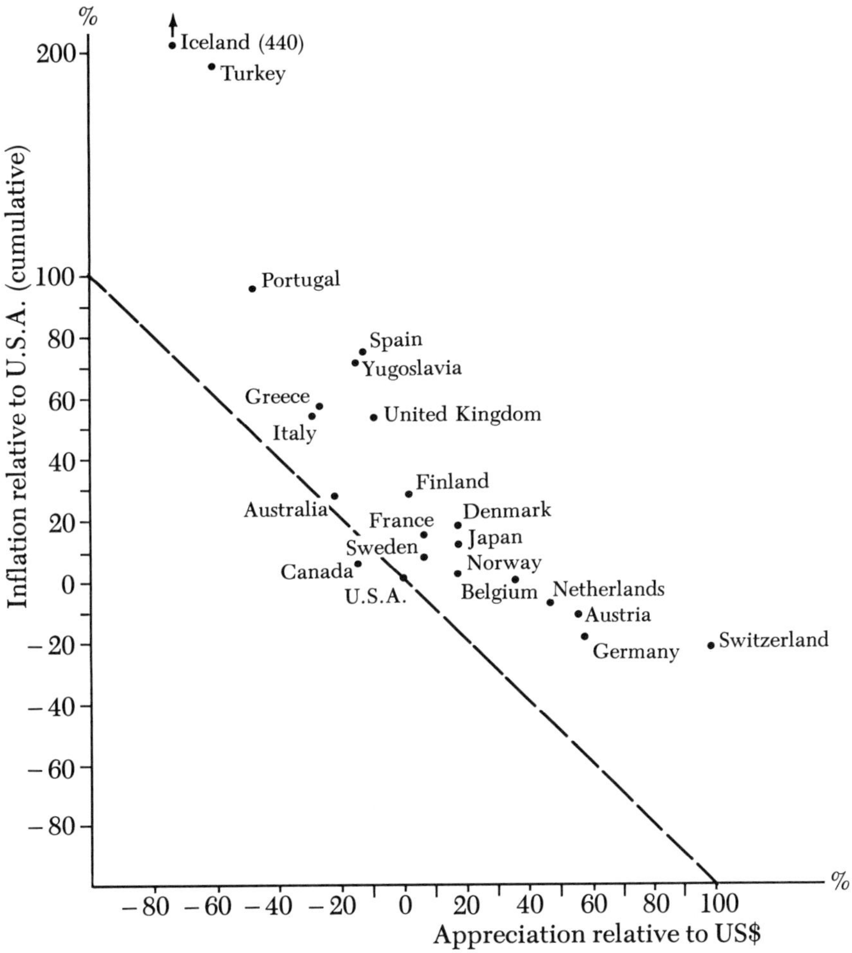

demand will not be affected much, if at all. In the short run, however, the exchange rate may be slow to respond because of other developments in the Capital Account, so there may be a substantial effect on net exports and a substantial impact on aggregate demand.

Figure 18–13 provides some evidence from the 1970s to back up our discussion. Figure 18–13 shows the cumulative price inflation for the OECD countries from 1973 (when most OECD countries adopted floating exchange rates) to 1979, relative to price levels in the United States. Relative inflation is plotted against the exchange rate appreciation of those same countries' currencies relative to the United States dollar. If relative price-level movements were exactly cancelled out by exchange rate movements, then a country like Switzerland, whose inflation rate was 20 percent less than the U.S.'s over this period, would have had a currency appreciation of 20 percent as well; the point for Switzerland in figure 18–13 would lie on the dotted 45-degree line. The OECD countries lie generally in a downward-sloping band, but there are substantial differences between relative inflation and relative exchange rate changes. There is room for a change in the domestic price level to have significant effect on aggregate demand without being offset by a change in the exchange rate, even over long periods.

Summary of price-level effects

In the short run, an increase in the domestic price level may well have an impact on aggregate demand. There may be a fall in net exports, if the central bank or some other market force delays adjustment of the exchange rate. There is likely to be some fall in consumption demand because of lower net wealth of households, especially in the form of pension wealth. There may be an increase in demand for real assets because of the greater inflation risk of fixed-nominal-value financial assets (a demand for inflation hedges). There may be a surge of capital-investment demand by firms and even households because of an easing of liquidity constraints, to the extent that higher prices reduce debt:equity ratios and do not generate other liquidity problems by causing higher nominal interest payments. The net effect on aggregate demand is likely to be negative except where a small group of liquidity-constrained investors responds with a vigorous expansion of investment demand; then the impact could be positive. We will assume in the next chapter that the net impact is negative, but bear in mind that the effect is uncertain.

SECTION 5 Summary

In this chapter we have explained the behavior of aggregate demand, up to a point. We have not generated a unique equilibrium level of aggregate demand for each domestic price level but instead a whole set of possible equilibria — one for each possible level of expected yields in the financial system. In chapter 19 we will add to our model an explanation of which set of expected yields is likely to occur at each price level and therefore which level of aggregate demand will be the unique equilibrium.

Our explanation so far has been a fairly straightforward Keynesian explanation, built upon the standard breakdown of aggregate demand into consumption, investment, government spending, and net exports. The result is a model of equilibrium demand behavior with the standard multiplier effects presented in introductory courses. We derived two versions of the *IS*-curve relationship between interest rates and equilibrium demand (or income) levels: the first assumed exchange rates fixed, and the second allowed for indirect effects of domestic interest rates on the exchange rate in a flexible-exchange-rate system. The second *IS* curve reflects a larger impact of interest rates on aggregate demand, since net exports as well as investment demand are stimulated by a fall in interest rates.

Dynamically, the adjustment of aggregate demand to a new equilibrium starts fairly quickly, though the adjustment path is not likely to be smooth or even stable in many cases. The behavior of investment demand, responding to changes in expected future sales and possibly to changes in expected future risks as well, is likely to amplify what would otherwise be a smooth adjustment process into one that approaches a new equilibrium cyclically or may even oscillate further and further away from it.

Even if the adjustment process itself were smooth and stable, aggregate demand as reflected in the *IS* curve is sensitive to so many different factors, some of them as volatile as future sales expectations, that aggregate demand would generally not be allowed to adjust for long without the occurrence of some new disturbance that would change the equilibrium level. Policy makers charged with managing aggregate demand are aiming at a continually moving target.

The price level can have an impact on aggregate demand and the *IS* curve through several channels. To the extent that price increases are expected, nominal interest rates will probably rise, but nevertheless real after-tax yields on financial assets are likely to fall. A higher price level may depress net exports and will probably depress consumption, but it may enable liquidity-constrained investors to finance greater investment in real capital. The effects of price-level changes on the net wealth of the private sector are clear (real net wealth is reduced, and consumption spending is reduced as a result), but it is not clear that the response of debtors exactly offsets the response of creditors for those debts of the private sector that are owed to other parts of the private sector. Because so many of the effects of price changes are in opposite directions, it is not likely that the net effect will be very large. We assume price increases will reduce aggregate demand, but we assume it with substantial uncertainty.

Questions for discussion

1. What difference would it make to the slope of the aggregate spending line in figure 18–4 or to the slope of the *IS* curve if we were to include specifically in our model a positive linkage between investment spending and income level?
2. Does the idea of an equilibrium level of demand imply that demand creates its own supply?

3. Does Tobin's q theory imply a wave of takeover bids in the stock market at a particular point in the business cycle? If so, at which point, and why?
4. Why is the equilibrium aggregate demand multiplier for government spending on goods and services different from that for government spending on transfer payments?
5. What would be the net effect on aggregate demand and on the *IS* curve of a tax-financed increase in government spending on transfer payments?
6. What determnines the slope of the *IS* curve?
7. What causes the *IS* curve to shift?
8. Does the effect of demand management policies occur quickly or slowly?
9. Would a change in the price level induce any change in your own level of demand? If so, why? Are you what Tobin calls a liquidity-constrained investor?

References

Branson, William H., and James M. Litvak. *Macroeconomics*. 2d ed. New York: Harper and Row, 1981.

de Bever, L., et al. "Dynamic Properties of Four Canadian Macroeconomic Models." *Canadian Journal of Economics*. May 1979, 133–94.

Dornbusch, R., S. Fischer, and G. Sparks. *Macroeconomics*. First Canadian Edition. Toronto: McGraw-Hill, 1981.

Tobin, James. "A General Equilibrium Approach to Monetary Theory." *Journal of Money, Credit, and Banking* 1 (1969), 15–29.

———. *Asset Accumulation and Economic Activity*. Yrrho Jahnsson Lectures; Chicago: University of Chicago Press, 1980.

Wilton, David, and David Prescott. *Macroeconomics: Theory and Policy in the Canadian Economy*. Don Mills, Ont.: Addison-Wesley, 1982.

CHAPTER 19

Aggregate Demand and Asset Markets

This chapter completes the explanation of aggregate demand behavior started in chapter 18. In chapter 18, spending behavior was analysed holding interest rates fixed. In this chapter I open up the model to include financial markets, and allow for interaction between real and financial markets that will cause interest rates to vary. I continue to discuss only equilibrium levels — of output, employment, and interest rates — but now I interpret equilibrium as requiring balance of supply and demand in both goods markets and financial markets.

The simplest version of the theory presented in this chapter is associated with Keynes; it is the widely used *IS–LM* model interpretation of Keynes' theory, put forward by Sir John Hicks in 1939. The more sophisticated explanation of asset-market behavior is associated with James Tobin and colleagues at Yale University and elsewhere; it corresponds more closely than the simpler model does to the picture of the Canadian financial system drawn in the first sixteen chapters of this book.

From this chapter you should understand:

1. the interaction of income levels and interest rates in a simple, three-asset financial system, as summarized by the *LM* curve,
2. the same interaction in a much richer financial system of the sort we discussed in the first half of the book,
3. simultaneous equilibrium in goods markets and asset markets, bringing together the *IS* and *LM* curves, and
4. the effects of the price level on this equilibrium.

SECTION 1 A simple asset-market model

In 1937, J. R. Hicks portrayed the core of the Keynesian model in (a) a simple version of the *IS* curve, presented in chapter 15, plus (b) a similar

LM curve, or asset-market equilibrium locus

equilibrium locus on the same diagram to describe the equilibrium behavior of a simple set of asset markets with only money and bonds (the *LM* curve).[1] The resulting *IS–LM* apparatus has been a very useful teaching and analytical device for almost half a century. The *IS–LM* apparatus has some limitations, but it is the starting point for almost every macroeconomist, and it is our starting point in this chapter. In this section I will present a modern version of the stripped-down financial-market model first used by Hicks in 1937 to derive the *LM* curve. I will add sophistication to the model in section 2.

Financial-market equilibrium requires that demand equal supply for each financial asset, subject to the constraint that total wealth be fully allocated. If there are only two assets, such as "money" (currency and bank deposits) and "debt plus equity," then the wealth constraint implies that, once the demand for money equals the supply of money, the demand for debt plus equity must equal the supply of debt plus equity as well. There cannot be an imbalance in any one financial market without an equal and opposite imbalance in other financial markets. The condition for financial-market equilibrium therefore boils down to the requirements that total wealth be allocated (that is, that total net wealth equal the total net value of all assets held) and that the demand for money equal the supply of money. We will look at those two conditions in turn.[2]

Private-sector wealth

In this model the net wealth of the private sector of the economy is the real value of privately held real capital assets (K), plus the net debt of the government. All privately issued debts are owed both by and to the private sector, so they make no contribution to the sector's net wealth. The government's debts are its bonds (B) and the cash reserve assets (R) issued by the government's central bank. Real private-sector wealth is therefore the sum of the real values of K, B, and R:

$$\frac{W}{P} = \frac{R}{P} + \frac{B}{P} + \frac{K}{P}.$$

Government bonds B have a total coupon payment b (the net interest paid by the government on the national debt) and a nominal value P_b per dollar of interest coupon. P_b is the present discounted value of a stream of $1 interest payments, discounted at the currently available yield on bonds (r). Using the formula for a perpetual bond, for convenience,

$$P_b = \frac{1}{r}.$$

---

[1]J. R. Hicks, "Mr. Keynes and the Classics: A Suggested Interpretation," *Econometrica* 5 (April 1937), 147–59.

[2]We could alternatively use the requirement that demand for debt plus equity equal the supply of debt plus equity. This is an exactly equivalent approach. Walras' law says that we need use only one of the two approaches, not both.

The real value of the private sector's bond holdings is therefore

$$\frac{B}{P} = \frac{b}{rP}.$$

The value of real capital assets held by the private sector likewise consists of an annual (expected) flow of net income k (total revenue less labor and materials expenses from all capital assets in use) and a price P_k per dollar of that revenue. P_k is the present discounted value of \$1 of capital-asset revenue per year forever, discounted at the yield currently available on real assets (r again, since debt plus equity is treated as a single asset in this model). Therefore $P_k = 1/r$, and

$$\frac{K}{P} = \frac{k}{rP}.$$

Total private-sector real wealth is

$$W = \frac{R}{P} + \frac{b}{rP} + \frac{k}{rP}. \tag{1}$$

Demand for money

Chapter 9 explained that the demand for money depends on real income, price levels, relative expected yields on money and other assets, relative risks, and wealth levels. That list has more variables than we want in a streamlined model, so we will adopt a simple linear version of money demand that explicitly acknowledges only real income (Y), prices, and the yield (r) on debt plus equity:

$$L = L_0 + hY - jr, \tag{2}$$

where L is the real demand for money, L_0 is a constant term, and h and j are constant coefficients. Since L is real demand for money, and the price level P does not appear in equation (2), we are assuming that changes in the price level affect the nominal demand for money proportionally and therefore do not affect the real demand for money at all. The constant term L_0 reflects the influence of excluded factors: relative risks, wealth levels, the yield on money itself, and the nation's payments habits. The yield on money is assumed fixed at zero. Wealth is assumed not to affect the demand for money, which implies that any extra wealth is put into the other asset, debt plus equity.[3]

[3]If wealth did affect the demand for money significantly, then, given that the price level affects real wealth as described earlier, we would expect to find that the price level affects the real demand for money; but we do not seem to find this, so real wealth must not have a significant effect on the demand for money.

FIGURE 19–1 Demand and supply of money

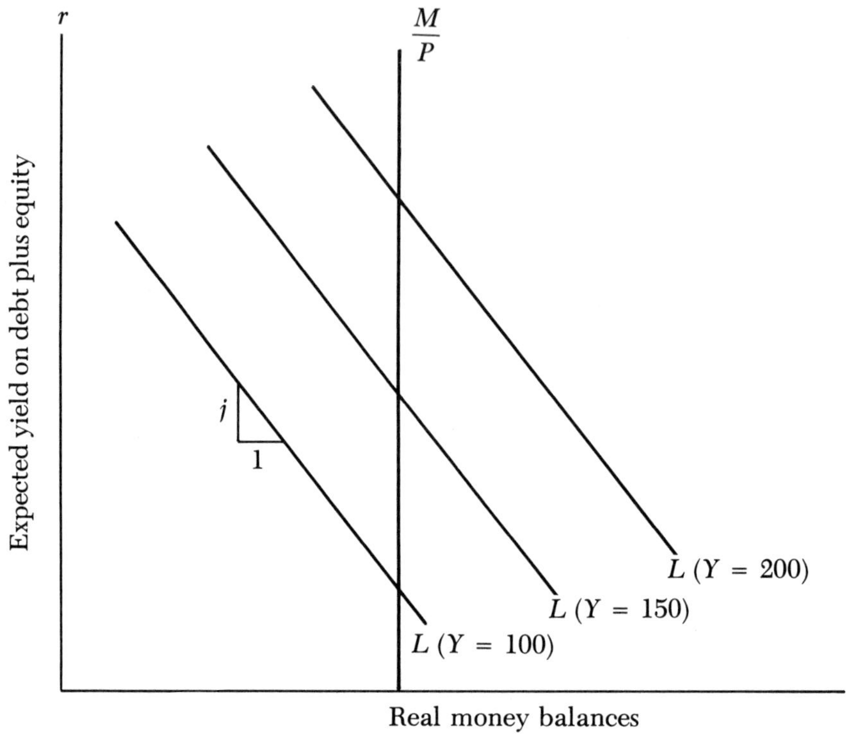

The demand for money is given as $L = L_0 + hY - jr$, so the horizontal intercept of the money-demand curves is $L_0 + hY$. Several demand curves are shown for different levels of Y. Supply of money in real terms is $M/P = \alpha R/P$. Real money supply is insensitive to interest-rate levels as long as the currency:deposit ratio is fixed, making the money-supply curve vertical.

Our money-demand relationship is illustrated in figure 19–1 for various levels of real income. Higher levels of the expected yield on debt plus equity reduce the demand for money because the opportunity cost of money is increased; firms and households get along with smaller cash balances and keep more of their wealth earning interest at each point of time. Higher real income levels increase the demand for money, but probably less than proportionally.

Supply of money

The nominal money supply consists of currency outside banks (C) and bank deposits (D) issued by the banking system. In principle the supply of bank deposits should depend on banks' behavior. Profit-maximizing banks want to issue deposits to the point where marginal asset revenue from investing deposit funds just equals the marginal interest and other costs of deposits. For the economy, therefore, the supply of deposits would normally depend on bank asset yields relative to bank deposit costs. In our simple model, this is not the case.[4] There are two reasons.

First, bank deposits in this model are all demand deposits and have zero yield (by custom, or collusion, or suggestion of the central bank). Second, banks are not allowed to reach what they would regard as their optimal deposit volume at a zero rate, because of a legal cash reserve requirement that ties cash reserve holdings to deposit levels, and a tight ceiling on the supply of available cash reserve assets. The cash reserve requirement is not variable in the short run, so the supply of deposits is determined mechanically by the level of cash reserve assets (R) rather than by banks' asset yields and debt costs.

Banks issue as many deposits as they can support with cash reserves, since they make profits at it when deposit interest costs are zero. The maximum level of deposits that the banks can support is $1/crr$ times the cash reserves available to the banks, where crr is the legal minimum cash reserve requirement. *Cash reserve assets* are currency and central-bank deposits, both issued by the government-owned central bank. Total nominal reserve assets available to the economy are the reserve base R, but banks do not get all of it: the public absorbs some of R in the form of currency holdings C. Banks' cash reserve holdings are therefore $R - C$, and banks supply deposits in the amount

Cash reserve assets

$$D = \frac{R - C}{crr}. \tag{3}$$

We assume as well that the public's demand for currency is a stable fraction cu of deposits (reflecting the fraction of grocery, liquor, illegal-drug, and other cash purchases in total spending). That is, $C = cuD$. This extra assumption allows us to relate the total money supply $C + D$ to the reserve base. Substituting $C = cuD$ in equation (3),

$$D = \frac{R - cuD}{crr},$$

which can be rearranged to give deposit supply as a multiple of the reserve base:

$$D = R\left(\frac{1}{crr + cu}\right).$$

[4]This approach to banks' supply of deposits was introduced by James Tobin in "Commercial Banks as 'Creators' of Money," in Deane Carson, ed., *Banking and Monetary Studies* (Homewood, Ill.: Irwin, 1963).

Because currency outside banks is the fraction *cu* of deposits outstanding, the money supply in total is

$$\begin{aligned} M &= D + cuD \\ &= D(1 + cu) \\ &= R\left(\frac{1 + cu}{crr + cu}\right). \end{aligned} \tag{4}$$

Money-supply multiplier

In equation (4), the term $(1 + cu)/(crr + cu)$ is the *money-supply multiplier*, which relates changes in the money supply to changes in the reserve base. The money-supply multiplier depends on the cash reserve ratio *crr* and the public's currency-to-deposit ratio *cu*. The larger *crr* and *cu* are, the smaller is the money-supply multiplier. If the cash reserve ratio *crr* is 0.10, and the currency:deposit ratio is 0.75 (the average ratio of currency to demand deposits in Canada), then the multiplier will be $(1 + .75)/(.10 + .75) = 2.1$. When the cashless society finally arrives and $cu = 0$, the money-supply multiplier will be $1/0.1 = 10$.

Equation (4) shows that the money supply does not depend on the level of expected yields on debt plus equity (r), so that if a real money-supply curve for M/P is superimposed over the money-demand curves in figure 19–1, the money-supply curve will be vertical.[5]

Since the money supply depends on the availability and use of the cash reserve base R, the money supply can be explained in terms of supply and demand for reserves. This approach is illustrated in figure 19–2. The supply of reserves by the central bank (R_s) is assumed to be fixed exogenously and does not vary with the level of deposits on the horizontal axis. Demand for reserve assets (R_d) comes from the public's demand for currency and from the banks' demand for cash reserves. Both demand curves are shown in figure 19–2, with slopes equal to *cu* and *crr* respectively. The total demand for reserves R_d is the vertical sum of the two partial demand curves, with slope $crr + cu$. Equilibrium in the "market" for cash reserve assets is at the intersection of demand and supply, yielding an equilibrium deposit level of $D^* = R_s/(crr + cu)$. Currency demand is the fraction *cu* of deposit demand, so equilibrium currency demand C^* is cuD^*, and the equilibrium money supply is

$$\begin{aligned} M^* &= D^* + C^* \\ &= D^*(1 + cu) \\ &= R_s\left(\frac{1 + cu}{crr + cu}\right). \end{aligned}$$

[5]If, as we suggested in chapter 2, the interest elasticity of currency demand is lower than the interest elasticity of deposit demand, then the ratio *cu* depends on the level of interest rates. Higher levels of the interest rate will increase the ratio of currency to deposits and raise *cu*. That reduces the money-supply multiplier and the money supply, for any given level of reserves. The M/P curve in figure 19–1 becomes downward-sloping instead of vertical.

FIGURE 19–2 Supply and demand for cash reserves

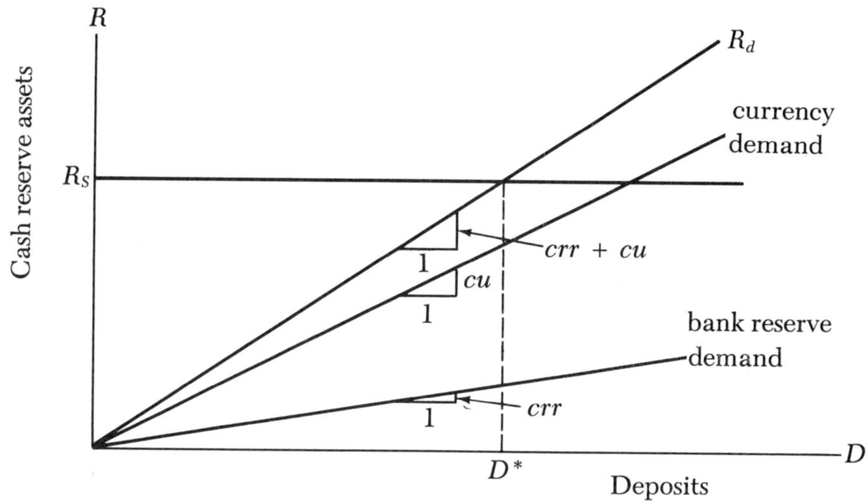

Supply R_s is fixed exogenously by the central bank. Demand for cash reserve assets R_d is proportional to deposits outstanding, but comes in two parts. Public currency demand is the proportion *cu* of deposits, and banks' demand for central-bank deposits is the proportion *crr* of deposits. Total demand R_d is therefore the proportion $cu + crr$ of deposits. The equilibrium deposit level is $D°$, where $R_s = R_d$.

Where *cu* and *crr* are constants, the money-supply multiplier is a constant. The money-supply relationship can then be summarized as

$$M = \alpha R,$$

where $\alpha = (1 + cu)/(crr + cu)$. The real money supply is similarly

$$\frac{M}{P} = \alpha\left(\frac{R}{P}\right). \tag{5}$$

The *LM* curve

Financial-market equilibrium occurs when wealth is fully allocated — so that $W = R/P + b/(rP) + k/(rP)$ — and when the real demand for money L equals the real supply of money M/P:

$$L = \frac{M}{P}.$$

Substituting for L and M/P from equations (2) and (5) gives

$$L_0 + hY - jr = \alpha\left(\frac{R}{P}\right), \tag{6}$$

which can be rearranged to produce an equation that relates r to Y:

$$r = \frac{L_0 - \alpha(R/P)}{j} + \left(\frac{h}{j}\right)Y. \tag{7}$$

Asset-market equilibrium locus, or *LM* curve

In equation (7), the first term, $[L_0 - \alpha(R/P)]/j$, is the vertical intercept, and the coefficient (h/j) of the second term is the slope of a line relating debt plus equity yields r to real income levels Y. This line, or *asset-market equilibrium locus*, is shown in figure 19–3. Since the equilibrium condition is that $L = M/P$, the short title for this line is the *LM* curve.

FIGURE 19–3 Derivation of the *LM* curve

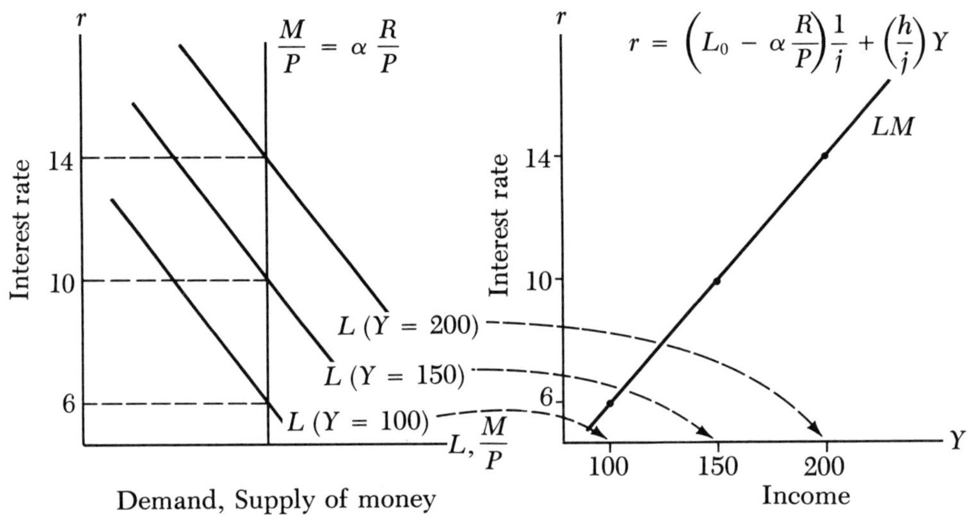

Different income levels generate different money-demand curves and therefore different equilibrium levels of asset yields. When the asset yields and the income levels are plotted together on the same diagram, the result is the *LM* curve.

The *LM* curve can be plotted from equation (7), or it can be derived graphically from a diagram of supply and demand for money as in figure 19–3. The intersections of various money-demand schedules (for various income levels) with the fixed, vertical money-supply curve produce a set of pairs of interest rate r and real income Y that trace out the *LM* curve when plotted on a diagram with r and Y instead of r and M/P.

The position of the *LM* curve depends on the ingredients of the intercept term in equation (7): the level of real reserves R/P, the currency-to-deposit ratio *cu* and the cash reserve ratio *crr* — which determine

FIGURE 19–4 Effect of higher real money supply

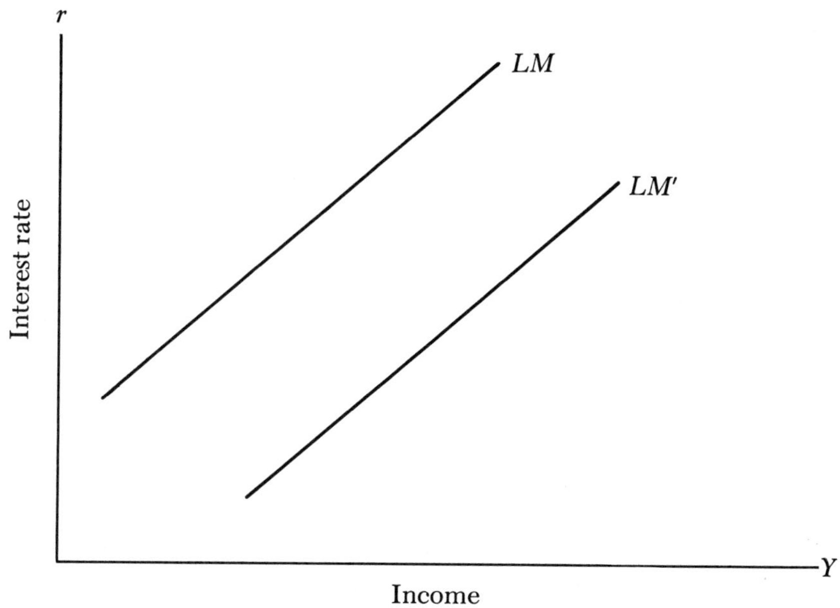

Higher nominal money supply or lower prices, or any increase in the money supply relative to the price level, will shift the *LM* curve to the right, so that each level of the interest rate is accompanied by a higher equilibrium level of real income *Y*.

α — and the relative risks and wealth levels, which are reflected only in the exogenous money-demand term L_0.

The slope of the *LM* curve is the ratio of income sensitivity to interest sensitivity of money demand. In chapter 9, we looked briefly at the evidence on demand for money, so we can use those results to give a rough estimate of the slope of the *LM* curve in Canada. The income elasticity of money demand is about 0.8, and the interest elasticity with respect to long-term rates is about −0.5. The implied ratio of linear coefficients h/j at a real income level of $350 billion and an interest rate of 10 percent can be calculated as[6] (0.8/0.5)(10/350), which is roughly 1/20. The slope of the *LM* curve in Canada is such that a $20 billion increase in real income and output is accompanied by a 1-percentage-point rise in long-term interest rates.

The effect of increasing the money supply *M* or of lowering the price level *P* (that is, of increasing *M* relative to *P*) is to shift the vertical *M*/*P*

---

[6]The income elasticity of 0.8 is $(dL/dY)(Y/L) = hY/L$. The interest elasticity of −0.5 is $(dL/dr)(r/L) = -jr/L$. Solving for both h and j and then dividing h by j gives $h = 0.8L/Y$, $j = 0.5L/r$, and $h/j = (0.8/0.5)(r/Y)$, as in the text.

schedule to the right in the first panel of figure 19–3. This has the effect of shifting the *LM* curve to the right also: each level of interest rate r will be accompanied, in equilibrium, by a higher level of income. Figure 19–4 illustrates such a shift. If the money supply grows faster than the price level over a series of years, the *LM* curve will be continually shifting to the right.

The *LM* curve when deposit yields are not fixed

Canadian banks introduced demand deposits with market-sensitive yields in July 1980, and their popularity is growing fast, so it is worth considering the impact of this change on our simple *LM*-curve model.

Assume that the deposit yield is set to clear the deposit market, instead of being fixed at zero. Higher income levels will still raise the demand for money and decrease demand for debt plus equity. The impact of this shift of asset demands is to raise the yield on debt plus equity and to lower the deposit yield.

There are two secondary responses to these changes in asset yields. First, households shift some of their deposits into currency as the deposit yield falls, which increases the demand for cash reserve assets even more. This process of demanding more currency and fewer deposits is known as *disintermediation*, since it involves a lessening of demand for the debts of intermediaries such as banks. Second, banks respond to the widening spread between debt yields and deposit interest rates by trying to expand their lending business. Banks try to expand by raising deposit yields to attract loanable funds.

Disintermediation

The initial results of higher real incomes are lower deposit rates and a worse shortage of cash reserve assets. The response of banks to their widening interest-rate spreads drives deposit rates back up to match the now higher yields on debt plus equity. Higher deposit yields cause the public to shift currency back into deposits again, lowering the currency:deposit ratio and easing the shortage of cash reserve assets faster than would otherwise have been the case. The net effect of higher income levels on debt-plus-equity yields is less than with fixed deposit yields, because a net increase of any size in deposit yields serves to reduce the currency:deposit ratio and ease the shortage of cash reserve assets.

The effect of variable deposit yields can be seen in a money supply and demand diagram such as figure 19–3. The currency:deposit ratio becomes sensitive to the level of interest rates, rising as interest rates (including deposit rates) fall. The money supply, which is $R_s\,(1 + cu)/(cu + crr)$, rises as cu falls, so the money supply rises as higher interest rates cause cu to drop. The real-money-supply curve M/P in figure 19–3 would become positively sloped rather than vertical as a result of variable deposit yields. Any increase in real income would therefore be associated with a smaller rise in interest rates, and the *LM* curve would be flatter than in figure 19–3.

Joint *IS–LM* equilibrium in the simple model

Together with the *IS* curve from chapter 18, the asset market equilibrium condition given in the *LM* curve gives us a unique equilibrium aggregate demand level. Figure 19–5 puts both *IS* and *LM* curves on the same diagram, with expected debt-plus-equity yields on the vertical axis and either aggregate demand (*AD*) or real income (*Y*) on the horizontal axis. At any point on the *IS* curve, $Y = AD$, so putting two different variables along the same axis is not a problem as long as the goods market remains in equilibrium.

FIGURE 19–5 The *IS–LM* diagram

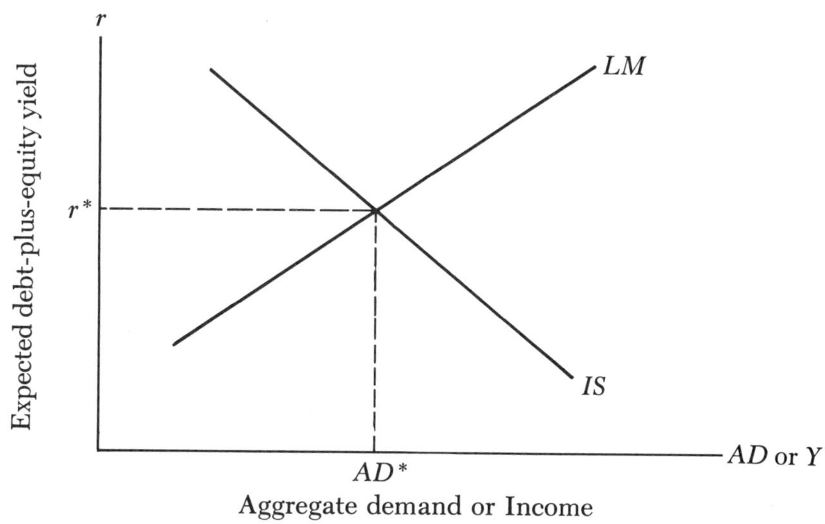

The *IS* curve gives all combinations of *r* and *AD* producing equilibrium in goods markets (that is, where $AD = Y$). The *LM* curve gives all combinations of *r* and *Y* producing equilibrium in asset markets. The intersection gives the unique levels of *r*, *AD*, and *Y* at which both goods markets and asset markets are in equilibrium. The equilibrium is conditional on the level of prices and all the other exogenous variables that determine the positions of the *IS* and *LM* curves.

The point of intersection of the *IS* and *LM* curves gives the only level of debt-plus-equity yields at which asset markets and the goods market are in equilibrium, and therefore gives the unique equilibrium level of aggregate demand on the horizontal axis. The demand level AD^* and the interest rate r^* are the equilibrium pair.

Not only are r^* and AD^* the equilibrium pair, but the equilibrium is stable as long as the goods market and asset markets respond to excess demand or supply at about the same speed. If the interest rate at any level of real income Y is above or below that on the *LM* curve, the interest rate r will be driven back toward the *LM* curve by the pressure of excess demand or supply in the market for debt plus equity. If aggregate demand at any level of interest rate r is greater or less than on the *IS* curve at that interest rate, there will be excess supply or demand, respectively, for goods; both output and demand levels will be driven back to the level on the *IS* curve by producers' adjustment of their output levels. Both adjustments (of interest rates and of output levels) will return the economy toward the equilibrium intersection in figure 19–5.

The *IS–LM* diagram is still the workhorse of aggregate demand theory and we will see it many more times in succeeding chapters, but it has its difficulties. The major difficulty is that the *LM* curve is designed to have a nominal yield on the vertical axis, while the *IS* curve is designed to have a real yield (on bonds, or on real capital assets) on that axis. For the *LM* curve what is needed is the opportunity cost of money; money has a fixed nominal yield of zero, so the opportunity cost of money is the entire nominal yield on other assets. For the *IS* curve, what is needed to explain investment demand is the expected real yield on capital assets.

The difference between nominal and real yields is mainly accounted for by expected inflation, as we discussed in chapter 14. Expectations of inflation are not likely to be stable over time and may be volatile even in the short run. The *IS* and *LM* curves therefore relate to different interest-rate scales on the vertical axis — scales that can move relative to one another.

The second major difficulty with the *IS–LM* apparatus that we have built so far is that its asset market is oversimplified. There is a whole structure of asset-market yields rather than just the one "debt-plus-equity" yield r. The *IS* and *LM* curves depend on different ingredients of that yield structure, so there are problems with *IS* and *LM* curves whenever the yield structure changes. The *LM* curve is designed to use a short-term, liquid-asset yield on the vertical axis, representing the yield on a close money substitute. Aggregate demand, and therefore *IS*-curve behavior, depends on several types of yields at once: mortgage loan yields affect housing demand, bond yields and yields on real capital affect other investment demand, and short-term liquid-asset yields affect the net capital outflows that (through the exchange rate) change net export demand.

A fall in debt-plus-equity yields would therefore imply a move along the *IS* curve in figure 19–5, but not necessarily along the *LM* curve as well. In other words, there is a problem whenever the structure of relative yields changes. Our discussion in chapters 14 and 15 suggests that yield structures are far from random, but they are still far from constant. For this reason we will find it useful to look at an extended model of asset markets that contains many more asset yields explicitly.

SECTION 2

Equilibrium in an extended asset market

The *LM* curve in figure 19–5 is a very useful first approximation for intermediate macro theory courses, but it does not reflect many of the financial interactions that earlier chapters have led us to expect. In this section we therefore extend the asset-market model by adding the main features of the Canadian financial system described in chapter 5. The result is still that higher levels of aggregate demand bring higher levels of expected yields, but the process by which this occurs is much less mechanical. The process is also more obviously prone to random disturbances — less certain than would appear from the simpler model used in section 1.

In this section we will first present the ingredients of the extended financial-market model, then sketch how higher aggregate demand levels are likely to affect its ingredients, and finally derive some more sophisticated *LM*-type relationships from it.

The extended asset-market model

Households and nonfinancial firms are lumped together as one sector in this model. The other two sectors are banks and the government (including its central bank). Banks engage in a wide enough range of lending and borrowing activities that we do not need to add other financial intermediaries, and there is little to be gained (except extra complexity) by adding a separate "rest of the world" sector.

Households and firms hold money (currency and demand deposits), time deposits, Treasury Bills, bonds, and real capital assets. Households may hold real capital assets directly (in the form of houses or family businesses) or indirectly by holding stocks and bonds of the company that has title to the real assets. Households and firms borrow by issuing loan notes and private (corporate) bonds.

Banks hold currency or central-bank deposits as cash reserves and invest the rest of their funds in Treasury Bills, loans, and bonds. Banks borrow with demand and time deposits. Demand-deposit rates are fixed at zero, but time-deposit rates are adjusted by banks to balance supply and demand in the time-deposit market. Currency and central-bank deposits are perfect substitutes as cash reserve assets, and the central bank stands ready at any time to convert one into the other on demand. Currency and central-bank deposits are essentially the same asset as far as banks are concerned.

The government as central bank holds Treasury Bills and government bonds and borrows by issuing currency and its own deposits. Central-bank deposits are held only by banks, whereas currency is held by banks and by the public. The rest of the government sector holds real assets and borrows by issuing Treasury Bills and government bonds to finance its asset holdings.

TABLE 19–1 Sectoral assets and liabilities in the extended model

HOUSEHOLDS AND FIRMS	
Assets	Liabilities
Money (currency and demand deposits)	Loans
Time deposits	Bonds
Treasury Bills	
Bonds	
Real capital assets	Wealth
BANKS	
Assets	Liabilities
Cash reserves (currency and central-bank deposits)	Demand deposits
	Time deposits
Treasury Bills	
Loans	
Bonds	Bank equity
GOVERNMENT SECTOR	
Assets	Liabilities
(a) Central bank	
Treasury Bills	Currency
Government bonds	Deposits of banks
(b) Other government	
Real capital assets	Treasury Bills
	Bonds

Table 19–1 summarizes these asset and debt holdings in a series of balance sheets for the three sectors. From these balance sheets we can easily construct a National Capital Account table showing which sectors are demanding and which are supplying in each asset market. Table 19–2 is such a table. Households and banks demand the currency and central-bank deposits supplied by the central bank. Households demand the demand deposits and time deposits supplied by the banks. Households and banks and the central bank demand the Treasury Bills supplied by the government. Banks demand the loan notes supplied by households. Households and the government demand real capital assets. Banks and the central bank and some households demand the bonds issued by the government and by some households.

The "Total private sector" column of table 19–2 shows the net holdings of each asset by the private sector (households and banks). There are no net holdings of demand and time deposits or of loans, because the private sector holds exactly as much of each in total as it owes. The only new asset that adds to private-sector net wealth is the stock of Treasury Bills, T. Real

TABLE 19–2 Demands and supplies in asset markets

Asset	Households and firms	Banks	Total private sector	Government: Central bank	Government: Other
Currency and central-bank deposits	demand	demand	R/P	supply	
Demand deposits	demand	supply	0		
Time deposits	demand	supply	0		
Treasury Bills	demand	demand	TB_s/P	demand	supply
Loans	supply	demand	0		
Bonds	net demand	demand	B_s/P	demand	supply
Real capital	demand		K/P		demand
TOTALS	net wealth W	bank equity	$R/P + TB_s/P + B_s/P + K/P$		

wealth of the private sector, the upper constraint on total asset demand, is therefore

$$W = \frac{R}{P} + \frac{T}{P} + \frac{B}{P} + \frac{K}{P}, \tag{8}$$

which can be written, as in section 2,

$$W = \frac{R}{P} + \frac{T}{P} + \frac{b}{r_b P} + \frac{k}{r_k P} \tag{9}$$

where r_b is the expected yield on bonds and r_k is the expected yield on existing capital assets. The last term in equation (9) can be written in any of three exactly equivalent forms:

$$\frac{K}{P} = k\left(\frac{1}{r_k P}\right) = k\left(\frac{P_k}{P}\right) = qk, \tag{10}$$

where q is Tobin's q ratio of market value to replacement cost of capital.

It is clear from equation (9) that the value of real wealth will fall as the price level rises and as either or both of r_b and r_k rise.

Behavioral structure of the extended model

In general, households' and firms' asset demand and borrowing depend on relative yields, relative risks, real income, prices, and the level of real wealth — just as expected from our analysis in chapters 8 and 10. I have explained what assets make up the net real wealth of the private sector and how the values of those assets are determined. We assume that the equity of banks is insignificant relative to the stock of other assets, so the wealth of the private sector in equation (9) is also the wealth of households and firms.

The relative risk of any asset reflects its relative covariance or degree of correlation with other assets and with debt costs. Higher real income and prices increase the demand for money (currency and demand deposits) and decrease the demand for all other assets at any given level of real wealth. Those effects describe the behavior of most of the asset demands and supplies in our extended model.

Banks' demand for cash reserves is still mechanical. Cash reserve requirements are assumed to be 10 percent for demand deposits and 3 percent for time deposits, and banks wish to hold no more than the legal requirements. Banks hold no significant excess reserves, because to do so is to forego profit unnecessarily. Banks' demand for other assets reflects relative yields, relative risks, and the quantity of deposits issued; the quantity of deposits issued serves as a financing constraint, playing the same role in bank asset demand as real wealth W does in household asset demand.

The quantity of deposits issued by banks in turn reflects relative yields on assets and deposits, the variances and covariances of deposit and asset yields, the banks' equity base, and bankers' degree of risk aversion — all exactly as described in chapters 10 and 11. In the short run, banks may not be able to increase or decrease their holdings of loans very quickly (customers may not be available in the necessary volume on short notice), in which case Treasury Bill investments take up the slack.

Banks supply demand deposits to all comers, at an unchanged interest rate of zero. Banks' supply of demand deposits is therefore infinitely elastic at a zero yield. Time deposits are supplied only to the point where marginal asset revenues equal marginal debt costs, and banks adjust their supply outstanding by changing their posted time-deposit rate. If available cash reserve assets are insufficient to support the profit-maximizing quantity of time deposits, given households' demand for demand deposits, banks will try to sell off holdings of Treasury Bills to secure the necessary extra reserves. Treasury Bill sales will continue until either time-deposit demand has decreased or currency and demand-deposit demand has shifted to time deposits, or both, in sufficient volume that actual reserves equal required reserves again.

Government and central-bank demands and supplies in asset markets are exogenous, the product of policy decisions made to stabilize the economy.

Table 19–3 provides an algebraic summary of the asset-market demand and supply behavior we have described for each financial market. For simplicity the relative-risk terms in the household and bank demand and supply functions have been left out. The demand and supply functions are in real terms, and the price level is assumed to affect all nominal demands proportionally, so the price level does not appear in any real demand and supply functions. The term E in table 19–3 refers to the set of relative yields on time deposits, loans, Treasury Bills, bonds, and real capital — all relative to the fixed zero yield on cash reserve assets and demand deposits.

TABLE 19–3 Equations of the extended model

Asset	Households and firms	Banks	Government	TOTAL
Cash reserve assets	$X_{dh}(Y/W, E)W$	$+ .1DD_s + .03TD_s$	$- R/P$	$= 0$
Demand deposits	$X_{dh}(Y/W, E)W$	$- DD_s$		$= 0$
Time deposits	$X_{dh}(Y/W, E)W$	$- X_{sb}(E)$		$= 0$
Loans	$-X_{sh}(Y/W, E)W$	$+ X_{db}(E)(TD_s + DD_s)$		$= 0$
Treasury Bills	$X_{dh}(Y/W, E)W$	$+ X_{db}(E)(TD_s + DD_s)$	$- TB_s$	$= 0$
Bonds	$(X_{dh} - X_{sh})(Y/W, E)W$	$+ X_{db}(E)(TD_s + DD_s)$	$- B_s$	$= 0$
Real capital	$X_{dh}(Y/W, E)W$		$+ K_{dg}/P$	$= K_T/P$

Definitional equations
Private-sector wealth: $W = R/P + TB_s/P + B_s/P + K/P$.
Relative price of capital: $q = 1/(r_k P)$.
Time-deposit supply: $TD_s = X_{sb}(E)$.

Note: E is the set of expected yields on time deposits, Treasury Bills, loans, bonds, and real capital assets (R_k). X_d and X_s refer to desired asset and liability proportions, respectively, of the sector's balance sheet. Subscripts h and b refer to households and banks. Y is real income, P is the price level, R is the nominal cash reserve base, DD_s is the supply of demand deposits, TB_s is the supply of Treasury Bills, B_s is the supply of government bonds, K_T is the total capital stock, and K_{dg} is the government's holding of capital assets (in nominal terms).

Equilibrium in the extended market model

Table 19–3 contains seven behavioral equations and three definitional equations (for time deposits, real wealth, and the relative price of capital) — enough to provide a solution for

1. an equilibrium set of relative yields on time deposits (r_{td}), Treasury Bills (r_{TB}), bonds (r_b), loans (r_1), and real capital (r_k),
2. the relative price of capital (q), and
3. real wealth (W) and the stock of time and demand deposits (TD_s and DD_s).

The set of equilibrium solution values is conditional on the values of the exogenous variables: prices (P), real incomes (Y), the cash reserve base (R), the zero yields on cash reserves and demand deposits, and the outstanding stocks of Treasury Bills, government bonds, and real capital.

Fortunately we need not wade through derivation of the equilibrium equations for all of the yields in our extended model, not even in an appendix. We can get the sense of the model without that.

Each of the expected yields will be determined by an equilibrium equation of the following general form (using the Treasury Bill yield as an example):

$$r_{TB} = r_{TB}(\overset{+}{r_{td}}, \overset{+}{r_b}, \overset{+}{r_1}, \overset{+}{r_k}, \overset{-}{W}, \overset{+}{Y}, \overset{-}{R}, \overset{+}{TB_s}), \tag{11}$$

where TB_s is the supply of Treasury Bills. The sign above each variable shows the direction of effect that the variable has on the level of r_{TB}. Higher yields on substitute assets decrease demand for Treasury Bills and raise r_{TB}. Higher time-deposit yields would also stimulate banks to issue fewer of them, which would give banks less funds to invest and decrease banks' demand for all assets including Treasury Bills; Treasury Bill yields would rise. Higher real wealth increases demand for all assets and depresses all yields. Higher real income shifts asset demand away from other assets toward money and pushes up yields on all of the other assets.

The equilibrium equations for the other yields have the same general shape, but with different supply variables to replace TB_s.

Each of the yield equations, such as equation (11), relates some asset yield to the level of real income, and always positively. Each such relationship gives an *LM*-type curve that can be plotted on a diagram with the expected yield on the vertical axis and real income on the horizontal axis. Each of those *LM* curves can then be used with an *IS* curve to determine aggregate demand. Before we take that final step, however, we need to put the flesh of understanding on the mathematical bones of our extended model of asset markets. We will do this by tracing through the sequence of effects when real income rises.

Asset-market responses to higher real income

Responses of assetholders and debtors to higher real income can be thought of as being in a series. There are impact effects first, followed by a series of feedback effects.

1. Higher real income levels mean higher transactions volumes and therefore higher demand for money — currency and demand deposits. Without extra supply of cash reserve assets R by the central bank, this increase in demand means excess demand for cash reserve assets. The banks in particular will be unable to support their previous volume of demand and time deposits when the public withdraws larger amounts of currency and transfers more of its wealth into demand deposits. Remember, demand deposits have cash reserve requirements three times as high as those on time deposits.
2. The public finances its extra currency and demand-deposit holdings by withdrawing funds from time deposits, selling off Treasury Bills, and taking out more loans — or trying to, at least. The banks react to their shortage of cash reserve assets by trying to sell off their holdings of

Treasury Bills. All of these actions depress asset prices and raise expected yields on the assets being sold off: Treasury Bills, time deposits, loans. If any bonds are sold off as well to provide extra money holdings, then bond yields will be driven up as well.

If the yield on money were variable, it would be lowered as the counterpart to raising yields of money substitutes, but in this model the yield on money is fixed at zero.

3. In response to higher expected yields on short-term assets such as Treasury Bills, time deposits, and loans, households and banks shift their portfolio demands from other assets into these short-term assets to take advantage of the higher relative yields. This is a standard portfolio substitution effect. Households will demand less money, and also fewer bonds and real capital. Some firms will shift their borrowing from loans to corporate bonds in order to take advantage of what are now relatively low debt costs on bond borrowing. This household and firm arbitrage will moderate the rise in short-term asset yields but also cause some rise in expected yields on bonds and real capital. Higher expected yields on real capital assets, r_k, lower the relative price q of real capital.
4. Banks have so far suffered an increase in debt costs for their time deposits, but they also have higher asset revenues on Treasury Bills and loans. Banks will shift their asset portfolio from bonds to Treasury Bills and loans to take advantage of the higher relative yields. Banks' extra selling pressure in bond markets will further depress bond prices and raise bond yields, causing further household substitution of bonds for real capital assets. The relative capital-asset price q will fall further, even though banks themselves hold no real capital assets to sell.
5. Banks would have to reduce their total asset portfolio size if the public continued to demand more currency and to hold a larger share of its total deposits in demand deposits. Larger public currency holdings mean that banks have fewer cash reserve assets available; a larger share of public deposits in demand deposits means that the average reserve requirement on total deposits is higher, since demand deposits have a 10 percent requirement and time deposits only a 3 percent requirement. However, higher yields on time deposits and on Treasury Bills and on loans persuade the public to make do with smaller money balances for the same aggregate demand and transactions volume. The pressure for higher short-term yields continues, and short-term yields will continue to rise, until the public's money demand has returned to its original level. At that original level, the banks have sufficient cash reserves to support their original volume of demand and time deposits, so there is no need for them to contract their total volume of asset holdings.

The effects of higher real incomes on asset markets so far can be summarized briefly. Short-term yields rise until money demand is restored to its original level. The higher short-term yields cause a series of portfolio substitution effects by both borrowers and lenders — effects that move long-term rates and long-term asset prices in sympathy with short-term yields and prices. Higher short-term yields will therefore be accompanied, as a sort of side effect, by higher mortgage rates and higher required yields on capital assets, producing lower house prices and lower share prices.

Exactly how much long-term yields will rise in sympathy with short-term yields was the subject of chapter 15, on the equilibrium structure of relative yields by term to maturity. The answer depends on expectations about future short-term yields, on relative risks of short- and long-term assets, and on degrees of risk aversion of household and institutional investors. Generally the response of long-term rates will be smaller than the response of short-term rates, but long-term asset prices are so much more volatile that the reponse of long-term asset prices will be much larger than the response of short-term asset prices. Stock-market prices in particular are likely to be seriously depressed by any significant increase in short-term interest rates, unless there are other forces at work increasing investors' expectations of the future net income flow from real capital assets. When stock-market prices are depressed, firms can expand more cheaply by buying up the stock of existing firms than by building new production facilities from scratch.

Wealth effects from higher real income

We have not yet considered wealth effects in our sketch of asset markets' response to higher real income levels. Higher long-term yields r_b and r_k reduce the market value of bonds and stocks, reducing households' real wealth. Lower real wealth holdings will in general reduce demand for assets. Supply of real capital and of government bonds is not affected at all, so the lower demand for assets will increase both short-term and long-term asset yields.

On the other hand, lower real wealth reduces demand for money. This reduction offsets some of the excess demand for cash reserves that initially unbalanced financial markets and drove up short-term yields. As a result, the increase in short-term yields will be smaller than it might have been.

With effects working in both directions, the net effect of lower real wealth levels is ambiguous in principle. In practice, wealth effects on the demand for money appear to be quite small (see the brief survey of empirical evidence on the demand for money in section 6 of chapter 9), so the second of the two wealth effects will be small. The major and net effect of lower real wealth is thus to reduce demand for nonmoney assets and raise their expected yields.

LM curves in the extended asset-market model

The asset-market responses in our extended market model produce a positive relationship between real income and asset yields, or equivalently

FIGURE 19–6 *LM*-type curves in the extended model

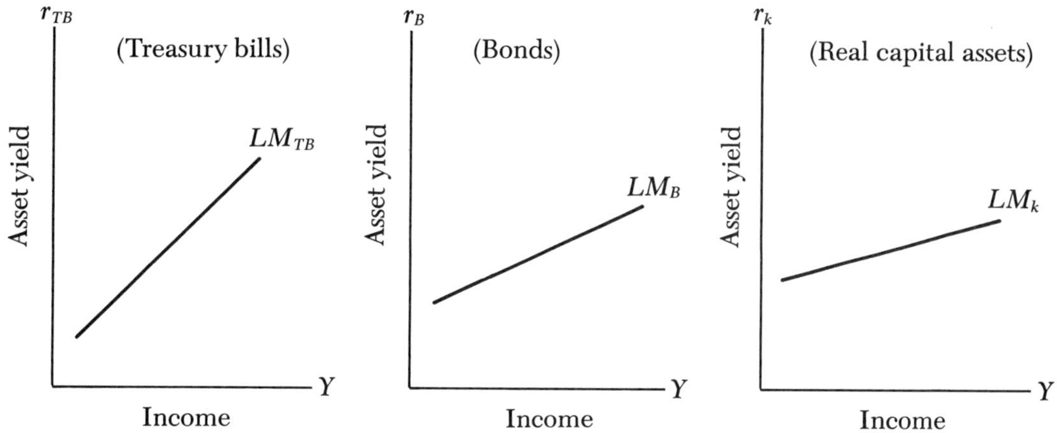

Higher real income pushes up the whole set of asset yields. Typically, short-term asset yields rise by more than long-term asset yields, so the *LM* curve for bond yields (LM_b) will be flatter than the *LM* curve for Treasury Bills (LM_{TB}).

a negative relationship between real income and relative asset prices such as q. Any one of those asset yields can be put together with the level of real income to produce an equilibrium locus that is similar in principle to the *LM* curves in figures 19–3 to 19–5. Figure 19–6 shows three of these "*LM*" curves. Each describes the relationship between real income and a particular asset yield, assuming that all other yields are allowed to adjust at the same time. Since the adjustment of short-term yields is usually larger than the adjustment of long-term yields, the *LM* curve using the Treasury Bill or the time-deposit yield will be steeper than the *LM* curve using bond or stock yields.

Figure 19–7 shows an "*LM*" curve relating aggregate demand to the equilibrium relative price of real capital (q). Just as higher aggregate demand raises the required yield on real capital, r_k, so it reduces the relative price of capital, q.

The position of each of the *LM* curves in figure 19–6 depends on the same set of factors as that of the *LM* curve in the simple model: real wealth levels (valued at constant yields), relative risks of different assets, degrees of risk aversion, cash reserves, prices, and the payments habits of households and firms. In practice the *LM* curves will also be sensitive to the range of other assets available. Introduction of more new near-money assets — by the creation of new financial intermediaries, for instance — will in general shift some demand away from money and in the process reduce expected yields on nonmoney assets; the *LM* curves in figure 19–6 will shift to the right.

FIGURE 19–7 Real incomes and capital-asset prices

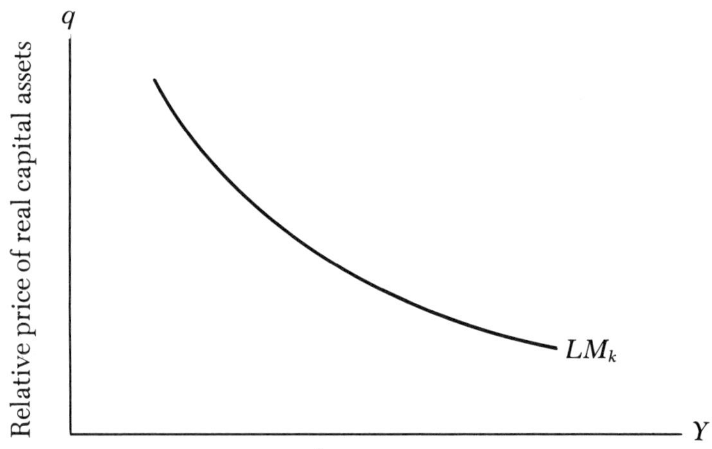

Higher real incomes push up equilibrium yields on real capital assets, r_k. This lowers the relative price of capital, $q = P_k/P = 1/(r_k P)$. The relationship between real income and q is therefore downward sloping, the inverse of panel (c) of figure 19–6.

The slope of the *LM* curve also depends on the same small set of factors as in the simple model. Expected yields must rise in both cases until (a) extra demand for money generated by higher real incomes has been offset exactly by (b) lower demand for money generated by higher yields on nonmoney assets. The slope of the *LM* curve therefore depends on relative sensitivities of money demand to real income and other asset yields.

Near-banks and the *LM* curve

We could have added near-banks to our extended model, but it would have made little difference to the behavior of asset yields. Near-banks do not have to hold cash reserves on their time deposits, so any shift of public asset demand from money to near-bank time deposits would reduce banks' required reserves by even more than a shift from money to bank time deposits. Introduction of near-bank time deposits would have two effects on the response of asset-market yields to higher income levels.

First, any increase in real income would cause shifts of asset demand from both bank and near-bank time deposits into money. Because near-bank time deposits have even smaller reserve requirements than bank time deposits, this shift would increase demand for cash reserves by more than without near-bank time deposits. By itself this increase would cause interest rates to rise by more.

FIGURE 19–8 *IS–LM* equilibrium in the extended model

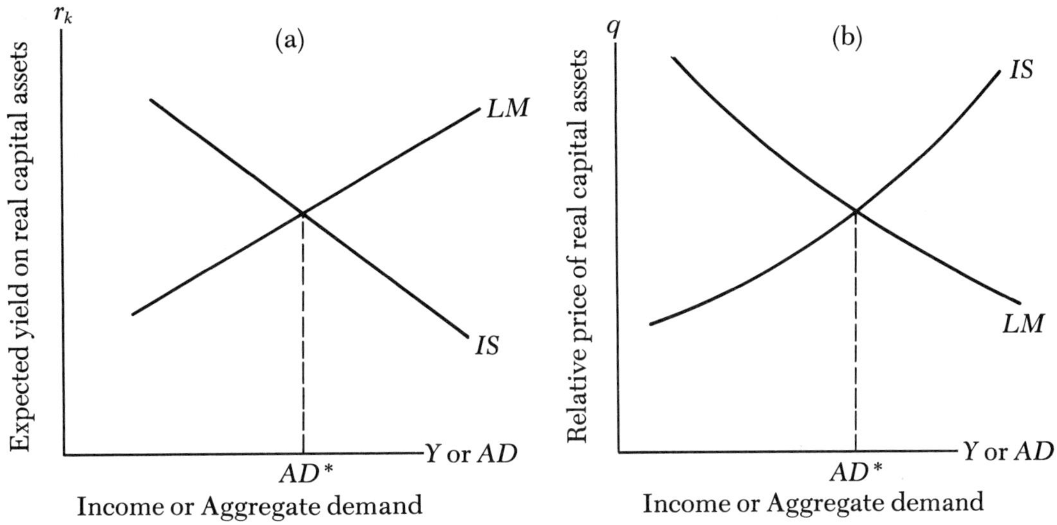

Panels (a) and (b) are alternative ways of presenting the same *IS* and *LM* relationships. In panel (a), the vertical axis measures the equilibrium yield on real capital assets, so the *LM* curve slopes upward and the *IS* curve slopes downward. In panel (b), the relative price of capital assets is measured on the vertical axis, so the slopes of *IS* and *LM* are reversed. The equilibrium level of aggregate demand, AD°, is the same in both cases.

The second effect of introducing near-banks and their time deposits would be that, as yields on time deposits rose along with other financial-asset yields, the public would shift out of money into both near-bank and bank time deposits. Because near-bank time deposits have even smaller reserve requirements than bank time deposits, this shift would reduce demand for cash reserves by more than if near-bank time deposits were not available. Thus, if near-banks were included in the model, demand for cash reserves would be increased faster by real income increases but reduced faster by increases in asset yields. Putting the two effects together, the response of asset yields to a rise in real incomes would be more or less unchanged.

SECTION 3 Joint *IS–LM* equilibrium

If each level of aggregate demand is associated with a particular set of financial-market yields, then we can find a unique equilibrium level of aggregate demand, for a given price level, by finding the aggregate demand level and financial-market yield structure at which both the goods market and the financial markets are in equilibrium. This means finding the level of aggregate demand that lies on both the *IS* curve of chapter 18 and the *LM* curves of section 2. Figure 19–8, for example, puts together the *IS* and *LM* curves using first the required yield on real capital (r_k) in panel (a) and then, in panel (b), the relative price of capital, q. Both panels produce the same equilibrium level of real income and aggregate demand AD^*.

The equilibrium level of *AD* can be found algebraically by substituting the value of the interest-rate terms from the *LM* curves into the *IS*-curve equation. This procedure is too cumbersome to be worthwhile for our extended model, but it is relatively easy for the simple model. The algebra provides a short and useful summary of asset-market feedback effects on goods-market demand levels. The *LM* equation in the simple model is equation (7):

$$r = \frac{L_0 - \alpha(R/P)}{j} + \left(\frac{h}{j}\right)Y. \qquad (7)$$

The *IS* equation, from chapter 18, can be written succinctly as

$$AD^e = \frac{A_0}{1-b'} - \left(\frac{c+g}{1-b'}\right)r, \qquad (12)$$

$$\text{where } A_0 = aW - bT_0 + I_0 + G + F_0 + gr_{US}, \qquad (13)$$

a collection of exogenous influences on aggregate demand. The coefficients of the *IS*-curve equation, for those who do not perfectly recall chapter 18, are as follows: $a = dC/dW$; $b = dC/dY$; $b' = dC/d(Y-T)$; $c = dI/dr$; $g = dF/dr_{US} = -dF/dr$; $h = dL/dY$; $j = -dL/dr$. Exchange rates are flexible in this model, so any change in net capital outflows F produces, via exchange rate changes, an equal change in net exports $X - M$.

Substituting for r in equation (12) gives the equilibrium level of aggregate demand as

$$AD^e = \frac{A_0}{1-b'} - \frac{c+g}{1-b'}\left(L_0 - \frac{\alpha R}{P}\right)\left(\frac{1}{j}\right) - \left[\frac{(c+g)h}{(1-b')j}\right]Y \qquad (14)$$

In equilibrium $AD = Y$, so (14) can be expressed as

$$AD^e + \left[\frac{(c+g)h}{(1-b')j}\right]AD^e = \frac{A_0}{1-b'} - \frac{c+g}{1-b'}\left(L_0 - \frac{\alpha R}{P}\right)\left(\frac{1}{j}\right)$$

so that

$$AD^e = \frac{A_0 - [(c+g)/j](L_o - \alpha R/P)}{1 - b' + (h/j)(c+g)} \qquad (15)$$

From equation (15) we can see that the level of AD^e depends on all of the exogenous variables carried over from the *IS* and *LM* equations (those variables in A_0 from the *IS* curve, plus L_0, R, and P from the *LM* curve). Since those exogenous variables are not constant in the real world, there are many sources of disturbance to aggregate demand. If the exogenous variables were all independent, we could expect that many of their random

FIGURE 19–9 Response to higher demand stimulus

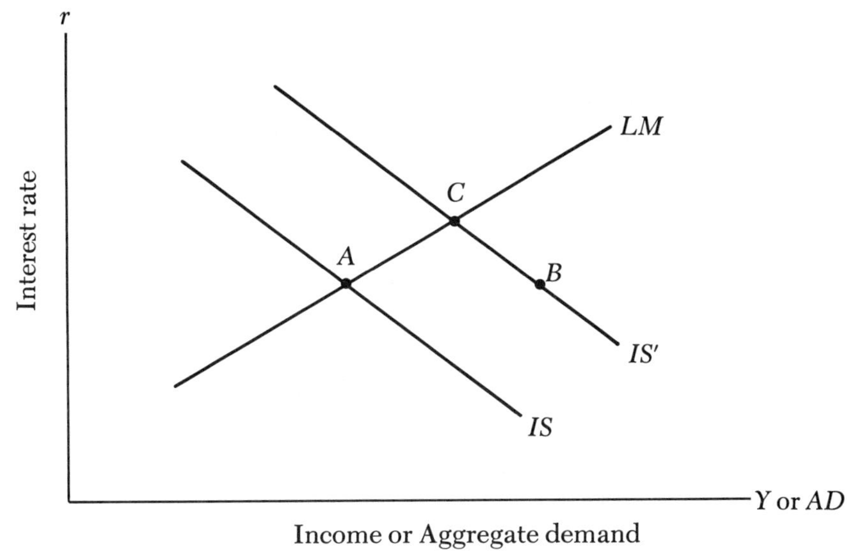

When a positive demand shock shifts the *IS* curve to the right, from *IS* to *IS′*, the new equilibrium does not move from *A* to *B*. Higher interest rates (along the *LM* curve) cause lower net exports and investment demand, offsetting part of the positive demand shock and producing a new equilibrium at *C*. Aggregate demand increases by less than if interest rates were held constant.

disturbances would cancel each other out and leave aggregate demand relatively stable, but we will see later that that is not the case.

At the same time, the response of AD^e to each of the exogenous variables in A_0 is now less than we found in chapter 18. We have added an extra feedback effect, one that serves to offset some of the effect of any change in exogenous variables. Higher aggregate demand levels now increase interest rates; the increase in interest rates moderates the increase in aggregate demand.

The extra feedback effect is easily seen in an *IS–LM* diagram like figure 19–9. Any increase in exogenous spending such as that by the government will shift the *IS* curve to the right. At an unchanged interest rate, the equilibrium aggregate demand would rise by an amount equal to the initial disturbance multiplied by the multiplier $1/(1 - b')$, as in chapter 18. Aggregate demand and the economy would move from *A* to *B* in figure 19–9.

Interest rates do not stay constant, however; they increase, by an amount determined by the *LM* curve. The economy therefore moves from an initial equilibrium at A to a final equilibrium at C in figure 19–9. The effect of the interest-rate increase is a shift in the equilibrium from B (where it would otherwise have been) to C. Aggregate demand is reduced.

Using the simple model, we can see the extra, interest-rate-feedback effect reflected in a smaller aggregate demand multiplier. In chapter 18, a \$1 change in A_0 for whatever reason would have increased aggregate demand by the multiplier factor $1/(1 - b')$. Now, equation (15) tells us that any \$1 change in A_0 will change aggregate demand by the factor $1/[1 - b' + (h/j)(c + g)]$. The extra term in the denominator is positive, because all of the coefficients are positive, so the factor as a whole is smaller than $1/(1 - b')$. The extra term represents an interest-rate-feedback effect, which can be written in terms of derivatives as

$$\frac{h}{j}(c + g) = -\frac{dr}{dAD}\left[\frac{dI}{dr} + \frac{d(X - M)}{dr}\right],$$

where dr/dAD is the slope of the LM curve (h/j), the amount by which an increase in aggregate demand drives up the interest rate. The feedback effect reflects impacts on aggregate demand induced by changes in r, which in turn are induced by changes in Y caused by the initial stimulus to aggregate demand. Any stimulus to aggregate demand is now reinforced by extra consumption spending (induced by income as in chapter 18) but is also partly offset by changes in investment and net export demand.

Interest-rate feedbacks in the extended model

In our extended model, with many different asset yields, we must be more specific about exactly which interest rates are involved in the feedback effects just discussed. There are three separate kinds of interest-rate feedback to be distinguished and then added up.

The first feedback effect is that an increase in Treasury Bill and time-deposit rates in Canada will open up a short-term interest differential in favor of Canada and reduce any net capital outflow. Demand for foreign currency will be reduced, the price of foreign currency will fall, and Canadian producers' competitive position will be weakened. Net export demand will fall. This feedback effect clearly depends on changes in short-term rates, since the most interest-sensitive capital flows are typically in short-term instruments like financial paper and term deposits. We discussed such capital flows in chapter 5, as part of our description of the money market.

The second interest-rate-feedback effect is that an increase in long-term rates on real capital will reduce the relative price q of capital assets and cause new construction activity to decline. That means less investment demand. This feedback effect depends on long-term yields' being affected by changes in real income.

The third feedback effect is an indirect effect, ignored in the simple model, that operates through changes in wealth. The effect is probably much smaller than the first two, but it requires more explanation. Higher expected yields on long-term assets depress the prices of bonds and real capital assets. Lower household wealth will reduce consumption spending. Lower capital-asset values also impair the balance sheets of many firms by raising their debt : equity ratios — an increase that will raise their borrowing costs and possibly limit the amount of credit available to them. Higher debt : equity ratios imply higher default risk for lenders, who logically insist on an extra risk premium in their lending rate to offset the extra expected default losses. Investment demand will be lowered as well as consumption demand. This third feedback effect reinforces the first two and depends mainly on long-term rates' being affected by higher real income levels.

In chapter 8 we looked closely at household asset portfolios to see whether any significant part of them is subject to market risk — that is, to fluctuations in prices caused by changes in yields, among other things. We concluded that few of the assets held directly by households in Canada are valued at market prices or are sensitive to fluctuations in market value. The exceptions are the family home and the value of pension fund entitlements. If measures of household wealth are not sensitive to interest-rate levels, then it follows that interest-rate-feedback effects on aggregate demand through impacts on household wealth will be small. Effects on firms' balance sheets and on investment demand are likely to be larger.

SECTION 4 Price-level impacts and the *AD* curve

The *IS–LM* diagram in figure 19–8 shows one equilibrium level of aggregate demand for a particular price level. The pair of values for AD^e and P give one point on an aggregate demand curve. In order to derive the others, we need to know what impact changes in the price level have on *IS* and *LM* curves. If there is no impact, then the aggregate demand curve will be vertical. If higher prices shift either or both of the *IS* and *LM* curves to the left, the aggregate demand curve will be downward sloping.

Prices and the *IS* curve

At the end of chapter 18 we discussed effects of price levels on the *IS* curve. Our conclusion was that higher price levels will shift the *IS* curve to the left — sometimes. Higher price levels reduce the real wealth of households by lowering the real value of money, bonds, and term-deposit holdings. Lower real wealth levels will in turn reduce consumption demand. However, higher price levels also reduce the real value of debts and improve debtors' balance sheets. Debtors are likely to borrow and spend more, other things equal. Debtors' extra spending could be greater than creditors' reduction in spending, even if creditors' wealth falls by more than debtors' wealth increases (by the margin of shrinkage in the real value of government bonds and the cash reserve base).

If higher prices are accompanied by higher expected future inflation, then nominal interest rates are likely to be higher as well (the Fisher effect, described in chapter 14). Higher nominal interest rates imply tighter cash flow constraints for debtors, particularly household borrowers, which in turn constrain borrowing and spending for capital assets such as housing.

Aggregate demand will be reduced by higher domestic prices to the extent that the competitive position of domestic producers is worsened. Higher domestic prices unaccompanied by an increase in the price of foreign currency will mean lower net exports and lower aggregate demand. We expect the price of foreign currency to move opposite to domestic price levels, however, just to keep the foreign exchange market in balance. Only if the exchange rate does not respond will there be a fall in net exports when the price level rises.

On balance, we can summarize the effect of P on the *IS* curve by saying that, although we would normally expect higher price levels to shift the *IS* curve slightly to the left, we should not be surprised to see a much larger shift on occasion, or even an expansion in aggregate demand.

Prices and *LM* curves

Price-level impacts on the *LM* curve are much more certain and also much larger. The first and strongest impact is on the level of the real cash reserve base, R/P. Higher price levels imply proportional reductions in the real value of the cash reserve base. The amount of real demand deposits that can be supported therefore shrinks proportionally as well. Higher price levels provoke excess demand for money in exactly the same way that lower cash reserve levels or higher levels of real income do. The result in all three cases is higher interest rates.

When the stimulus is higher real income, the result is described as a shift along the *LM* curve, because aggregate demand is measured along the horizontal axis. When the stimulus is higher prices, the effect is a shift of the *LM* curve to the left, producing higher interest rates or lower capital-asset prices q at each level of aggregate demand.

The effect of lower real values of R/P is reflected in equation (15), the equation for equilibrium aggregate demand in the simple model. From that equation, the effect of price level on AD^e is

$$\frac{dAD^e}{dP} = \frac{\left[(c + g)/j\right]\left[\alpha\frac{d(R/P)}{dP}\right]}{1 - b' + (h/j)(c + g)} \tag{16}$$

Because $d(R/P)/dP$ is negative, so is dAD^e/dP.

A second possible but once-only effect of price levels on asset markets will occur if higher price levels are accompanied by greater uncertainty about future price levels. Generally, greater inflation risk will increase the relative risks of nominal versus real assets. Households will demand more of assets seen as a hedge against inflation and less of everything else. The structure of relative yields will change: yields on capital assets will fall, while bond yields will rise. The q ratio will rise and stimulate investment demand, but the cost of borrowed funds will also rise and discourage investment demand. The *LM* curve relating real income and r_k will shift to the right, while the *LM* curve relating real income and r_b will shift to the left. The net effect on aggregate demand is unclear. Since the net effect is unclear, we will ignore it except to add it to our long list of sources of uncertainty about macroeconomic behavior.

A third possible price-level impact on *LM* curves is via changes in real wealth. Higher prices mean lower real values of Treasury Bills and government bonds and cash reserves and therefore lower real net wealth of the private sector. Private-sector asset demand must be smaller in total. Demand for money is not affected in real terms by changes in the price level, so other assets must bear the brunt. In general, asset prices will be reduced and expected yields driven up for all assets other than the government bonds and Treasury Bills whose real supply will have shrunk by even more than demand. The effect may be mild, but some general increase in expected yields on capital assets is to be expected. Aggregate demand will be lowered as the *LM* curves shift to the left.

Aggregate demand curves

Figure 19–10 shows the impact of a higher price level on aggregate demand if it shifts both *IS* and *LM* curves to the left. The price level starts at 100, with equilibrium aggregate demand at AD^* panel (a). This produces point A on the aggregate demand curve in panel (b). With a price level of 120, both the *IS* and *LM* curves lie farther to the left, so the equilibrium falls from AD^* to AD' The combination of higher price level $P = 120$ and lower demand level AD' produces a second point, B, on the aggregate demand curve. By considering many more price levels we can derive all of the other points on the aggregate demand curve and plot them all as in panel (b).

The aggregate demand curve in figure 19–10 is defined by its slope and position. The slope depends on impacts of price levels on *IS* curves and *LM* curves, as we have discussed. The position depends on all of the factors that determine the position of the *IS* and *LM* curves, except the price level itself (the influence of the price level is already reflected in the slope of the demand curve). The list of factors includes government spending, the level of nominal cash reserves, the exogenous portion of net capital outflows, tax rates, relative risks, expected future interest rates, and many more factors less likely to change in the short run.

Changes in any of the variables affecting either the *IS* or the *LM* curves will shift the aggregate demand curve to right or left. For instance, a defence spending boom would shift the *IS* curve to the right: at each possible interest rate, the level of aggregate demand would be bigger. On

FIGURE 19–10 Derivation of the aggregate demand curve

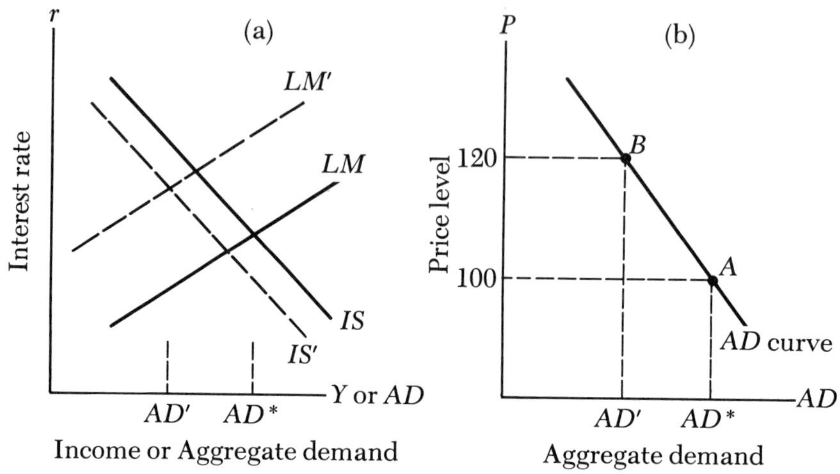

A price level of 100 in panel (a) yields an equilibrium aggregate demand level of $AD°$, at the intersection of *IS* and *LM*. That is plotted as point *A* in panel (b) — one point on the aggregate demand curve relating prices and *AD*. When the price level rises to 120, the *IS* curve is shifted to *IS'*, and the *LM* curve to *LM'*. The new aggregate demand equilibrium is at the intersection of *IS'* and *LM'*, at *AD'*. That produces point *B* in panel (b). Repeating this exercise for many different price levels gives all the points on the *AD* curve in panel (b).

an *IS–LM* diagram, the equilibrium levels of demand and interest rate would be bigger, for the same price level. On an aggregate demand diagram, therefore, the level of equilibrium aggregate demand associated with each price level would be greater than before; the aggregate demand curve would have shifted to the right.

A lower level of cash reserve assets would shift the *LM* curve to the left. Each price level would be associated with a lower equilibrium level of aggregate demand and a higher interest rate. The aggregate demand curve would shift to the left.

Aggregate demand with the exchange rate fixed

We have assumed so far that the central bank takes no action to maintain the exchange rate at any particular value. The central bank is therefore not involved in the foreign exchange market consistently as either buyer or seller of assets. In practice, central banks are not indifferent about the level of the exchange rate, as our model implies. Often the central bank in

Canada has expressed a desire not to see the exchange rate fall, for fear that that would drive up the domestic cost of imports and worsen inflation.

When the central bank takes a position on the exchange rate, there are two important changes in the way our aggregate demand model works. First, changes in domestic price levels affect domestic producers' competitive position proportionally, with no offsetting effects from exchange rate changes. This extra impact of price level on net exports increases the total effect of price on aggregate demand, flattening the aggregate demand curve. Second, the central bank may not be able to keep the level of cash reserves fixed exogenously; the size of R and of the money supply may be tied to the foreign exchange market and therefore endogenous. This second effect is important and deserves further explanation.

The central bank can maintain a particular level of the exchange rate $P_{US\$}$ by supporting the price, with exactly the same technique that the agriculture department would use to support the price of potatoes: the central bank stands ready to buy up any excess supply and to satisfy any excess demand by selling off foreign exchange from its own reserves.

Central-bank purchases of foreign exchange assets will by themselves increase total central-bank deposits outstanding, because the central bank pays for any asset purchases by issuing drafts (cheques) against itself. The drafts are deposited in banks, which present them to the central bank and receive extra central-bank deposits in settlement. Central-bank sales are paid for by cheques on banks; when the central bank presents those cheques, the banks accept a reduction in their central-bank deposit accounts in settlement. Increases and decreases in central-bank deposits of course change the level of the cash reserve base and hence the money supply and all *LM* curves.

The question is, under what conditions can we expect the foreign exchange market to cause central-bank purchases of foreign exchange and therefore to lower domestic interest rates? Under what conditions can we expect the opposite?

Central-bank purchases of foreign exchange are triggered by any Balance of Payments surplus. That in turn can be caused by lower domestic price levels (relative to foreign price levels) or by higher foreign demand levels (relative to domestic demand levels) or by a larger interest differential in favor of Canada. If a fall in domestic price levels leads to central-bank purchases, and therefore to a larger cash reserve base and to lower domestic interest rates and higher levels of aggregate demand, then lower price levels are associated with higher aggregate demand. The higher cash reserve base shifts the *LM* curve to the right, and aggregate demand increases along the *IS* curve. This extra effect of prices on aggregate demand via cash reserves would make the aggregate demand curve flatter than otherwise, as long as central-bank operations to stabilize the foreign exchange rate are allowed to affect the level of R.

The central bank is not always or even usually constrained to allow its foreign exchange transactions to affect the cash reserve base. The central bank can, for instance, buy foreign exchange assets and at the same time sell government bonds. Its total assets are then not affected, and neither is R. If R is not affected, neither is the LM curve or the general level of domestic interest rates. Alternatively, the central bank could sell foreign exchange assets and buy government bonds. This kind of operation is known as *sterilization* because it manages foreign exchange operations while sterilizing all side effects on the domestic money supply.

Sterilization

In general the central bank will want to sterilize its foreign exchange operations; the requirements of the foreign exchange market will not normally coincide with the requirements of domestic stabilization policy, and only by sterilization can the central bank achieve both exchange rate and domestic objectives. The central bank will admittedly not be able to sterilize foreign exchange purchases if it runs out of government bonds to sell, but that limit is easily removed by the central bank's arranging with the government to swap bonds for central-bank deposits.

To summarize this section on the aggregate demand curve with a fixed exchange rate, there will definitely be a stronger impact of price-level changes on aggregate demand than when the exchange rate is left to float freely. If the cash reserve base is affected, then the aggregate demand curve will be flatter still.

SECTION 5 Summary

In this chapter we considered how the level of interest rates is determined, for given levels of aggregate demand in goods markets. The explanation used two streamlined models of the full asset-market equilibrium from chapter 14. The first is a simple, two-asset model with only money and bonds, which produces the LM-curve relationship between interest rates and aggregate demand. The condition for asset-market equilibrium boils down to the requirement that demand for money equal supply of money. Demand for money was explained at length in chapter 9. Supply of money becomes a constant multiple of the available cash reserve base R, under plausible assumptions about the public's desired currency-to-deposit ratio.

The main conclusions of the simple model remain when we extend the asset-market model to include a wider range of assets and much more borrower and lender discretion. Higher aggregate demand levels still produce higher interest-rate levels because of excess demand for cash reserves and money, since the yield on cash reserves and demand deposits is arbitrarily fixed at zero. Instead of the yield on cash reserves and money being lowered, yields on all other assets are increased. The yields most affected initially are short-term, liquid-asset yields, but a series of portfolio substitution effects causes long-term asset yields to move in the same direction.

Putting together the equilibrium conditions for the goods market and for financial markets produces a unique equilibrium level of aggregate demand for each price level. Different price levels of course imply different equilibrium aggregate demand levels and therefore a schedule of different demand and price levels that traces out the aggregate demand curve. The slope of the aggregate demand curve reflects the impact of price level on both *IS* and *LM* curves. Of the two, the *LM* curve is more obviously affected by price levels, because the level of cash reserve assets R is fixed in nominal terms and must shrink proportionally as the price level P rises. Higher price levels therefore imply excess demand for cash reserve assets in financial markets, higher levels of interest rates, and lower levels of aggregate demand. There may also be wealth effects, as higher price levels shrink real wealth, and there may be some competitive effects on net export demand if domestic price-level changes are not accompanied by offsetting changes in the exchange rate. The end result is a downward-sloping aggregate demand curve, but one whose slope is likely to vary over time.

Questions for discussion

1. Why does the condition for financial-market equilibrium require only that wealth be allocated and that money demand equal money supply, in the simple asset model of section 1?
2. How is household wealth affected by the level of interest rates? How does this change in household wealth affect the level of aggregate demand?
3. What causes shifts of the *LM* curve?
4. Why is the money-supply multiplier not just $1/crr$, as in many introductory textbooks? Explain in words. What would it be if the public's currency demand were fixed?
5. What is the situation in financial markets when the economy is above its *LM* curve? What will happen in such a case?
6. What is the effect on an *IS–LM* diagram of higher expected inflation?
7. List five sources of uncertainty about the response of aggregate demand to a change in the level of cash reserves.
8. Under what circumstances could the aggregate demand curve be vertical?
9. What causes shifts of the agregate demand curve?

References

Dornbusch, R., S. Fischer, and G.R. Sparks. *Macroeconomics*. Toronto: McGraw-Hill, 1981.

Laidler, David E.W. *The Demand for Money*. 2d ed. New York: Dun-Donnelly, 1977, parts 1 and 2.

Smith, Gary N. *Money and Banking: Financial Markets and Institutions*. Reading, Mass.: Addison-Wesley, 1982.

Tobin, James. "Commercial Banks as 'Creators' of Money." In Deane Carson, ed. *Banking and Monetary Studies*. Homewood, Ill.: Irwin, 1963.

———."A General Equilibrium Approach to Monetary Theory." *Journal of Money, Credit, and Banking* 1 (1969), 15–29.

Wilton, David A., and David M. Prescott. *Macroeconomics*. Don Mills, Ont.: Addison-Wesley, 1982.

CHAPTER 20

Aggregate Supply

The aggregate model of the economy presented in chapter 17 consists of an aggregate demand curve and an aggregate supply curve. Chapters 18 and 19 have explained the behavior of aggregate demand, which is summarized in the aggregate demand curve. This chapter does the same for aggregate supply. The supply side of the economy consists of the aggregate supply curve, with the markets for labor and other inputs behind it, so this chapter must (a) explain the behavior of those input markets and (b) derive the implications for output and prices at various possible levels of demand. I initially derive and explain an aggregate supply curve in both short and long run in a static economy, since that is the simplest kind of economy to work with. Then I extend the concept of aggregate supply to fit the more realistic context of a dynamic economy in which wages and prices change persistently along some expected trend.

SECTION 1 Aggregate supply in a static economy

In this section we want to understand what determines how much will be produced at each price level or, equivalently, how high a price will be charged for each output level.

The two methods of posing the question introduce a convenient distinction in macroeconomics, between flex-price sectors and fix-price sectors.[1]

Flex-price markets

In *flex-price markets* (auction markets, mainly) the price of output is determined from day to day by the interplay of supply and demand; an example is the price of metals on the London Metals Exchange. In these markets, producers respond to price signals and adjust their output levels

[1]Sir John Hicks introduced this convenient distinction between flexible and fixed-price markets, in *Capital and Growth* (Oxford: Oxford University Press, 1965), 76–83.

according to essentially marginal cost information — the costs of inputs and their marginal productivity. In *fix-price markets* — and these include markets for most items we buy — the price of output is set by sellers as a more or less fixed markup over production costs.[2] In fix-price markets, producers respond to quantity signals (they satisfy all demand that comes in the door) and later set prices essentially on the basis of average cost information — prices of inputs, and average productivity. In both markets, cost information will be crucial in determining the level of prices, but in flex-price markets the level of demand will have an impact even in the short run.

Fix-price markets

Often the producer's price will be set as a markup over labor costs; when wholesalers and retailers add their own markups, and governments add their sales tax markup, the final consumer price is determined in the short run by labor costs alone. To be sure, markups have some flexibility and will be squeezed in a severe recession (during special clearance sales, or even going-out-of-business sales), but in the short run goods sold in fix-price markets will have prices determined almost solely by input prices.

Labor costs will dominate price setting, because labor costs amount to almost two-thirds of total production costs in national income. Labor costs in turn reflect wage rates and labor productivity. Average labor costs per unit of output (known as *unit labor costs* in the business world) are simply wage rates divided by average labor productivity. Where W_a is the nominal wage rate, N is hours of employment, and PY is nominal output, average labor productivity is PY/N and

$$\text{unit labor cost} = \frac{W_a}{PY/N}. \tag{1}$$

If prices are a multiple of unit labor costs, then prices are a multiple of $W_a/(PY/N)$ as well.

It follows from what we have said that, if extra inputs are available at constant prices, extra output will be available at constant prices as well (unless there are decreasing or increasing returns to scale in production);

---

[2]Arthur Okun referred to these markets as *price-tag markets*, which gives an idea of their prevalence. Almost all markets in which goods have price tags will have prices fixed by some sort of markup formula just because calculating prices by any other method would be more expensive. When inventory builds up because of a slump in demand, there is a temporary "big bargain sale" when all price tags are marked down — by a markdown formula. *Prices and Quantities* (Washington, D.C.: Brookings Institution, 1981), 263ff. Maurice Levi and Albert Dexter note that in Canada many of our prices are set explicitly by regulatory authorities such as public utility commissions, which are even slower to respond to the level of demand than the rest of the fix-price sector. "Regulated Prices and Their Consequences," *Canadian Public Policy*, March 1983, 24–31.

FIGURE 20–1 Possible aggregate supply curves in fix-price markets

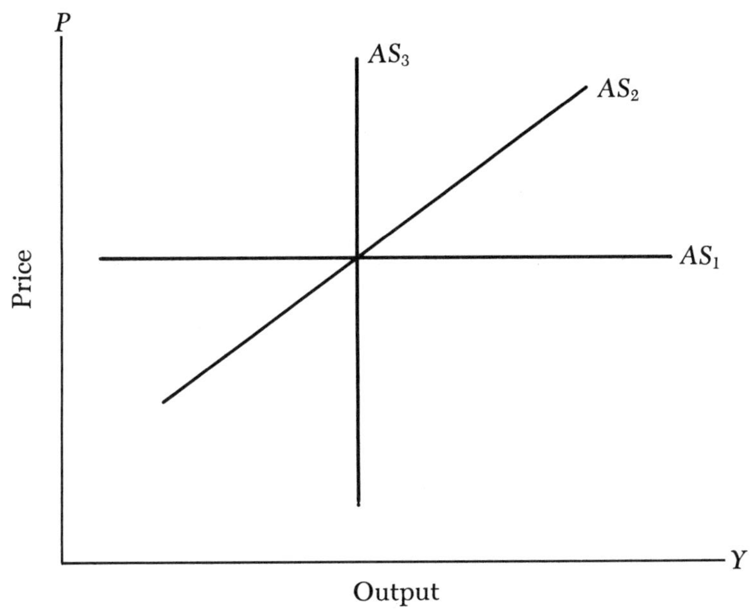

If inputs are available at constant cost, the aggregate supply curve is flat like AS_1. If extra inputs are available only at increasing cost, the aggregate supply curve will slope upward like AS_2. If extra inputs are not available at all, the aggregate supply curve will be vertical like AS_3.

the aggregate supply curve will be flat, like AS_1 in figure 20–1. If inputs are available only at increasing prices, then output will be available only at increasing prices because producers will pass along input-cost increases in price increases through their markup pricing, as on AS_2 in figure 20–1. If extra inputs are not available at all, even at sharply higher wages or capital costs, then extra output will not be available at all, even at sharply higher prices; the aggregate supply curve will be vertical, like AS_3 in figure 20–1. Finally, if technology improves and unit labor costs fall, the same markup pricing rule will pass along the benefit in lower consumer prices as long as there is sufficient competition. Each of the three *AS* curves in figure 20–1 will shift to the right or downward by the amount of the productivity increase.

We clearly need to know how supplies of inputs respond to extra input demand, and labor supply is the key. That brings us to a fork in the road, since labor-supply behavior in the long run is different from what it is in the short run. We will start with the long-run behavior.

Labor markets in the long run

Standard neoclassical labor-market theory tells us that labor demand and labor supply will both depend on the level of the real wage w ($w = W_a/P$). Each employer will hire labor to the point where labor's marginal product is equal to the real wage, and workers will supply labor to the point where the marginal rate of substitution of labor for leisure equals the real wage rate. Figure 20–2 shows both demand and supply curves in a traditional labor-market diagram. There is only one possible equilibrium in figure 20–2, at the intersection of demand and supply. The equilibrium gives a unique level of labor inputs into production, N^*, and a unique level of the real wage w^*. Note that it does not tell us the level of nominal wages W_a, so we cannot figure out the price level using the markup formula.

FIGURE 20–2 Neoclassical, long-run labor market

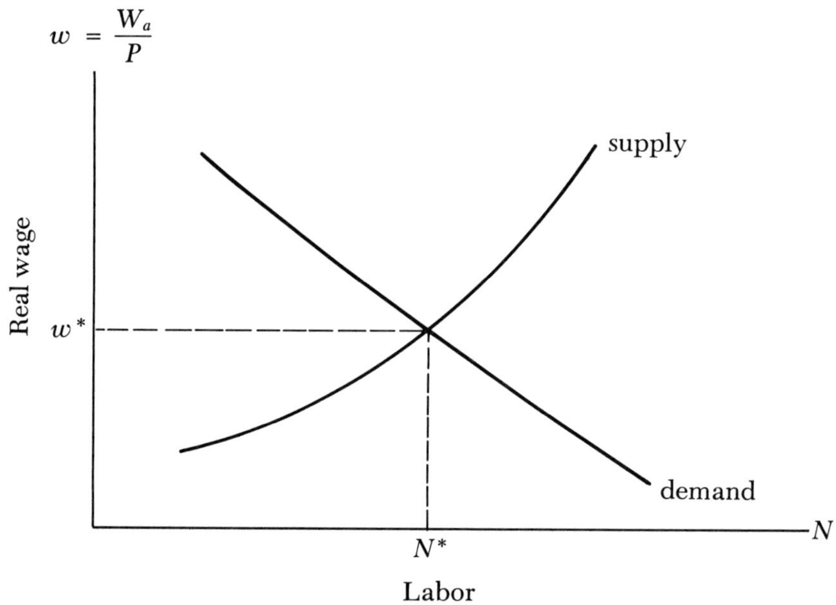

Labor is demanded until the marginal product of labor equals the real wage rate w, so the demand curve is the marginal-product-of-labor curve. Labor is supplied to the point where the marginal utility of leisure (relative to the marginal utility of extra income) just equals the real wage rate. Supply equals demand at $w = w^*$ and $N = N^*$.

The equilibrium real wage in figure 20–2 could be reached either by changes in nominal wages or by changes in prices. If the real wage is initially too high, it can be lowered either by a series of nominal wage cuts or by workers' not demanding extra nominal wages when the price level rises. The second adjustment process has the decided advantage that it

TABLE 20–1 Wages, prices, and real wages in Canada, 1975–82

Year	Average hourly earnings ($)	Price level (1975 = 100)	Real wage level in 1975 dollars
1975	5.06	100.0	5.06
1976	5.76	107.5	5.36
1977	6.38	116.1	5.50
1978	6.83	126.5	5.40
1979	7.43	138.1	5.38
1980	8.19	152.1	5.38
1981	9.17	171.0	5.36
1982 (August)	10.42	192.1	5.42

Source: Bank of Canada Review.

FIGURE 20–3 Adjustment in the neoclassical labor market

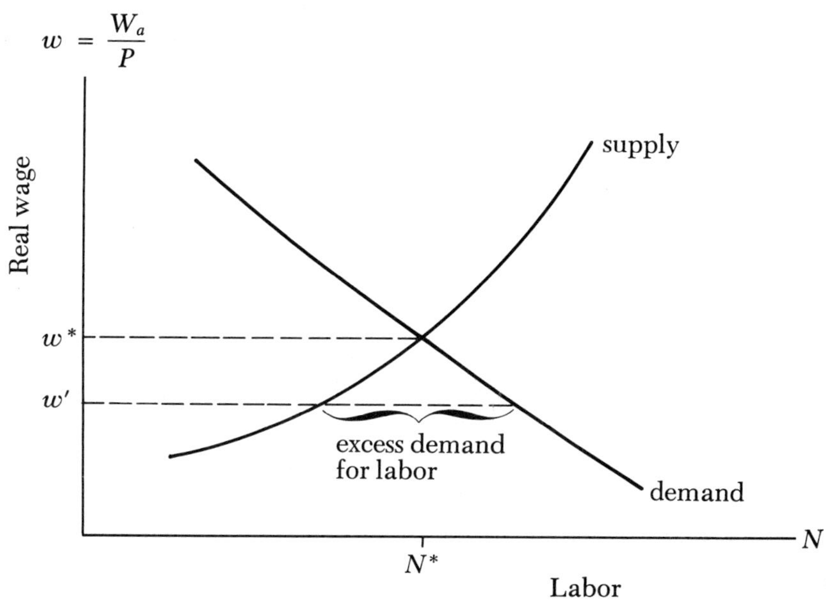

An increase in the demand for goods raises goods prices; higher goods prices lower the real wage level from w^* to w'. At w' there is excess demand for labor, so the nominal wage is driven upward. As nominal wages rise, the real wage rises toward w^* and the excess demand for labor is reduced. The process continues until the market is once again in balance at $w = w^*$ and $N = N^*$.

would lower all real wages together and therefore not disturb relative wages, so it is a plausible possibility. Table 20–1, for instance, shows what happened to nominal wages, prices, and real wages in Canada over the years 1975–82. Real wages fell from 1977 to 1979, and again from 1980 to 1981 (though not by much for the typical wage-earner). If the economy were allowed enough time free of other disturbances, the labor market could be expected to settle more or less at the equilibrium in figure 20–2. There would be full employment, in the sense that all those who wanted work at the prevailing real wage would have it, and only those who wanted to stay home (or deal in the underground economy) would not work.

Now imagine an increase in aggregate demand in goods markets. Inventories of finished goods are run down, and producers receive more orders to replenish them. Sooner or later, if output is not increased, prices of goods will increase — sooner in flex-price markets, later in fix-price markets. With higher output prices, the real wage of labor is lower — at w_1 instead of w^* in figure 20–3. Quantity of labor demanded is larger and there is excess demand for labor. The result is that nominal wages W_a are bid up until the excess demand is removed, which brings real wages back to their original level. With higher nominal wages, producers no longer want to increase output levels, and the original equilibrium output level is restored. Aggregate supply has not increased despite the increase in output prices. The aggregate supply curve remains vertical.

Figure 20–4 illustrates this argument with a three-part diagram. The equilibrium level of labor inputs in panel (a) is insensitive to the price level because higher prices simply increase nominal wages by the same proportion and labor supply responds only to the real wage level. There is therefore only one possible level of labor input, N^*, at all price levels. Panel (b) relates labor inputs to output levels via the production function.[3] Higher labor input levels generate higher output levels, but if there is only one possible labor input level N^*, then there is only one possible output level. This is shown as Y^* in panel (c), for all price levels. Output will increase only if the labor supply grows (shifting the labor-supply schedule in panel (a) to the right) or if technological improvements shift the production function upward in panel (b). The price level will not change the output level by itself.

In the long run, therefore, neoclassical analysis suggests that aggregate demand will not be able to influence the output level unless somehow

---

[3]This production function is drawn with some assumption about supplies of other inputs. If other inputs are assumed fixed, then only labor is added to produce the extra output, and the production function can be expected to flatten out because of diminishing returns to labor. If other inputs are assumed to be combined with extra labor in more or less fixed proportions, then there need not be diminishing returns to labor, and the production function need not flatten out. In the long run neither of these assumptions makes any difference to the slope of the aggregate supply curve. The aggregate supply curve is vertical because with only one level of labor input, only one point on the production function is ever used.

FIGURE 20–4 Determination of aggregate supply

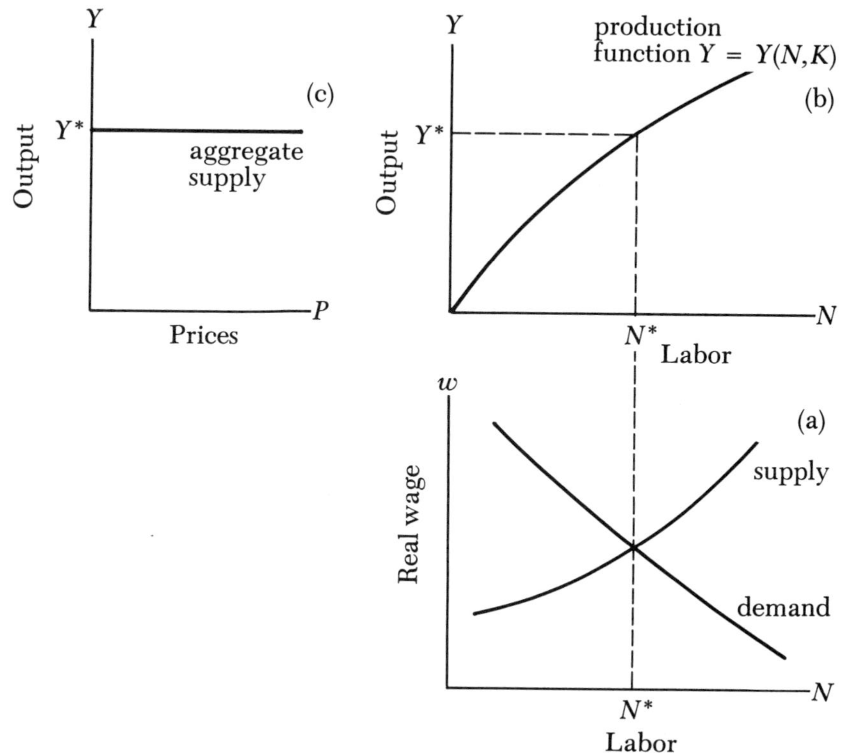

Panel (a) shows the unique equilibrium level of employment N^*. Panel (b) relates output level to labor inputs with a production function. With labor input set at N^*, output can only be Y^*. If the price level does not affect employment, then it does not affect output either, as in panel (c).

aggregate demand can influence technology or labor supply. Instead, aggregate demand will determine just the price level. Figure 20–5 illustrates the proposition.

We can see the adjustment process on a simple *IS–LM* diagram if we just add a vertical supply curve to it at output level Y^* and assume that the price level does not cause that supply curve to shift. In figure 20–6 the demand equilibrium is initially at *AD*, below the supply level Y^*. Excess supply in goods markets causes the price level P to fall, eventually. As P falls, real wages rise and excess supply develops in the labor market; nominal wages therefore fall as well. Falling prices shift both the *IS* and the *LM* curves to the right, until demand equilibrium *AD* coincides with the supply of output at Y^*. The end result is still Y^*, but a lower price level.

FIGURE 20–5 Long-run aggregate supply and aggregate demand

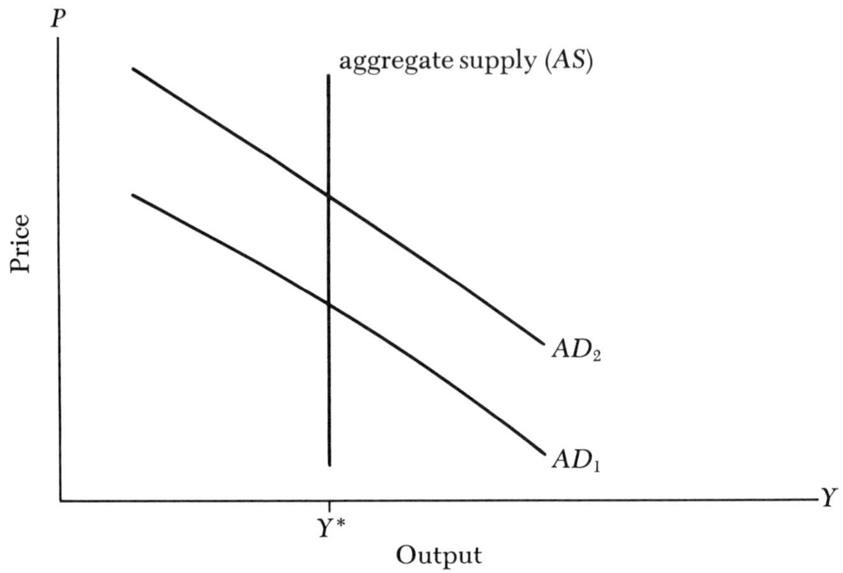

In the long run, the aggregate supply curve *AS* is vertical and insensitive to price levels. The intersection of aggregate demand and aggregate supply curves still determines equilibrium, but all aggregate demand curves (such as AD_1 and AD_2) will yield the same output level $Y°$. Aggregate demand therefore determines only the price level.

The short run

In the short run, we acknowledge that there is considerably more to wage determination than simple market-clearing at the equilibrium real wage level. First, workers are concerned at least as much with their relative wages as with their real wages (relative to those of similar workers in other regions, or other occupations, or just in other firms).

Second, wages in labor markets are closer to being fixed than flexible in the short run. Labor markets are also fix-price markets, as a rule. For labor employed in "career" jobs expected to last a long time, there is a long-run relationship between worker and employer that neither wants to disturb.[4] The employer does not want to have to train new workers; the training costs money, and so do the repairs to equipment (or perhaps customer relations) accidentally abused by inexperienced workers. Employees, for their part, want to keep steady jobs that use their training; they want to avoid the stress of changing workplaces and possibly uprooting their

[4]For the best discussion of career- and casual-labor markets, see Arthur Okun, *Prices and Quantities* (Washington, D.C.: Brookings Institution, 1981), 81ff. Another good discussion is Daniel J. B. Mitchell, *Unions, Wages, and Inflation* (Washington, D.C.: Brookings, 1980).

FIGURE 20–6 Supply and demand adjustment in the long run

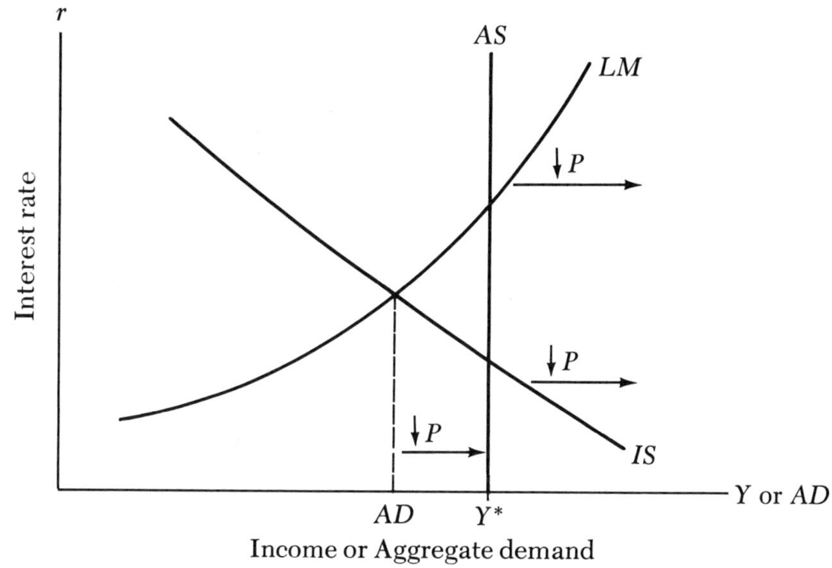

If demand equilibrium at *AD* is less than equilibrium supply at $Y°$, price levels fall. Since nominal wages fall as well and real wages are constant, aggregate supply does not change. Lower prices shift both the *IS* and *LM* curves to the right, however, until *AD* coincides with $Y°$.

families. Employees also do not want to forfeit accumulated pension entitlements.

Employers therefore do not slash wages in career-labor markets whenever there is an increase in unemployment, and career workers do not leave en masse whenever their wage rate does not keep up with the latest increase in the Consumer Price Index. Career wages are cut only when survival of the firm is at stake — that is, when both employers and employees would otherwise lose their long-standing relationship. On the other hand, wages will still rise when there is strong demand for labor in any market. Workers prefer to stay with their current employer, other things equal, but if the price is right they will move. Furthermore, the workers who stay will expect the employer to come close to matching wages paid elsewhere, just as a matter of equity; if workers are to be loyal and generate profits for shareholders, the shareholders are to reciprocate with "fair" wage levels.[5]

[5]The importance of equity in wage setting is most easily seen in management and clerical salary determination, where outside compensation specialists such as McKinsey and Co. are often brought in precisely to tell employers what the prevailing salary levels are for particular jobs.

The other category of labor besides career labor is casual labor. Casual labor is usually unskilled and easily replaceable and has a high turnover rate. Neither employer nor employee has a commitment to the job, so wages do tend to respond to unemployment. Even here, though, legal minimum-wage floors set limits to wage cuts and give rise to excess supply disequilibria in casual-labor markets when demand falls off.

The average wage, which reflects both casual and career wages, will therefore fall with higher unemployment to the extent that casual wages fall.

The labor market cannot generally be in equilibrium in the short run if wage levels are sticky downward. Disequilibrium will be the rule. Generally there will be excess supply of labor at prevailing wage rates, since wages are sticky downward but not upward. Those parts of the labor market with strong demand growth will therefore have wage increases that generally balance supply and demand. Parts of the labor market with particularly weak demand will have high unemployment levels but no wage decreases. (As this is written, the unemployment level among field geologists is reported to be about 50 percent, but the wage levels for those employed has not fallen much behind relative to wage levels elsewhere.) The other sectors of the labor market with only normal excess supply will tend to have an upward wage drift to match the wages of the sectors in strong demand, so the average wage level will tend to be above the market-clearing level.

Figure 20–7 illustrates the typical disequilibrium labor-market situation. It is clear from the figure that an increase in demand for labor (because of higher output prices or, more likely, because of higher expected sales volume per worker) will now cause increased employment of labor. Increased employment of labor implies increased output level, so the aggregate supply curve is not vertical as in the long run.

How steep the aggregate supply curve is depends on how much nominal wages increase as employers increase their demand for labor. In general, any increase in aggregate demand will not be evenly spread across all sectors but will cause shortages in particular labor markets. Engineers, construction workers, computer specialists, or some such group of workers is sure to become relatively scarce. Wage levels for these groups will be increased by a surge of aggregate demand, even if the typical labor market still has some slack. The average wage level will therefore increase as aggegate demand rises. Further, the number of labor-market sectors that are tight will increase as the level of demand rises, so the average wage will rise by more, the larger the increase in aggregate demand. In the few casual-labor markets, wages come closer to equilibrium and will therefore rise and fall with demand like any market-clearing price. Figure 20–8 shows the short-run aggregate supply curve that is implied in an economy with both fix-wage and flex-wage labor markets.

We can turn the aggregate supply curve around and present it in a different way that will help later on. The wage level in labor markets rises

FIGURE 20–7 Keynesian short-run labor markets

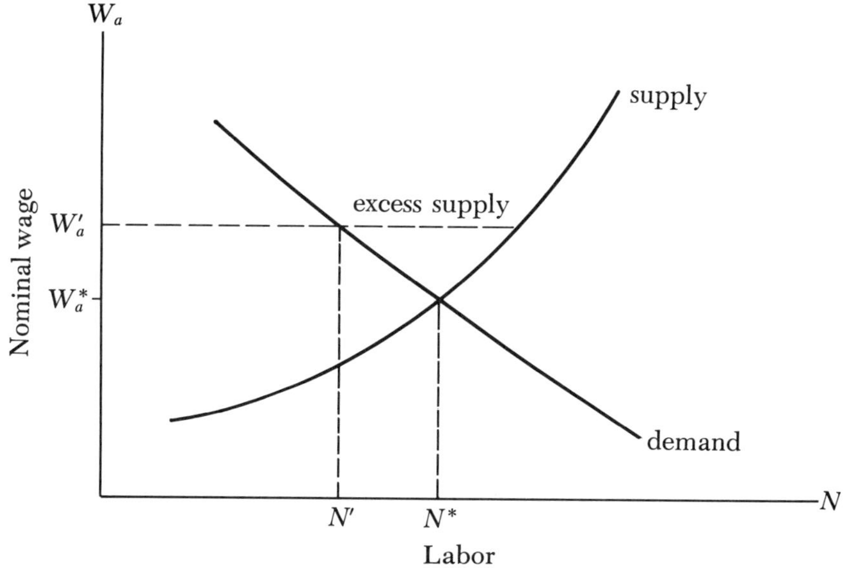

The nominal wage is at W'_a, which is above the equilibrium nominal wage W°_a. As a result, employment is at N', below the equilibrium level N°, and there is excess supply of labor (unemployment). Wages do not fall, because the nominal wage W'_a is sticky downward. The level of employment will change with shifts in the demand curve.

and pushes up prices as aggregate demand for output increases, because extra output employs more and more of the excess supply of labor in each labor market. The total unemployment rate of the economy is a rough proxy for the level of excess labor supply, so we can regard the aggregate supply curve in figure 20–8 as reflecting essentially a relationship between the price level and the level of unemployment. Alternatively, we could measure the level of output in figure 20–8 as a fraction of full capacity output (Y/Y_c) and describe aggregate supply as relating the price level to the rate of capacity use Y/Y_c. Labor and capital are normally used in more or less fixed proportions in the short run, so output capacity use is a good proxy for use of labor and use of capital available to the economy.[6] Figure 20–9 illustrates both of these ways of looking at the short-run aggregate supply curve.

[6]Layoffs of capital are not as obvious as layoffs of workers when recession hits (except to firms renting out capital equipment on short-term leases), but capital layoffs are the rule rather than the exception. When firms drop to a single shift, for instance, they idle their equipment at the same time that they idle their workers. When workers are rehired, the equipment is brought back into service. The labor:capital ratio is flexible, to be sure, but mainly in the long run.

FIGURE 20–8 Short-run aggregate supply

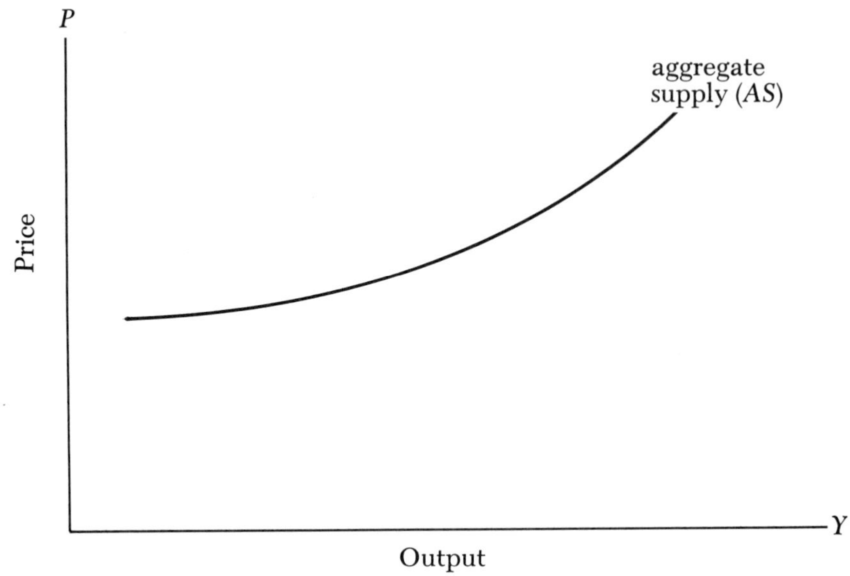

Higher output levels imply increased employment, which uses up excess supply in labor markets. As more individual labor markets become tight, more wages are driven up above "normal" levels. Prices increase to pass on those wage increases to consumers, thus preserving profit margins.

The aggregate supply curve in figure 20–8 does have one peculiar feature not normally found in supply curves in microeconomic theory. It has a ratchet mechanism that makes the slope steeper for increases in aggregate demand than for decreases in aggregate demand.[7] Adjustment of wages in career-labor markets is asymmetric: wages will rise when demand increases but will not fall again when demand for labor falls. The price of output produced by career labor will increase when aggregate demand rises but will not fall again when aggregate demand falls off and unemployment rises. Only prices of output produced by casual labor, and output sold in auction markets, will fall significantly in the short run as demand falls off.

The aggregate supply curve is therefore steeper when we move upward along it than when we move downward along it. In figure 20–10, for

[7]Richard Lipsey suggests that belief in a ratchet mechanism, an asymmetry of adjustment of prices to increases and decreases in demand, is one of the beliefs that separate monetarist from Keynesian economists. The two groups overlap so much that even this is not a hard-and-fast dividing line. "The Understanding and Control of Inflation: Is There a Crisis in Macro-economics?" *Canadian Journal of Economics*, Nov. 1981, 545–76.

FIGURE 20–9 Alternative views of aggregate supply

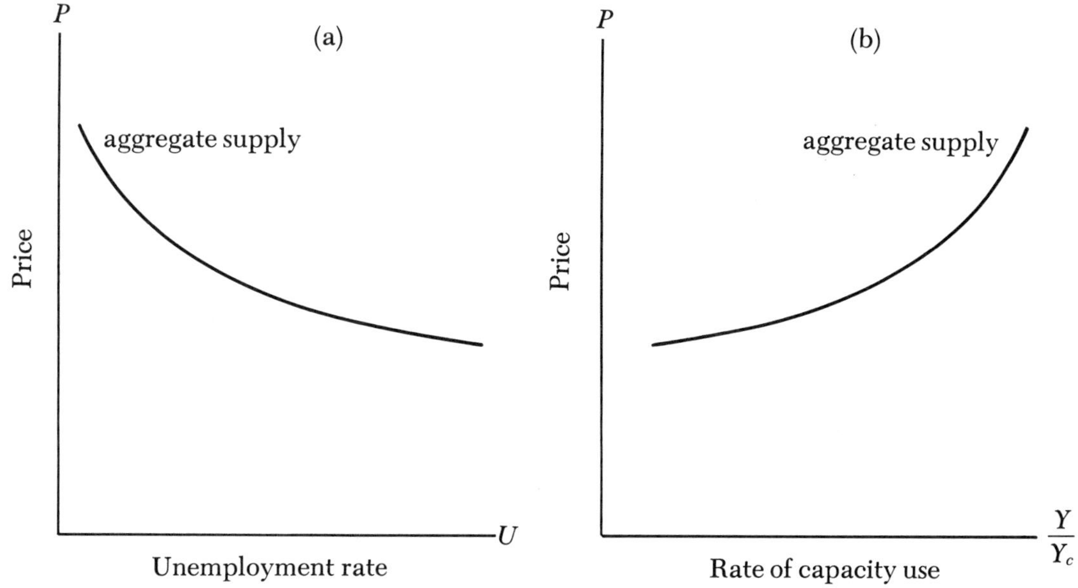

Since higher output levels are associated with lower unemployment levels and higher capacity use rates, we can replace the horizontal axis of figure 20–8 with either the unemployment rate, in panel (a), or the capacity use rate, in panel (b). These are two different ways of looking at essentially the same relationship as in figure 20–8.

instance, aggregate demand first shifts from AD to AD' and then returns to AD. The price level first increases from P to P' along the original supply curve AS, and output increases from Y to Y'. As actual output rises, the aggregate supply curve becomes flatter for all lower output levels, so that when demand falls the economy moves backward from Y' along a new supply curve AS'. The result is a new short-run equilibrium price level P'' that is higher than the original price level P, and a new equilibrium output level Y'' that is lower than the original output level Y.

To summarize short-run aggregate supply, it is less than vertical. Extra output will be made available if demand increases. The price increase necessary rises with the size of the demand increase and will be larger with higher starting rates of capacity use. The supply curve will depend on such supply-side factors as the level of technology, the size and composition of the population, the education level of the labor force, and availability of other inputs besides labor.

FIGURE 20–10 The ratchet mechanism in aggregate supply

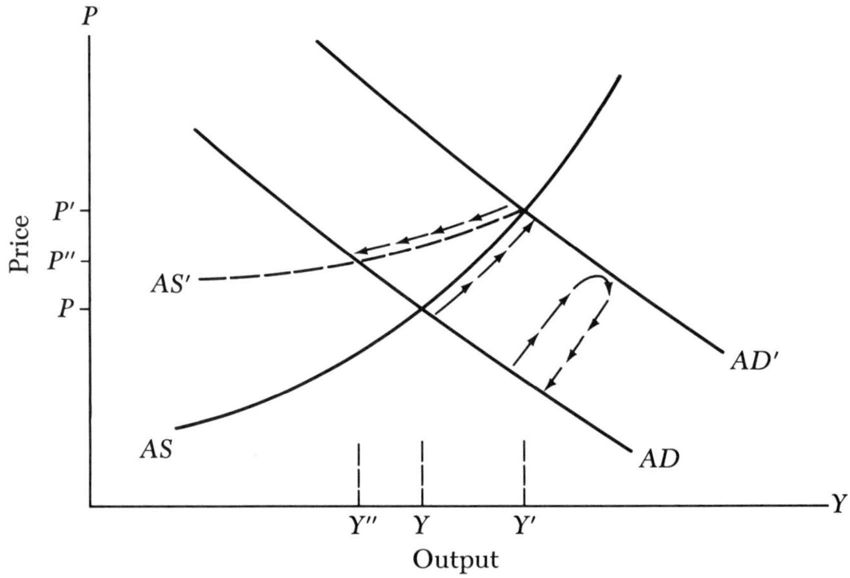

Aggregate demand shifts first from *AD* to *AD′* and later back again to *AD*. The economy first moves from *P* and *Y* to *P′* and *Y′* when demand increases, along *AS*. When demand falls again, wages are sticky downward in career-labor markets, so the economy moves along a flatter supply curve *AS′* and ends up back on *AD* at *P″* and *Y″*. The final price level is higher than at the start, and the output level is lower.

SECTION 2

Aggregate supply in motion: the Phillips curve

It is possible — even easy — to adapt the short-run and long-run analyses of the preceding section to a world where prices and wages are on the move.[8] Wages and prices are not static but rather are expected to rise continually over time. This adaptation makes the entire supply and demand apparatus much more readily applicable to the real world, so the effort is well spent. We will start with the short run, since that is the analysis that is fresher in our memory.

[8]Richard Lipsey suggests that Phillips himself saw the Phillips-curve explanation this way. Lipsey, "Understanding and Control of Inflation," 556.

The short run

In the short run, workers care most about relative wages, about not falling behind other unions, companies, or regions. That concern implies that wage increases in any one union or firm will have to be comparable to wage increases in other unions or firms or regions, or else workers will cut back on labor supply (they will strike, or try to move to where wage levels are getting ahead). When their particular kind of labor skill is in hot demand, workers will want above-average wage increases. When their type of labor skill is in excess supply, however, career workers will expect employers not to take advantage of their weakness by offering much less than the going rate of wage increase. Some employers will slash wage increases, but if the company's survival is not at stake to justify the cuts, labor turnover will rise and retraining costs will rise by more than the wage cuts would have saved. Only in industries using casual labor (unskilled, easily replaced labor) will such a "flex-wage" strategy be worthwhile.

In other words, the rate of wage increase will be sticky downward, for exactly the same reasons that we earlier suggested make the wage level sticky downward. We have simply applied to the rate of change in wages the reasoning we used to explain the wage level.

The rate of wage increase will rise as the level of unemployment falls, for the same reason that the wage level rose in section 1. More labor markets become tight as aggregate demand increases, so more workers demand and get above-average wage increases. The other sectors try to keep up, and the average wage increase rises. This relationship is well known in macroeconomics as the Phillips curve, after the British economist A. W. Phillips, who drew the first curve through a scatter of points depicting unemployment rates and wage increases in Britain from 1861 to 1957.[9] A typical Phillips curve is shown in figure 20–11. A general equation for the Phillips curve is

$$\frac{dW_a}{W_a} = H(U); \frac{dH}{dU} < 0, \qquad (2)$$

where U is unemployment, and $H(U)$ is a functional relationship illustrated in figure 20–11. Figure 20–11 is very similar to the static aggregate supply curve in panel (a) of figure 20–9, but with the rate of wage change rather than the price level on the vertical axis. The logic behind the two is the same.

[9]A.W. Phillips, "The Relation between Unemployment and the Rate of Change of Money Wages in the United Kingdom, 1861–1957," *Economica*, Nov. 1958, 283–99. For a modern specification of this relationship in Canada, see W.C. Riddell and Philip Smith, "Expected Inflation and Wage Changes in Canada," *Canadian Journal of Economics*, Aug. 1982, 377–94.

FIGURE 20–11 The Phillips curve

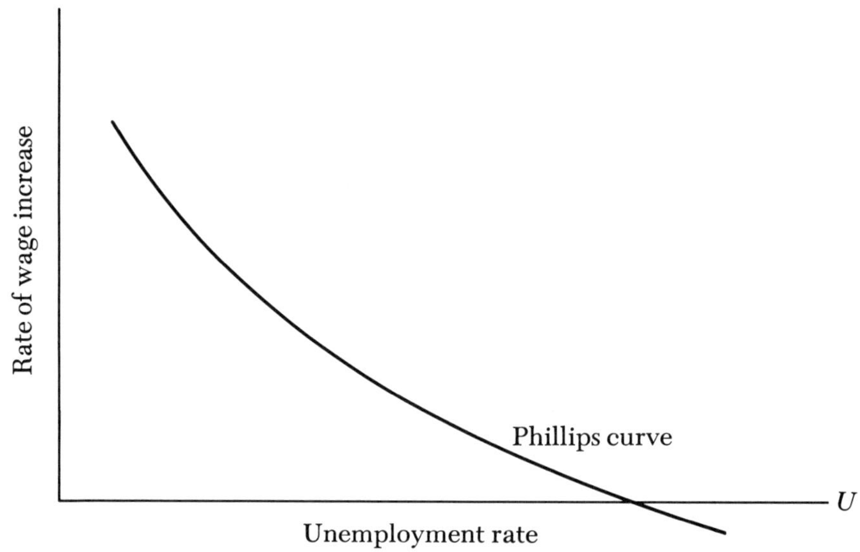

Higher unemployment rates cause fewer labor markets to be tight, so fewer workers receive above-normal wage increases. Few workers ever receive below-normal wage increases, so wage increases fall more slowly as unemployment rises. Only in casual-labor markets with unskilled, easily replaceable workers will wages ever fall (unless firms are threatened with bankruptcy).

In a world of markup pricing, higher rates of wage increase mean higher rates of price increase, though the two will generally not be equal.[10] The rate of price increase dP/P will generally be equal to the rate of increase in unit labor costs, which is the difference between the rate of nominal wage increase (dW_a/W_a) and growth in labor productivity (dt/t):

$$\frac{dP}{P} = \frac{dW_a}{W_a} - \frac{dt}{t}.$$

Substituting our explanation of the rate of wage increase from equation (2) gives

$$\frac{dP}{P} = H(U) - \frac{dt}{t}. \tag{3}$$

[10] R.G. Lipsey, "The Relation between Unemployment and the Rate of Change of Money Wages in the United Kingdom, 1862–1957: A Further Analysis," *Economica*, Feb. 1960, 1–31.

Equation (3) gives us a short-run relationship between the inflation rate and the level of unemployment. Unemployment is almost an inverse index of the rate of capacity use, so we can re-express inflation in equation (3) as depending on capacity use Y/Y_c rather than on unemployment U. That revision gives us a short-run aggregate supply curve that relates inflation to the rate of change of technology, dt/t, and to the rate of capacity use Y/Y_c:

$$\frac{dP}{P} = H'\left(\frac{Y}{Y_c}\right) - \frac{dt}{t}; \frac{dH'}{d(Y/Y_c)} > 0. \tag{4}$$

The aggregate supply curve in equation (4) is derived from equation (3) in the manner shown in figure 20–12. Panel (a) shows the relationship in equation (3), with unemployment on the vertical axis. Panel (b) shows the inverse relationship between capacity use and unemployment — a relationship known as Okun's Law. This relationship serves to convert unemployment into equivalent levels of capacity use. Panel (c) then connects the inflation levels from panel (a) — bent 90 degrees by the 45-degree line in panel (d) — to those equivalent capacity use levels. The aggregate supply curve in panel (c) is the same as equation (4).

The short-run aggregate supply curve in panel (c) of figure 20–12 will shift upward whenever the rate of technological change slows down and whenever the rate of wage change increases at any given level of unemployment. An increase in the markup of prices over labor costs will also increase the price level, but only once, at the time of the markup increase.[11] One source of higher markups is extra monopoly power in the hands of producers; others, less Machiavellian but more relevant to this book, are higher nominal interest-rate charges on borrowed funds and higher extraction costs for basic raw materials.

We noted in section 1 that because of asymmetry in wage adjustment there is a ratchet mechanism at work in the aggregate supply relationship. The same is true when we discuss rates of price change instead of price levels. An increase in aggregate demand will raise capacity use and inflation in the short run, but the same decrease in aggregate demand will not return the economy to its original position. Instead, the reduction in demand will lower inflation by less and capacity use by more. The economy would end up with more inflation and more unemployment as a result of a temporary increase in aggregate demand. This process can be illustrated with a diagram very similar to figure 20–10.

[11] Monopoly power is often alleged to be the cause of inflation. Monopoly power, if exercised, increases the markup over unit labor costs at the time it is exercised (it was exercised by OPEC, for instance, in 1973–74 and again in 1979–80). The increased margin increases prices once, and after that just keeps them higher. Inflation is therefore affected once only, at the time the extra monopoly power is exercised. In figure 20–12, the aggregate supply curve is shifted upward, but only for one period. After that it will shift back down again to its original position if all other things remain equal (a big if).

FIGURE 20–12 Derivation of a relationship between inflation and capacity use

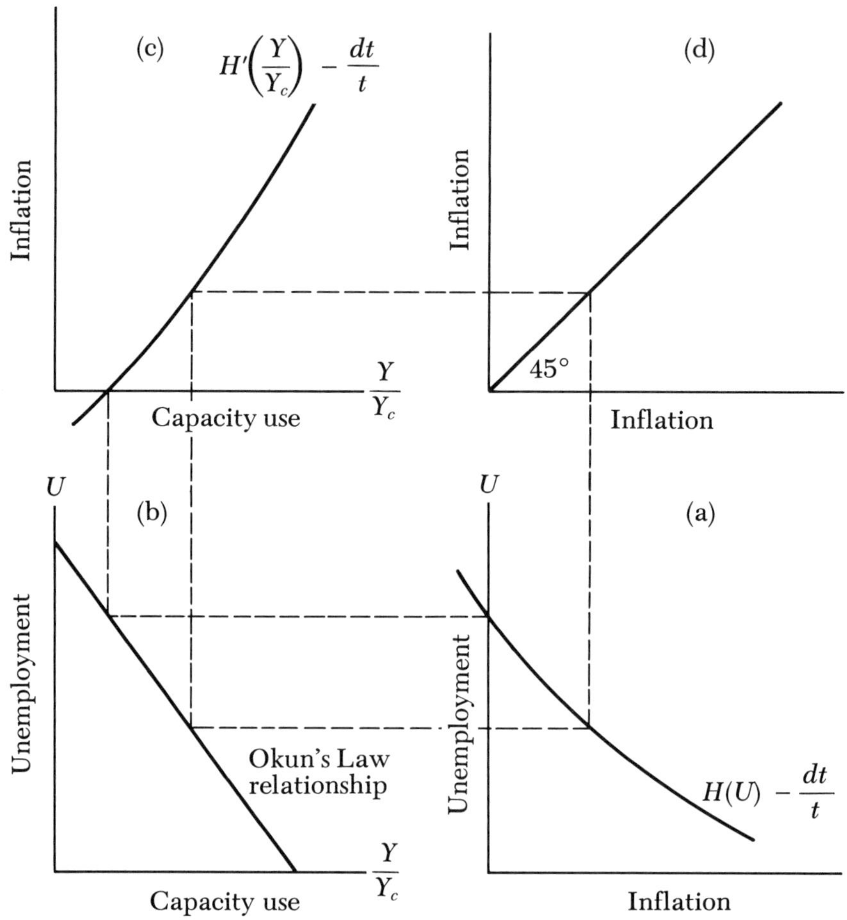

Panel (a) shows the short-run Phillips-curve relationship. Panel (b) shows the "Okun's Law" relationship between unemployment and capacity use. Panel (c) relates the capacity use associated with each unemployment rate to the inflation rate also associated with it — from panel (a) via the 45-degree line in panel (d).

The long run

Phillips' relation between unemployment and inflation was designed to explain only the short run. Keynes in particular felt that the long run was irrelevant, only partly because, as he put it, "in the long run we are all dead." A more cogent reason is that a series of short runs do not necessarily lead to a long-run equilibrium solution. However, the long-run solution does shed some light on the range of short-run solutions that are likely. We will therefore look at what sort of inflation rate and supply response would be likely if the world were allowed to adjust to a demand increase undisturbed for an eon or two.

In the long run, any rate of wage increase different from the rate of price increase implies a continually changing real wage. If increases in real wages were not offset by improvements in labor productivity, then the level of unit labor costs would rise continually in real terms. Demand for labor would gradually fall to zero, so nominal wages would be forced down relative to prices until real unit labor cost levels were constant again. If growth of labor productivity were greater than the rate of growth of real wages, then the level of unit labor costs would have to fall continually. Demand for labor would then grow continually, driving nominal wages up relative to prices until the excess demand for labor was removed. In a long-run equilibrium, therefore, the rate of growth of real wages must equal the rate of growth of labor productivity.

If productivity growth is constant, which we assume here for simplicity, then real wage growth must be constant as well. That implies that any extra growth of prices must be exactly offset by extra growth of wages and that there will be no change in growth of real wages and no change in demand for labor. With no change in demand for labor, there can be no change in output, and the aggregate supply level must be insensitive to the rate of inflation in the long run. The long-run aggregate supply curve will therefore be vertical as in figure 20–13. The level of output at which the supply curve is vertical will increase over time with technological change and growth of the labor force, but the rate of capacity use and the rate of unemployment will not change. The level of output Y^* in figure 20–13 is known as the *natural rate of output*, and the level of unemployment and capacity use associated with it as the *natural rates of unemployment and capacity use*. We will return to these concepts in the next chapter when we discuss the dynamics of the business cycle.

Natural rates of output, unemployment, and capacity use

In a long-run equilibrium, therefore, the level of output depends on the size of the labor force, the rate of growth of technology, and the stock of other inputs available to be used with labor. Neither capacity use nor unemployment is sensitive to the inflation rate. In short-run disequilibrium, decreases in the unemployment rate are associated with increases in inflation at increasing rates, and the return to higher unemployment rates does not return the economy to the original inflation rates associated with high unemployment.

FIGURE 20–13 Long-run aggregate supply

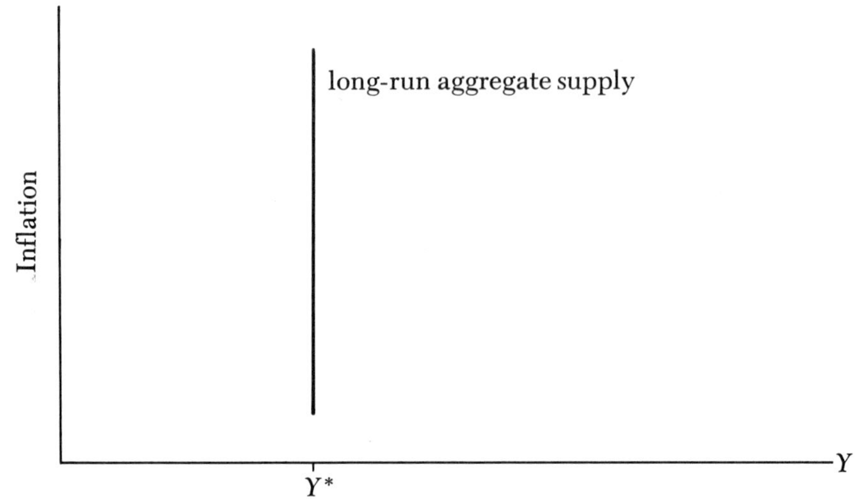

In the long run, real wage growth must equal productivity growth, or else demand for labor will be continually growing or falling. Real wage growth is unaffected by the rate of inflation, since nominal wage growth will adjust equally whenever price inflation changes. With constant real wage growth, the employment level is fixed and the output level is determined by the employment level at Y^*, called the natural rate of output.

Evidence in Canada, 1954–83

It is always risky to jump from incomplete models to the real world, since there are factors at work in the real world that have not yet appeared in the model, but the experience of Canada since 1954 tends to confirm both the long-run and short-run predictions of our aggregate supply models. Figure 20–14 shows the combinations of unemployment (of prime-age males) and inflation (of the Consumer Price Index excluding food) that we have had in Canada since 1954, with successive years connected. There have been disturbances in individual years because of supply disturbances (good and bad weather, strikes, OPEC collusion on oil prices, tax changes, and the like), so at this point we are interested only in broad impressions.

The average unemployment rate has not fallen for prime-age males over the last thirty years, despite a commitment by the federal government to high employment. Instead there has been an upward drift in unemployment rates, most of which is apparently accounted for by increases in unemployment-insurance benefits relative to average wages (that is, increases in the reward to leisure and job search relative to continued

FIGURE 20-14 Unemployment and inflation, 1954–83

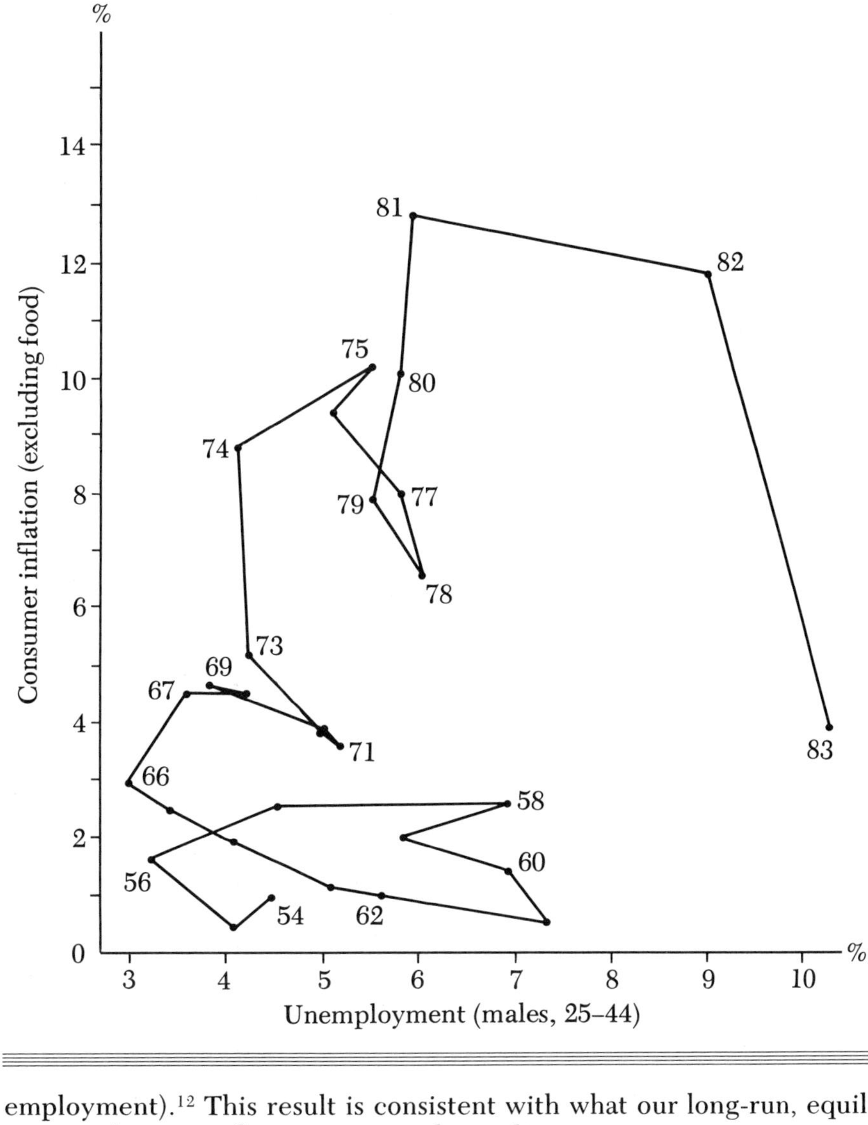

employment).[12] This result is consistent with what our long-run, equilibrium explanation of aggregate supply predicts.

[12]Frank Reid, "Unemployment and Inflation: An Assessment of Canadian Macroeconomic Policy," *Canadian Public Policy*, 1980, 283-99; Frank Reid and N. Meltz, "Causes of Shifts in the Unemployment-Vacancy Relationship: An Empirical Analysis for Canada," *Review of Economics and Statistics*, 1979, 470–75; C. Green and J.-M. Cousineau, *Unemployment in Canada: The Impact of Unemployment Insurance* (Ottawa: Economic Council of Canada, 1976); H. Grubel, D. Maki, and S. Sax, "Real and Insurance-induced Unemployment in Canada," *Canadian Journal of Economics*, 1975, 174–91.

At the same time, there have been several episodes in Canada of sustained decreases in unemployment. They have been accompanied by moderate increases in inflation, exactly as predicted by our short-run, disequilibrium explanation of aggregate supply. The years 1954 to 1956, and the years 1961 to 1966, provide good examples over significant periods of time. Furthermore, when unemployment rose again after each of these periods, the inflation rate did not drop to its original level. Both instances confirm the short-run aggregate supply model's predictions. The period since 1971 has been too confused by shifts in the supply relationship in Canada to yield such easy demonstrations, though the recovery from 1975 to 1979–80 in the United States essentially repeats the performance of 1961–66 in Canada (at a higher average level of inflation).

If the short-run results are correct, and the long-run results are correct as an average, how can the two of them be reconciled? Why is it that increases in capacity use are possible in the short run with moderate increases in inflation, but are somehow reversed in the long run? To put it differently, why is the goal of full employment achievable only in the short run? In order to answer this question, we need to look at the medium-run performance of the economy and at the dynamics of demand and supply movements over time. Those are the topics of the next chapter.

SECTION 3 Summary

In this chapter we added an explanation of aggregate supply to our explanation of aggregate demand from chapters 18 and 19. Aggregate supply does not depend significantly on what happens in financial markets, so our treatment of it was brief.

Aggregate supply reflects the supply of inputs into production, especially the supply of labor. In the long run, the supply of labor will depend on the real wage level, and changes in the price level will not have the power to influence real wages. In the long run, aggregate supply will therefore not be sensitive to the price level at all. The aggregate supply curve will be vertical.

In the short run, it is agreed that relative wages matter at least as much and probably much more than real wages. Wage agreements in unions and implicit, long-standing relationships between other workers and employers make nominal wage levels of most workers in career jobs (as opposed to casual labor) relatively insensitive to actual prices in the short run. Nominal wage levels will rise as capacity use rises (that is, as unemployment falls) but will not fall significantly as capacity use falls. Labor markets are characterized by disequilibrium and some excess supply most of the time. In the short run, therefore, aggregate supply does increase with extra demand, and with only moderate price increases.

The aggregate supply relationship can be thought of as a relationship between output levels and price and wage levels, in a static economy, or alternatively between output levels and rates of price and wage increase in a dynamic economy. In labor markets particularly, the latter is more realistic and only slightly more complicated. The logic of static aggregate supply relationships transfers fully and easily to the dynamic setting, both in the short run and in the long run, with the same conclusions: changes in output and employment do not accompany changes in inflation in the long run, but they do (asymmetrically) in the short run.

Questions for discussion

1. Give three examples each of flex-price and fix-price markets.
2. If there are increasing returns to scale, does it follow that the (static) aggregate supply curve must slope downward?
3. Neoclassical analysis suggests that aggregate demand will not be able to influence the output level unless somehow it affects technology or labor supply. Is either of these extra effects likely?
4. Which is more important to you in picking a summer job (assuming you have a choice, that is) — relative wages or real wages? Which is more important to your parent or parents in their jobs?
5. How does the Canadian evidence since 1954 support the long-run theory of aggregate supply given in this chapter?

References

Dornbusch, R., S. Fischer, and G. Sparks. *Macroeconomics*. Toronto: McGraw-Hill, 1981.

Lipsey, Richard G. "The Understanding and Control of Inflation: Is There a Crisis in Macro-economics?" *Canadian Journal of Economics*. Nov. 1981, 545–76.

Mitchell, Daniel J.B. *Unions, Wages, and Inflation*. Washington, D.C.: Brookings Institution, 1980.

Okun, Arthur. *Prices and Quantities*. Washington, D.C.: Brookings Institution, 1981. A very readable account of disequilibrium labor-market theory.

Tobin, James. "Inflation and Unemployment." *American Economic Review*. March 1972, 1–18.

Wilton, David A., and David M. Prescott. *Macroeconomics*. Don Mills, Ont.: Addison-Wesley, 1982.

CHAPTER 21

The Business Cycle

Chapters 18 to 20 have derived the aggregate demand and aggregate supply curves, which make up the basic macro model of the economy presented in chapter 17. In chapter 20 we also looked at short-run and long-run equilibria for the economy by putting the demand and supply sides together. In the context of stabilization policy, however, neither short run nor long run is particularly appropriate. Policy makers must consider more than the short-run impacts, and yet they cannot focus exclusively on the long-run effect of their policies. They must consider the medium-term effects as well — the time path of moving short-run equilibria that the economy produces on its way from the short run to the long run. In advanced industrial economies this time path is usually a cyclical one, tracing out a process known as the business cycle. It is this cycle that stabilization policy is supposed to counter.

In this chapter I use the model developed in chapters 18, 19, and 20 to explain the business cycle. Following that explanation, we can turn our attention to the stabilization policies that the government must use to counter the economy's cyclical response. In this chapter, your task is to learn:

1. why the short-run aggregate supply curve shifts beyond the short run,
2. how instability of the aggregate supply curve causes a cyclical response of both inflation and unemployment once the economy is disturbed from equilibrium, and
3. what the potential role of stabilization policy is in such an economy.

SECTION 1 Instability of aggregate supply

The short-run explanation of aggregate supply focusses on relative wages as dominating wage negotiations and producing downward wage rigidity. The long-run explanation focusses on real wages as the important variable. In the medium-run explanation we must essentially add the real wage to the short-run explanation. Edmund Phelps and Milton Friedman both added this extra ingredient to macroeconomic thinking in 1967, and it quickly became part of a mainstream macroeconomic model known (for reasons that will become apparent later) as the *accelerationist model*.[1]

Accelerationist model

The basic idea that must be added to the short-run explanation of aggregate supply is this: as lower unemployment and higher capacity use drive up the rate of wage and price increase, workers come to accept higher rates of wage and price inflation as normal and to insist upon the higher rates of wage increase even if unemployment increases. The explanation comes in two parts, each of which forms part of the truth.

The first part of the explanation is that accelerating inflation is likely to leave significant groups of workers behind in real terms: some of them are locked into three-year contracts negotiated before inflation accelerated, and therefore suffer falling real incomes for two years before they can renegotiate their contracts; others are in such excess supply at the start that they cannot keep up with inflation initially. All of these workers want to catch up with the faster inflation and if possible stay ahead of it in the future.[2] Workers are willing to take real wage cuts due to inflation for one year, but not for five years in a row. Real wages therefore do matter once we are beyond the short run.

The second part of the explanation is that wage increases are based to a large extent on what is considered a "normal" rate of wage increase in the economy. As price and wage inflation rise with strong demand, workers' and employers' conception of what is normal slowly rises too. Our expectations adjust to our reality, and what is normal is essentially what is expected.

The short-run Phillips curve and the short-run aggregate supply curve therefore gradually shift upward over time as actual wage and price inflation persist at rates faster than was normal in the recent past. Each level of capacity use is then associated with a higher rate of inflation. Figure 21–1 illustrates the effect. Similarly, a prolonged bout of low capacity use will lead to slower rates of wage and price increase, which will slowly lower the "normal" rate of wage and price inflation. Short-run aggregate supply curves will shift downward.

---

[1]Edmund S. Phelps, "Phillips Curves, Expectations of Inflation, and Optimal Unemployment over Time," *Economica*, Aug. 1967, 254–81; and Milton Friedman, "The Role of Monetary Policy," *American Economic Review*, March 1968, 7–11.

[2]D. A. Wilton, "The Wage Determination Process in Canadian Manufacturing Industries, 1962–75" (Economic Council of Canada Discussion Paper, 1977); L. N. Christofides, R. Swidinsky, and D. A. Wilton, "A Microeconometric Analysis of the Canadian Wage Determination Process (1966–75)" (Economics Dept., University of Guelph, 1978, mimeo).

FIGURE 21–1 Changes in the normal rate of inflation

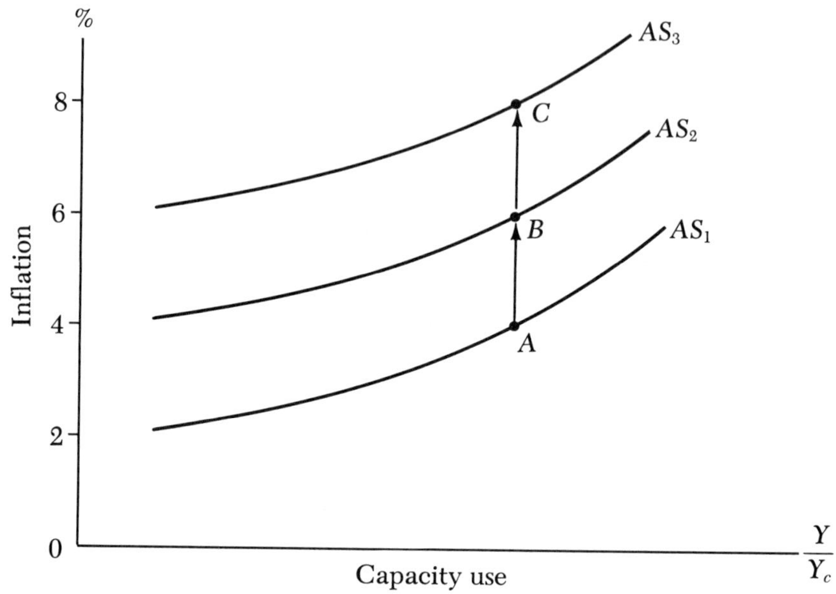

If on AS_1 capacity use stays at A so that inflation is 4 percent, when 2 percent is perceived as normal (consistent with wage inflation of 6 percent and productivity growth of 2 percent), then gradually the normal rate of inflation will come to be seen as 4 percent also. By the time that has occurred, the economy will be on AS_2, and if capacity use is still the same, actual inflation will be at 6 percent instead of 4 percent. If this process persists, the economy will move gradually to AS_3, and so on upward.

Our short-run supply curve equation must be modified to take this new factor into account. The aggregate supply curve from chapter 20 was written in a dynamic context as

$$\frac{dP}{P} = H'\left(\frac{Y}{Y_c}\right) - \frac{dt}{t},$$

where $H'(Y/Yc)$ is the Phillips-curve relationship between wage inflation and capacity use. Now we need to add to that Phillips curve the idea of normal or expected inflation. If $H'(Y/Yc)$ shifts with changes in the normal or expected future inflation rate, which is described algebraically by the function $G(dP/P)$, then the aggregate supply curve becomes

$$\frac{dP}{P} = H'\left(\frac{Y}{Y_c}\right) + G\left(\frac{dP}{P}\right) - \frac{dt}{t}. \tag{1}$$

Expectations-augmented Phillips curve

The first two terms on the right-hand side make up what is known as an *expectations-augmented Phillips curve*, so equation (1) could be described also as an expectations-augmented, short-run, aggregate supply curve. $G(dP/P)$ is based partly on past inflation as a measure of what must be caught up on, and partly on expected future inflation. Expected future inflation may also be based heavily on recent past inflation, where people form their expectations by extrapolating from the recent past. To the extent that wage inflation dW_a/W_a reflects "patterning" (setting wage increases equal to those of some other wage agreement) after those groups whose wage settlements have a cost-of-living-adjustment (*COLA*) clause, the normal rate of wage increase will reflect the current rate of inflation with no lag at all.

Cost-of-living-adjustment (COLA) clause

There is a lag between faster inflation and upward shifts of the aggregate supply curve. The shift is not immediate and may not occur at all if the faster inflation lasts for only one year. Many workers' wages are determined by three-year collective agreements, so wages cannot be adjusted to actual inflation until the agreement expires (unless the agreement has a cost-of-living adjustment that works automatically). It follows that the average rate of wage increase will respond only slowly even if new wage settlements respond immediately. New settlements will be based heavily on past settlements, however (that is, on what is considered normal), so even new settlements are unlikely to change abruptly.[3]

The accelerationist result

In the medium run, adding the concept of a movable "normal" rate of inflation that tracks behind actual inflation produces steady acceleration or deceleration of inflation whenever unemployment or capacity use deviates consistently from the natural rate. The reason is simple. As long as actual inflation is consistently above the normal rate $G(dP/P)$, the normal rate will always be adjusting toward the actual rate and in the process pushing the actual rates of both wage and price inflation upward by the same amount. This positive feedback process continues for as long as actual inflation remains ahead of the normal rate. The opposite happens if inflation is consistently below the normal level. Figure 21–2 illustrates the idea.

It follows immediately that the only stable long-run rate of unemployment or capacity use is at the natural rate. Indeed, this is true by definition, since the definition of the natural rate is the rate at which inflation will neither accelerate nor decelerate. Many economists prefer the bulky term

---

[3]For a discussion of the source of wage rigidities in the Canadian economy, see W.C. Riddell, "The Responsiveness of Wage Settlements in Canada, and Economic Policy," *Canadian Public Policy*, March 1983, 9–23. For an unflattering comparison of the Canadian and foreign economies in this respect, see C.L. Barber and John C.P. McCallum, *Controlling Inflation* (Toronto: James Lorimer, for the Canadian Institute for Economic Policy, 1982), chaps. 4 and 5.

FIGURE 21–2 The accelerationist hypothesis

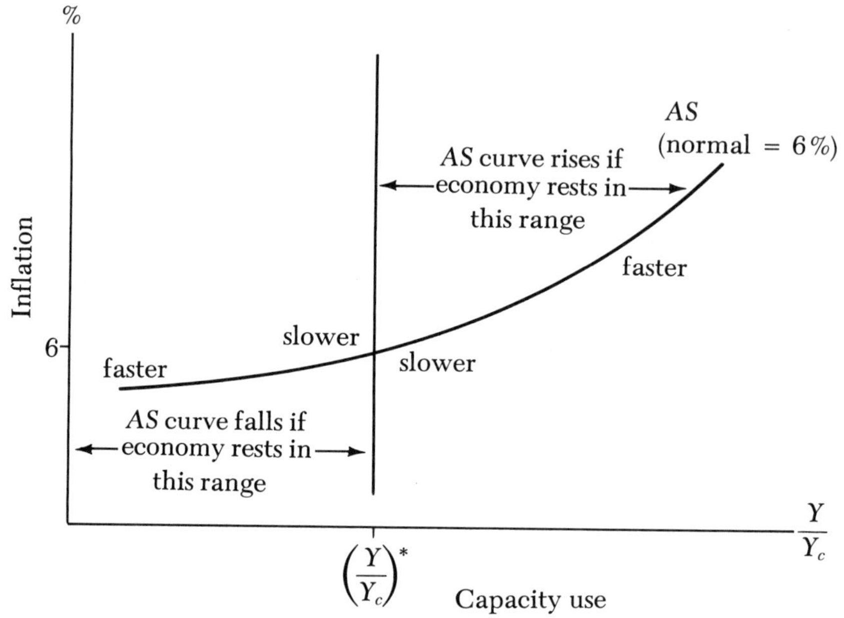

If actual inflation persists at rates above the normal rate of 6 percent in this diagram — that is, to the right of the natural rate of capacity use $(Y/Y_c)^*$ — then the *AS* curve will shift upward as the normal rate is revised upward toward the actual rate. Inflation will accelerate. If the economy rests instead on *AS* to the left of $(Y/Y_c)^*$, the normal rate of inflation will decline (slowly), and the *AS* curve will shift downward. Inflation will decelerate.

Non-accelerating inflation rate of unemployment (NAIRU)

non-accelerating inflation rate of unemployment (NAIRU) to *natural rate of unemployment* for just this reason. At capacity use rates above the natural rate, the short-run supply curve shifts continually upward. Below the natural rate, it shifts continually downward.

The rate of change of $G(dP/P)$, and therefore the rate of shift of the short-run aggregate supply curve, depends on how far actual inflation is above or below the previous normal rate, so the acceleration or deceleration of inflation is quicker as capacity use deviates further from the natural rate of capacity use. It is as though the economy were a weather balloon being sent into a hurricane: the farther out from the eye of the hurricane the economy is, the faster the economy will be moving once the hurricane's wind currents have seized it.

Also, the downward shift of aggregate supply will generally be slower for a given deviation of capacity use from normal, because decreases in capacity use have less effect on actual inflation than do increases in capacity use. In figure 21–2, therefore, the acceleration of inflation is faster typically than the deflation, and both occur faster with increasing distance of the economy from the natural rate of capacity use.[4]

SECTION 2

Aggregate demand and inflation

What happens to aggregate demand as inflation accelerates and decelerates? Accelerating inflation means that the price level gets higher and higher (faster and faster) and that it is expected to do so in the future as well. Higher price levels reduce aggregate demand by shrinking the cash reserve base R/P and driving up interest rates, by worsening the competitive position of domestic producers if the exchange rate does not adjust to compensate, and by reducing the level of real private domestic wealth. Higher expected inflation will also tighten the cash flow constraints on debtors by increasing nominal interest rates for any given real interest rate; debtors will therefore reduce their externally financed spending. We discussed all of these effects in chapters 18 and 19.

Aggregate demand therefore falls as the price level rises. To put that in a dynamic context, the level of aggregate demand will continue to shrink when inflation is positive. Even if cash reserves are growing at the same rate as prices, so that R/P is constant and real interest rates are not forced upward, the higher prices and higher nominal interest rates will still have wealth and cash flow effects that reduce aggregate demand. Inflation will therefore reduce aggregate demand once the inflation has risen close to the rate of reserve growth. If inflation raises prices faster than cash reserves are growing, R/P will continue to shrink, and real interest rates will rise continually. Aggregate demand will then continue to fall because of wealth, cash flow, and real interest-rate effects. That is, corresponding to the idea of continual acceleration of inflation when capacity use exceeds the natural rate is the idea of continual decreases in demand when inflation is significantly higher than growth of reserves.

Deceleration of inflation to a rate below the rate of growth of nominal cash reserves dR/R will cause real interest rates to fall. When the gap between inflation and cash reserve growth is large enough, increasing R/P will just offset the depressing effect of lower real net wealth and tighter cash flow constraints for debtors from inflation and nominal interest rates. Once inflation has fallen below that level, aggregate demand will start to rise, and capacity use will rise with it. This effect, like that described in the

[4]It follows that five years of high capacity use followed by five years of low capacity use will typically leave the economy at a higher rate of inflation than it started with. This outcome is the result of asymmetrical adjustment of wage inflation to unemployment. See James Tobin, "Inflation and Unemployment," *American Economic Review*, March 1972, 1–18. In our hurricane analogy in the text, the entire hurricane drifts in one direction because the wind is stronger on one side than the other.

TABLE 21–1 Inflation, real money supply, and capacity use in Canada, 1977–83

Year	Actual inflation	Recent inflation $G(DP/P)$	Short-term interest rate	Real money-supply Growth	Capacity use at year-end
1977	7.1	10.2	7.35	1.2	82.6
1978	6.5	8.3	8.59	3.5	84.0
1979	10.3	6.8	11.55	−3.0	83.6
1980	11.0	8.4	12.75	−3.5	79.5
1981	10.1	10.7	17.77	−5.6	74.5
1982	10.1	10.6	13.81	−9.4	65.5
1983	5.1	10.3	9.31	7.3	75.0

Note: "Recent inflation" is an average of inflation in the previous two years.

Source: Bank of Canada Review.

preceding paragraph, operates continually for as long as inflation stays much below the rate of cash reserve growth.

There is therefore a critical level of inflation, slightly below the rate of growth of cash reserves, at which aggregate demand and the rate of capacity use will be stable. Below that critical rate of inflation $(dP/P)^*$, capacity use will increase, and above it demand and capacity use will decrease.

The effect of inflation on aggregate demand and capacity use is easily seen in the Canadian experience of 1977–83, when the central bank pursued a policy of explicitly restricting the growth of narrow money M1 (which is a reasonable proxy for the cash reserves supporting narrow money) below the rate of inflation. Table 21–1 gives the data for these years. As time passed, short-term interest rates rose higher and higher, and eventually aggregate demand slumped. The economy was moved from high rates of capacity use to low rates of capacity use.

A counterclockwise business cycle

Adding together the behavior of demand and supply makes our earlier analogy to a hurricane even more appropriate. Figure 21–3 puts them together in a phase diagram, which shows the movements to be expected from inflation (vertically) and capacity use (horizontally) when the economy is at various points on the diagram. Inflation accelerates to the right of the natural rate of capacity use and decelerates to the left of it. Aggregate demand, and therefore capacity use, falls when inflation exceeds $(dP/P)^*$ and rises when inflation is below that rate. The actual path of the economy

FIGURE 21–3 Dynamic time path of inflation and capacity use

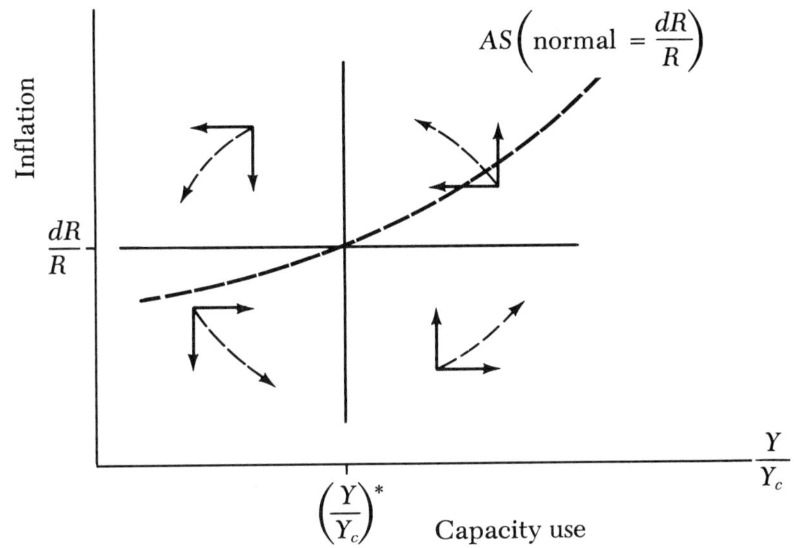

Inflation accelerates to the right of $(Y/Y_c)^*$ and decelerates (more slowly) to the left of it, because of shifts in aggregate supply. Capacity use falls when inflation exceeds dR/R and increases when inflation is below that, because of shifts of aggregate demand. The economy therefore follows a counterclockwise path in this diagram.

(a combination of inflation-rate changes and capacity rate changes) will be in a counterclockwise cycle around the economy's rest point at $Y/Yc = (Y/Yc)^*$ and $dP/P = (dP/P)^*$. Inflation and capacity use will be constant only if actual inflation is just below the rate of growth of cash reserves and if actual capacity use is at the natural rate.

The economy can easily be dislodged from the stable point in the middle of the hurricane in figure 21–3. Whenever it is dislodged, it starts to spin around in a counterclockwise cycle. The forces causing the hurricane's wind currents are changes in normal inflation (pushing inflation) and changes in real cash reserves available to the banking system (pushing capacity use). The cyclical effect does not require a particular kind of disturbance to get started; any disturbance will do.

Demand and supply shocks

The initial impact on the economy does depend on whether the disturbance is in demand or in supply. Demand disturbances affect the aggregate demand curve, whereas supply disturbances affect the aggregate supply curve and often come from changes in labor-market behavior. A positive

FIGURE 21–4 Demand and supply shocks in the short run

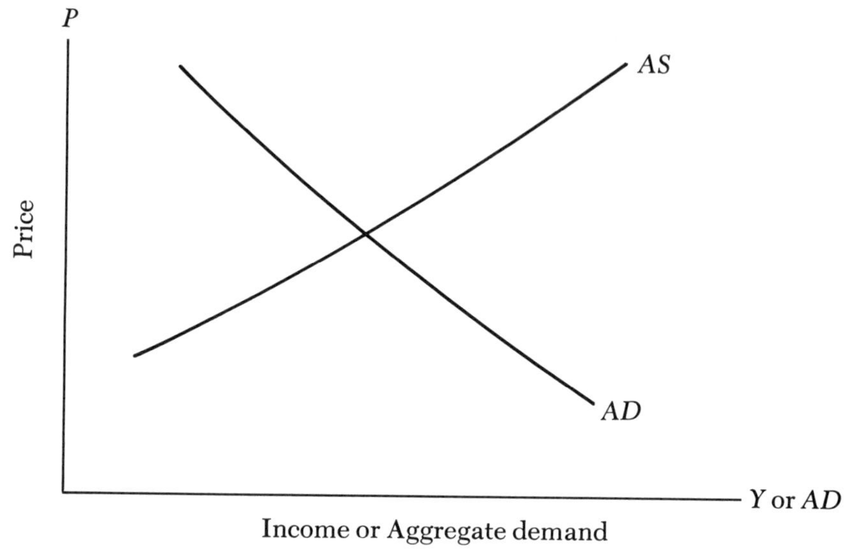

A demand shock shifts the aggregate demand curve to the right (for a positive demand shock) or to the left (for a negative demand shock). A supply shock shifts the aggregate supply curve to the right (if the shock is favorable) or to the left (if the shock is adverse). The short-run effect on *P* and *Y*, and therefore the impact effects on inflation and capacity use, can be seen from what happens to the equilibrium intersection in the figure when either curve shifts.

demand shock (a disturbance, such as higher investment spending, that shifts the aggregate demand curve in figure 21–4 to the right) will initially increase both capacity use and inflation, moving the economy along its short-run aggregate supply curve. In figure 21–5, the economy would be moved to the northeast. A negative demand shock (such as would be generated by a decrease in the rate of growth of nominal cash reserves, dR/R) would move the economy in the opposite direction, to the southwest.

An adverse supply shock (such as tighter collusion by a group of input suppliers) would shift the aggregate supply curve to the left in figure 21–4, causing a movement upward along the aggregate demand curve. Capacity use would fall and inflation would increase, because of the higher price levels that accompany higher costs. The economy would be moved to the northwest in figure 21–5. A favorable supply shock (such as a fall in business taxes) would move the economy in the opposite direction, to the southeast.

The different types of disturbance will cause the economy to be pushed into different parts of the hurricane to start with, but the currents that

FIGURE 21–5 Initial effects of demand and supply shocks

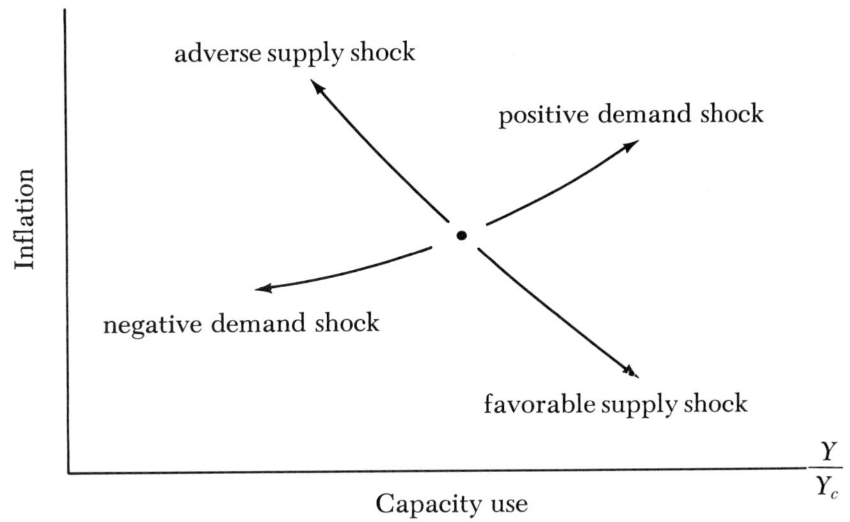

Demand shocks shift capacity use and inflation in the same direction, along the economy's short-run aggregate supply curve. Supply shocks shift capacity use and inflation in opposite directions, along the economy's aggregate demand curve. Subsequent effects are illustrated in figure 21–3.

operate thereafter, pushing the economy in a counterclockwise cycle, are the same in all parts of the storm. If an economy is already in the hurricane, engaged in a cyclical response to some past demand or supply shock, new demand and supply shocks will simply push it in the direction shown in figure 21–5. The economy's changes in capacity use and inflation between one year and the next will increase with the distance of the economy from its resting point at $(Y/Yc)^*$ and dP/P^*. Demand and supply shocks that nudge a moving economy away from that point will therefore cause wider cyclical swings, while shocks that nudge a moving economy closer to the rest point will cause smaller cyclical swings.

Combinations of demand and supply shocks will, like cross-winds, produce combination results. For instance, if an adverse supply shock such as the raw material and food shortages of 1972–74 is combined with the expansionary demand policies of the period, the result is the net of two separate impacts. According to our theory, the adverse supply shock will increase inflation and reduce capacity use, and the demand shock will increase inflation and increase capacity use. The net impact on capacity use will thus be small, and the impact on inflation large. That is exactly what happened in Canada in 1972–75.

As another example, consider the two policies followed by the government of Margaret Thatcher in the United Kingdom in 1979–81. The government practised severe monetary restraint and at the same time shifted much of the tax burden from income taxes to a form of sales tax (the value-added tax). Monetary restraint is a negative demand shock, lowering both capacity use and inflation. A shift of the tax burden into sales tax significantly increases an economy's costs because sales taxes are part of total costs whereas income taxes are not; that adverse supply shock will serve to increase inflation and also to reduce capacity use. The results of both policies at once should be a small net impact on inflation and a large decrease in capacity use (a large increase in unemployment). Those were precisely the outcomes in the United Kingdom.

Rational-expectations behavior

The length of time required for the cyclical process depicted in figure 21–3 depends partly on how fast the normal rate of inflation adjusts to actual inflation. If the adjustment of normal inflation depends heavily on people's expectations of future inflation, then the speed of the cycle will depend on how fast expectations of inflation adjust. Here is where the concept of rational expectations may make a difference.

We encountered the idea of rational expectations in chapter 14 when we discussed the efficient-markets hypothesis. There we concluded that, in forming expectations about future asset prices, participants in organized auction markets such as the stock market take into account all available information with no appreciable delay — not even of a day. If the same is true of union leaders and firms in forming expectations about future inflation of goods and labor prices, then there is reason to expect inflation to accelerate more rapidly than otherwise. At the extreme, if adjustments of expectations were the only source of lags in upward shifts of the aggregate supply curve in figure 21–1, then with rational expectations the aggregate supply curve would shift upward almost immediately following a positive demand shock; the upward shift of aggregate supply would choke off the demand stimulus almost immediately by raising prices and reducing the real cash reserve base R/P. Capacity use would hardly be affected at all. Even in the short run, the aggregate supply curve would be almost vertical.

Our explanation of wage- and price-setting behavior, however, does not suggest that the lag in adjustment of inflation depends heavily on lags in adjustment of expectations, so even an acknowledgment that expectations are formed rationally and adjusted at the speed of light still does not eliminate the business cycle. What such an admission does do is complicate stabilization policy.

SECTION 3 Some implications for stabilization policy

In the next three chapters we will discuss the use of stabilization policy to moderate the cyclical process described in this chapter. Before we plunge into discussion of the policy tools available to the government, it will be useful to stand back and look at the major policy implications that flow from our model.

1. Demand and supply shocks have long tails, like Halley's comet. Any disturbance to the economy sets off a potentially endless cycle of changes in capacity use and inflation. We do not know whether the cycle is such as to be damped quickly, though our historical experience in Canada suggests it is not. Policy changes must therefore be thought through with an eye to possible effects a long way down the road — even if the multiplier impacts of the policy change on aggregate demand are felt quite quickly. This chapter has shown that the multiplier impacts of a policy on aggregate demand are just the initial effect on the economy.
2. Domestic policies that affect demand and supply levels can be used to offset demand and supply shocks from outside the economy, as well as to cause new shocks. In other words, there are good shocks and bad shocks.
3. Government policies are themselves ingredients in the public's expectations about the future. Unpredicted changes in government policy will therefore upset the private sector's plans in some way. Unless the government is reasonably certain the surprise will be appreciated, there is a case for doing just what is expected. Alternatively, there is a case for making sure the policy is understood in advance and is not a surprise.[5]
4. The public's expectations about government policy can themselves be important to the success of that policy. For instance, many economists argued in 1982 that government policies of restraint would bring down inflation much faster than past experience would have suggested, because there would be a *credibility effect*. They reasoned that, if the public believes the government will cause and then prolong a recession long enough to wrestle inflation to the ground (crushing many innocent bystanders in the process), then the public's conception of "normal" inflation will drop abruptly, and the policy will succeed quickly. A prolonged recession will not be necessary. If the government is not believed to be that draconian, then the policy will not work quickly; the recession will be prolonged, and the policy will be painful (symmetrically, that should be called an *incredibility effect*).

Credibility effect

---

[5]The Bank of Canada's monetary policy of 1975–82 is a prime example of a policy carried out with frequent warnings to the private sector. Government budgets, by contrast, are prepared in great secrecy.

Policy impacts

The impact of particular stabilization policies can be hard to isolate, since a sensible government will use more than one policy tool at a time, but we can use two possible strategies for monetary policy to illustrate the power of stabilization policy for good or ill.

A political feedback rule for cash reserve growth

The least plausible part of the cyclical process in figure 21–3 is the assumption that the central bank will leave dR/R fixed throughout the cycle.[6] Let us consider whether that assumption is at all critical. One logical alternative is for the central bank to follow a "political" feedback rule, combatting the acceleration of inflation by lowering dR/R and combatting high unemployment with faster dR/R. This rule makes dR/R inversely related to capacity use Y/Y_c.

$$\frac{dR}{R} = a - b\left(\frac{Y}{Y_c}\right). \tag{2}$$

The lower is capacity use, the faster is cash reserve growth. The result can be seen in figure 21–6, where the critical level of inflation at which aggregate demand is stable now varies with capacity use.

$$\left(\frac{dP}{P}\right)^* = a - b\left(\frac{Y}{Y_c}\right). \tag{3}$$

The boundary separating the zone of increasing aggregate demand from the zone of decreasing aggregate demand is now tilted instead of flat. Aside from that tilt, figure 21–6 is no different from figure 21–3. The phase-diagram arrows are the same, and the economy will follow a counterclockwise path just as before. The cycles might be more or less damped than otherwise, however, depending on the specific timing of the changes in cash reserve growth. The cycle is not stopped or eliminated if cash reserve growth is not constant, but it is changed.

An accommodating policy rule

There is one kind of monetary-policy reaction that will have a dramatic effect on the cycle. That is a policy of adjusting cash reserve growth dR/R to accommodate inflation dP/P. This is the kind of policy that produces hyperinflation if other policies are such as to keep capacity use high. When capacity use is high and inflation is accelerating, it is mainly shrinkage of R/P that puts an end to the acceleration of inflation by bringing on a

---

[6]Milton Friedman has suggested for the last few decades that the central bank should in fact fix the growth of the money supply at 4 percent and leave it there, so the fixed rate of growth of R is not as unlikely as it looks at first glance. We will discuss the logic of Friedman's monetary rule in chapter 24.

FIGURE 21–6 Effect of a countercyclical monetary rule

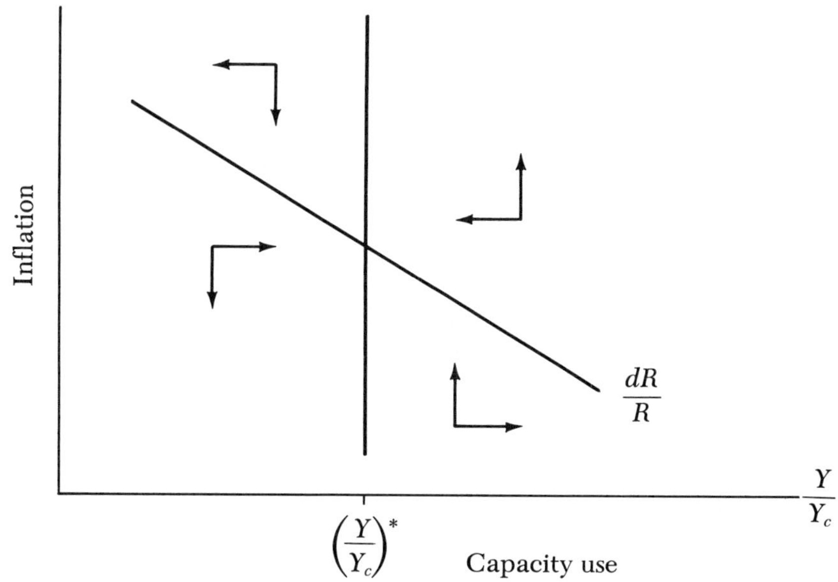

If growth of cash reserves R is lowered to counter accelerating inflation — that is, whenever Y/Y_c is to the right of $(Y/Y_c)^*$ — and raised to counter low capacity use rates, dR/R becomes a decreasing function of capacity use, and the critical line separating zones of increasing demand and capacity use from zones of decreasing demand and capacity use becomes tilted instead of flat. The economy still follows counterclockwise cycles, as the direction of the arrows suggests.

recession through higher real interest rates. When R is increased in step with P, that check does not occur. In figure 21–6, the critical rate of inflation $(dP/P)^*$ disappears: there is no longer any inflation rate above which real interest rates are forced upward. Inflation can accelerate as long as the central bank's printing press for money does not wear out.[7]

This chapter has given an idea of the economic process that is to be stabilized by government policy, particularly by policies operating through the financial system. Chapters 22 and 23 will explain what tools of stabilization policy the government can use to counteract the business

[7]In the German hyperinflation of 1922–23, the rate of growth of the money supply reached 1300 percent per month in the worst month. In Hungary, the world-record holder for its performance in 1945–46, growth of the money supply reached 1.03 million billion percent. Price inflation in the peak months was 32 400 percent in Germany and 42 million billion percent in Hungary. For further details, see Philip Cagan, "The Monetary Dynamics of Hyperinflation," in Milton Friedman, ed., *Studies in the Quantity Theory of Money* (Chicago: University of Chicago Press, 1956).

cycle, and chapter 24 will then consider at some length how the government should go about using those tools.

SECTION 5

Summary

In the medium run, which is relevant for stabilization policy, the short-run aggregate supply curve is misleading. Over time, a high level of capacity use, which initially raised inflation by only a moderate amount, will gradually produce accelerating inflation, as everybody revises upward their idea of what is a normal inflation rate. In the medium run, aggregate supply curves shift continually upward if capacity use is high and adjust continually downward if capacity use is low. The adjustment process may be slow, however, especially if inflation had been stable for a long time before that.

Since aggregate demand responds cumulatively to inflation where the inflation is greater than the growth of cash reserves, a continual acceleration or deceleration of inflation cannot last long. Acceleration of inflation will soon produce such tight financial markets that aggregate demand will be choked off; boom will turn to recession, and capacity use will fall.

The combination of aggregate supply and aggregate demand adjustment to actual inflation produces a cyclical process of adjustment of inflation and capacity use. The cyclical process can be started by any disturbance to aggregate demand or supply. Demand shocks will initially change capacity use and inflation in the same direction, while supply shocks will initially change them in opposite directions, but the subsequent cyclical response will be the same for both types.

The cyclical process can be changed in midstream by new demand or supply shocks, and usually is. The government may be a major source of such shocks, and there is reason to expect that appropriately administered demand and supply shocks could dampen the cyclical process. At the same time, the public's expectations affect the cyclical process in important ways.

Questions for discussion

1. What do you expect to happen to tuition fees next year? On what do you base your expectations?
2. Must increases in the normal inflation rate always push up actual inflation by the same amount? Why or why not?
3. What is the definition of the natural rate of inflation? How would you go about estimating it?
4. Why is the critical rate of inflation, at which capacity use neither rises nor falls, slightly below the rate of cash reserve growth?
5. What is the impact effect of a combination of favorable supply shock and positive demand shock?

References

Dornbusch, R., S. Fischer, and G. Sparks. *Macroeconomics*. Toronto: McGraw-Hill, 1981.

Lipsey, Richard G. "The Understanding and Control of Inflation: Is There a Crisis in Macro-economics?" *Canadian Journal of Economics*. Nov. 1981, 545–76.

Okun, Arthur. *Prices and Quantities*. Washington, D.C.: Brookings Institution, 1981. A very readable account of disequilibrium labor-market theory.

Tobin, James. "Inflation and Unemployment." *American Economic Review*. March 1972, 1–18.

Wilton, David A., and David M. Prescott. *Macroeconomics*. Don Mills, Ont.: Addison-Wesley, 1982.

PART SIX

Stabilization Policy in Canada

CHAPTER 22

Stabilization Policies

Chapters 18 to 21 described the macroeconomic system within which stabilization policies must work. That macroeconomic system is characterized by long, cyclical, asymmetric adjustment processes that involve swings in both unemployment and inflation once the economy is disturbed from equilibrium by either demand or supply shocks. Some demand and supply shocks are under the government's control (this entitles them to the name *policies* instead of *shocks*), and they can in principle be used to offset other demand and supply disturbances in the economy. Government stabilization policy consists of using government-induced supply and demand shocks to nudge the economy closer to a position of stable inflation and stable unemployment, which means moderating the business cycle.

Your task in this chapter is to learn:

1. the range of aggregate demand shocks that the government can induce,
2. the sorts of impact to be expected from each type of policy,
3. how the financial system affects one indicator of the government's demand-management position, the government deficit,
4. the range of supply-management tools available to governments, and
5. how incomes policies in particular would operate.

The next chapter will discuss how monetary policies work, and chapter 24 will address the question of how those policies ought to be combined to form an optimal stabilization policy.

SECTION 1 Demand-management tools

A *demand-management tool* is best described as anything the government can manipulate to shift the aggregate demand curve derived in chapter 19. This is a broad definition that probably includes some government actions not intended specifically for stabilization purposes. Demand-management actions must influence one or more of consumption, investment, government spending, and net exports — since those are all there is to aggregate demand. Chapter 18 explained what each of these categories of demand depends upon, so we need only review the list to see which of the determinants might be subject to government influence.

Government spending

Government spending on goods and services (both current and capital) is the most obvious demand-management tool. It is totally under government control. Changes in government spending on domestic goods and services have a direct and immediate dollar-for-dollar impact on *AD* (that is, they have an impact multiplier of 1.0). Government spending programs can be varied so they have different impacts in different regions — even in different constituencies. The subsequent effects of government spending on consumption and possibly on investment cannot be so specifically allocated across regions, but in Canada the impact effect accounts for about half of the total effect on demand. Being able to allocate half of the total effect between regions is a real advantage.

TABLE 22–1 Government spending and transfer payments, 1982 (percentage of GNE)

	Federal	Provincial	Municipal and hospitals	Row total
Spending				
Current goods and services	4.7	5.8	9.0	19.9
Capital goods and services (gross)	0.4	1.1	1.4	3.0
TOTAL SPENDING	5.1	6.9	10.4	22.9
Transfer payments				
To other governments	4.5	6.7	—	—
To persons	5.8	3.7	0.1	10.4
Interest on debt	3.3	1.4	0.6	5.4
Subsidies, capital assistance	2.4	0.5	—	3.0
TOTAL TRANSFERS	16.0	12.3	0.7	18.8
TOTAL CASH OUTLAYS	21.1	19.2	11.1	40.9

Source: Statistics Canada, *National Income and Expenditure Accounts.*

What is often not réalized about government spending in Canada is the extent to which it is divided among the many different governments.[1] Table 22–1 gives a breakdown of government spending by type and level for 1982. Total government spending is almost a quarter of GNP. Total cash outlays including transfer payments are over two-fifths of GNP if intergovernmental transfers are excluded, and over half of GNP if they are included. Although the federal government generates almost half of total government cash outlays, little of that is actual spending on goods and services, so the federal government accounts for only 5 percent of aggregate demand. The twelve provincial governments account for 7 percent, and the hundreds of municipal governments and hospitals account for 10 percent. In other words, federal government demand for goods is less than a quarter of total government demand, and the rest is well spread out among lower governments.

Transfer payments are much more concentrated in federal hands, but transfer payments merely reroute income flows; they are not in themselves part of aggregate demand for current output.

If each government's spending is independent of other governments' spending, then spreading around government spending powers is akin to diversifying an asset portfolio across a large number of assets: the average or total government spending is made more stable than if the spending power were more concentrated in a single central government, as in the United Kingdom. Where government spending is to be used as a stabilizing device, however, spending allocations must be flexible, able to adjust up or down when other demands move in the opposite direction. Stability of total government spending therefore could mean inflexibility and could be undesirable from the point of view of stabilization policy.

If different governments typically changed their spending in opposite directions, total government spending would be even more stable and inflexible. Over the period 1951–80, that is what tended to happen. The correlation of federal and nonfederal government spending was –0.67 — nowhere near zero. The two levels of government showed the same pattern of real spending growth on average, but the year-to-year variations were offsetting rather than reinforcing.

Consumption

Consumption spending depends on real household wealth and real personal disposable income levels in the short run. The government directly influences consumption spending by its taxes and transfers, which change real disposable income for a given level of GNP. Extra indirect taxes and

[1]This issue is discussed at length in two discussion papers by Pierre Fortin for the Economic Council of Canada, "The Comparative Size of the Federal and Provincial Budgets and Economic Stabilization" and "Provincial Involvement in Regulating the Business Cycle: Justification, Scope, and Terms"(Economic Council of Canada Discussion Papers 211 and 213, Feb. 1982).

extra depreciation allowances, for instance, reduce the share of national income in GNP, since national income is defined as GNP less depreciation and indirect taxes. Extra corporate income taxes will reduce personal disposable income to the extent that before-tax corporate profit margins are increased to cover the tax liability (that is, to the extent that the tax is passed on to customers in the form of higher prices). Reduced transfer payments to households reduce the share of personal income in national income, and extra personal income taxes reduce the share of personal disposable income in personal income.

Consumption spending responds only gradually to changes in disposable income unless the changes are immediately believed to be permanent, so income tax increases will generally produce a negative but gradual demand shock. Tax changes have the political disadvantage of not being quickly adjustable: stability of tax treatment is seen as desirable by the electorate, and elected politicians take heed. Temporary surtaxes and temporary tax concessions, being easily adjustable, are the exceptions, but they too affect aggregate demand only gradually.

The government can also influence consumption by changing the value of net private real wealth. Monetary-policy actions will change real wealth by changing interest rates and asset prices, but we are deferring discussion of monetary policy until chapter 23. Government spending will change net private real wealth by changing the outstanding government debt.[2] Remember, we defined real private wealth in chapter 18 as the net debt of government to the private sector plus the private sector's real capital assets.

There is some question about the wealth effect of government bond issues. Some economists maintain that, because households' expectations are rational, there will be no wealth effect at all. Realizing that greater current bond issues imply greater future taxes to pay the interest and repay the principal, households will not anticipate a net increase in disposable income and therefore will not increase their consumption. If this is so, the net wealth effect of government bond issues on aggregate demand might be zero.[3] The evidence seems to show, however, that the prospect of greater future tax liabilities does not offset the effect of greater future interest receipts, so the public still perceives some increase in net private wealth.[4] The impact of new government bond issues is uncertain and unreliable and therefore not to be counted on for stabilization policy.

---

[2]When there is inflation, real government debt (and real household wealth with it) will shrink over time even if there is no deficit. To keep real wealth constant, there must be an annual deficit equal to iB, where i is the inflation rate and B is the nominal value of the outstanding stock of government debt.

[3]See, for instance, Neil Bruce, "The *IS–LM* Model of Macro-economic Equilibrium and the Monetarist Controversy," *Journal of Political Economy*, 1977, 1049–62.

[4]It may be that future taxes are discounted at a higher rate than future benefits, as though payment of those taxes were less certain. More plausibly, the taxes are spread more broadly than the benefits and are therefore likely to be ignored by a larger portion of those affected.

Investment spending

Investment spending depends on relative yields and relative risks of real assets versus financial assets, and on available equity. The government can influence all three factors.

Monetary policy influences financial-asset yields and may over time have large effects on relative risks. We defer discussion of monetary policy until chapter 23.

Tax and spending policy (that is, fiscal policy) affects the level of investment demand by affecting future expected revenues from real capital assets, the current replacement cost of capital assets, and the degree of risk involved. Special government assistance for companies in trouble greatly reduces the risk of real assets (stocks) relative to bonds and deposits, for instance.

Accelerated depreciation allowances affect investment demand by allowing firms to defer corporate income tax longer and therefore to raise the expected return to equity; lower corporate income tax rates increase investment demand by increasing the after-tax return on real capital assets at each level of before-tax return.

Net exports

Net exports are determined by relative prices, incomes, and interest rates at home and abroad, by the exchange rate, by relative risks for investors, and by the level of tariff and nontariff barriers to trade and capital flows. When the exchange rate floats freely, it will find a level at which net exports have become equal to net capital outflows, so changes in net capital outflows will indirectly cause changes in net exports. Because we operate under a flexible exchange rate system, it is the determinants of net capital outflows that matter most.

Monetary policy has strong effects on net capital flows by causing changes in interest differentials between Canada and abroad. Government tax policies and foreign-investment review policies affect net foreign investment in Canadian real assets, but these are not usually policies that can be used for reliable short-run impact on aggregate demand. Over short periods, the government can influence the exchange rate directly by making purchases and sales in the foreign exchange market. The government can also use implicit or explicit exchange controls, as it did in the summer of 1981: the Minister of Finance and the Governor of the Bank of Canada asked bankers directly to curtail lending for foreign takeovers, in order to reduce capital outflows and support the falling value of the Canadian dollar.

The government can and does change net exports even in the short run by raising and lowering trade barriers for specific sectors (such as the shoe-, textile-, or beef-producing sector).

Demand-management tools: summary

To summarize this section: the government has at its disposal four kinds of demand-management tools: (1) government spending on goods and services, (2) tax and transfer policy, (3) monetary policy, and (4) exchange rate policy. These policy tools differ in the parts of aggregate demand they affect directly, in degree of adjustability, and in uncertainty and timing of effect. For stabilization policy, all of these attributes are important. We will look briefly at some of them in the next section.

SECTION 2 Multipliers, crowding out, and lags

Any reader who has not just parachuted directly into this chapter will know by now that demand shocks generated by government demand-management policy will have multiplier effects. In the *IS* model of aggregate demand in chapter 18, the multiplier is $1/(1 - b')$, where b' is the marginal propensity to consume out of GNP (rather than out of personal disposable income). By chapter 19 the multiplier had shrunk somewhat: with interest-rate and exchange-rate feedback effects added, higher aggregate demand levels push up interest rates and in the process reduce both investment demand and net exports.

In this chapter, we can include as well the feedback effects of changing price levels. We know from chapter 21 that higher price levels reduce aggregate demand by forcing interest rates up even more, and possibly by reducing net private-sector wealth as well. Multiplier effects of demand shocks will therefore be smaller in the more complete analysis of this chapter than in chapter 19.

How much will changing price levels reduce aggregate demand multipliers? The answer clearly depends on the length of time allowed. Demand shocks generate price changes by shifting the aggregate demand curve along the aggregate supply curve, as shown in figure 22–1. In the long run, the aggregate supply curve is vertical, so the price increase is enough to choke off any demand shock and leave a demand multiplier of zero. This long-run result is hardly relevant for stabilization policy, however, since the cycle of unemployment and inflation that is to be stabilized is a short- to medium-run phenomenon. In the short to medium run, the aggregate supply curve is less than vertical. For the first few years after a demand shock, the demand multiplier is still positive even though prices do rise. At some point inflation pushes interest rates up by enough that the decrease in investment and net export demand more than offsets the initial demand shock, and output levels fall below where they started; at this point, demand multipliers are negative. Eventually, the lower rates of capacity use will lower inflation to the point where real money supplies, investment spending, and net exports start to expand again; for a while, output multipliers will become positive.

FIGURE 22–1 Short- and long-run crowding out

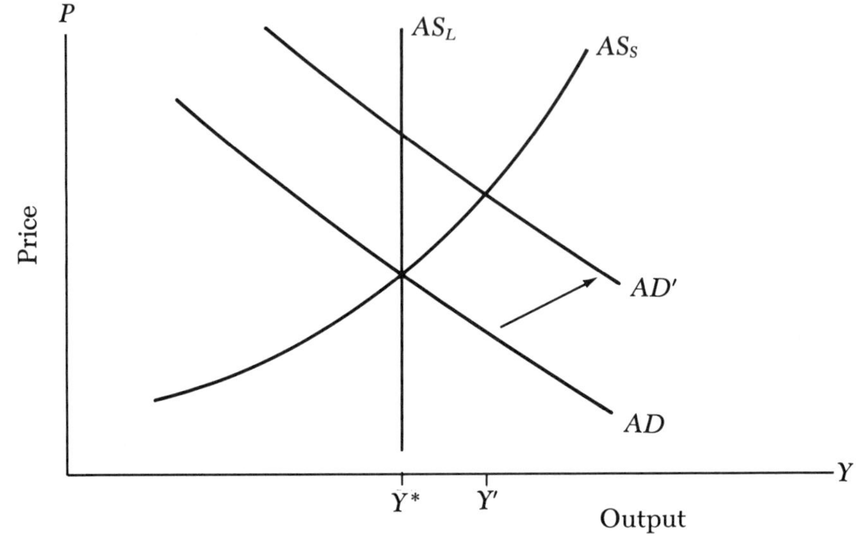

In the short run, a positive demand shock shifting the aggregate demand curve from *AD* to *AD'* will move the economy along its short-run aggregate supply curve AS_s, causing output to increase from Y° to Y'. There is some crowding out because of the price increase, since output would have increased by the full horizontal shift of the aggregate demand curve had the supply curve been horizontal. In the long run, the economy merely moves up its long-run aggregate supply curve AS_L; the price increase is sufficient to crowd out all of the demand shock.

Evidence on multipliers

As evidence of how long it takes for price feedback effects to occur, consider the results in figure 22–2. Each panel shows aggregate demand multipliers from four large econometric models of Canada, for ten years after a positive demand shock (a surge of government spending, maintained for ten years). The bottom panel shows multipliers for nominal aggregate demand. The price feedback effects increase nominal aggregate demand but decrease real aggregate demand, so whenever the real and nominal aggregate demand multipliers in figure 22–2 move in opposite directions, they do so because of higher prices.

The models whose simulations are recorded in figure 22–2 were constrained to hold the exchange rate constant (by central-bank purchases and sales of foreign exchange, which were sterilized to prevent effects on the money supply), so any price increase worsens the competitive position of domestic producers by more than if the exchange rate were allowed to compensate. On the other hand, holding the exchange rate fixed prevents any interest-rate feedback effects on net exports, so the aggregate demand multiplier before price effects is larger than with flexible exchange rates.

In figure 22–2, the nominal and real aggregate demand multipliers are roughly equal for the first two years. Nominal multipliers are higher, but

FIGURE 22–2 Real and nominal output multipliers

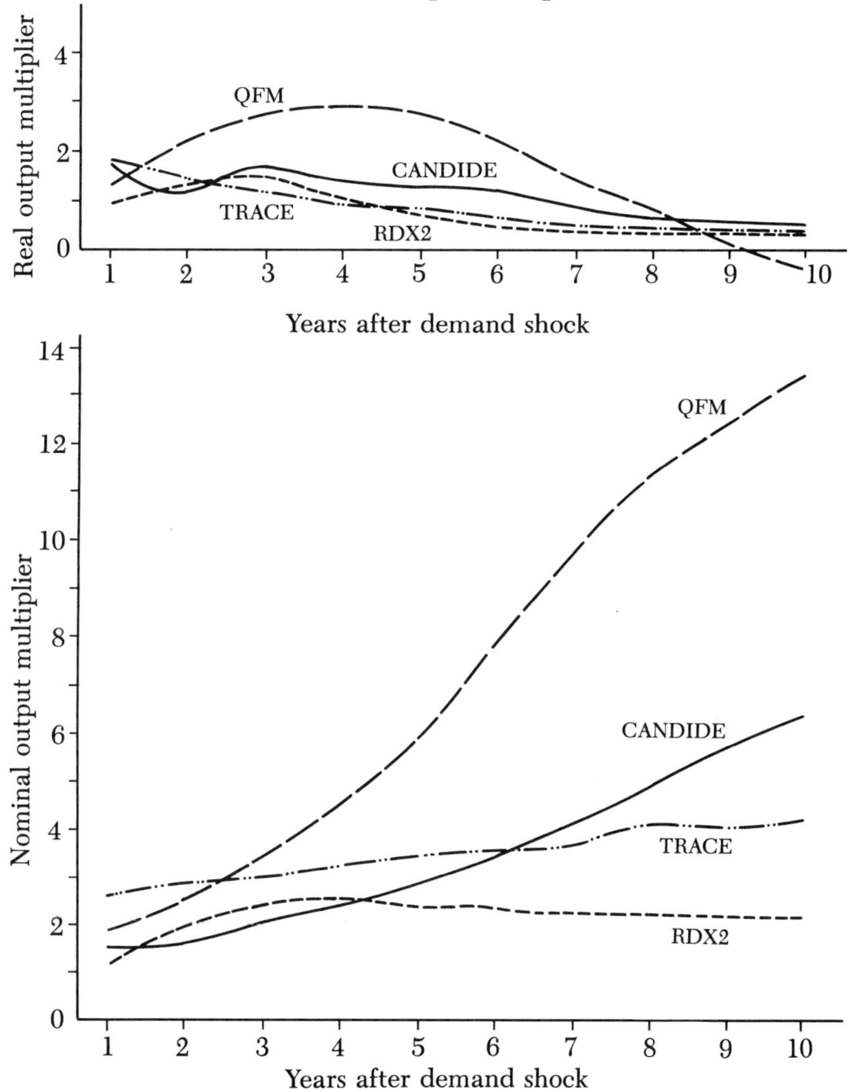

QFM is the Quarterly Forecasting Model (University of Toronto); TRACE is the Toronto Annual Canadian Econometric Model (University of Toronto); CANDIDE was developed by the Economic Council of Canada; RDX2 was developed by the Bank of Canada.

Source: John F. Helliwell et al., "Comparing the Dynamics of Canadian Macromodels," *Canadian Journal of Economics*, May 1979, 185.

not by much. By the third year, real multipliers are falling while nominal multipliers keep on rising;[5] this shows that price feedback effects are becoming important. With floating exchange rates, the reduction in real demand multipliers would be even slower.

Note that in the econometric-model simulations in figure 22–2 only one of the simulations (that of the Quarterly Forecasting Model) produces a negative real demand multiplier, and the other three converge within about seven years on what looks like a stable real output level (with continuing inflation in two of the models but a stable price level in the Bank of Canada's RDX2 model).

The multiplier patterns do not show any sign of a cyclical response to demand shocks such as we predicted in chapter 21 and such as the Canadian economy has actually followed since 1953. Part of the reason for lack of cyclical responses is that these econometric models do not have the property of a vertical long-run supply curve, which we built into our thinking in chapter 20. Part of the reason for lack of cyclical response is that the reaction of governments in the econometric models is less extreme than actual government responses since 1953. In Canada we have had repeated swings of demand stimulus and demand restraint, from monetary and fiscal policy as well as from outside shocks. Canada's performance has as a result been more cyclical than in a controlled simulation path.

The evidence for Canada, in figure 22–2, is roughly similar to that for the U.S. Fromm and Klein surveyed eleven large-scale models in the early 1970s and concluded that "most of the models here show [real GNP multipliers] reaching a peak in two or three years and then declining thereafter in fluctuating paths."[6]

These real multiplier results provide an answer to a claim, advanced by some monetarists in the eary 1970s, that any positive demand stimulus from government spending would merely crowd out private spending of roughly the same amount and have no net impact on aggregate demand by the end of one or two years.[7] The *crowding-out* mechanisms envisaged were those we have already considered (interest-rate and price-level feedback effects), and they were expected to work quickly. The evidence

Crowding out

[5]In the large-scale models whose simulation results are shown in figure 22–2, the pattern of response at the end of the first and third years is described this way: "During the first year ... the [aggregate demand] multiplier dominates the response pattern. Factor inputs, especially of fixed capital, have not adjusted fully. Wages and prices have barely begun to react. ... Interest rates have not fully adjusted, so that the dampening effect of monetary policy is as yet hardly perceptible. By the third year the wage-price interaction builds up, factor inputs adjust to their new desired levels, and the effects of financial variables [interest rates and wealth levels] become important to a degree varying from model to model on account of different lags." John F. Helliwell et al., "Comparing the Dynamics of Canadian Macromodels," *Canadian Journal of Economics*, May 1979, 182.

[6]Gary Fromm and Lawrence R. Klein, "A Comparison of Eleven Econometric Models of the United States," *American Economic Review*, May 1973, 393.

[7]This topic is surveyed in Keith Carlson and Roger W. Spencer, "Crowding Out and Its Critics," *Federal Reserve Bank of St. Louis Review*, Dec. 1975, 2–15.

suggests that the monetarist view on this point was exaggerated (perhaps *accelerated* would be a better word). There is crowding out of any demand shock in the long run, but it occurs only gradually.

Demand-management policies can be divided into groups by the directness with which they influence demand. Government spending is the most direct; transfer payments and personal tax changes are the next most direct; and changes in subsidies, depreciation allowances, and interest rates are the least direct. Directness of effect is likely to be correlated with certainty of effect — both certainty of total cumulative effect and certainty of timing. Effects operating through interest rates are likely to be the least certain, both because the impact of interest-rate changes is uncertain and because the actual impact of policy on interest rates is itself uncertain; many other things that remain equal in our models do not remain equal in real life, and we cannot foresee and allow for all of the possible changes.

SECTION 3 Deficits and the financial system

We have paid little attention so far to a basic proposition about government spending increases and tax cuts as demand-management policies: they must be financed. If spending increases or tax cuts are not financed by revenue increases of some sort, they give rise to deficits. In this section we will consider the interaction between deficits and the financial system.

There are many intricacies involved in measuring the government-sector deficit that have to do with the differences between national-income accounting and public-sector accounting. These intricacies do not concern us. The version of the public-sector budget referred to here is the national-accounts budget, which is compiled on a calendar-year basis just like the national income accounts. Only transactions that involve flows into GNE or uses of GNP are included in the national-accounts budget. Non-budgetary transactions such as loans to farmers or purchases of foreign exchange (which do not cause direct increases in aggregate demand) are excluded.

The budget deficit is always financed either by net new issues of bonds and Treasury Bills (over and above debt issues that merely refinance maturing issues of already outstanding bonds) or by running down of the government's cash balances. Neither of these actions necessarily implies an increase in the money supply, but both of them could. The federal government holds its operating account in the Bank of Canada, and as we will see in the next chapter, any use of that account to make payments serves to increase the amount of Bank of Canada deposits held by chartered banks. The federal government also holds accounts (far larger accounts) in the chartered banks, and use of those accounts has no effect on the cash reserve base; the only monetary impact of the government's running down those deposits is freeing up of cash reserves so that banks can support a larger volume of privately held deposits. The federal government actually makes its payments from the Bank of Canada account, but the Bank of Canada regularly transfers funds from the other government accounts in chartered banks to cancel out any effects of government spending on the cash reserve base.

Federal government bond issues will lead to increases in the cash reserve base if any of the bonds are bought by the Bank of Canada. Otherwise, government bond issues have almost the same impact on financial markets that corporate bond issues of the same size have; the only difference between the two is the extra wealth effect that extra government-sector debt has — an effect we considered earlier.

Factors affecting budget deficits

Budget deficits are often used as indicators of the extent to which governments are stimulating demand. The financial system has an impact of its own on budget deficits, however, so the government deficit is a poor index of government demand stimulus. This impact is from the inflation premium in nominal interest rates, caused by expected inflation.

We saw in chapter 14 that higher expected inflation leads to higher nominal interest rates, by an amount at most equal to the extra expected inflation. The inflation premium offsets loss of real value of the debt due to inflation, so that with both inflation and inflation premiums, lenders and borrowers are about as well off as with no inflation and no inflation premium. The inflation premium, however, appears in the government budget as part of current spending, and therefore the inflation premium swells the budget deficit.[8] No account is taken, anywhere in the budget, of the lower real value of the government's debt.

Because inflation is part of the economy's business cycle, the inflation premium is also part of that cycle and can be expected to rise and fall with the cycle.[9] A measure of the government deficit intended to reflect only discretionary demand stimulus would attempt to remove the inflation premium from the deficit.

There have been several attempts to estimate the inflation premium in interest payments on the public debt and to produce deficit measures with that removed.[10] Figure 22–3 shows one set of estimates produced by

---

[8]Extra interest on the public debt appears as an extra transfer payment in the government budget, since interest on the public debt is not classified as a payment for the services of capital.

[9]Since coupons on outstanding bonds do not rise (following an increase in prevailing bond yields due to extra expected inflation) until they mature and are replaced, the government's inflation premium will rise slowly and for a long time after inflation speeds up, and fall equally slowly as expected inflation subsides.

[10]The earliest was by C.L. Barber and J.C.P. McCallum, *Unemployment and Inflation: The Canadian Experience* (Toronto: James Lorimer, for the Canadian Institute for Economic Policy, 1980). Later the Department of Finance prepared its own estimates, in its annual *Economic Review*. Most recently estimates appeared in Henri-Paul Rousseau, "The Dome Syndrome: The Debt Overhanging Canadian Government and Business," *Canadian Public Policy*, March 1983, 37–52, and in Neil Bruce and Douglas Purvis, "Fiscal Policy and Recovery from the Great Recession," *Canadian Public Policy*, March 1983, 53–70.

Henri-Paul Rousseau in March 1983. The effect of inflation on budget deficits is large after 1974 and growing as (a) more and more outstanding debt is rolled over at the newer, higher interest rates and (b) the government debt grows relative to GNE.

FIGURE 22–3 Government deficits and inflation adjustments, as shares of GNP, 1962–82

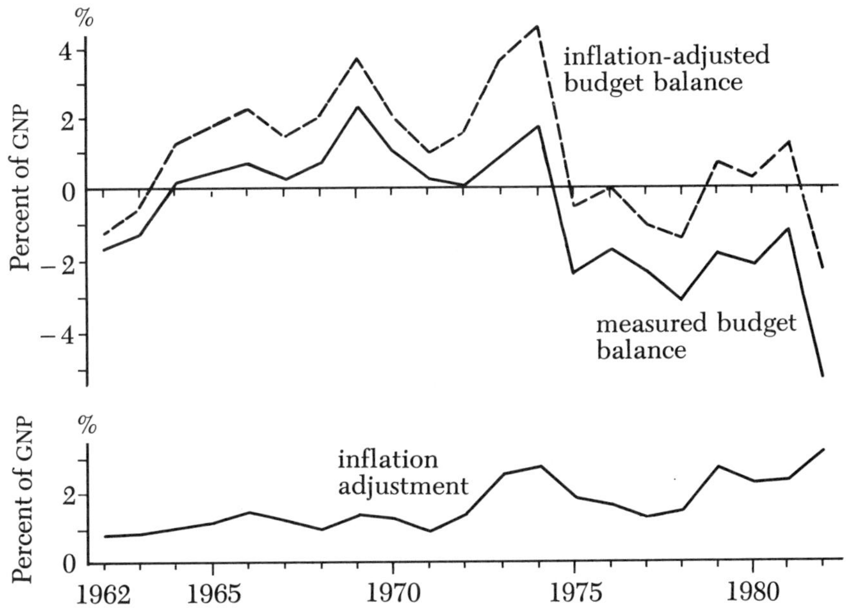

Source: Henri-Paul Rousseau, "The Dome Syndrome: The Debt Overhanging Canadian Government and Business," *Canadian Public Policy*, March 1983, 44f.

It is worth noting that the inflation premium in the recorded deficit does not by itself raise the ratio of debt to GNE. Inflation increases GNE in the same proportion that (by the inflation premium) it adds to the debt.

SECTION 4

Supply-management policies

Supply-management policy

We identified the supply side of the economy in chapter 20 as consisting of the aggregate supply curve and the markets for inputs — particularly labor. *Supply-management policies* are those designed to affect the supply side of the economy. For the purposes of stabilization policy, a supply-management tool must affect the supply side in the short run and should be adjustable rather than permanent.

The government has as large an influence over the supply side of the economy as over the demand side, but little of its influence can be used in the short run to counteract adverse supply shocks temporarily with a favorable supply shock. Government regulations for work safety, pollution abatement, crime prevention, and consumer information all affect the level of production costs, for instance, but these programs cannot be flipped on and off to suit the needs of anti-inflation policy.

Labor-supply policies

The government influences labor costs, the most important ingredient of total production costs, in many ways. The government controls the mix of formal training of the labor force through the technical schools, community colleges, and universities, thereby influencing both labor productivity and the availability of labor for particular occupations. Job-training programs and immigration policy are both used to adjust particular kinds of labor supply in the short run. Minimum-wage laws, unemployment-insurance contribution and benefit rates, and employment subsidies all influence the labor market and are adjustable (which makes them supply-management policies).

Capital-supply policies

Supply of capital inputs is affected in the medium run by all of the policies we have discussed that are designed to stimulate investment demand in the short run. Today's investment demand is tomorrow's extra supply of capital goods. The Reagan administration in the United States chose to play up the capital-supply effects of its accelerated depreciation allowance schemes, earning a reputation as a "supply-side" administration, whereas the same sorts of investment-stimulating measures taken by previous administrations were regarded as demand-management policies to create jobs.

Because of the supply impact of investment-stimulating policies, many economists regard the investment share of GNP as a useful criterion for stabilization policy: "good" policies are those that not only stabilize output and inflation but also generate high investment to leave us with more productive capacity in the future.[11] For the same reason, all long-run growth models give a key role to the investment share.

Tax policies

Indirect taxes

The government has direct impact on costs through its indirect taxes. Indirect taxes are those levied on goods and assets rather than directly on taxpayers, so *indirect taxes* are built into the prices of goods by whomever

[11]Robert E. Hall, "Stabilization Policy and Capital Formation," *American Economic Review*, May 1980, 157–63.

pays the taxes. Sales taxes, excise taxes, and property taxes are the main forms of indirect tax. All three could be used as supply-management tools. Finance Minister Chrétien reduced the manufacturer's sales tax by 3 percent in November 1978 as an exercise in supply-management policy, but the other taxes have not been used in this way.

Exchange-rate policies

Exchange rates affect the cost of imported goods and therefore represent a source of possible supply shocks. Exchange-rate policies and monetary policy generate a favorable supply shock when they cause the price of foreign currency to fall and an adverse supply shock when they cause the exchange rate to rise.

Incomes policies

Incomes policy

The most dramatic and direct supply-management policy is *incomes policy*, a special set of laws and regulations designed to modify or constrain the results of collective bargaining and price-setting behavior in the public and private sectors.

Incomes policies are designed solely as anti-inflation tools. Their impact on unemployment is only that if they do work (a matter of some dispute) it will be possible to reduce inflation with less unemployment and recession than would otherwise be needed. Recently incomes policies have been seen by many as a logical substitute for, or at least a complement to, restrictive monetary policy, so it will be worthwhile to discuss them in more detail than the other stabilization policy tools.

Readers will have noted in chapters 20 and 21 that the wage- and price-setting process in Canada has a lot of momentum or inertia — enough to prevent quick adjustment of wage inflation to excess supply of labor. Wages are set in the short run with an eye on other wages of comparable groups, and wages are often set in multi-year contracts. Many prices are set by markups over wages and other costs. Prices and wages will adjust eventually to excess supply, but eventually can be a long time coming.

Incomes policies are designed to cut through that inertia by modifying or setting aside the usual factor-market processes for determining incomes. Incomes policies come in two variants: mandatory and voluntary.

Mandatory policies: controls

Mandatory incomes policies

Mandatory incomes policies are either wage and price controls or just wage controls. These policies work by setting a maximum allowable rate of increase for wages in collective agreements or private bargains and by giving a regulator power to order roll-backs in any agreements over the set limit. If price controls are also in place, they typically call for justification of price increases in terms of cost increases in basic materials and labor, with no allowance for profit-margin increases.

The simplest form of wage and price controls is the ninety-day wage and price freeze, where the limits and procedures are simple and obvious. For longer periods there must be greater flexibility, so wages are usually tied to some predicted rate of growth of productivity, and a wage-increase limit is applied to the average wage level for the whole firm.

In the Canadian wage-and-price-control scheme introduced in October 1975 (administered by the Anti-Inflation Board [AIB] until early 1978), the ceiling rate of wage increase was initially set at 12 percent per year, way above any estimate of productivity growth, and was to be lowered by 2 percent per year.[12] The price controls of the AIB experiment operated indirectly through profit controls: firms were required to keep their profits down to a past average level, so any savings in labor costs achieved through the wage controls had to be either passed on in price reductions or else squandered in excess costs. The government had no direct control over excess costs and had to rely on competition to police that escape route.

The problems with mandatory incomes policies are few but huge. First is the problem of enforcement. Unless the controls are to be imposed on only a handful of unions and firms, a large bureaucracy is needed, and needed quickly. Furthermore, even though the controls may have widespread public support, each firm or union will have some grounds for believing that its case is different from the others and justifies special treatment. Most of these special claims must be denied, giving rise to accusations of government inequity.

Second, wage and price controls give rise to distortions in the economy. These are very small to start with but rise exponentially as the controls are left in place. Markets work in allocating resources because changes in relative prices and incomes attract and repel new workers and new firms to and from various sectors. Prices may be rigid in the short term, but they are more flexible when seen over a five-year horizon. Wage and price controls greatly reduce that flexibility of prices, and especially of incomes. Add to this distortion the more or less random effects of some firms and unions' being more successful than others in getting around the regulations by various legal and illegal strategems such as income in kind, job reclassification, deferred compensation, changes in working conditions, and kickbacks. With the market system's message system thus fouled up, it is to be expected that shortages and surpluses will begin to appear.

---

[12]For the details of the Anti-Inflation Board experiment, see Allan H. Maslove and G. Swimmer, *Wage Controls in Canada, 1975–78: A Study of Public Decision Making* (Montreal: Institute for Research on Public Policy, 1980); or Frank Reid, "Price and Wage Controls in Canada," in John C. Anderson and Morley Gunderson, eds., *Union-Management Relations in Canada* (Don Mills, Ont.: Addison-Wesley, 1982); or Reginald S. Letourneau, *The Impact of the Anti-Inflation Programme: A Framework for Analysis* (Ottawa: Conference Board in Canada, 1979). For discussion of its effects, see Frank Reid, "The Effect of Controls on the Rate of Wage Change in Canada," *Canadian Journal of Economics*, May 1979, 214–27, or D.A.L. Auld et al., "The Impact of the Anti-Inflation Board on Negotiated Wage Settlements," Canadian Journal of Economics, May 1979, 195–213.

Voluntary incomes policies

Voluntary incomes policies

Voluntary incomes policies also set guidelines for wage and sometimes price increases, but they leave to individuals' discretion whether to follow the guidelines. In the weakest form of incomes policy, the only sanction is jawboning — that is, attempted persuasion by some government official or politician. Few unions or firms are easily persuaded by government officials that they should step out of line with their peers in wages or profit margins. The official doing the jawboning is not able to give unions and firms the assurance they need that other negotiators will be following their lead, that they will not be the only union or firm to depart from the norm. It is partly a problem of trust and confidence, as intractable here as in most other situations where people must act independently but co-operatively.

To strengthen the jawboning process, the government can threaten to impose mandatory controls. With a centralized wage-bargaining setup, it is credible to the participants that their behavior might provoke government imposition of controls. In a decentralized bargaining system such as ours in Canada, it is not credible to any one union or employer that its settlement might be the straw that breaks the camel's back, so the threat of government controls will have little influence.

Tax-based incomes policy (TIP)

The alternative to jawboning is bringing closer to home the consequences of not following the guidelines. A *tax-based incomes policy*, or TIP as it is called, has been suggested as a possibility.[13] Under a TIP, either the personal or the corporate income tax is used to provide carrots and sticks to the participants in the wage-bargaining process. If it is the personal income tax, then those receiving wage increases above the guidelines are penalized with a tax surcharge; those whose increases are below the guidelines are rewarded with a tax credit. The carrots and sticks are adjusted to fit each individual's situation, though mostly through the withholding tax levied at the place of employment (a mechanism that greatly reduces the difficulties of locating individuals who have made large wage settlements). If the corporate income tax is used, then it is the firm that gets the carrots and sticks. Below-average wage settlements are rewarded with corporate tax rebates, while excessive wage increases bring tax surcharges.

In addition, the government can tie its own extensive contracting in many sectors to observance of the guidelines.

Problems of voluntary incomes policies are less serious than those of the mandatory policies, but they are still serious. First, most incomes policies would have to be nationwide to be both fair and effective, but the whole area of wage contracts is under provincial jurisdiction. Second, the Income Tax Act would have to be revised and new means found for enforcing it if we were to adopt a TIP scheme; both changes present serious administrative difficulties.

---

[13]For an enthusiastic account of the benefits of a TIP, see Ronald G. Bodkin, "The Challenge of Inflation and Unemployment in Canada during the 1980s: Would a Tax-based Incomes Policy Help?" *Canadian Public Policy*, Supplement, 1981, 204–14.

Third, there is the political problem of any TIP: the attitude of labor. Because TIP schemes are aimed squarely at labor income rather than at property income, unions feel that such schemes discriminate against union members to protect the real income of bosses. TIP schemes *must* be aimed at labor income, though, because labor income is such a large share of national income — over 75 percent in 1982 and over 70 percent since as long ago as 1965. And control over labor income yields control over much property income as well, because much of the latter is generated from product prices, which are determined by a markup over labor costs of producing those products.

It could be argued that the extra cost of monitoring all property income explicitly would be far too large for the small benefit of extra price control. But it is no less plausible to argue that incomes policies that explicitly control only wage income are biased against labor, and such a charge is politically dangerous for the government.

The function of incomes policies is to speed up the process of lowering expectations or norms for wage increases. The previous adjustment process is temporarily replaced during the incomes policies by a new one in which firms or unions are given either incentives to lower their rate of price or wage increase, or else no choice at all.

Success of the voluntary policies depends on how credible the incentives are. We have discussed the jawboning method of inducing compliance with voluntary incomes policies. Under a TIP that used the corporate income tax, participants might well conclude that no firm was going to risk souring relations with all of its employees for some benefit in the corporate income tax; the cost in worker turnover would be far greater than the tax benefits. This logic is independent of whether the employees are unionized.

For the TIP system based on the personal income tax, the benefits of moderation would at least be shared by firm and employees, satisfying some canon of fairness. Such a scheme would therefore be more believable, and purely as a result of that (a credibility effect) it might work. Participants might well revise their norms for wage increases downward faster than before.

Under mandatory wage controls, there is no question that expectations would fall as long as the controls were seen as enforceable.

Demand Management under incomes policies

If inflation is to stay down after the mandatory controls are removed, expectations or norms for nominal wage increases must stay low after controls are removed. Let us take it as given that the mandatory controls must be removed at some point within six years after their introduction, though a TIP scheme could be kept on longer. Under both mandatory and voluntary incomes policies, rational expectations of inflation or of wage increases will not stay low after the end of the controls period if there is evidence that demand will be excessive, or if there are shortages to be eliminated. Under mandatory controls, of course, there are sure to be some shortages to be eliminated after the controls are removed, so there is bound to be upward pressure on some prices and wages. The higher the average rate of capacity use during the controls period, the greater the number of these sectors and the larger the shortages.

The implication is that policy makers are not free to raise the rate of capacity use far, if at all, during a period of wage controls, if they do not want inflation to erupt again as soon as the controls are lifted. Incomes policies are a supplement to other supply-management policies and to demand-management policies, not a replacement for them. The benefit from incomes policies is merely that they speed up the downward phase of the counterclockwise cycle explained in chapter 21, thereby allowing the economy to spend a shorter time in the purgatory of low capacity use but falling inflation. Purgatory can be shortened, but not bypassed.

SECTION 5 Summary

This chapter has briefly surveyed the policy levers, other than monetary policy, available to governments to manipulate the economy. The policies divide naturally into (a) demand-management tools, which shift the aggregate demand curve, and (b) supply-management policies, which shift the aggregate supply curve.

Demand-management policy tools include monetary policy, government spending, transfers, taxes, and exchange-rate policy. There are many different types of taxes and spending, each with a particular impact on demand. Government spending in Canada is split up among many governments; a result is that federal policy changes can be and have been offset by opposite changes in provincial and local government spending.

All demand shocks have multiplier effects on output; the multiplier effects will vary with type of policy (since different policies have different types and sizes of impact effects) and with the length of time allowed for multiplier effects to occur. The longer the time horizon, the more powerful the offsetting forces set up by changes in interest rates, exchange rates, and prices. In the long run, the output multipliers will all be close to zero. The long run is probably several decades off, however, so it is the short- and medium-run multipliers that matter for policy.

Government budget deficits have an impact on the financial system and are affected in turn by the financial system. Budget deficits must be financed somehow, and some methods (running down Bank of Canada deposits or selling bonds to the Bank of Canada) will increase the cash reserve base of the banking system. The other methods (running down deposits in the chartered banks or selling bonds to the public) will not affect the cash reserve base.

The financial system affects deficits in that higher expected inflation will raise nominal bond yields and greatly swell the interest costs of large net debtors like the government sector. Actual deficits will therefore be inflated during inflationary periods.

Supply-management policies include all government incentives to labor and capital supply (such as investment incentives, job-training schemes, low income tax rates) and indirect taxes. Exchange-rate and interest-rate policy have significant supply-side impacts as well as demand impacts. The most important supply-management policy is an incomes policy.

Incomes policies serve to reduce expectations of inflation, either by legislating ceiling rates of wage increase or by providing incentives for lower rates of wage increase. The power of the incomes policy depends on its credibility. If incomes policy is to lower inflation permanently, it must be supplemented with a demand-management policy that prevents shortages; otherwise the eventual relaxation of controls will be accompanied by renewal of inflation (a "postcontrols bubble") at close to or above the old rates.

Questions for discussion

1. What is the difference between a demand shock and a demand-management policy initiative, if any?
2. Does the negative correlation of federal and nonfederal spending contribute to economic stabilization or not? Make a case for both answers.
3. Is monetary policy a demand-management or a supply-management policy?
4. Why must multiplier effects of stimulatory aggregate demand policies be negative at some point of time after the initial impact? Why does the crowding out occur?
5. Under what circumstances would a government deficit "cause" faster growth of the money supply? Why is that outcome not inevitable?
6. What is the benefit from use of incomes policies?

References

Bank of Canada. *Annual Report*. Annual.
Department of Finance. *Economic Review*. Annual.
Minister of Finance. *Budget Speech*. Occasional.

The Financial Post, the "Report on Business" in *The Globe and Mail*, and The *Financial Times* all have commentary from time to time on stabilization-policy actions of governments, especially just before and after budget speeches.

CHAPTER 23

The Tools of Monetary Policy

So far in our discussion of stabilization policy we have taken a very simplified view of monetary policy: in financial markets, the Bank of Canada controls the level of nominal cash reserve assets R. Control of R gives the Bank of Canada influence over the position of the LM curve at each price level and therefore influence over the level of aggregate demand. In fact, the arsenal of monetary-policy weapons includes more than just control of the cash reserve base, and the Bank of Canada has several different ways of controlling the reserve base. All of the Bank of Canada's stabilization tools will be described and discussed in this chapter. Chapter 24 will present the appropriate strategy for using those tools.

Your task in this chapter is to learn:

1. what powers and organization the Bank of Canada has that affect its ability to conduct monetary policy,
2. how the Bank of Canada goes about cash reserve management,
3. the logic of the Bank's intervention in the foreign exchange market,
4. the impacts of the Bank's other policy levers, and
5. the expected relationship of cash reserve changes to money-supply changes, and why that relationship is uncertain.

SECTION 1 The Bank of Canada

The organization, functions, and powers of the Bank of Canada were well stated in the Bank's own submission to the Royal Commission on Financial Management and Accountability in March 1978. This section quotes extensively from that submission and its appendix (both reprinted in the *Bank of Canada Review*, June 1978).

Organization of the Bank of Canada

The Bank of Canada was set up in 1934 by the Bank of Canada Act and has been owned entirely by the government since 1938. Each year the Governor of the Bank reports to the Minister of Finance, and each year the Bank's considerable profits (entirely from seigniorage, the printing of money) flow directly into the government's coffers.

> The responsibility for the affairs of the Bank of Canada rests with a Board of Directors composed of the Governor, the Senior Deputy Governor, and twelve directors appointed from diversified occupations for three-year terms by the Minister of Finance with the approval of the Governor-in-Council [that is, Cabinet]. The Deputy Minister of Finance is also a member of the Board but does not have the right to vote. ... No director can be a director, officer, or shareholder of a chartered bank, a bank to which the Quebec Savings Bank Act applies, or an investment dealer that acts as a primary distributor for new Government of Canada securities. The directors appoint the Governor and the Senior Deputy Governor, also with the approval of the Governor in Council, for seven-year terms during good behaviour. ... The Board normally meets seven times a year. Between its meetings an Executive Committee, composed of the Governor, the Senior Deputy Governor, two other directors and the Deputy Minister of Finance (without a vote), acts for the Board and has all the powers of the Board.
>
> The presence of the Deputy Minister of Finance on both the Board of Directors and the Executive Committee provides a formal channel of communication between the Bank of Canada and the Department of Finance. It is supplemented by many other close contacts of a less formal character.
>
> The Governor is Chairman of the Board and Chief Executive Officer of the Bank and handles the direction and control of the Bank's affairs on behalf of the Board.

These passages give the impression of a central bank run by a board of directors, much like other corporations.

> A number of factors tend, however, to focus responsibility on the Governor. ... Since other directors [other than the Governor and Senior Deputy] are expected to devote only a small part of their time to the affairs of the Bank and are not required to be expert in the field of monetary policy, it would not be reasonable to look to them to formulate monetary policy. ... In practice, the Governor and the Senior Deputy Governor, with the assistance of their senior officers, formulate and conduct monetary policy, direct the other business of the Bank, and report to the Board and Executive Committee at the regular meetings. On the basis of these reports ... the Board has the

> responsibility for satisfying itself that the Bank is being well run in all major respects or for taking initiatives to improve the situation.

The preceding passages give the impression that monetary policy is the preserve of the Governor and the Senior Deputy Governor. In almost all circumstances this is accurate. However,

> the fact that the Bank of Canada operates with a large measure of independence does not mean that the Government can be relieved of the ultimate responsibility for monetary policy. ... The [Bank of Canada] Act now provides for regular consultation between the Governor and the Minister of Finance and for a formal procedure whereby, in the event of a disagreement between the Government and the Bank which cannot be resolved, the Minister with the approval of the Governor-in-Council may issue a directive to the Bank as to the monetary policy it is to follow.[1] The directive must be in writing, in specific terms, applicable for a specified period and published forthwith. This provision of the Act makes it absolutely clear that the Government must take the ultimate responsibility for monetary policy but the Bank is in no way relieved of its responsibility so long as a directive is not in effect....
>
> Although it is not possible to foresee all of the conditions which might give rise to the issuance of a directive to the Bank, it seems most likely that one result would be the resignation of the Governor since a directive would hardly be necessary if he felt he could in good conscience carry out the policy favoured by the Government. For the independent status of the Bank to be meaningful, therefore, the Governor must be prepared at all times to insist on the policies which the Bank believes to be right and to be ready to resign in the event that he is overruled by a directive.

The net result of this special procedure for a directive to the Bank (a procedure that has never been used) has been to make the Minister of Finance very cautious about publicly expressing anything but support for the policies of the Bank. Any hint of disagreement, publicly expressed, might force the Minister into using a directive. Use of a directive would bring about the Governor's resignation and start a crisis that would do serious damage to the Minister's political career. That is a cost Ministers of Finance will incur only if completely convinced the Bank is in serious error. Under all other circumstances the Governor is free to formulate and defend his monetary policy unopposed (in public) by the Department of Finance.

---

[1]This provision was put into the Bank of Canada Act in 1967, following a misunderstanding between Governor James Coyne and the Diefenbaker government in 1960–61 over who had the final responsibility for monetary policy. The effect of the provision, paradoxically, has been to give the Governor of the Bank greater discretion than before. See J.L. Granatstein, "The Untouchables," *Saturday Night*, April 1983, for a clear and colorful account of how central bankers have interacted with governments in Canada.

Any objections the government has will be conveyed privately through the Deputy Minister's participation on the Board and Executive Committee, or through the regular consultations of the Governor with the Minister of Finance.

Internally, the Bank has several operating departments to carry out its day-to-day securities business, and several research departments to decipher the true functioning of the various parts of the economy that the Bank must attempt to influence. A large, well-qualified staff in these departments (including many of the brightest graduates of money and banking courses) generate a flood of research memoranda and regular forecasts from several large-scale econometric models of the economy. Each Monday morning all of the Bank's senior staff (Governor, Deputy Governors, Advisors, and department chiefs) assemble to review the state of the economy and discuss the current policy stance in the light of it. It is in this body of well-informed experts that monetary-policy initiatives are formulated.

Objectives and functions

The objectives of the Bank of Canada are described in the preamble to the Bank of Canada Act:

> To regulate credit and currency in the best interests of the economic life of the nation, to control and protect the external value of the national monetary unit and to mitigate by its influence fluctuations in the general level of production, trade, prices, and unemployment, so far as may be possible within the scope of monetary action, and generally to promote the economic and financial welfare of the Dominion.

The Bank of Canada also has fiscal-agency functions for the federal government. These functions are mostly irrelevant to monetary policy, except that they give the Bank extra means of influencing the financial system. Fiscal-agency functions include:

1. handling all federal government receipts and payments, as holder of the government's chequing account,
2. transferring the government's deposit funds between its chequing account (in the Bank of Canada) and its nonchequing, interest-bearing deposit accounts (in the chartered banks),
3. issuing and underwriting all government bond and Treasury Bill offerings, and
4. buying and selling foreign-currency assets in the name of the Exchange Fund Account, a fund held in the name of the Minister of Finance. (The fund was discussed in chapter 18 and will be discussed again in chapter 25.)

The Bank of Canada functions as the bank of settlement for the Canadian payments system. This means that the Bank of Canada holds deposits of all clearing members of the payments system with which net clearing balances can be settled at the end of each day.[2]

The Bank of Canada also functions as a backstop to the financial system, as lender of last resort to chartered banks and other members of the Canadian Payments Association and to federal and provincial governments. This function allows the Bank to keep default-risk levels low but does not have much relevance for stabilization policy.

TABLE 23–1 Balance sheet of the Bank of Canada, December 31, 1982

Assets	Millions of dollars	Percentage of total
Treasury Bills	2 427	12.5
Government of Canada bonds		
3 years and under	4 697	24.2
over 3 years	8 248	42.5
Advances to banks	143	0.7
Foreign-currency deposits	264	1.4
Other assets	3 644	18.8
TOTAL ASSETS	19 423	100.0
Liabilities		
Notes outstanding		
held by banks	2 228	11.5
in circulation outside banks	10 491	54.0
Canadian-dollar deposits		
due government of Canada	81	0.4
due chartered banks	4 838	24.9
due foreign central banks and international institutions	123	0.6
other	40	0.2
Foreign-currency liabilities	81	0.4
Other liabilities	1 541	7.9
TOTAL LIABILITIES	19 423	100.0

Source: Bank of Canada Review.

The Bank of Canada is a financial intermediary, although a special one charged with a range of extra service functions as the government's fiscal agent. Table 23–1 shows the composition of the Bank of Canada's balance

[2]Some smaller members of the Canadian Payments Association will have their cheque-clearing losses settled through a clearing member, rather than through the Bank of Canada. The smaller members keep their clearing balances with the clearing member instead of with the Bank of Canada.

sheet at the start of 1983. Almost all of its assets are in interest-earning debts of the federal government, acquired either through purchase in the secondary bond market or through subscription at time of issue. All of the Bank's debt is non-interest-bearing debt, so the Bank of Canada's interest spread is enormous. Profit is not in any way the goal of the central bank, but central banking has always been very profitable, even after allowing for large research departments, extensive unpaid fiscal-agent operations, and even subsidized cafeterias. In 1981, for instance, the Bank of Canada alone made more profit than all eleven domestically owned chartered banks put together.

Note in table 23–1 that foreign-currency liabilities and assets of the Bank of Canada are small, even though it is the Bank of Canada that carries out all official intervention in the foreign exchange market. About 95 percent of Canada's official foreign exchange reserves are held in the name of the Department of Finance in the Exchange Fund Account and therefore do not appear in the Bank's balance sheet. Note also that the federal government's deposit account in the Bank of Canada is very small relative to its accounts in the chartered banks. The former is shown as $81 million in table 23–1, while the latter amounted to $7818 million on the same date. The two accounts have been imbalanced in this way since at least 1961.

SECTION 2 Cash reserve management

The Bank of Canada has an effective monopoly of cash reserve assets. As you learned in chapter 11, the Bank Act specifies that chartered banks must hold a certain legal minimum amount of cash reserve assets per dollar of each type of deposit liability. By varying the total of cash reserve assets available relative to the total required by the banking system — an action known as *cash reserve management* — the Bank of Canada can influence the level of short-term interest rates and the amount of deposit liabilities that banks make available to the rest of the economy. In this section we will look at how the Bank of Canada manages the level of cash reserves of the banking system, and how banks can react.

Cash reserve management

Sources and uses of cash reserve assets

We can see how the Bank manages cash reserve assets, or the monetary base, by looking again at the Bank of Canada's balance sheet from table 23–1, reclassified more simply in table 23–2. The monetary base (MB) consists of notes in circulation (N) and chartered-bank reserves (R). The monetary base plus the other liabilities (OL) and the government's deposit (GD) make up total liabilities, which must by definition equal total assets: government bonds (B) plus advances (A) plus foreign-currency deposits (FCD) plus other assets (OA).

TABLE 23–2 A simplified Bank of Canada balance sheet

Assets (percentage of total)		Liabilities (percentage of total)	
Government bonds (*B*)	79	Notes in circulation (*N*)	54
Advances (*A*)	1	Notes in banks and bank deposits = chartered-bank reserves (*R*)	36
Foreign-currency deposits (*FCD*)	1	Government deposit (*GD*)	1
Other assets (*OA*)	19	Other liabilities (*OL*)	9
TOTAL	100	TOTAL	100

Source: Data are from *Bank of Canada Review*.

Rearranging this equation to isolate the monetary base gives

$$MB = B + A + FCD + OA - GD - OL. \quad (1)$$

Managing the monetary base is therefore equivalent to managing the items on the right-hand side of equation (1).

An alternative way of looking at cash reserve management is to focus just on bank reserves, *R*. These are by definition equal to the monetary base less notes in circulation (outside banks, that is), so we can derive a bank reserve equation from equation (1) just by subtracting *N* from each side:

$$R = B + A + FCD + OA - GD - OL - N. \quad (2)$$

Defensive operations

Dynamic operations

Management of either *R* or *MB* reduces to two types of operations, called defensive and dynamic. *Defensive operations* consist of changing the items on the right-hand sides of (1) and (2) that the Bank of Canada can control, in order to offset changes in other items it cannot control and keep *MB* and *R* unchanged. *Dynamic operations* consist of changing the items the Bank controls in order to cause changes in *MB* or *R*.

Controllable and uncontrollable items

The Bank controls its bond purchases, most of its foreign-currency deposits, its other assets, and the government deposit. The Bank does not control advances (either to money-market dealers through purchase and resale agreements, or to members of the Canadian Payments Association through outright advances) and other liabilities. The Bank does not have complete control over its foreign-currency deposits or other liabilities, because a foreign central bank might want to increase or decrease its foreign-currency deposit with the Bank of Canada, and the Bank could hardly refuse. In that situation, however, the Bank's other liabilities would change by the same amount as its foreign-currency deposits, and neither *MB* nor *R* would be affected.

On the surface, the government deposit does not look as though it is controlled by the Bank of Canada. All payments from or to the government first go into or out of the government's account in the Bank of Canada. This happens whether the payments are for current taxes and expenditures, for redemptions of maturing bonds or Treasury Bills, or for purchases of newly issued bonds. Purchases and sales of foreign exchange by the government's Exchange Fund Account also cause large flows into and out of the government's deposit account in the Bank of Canada and must be offset if they would otherwise cause inappropriate changes in the cash reserve base. However, the Bank of Canada has no trouble in keeping track of these deposit changes in its role as the government's banker. Each of them can be offset the same day simply by transfer of exactly the same amount in the opposite direction between the government deposit in the Bank of Canada and its notice deposits in the chartered banks. This is done every day.

Defensive operations

Because of variations in items on its balance sheet that it does not control, the Bank of Canada needs defensive operations. Defensive operations are needed to counter (a) changes in advances, made by dealers or banks or other members of the Canadian Payments Association, which affect both *MB* and *R*, and (b) shifts in the public's desired currency-to-deposit ratio, which change N/R and affect *R* but not *MB*. One could say that a third type of defensive operation is to counter changes in the government deposit caused by federal payments or receipts, including purchase of foreign exchange on behalf of the Exchange Fund Account.

Of these, the Bank need not be much concerned with advances. They are typically zero for banks, and not much larger for the money-market dealers; in any case they are very short-term arrangements unwound in one or two weeks.

Shifts in the public's desired currency-to-deposit ratio are only a bit more troublesome. Such shifts are partly predictable (such as around Christmas and during the summer) and partly random. The public's currency holdings are six times as large as bank holdings, so small changes in the public's holdings matter to bank reserves. Fortunately, currency in circulation outside banks does not fluctuate randomly from month to month by much more than 1 percent of total bank cash reserve holdings. Seasonal fluctuations of public currency holdings are much bigger but also much more predictable.

Dynamic operations

The Bank of Canada can change the monetary base, or reserves, by changing any of the four items it controls: government bond holdings, foreign-currency assets, other assets, and the federal government deposit.

In practice, almost all dynamic operations are done either by changes in bond holdings, via purchases and sales known as *open-market operations*, or by transfers of federal government deposits.

Open-market operations

Recall that cash reserve assets are all liabilities of the Bank of Canada, whether they are currency or Bank of Canada deposits. The first way of increasing cash reserve assets of banks is to issue more currency or more deposits. The Bank of Canada cannot just print more currency and distribute it free by helicopter. The Bank must receive something in exchange. The Bank puts extra currency or deposits into circulation by buying extra federal government bonds and Treasury Bills. Bonds are almost always bought at time of issue, not in the secondary market. Treasury Bills are bought in the weekly auction of new issues, but also during the week in the secondary Treasury Bill market. The whole set of transactions is included in the term *open-market operations*. All involve changing the term B in our equations (1) and (2).

Open-market operations

To see how open-market operations work we will follow the initial stages of an open-market purchase of \$10 million of Treasury Bills by the Bank of Canada. The purchase is from some existing holder, say a large industrial corporation that had invested a temporary cash surplus in Treasury Bills. The corporation gives up the Treasury Bills and receives in turn a draft (a cheque, basically) drawn on the Bank of Canada. The draft is immediately deposited in the corporation's bank account so that now a chartered bank is involved. The chartered bank has received a draft on the Bank of Canada, which is presented for payment to the Bank of Canada and converted to either currency or, more likely, an extra \$10 million credit in that bank's deposit with the Bank of Canada. Either conversion will increase the bank's cash reserve assets by \$10 million.

An open-market sale by the Bank of Canada works the same way but in reverse: the draft to pay for securities bought is drawn by the corporation on its chartered-bank account and given to the Bank of Canada instead of vice versa; in settlement, the chartered bank's deposit with the Bank of Canada is drawn down by the amount of the cheque.

Open-market operations change banks' cash reserve assets by the amount of the transaction. Excess reserves are changed in the same direction but not by quite so much, since open-market operations also involve a change in banks' deposits by the same amount as the change in cash reserves (and in the same direction). When banks' deposits fall, their required reserves also fall; this decrease tends to increase banks' excess reserves. As a result of the open-market purchase just described, the receiving bank's reserves and deposit liabilities both rise by \$10 million. With \$10 million more of deposit liabilities, the bank will experience an increase in required reserves of \$1 million if the deposits are all demand deposits, so that only \$9 million of the extra cash reserves will be excess reserves.

Federal deposit transfers

For several reasons, the Bank of Canada now prefers to use federal deposit transfers rather than open-market operations for changing the monetary base and bank cash reserves. *Federal deposit transfers* involve shifting part of the federal government's wealth between deposits in the Bank of Canada and deposits in the chartered banks. This transfer of deposits is no different in principle from any individual's shifting funds from one type of deposit to another. However, because one deposit is in the Bank of Canada and the other is in chartered banks, transfer of federal deposits will change total bank cash reserve assets. Transfers to federal deposit accounts in chartered banks will increase bank cash reserves; transfers to the federal deposit account in the Bank of Canada will decrease bank cash reserves. In each case cash reserves will change by the amount of the transfer.

Federal deposit transfers

An example of a federal deposit transfer will show how bank cash reserve assets are affected. Imagine that the Bank of Canada moves \$10 million from the federal deposit in the Bank of Canada to the various federal deposits in chartered banks. Each chartered bank accepts an extra deposit liability (to the federal government) and in exchange gets an equal increase in its deposit account with the Bank of Canada. The latter increase is an addition to its cash reserves — an addition that must add up to exactly \$10 million for all chartered banks together. The only changes on the Bank of Canada's balance sheet are that the deposit owing to the federal government — *GD* in equations (1) and (2) — is reduced by \$10 million and the deposits owing to the chartered banks rise by \$10 million. There is no change in the Bank of Canada's assets; there is merely a change in the pattern of the central bank's liabilities. Both *MB* and *R* rise.

Federal deposit transfers are more frequently used in Canada than open-market operations, for several reasons. First, in using federal deposit transfers the Bank of Canada does not intervene directly in any financial market to buy or sell, so it does not run the risk of causing a distortion in relative yields. Such a risk is always present for large open-market operations, since the Bank of Canada cannot spread its purchases and sales over a wide range of different assets such as commercial paper or provincial bonds. Second, federal deposit transfers cause more or less proportional cash reserve changes across all banks, discriminating against none. To the extent that some banks are regionally concentrated, diffusion of the policy's impact across all banks ensures diffusion across all regions as well. Finally, federal deposit transfers are easy, they affect bank cash reserves the next day, and their effect is certain, totally within the central bank's control. All three features are desirable.

Foreign exchange swaps

There is a limit to the size of federal deposit transfers that is possible if one of the types of deposit account is very small. Transfers out of the federal account in the Bank of Canada cannot be large if the account itself is not very large. Typically, that account has not been large; yet the Bank of Canada's main need has been to increase bank cash reserves, which calls for federal deposit transfers out of the Bank of Canada account. Foreign exchange swaps with the federal government's Exchange Fund Account (EFA) are one answer to this problem.

Foreign exchange swaps serve to boost the federal government's account in the Bank of Canada without need for extra taxes or bond issues. The Bank of Canada merely buys up some of the foreign-currency reserve assets held for the government by the Exchange Fund Account. This purchase increases *FCD* in equations (1) and (2). Normally, one would expect the EFA's Canadian-dollar account to be increased by the value of the foreign-asset sale, but the EFA holds no Canadian dollars. Instead, any Canadian funds received by the EFA are automatically repaid to the government to reduce the EFA's debt to the government (the debt that "finances" the EFA's entire holding of foreign-currency assets, in an accounting sense), so the funds received by the EFA end up increasing the government's account in the Bank of Canada — item *GD* in equations (1) and (2). Neither *MB* nor *R* is affected yet, but the purpose of the swap has been achieved: the Bank of Canada can now arrange a larger federal deposit transfer than before.

Cash reserve requirements in detail

At the start of this section we said that what the Bank aims to do with cash reserve management is change the banks' excess cash reserves in order to change their activity in the money market and thereby change short-term yields in the economy. Thus, what matters in cash reserve management is not the absolute level of cash reserves but only whether cash reserves are above or below the level the banks wish to hold. The level Canadian banks wish to hold is easy to describe: just high enough to meet the legal cash reserve requirement, and no higher. In the United States, commercial banks as a rule hold more than they are required to by law, but not in Canada. Cash reserve assets earn no interest, so chartered banks try to keep all excess cash reserves invested in interest-earning, nonreserve assets. The banks are remarkably successful at it.

Cash reserve requirements are specified in the Bank Act as various percentages of deposit liabilities outstanding. Up to February 1981 the percentages were 12 percent of Canadian-dollar demand deposits, 4 percent of all Canadian-dollar term and notice deposits, and 0 percent of all other (that is, foreign-currency) deposits. In February 1981 the percentages started changing gradually toward the new levels that will be reached in September 1985. These new requirements are 10 percent of Canadian-dollar demand deposits, 3 percent of foreign-currency deposits held by Canadian residents, 2 percent of reservable Canadian-dollar term and notice deposits, plus 1 percent more for amounts over $500 million, and 0 percent for all other deposits. *Reservable* term and notice deposits are defined to exclude all term deposits that at time of issue were not redeemable within one year of the date of issue. The effect of the new cash reserve ratios is to lower the average cash reserve requirement from $5\frac{1}{2}$ percent to under 4 percent of total reservable deposits. The ratio relative to total deposits of all types, reservable and otherwise, will fall eventually from 2.85 to 2.30 percent.

Regulations issued under authority of the Bank Act spell out exactly how cash reserve requirements are to be met. The effect of current regulations is that current required reserves are based on deposit and vault-cash measures as of roughly six weeks earlier. For instance, the statutory deposit totals to be used in calculating required cash reserves for January are the average of Wednesday deposit totals from the second half of November and the first half of December. The statutory level of vault cash to be counted toward meeting January's cash reserve requirement is to be calculated as the average of actual vault-cash holdings on those same four Wednesdays. Only holdings of Bank of Canada deposits are calculated using a current measure.

It may help to see cash reserve requirements in equation form. Ignoring the detail about the first $500 million of reservable notice and term deposits, the cash reserve requirement by September 1985 will be

$$BCD + VC^* \geqslant .10DD^* + .03FCD^* + .03TND^*, \tag{3}$$

where *BCD* is Bank of Canada deposits, *VC* is vault cash, *DD* is Canadian-dollar demand deposits, *FCD* is foreign-currency deposits of residents, *TND* is reservable Canadian-dollar term and notice deposits, and the asterisk denotes statutory (that is, lagged) measurement. Subtracting VC^* (the statutory measure of vault cash) from both sides of relation (1) gives the cash reserve constraint for *BCD*, the only cash reserve asset that banks can adjust during the current month:

$$BCD \geqslant (.10DD^* + .03FCD^* + .03TND^*) - VC^*. \tag{4}$$

Chartered banks must keep at least enough Bank of Canada deposits on hand to make up the difference between total required reserves and statutory vault cash. Both required reserves and statutory vault cash are known for each month before the month begins.

Reserve averaging periods

Reserve averaging period

The Bank Act and its regulations further specify that the Bank of Canada deposit holdings of each bank need satisfy equation (4) only on average over each of two two-week *reserve averaging periods* in the month. Bank of Canada deposits can be below the requirement on some of the days, provided that for the whole averaging period the cumulative excess holding is positive. Equation (4) is therefore better described in this way: the cumulative sum of excess cash reserve holdings over the whole averaging period must be greater than or equal to zero;

$$\sum_{t=1}^{n} [BCD - (.10DD^{*} + .03FCD^{*} + .03TND^{*} - VC^{*})] \geqslant 0, \qquad (5)$$

where n is the number of days in the averaging period (somewhere between 13 and 16, depending on the month).

Cash reserve strategies of chartered banks

Each chartered bank thus knows in advance of each month exactly what the minimum average level (or total cumulative level) of its Bank of Canada deposits must be to meet the cash reserve requirement, and each bank directs its liquid-asset management toward ensuring that the constraint is met with only the minimum to spare. Banks are always subject to unexpected daily gains and losses of Bank of Canada deposits as a normal result of cheque clearing, so Bank of Canada deposits cannot be controlled down to the penny. When the cumulative sum of daily excess cash reserve holdings rises or falls relative to the desired amount, the chartered bank normally adjusts reserve holdings by purchases or sales of money-market assets that take effect the next day. For the last day of the averaging period, next-day adjustment is not good enough; clearing losses that reduced the cumulative excess to below zero would have to be made up on the same day by expensive borrowing from the Bank of Canada. "Each bank therefore tries to accumulate over the averaging period a cushion of cumulative excess cash reserves greater than or equal to the largest random clearing loss it anticipates on the last day of the averaging period."[3]

Figure 23–1 shows what chartered banks actually did in managing their cash reserves in the first half of 1981, a period of monetary tightness and steeply rising interest rates. In the first half of each two-week averaging period the banks typically let their Bank of Canada deposits fall below the required average assets. In the second half of each period they raised Bank of Canada deposits to bring the average for the whole period just above the required minimum. Usually the means of accomplishing this was a temporary transfer of vault cash to Bank of Canada deposits.

The striking feature of figure 23–1 is how little excess cash reserves the banks do hold. The only exception is in the second half of October, when the year-end balance sheet is struck for the annual report. Then the banks hold twice as much in excess cash reserves as during the rest of the year. The reason is to avoid even the smallest chance of being forced by a last-day clearing loss to borrow from the Bank of Canada. A Bank of Canada advance would not look good on the balance sheet and might invite anxious

[3]W. R. White, *Management by the Canadian Banks of Their Domestic Portfolios, 1956–1971: An Econometric Study* (Ottawa: Bank of Canada, 1975), 124.

questions from shareholders about the quality and prudence of the management.

FIGURE 23–1 Excess cash reserves within two-week averaging periods in percent of statutory (reservable) deposits

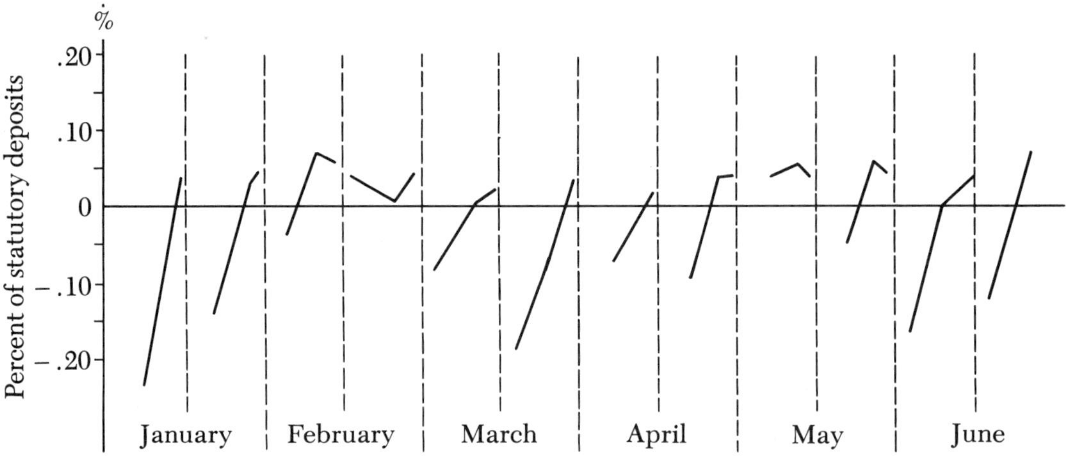

Source: Bank of Canada, *Weekly Financial Statistics*, 1981.

Summary of cash reserve management

To summarize this section on cash reserve management: the Bank of Canada typically increases cash reserves of banks directly by transferring federal deposits into the chartered banks and crediting the chartered banks' own deposits with the Bank of Canada. This transfer spreads the reserve increase over all banks. If the reserve increase causes banks to hold more excess cash reserves than they wish to hold at that point in their two-week averaging period, they will try to invest the surplus either in interest-earning liquid assets or, as customers become available, in general loans. Chartered banks will not hold significant amounts of any increase in reserves in the form of excess cash reserves.

In deciding on the amount of deposit transfer that will manage cash reserves properly, the Bank of Canada must keep track of or "defend against" several other influences on cash reserves in chartered banks, such as fluctuations in public currency holdings, government payments and receipts, borrowing from the Bank by money-market dealers and chartered banks, and any open-market sales or purchases of bills or foreign exchange that the Bank may have undertaken for other reasons. The remaining deposit transfer undertaken by the Bank of Canada is just the residual needed to bring the total adjustment up to that desired by the Bank.

SECTION 3 Exchange rate management

Exchange rate management is a simple policy tool. It involves the Bank of Canada's buying and selling foreign-currency assets in the foreign exchange market to stabilize the price of foreign currency, just like any other price-support agency. The Bank of Canada places its orders to buy and sell through the interbank foreign exchange market operated by the brokers of the Canadian Bankers' Association, in the same way that the chartered banks' foreign exchange traders do.

Usually the Bank intervenes in the foreign exchange market only to slow down changes in the exchange rate, without trying to prevent the rate from reaching its eventual equilibrium. If the Bank feels a change in the exchange rate is called for, its normal method of achieving the new level is by changing domestic interest rates relative to foreign interest rates. For instance, in August 1981, when the U.S.-dollar exchange rate rose above C$1.25 and the Bank wished to prevent its rising any further, the Bank raised Canadian interest rates three percentage points above U.S. rates.

As we discussed in chapter 19, foreign exchange operations will change the cash reserve base if they are not sterilized. If the Bank of Canada buys U.S.-dollar deposits for itself, then the Bank of Canada's draft in payment will find its way into a chartered bank and be used by the chartered bank to increase its deposit in the Bank of Canada; *FCD* and the monetary base will have increased, in equation (1). If the Bank of Canada instead buys foreign exchange for the Exchange Fund Account, then the EFA pays essentially by writing a draft on the government's account in the Bank of Canada (adding to its own debt to the government in the process). The EFA's draft on the government's deposit account in the Bank of Canada finds its way into a chartered bank fairly quickly and is used by that bank to increase its own deposits in the Bank of Canada; *GD* falls in equation (1), and the monetary base is increased in this case also.

The increase in cash reserves can be prevented in either case if the Bank of Canada at the same time sells off some of its bonds or Treasury Bills, or else transfers some of the government's funds from chartered-bank deposits to the Bank of Canada account in a normal defensive operation.

The impact effects of exchange rate management are relatively small, if all the Bank is doing is stabilizing the exchange rate around a level it would have stayed close to anyway. However, exchange rate management is useful in stabilizing aggregate demand only if the Bank keeps the exchange rate at a level different from what the equilibrium would be without central-bank intervention. The impact of such a policy is on net exports, and possibly on aggregate supply through the cost of imported goods and components. Impacts on cash reserves are not inevitable, as they can easily be prevented by the Bank, so such effects are better regarded as part of cash reserve management than as part of exchange rate management. However, as mentioned, the Bank is likely to adjust the exchange rate to new levels mainly by changing domestic interest rates rather than by exchange rate management itself.

SECTION 4

Other policy tools

The other policy tools are (1) changing the secondary reserve requirement imposed on chartered banks (note the word *secondary*; the Bank of Canada cannot change the primary, or cash, reserve requirement, so that is not a policy tool), (2) setting the Bank Rate, (3) advising the federal government on debt-management policy (that is, on adjusting the relative supplies of various maturities of federal debt), and (4) using moral suasion to produce or prevent certain specific lending or borrowing practices by banks and other intermediaries.

Secondary reserve requirements

Secondary reserve assets

Secondary reserve requirement

Banks are required to hold an amount of secondary reserve assets at least equal to a specified percentage of their Canadian-dollar deposit liabilities. *Secondary reserve assets* include excess cash reserve assets, federal Treasury Bills, and day loans to money-market dealers. *Secondary reserve requirements* have existed since 1955 (when they were introduced informally by the Bank of Canada, using its powers of moral suasion) and have been included in the Bank Act since 1967. The Bank's power is limited to raising or lowering the percentage specified for the secondary reserve requirement. Changing the secondary reserve requirement has limited effect and is not in accord with the way the Bank currently feels it ought to be conducting monetary policy, so no use has been made of this monetary-policy tool since 1977.[4]

An increase in the level of the secondary reserve requirement forces a reallocation of chartered banks' asset portfolios away from other assets and into secondary reserve assets. In effect this means a move into Treasury Bills and out of general loans. Equilibrium yields will fall for Treasury Bills and rise for bank loans.

Any change in relative yields causes offsetting changes in financial flows, and this change is no exception. Lower Treasury Bill yields will cause a shift of demand to other money-market assets, including term deposits, bankers' acceptances, and commercial paper. On the other hand, higher general loan yields will stimulate near-banks to expand their lending and issue more term deposits, while large and medium-size firms will shift their borrowing from general loans to commercial paper and bankers' acceptances. The net effect on money-market yields is likely to be only a slight widening of the differential between Treasury Bill yields and general loan yields. It is not clear that money-market yields as a whole will be affected at

[4]Effective December 1981, the Bank lowered the secondary reserve ratio from 5 to 4.0 percent, but purely because otherwise the requirement might have become restrictive. With heavy sales of Canada Savings Bonds in the fall of 1981, the federal government did not need to issue as many Treasury Bills as usual, so the supply of secondary reserve assets grew more slowly than usual. Lowering the secondary reserve requirement allowed the demand to grow more slowly as well.

all, on average. Impacts of changes in secondary reserve requirements on long-term yields and the relative price of real capital assets are likely to be invisibly small.

Even general loan yields may well be unaffected. With unchanged term-deposit costs, there will be some limited amount of credit rationing if loan rates do not rise, but the borrowers most likely to suffer are precisely those most likely to be taking advantage of the now cheaper borrowing opportunities with commercial paper and bankers' acceptances.

Most of any remaining credit rationing by banks as a result of increased secondary reserve requirements will also be offset by expansion of other nonbank credit sources such as credit unions and trust companies. Even use of life insurance policy loans will increase.

Originally the logic behind secondary reserve increases was that they could be used to impound excess liquidity in bank asset portfolios, in order to prevent banks from increasing the volume of their loans. Over time the Bank of Canada's strategy has changed to one of attempting solely to change yields and not to change credit volumes directly, so the power to impound liquidity has come to be considered useless. Nevertheless, the Bank argued to keep the power when the Bank Act was revised in 1980.

The Bank Rate

The *Bank Rate* is the minimum rate at which the Bank will make advances to members of the Canadian Payments Association. In practice, the Bank makes few such advances (see table 23–1, where Bank of Canada advances are shown to be tiny). Such loans are intended to be last-resort financing, to be used only when other liquidity adjustments are exhausted. To reinforce this intention, the Bank Rate is made a penalty rate, higher than can be earned on Treasury Bills.

Until March 1980 (except for the years 1956–62) the Bank Rate was set and adjusted explicitly by the Bank of Canada. The rate must be made known to the public, so every adjustment was the occasion for a press release. This system caused some unnecessary problems. In the words of a financial columnist, "One major pitfall was that changes by the Bank were subject to a number of conflicting assessments by the money market. Among key questions the market had to decide were: Was the rate adjustment a lagged response to changes in market rates? Was the rate change an indication from the Bank of what it thought rates should be or was it where it thought rates would be in time?"[5] Even if the Bank did not change the Bank Rate there was uncertainty whenever market interest rates moved significantly. The press releases themselves usually discussed the rate change in relation to movements of market rates, but they often did not provide clear answers to the questions of the money market.

---

[5]Barry Critchley, *The Financial Post*, March 14, 1981, 32.

Furthermore, said the same columnist, "previous Bank Rate changes were announced under the lights and the message flashed across the box to all Canadians. The next day, Parliament, with great fanfare, would debate the merits of this change and interest rates became very much part of the political world." On March 10, 1980, the Bank of Canada announced it would float the Bank Rate automatically every Thursday at a quarter of one percent (25 basis points) above the average yield in the latest Treasury Bill auction. Changes in the Bank Rate are now more frequent and also smaller than before, and timing of Bank Rate changes relative to market rate changes is no longer uncertain. Perhaps most important, the Bank Rate is no longer looked at as a signal of monetary policy. Instead, monetary-policy signals are picked up from listening to the Bank's senior officers explaining their policy in speeches, in testimony before Parliamentary committees, and in the Governor's Annual Report. The Bank Rate is given the little emphasis it deserves as a policy tool.

Not entirely incidentally, the Governor of the Bank of Canada probably takes less political flak for high interest rates than he would if the Bank Rate did not float. In the past, it often seemed to the public that Bank Rate changes were caused entirely by the Bank of Canada. Since chartered-bank prime rates usually went up immediately after Bank Rate changes, and by the same amount, many prime-rate increases were blamed on the Governor as well. Now it is clear that the Bank of Canada is not the only force influencing interest-rate levels. In fact, it is probable that most of the voting public now underestimates the Bank's influence on money-market rates. In the money market itself, a trader commented right after the change: "There is now one less surprise I have to contend with when I plan what my activity will be over the next one to two weeks. In the past, the market would often be surprised by the timing of a Bank Rate change."[6]

Debt management

As fiscal agent of the federal government, the Bank of Canada advises on the proper structure of the public debt and the proper composition of current borrowing. This advice can be used as a vehicle for interest-rate management, since changes in the relative amounts of various types of debt outstanding will influence relative interest rates in financial markets. At least in principle it will. In practice, the term structure of the federal debt has so far made little difference to the term structure of interest rates on federal debt. In chapter 15 we reviewed evidence on the behavior of relative interest rates in short- and long-term parts of government debt markets. The evidence shows that arbitrage between short- and long-term debt markets is large enough to cancel out almost all of the initial impact effects of changes in relative supplies of short- and long-term debt instruments.

---

[6]Cited in Critchley, *Financial Post*.

Even if it were clearly established that changing the structure of the federal debt would have definite effects on relative interest rates, it would still not be clear that the policy tool was worth using. First, the scale of debt-shifting necessary to bring about a large change in relative interest rates might be such as to cause disorderly markets. Such disorder occurred in 1960 after the mammoth conversion from short- to long-term debt in the Conversion Loan episode.[7]

Second, debt-management policy has very little effect on the average level of interest rates. Some rates go up, but others go down. For the policy to be effective, the Bank must know which interest rates affect spending in the real sector, and how. Such precise knowledge is not available. Many economists believe that it is the return on equity that matters most to spending on new investment in the real sector, and Tobin showed long ago that theory does not clearly specify what effect a rise in the relative quantity of long-term debt would have on equity yields. If long-term debt and equity were close substitutes, the equity yield would rise. If they were not close substitutes, the yield on equity would fall.[8]

Moral suasion

As a tool of monetary policy, *moral suasion* is vaguely defined. In 1978 the Governor of the Bank described it and its use in these terms:

> Moral suasion consists in requesting the banks, and possibly other financial institutions and market participants, to allocate credit, set interest rates, or otherwise conduct their operations in conformity with particular, specified monetary policy objectives rather than solely in the light of their own assessments of current market conditions. ... So far as I am concerned, the Bank of Canada does not now, and probably will not in the future, rely to any great extent on moral suasion. ... Moral suasion is only useful for a short period of time, and in unusual circumstances in which the need for some special type of action is evident to the affected parties and is ultimately in their own best interest.[9]

This passage suggests that moral suasion would not be very effective if it ran counter to the profitability of banks. Most recorded uses of moral suasion have not done so. In fact, many uses of moral suasion have had the effect of increasing bank profits by reducing the extent of price competition among banks. After the 1967 Bank Act revision, the Bank of Canada

---

[7]See C.L. Barber, "The Canadian Economy in Trouble" (Brief to the Royal Commission on Banking and Finance, unpublished, 1962); or John S. McCallum, "The Canadian Conversion Loan: A Remembrance," *Journal of Bank Research*, Spring 1980, 54–57.

[8]James Tobin, "An Essay on Principles of Debt Management," in Wm. Fellner et al., *Fiscal and Debt Management Policies* (Englewood Cliffs, N.J.: Prentice-Hall, 1963).

[9]"Opening Statement by Gerald K. Bouey, Governor of the Bank of Canada, before the House of Commons Standing Committee on Finance, Trade, and Economic Affairs, 28 November 1978," *Bank of Canada Review*, Dec. 1978, 3–8.

frequently intervened in vigorous competition between chartered banks for large-scale term deposits, to ask the big banks to compete less vigorously. In May of 1972 the intervention took the form of the Winnipeg Agreement: banks agreed to observe a ceiling on interest rates on large term deposits of up to one year to maturity. This ceiling was raised many times and finally removed entirely in January 1975.

On occasion moral suasion has been used to limit the spillover effects of tight U.S. monetary policy. The major banks have been asked repeatedly to keep flows of credit available to their domestic borrowers, in order to avoid having them squeezed to the wall by foreign firms trying to get around tight credit conditions in the United States.

Another use of moral suasion has been to help the government in its short-run stabilization of the exchange rate. When U.S. interest rates have been rising sharply the Bank has frequently asked the chartered banks not to facilitate short-term capital outflows by Canadian residents by offering swapped deposits (foreign-currency deposits with prearranged forward cover). In July 1981 both the Minister of Finance and the Governor of the Bank of Canada asked the major banks to lower or cut out their financing of foreign takeover bids by Canadian companies, in order at least to delay a large flow of direct investment abroad. The motive in both cases was to ease pressure on the exchange rate and reduce the need for further increases in already high domestic interest rates.

Moral suasion has generally been effective. There have been exceptions, however. For instance, in 1970 the Minister of Finance gave his opinion that the banks should not engage in equipment leasing, either directly or through subsidiaries. In 1973 the banks started buying into leasing companies anyway, getting around the Bank Act restriction on ownership of nonbank companies by using only companies with a share capital of less than $5 million.[10] On other occasions the Bank has attempted to use moral suasion on other groups of intermediaries, but with little success.

SECTION 5 Cash reserve management and money-supply measures

Discussion of monetary policy is often conducted in terms of what happens to the money supply, rather than what happens to the cash reserve base, so it will be helpful to discuss the connection between cash reserves and money-supply measures.

---

[10]Cf. H.H. Binhammer and Jane Williams, *Deposit-taking Institutions: Innovation and the Process of Change* (Ottawa: Economic Council of Canada, 1976), 80.

Interest rates and the money-supply equation

Recall that in Canada there are four money-supply measures: M1, M1A, M2, and M3. They were defined in chapter 9; basically M1 and M1A are currency plus chequable Canadian-dollar bank deposits, whereas M2 and M3 include some nonchequable deposits as well. M2 includes personal, Canadian-dollar term and notice deposits; M3 includes all deposits except foreign-currency bank deposits held abroad or held by nonresidents.

Recall also, from chapter 19, that where there is only one kind of deposit, the relationship between cash reserve base R and money supply M is given by

$$M = R\left(\frac{1 + cu}{cu + crr}\right), \tag{6}$$

where cu is the ratio of currency to demand deposits desired by the public, and crr is the banks' cash reserve ratio. With cu and crr constant, equation (6) makes the money supply a constant multiple of the cash reserve base.

If the public's desired currency-to-deposit ratio is sensitive to levels of interest rates on other assets, then the money supply will be a varying multiple of the reserve base. For instance, it is likely that currency demand is less sensitive to money-market yields than is bank deposit demand. Higher money-market yields will therefore lower bank deposit demand by relatively more than currency demand and raise the currency-to-deposit ratio; at any level of reserves, the money supply will be smaller. A decrease in the reserve base by x percent will therefore decrease the money supply by more than x percent precisely because the decrease in reserves will raise yields on money-market assets.

When there are two or more kinds of deposits, as there are in Canada, the response of money supply to changes in reserves depends on the definition of money being used. Narrow money (M1 or M1A) is a multiple of the part of cash reserves R not tied up supporting term deposits. The volume of term deposits held rises and falls with the level of relative yields on term deposits (relative to yields on narrow-money assets, among others); lower term-deposit yields attract fewer term depositors and leave more of the total cash reserve base available to support demand deposits.

An increase in reserves R decreases money-market yields and reduces demand for term deposits. More of the original reserves are now available to support M1, so M1 can grow faster than did R. Conversely, when R contracts M1 must contract even faster.

The behavior of broad money and reserves is best explained as an analogue of the case of a single type of deposit. Imagine term and demand deposits lumped together, with a cash reserve requirement that is a weighted average of 10 percent on demand deposits and 3 percent on term deposits. Broad money would then be related to the reserve base as in equation (6). The weighted-average cash reserve requirement depends on the relative sizes of demand deposits and term deposits, which in turn depend on yield levels. For instance, an increase in cash reserves would lower money-market yields and term-deposit yields; those changes would shift asset demand from time deposits to demand deposits and raise the average cash reserve requirement. By itself, an increase in the average cash reserve requirement will reduce the money supply, so cash reserve growth of x percent would be followed by broad-money growth of less than x percent. Only if the lower yields also raised the currency-to-demand-deposit ratio (as we suggested earlier) would broad-money growth change as much as cash reserve growth.

Even this much analysis of money-supply responses quickly brings out the idea that any change in R can be accompanied by several different changes in M depending on how relative yields change and how they influence asset demands. Term-deposit demand in particular is quite sensitive to small changes in relative yields (as well as to relative risks and wealth changes), so response of broad money to cash reserve changes is likely to vary substantially over time.

Table 23–3 illustrates the uncertainty of the connection between cash reserve growth and money-supply growth over a series of three- and six-month periods from 1978 to 1982.

Borrowed reserves

There is one further source of unreliability in the connection between cash reserve management by the Bank of Canada and money-supply measures. That source is the potential use by banks of borrowed reserves to supplement cash reserves made available directly by the Bank of Canada. If chartered banks vary their amount of borrowed reserves to offset Bank of Canada cash reserve management, total reserves will be made more stable and so will interest rates and the money-supply measures.

In the United States, borrowed reserves are a significant source of uncertainty in regulation of the money supply. U.S. banks often make use of Federal Reserve lending facilities, often to offset tight money policies. In Canada there is less reason for concern over this issue, because chartered banks have not made extensive use of borrowed reserves. However, money-market dealers do make extensive use of their purchase and resale (that is, borrowing) facility with the Bank of Canada.

A purchase and resale agreement between the Bank of Canada and a money-market dealer has the same effect on cash reserves as an explicit advance to a chartered bank; further, the chartered banks can strongly influence how much of that type of borrowing is done by the money-market dealers. For instance, chartered banks can and do use excess cash reserves to extend more day-to-day loans to money-market dealers, who in turn could use the funds to replace purchase and resale agreements with the Bank of Canada. The net result would be to cancel at least part of the increase in cash reserves, just as surely as if the banks had repaid debts of their own to the central bank.

TABLE 23–3 Monetary growth rates 1978–82
(three- and six-month changes at annual rates)

Quarter ending	Chartered-bank cash reserves	Demand deposits	Demand and personal savings deposits	Total reservable deposits
1978 Feb	28.0%	– 6.6%	2.0%	– 1.9%
May	18.9	7.5	14.5	28.0
Aug	4.5	35.9	17.5	19.9
Nov	21.1	17.5	21.9	28.2
1979 Feb	10.6	–21.7	5.3	9.3
May	13.1	4.6	18.8	26.7
Aug	–9.1	39.0	26.0	22.5
Nov	38.3	–16.1	21.7	16.1
1980 Feb	–30.0	0.2	16.0	8.7
May	100.3	–10.0	17.9	18.4
Aug	–19.4	51.9	19.4	9.9
Nov	44.2	14.8	16.3	5.5
1981 Feb	–17.8	–21.6	3.4	16.2
May	–9.5	14.4	18.8	13.2
Aug	1.2	21.7	25.1	12.9
Nov	–3.2	3.1	19.9	8.6
1982 Feb	8.7	–31.5	5.6	17.7
May	–64.2	—	—	–38.8
Six months ending				
1978 Aug	11.5	20.8	16.0	23.9
1979 Feb	15.7	–4.1	13.3	8.4
Aug	1.4	20.6	22.4	24.6
1980 Feb	–1.6	– 8.3	18.8	12.3
Aug	27.1	16.9	18.6	14.1
1981 Feb	8.8	–5.1	9.7	10.7
Aug	–1.0	18.4	22.5	13.3
1982 Feb	15.7	17.1	12.9	13.3

Source: Bank of Canada Review.

Alternatively, the banks could respond to a tight cash reserve situation by calling in day-to-day loans from money-market dealers, forcing the latter to make greater use of the Bank of Canada's purchase and resale facility. This would cause cash reserves temporarily to rise above the level desired by the Bank of Canada.

How serious a threat are borrowed reserves to the Bank of Canada's ability to control the level of cash reserves? Neither day-to-day loans nor the average amount of outstanding purchase and resale agreements is large. At month-ends in 1980 the averages outstanding were only $133 and $140 million respectively. Both totals are volatile, with fluctuations of $200 million either way being common between weeks. To put that in perspective, $200 million is 0.16 percent of reservable deposits. Such fluctuations could easily be used to provide (temporarily) the extra cash reserves needed for a larger deposit expansion than the Bank of Canada desired. However, there is no evidence that fluctuations have been engineered with that in mind except for periods of a few weeks. In particular, banks have not responded to prolonged tight cash reserve situations by running down day-to-day loans and forcing the money-market dealers to greater and greater use of the Bank of Canada's purchase and resale facility. For instance, both totals were as large at the end as at the beginning of 1980, a year of tight credit. Banks adjust day-to-day loans only as a very short-term form of liquidity management, designed to allow time for more appropriate changes in other liquid assets and deposit growth rates.

SECTION 6 Summary

The Bank of Canada is the body charged with primary responsiblity for designing and carrying out monetary policy in Canada, in pursuit of fairly general objectives set out in the Bank of Canada Act. The Governor and his senior administrative staff bear most of the burden; a government-appointed Board of Directors serves mainly as a watchdog. At the same time, the Minister of Finance shares responsibility with the Governor; the Minister has both the power and the responsibility to overrule the Governor should the Minister ever conclude that monetary policy was in serious error.

The Bank of Canada has several powers that make it, rather than the Department of Finance, the logical wielder of monetary policy. The Bank serves as banker, securities underwriter, and fiscal agent for the federal government. The Bank is lender of last resort to banks, to governments, and (indirectly) to money-market dealers. The Bank is the issuer of the monetary base of cash reserve assets (currency and Bank of Canada deposits) for the economy.

The main monetary-policy tools are regulation of the cash reserve base and intervention in the foreign exchange market. The Bank of Canada can also adjust the secondary reserve requirement, change the Bank Rate (the Bank of Canada's minimum lending rate for advances to banks), change the structure of federal debt outstanding, and use the Bank's influence, reputation, and persuasive powers to persuade banks and others to adopt particular lending policies. Of these tools, regulation of cash reserves is by far the most important. Of the other tools, only moral suasion is used with any frequency. Moral suasion is generally used either to effect minor changes in bank credit allocation or else to damp down vigorous bank competition for loan or deposit business.

Cash reserve management involves raising and lowering available cash reserve assets (currency and Bank of Canada deposits) relative to (a) the amount required by chartered banks under the legal cash reserve requirements set out in the Bank Act plus (b) the amount absorbed by other uses such as currency in circulation and deposits of governments and international bodies. Excess cash reserves above amounts (a) and (b) will be invested immediately by chartered banks, which try to keep excess reserves earning interest instead.

The Bank of Canada can raise or lower cash reserve asset totals by buying and selling assets (typically Treasury Bills, but also foreign-currency assets and occasionally federal government bonds). These transactions are collectively known as open-market operations. Alternatively, the Bank of Canada can raise or lower the banks' cash reserves by transferring federal deposits between the federal account in the Bank of Canada and federal deposit accounts in the chartered banks. For several reasons transfer of federal deposits is the preferred method of cash reserve management.

Changing cash reserves at any rate will change the various money-supply measures in Canada in the same direction, but not at the same rate. The money-supply multiplier that relates cash reserves to the money supply is affected by the average level of short-term interest rates for two reasons: first, the public's desired currency:deposit ratio will rise with interest rates if, as seems probable, currency is less sensitive than demand deposits to other yields. Second, the share of demand deposits in total deposit demand will fall as yields on other assets rise, so the weighted-average cash reserve requirement for all deposits taken together will fall. Changes in relative yields and relative risks on individual short-term deposits and other assets will also affect the ratio of demand to time deposits, so the money-supply multiplier will not be particularly stable over time.

Questions for discussion

1. What control, implicit or explicit, does the government have over the Bank of Canada?
2. Why is the Bank of Canada so profitable?
3. Bond holdings of the Bank of Canada are very large, and the federal deposit is very small. Does it follow that the Bank relies more on open-market operations than on federal deposit transfers to increase the monetary base?
4. List four sources of uncertainty facing the Bank in its attempts to control the money supply by controlling the monetary base.
5. What uncertainty faces banks in meeting their legal cash reserve requirement?

6. What is the effect on the Canadian monetary base of the German central bank's withdrawing some of its deposits in the Bank of Canada (and being paid in Deutsche Marks)?
7. How could exchange rate management modify the business cycle (for example, a boom with rising inflation)? Is this a demand-management or a supply management tool?
8. What are the similarities between the effects of a change in secondary reserve requirements and the effects of a change in debt-management policy?
9. How is moral suasion different from collusion in an informal cartel? How do you think moral suasion would be affected by the entry of fifty-eight new, small, foreign-owned banks?

References

Binhammer, H.H. *Money, Banking and the Canadian Financial System*. 4th ed. Toronto: Methuen, 1982, part 4.

Binhammer, H.H., and Jane Williams. *Deposit-taking Institutions: Innovation and the Process of Change*. Ottawa: Economic Council of Canada, 1976.

Boreham, G.F. *Money and Banking: Analysis and Policy in a Canadian Context*. 2d ed. Toronto: Holt, Rinehart and Winston, 1979, part 3.

Clinton, Kevin, and Kevin Lynch. "Monetary Base and Money Stock in Canada." Bank of Canada Technical Report 16, July 1979.

Galbraith, John A. *Canadian Banking*. Toronto: Ryerson, 1970.

Granatstein, J.L. "The Untouchables." *Saturday Night*. April 1983.

"Opening Statement by Gerald K. Bouey, Governor of the Bank of Canada, before the House of Commons Standing Committee on Finance, Trade, and Economic Affairs, 28 November 1978." *Bank of Canada Review*, Dec. 1978, 3–8.

Tobin, James. "An Essay on Principles of Debt Management." In Wm. Fellner et al., *Fiscal and Debt Management Policies*. Englewood Cliffs, N.J.: Prentice-Hall, 1963.

White, W.R. *Management by the Canadian Banks of Their Domestic Portfolios, 1956–1971: An Econometric Study*. Ottawa: Bank of Canada, 1975.

CHAPTER 24

Rules for Stabilization Policy

In chapter 21 we discovered that the behavior of inflation, output, and employment in a modern open economy is described by slow cycles. Even without policy changes, the full cycle from boom to boom might take a decade or so. The economy is also subject to many types of exogenous shocks, including shocks from abroad. Finally, the pattern of response to those shocks is uncertain and variable. Expectations play a big part in patterns of response, and expectations can be particularly volatile in the short run.

In order to stabilize the economy and moderate the cycles for private individuals, the government uses the range of policy tools discussed in chapters 22 and 23. Each major policy tool, and how it affects (or does not affect) the economy, was described. What remains is to explain how the government should go about applying and co-ordinating the tools of stabilization policy — that is, to explain the logic of optimal stabilization policy.

Your task is to learn:

1. the benefits and costs to society of the different, competing goals of stabilization policy,
2. the effect of uncertainty on optimal policy responses to unexpected shocks,
3. the alternative rules for conduct of monetary and exchange rate policy, and
4. which rules are being or have recently been used by the Bank of Canada, and why.

SECTION 1 Policy environment and policy goals

The government and its agency, the central bank, are charged with stabilizing the economy; in carrying out that mandate, they face several kinds of uncertainty. Government policy makers are uncertain about exactly how the economy works, despite the conviction with which many economists put forth their own explanations. The government is not sure of the size of aggregate demand multipliers, the size of supply responses, or the speed of either. Since the government cannot be sure of the levels of many of the exogenous variables in its own economic forecasting models, it must be ready to meet unexpected demand and supply shocks. Policy makers know there are lags in response of output, employment, and price levels to both demand and supply shocks, but they do not know how long those lags will be. Finally, measurement of aggregate demand and output levels occurs so slowly and is subject to so much revision that the government and the Bank of Canada are uncertain about even the current state of the economy; their measurements lag several months behind.

Policy objectives

There are two approaches to analysis of policy objectives. One is the Machiavellian, public-choice approach pioneered by James Buchanan and Ronald Coase. In this approach, governments and government bureaucracies are seen as pursuing their own objectives with the tools of public policy, basically minimizing the risk of losing office by doling out the favors of public policy to influential constituents. Because of their risk aversion, bureaucrats in this view often tend to be vague or even secretive about their objectives; secrecy enlarges their discretion and reduces the chance of their being evaluated and found wanting by the public. Professors Acheson and Chant have evaluated the Bank of Canada from this viewpoint.[1]

The second and more traditional approach to thinking about government policy objectives is what Buchanan labels the "naive" social-welfare approach.[2] This approach assumes that the government is trying to maximize social welfare. Subsidiary, or operational, goals are then derived from that grand premise. Policy derived from this approach can claim to be optimal policy. Governments are assumed to know that voters will turf them out of office if such optimal policies are not followed. Civil servants are assumed to be disinterested servants of the public good.

We will follow the second approach, despite its limitations, but we will keep the first approach in mind as a possible subplot to the chapter.

Objectives under certainty

Under certainty (certainty for government, at least) the basic goals of stabilization policy are to produce levels of output Y and prices P that are

---

[1]Keith Acheson and John Chant, "The Choice of Monetary Instruments and the Theory of Bureaucracy," *Public Choice*, Spring 1972, 13–33.

[2]James Buchanan, "The Political Ambiguity of Reagan Economics: Marginal Adjustment or Structural Shift?" *Journal of Monetary Economics*, Nov. 1982, 287–96.

close to target levels Y_T and P_T respectively. Y_T will be on a steadily growing trend line, and P_T will be either constant or inflating at a steadily declining rate (for a gradual return to price stability). Achievement of the targets implies stability rather than cyclical behavior of the economy. It does not matter much whether the level of employment, unemployment, or capacity use is substituted for the level of output in the short run, since those four behaviors track one another fairly closely.

A formal way of expressing such goals is to say that policy makers want to minimize a loss function L that rises with the gaps between actual and target levels of Y and P. Particularly if the public expects levels Y_T and P_T, it is likely that the loss to society rises more than proportionately with the gap between target level and actual economic performance; larger gaps, or "errors," between target and performance will increase the frustrations of individuals trying to plan their finances and business ventures, and at an increasing rate. Professor Henri Theil has suggested a quadratic loss function as a good approximation of the government policy makers' loss function:

$$L = a_1(Y - Y_T)^2 + a_2(P - P_T)^2, \tag{1}$$

where the coefficients a_1 and a_2 are both positive.[3]

Objectives under uncertainty

Where policy makers are uncertain about the economy and about the effects of their policy, it is best to think of their objectives as a combination of maximizing the expected outcome and minimizing the variance of possible outcomes around that expected outcome. This is exactly the same approach as in chapter 8, where rational investors maximized a utility function that depended on expected portfolio yield and variance of possible yields around the expected yield. With this approach, policy makers will be concerned about expected gaps between targets and performance for real output and price levels, and about the variance of real output and price levels around their expected levels.[4]

Policy makers are also likely to be concerned about variances in interest rates and exchange rates, since these "prices" are particularly important to financial plans of households and firms in society. There is not likely to be any social target for the interest rate or the exchange rate, but large changes in either are likely to be considered undesirable.

---

[3]Henri Theil, *Economic Forecasts and Policy* (Amsterdam: North Holland, 1961).

[4]Where the policy maker has a single objective of minimizing $L(Y - Y_T)^2$ under certainty, the rational response under uncertainty is to minimize the expected loss. It is easy to show that when L is quadratic, minimizing $E[L(Y - Y_T)^2]$ is equivalent to minimizing $L'[E(Y - Y_T)^2, Var(Y)]$. Where there are two or more objectives, it is more complex. This logic is the basis of the mean-variance approach to portfolio theory and is discussed in appendix 1 to chapter 8.

A full objective function for stabilization policy makers is therefore likely to contain six ingredients, as in equation (2):

$$L = a_1E(Y - Y_T)^2 + a_2E(P - P_T)^2 + a_3Var(Y) + a_4Var(P) + a_5Var(r) + a_6Var(P_{US\$}), \quad (2)$$

where all of the coefficients are positive (all of the arguments are social "bads").[5]

The weights given to each argument in equation (2) will vary over time, but they will reflect roughly the relative social costs imposed by high levels of each ingredient. We will take a brief detour to look at the costs involved, since there are many times when makers of stabilization policy must choose between hitting output targets and hitting inflation targets.

The costs of slow output growth

The costs of slow output growth (when $Y < Y_T$) are basically the foregone value of output that could have been produced had unemployed labor and idle capital resources been fully used instead. When capacity output is $400 billion, as it is in Canada, each 1 percent shortfall in output is $4 billion of waste for every year the shortfall continues. The recession of 1981–82 produced a drop in output of 8.6 percent from an already slack level, so the waste implied is around $34 billion per year — over $1000 per capita. The total costs of a recession are clearly very large.

That is only a rough estimate of the cost of output slack. A more sophisticated measure will include several adjustments.[6] Allowance will be made for nonrenewable resources that are saved for the future as a result of lower current output. Allowance will be made for the value of nonmarket activity (painting the house, spending more time with the children, and so on) that the unemployed may engage in during a period of unemployment. Allowance will also be made for the loss of job skills by the unemployed and for the greater uncertainty unemployment adds to their lives and to the lives of all others who may feel their job security threatened (there is ample

---

[5]An alternative version of equation (2) that is often encountered is the suggestion that policy makers attempt to minimize the variance of nominal income (*PY*) around some desired trend. In a medium-run context, this formulation implies that offsetting fluctuations in prices and real incomes leave society unaffected, which is not plausible. In a short-run context and with the proviso that price levels are undisturbed by supply shocks, this version of policy makers' goals amounts to stabilizing real output around its trend. Equation (2) is more explicit and more general. See W.R. White, "Alternative Monetary Targets and Control Instruments in Canada: Criteria for Choice," *Canadian Journal of Economics*, Nov. 1979, 591.

[6]For a good discussion of these adjustments, see Arthur Okun, *Prices and Quantities* (Washington, D.C.: Brookings Institution, 1981), 297–98, or D.A. Wilton and D.M. Prescott, *Macroeconomics* (Don Mills, Ont.: Addison-Wesley, 1982), chap. 3, or Orley Ashenfelter, "The Withering Away of a Full Employment Goal," *Canadian Public Policy*, March 1983, 114–25.

evidence from sociologists that extra unemployment is a powerful source of despair and, in a significant number of cases, pushes people to suicide). It is likely that extra slack in the economy also lowers the rate of capital formation; with less capital per worker, output per worker will be lower for all future periods. Finally, allowance could be made for the fact that with extra slack there are fewer shortages in the economy — themselves a source of both inefficiency and uncertainty. The net result of all the extra allowances is probably close to a saw-off, leaving the loss of foregone output as a reasonable estimate.

The costs of slack and unemployment are of course borne mainly by the unemployed. Society reallocates some of the burden of a shortfall in output growth by handing out unemployment-insurance benefits, and occasionally by government bailouts of firms on the brink of bankruptcy, but that assistance only repairs a fraction of the damage done and does not reduce the total burden on society.

The cost of inflation

The costs imposed by inflation are less visible and therefore harder to describe. They are also, in many economists' estimation, much smaller than the costs of recession. The costs of inflation come from inefficient financial arrangements, reduced incentives to invest in long-term capital assets, undesirable income redistribution, and greater uncertainty in contractual arrangements.

Shoe-leather costs

Inflation tax

Inflation makes financial arrangements inefficient by putting a tax on money, the so-called *inflation tax*. Because money pays no interest, inflation reduces its real value each year. Rational money-holders respond by shifting their portfolios out of money and into interest-earning assets. In corporations (which hold most of the money supply in Canada) this adjustment is known as tighter cash management. Financial vice-presidents hire more assistants to collect the firm's revenues faster and to keep the funds invested in Eurodollar deposits and other exotic investments right up to the time the money is needed for purchases. Banks co-operate by setting up computer routines that invest corporations' excess demand-deposit balances overnight.

In early discussions of the costs of inflation, the main extra cost of such transactions was thought of as extra trips to the bank, so the costs have come to be known as *shoe-leather costs*. The transactions costs could be approximated roughly by the annual salary costs of all the extra financial staff of Canadian corporations added since 1960, over and above those needed just to service a growing volume of real output. The entire finance, insurance, and real estate sector employs only 4 percent of the labor force, so this extra cost has to be a tiny share of GNP.

Wealth distortions

Because of the inflation tax on money, some investors are persuaded to shift more of their wealth from money into real assets. If the real assets are used in production, society has a net gain in output capacity. If the real assets are barren — that is, if they are held just because of their anticipated capital gains and are not used in either production or consumption — society has wasted resources in producing them. Without inflation, the demand for those real stores of value could have been met instead by money, which is costless to produce. This effect of inflation is as though we were all persuaded by some slick salesperson that we should breathe our air through oxygen masks instead of directly from the atmosphere. The cost of this inflation-induced inefficiency could be approximated by the total opportunity cost of mining all the gold and silver and producing all of the other real assets used as hedges against inflation.

The response of lenders to rising inflation has been to shorten the average term of their lending. That, plus the "tilt" in real loan repayments (discussed in chapter 6, in connection with household mortgage loans) causes firms to concentrate on capital assets that generate revenues in the near rather than the distant future, so that investment in the economy emphasizes equipment rather than structures and other long-term investments like pipelines and rail beds. This distortion produces an inefficient pattern of capital investment and therefore a lower growth rate for the economy.[7]

Income redistribution

Inflation redistributes income by taxing net creditors with fixed-yield assets and subsidizing net debtors with fixed-yield debts. We saw in chapter 14 that nominal yields do adjust to compensate for expected inflation, though apparently real yields fall a bit before tax and a lot more when taxes are taken into account. Nominal yields do not adjust at all for unexpected inflation. Further, nominal yields cannot adjust on existing fixed-yield assets; the holders and issuers adjust their nominal yields only when the asset matures and is replaced.

We noted in chapters 11 to 13 that financial intermediaries generally do not suffer from this effect of inflation, because they typically have fixed-interest assets offset by fixed-interest debts. The major identifiable group that suffers from inflation is retirement savers. Pension annuities are typically not indexed against inflation (though the Canada Pension Plan, the Old Age Security pensions, and the federal civil service pensions are indexed). There are ad hoc adjustments to private-sector (company) pensions that on average seem to compensate pensioners for about half of the

---

[7]Dr. Barry Bosworth of the Brookings Institution has investigated for the U.S. the claim that inflation causes a distortion of investment spending away from long-lived assets and has found the distortion to be insignificant for the 1970s. "Capital Formation and Economic Policy," *Brookings Papers on Economic Activity*, 1982:2, 273–26.

impact of inflation (this fraction seems likely to increase over time). Pension funds have been big investors in fixed-interest, long-term assets, the very assets that suffer most from inflation, so pension funds have not been able to provide much protection to pensioners.

There are further windfall gains and losses to owners of particular assets that apppreciate faster or slower than inflation. In the 1970s, the main asset appreciating faster than inflation was the family home. Fortunately, the retired group as a whole contains a disproportionate number of home-owners, so this benefit partly or wholly compensated some of the retirees for erosion of the real value of their pension benefits.

Extra uncertainty

An even less visible effect of inflation is the undermining of confidence in contractual or customary arrangements with fixed nominal terms. Okun has argued that many business and consumer relationships are based on long-term contracts, explicit or implicit.[8] Shoppers have a few reliable suppliers, whom they trust to provide a good deal. This trust saves a great deal of effort, since continually shopping around for everything would consume far too much time and money. Similarly, employees have an explicit or implicit contract with employers that employers will continue to treat them fairly (relative to other employers' wages and working conditions) so employees will not need to search out and compare alternative jobs each morning.

Inflation undermines such trust and confidence because it changes all prices and wages, and in particular because it does not change them evenly and at the same time. Different firms will raise their prices at different times, and wages are typically adjusted at different times of year for each firm or union. At any point of time, shoppers will be less certain that their regular supplier is offering the best deal, so they will have greater incentive to search out other suppliers — just because of the extra uncertainty. Formal wage and supply contracts will be renegotiated more frequently. Since inflation provides no greater expectation that time spent in extra search will be successful, the extra effort is just a waste.

Costs of uncertainty

It is a basic assumption of this book that extra risk is undesirable. Individuals and firms wish to avoid it. Some uncertainty adds spice to life, but there is more than enough uncertainty to go around for most of us, so its marginal utility is decidedly negative — especially when it affects our financial planning. Uncertainty of future output, employment, price levels, interest rates, and exchange rates (especially for those Canadians planning to retire to Florida and live off income in Canadian dollars) increases the chance of large errors in financial plans. Some of the errors would work to our

---

[8]Okun, *Prices and Quantities*, 278ff.

advantage, of course, and the expected error might be exactly zero. Nevertheless, the extra satisfaction from errors in our favor is generally not enough to compensate for the prospect of lost satisfaction from errors in the opposite direction.

The costs of uncertainty are probably not nearly as large as the costs of unemployment. One way to estimate the costs of uncertainty is to look at what people will pay to have uncertainty removed: the cost of insurance of various kinds. Unemployment insurance is the scheme designed to remove some of the financial uncertainty associated with uncertain employment. The full unemployment-insurance contribution is not a measure of what we pay to remove uncertainty, because most of that contribution is just transferred from the employed to the unemployed; only the cost of operating the unemployment-insurance system (salaries and supplies for the Unemployment Insurance Commission, essentially) should be included.

Similarly, we pay the cost of mining gold and silver and other hedges against inflation, just to remove some of the risk of uncertain inflation. If we are rational, the cost of inflation uncertainty must be at least equal to the cost of producing inflation hedges.

For uncertainty of interest rates and exchange rates, we do have futures markets in which the risks can be offset. The costs of operating those markets serve as a minimum estimate of the costs of interest-rate and exchange-rate uncertainty. Most investors exposed to interest-rate and exchange-rate risk do not make use of the futures markets, however, so the full cost of this uncertainty is surely many times higher than just the operating costs of the futures markets. Our concern over interest-rate risk is reflected in the fact that in late 1983 the federal government announced an interest insurance scheme for home-buyers.

Uncertainty about the exchange rate is likely to discourage some foreign trade and produce inefficient patterns of output if traders and producers are confused by fluctuating relative price signals.[9] If prices are sticky downward but not upward, merely fluctuating exchange rates (with no upward trend at all) could raise the inflation rate in an open economy dependent on many imported components.

Uncertainty of the interest rate increases income risk and market risk of financial assets, so many investors will prefer to hold real assets instead. Large interest-rate variations also generate severe cash flow problems for mortgage borrowers and business firms, which are inevitably followed by an increase in the rate of bankruptcies.[10]

---

[9]A recent study of the behavior of international firms under flexible exchange rates suggests that such firms were not much affected by the extra exchange rate risk of the 1970s: they did not reduce their investment, though they did do much more hedging in forward-exchange markets and they took foreign exchange risk into account in deciding on their financing strategy. John Blin, S.I. Greenbaum, and D.P. Jacobs, *Flexible Exchange Rates and International Business* (Washington, D.C.: British North American Committee, 1981).

[10]White, "Alternative Monetary Targets," 591.

SECTION 2 Optimal responses

Assignment of policy tools

The government has a wide range of policy tools to use in achieving its stabilization objectives. We noted in chapter 17 that at least one tool is needed for each objective. We also noted that the government is not free to assign tools to objectives just any old way, and wouldn't be even in a world where policies had perfectly predictable effects. The policy tools must be allocated to achievement of specific objectives in a specific way if the economy is to be stable. Mundell's assignment theory essentially requires that policy tools be used mainly to influence those goal variables that they are comparatively efficient at affecting. This is simply the doctrine of comparative advantage from the theory of international trade, applied to the use of policy tools instead of to the use of society's resources in production.

If monetary policy is used to achieve employment targets while fiscal policy is used to stabilize interest rates, for instance, both employment and interest rates may be destabilized. Monetary policy would cause large changes in interest rates in attempting to achieve satisfactory employment, while fiscal policy would cause large changes in employment by attempting to keep interest rates stable. Neither policy could be effective because of the side effects of the other. An extreme analogy would be using the accelerator to control a car's direction (by causing the back end to skid to one side or the other) and the steering wheel to control speed (by wobbling the front wheels to cause more or less friction on the road surface). The car would end up in a ditch. Use of policy tools must be better allocated than that.

Professor Pierre Fortin of Laval University has argued that the comparative advantage of monetary policy in an open economy like Canada's lies in controlling inflation and the exchange rate, while the comparative advantage of fiscal policy is in controlling employment.[11] When the available set of policies is enlarged to include incomes policies and exchange rate management, the comparative advantage of monetary policy is less clear. Over periods longer than a few months, however, monetary policy would be needed to supplement exchange rate management to keep the exchange rate stable, or else foreign exchange reserves could be exhausted. Monetary policy would also be needed to supplement incomes policies in any attempt to reduce inflation, since incomes policies do not work well on their own.

[11] Pierre Fortin, "Monetary Targets and Monetary Policy in Canada: A Critical Assessment," *Canadian Journal of Economics*, Nov. 1979, 625–46.

Assignment in practice

In practice, monetary and fiscal policies in Canada have been used at cross-purposes most of the time since 1979, which is obviously inefficient.

The government made little use of incomes policies until the 1981–82 recession was well under way, while monetary and fiscal policy were trying to push aggregate demand in opposite directions.[12]

Policy makers had decided that inflation was enemy number one and that it was to be fought by temporary restriction of output growth — that is, by a negative demand shock. There was some attempt to use supply-management policies to generate favorable supply shocks, but not much.[13] The Bank of Canada pursued a monetary policy that reduced money-supply growth below that of nominal income and pushed up real interest rates. This policy, which matched the policy followed in the United States by the Federal Reserve Board, succeeded in bringing on a recession in mid-1981. Federal fiscal policy, on the other hand, was on the whole expansionary during this period. Only by 1981 was the cyclically adjusted and inflation-adjusted budget in surplus, though the government-sector budget as a whole was in surplus from 1979 on.

Furthermore, the federal and several provincial governments set up interest-subsidy schemes in 1981 to alleviate the cash flow problems of home-owners and small businesses caused by tight monetary policy; these schemes directly undermined the main thrust of monetary policy, which was to reduce aggregate demand.

Effect of uncertainty

The certainty-equivalent rule

There is a good theoretical basis for propositions that certain kinds of uncertainty do not matter to the conduct of stabilization policy. These kinds of uncertainty increase risks in the economy, but the risks are not affected by the conduct of stabilization policy. Uncertainties about the levels of all exogenous variables (future wealth, foreign interest rates, expectations of investors, and so on) are of this type. Optimal policy strategy in the face of this type of uncertainty is to make an unbiased estimate of the effects of policy changes on the target variables and then to proceed as if that estimate were known for certain; for obvious reasons, this

---

[12]The federal government did introduce a wage and price restraint program in the federal public sector in June 1982 but was not able or willing to extend it to the private sector.

[13]The restraint program included restrictions on public price-setting agencies such as public utility commissions, but these did not prevent provinces, for instance, from raising sales and excise taxes, or even from imposing payroll taxes. The federal government also raised unemployment-insurance contribution rates, which are a form of tax on labor costs. An initiative to reduce the burden of regulation never got past the study stage. Meanwhile, the federal and Alberta governments agreed in 1981 on a massive increase in oil and natural gas prices.

Certainty-equivalent approach

is known as the *certainty-equivalent approach*.[14] Theil has shown that, even where changes in the policy or in exogenous variables affect output and inflation with long and possibly uncertain lags, the errors from the certainty-equivalent approach will be less serious than the errors from any other approach.

Brainard's rule of caution

Optimal stabilization policy is affected if there is uncertainty about the effect of policy tools. This type of uncertainty matters because the level of uncertainty about economic performance of the economy must increase as the size of policy change increases. William Brainard of Yale University demonstrated in 1967 that optimal policy will be more cautious in the face of this type of uncertainty.[15] His demonstration is worth repeating both because of the light it sheds on optimal policy making and because it is a useful application of the mean-variance approach to decisions outside the area of portfolio choice.

In the simple case with only one policy tool (and therefore only one target as well), let Y be the target variable and P the policy tool. Policy affects the target variable as follows:

$$Y = aP + u, \tag{3}$$

where u is a random error term reflecting uncertainty about all other exogenous variables affecting Y. The term u has a probability distribution with expected value $E(u)$ and variance $Var(u)$. The policy coefficient a is uncertain, with expected value $E(a)$ and variance $Var(a)$.

Assume that policy makers want to increase expected performance and decrease the standard deviation of performance. Expected performance is $E(Y) - Y_T$, where

$$E(Y) = E(a)P + E(u) \tag{4}$$

and Y_T is the target level of income.

The variance of Y depends on the variances of a and u, on their covariance $Cov(a,u)$, and on the level of the policy P:

$$Var(Y) = P_2 Var(a) + Var(u) + 2PCov(a,u). \tag{5}$$

Assume that Y will be less than the target level Y_T if no policy action is taken, so the optimal level of P will be positive. Increases in P will therefore raise $E(Y)$ toward the target Y_T at the rate $E(a)$ but will also raise the level of uncertainty $Var(Y)$.

The effect of policy on $E(Y)$ and $Var(Y)$ is most easily seen in the simple case where $Var(u)$ is zero. In this case, $Var(Y) = P_2 Var(a)$, so the standard

[14] Theil, *Economic Forecasts and Policy*. See also Fortin, "Monetary Targets," 631; Fortin suggests on the basis of U.S. results that Canadian forecasters may well produce unbiased forecasts of real GNP growth up to four quarters ahead.

[15] William C. Brainard, "Uncertainty and the Effectiveness of Policy," *American Economic Review*, 1967, 411–25.

deviation of the target variable, $S(Y)$, equals $PS(a)$. The expected value of Y when P is zero is simply $E(u)$, shown on the vertical axis of figure 24–1. Higher levels of P raise $E(Y)$ at the rate $E(a)$ and raise the standard deviation of Y at the constant rate $S(a)$. Policy makers therefore have an opportunity set given by the straight line from $E(u)$ in figure 24–1.

FIGURE 24–1 Optimal policy with uncertain policy effects

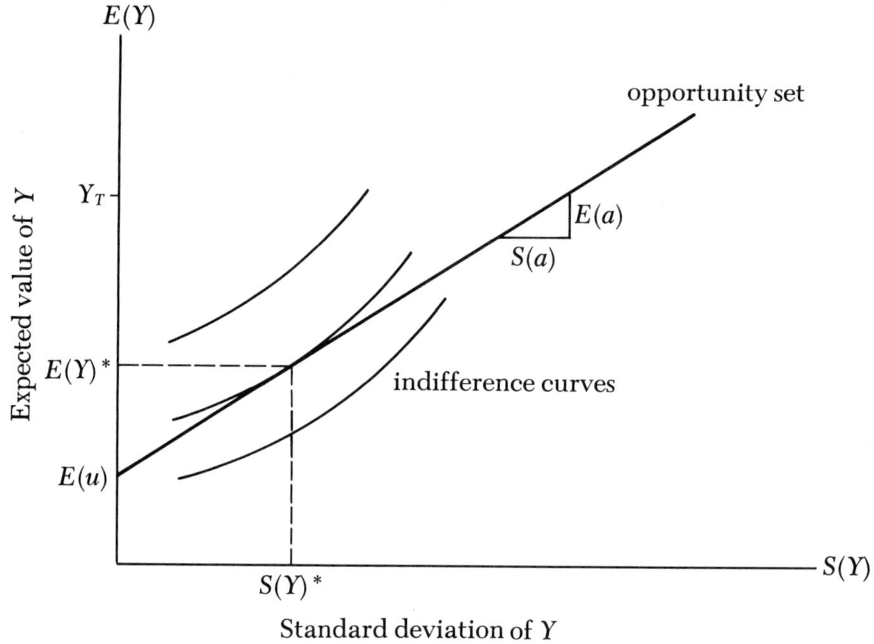

The policy maker increases both the expected outcome and the variance of the outcome by increasing the policy size. The optimal policy is therefore at the point of tangency of the opportunity set and the highest indifference curve, where the marginal rate of substitution of extra $S(Y)$ for extra $E(Y)$ (the slope of the indifference curve) is equal to $E(a)/S(a)$ (the slope of the opportunity set). $E(u)$ is the level of $E(Y)$ that would occur at the expected level of all other exogenous variables if the policy variable were set at zero.

Optimal policy is the level of P at the point of tangency of the opportunity set with the highest indifference curve in figure 24–1. This is the level of P that produces $E(Y)^*$ on the vertical axis and the level $S(Y)^*$ on the horizontal axis.

The optimal policy falls short of the level that would achieve the target Y_T exactly. Optimal policy is tentative, cautious in the face of uncertainty about policy effects, because more aggressive policy adds to uncertainty. The extent to which optimal policy falls short will depend on how risk-averse policy makers are, how powerful the policy is — that is, $E(a)$ — and how uncertain the effect of policy is — that is, $Var(a)$.

If we relax the requirement that all the rest of the world be certain, so that $Var(u)$ is no longer zero, the effect of extra policy doses on the variance of Y changes. The rate of change of $Var(Y)$ with respect to P is

$$\frac{dVar(Y)}{dP} = 2PVar(a) + 2Cov(a,u).$$

Policy will increase uncertainty by less as the covariance of a and u becomes smaller. If uncertainty about policy effects and about exogenous variables is negatively correlated, policy could even reduce uncertainty about Y over some initial range of P values. For instance, if monetary policy were expected to have large effects whenever net export demand fell, monetary policy could be used more aggressively than without such an expectation. In figure 24–1, such negative covariance would cause a steeper opportunity line and lead to greater levels of $E(Y)$. With the same level of $E(a)$, that would imply less caution in the use of policy.

Diversification of policies

When there is more than one policy instrument available, policy makers can diversify in the same way that investors diversify asset portfolios, and with the same effect. If several policies are used to achieve the same level of $E(Y)$, the variance of Y due to uncertainty of policy effects is greatly reduced. In the special case where $Var(u)$ is zero, where all the policy coefficients have the same but independent variances, and where all policies are used in equal amounts, the variance of real income $Var(Y)$ is just the fraction $1/n$ of what it would have been if only one policy had been used. More generally, the reduction in variance of Y will depend on the pattern of covariances among coefficients of various policy tools, just as variance of portfolio yield depends on the pattern of covariances among yields on various assets in an asset portfolio.

In general, uncertainty of outcome will be minimized if all available policy tools are used to achieve the objective. This may have been part of the logic behind the Porter Commission's recommendation in the fall of 1964 that all stabilization policy tools be used to push the economy in the same direction.

By contrast, Milton Friedman has argued long and hard, ever since 1953, that monetary policy has effects on aggregate demand with such long and variable lags that the best policy for human policy makers in an uncertain world is to set money-supply growth at a trend rate of 4 percent and not to attempt any countercyclical variation at all.[16] Friedman's suggestion is optimal in Brainard's context only if (because of mistakes in estimating the lag in effect, for instance) the expected contribution of policy P to reducing $E(Y) - Y_T$ is zero.

[16]M. Friedman, "The Effects of a Full-employment Policy on Economic Stability: A Formal Analysis," *Essays in Positive Economics* (Chicago: University of Chicago Press, 1953). See also Friedman, *A Program for Monetary Stability* (New York: National Bureau of Economic Research, 1959).

Brainard's analysis raises the important and largely unanswered question of which policies have the most certain impact. Certainty of impact is likely to be associated with directness of impact and with accumulated experience in use of the policy instrument. Government spending, for instance, has a closely predictable effect on aggregate demand;[17] monetary policy does not, because monetary policy affects aggregate demand only indirectly through effects on interest rates, exchange rates, and wealth.[18] On the other hand, Milton Friedman and Anna Schwartz sought to increase the perceived reliability of monetary policy by documenting the effects of money-supply changes over more than a century of U. S. history.[19] The world has little experience with incomes policies, by contrast, so even their staunchest advocates are uncertain about how effective they would be.

Professor Robert Lucas of the University of Chicago has pointed out that any policy action that affected the structure of the economy (such as switching from an income tax to a consumption tax) would make the economy's past responses irrelevant as guides for future policy.[20] We could not be certain of the effects even of policies used before, until we had established exactly how the structure of the economy had changed. Since expectations-formation processes are an important part of the economy's structure for macroeconomic policy, and they are unobservable, it is very hard to establish what changes in structure are caused by various policy actions. Lucas' message is therefore that policy effects are bound to be more uncertain than our econometric estimates suggest.

SECTION 3 Choice of policy rules

Monetary economists waged a fierce debate throughout the 1960s on the relative merits of rules and discretion as guidelines for the use of monetary and fiscal policy. This debate is not quite over, but one principle has been firmly established as a result of the work of the rational-expectations

---

[17]Government spending itself has long been considered relatively unpredictable, however, because of the unpredictability of the U.S. Congress in amending the President's budget proposals. In Canada, with majority government in command of the legislature, this problem is usually much less serious than in the United States. In Canada, however, there is extra uncertainty about whether provincial policy will be used to counteract federal fiscal policy.

[18]Monetarists have sometimes argued that monetary policy has direct effects on aggregate demand, independent of interest rates. The Bank's view is that it "has never uncovered any links between the supply of base money (or any other measure of the money supply) and the price level or the rate of economic activity that are not attributable, directly or indirectly, to the movement of interest rates or the exchange rate." Gordon Thiessen, "The Canadian Experience with Monetary Targetting" (Ottawa: Bank of Canada, May 5, 1982), 2.

[19]M. Friedman and A. Schwartz, *A Monetary History of the United States, 1867–1960* (Princeton: Princeton University Press, 1963).

[20]Robert E. Lucas, Jr., "Econometric Policy Evaluation: A Critique," in Karl Brunner and Alan H. Meltzer, eds, *The Phillips Curve and the Labor Market* (Amsterdam: North Holland, 1976), 19–46.

school:[21] where the objective of policy makers is to reduce uncertainty for the rest of the economy, it does not help to keep the use of policy tools secret. Use of monetary and fiscal levers on the economy generates extra demand or supply shocks; if use of these policies is kept secret until after the fact, then the shocks must be unexpected by the private sector and must necessarily increase the general public's uncertainty about the future. Instead, policy should be used according to rules of some sort, known in advance by the public. Policy-induced shocks should be expected. The debate over rules versus discretion has therefore shifted to a debate over simple rules versus complex rules, or possibly even constant-growth rules versus feedback rules.

Choice of policy rules essentially determines which exogenous shocks will be allowed to affect real output, inflation, interest rates, and exchange rates and which will be automatically offset by policy changes. The *optimal policy rule* for any policy tool is defined as the one that produces the lowest variance of the target variable.

Optimal policy rule

Optimal monetary rules

The logic of optimal policy rules is best developed in the context of managing aggregate demand and is based on the work of Professor William Poole of Brown University.[22] We will first present Poole's approach in that context and then extend the approach to management of real output and inflation with both demand and supply shocks.

The IS curve

Policy makers face uncertainty from two sources in managing aggregate demand. The *IS*-curve relationship is uncertain, and so is the *LM*-curve relationship. For convenience I will repeat the equations for the *IS* curve from chapter 18:

$$AD^e = \left(\frac{A_0}{1 - b'}\right) - \left(\frac{c + g}{1 - b'}\right)r \tag{6}$$

$$\text{where } A_0 = aW - bT_0 + I_0 + G + F_0 + gr_{US}. \tag{7}$$

F_0 and gr_{US} reflect the Capital Account of the Balance of Payments (which affects the exchange rate, and therefore net exports), while the coefficient g in the numerator of the second expression reflects the influence of domestic interest rates on net exports via the Capital Account and the exchange rate. The multiplier is $1/(1 - b')$ rather than $1/(1 - b' + m)$,

[21]This school includes the work of Robert Lucas, Thomas Sargent, Neil Wallace, and others. For a summary and evaluation, see Michael Parkin, *Modern Macroeconomics* (Toronto: Prentice-Hall, 1982), part 5.

[22]William Poole, "Optimal Choice of Monetary Instruments in a Simple Stochastic Macro Model," *Quarterly Journal of Economics*, 1970, 197–216. This approach to stabilization policy has been extended to an open economy by Gordon Sparks, in "The Choice of Monetary Policy Instruments in Canada," *Canadian Journal of Economics*, 1979, 615–25.

because we assume that any rise in imports is offset, after a rise in the exchange rate, by an equal change in net exports.

Even this brief sketch of the *IS*-curve relationship is enough to remind us that it is uncertain at many points. All items in equation (7), even G and T_0, are subject to unexpected disturbances (remember, government spending and taxation in Canada are not under the control of any one government). Variations in real wealth, sluggishness in response of the exchange rate (or the opposite, overresponse), changes in the pattern of interest rates in the financial system — all of these and more will affect the level of aggregate demand.

The LM curve

The *LM* curve from the simple, two-asset model of chapter 19 looks simpler than the *IS* curve, but it is also uncertain. When the cash reserve base is fixed, the *LM*-curve relationship is

$$r = \frac{L_0 - \alpha(R/P)}{j} + \left(\frac{h}{j}\right)Y. \tag{8}$$

The constant term L_0 reflects the impact of real wealth and relative risks on demand for money. R/P is the real cash reserve base. The money-supply multiplier α reflects the cash reserve requirement and the public's desired currency:deposit ratio. The coefficient ratio h/j is the ratio of income to interest sensitivity of the demand for money.

Most of the uncertainty in equation (8) is likely to come from the terms L_0 and α. If positive "errors" in the one are typically associated with positive "errors" in the other, then they will offset each other and have little net effect on interest rates, but there is little reason to expect any such pattern of correlation.

Alternative rules for cash reserve management

Now that we have recalled what we need to know about *IS* and *LM*, let us return to monetary rules. There are two simple alternative rules for the conduct of cash reserve management, the major tool of monetary policy. The first rule is to hold nominal reserves R fixed (or to increase R at a fixed rate, in a growing economy; here we ignore economic growth for simplicity). In that case the interest rate is determined as in equation (8), and the *LM* curve is like LM_R in figure 24–2. The second rule is to instruct the Bank of Canada's money-market trader to buy and sell Treasury Bills or to transfer federal deposits, so that money-market interest rates are kept at a target level. This rule fixes the interest rate but allows the level of R to be determined by market forces. Equation (8) can be rearranged to reflect this change, isolating R on the left-hand side:

$$R = \frac{P}{\alpha}(L_0 - jr + hY). \tag{9}$$

FIGURE 24–2 Alternative *LM* curves

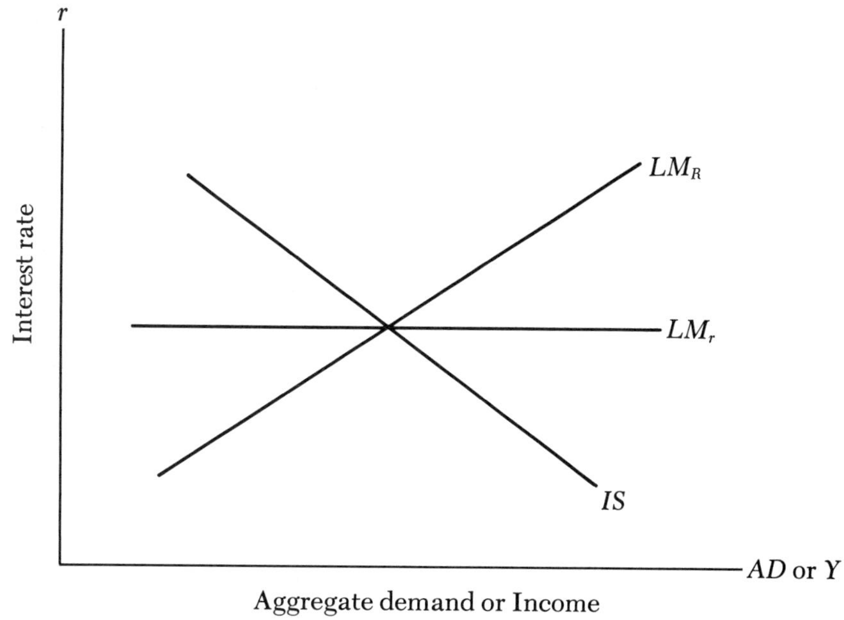

If the cash reserve base is fixed, then increases in Y will raise money demand and push interest rates up. The *LM* curve will have a positive slope, like LM_R. If the interest rate is fixed, then higher Y levels will lead to higher cash reserves sufficient to prevent any upward movement of interest rates. The *LM* curve will therefore be flat, like LM_r.

When the interest rate is fixed and R is variable, the *LM* curve becomes a flat line on an *IS–LM* diagram, such as LM_r in figure 24–2.

Now consider the response of aggregate demand, for a given price level, to any of the possible disturbances in either *IS* or *LM* curves. Figure 24–3 shows both types of *LM* curves (LM_R if reserves are fixed; LM_r if the interest rate is fixed), intersecting at $r = r^*$ to achieve the target AD_T. The target AD_T will occur if the *IS* curve is in its expected position IS^e. However, random disturbances to the *IS* curve could produce actual demand levels and *IS* curves to the right or left of IS^e as shown in the figure. With reserves fixed (along LM_R), surges of demand for goods are partly choked off by rising interest rates (which lower investment demand and indirectly lower net exports as well). With the interest rate fixed (along LM_r), there is no such offsetting effect; the range of possible aggregate demand outcomes is correspondingly wider. That is, a monetary rule fixing R will offset more of any exogenous shocks to the *IS* curve than the rule of changing R to keep the interest rate constant.

FIGURE 24–3 Effect of shocks to the *IS* curve

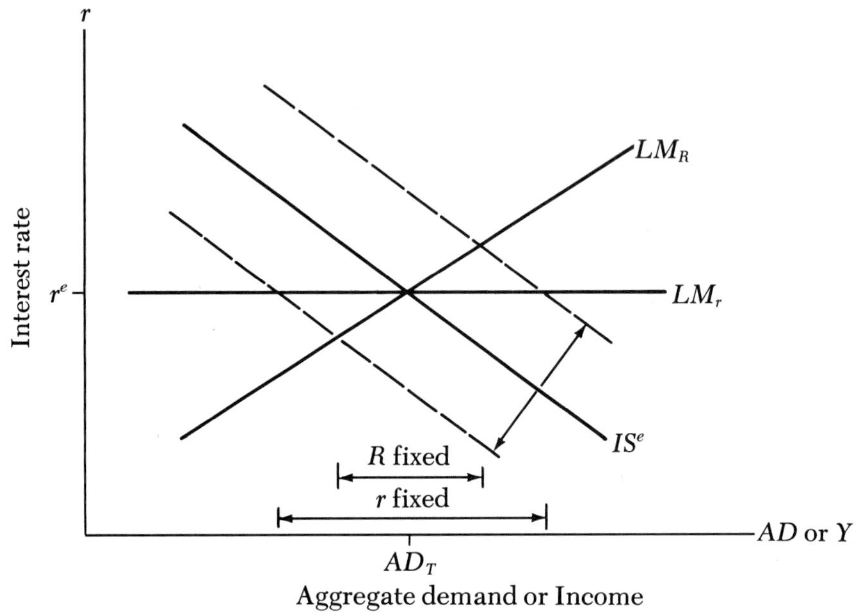

Shocks to the *IS* curve shift it horizontally in either direction from its expected position IS^e. With cash reserves fixed, the resulting changes in equilibrium aggregate demand are much smaller than if the interest rate were fixed, because the interest-rate feedback serves to dampen demand shocks.

When the disturbances are in the *LM*-curve equation, it is the fixed-interest rule that comes off better. Figure 24–4 shows the result of changes in L_0 when the *IS* curve is certain. With the level of cash reserves fixed, any increase in L_0 shifts the *LM* curve to the left and drives up the interest rate. Higher interest rates reduce investment demand and net exports, depressing aggregate demand. With the interest rate fixed instead, the disturbance in L_0 is automatically offset by changes in cash reserves. There is no change in interest rates and therefore no change in aggregate demand. The fixed-interest rule completely offsets exogenous shocks in the financial system, whereas the fixed-reserve-base rule transmits them to the real sector.

Which strategy is optimal clearly depends on the relative size and frequency of shocks in the real and financial sectors.

Recognizing shifts of IS and LM curves

Impatient readers may raise the objection at this point that there really is no issue here, because the central bank can easily distinguish between

FIGURE 24–4 Effects of shocks to money demand

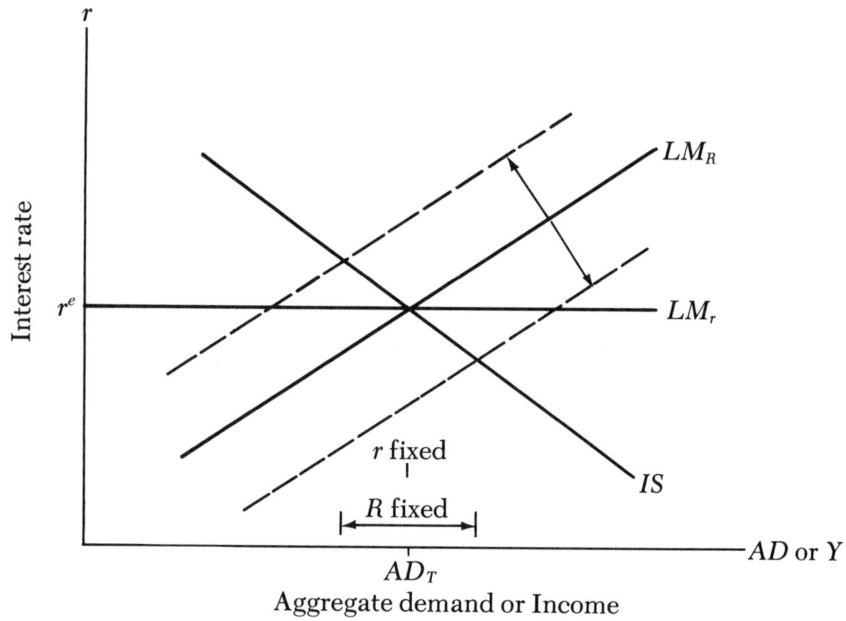

Shocks to money demand shift the LM_R curve to the right or left but are completely offset by changes in the reserve base if the interest rate is fixed so that LM_r does not move at all. Equilibrium aggregate demand thus does not move at all if the interest rate is fixed.

shifts of *IS* and shifts of *LM* curves as they occur. After all, shifts of the *IS* curve cause interest rates and aggregate demand to move in the same direction, whereas shifts of the *LM* curve cause them to move in opposite directions. The central bank need only watch what is happening to both interest rates and aggregate demand. Alas, the central bank cannot use this simple rule, because aggregate demand is not known until several months after the fact. Statistics Canada works long and hard but is able to produce estimates of "current" aggregate demand only in the middle of the following quarter; even those estimates are subject to large and frequent revisions later on.

An optimal rule for cash reserve management

The Bank of Canada can use a combination of fixed-interest-rate and fixed-reserve rules for monetary policy, and in general such a combination will be better than either of the two rules alone. Choosing the optimal combination is best explained by imagining the Bank as (a) knowing that both goods and financial markets are subject to shocks and (b) able to detect these shocks only by their effect on interest rates (timely estimates of current aggregate demand not being available).[23] Imagine the Bank to be expecting the interest rate r^e and selecting the appropriate level of R in figure 24–5 to cause the aggregate demand level AD_T, but actually observing the interest rate r'.

FIGURE 24–5 The optimal monetary rule

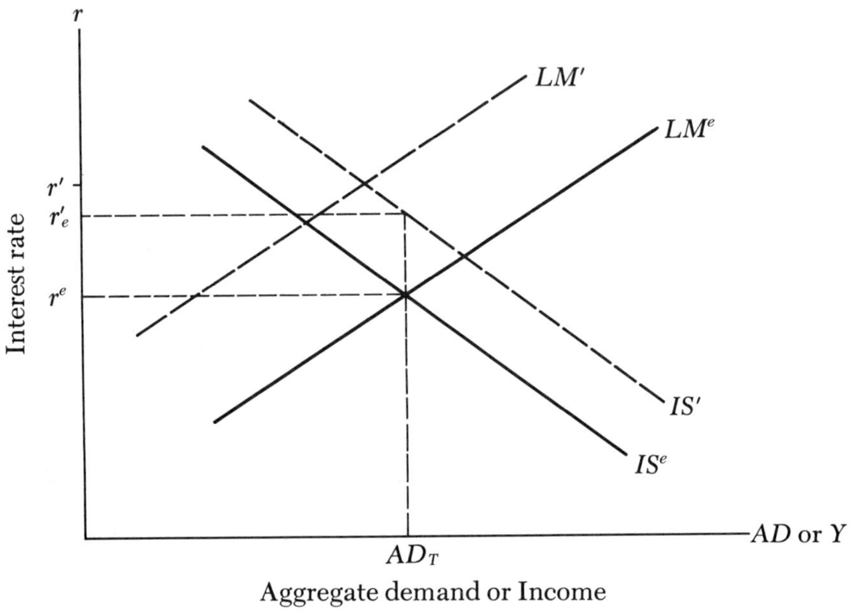

The Bank expects *IS* and *LM* curves to be in the positions IS^e and LM^e, generating interest rate r^e and achieving the target demand level AD_T. During the policy period the Bank observes an actual interest rate of r' instead of r^e. The Bank infers from past volatility of *IS* and *LM* that some of the increase in r is due to an increase in aggregate demand (which shifted the *IS* curve to *IS'*) and that the rest is due to a financial disturbance that shifted the *LM* curve to *LM'*. Optimal policy to maintain AD_T is to adjust the interest rate to r'_e, by increasing the cash reserve level to shift the *LM* curve until it again intersects the *IS* curve above AD_T.

The rate r' lies above the level that would be caused by the Bank's expectations of *IS* and *LM* curves (the ones shown in figure 24–5), so clearly one or both of the *IS* and *LM* curves have shifted. But which one? If the *IS* curve is to blame, then the cash reserve base should not be increased; interest rates should be allowed to stay high, and maybe should even be raised further by a reduction in the reserve base. If the *LM* curve is to blame, then cash reserves should be increased to offset it, or else the Bank

[23]This explanation of the logic of Poole's approach is given by Stephen F. Leroy and David E. Lindsey, "Determining the Monetary Instrument: A Diagrammatic Exposition," *American Economic Review*, Dec. 1978, 929–34.

will find that aggregate demand has fallen below AD_T because of higher interest rates, and the Bank will be accused of allowing a financial disturbance to cause recession.

The Bank of Canada's best guess is to assume that the change in interest rate is due to shifts in both *IS* and *LM*, in proportions determined by the relative stability of the *IS* and *LM* curves in the past. The larger the relative past instability of the *IS* curve, the more of the rise in r is blamed on the *IS* curve and the less of it is offset by changes in cash reserves. The larger the relative volatility of financial markets, the more of the rise in r is blamed on the *LM* curve and the more it is offset by monetary policy. That is, optimal policy requires making the inference about the new position of the *IS* curve on the basis of observation of r' instead of r^e and then adjusting the level of the target interest rate from r^e (or the target cash reserve base from its previous level) to produce the same AD_T from the new *IS* curve.

The weakest part of our story so far has been the assumption that the Bank can detect that there has been a shock only by the change in interest rate. In fact, the Bank has its corporate ear constantly to the ground and will have a flood of other information to help it discriminate between financial and real demand shocks. Its optimal policy rule is to counter real shocks by holding R fixed (or even reducing R when aggregate demand increases, if the volatility of interest rates does not matter) and to cancel out financial shocks by adjusting the cash reserve base. With sufficient information, this combination policy is less uncertain than our analysis has suggested. However, such a combination policy rule is hard to explain to the public and does little to reduce their uncertainty.

Optimal rules for exchange rate management

The Bank has a choice of policy rules for managing the exchange rate, since it influences the exchange rate through its purchases and sales of foreign exchange assets. Essentially the Bank can buy and sell currencies to keep the exchange rate stable, or the Bank can let the exchange rate float freely without intervention. There are limits to the Bank's power to stabilize the exchange rate without using domestic interest rates as well, but use of foreign exchange reserves will be effective in the short run.[24] The question is, what use should be made of this power in the short run? Which rule will most reduce uncertainty?

Whether the exchange rate is fixed or flexible in the short run has a big effect on the slope and behavior of the *IS* curve and therefore on the slope and behavior of the aggregate demand curve for the economy. These effects are visible in the two alternative equations for the *IS* curve, under

[24]The Report of the Working Group on Exchange Market Intervention, commissioned at the Versailles Summit of 1982, concluded that exchange-market intervention had little impact unless it was unsterilized — that is, accompanied by changes in the domestic monetary base (Paris, March 1983, 69).

flexible and fixed exchange rates. Under flexible exchange rates, our equation for the *IS* curve is

$$AD^e = \left(\frac{A_0}{1 - b'}\right) - \left(\frac{c + g}{1 - b'}\right)r, \tag{6}$$

where $A_0 = aW - bT_0 + G + I_0 + F_0 + gr_{US}$. (7)

The terms F_0 and gr_{US} in equation (7) reflect capital-market influences on the exchange rate. Note that equations (6) and (7) contain no exogenous variables reflecting the Current Account of the Balance of Payments, since Current Account fluctuations are automatically offset by exchange rate fluctuations. The numerator term $(c + g)$ in equation (6) reflects the influence of interest rates on both investment (through c) and net exports (through g).

Under fixed exchange rates, the similar equation for the *IS* curve is

$$AD^e = \frac{A_0'}{1 - b' + m} - \left(\frac{c}{1 - b' + m}\right)r, \tag{10}$$

where $A_0' = aW - bT_0 + G + I_0 + X_0$. (11)

The *IS* curve in equation (10) has an intercept term that depends on fluctuations in the Current Account and not on those in the Capital Account; X_0 replaces $F_0 + gr_{US}$ from equation (7). The *IS* curve in equation (10) has a smaller aggregate demand multiplier term $1/(1 - b' + m)$, so changes in A_0' have less total effect on demand than do changes in A_0 in equation (6). Finally, the *IS* curve in equation (10) is steeper not only because of the smaller multiplier but also because the interest rate is allowed to affect only investment demand (through c) and not both investment and net export demand.

Figure 24–6 illustrates the impact of a random change in exogenous demand (that is, in A_0 or in A_0') with both types of *IS* curve and a single, certain *LM* curve. IS_1^e is the expected *IS* curve with fixed exchange rates, and IS_2^e is the expected *IS* curve with flexible exchange rates. The unexpected increase in A_0 shifts IS_2 to the right by the factor $1/(1 - b')$. The same increase in A_0' shifts IS_1 to the right by the smaller factor $1/(1 - b' + m)$. If the cash reserve base is held constant, however, the increase in interest rates will offset this exogenous demand increase at a faster rate for IS_2 than for IS_1, so the new equilibrium level of aggregate demand will not necessarily be bigger under flexible exchange rates than under fixed exchange rates. In short, there is nothing much to choose between the two policy rules on grounds of stabilizing aggregate demand.

The other difference between the two exchange rate rules is that aggregate demand is made sensitive to changes in the Capital Account under flexible exchange rates and to changes in the Current Account under fixed exchange rates. If the economy is to be insulated from both, then a combination policy is needed. Such a policy is called a *managed float*. The government will want to allow the exchange rate to respond whenever the

Managed float

Current Account is disturbed and to prevent the exchange rate from changing when the Capital Account is disturbed.

FIGURE 24–6 Effect of exchange-rate policy on demand shocks

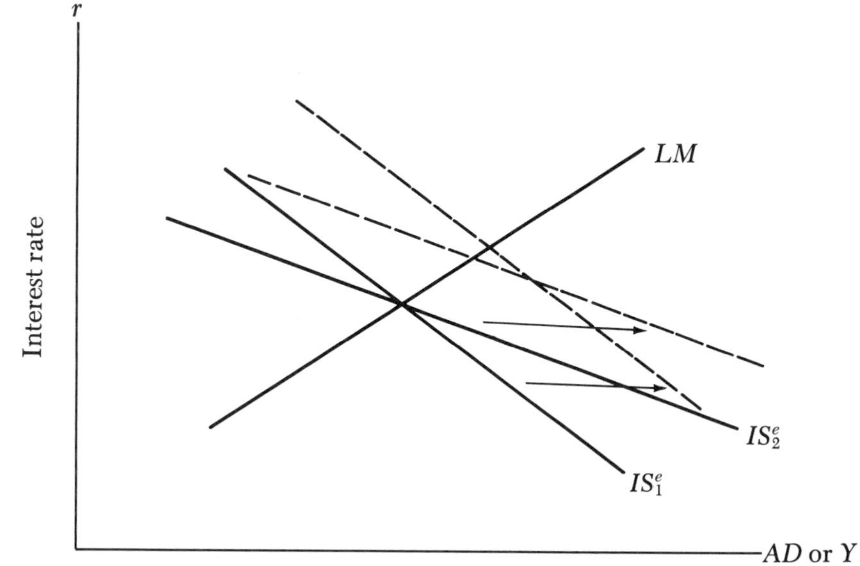

With floating exchange rates, the *IS* curve is flatter (IS_2) and shifts more in response to disturbances in exogenous demand components. The combination of greater volatility of the *IS* curve and a more powerful interest-rate feedback mechanism means that the net effect of floating exchange rates on demand volatility is not clear.

Supply shocks

The problem in choosing an optimal policy rule is choosing between an interest-rate rule and a cash-reserve-base rule to stabilize real output growth and inflation in an economy with both demand and supply shocks. We have seen that fixing cash reserves is better for shocks to the *IS* curve, but fixing interest rates is better for other disturbances to the demand side. What difference does it make, if any, if there are supply shocks as well?

Figure 24–7 shows aggregate demand and aggregate supply curves as derived in chapters 18 and 19. There are two aggregate demand curves, because the choice of monetary-policy rule affects the slope and behavior of the *AD* curve just as it affects the *LM* curve. With fixed cash reserves, higher prices reduce real cash reserves and drive up interest rates; the higher interest rates depress investment demand and net exports. Aggregate demand is thus sensitive to the price level. When the interest rate is fixed instead, higher prices are accompanied by higher cash reserves. Real cash reserves are not affected by inflation, and neither is the interest rate. With no effect on the interest rate, aggregate demand is not sensitive to prices. The aggregate demand curve is vertical.[25]

FIGURE 24–7 Aggregate demand curves and supply shocks

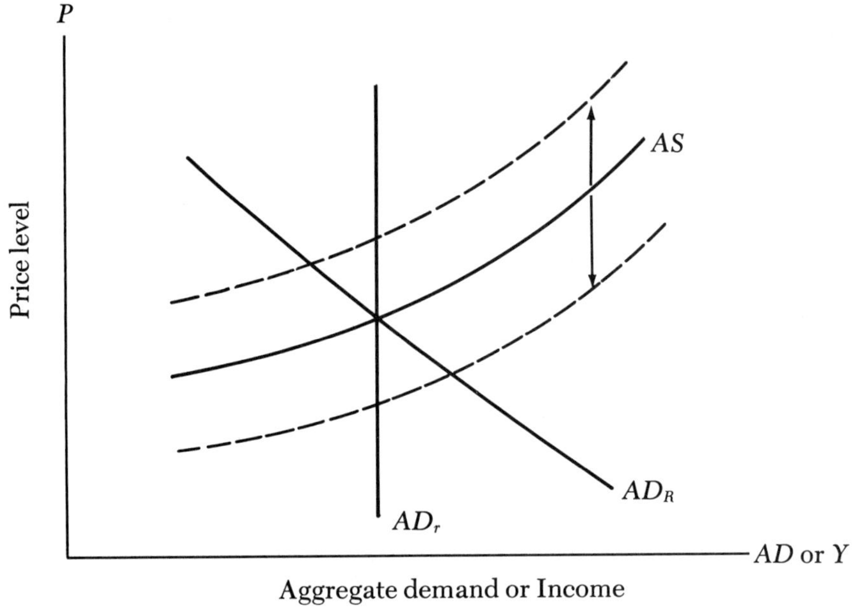

With cash reserves fixed, higher price levels cause higher interest rates and therefore lower aggregate demand, as along AD_R. With the interest rate fixed, there are no interest-rate feedback effects, so aggregate demand is not sensitive to price levels, as along AD_r.

Supply shocks that shift *AS* up and down will merely affect price levels if the interest rate is fixed. If cash reserves are fixed, price levels will be less affected and output levels will be more affected. The flatter the *AS* curve in the short run, and the flatter the *AD* curve, the larger will be the output variations when the cash reserve base is fixed.

Now imagine fluctuations in aggregate supply due to unexpected supply shocks, producing the shifts of *AS* in figure 24–7. Clearly the fixed-cash-reserve rule yields less price volatility but more output volatility than the fixed-interest-rate rule. Which is more desirable depends on the relative social costs of the two kinds of volatility.

Figure 24–8 illustrates the effect of the two policy rules in the event of unexpected demand shocks. With fixed cash reserves, an increase in any exogenous demand component such as I_0 has a smaller multiplier effect on aggregate demand and shifts the *AD* curve by less, because the initial

[25]If the price rises for long enough, inflationary expectations may rise as well. In that case, a constant nominal interest rate will mean a lower real interest rate, so aggregate demand may well increase; the aggregate demand curve may be positively sloped. Some Bank critics argue that this is precisely what happened in 1973–75 as a result of Bank policy.

stimulus is partly offset by the interest-rate feedback mechanism. Higher price levels cause even more interest-rate feedbacks by reducing real cash reserves, so aggregate demand is lowered by higher prices as well, and the net impact of the demand shock produces relatively small changes in both output and prices. With fixed interest rates, on the other hand, the *AD* curve shifts further to the right for the same exogenous demand shock and is less offset by price increases. With fixed interest rates, in other words, both prices and output levels are more sensitive to demand shocks. Only the interest rate is more stable.

FIGURE 24–8 Aggregate demand shocks and monetary rules

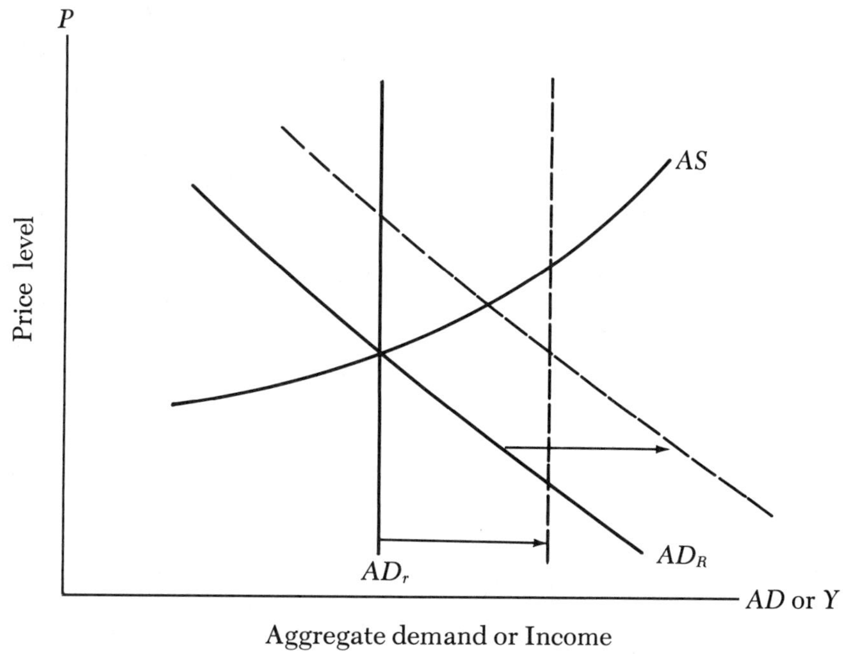

With interest rates fixed, aggregate demand shocks are not offset by any interest-rate feedback mechanism, so the AD_r curve is more volatile than if cash reserves were fixed and the interest rate were allowed to vary. Price changes have less offsetting effect along AD_r, so the volatility of both prices and output levels is greater if interest rates are fixed in the presence of demand shocks.

The appropriate conclusion is that, for stabilizing inflation, the fixed-reserve-base rule is better for both demand and supply shocks. For stabilizing output, the fixed-interest rule is better for aggregate supply shocks and for all other shocks affecting the financial system. If the Bank of Canada can discriminate clearly between aggregate demand and aggregate supply shocks, a combination strategy will be better than either rule by itself.

It will come as welcome news that the Bank's actual strategy has much in common with the optimal strategies we have discussed in this section. Unfortunately, it does not always look that way, and the Bank's strategy differs in some important and controversial ways.

SECTION 4

The Bank of Canada's approach

The Bank of Canada has consistently adopted a strategy of fixing the interest rate in the very short run and of managing the exchange rate to varying extents. The level of cash reserves has been adjusted, by open-market operations and federal deposit transfers, to whatever level is needed to maintain target interest rates. That level is determined essentially by what happens to the demand for money, which in turn depends mainly on nominal GNE and on interest rates. Over periods longer than a few months, the Bank adjusts the level of interest rates in light of what it thinks has happened to the excess of actual over desired aggregate demand. The Bank's officials look at everything that might help them make the correct inference about what is happening to actual aggregate demand.

Any discussion of the Bank's strategy must start with the Bank's stated objectives. In the words of a senior Bank official, writing in May 1982, "In recent years the primary objective of monetary policy in Canada has been to bring down the rate of inflation."[26] Another official of the Bank has given as subsidiary objectives the prevention of large changes ("disorder") in financial and exchange markets. The Governor of the Bank has frequently argued that lowering inflation is a prerequisite to resumption of healthy output growth, which makes lowering inflation in the short run the primary goal regardless of its temporary effect on the level and variability of real output and employment.

The Bank has attempted to lower and stabilize inflation through a combination of increasing monetary stringency and managing the exchange rate (with foreign exchange reserves and on occasion with interest rates as well) to prevent shocks in the exchange market from pushing up domestic costs and therefore prices. The Bank has also tried, by loudly announcing a simple and explicit anti-inflationary strategy, to influence inflationary expectations directly; this is an attempt to lower the aggregate supply curve. Some Bank critics are sceptical about the effect of such a psychological venture, but it is almost impossible to tell whether this strategy had any effect.

Since the Bank was attempting not just to stabilize inflation but also to lower it, the Bank purposely acted to reduce aggregate demand below desirable long-run levels, by fixing target interest rates higher than desirable long-run levels. The Bank's attempt to lower and stabilize inflation

[26]Thiessen, "Canadian Experience with Targetting," 2f.

rates therefore implied that the level of output growth and employment would temporarily be lowered and destabilized, but the Bank's policy had at least the tacit support of the federal Cabinet. The government put the Anti-Inflation Board in place from October 1975 to April 1978, to help the Bank in this task, and attempted restraint of various sorts in federal spending, but in most years federal spending seemed to be attempting to stem the unemployment consequences of restrictive monetary policy. Table 24–1 shows the major stances of monetary and fiscal policy for the years from 1975 to 1983: interest rates, changes in real cash reserves and in real M1, and the cyclically adjusted deficit of the government sector.

TABLE 24–1 Monetary and fiscal policy measures, 1975–83 (percent)

		Change in real values		Cyclically adjusted deficit (% of GNP)	
	Treasury Bill yields	M1	Cash reserves	Federal	All government
1975	7.4	2.7	4.7	1.9	2.0
1976	8.9	−1.4	0.0	1.8	1.8
1977	7.4	1.2	4.9	2.9	1.6
1978	8.6	3.5	5.3	3.9	2.3
1979	11.6	−3.0	−1.4	3.0	1.1
1980	12.8	−4.1	−0.8	2.3	1.0
1981	17.8	−5.6	−7.3	1.2	−0.1
1982	13.8	−7.6	6.0	2.5	1.0
1983	9.2	5.3	12.6	2.6	0.6

Sources: Department of Finance, *Economic Review*; *Bank of Canada Review*.

Because it was attempting to use monetary policy to lower inflation by lowering demand, while fiscal policy was attempting in various ways to keep demand high, the Bank of Canada had to raise domestic interest rates much more than was originally anticipated to achieve its goal of a recession large enough to moderate wage and price increases. From 1975 to 1982, Canadian interest rates were much more volatile than the Bank really desired, and would have been volatile even if U.S. interest rates had not been extremely unstable in 1980–81. Figure 24–9 shows the pattern of U.S. and Canadian short-term interest rates from 1977.

The strategy of gradualism

In its policy making, the Bank does not observe levels of real output in time for these observations to be of much use, so it has the inference problem discussed in section 3. Bank officials therefore make use of all possible information, including observations of any series that appears from the past to be correlated with output levels but is measured more quickly. Manufacturing shipments, changes in inventories and price levels, cheques cashed in major clearing centres, and movements of monetary aggregates are all pressed into service as indicators, in addition to changes in interest rates and exchange rates.

FIGURE 24–9 Canadian and U.S. ninety-day Treasury Bill yields

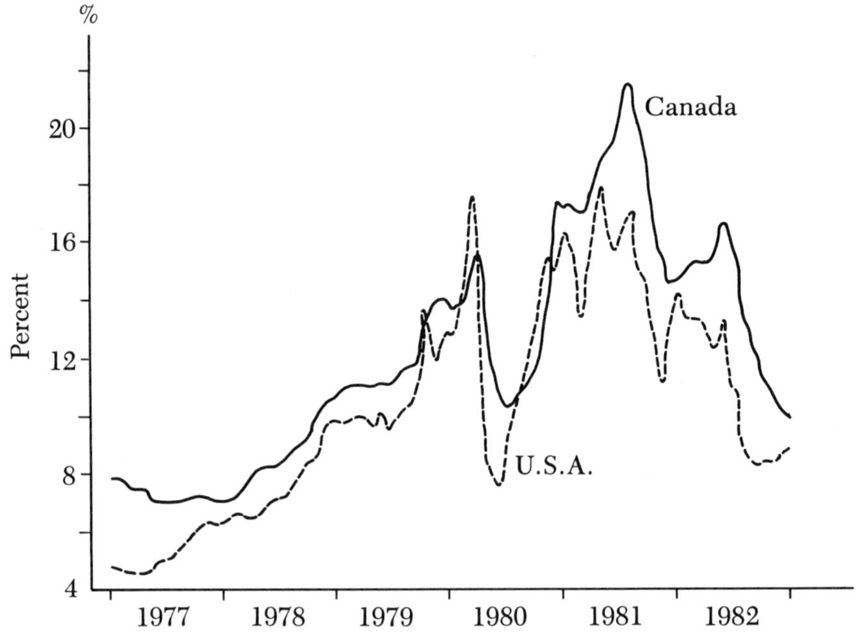

Source: Bank of Canada Review.

From September 1975 to early 1982, the Bank elevated movements in M1 to a special place among its indicators of real output behavior. The Bank even formulated its policy (or at least explained its policy) in terms of what it desired for M1. In the belief that movements in M1 were closely correlated in the short term with those of real output, prices, and short-term interest rates, the Bank proposed to slow down inflation and stabilize growth of *nominal* GNP (the product of the price level and the real output level) by adjusting short-term interest rates so as to keep M1 growth within a target growth band two percentage points wide. The Bank also planned to lower the target band gradually over time. Because of the idea that the growth targets for nominal GNP should be lowered only gradually, rather than all at once, the Bank's policy was known as the *strategy of gradualism* (to distinguish it from a *cold turkey* strategy). Some have called it the M1 strategy, and on occasion it is referred to as the Bank's monetarist strategy.

Strategy of gradualism

One of the more remarkable features of the Bank's M1 strategy was that it was so explicit. Previously, the Bank's policy had not been expressed in terms of any quantitative measures, but rather had consisted of using the Bank's discretion to find the "right" interest rate and other credit-market conditions to maintain the "right" degree of demand pressure or restraint in the economy. To the extent that uncertainty about stabilization policy contributes to the uncertainty under which people must make their future plans, the Bank's M1 strategy announcement in September 1975 must have reduced that uncertainty.[27]

FIGURE 24–10 Money-supply growth, 1975–82

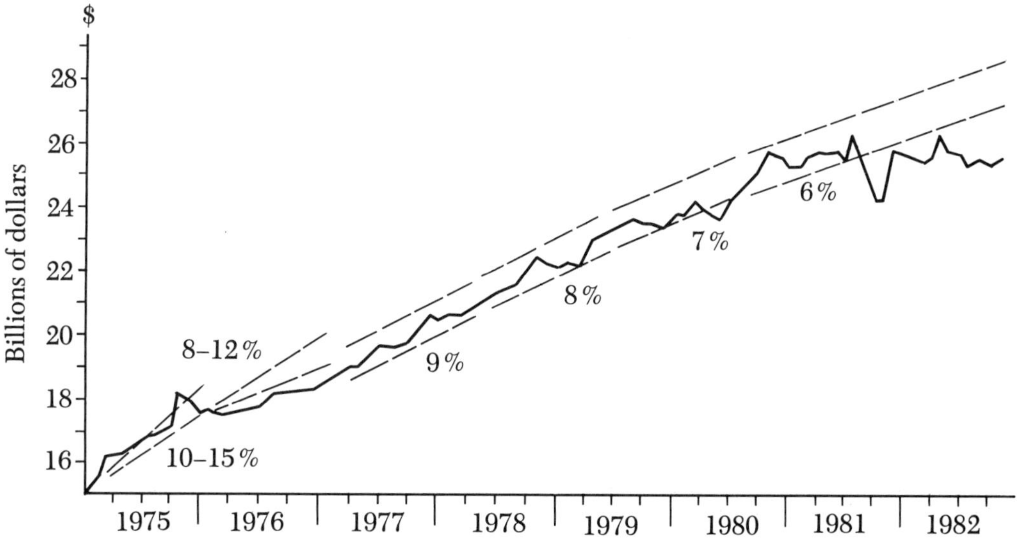

The dotted lines on either side of the money-supply growth path indicate the bounds within which the Bank aimed to keep the money supply. The range, or the midrange target growth rate, is given below each set of bands.

Source: Bank of Canada Review.

Figure 24–10 shows what actually happened to M1, as well as the upper and lower target bands. The Bank was able to achieve more or less what it sought for M1, until 1981–82. Professor Fortin has noted that M1 growth was not only reduced, but also made much more stable.[28] He developed table 24–2 to show what M1 growth had been before 1975: much more erratic, much less stable, following a definite stop-go pattern.

[27]Professor Thomas Courchene has labelled the announcement (by the Governor in a speech in Saskatoon) the "Saskatoon Manifesto." It is undoubtedly the Governor's best-known speech. *Monetarism and Controls: The Inflation Fighters* (Montreal: C.D. Howe Research Institute, 1976), 24.

[28]Fortin, "Monetary Targets," 626ff.

The Bank's policy was neither as blind nor as single-minded (not as consistent, some critics would say) as this description suggests. In 1978 and again in the summer of 1981 the Bank abandoned its target of M1 growth to help manage the exchange rate, when mere buying and selling of foreign exchange was not enough. The Bank was concerned both about the cost impact of further increases in the exchange rate, which would have constituted an adverse supply shock, and about the extra uncertainty that its benign neglect of the exchange rate might cause in the foreign exchange market. Apart from those episodes, the Bank did raise or lower domestic interest rates as needed to cause M1 to grow within its band, and hoped that in the process it was causing nominal GNP growth to slow down as well.

TABLE 24–2 M1 growth rates, 1965–74 (percent)

Period	Mean annual increase
4th quarter 1965 to 2nd quarter 1967	10.3
2nd quarter 1967 to 2nd quarter 1968	1.7
2nd quarter 1968 to 2nd quarter 1969	10.8
2nd quarter 1969 to 2nd quarter 1970	0.6
2nd quarter 1970 to 2nd quarter 1974	13.0

Source: Statistics Canada, CANSIM databank; first produced in Pierre Fortin, "Monetary Targets and Monetary Policy in Canada: A Critical Assessment," *Canadian Journal of Economics*, November 1979, 629.

In November 1982 the Bank formally abandoned its reliance on M1. Informally, the Bank abandoned it about six months earlier.[29] The relationship between M1 and nominal spending had shifted downward during 1981 for several reasons, but the Bank was denied the opportunity to make a reliable estimate of the extent of the shift, by a change in its data due to the introduction of the revised Bank Act in December 1980. The Bank did not know where its M1 target band should be moved to, and therefore gave up the target-band idea entirely. By then the Bank was also clearly disappointed that slowing the growth of nominal GNP was resulting mainly in a decline of output rather than slow growth of price levels. The reason may have been a series of food and energy price shocks after 1977, as well as the standard asymmetrical response of inflation to capacity use that Keynesian economists had claimed all along.

The strategy of gradualism had been intended to move Canada down from high to low inflation with little of the traumatic recession that other countries had experienced from less gradual monetary policies, but the

[29]See the Bank of Canada's Annual Report for 1982 (Ottawa, 1983), 25–30, for a discussion of the reasons for abandoning monetary targets; or see Thomas J. Courchene, *No Place to Stand?* (Montreal: C.D. Howe Research Institute, 1983).

strategy failed in that respect. The traumatic recession was only deferred. In 1982 the Bank returned to a less contentious policy of inferring the behavior of aggregate demand and supply from a wide range of indicators and choosing the proper short-term interest rate in light of an assessment of where the *IS* curve lies. This is essentially the optimal combination policy response discussed in section 3. It should be noted, however, that the Bank's primary objective is still to reduce inflation, so it still wishes to see aggregate demand restrained below its long-run trend level.

Evaluation of the M1 strategy

The Bank's M1 strategy was contentious for several reasons, some of which are relevant for future policy. This controversy exists despite agreement by almost all economists that slow growth of monetary aggregates is a necessary condition in the long run for low inflation rates, and despite recognition of the benefits of a clearly announced rule for conduct of stabilization policy.

The first ground for contention with the M1 strategy is that a policy of slowing inflation by causing recession (however gradually) is very expensive to society (see the description of costs of slow output growth, in section 1). If there is a much cheaper alternative not being used, then a recessionary strategy is not only expensive, but also inefficient. Many economists, but not all, feel that various forms of incomes policy plus mild restraint of demand would reduce inflation significantly at much lower cost than massive recession alone.[30] Such an alternative would not eliminate the need for demand restraint, but it would shorten the necessary period of restraint and allow higher average capacity use.

The second ground for contention is that slowing and stabilizing nominal GNP growth is not the same thing as stabilizing output and price levels. If inflation is not sensitive to unemployment in the short run, then the policy of gradual monetary restraint will produce ever slower growth of output until a recession occurs, and only at that point will inflation subside at all quickly. When inflation has subsided, then and only then will real output grow again. Neither path is a picture of stability. The only benefit is that inflation is lower at the end than at the beginning.

Furthermore, the higher interest rates needed to bring M1 back into its target band may not be enough to bring nominal spending back on track. The interest-rate increase required to do that would come only gradually if aggregate demand is not very sensitive to interest rates. This interest-rate increase would occur only gradually as continued rapid nominal demand growth continued to push M1 growth above its target band year after year. Each year that M1 growth exceeded the target rate, the Bank would raise

---

[30]Some eighty-one economists signed a petition to this effect in the fall of 1982 and sent it to *The Globe and Mail* as well as to the Minister of Finance.

interest rates further. Eventually, but not necessarily quickly, nominal spending would respond. Only if the interest elasticity of money demand and of aggregate demand were identical would the two have followed the same stable path.

Figure 24–11 shows the logic of this argument for Canada. Panel (a) records M1 growth, nominal GNE growth, and the change in interest rates from January to December for each year from 1975 to 1982. Panel (b) breaks down nominal GNE growth into real growth and inflation. Clearly, the Bank's operating strategy required continual increases in interest rates to keep growth of M1 demand on target (for every year in which nominal GNE growth exceeded the desired M1 growth), but nominal GNE growth hardly responded at all for the first five years. Adverse supply shocks worsened the situation, undoubtedly, but they do not account for all of the slow response of nominal GNE.

The third ground for contention with the Bank's strategy of gradualism is that it implies a nonaccommodating response to supply shocks. Adverse supply shocks will raise prices, and with no adjustment of monetary growth, the real money supply and real cash reserve base will shrink, so interest rates will be driven up and aggregate demand will be lowered. If this reduction in demand lowered domestic prices again, the supply shock would be offset and the price and output levels would be kept stable. If instead prices did not respond to lower demand by rolling back in the short run, then both inflation and unemployment would be raised. Neither prices nor output would be kept stable. The evidence suggests that price inflation does not respond quickly to changes in aggregate demand, so the second of these two results is more likely. Nonaccommodation of adverse supply shocks thus destabilizes output levels in the short run. Exactly the opposite reactions of prices, real cash reserves, aggregate demand, and unemployment occur in the event of favorable supply shocks. Only if supply shocks are expected to be adverse, and if the goal is to lower inflation, will this be an optimal policy.

The Bank has formally abandoned its M1 strategy in the sense that it is no longer expressing its policy in terms of keeping M1 growth within a specific band. There is still a role for M1, however, which Professor Benjamin Friedman has described as follows.[31] The Bank of Canada always has forecasts (Y^*) of the current real income level from past data, and it has forecasts ($M1_d^*$) of the current demand for M1 based on those same data. If the prediction error in M1 ($M1_d - M1_d^*$) is highly correlated with the prediction error in real output ($Y - Y^*$), then a policy of minimizing the sum of squared prediction errors of M1 (that is, stabilizing M1 growth about a trend line) will be almost equivalent to minimizing the sum of squared prediction errors for real output (that is, stabilizing real output around its trend).

---

[31]Benjamin Friedman, "The Inefficiency of Short-run Monetary Targets for Monetary Policy," *Brookings Papers on Economic Activity*, 1977:2, 293–335.

FIGURE 24–11 GNE, M1, and interest-rate changes, 1970–82

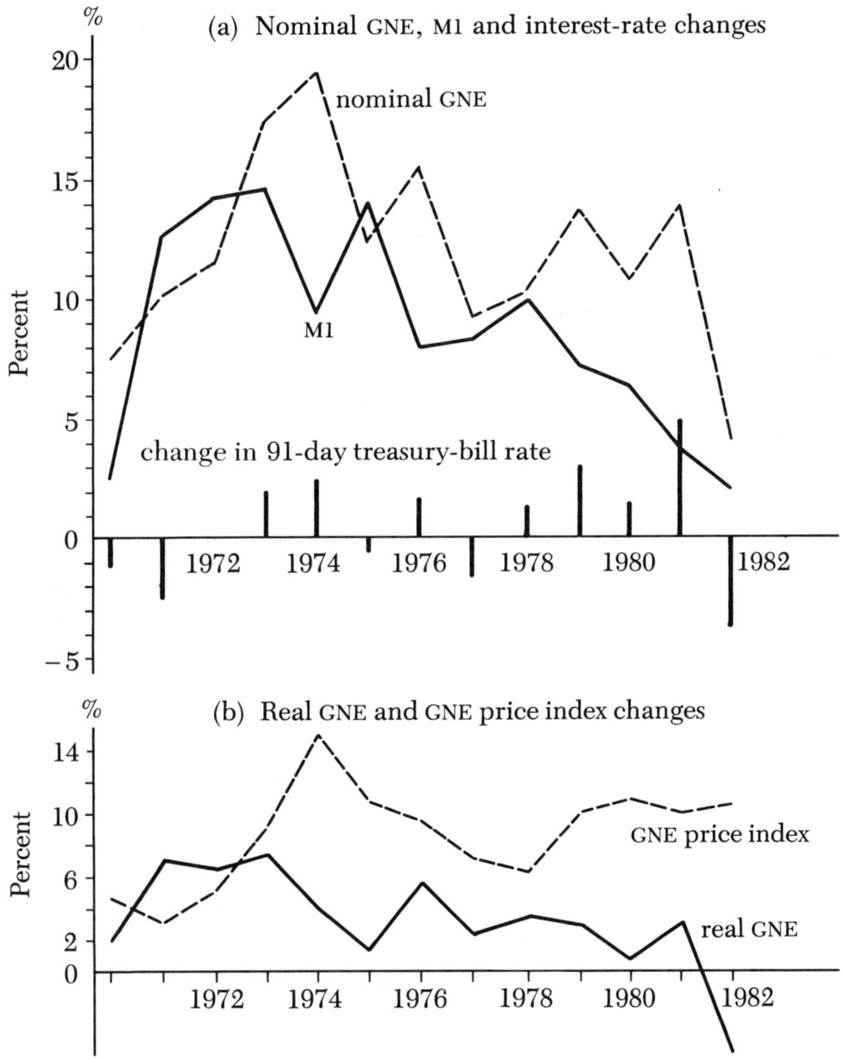

Where demand for money rises more or less proportionally with nominal GNE, then excess demand for money is generated whenever nominal GNE grows faster than M1 supplied, and interest rates are forced upward. Panel (a) shows the evidence. Panel (b) breaks down nominal GNE growth into price inflation and real spending growth — a breakdown that is useful if elasticities of money demand are different for prices and real income.

What is required is close correlation of prediction errors for M1 and real output, so that a positive prediction error for M1 can reliably be interpreted by the Bank as evidence that real output is above its predicted level. The more unpredictable is M1, the less value this strategy has. During 1981 and 1982, M1 demand shifted downward substantially, but it is possible that those shifts will be of the once-only kind. When M1 demand has adjusted, its prediction errors may once again be useful in the conduct of monetary policy.[32]

SECTION 5 Summary

The Bank of Canada must choose its policy strategy in an environment that is subject to several different types of uncertainty. The Bank is uncertain about all of the exogenous variables affecting aggregate demand and supply, about many of the impacts of its own policies, and often about the use that will be made of other stabilization policies. In principle and under certainty, each policy tool should be directed toward controlling that objective that it can influence relatively efficiently, but that policy-assignment rule is often violated.

The objectives of stabilization policy are generally conceived to be stabilization of output, employment, and inflation, at high levels for output and employment and at low levels for inflation. Stability of the interest rate and the exchange rate are also desirable to reduce uncertainty of important parameters in private-sector decisions.

Uncertainty about exogenous variables, undesirable though it is, presents no special problems for stabilization policy. Policy makers will do the least damage to the economy by proceeding on the basis of their best estimates of where exogenous variables will leave the target variable. If the effect of policy itself is uncertain, then policy makers will find it desirable to be cautious in their policy actions. Also, uncertainty about the effects of policies will cause policy makers to want to use more rather than fewer policies, in order to spread the risks over many policy tools so that much of the uncertainty will cancel itself out.

Each policy tool should be used according to an explicit rule of some sort, just to reduce the uncertainty of the public about policy shocks. The choice of optimal rules depends on the extent to which each offsets outside disturbances. For instance, a policy rule of fixing the reserve base has an automatic stabilizing property for disturbances affecting the *IS* curve, whereas a policy rule of fixing the interest rate has the same stabilizing property for disturbances affecting the financial system. Where both types

---

[32]The changes have been caused by such events as the spread of corporate cash management services of banks from just the large customers to some of the medium-size customers; by the introduction of interest-bearing chequing deposits; and by introduction of daily-interest savings deposits, which reward even short-term deposits during the month. The effects of these changes on the demand for money were analysed in chapter 9.

of disturbances abound, a combination policy is the best; the weights given to each type of rule will depend on the relative expected frequency and size of each type of disturbance. Fixing the reserve base will reduce both price and output volatility in the face of aggregate supply shocks.

The Bank of Canada has followed a policy basically of fixing interest rates in the very short run, but then adjusting interest rates either when aggregate demand is believed to have shifted or else when the Capital Account of the Balance of Payments is disturbed enough to threaten the exchange rate (for example, by large changes in U.S. interest rates). The Bank infers changes in the unobservable level of current aggregate demand from all relevant data it can find.

For the period 1975–82 the Bank used M1 as an indicator of nominal aggregate demand and even expressed its policy targets in terms of maintaining a stable but declining growth rate of M1. By November 1982 the Bank had to abandon that strategy formally because of instability of the relationship between M1 and real output levels.

Questions for discussion

1. What weights would you give to the various components of the social-loss function in equation (2) of this chapter? Would your weights as Minister of Finance be influenced by lobby groups? Which lobby groups would you expect to push for higher weights for price stability? For stability of real growth?
2. Is it plausible that the value of extra leisure-time activities could ever exceed the value of output foregone as a result of extra unemployment?
3. Are the costs of unemployment reduced by unemployment insurance?
4. If it is possible to remove inflation by reducing aggregate demand, how long will the costs and the benefits last from doing so?
5. Does the assignment rule suggest that stabilization policies can be handled separately, without co-ordination?
6. Is uncertainty a sufficient reason for doing nothing with stabilization policy?
7. Professor Lucas has argued in a famous critique of policy simulations that the policy itself changes the structure of the economy. How does this argument undermine the logic of Poole's optimal (combination) monetary rule, if at all?
8. In what sense could a monetary policy of restraint be inefficient?
9. What was gradual about the strategy of gradualism? What were the alternatives? Which was preferable, in retrospect?

References

Brainard, William C. "Uncertainty and the Effectiveness of Policy." *American Economic Review*. 1967, 411–25.

Courchene, Thomas J. *Money, Inflation, and the Bank of Canada*. Montreal: C.D. Howe Research Institute, 1975.

———. *Monetarism and Controls: The Inflation Fighters*. Montreal: C.D. Howe Research Institute, 1976.

———. *The Strategy of Gradualism*. Montreal: C.D. Howe Research Institute, 1977.

———. *Money, Inflation, and the Bank of Canada*. Vol. 2. Montreal: C.D. Howe Research Institute, 1981.

———. *No Place to Stand? Abandoning Monetary Targets: An Evaluation*. Montreal: C.D. Howe Research Institute, 1983.

Leroy, Stephen F., and David E. Lindsey. "Determining the Monetary Instrument: A Diagrammatic Exposition." *American Economic Review*. Dec. 1978, 929–34.

"Monetary Policy in Canada: A Symposium." *Canadian Journal of Economics*. Nov. 1979, 590–646. With papers by William R. White, Thomas Courchene, Gordon Sparks, and Pierre Fortin.

Poole, William. "Optimal Choice of Monetary Instruments in a Simple Stochastic Macro Model." *Quarterly Journal of Economics*. 1970, 197–216.

PART SEVEN

The International Financial System

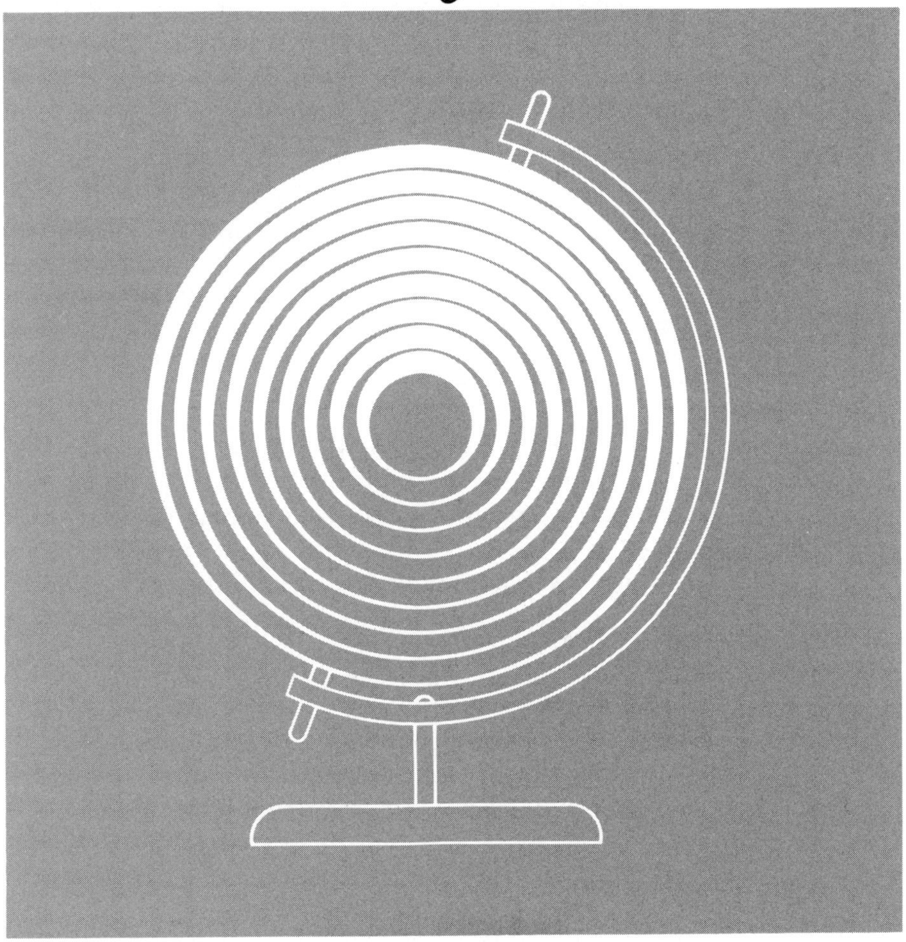

CHAPTER 25

The International Financial System

Previous chapters have discussed various aspects of the international financial system. The role of banks in Eurocurrency markets was discussed in chapter 11. Forward-exchange markets were discussed in chapters 8 and 15 as examples of hedging markets — hedging against foreign exchange risk. The activity of money-market dealers in soliciting international arbitrage was mentioned in chapters 5, 7, and 15. The behavior of floating exchange rates and their effect on the domestic economy were built into the discussion of demand behavior in the macroeconomic theory of chapter 19 and formed an important part of our optimal policy discussion in chapter 24. No one could have read this far without realizing that Canada's is an open economy with an open financial system. Canada is influenced by what goes on in the international financial system and influences the international economy in turn.

What makes Canada unique as an open economy is the strong influence exerted on it by just one other economy — that of the U.S. Instead of being subject to a diversified "portfolio" of outside disturbances such as changes in foreign interest rates, Canada is subject to shocks mainly from just one country.

Canada's financial integration with the rest of the world shows clearly in table 25–1, which summarizes information from chapters 5 and 7 on the role of the rest-of-the-world sector in Canadian financial flows and stocks. Canadians borrow extensively from foreigners, and foreigners borrow extensively from us. We buy foreign-currency assets both for short and long terms, and foreigners buy Canadian-dollar assets for short and long terms. In addition, there are very large flows of foreign-currency payments and receipts to pay for exports and imports of goods and services; for 1981, the combined total of these flows was over $200 billion, almost two-thirds of gross national product. Almost all of these payments and receipts are in U.S. dollars, the key currency of international trade. The terms on which these foreign-currency payments are made, and in particular the rate at which foreign currency is exchanged for domestic currency, have large and important effects on Canadian output and inflation.

TABLE 25–1 Role of foreign (rest-of-the-world) sector in the Canadian financial system (millions of dollars)

	1981 flows	End of 1980 stocks
Net borrowing, by issue of		
international reserve assets	382	4 811
deposits	4 427	22 442
loan notes	4 277	19 750
stocks sold to affiliates	7 088	37 074
TOTAL (NET) BORROWING	16 124	95 047
Net lending, by purchase of		
deposits	11 111	46 777
loan notes	3 213	7 143
Treasury Bills and short-term paper	1 189	4 274
mortgage loan notes	—	1 610
bonds	11 736	46 149
stocks	4 980	79 085
TOTAL (NET) LENDING	32 229	190 080

Note: 1981 flow figures are provisional.

Source: Statistics Canada, *Financial Flow Accounts*, Cat. 13–002, Fourth Quarter, 1981.

This chapter does not need to explain the impact of the rest of the world on the Canadian economy; that has been done in the appropriate places in previous chapters. What the chapter does need to do is pull together the bits and pieces of previous discussions and fill in some gaps, in order to provide a comprehensive view of the international financial system. Understanding this system is important, especially to those in open economies, because the international financial system is to the world trading economy what Canada's domestic financial system is to its domestic economy. That the world's financial system is currently a bit creaky and in need of repair makes an understanding of it that much more vital.

Your task in this last chapter is therefore to learn:

1. the major parts of the international financial system,
2. the links between the international financial system and domestic stabilization policy, and
3. the criteria for assessing the performance of the world financial system.

SECTION 1

Elements and functions of the world financial system

All of us participate in the world financial system whenever we buy a U.S.-dollar money order to buy something out of a foreign mail-order catalogue. Mostly we just use the international payments mechanism and do not add to Canada's foreign-currency assets or run up foreign-currency debts. However, countries with Current Account surpluses must build up their stock of foreign-currency assets by the amount of that surplus, so the individuals, corporations, and central banks in those countries must as a whole have been lenders in the international financial system. For countries with Current Account deficits, individuals and corporations and central banks must as a whole have borrowed in the international financial system.

In the middle of the international financial system are the intermediaries, as usual, making it possible for lenders to buy a sort of asset different from the promissory notes supplied by the borrowers. Almost all of the intermediaries in the international financial system are banks of some sort, dealing in assets and debts with relatively short maturities. The only major financial institutions engaging in long-term international lending are official international lending agencies like the International Bank for Reconstruction and Development, better known as the World Bank.

Figure 25–1 gives a flow chart of the international financial system that is basically the same as the one for the Canadian financial system (see figure 2–1). Funds flow from surplus groups to deficit groups either directly or indirectly. The indirect flows may go through one or several different financial intermediaries on the way from lender to borrower. Participants in this world financial system, as both lenders and borrowers, are individuals, corporations, central banks, and governments. Within each nation there are always some individuals and corporations lending in the world financial system, and others borrowing. The nation's Balance of Payments records all of these transactions, and the Current Account surplus or net capital outflow (including official lending) represents the net lending of members of that nation in the world financial system.

World money

One of the assets held in this world financial system is *world money*: U.S.-dollar demand deposits held in U.S. banks and used for international payments. Another, less important asset, available to central banks only, is Special Drawing Rights balances held in the International Monetary Fund. The vast bulk of assets held in the world financial system are near-moneys, denominated usually in U.S. dollars but sometimes in German marks, French francs, or British pounds (sterling). Some of the near-moneys are simply U.S. money-market assets such as U.S. government Treasury Bills or short-term corporate paper. Most of the near-moneys are term deposits

Eurobanks

issued by *Eurobanks* (banks operating in the Eurodollar market) or by banks in the U.S. The intermediaries in figure 25–1, mainly banks, hold as

FIGURE 25–1 Flows in the world financial system

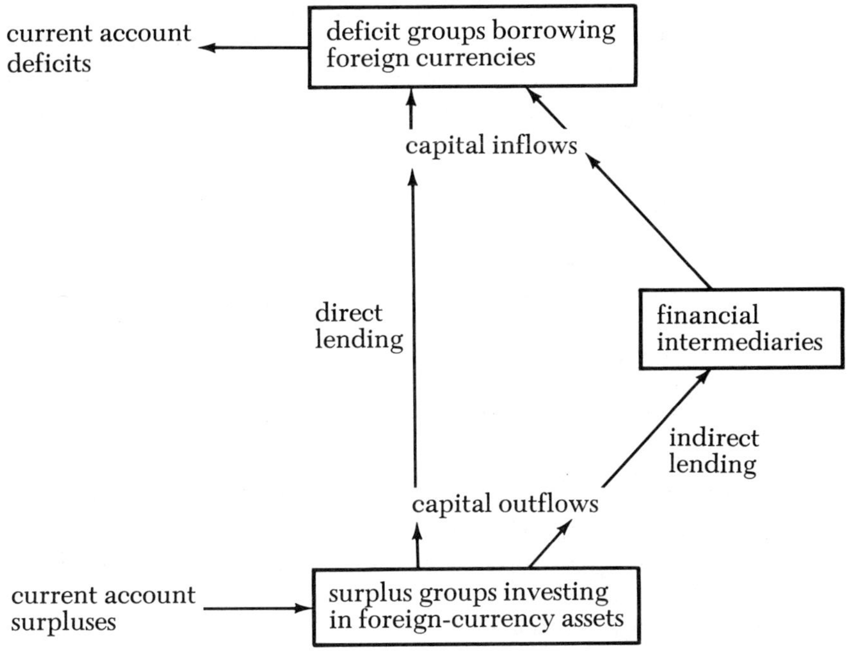

assets either the term deposits issued by other banks or the promissory loan notes issued by traders, resource development corporations, and governments that borrow in the world financial system. The term deposits in the international financial system have terms ranging from overnight to five years, as do the loans. The average term of loans is longer than the average term of deposits, but most of the loans have floating interest rates tied to a benchmark deposit rate known as *LIBOR* (for London Inter-Bank Offer Rate), so a mismatch of asset and liability maturities does not mean great volatility of interest spreads.

LIBOR (London Inter-Bank Offer Rate)

One of the confusing aspects of the world financial system is its overlap with the U.S. domestic financial system. The U.S. dollar is the key currency of international trade transactions, and U.S.-dollar demand deposits are the main medium of exchange in world trade. As a result, all U.S.-dollar near-moneys are also world near-moneys. There is no clear dividing line, but essentially the demand for U.S. dollars for domestic transactions by U.S. residents is not part of the world financial system, and the demand for U.S. dollars for transactions with nonresidents is.

The role of the world financial system in channelling savings from surplus groups to deficit groups is clear in figure 25–1. This role was dramatic in the years 1974–76 and 1979–82 as the OPEC nations became a huge surplus group almost overnight and as a host of less-developed countries became a huge deficit group, borrowing to finance their basic consumption needs for oil. The channelling of funds involved much strain, with more strain still to come. Many nations have already used up their credit limits and are dependent on the World Bank and other official lending agencies for aid and for "soft" loans (at less than market rates) just to service their existing debt.[1]

Figure 25–1 does not show the role of the world financial system in providing an international payments mechanism to allow you and me to buy a U.S.-dollar money order without a lot of fuss, and it does not show how growth of the world money supply is arranged. We will postpone the topic of world money-supply growth until section 3, but we will deal with the world payments mechanism here.

The world payments mechanism

The currency of world trade is the U.S. dollar, usually in the form of demand deposits issued by U.S. banks and transferred by cheque or bank draft. Some German-mark deposits are used, some French francs, some sterling deposits, even some Canadian-dollar deposits, but the vast bulk are U.S.-dollar demand deposits.

Individuals and corporations in each nation have access to U.S. dollars mainly through their own domestic foreign exchange market, which is usually run by the private banks and some private foreign exchange brokers. In countries with foreign exchange controls, the foreign exchange market may be effectively a department of government or the central bank instead. Private-sector banks in turn buy and sell foreign exchange at a wholesale level among themselves, with the central bank's traders, and with traders in other nations' foreign exchange markets. Central banks have a set of international arrangements to help stabilize the exchange rates that these exchange markets produce. In addition to all of this is the Eurodollar, or Eurocurrency, market. We will deal with each part of the world payments system in turn.

The Canadian foreign exchange market

Each nation's foreign exchange market is a little different from that of other nations. In Canada, the difference is that we have few private foreign exchange brokers acting as agents; the major banks run the foreign

---

[1]The list of countries that "might have trouble paying back" their Eurodollar loans is given in Adam Smith's *Paper Money* (New York: Dell, 1981): Brazil, the Philippines, Korea, Turkey, Thailand, Poland, Pakistan, Nicaragua, Panama, Egypt, Jamaica, Ethiopia, Kenya, Morocco, Yugoslavia, Sudan, and Zaire (p. 302). There are many others whose low credit standing prevented their getting a Eurodollar loan in the first place.

exchange market as principals through an interbank market whose brokers are salaried employees of the Canadian Bankers' Association.[2]

Most foreign exchange is bought and sold in Canada within individual banks. Exporter customers sell their foreign exchange to their regular bank, which then resells it to importer customers at a price higher by $\frac{1}{2}$ to 1 percent (the bank's expense and profit margin). When exporter customers bring in for sale exactly the amount and mix of currencies that the importer customers want to buy, the bank need never look outside itself in its foreign exchange dealings.

However, it is unlikely that any one bank will have coming in from export customers each day exactly the amount and mix of currencies it needs for its import customers. When there is a mismatch, the individual bank will allow its inventories of individual currencies to be run up or run down, but within narrow limits. Outside those limits the bank will go to the interbank market to sell off excess currency holdings and replenish inventories that are too low. The "currency" holdings are not usually paper bank notes; instead, banks' foreign-currency assets consist mainly of hundreds of deposits held in foreign correspondent banks. Such deposits can be converted into bank notes to pay import bills, but usually import bills are paid with bank drafts instead.

The interbank market consists of individual banks (Canadian and foreign), the Bank of Canada, investment dealers, some near-banks, and salaried brokers hired by the Canadian Bankers' Association. All the traders have, displayed on their computer screens, current information on the latest bids and offers. To *hit* a bid or *take* an offer, they telephone the CBA brokers, who then give the name of the other party to the transaction. The *hitter* or *taker* then specifies a new bid or offer rate, which is again displayed on the video screen. The interbank market is not only for spot (immediate) exchange transactions but also for forward exchange. The display of bid and offer rates for the various currencies includes bids and offers for spot delivery and for assorted future delivery dates.[3]

Canada's interbank foreign exchange market is only one of a world network of foreign exchange markets, all buying and selling the same currencies. The banks' traders in Canada, and other traders elsewhere, constantly engage in arbitrage transactions to profit from any differences in exchange rates for the same currency and delivery date. This action keeps exchange rates in unison around the world.

---

[2]One private foreign exchange broker set up shop in Toronto in 1975. Two more started business in 1978. They operate on commission (.025 percent for large transactions); the interbank market has no commission, but banks operate on spreads generally larger than that. For a recent survey of this market, see *Bank of Canada Review*, November 1983.

[3]The Toronto, Winnipeg, and Chicago futures markets deal in foreign-currency futures as competitors to the interbank forward-exchange market. The futures contracts are standardized and have commission charges. Forward-exchange arrangements are more customized, are paid for by spreads, and are generally not available to speculators. Forward-exchange contracts are available even in retail amounts as small and as specific as $3647.

Today the Bank of Canada sits on the sidelines of Canada's foreign exchange market, basically just leaning against any strong trends in exchange rates in order to slow them down. However, for the period 1962–70 the Bank of Canada accepted a responsibility under the Bretton Woods system to intervene as often as necessary to keep the exchange rate within a small range relative to the U.S. dollar. Under that system central banks were the centre of each nation's foreign exchange market. The main world storehouse of central-bank foreign exchange reserves was (and still is) the International Monetary Fund, which is therefore the centrepiece of the world payments mechanism.

Bretton Woods, GATT, and the IMF

At the Bretton Woods conference in Bretton Woods, New Hampshire, in 1944, forty countries agreed to an organization of international payments that would prevent the self-defeating cycle of currency devaluations, and the erection of import barriers, started in the 1930s to combat each country's depression. The nations agreed that exchange rates should be pegged within 1 percent of a parity rate and maintained there by central banks' buying or selling foreign exchange to meet any excess demand or supply. That is, central banks were to run a two-way price-support scheme for the price of their currency. Only if the nation had a "fundamental disequilibrium" at the central parity rate would the parity rate be changed. This system was maintained with increasing difficulty until early 1973, when most of the major trading nations abandoned defense of any central parity rate and let their currencies float.

Interestingly, Canada abandoned the system of pegged exchange rates as early as October 1950, joined it again in May 1962, and then abandoned it again in May 1969, well before the Bretton Woods system collapsed. Canada was an international maverick in this respect.

General Agreement on Tariffs and Trade (GATT)

The *General Agreement on Tariffs and Trade (GATT)* is an outgrowth of the Bretton Woods conference that sets out acceptable codes of conduct for trade in goods and services. It is an executive agreement of the participating governments that prohibits import controls and quotas, export subsidies, and barriers to the free international movement of capital funds. Not all members live up to the code at all times, but GATT does reduce the chances of a round of self-defeating attempts by member nations to protect domestic jobs at the expense of employment in the economies of their trading partners (that is, attempts to export domestic unemployment to their trading partners).

International Monetary Fund (IMF)

The *International Monetary Fund (IMF)* was started in 1947 as a specialized agency of the United Nations to monitor and assist in setting and maintaining central parity exchange rates. The participating nations realized that defense of parity exchange rates would require each central bank to have adequate reserves, so the International Monetary Fund was set up as a central pool of foreign exchange reserves upon which all nations could draw. Each member nation contributed some gold or other convertible foreign exchange, plus a larger amount of its own currency. In return, each nation could borrow foreign exchange up to and later beyond its total contribution, or *quota*, though under increasingly stringent conditions as its borrowings increased.

Many further arrangements have been made since 1947 that increase the ability of central banks to intervene in foreign exchange markets. The purpose of the Bretton Woods scheme was to enable central banks to defend fixed exchange rates, in order to give national governments time and elbow room for whatever domestic adjustments were needed to remove Current Account deficits. Now, with floating exchange rates, the purpose of the IMF borrowing privileges is to allow central banks to slow down or delay exchange rate movements. The rationale is still that national governments should be given the time and elbow room to take steps other than currency devaluation to reduce Current Account deficits.

Table 25–2 gives a list of the various arrangements made since1947 to increase central banks' liquidity. Not surprisingly, many of the arrangements take the form of extra stand-by credit facilities, which are less expensive than increases in total reserves. In a closed world financial system where excess supply of one currency generally means excess demand for another, there are always stand-by lenders to match the stand-by borrowers.[4]

As well as resorting to official stand-by arrangements, many central banks and governments have also borrowed foreign exchange reserves from Eurobanks. For instance, the Canadian government arranged $5.5 billion in stand-bys in 1977 and 1978, in addition to borrowing $2.2 billion dollars and German marks from the international bond markets.[5]

Special Drawing Rights (SDRs)

From a longer-term perspective, the most important change shown in table 25–2 is the introduction of *Special Drawing Rights*. These "deposits" with the International Monetary Fund were originally redeemable at a fixed price in gold, then in U.S. dollars, and now in a basket of currencies. They are still available only to central banks and a few other international institutions, but their convertibility enables central banks to economize on other forms of foreign exchange reserves. The most important aspect of SDRs is that they are issued by a stroke of the pen. They are a world paper money issued by a world central bank. SDRs are an important advance for the world financial system just as the development of central-bank fiat currency was important for Canada's domestic financial system. Use of SDRs is still relatively small, but so was the use of Dominion Notes when the

[4]For instance, the IMF used the General Agreement to Borrow to raise US $3.9 billion to help the United Kingdom in January 1977.

[5]The major central banks agreed in 1971 not to hold their foreign exchange reserves in the Eurodollar market, despite its higher interest rates. The purpose of the agreement was to keep tighter control of world liquidity (that is, to force greater adjustment of Current and Capital Accounts on deficit nations, since that is the alternative). Many central banks and governments of Third World nations still keep official reserves in Eurobanks. Andrew Crockett, *International Money* (Sunbury-on-Thames: Nelson, 1977), 171.

TABLE 25–2 International liquidity increases, 1947–82 (billions of U.S. dollars)

	Drawings to March 1982
1. IMF quotas established 1947 (usable up to 100% by any country, with increasingly stringent conditions on repayment and internal adjustment).	28.9
2. Standby arrangements established 1952, providing automatic, line of credit facilities under pre-agreed conditions.	2.8
3. IMF quotas raised by 50%, 1959.	
4. General Agreement to Borrow (GAB) set up in 1962 among Group of Ten industrialized countries and Switzerland, authorizing IMF to borrow up to $7.7 billion to finance drawings under its financing facilities.	
5. Compensatory Financing Facility established 1963 for longer-term adjustment needs, repayable in 3 years, for up to 50% of quota; for primary exporting countries.	8.3
6. IMF quotas raised by 25%, 1965–66.	
7. IMF quotas raised by 25%, 1970–71.	
8. Special Drawing Rights created and allocated to each IMF members' reserves in the amount of $9.3 billion, 1970–72.	
9. Buffer Stock Financing Facility created for developing countries contributing to international buffer stocks for up to 50% of quota.	0.1
10. Extended Fund Facility established 1974 for medium-term loans, repayable in 4–10 years, for up to 140% of quota.	2.6
11. Oil Facility established June 1974 for loans to Third World nations financing oil deficits. Fully used by May 1976. Financed largely by borrowing from OPEC countries. Repayable in installments over 7 years.	7.8
12. Liberalization of terms and amounts of Compensatory Financing Facility (established 1963) to 125% of quota.	
13. Creation of Subsidy Account in 1975 to aid poorest nations in using the Oil Facility.	
14. IMF quotas raised by 23.4% in 1978.	
15. Special Drawing Rights created, $4 billion each in 1979, 1980, 1981, all credited to members' reserve accounts, bringing the total to 21.4 billion SDRs, valued at US$24.1 billion.	
16. Supplementary Financing Facility established Feb. 1979 to provide longer-term assistance, with a maximum of US$8.8 billion. Repayable in 3½ to 7 years.	4.5
17. IMF quotas raised by 50% in 1980, to a level of US$68.2 billion.	
18. Enlarged Access Policy established May 1981 to provide supplementary financing for short and long (more than 3½ years) periods, up to US$10.5 billion. Repayable in 3½ to 7 years.	1.1

Source: International Monetary Fund, *International Financial Statistics*, May 1982.

Canadian government first issued them at the time of Confederation. Now at last the world has in place a mechanism that can adapt the stock of world money cheaply and reliably to meet the needs of world trade.

The Bank for International Settlements

Bank for International Settlements (BIS)

The *Bank for International Settlements (BIS)* in Basel, Switzerland, is older than the IMF. It was set up in 1930 by central banks of the industrialized countries, who remain its directors. It is essentially a central bankers' co-operative bank designed to do collectively what the central banks by themselves would find difficult. The BIS handles and co-ordinates foreign exchange swaps between member central banks, and it extends collective but limited guarantees to act as a lender of last resort for the Eurocurrency-market banks. Because the latter are playing an ever larger role in the world financial system, the lender-of-last-resort function is increasingly important for world financial confidence, and in the financial world, confidence is necessary for performance.

The Eurocurrency markets

Eurodollar deposit

Eurodollar, or Eurocurrency market

Eurodollars, Euromarks, even Euroyen — they sound exotic, quite different in some mysterious way from ordinary dollars, marks, and yen. In fact, the only difference is location. A U.S.-dollar deposit would normally refer to a deposit issued by a bank in the U.S. A *Eurodollar deposit* is the same sort of deposit issued by a bank outside the U.S. A Euromark or Euroyen deposit is a German-mark or Japanese-yen deposit issued by a bank outside Germany or Japan. The Eurocurrency markets are not actually markets for currencies, however, nor even for demand deposits denominated in those currencies. Rather, the *Eurocurrency markets* are markets for short- to medium-term deposits denominated in currencies other than that of the host country.

Eurobond

The long-term part of the Eurocurrency market is the *Eurobond market*. Sixty percent of Eurobonds and 75 percent of Eurocurrency deposits are in U.S. dollars. "Short to medium term" stretches from overnight to five years, with nearly 90 percent at six months or less. London is the biggest centre; others include Zurich, Frankfurt, Paris, Brussels, Amsterdam, Luxembourg, Hong Kong, Singapore, Tokyo, Panama, and more recently Bahrain, as well as centres in the Carribbean. Many U.S. banks participate through subsidiaries chartered in the Caribbean but operating out of New York. Depositors are other banks, OPEC and Third World governments and central banks, and some industrial corporations. Borrowers are mostly public-sector companies and governments.

Because the banks are generally transacting with foreigners and in a currency not that of the host country, the host countries have not felt much need to regulate the bank intermediaries, so the costs of doing Eurocurrency business are small. There are no reserve requirements where the deposits are held in foreign subsidiaries, no deposit-insurance premiums, few reporting requirements, loose capital restrictions, few taxes, and intense competition. Margins between loan rates and deposit rates are therefore very small (0.5 to 1.0 percent), and deposit rates are often considerably higher than in domestic markets. When the reserve requirement in domestic financial markets is 3 percent, for instance, and loan assets yield 15 percent, the reserve requirement lowers average asset earnings for domestic assets (loans plus reserves) by 0.45 percent; domestic-deposit yields must be 0.45 percent lower just to give the domestic bank the same spread as on Eurocurrency business. For large-scale accounts of many millions, 0.45 percent is a large difference. It is understandable that intermediaries have flocked to the Eurocurrency markets to do their international business.

As a credit facility, the Eurocurrency markets are an important adjunct to the various national credit markets. Total external assets of Eurocurrency banks in 1980 were $810 billion.[6] Participation of banks from many nations enables much pooling of funds, which is helpful in financing large-scale energy projects. The presence of so many banks makes it easier to syndicate difficult loans, and syndicating loans reduces risk for individual lenders and possibly also increases the chances of repayment (by increasing the number of nations that would be offended if the borrower defaulted!). The functions of the Eurocurrency markets could be performed by groups of banks in national credit markets, but only with difficulty, and some of the transactions would be so expensive that the borrowing and therefore the investment projects would never be undertaken.

The Eurocurrency market is not particularly important as a creator of money in the narrow sense. The deposits issued in Eurocurrency markets are all time deposits rather than demand deposits (though one-third are for maturities of eight days or less). Those Eurocurrency deposits held by Canadian residents and booked in Canada do form part of our broad-money measure M3 but not part of our narrow-money measure M1.

What makes the Eurocurrency markets so confusing is mostly the layering of deposits between lender and borrower. In many cases the original deposit (for example, of a cheque on a New York bank) in a Eurobank account will be loaned out by that bank to another bank (redeposited) and possibly then to a third or fourth bank before being loaned out through a syndicate arrangement to some primary borrower such as a debtor country or an investment project contractor. Because of this layering, over one-third of the gross assets of Eurocurrency banks are deposits in other banks.

In each stage of the redepositing-relending process, the bank margin is tiny (but sufficient), so the eventual cost of the Eurodollar credit to the

[6]Of this $810 billion, which excludes all deposits in other banks, the bulk is held in European banks. See Bank for International Settlements, Annual Report for 1980–81, 105.

primary borrower is still less than would be available in the U.S. from banks subject to deposit insurance and reserve requirements. In all cases the end result, as in the domestic financial system, is transfer of funds from savers to borrowers. Within the Canadian financial system the same sort of thing happens when funds deposited in a credit union are reloaned to the credit union central and then to a trust company and then to a bank, before being finally loaned out to a business firm for real investment spending.

SECTION 2 The Rest of the World and stabilization policy

In analysing macroeconomic behavior in chapters 17 to 21, and optimal policy in chapter 24, we generally assumed the current institutional arrangement of a managed float for the exchange rate. In the very short run of a few months, the government can stabilize the exchange rate by adding to or selling off its foreign exchange reserves, but those reserves are not large enough to withstand for long a significant excess demand for foreign exchange; over periods longer than a few months, therefore, the exchange rate floats.

The central bank can affect this float even over long periods by directing its interest-rate management at the Capital Account of the Balance of Payments rather than at domestic aggregate demand. The Bank of Canada did just this in July and August 1981 when it pushed short-term Canadian interest rates up 300 basis points. The purpose was to generate a large short-term capital inflow that would offset direct capital outflows and prevent the exchange rate from sinking further.

Such actions by central banks are a temporary return to the situation that all central banks faced under the system of pegged exchange rates. Pegged exchange rates were abandoned by many countries in 1973, but there are still dozens of countries with pegged exchange relationships of various sorts.[7] The best-known and most important arrangement is the European Monetary System (EMS), or *snake*, in which West European currencies are pegged to one another but collectively float relative to other currencies such as the U.S. dollar. The reprinted news article describes some of the difficulties the members of the EMS have in maintaining even that limited type of pegged-exchange-rate system.

[7]Canada has been on a fixed-exchange-rate system for most of our history. We were formally on the gold standard from 1853 to 1914, and then from July 1926 to January 1929. Our currency was pegged to the U.S. dollar in World War II and afterward (at parity, then 90.9 cents U.S., then parity) to 1950, and then again from 1962 to 1970 (at 92.5 cents U.S.). Currently, 103 member countries of the IMF still have fixed exchange rates, though they account for only 20 percent of world trade. See *International Financial Statistics*, published by the IMF, for the latest data.

EEC talks to focus on possible realignment of EMS

BRUSSELS (Reuter) — European Economic Community finance ministers will meet in Brussels this weekend to discuss a possible realignment of the European Monetary System, according to monetary sources.

A senior official of the Bank of Italy in Rome said the meeting would begin this afternoon. However, monetary sources in Brussels said it would start either tonight or tomorrow, depending on progress at a prior meeting of the community's Monetary Committee, which normally works out the technical details of any realignment.

The EMS limits the extent to which its eight member currencies can fluctuate against each other, while floating against outside currencies, thereby facilitating trade. All EEC countries except Britain and Greece belong.

The meeting comes after two weeks of uncertainty in foreign exchange markets that has led to a dramatic rise in the value of the West German mark and heavy pressure on the French franc and other weaker currencies in the system.

Earlier yesterday, a resurgence of speculative purchases of the strong West German mark sent the French and Belgian francs, the Irish pound and the Danish crown crashing to their EMS floors, currency dealers said.

French Finance Minister Jacques Delors said West Germany should revalue the mark upward in order to maintain the EMS. But West Germany has been resisting an upward valuation that might damage the competitiveness of its exports.

In the past few days, the West German mark has frequently touched the top of the system's limit levels, forcing central banks to intervene to keep its price down.

Monetary officials said West Germany called the meeting.

One minister, who refused to be named, said it was difficult to predict the outcome of the meetings, but expected the talks to be long and difficult.

Apart from West Germany, other governments have been spending billions of dollars in the market to bolster the values of the weaker currencies.

Foreign exchange dealers said they expected the mark to be revalued and the French franc devalued by a margin of up to 10 per cent of their present parities.

Belgium and Luxembourg, however, would resist devaluation of their currencies in any realignment, senior political sources said in Brussels.

Source: The Globe and Mail, Toronto, March 19, 1983.

Fixed versus flexible exchange rates

The choice between fixed and flexible exchange rate systems greatly affects the real and financial links between economies. The choice also affects the degree of autonomy of domestic monetary policy, so it is a topic you should understand before arriving at the back cover of this book.

We have already examined the effect of domestic monetary policy on the Balance of Payments under flexible exchange rates. Higher domestic interest rates lower net capital outflows; the induced fall in the exchange rate $P_{US\$}$ reduces net exports. A lower exchange rate also lowers the cost of imported goods and therefore constitutes a favorable supply shock for the economy as well as a negative demand shock.

For other nations, Canada's domestic policy of higher interest rates has the opposite effects. Their exchange rates (the price of Canadian currency in terms of their own) rise, their net exports are stimulated, and their costs of imported Canadian goods go up. Canada thus lowers its demand and its costs partly by increasing demand and costs in the rest of the world.

At the same time, flexible exchange rates typically insulate economies from changes in relative inflation rates. This insulation is not very reliable over short periods, but it is much more so over periods of several years where the price inflation is basically the result of different monetary-growth rates.

Flexible-exchange-rate systems thus allow countries to run independent domestic monetary policies with different domestic inflation rates, but domestic monetary policies essentially shift demand (and cost pressures) to and from the rest of the world.

Fixed-exchange-rate systems do not provide the same autonomy. Under fixed exchange rates different economies are constrained to have similar interest rates and similar inflation rates. Monetary policy is powerless to shift domestic aggregate demand to and from the rest of the world, but inflation becomes a worldwide phenomenon.

The central property of a fixed-exchange-rate system is that changes in official reserves by themselves change the monetary base in the same amount unless sterilized. Disturbances in the Balance of Payments can therefore feed back to disturb domestic monetary policy. In order to see the many effects of this extra feedback to the monetary base, we will look at several different shocks: an expansionary monetary policy, higher foreign interest rates, and higher foreign price levels.

Expansionary monetary policy

An increase in cash reserves lowers domestic interest rates and therefore increases investment spending. A lower interest rate also increases the net capital outflow and puts upward pressure on the exchange rate. With a fixed exchange rate, the Bank of Canada must sell off official reserves to keep the value of foreign currency constant; the Bank's sales lower the cash reserve base and therefore partially offset the original policy action. The net impact of monetary policy will be smaller as the response of capital outflows is larger, since it is the capital-outflow response that determines how much of the official reserves must be sold off. Monetary policy can therefore be very weak or even completely offset when capital flows are very interest-sensitive. Independent domestic monetary policy becomes impossible unless capital flows are impeded somehow.

Higher foreign interest rates

The example of expansionary domestic monetary policy shows that it is difficult to move Canadian interest rates away from world interest rates under a fixed-exchange-rate system. The other side of this coin is that it is difficult to prevent Canadian interest rates from moving when world interest rates change. Consider for instance the effects of a surge of U.S. interest rates (U.S. interest rates are a good proxy for "world" rates as far as Canada is concerned). Higher U.S. interest rates stimulate a larger net capital outflow. The excess demand for U.S. currency generated by a larger net capital outflow is met by the Bank of Canada's selling off foreign exchange reserves. This sale reduces the monetary base, which drives up Canadian interest rates either until they are equal to U.S. rates or until the net capital outflow stops. The contrast with a flexible-exchange-rate system is striking. Under flexible exchange rates, demand in the Canadian economy is stimulated by higher U.S. interest rates as though tighter U.S. monetary policy merely exported part of U.S. demand and employment to Canada. Under fixed exchange rates, U.S. monetary policy itself is exported to Canada. In the end we, too, have tighter monetary policy.[8]

Higher foreign price levels

Higher foreign price levels improve the competitive position of Canadian producers and increase net exports. Under fixed exchange rates, the surge of net exports is not offset by falling foreign-currency values. Instead, the Bank of Canada buys up the extra supply of foreign exchange from the exporters. The monetary base in Canada expands, and the effect of monetary expansion is added to the effect of trade-sector expansion. Effectively, higher inflation abroad is exported to Canada as a surge of demand. If our economy is close to capacity, inflation speeds up in Canada as well. Inflation therefore becomes a worldwide concern under fixed exchange rates; no country can avoid inflation if its major trading partners pursue very expansionary monetary policies. This is part of the story of the early 1970s.

---

[8]Clearly, under fixed-exchange-rate regimes monetary policies must be co-ordinated among trading partners. This requirement is explicitly recognized by the eight countries participating in the European Monetary System, who are attempting to keep their exchange rates stable relative to each other but not relative to the rest of the world.

SECTION 3

Conduct and performance of the world financial system

The international financial system poses both microeconomic and macroeconomic problems, quite apart from the problem each member nation has in deciding whether to fix or float its exchange rate. In this last section we will consider these problems, by looking at the goals of an international financial system and then seeing how they are or are not met.

There could be many different goals for the world financial system, but minimum goals must include the following:

1. It should provide an efficient payments mechanism for international transactions;
2. It should transfer savings efficiently from surplus groups to deficit groups, with at least no worsening of the world's distribution of incomes and wealth;
3. It should at least not reduce what equity there is in the world distribution of income and wealth; and
4. It should provide for adequate growth of the world money supply in line with the needs of world trade.

Some of these goals have been met more satisfactorily than others.

Efficiency of the payments mechanism

The payments system is efficient. The use of a single currency for almost all international trade provides all of the benefits of a single unit of account. With a single currency, traders are more easily able to keep track of relative values of goods and services from different economies, so there is a saving in information costs. Use of the currency of the major trading nation as that single, key currency enables still more savings. When the pound sterling was the major international currency, before World War I, world traders could make use of the existing British banking system to handle payments and receipts. No separate world banking structure was needed. After World War II, the U.S. dollar became the key international currency because the U.S. was the largest trading nation. Payments in world trade are made mostly by transfers of U.S.-dollar demand deposits in New York banks, so the existing U.S. financial system handles most of the payments mechanism. The international trade still conducted in pounds sterling or in French francs is similarly paid for through the British and French banking systems.

The system of payments by transfer of demand deposits is relatively efficient and is becoming more efficient. Most transfers are still by cheque, bank draft, or telex, but many of the large-scale transfers are electronic through the SWIFT system (Society for Worldwide Interbank Financial Telecommunication). With almost all major banks now recording their deposit balances on computers, most international payments will soon be made electronically at almost zero marginal cost. This is a far cry from sending gold under armed guard to settle international debts, as was once done.

Gold has largely been replaced as a medium of exchange in international trade. It is still very important as a store of value internationally and will likely continue to be so for many decades, but it is not used much for making payments, even among central banks.[9] Given the relative social costs of adding to world reserves of gold versus adding to stocks of paper money, this is an efficient development.

The most significant innovation in the world payments mechanism has been the introduction of Special Drawing Rights on the International Monetary Fund as an international paper money for payments among central banks. There is no world government with the power to declare SDRs as legal tender, which would ensure their acceptability as media of exchange, but the IMF members have agreed on a set of rules for holding and transferring SDRs that do more or less the same thing.[10] The SDR is valued at the average of a basket of currencies and is therefore automatically more stable than the value of the typical currency in that basket. Fifteen countries take advantage of this stability and peg their currencies to the SDR.[11] Currently the SDR balances of central banks are to world money what the Bank of Canada deposits of chartered banks are to the domestic Canadian money supply, but the SDR's role could easily be expanded should there be a need to take pressure off some of the other assets serving as international moneys (U.S. dollars in particular).

The other consideration in the international payments mechanism, besides its efficiency, is its risk level. Some foreign exchange rates are not tied together. Where the risk is worth it, traders can cover in forward-exchange markets for periods that now stretch up to five years into the future. Most international trade transactions require only a few months

---

[9]In September 1975 the members of the International Monetary Fund agreed to abolish the official price of gold and to sell off or give back one-third of the IMF's total gold holding. The proceeds of gold sales have been used to set up the IMF Trust Fund for soft loans to developing countries. US $3.4 billion has been loaned from this Fund as of March 1982.

[10]Central banks can use their allocated SDR quotas to buy whatever foreign currencies they wish. Canada had used SDR 630 million of its 780 million quota in this way as of April 1982. We are not obligated to buy those SDRs back from the other central banks to which we have transferred them, but on average over a five-year period our SDR holdings must be at least 15 percent of our allocated quota. For Canada this means SDR 117 million at our current quota level. On the other side, no country is obligated to accept SDRs in exchange for its own currency in an amount greater than three times its allocated quota. There is a charge for use of SDRs, and an interest payment on SDR holdings above the quota.

[11]There have also been several Eurobond issues denominated in SDRs. These represent use of the SDR merely as an international unit of account, not as a medium of exchange or a store of value.

of forward cover, between arranging the transaction and receiving payment, and for such short periods the forward-exchange markets have generally functioned smoothly and reliably.

Efficiency in transfer of savings

At first blush, the world financial system seems amazingly efficient compared to national financial systems. The Eurocurrency market in particular is subject to intense competition by dozens of large banks from many countries. These banks operate on the slimmest of margins and make reasonable returns on equity only because of large leverage.[12]

It is possible that the Eurocurrency banks have taken more risks than their depositors would really like. Depositors are not in a position to press for safeguards because there is not a supervisory international government or other body to turn to for appropriate regulation.[13] On the other hand, depositors have alternatives in various domestic financial systems that are regulated for greater safety, so one can only assume that risks taken on by Eurocurrency investors are taken on voluntarily.

The job of channelling surpluses from primary lenders to primary borrowers is more complicated for the world financial system than for any national financial system. The reason is that in the 1970s and early 1980s there were dramatic changes (which will probably continue throughout the 1980s) with respect to which nations had the surpluses and which nations had the deficits to be financed. With the quadrupling of oil prices by OPEC in 1973, the OPEC nations found themselves with enormous surplus revenues they could not begin to spend quickly. Among the industrialized nations and particularly among Third World nations, non-oil producers had large payments deficits they could not quickly reduce. Some way was needed to transfer the OPEC surplus from the OPEC countries to the deficit countries. Yet the OPEC countries did not feel like lending all that money directly to Third World countries, for the very good financial reason that many of the latter were not good risks. There were substantial chances of the loans' not being repaid.

The method of financing used was for the OPEC nations — particularly the ones with little population to absorb the extra oil revenues in extra

---

[12]Margins between prime loan rates and deposit rates in London were roughly $1\frac{1}{4}$ percent for developed countries and $2\frac{1}{2}$ percent for less-developed countries in 1974–76. By the 1979–81 period, competition had slimmed these margins to only 0.5 percent and 0.68 percent respectively. Smith, *Paper Money*, 300.

[13]Each national government is willing to regulate, but each knows that if it did, the banks would move their head offices to more permissive places like Singapore, the Isle of Man, Luxembourg, and the Cayman Islands. In recognition of this, the U.S. has passed legislation allowing U.S. international banking subsidiaries to be incorporated in the U.S. without being subject to most U.S. restrictions.

spending on goods and services — to put the revenues in short-term U.S.-dollar bank deposits, chiefly but not wholly in Eurodollar banks. The banks in turn loaned the money out in syndicate loans to traders, to the deficit countries, and to corporations financing large-scale energy or construction projects in the OPEC countries themselves.[14] The loans were for longer terms than the deposits (up to ten years) but at rates adjusted to market interest rates every three to six months, so that the banks did not need to worry about positive spreads turning negative.

The main concern of bankers holding large amounts of petrodollar deposits was the possibility of their withdrawal — for instance, if OPEC depositors wished to transfer part of their deposit portfolio to German-mark deposits instead. In that case the banks would have had to expose themselves to foreign exchange risk or else bid U.S.-dollar deposit rates up substantially. During the first petrodollar crisis of 1974–76 the U.S. dollar was still the only feasible international money that could absorb that large a scale of investment, so the OPEC investors had few alternatives, and the bankers' fears were not realized. Today there are more alternatives, though the U.S. dollar is still the main international money.

There is still the possibility that further large oil-price increases will occur in the late 1980s, as world demand for oil recovers. Each price increase will repeat some of the main financial effects of the previous increases: a large, temporary increase in revenues for oil-producing nations, at least temporarily resulting in a large extra surplus savings flow to invest, and large, compensating deficits of industrialized and Third World countries to be financed. Banks in the international financial system will continue to be the main intermediaries, but with increasing difficulty. The reason for the difficulty is that the borrowers are always the same, and their debts accumulate. Depending on the speed with which oil prices increase, debts may increase faster than the debtors' incomes, and repayment will become impossible.[15] Many less-developed countries have already had their debts extended; a further crisis could lead some nations to default just as domestic corporations and individuals occasionally do. For the international banks, of course, whose business has small margins and large leverage because of intense competition, this risk of default raises asset risks substantially. The situation is not healthy, even for the oil-producing nations.

---

[14]In the period 1974–80 the non-oil-producing less-developed countries had cumulative Current Account deficits of US$210 billion and borrowed a net total of $93 billion from the Eurocurrency banks. Over the same period the OPEC countries invested $82 billion in those same banks. Bank for International Settlements, Annual Report for 1980–81, 108.

[15]Between 1973 and 1980 the net debt of non-oil-producing less-developed countries to Eurocurrency banks alone soared from US$4.5 billion to US$102.3 billion. The gross debt (not subtracting the Eurocurrency deposits held by some of these countries) was US$195 billion at the end of 1980. These countries owed a further US$183 billion to the World Bank. The bulk of the $195 billion was due by the end of 1983.

Contribution to equity in the world distribution of income and wealth

In the Canadian economy there is a general presumption that income redistribution should be done mainly through taxes and transfer payments and that the financial system should merely be neutral, providing equal access to all and discriminating only by credit risk.

For the world financial system this presumption does not hold. Income disparities between nations are huge, and there is no tax or transfer mechanism to remove those disparities. There is only world aid and the provision of soft loans on relatively generous terms. The world financial system is therefore under pressure to be very nonneutral, on humanitarian grounds.

The Eurobanks have little room in their interest spreads for consideration of factors other than credit risks of borrowers. The other international lenders are official institutions, which are more capable of bias toward poorer countries. The World Bank, for instance, was set up for just this purpose.

The International Monetary Fund has been the subject of pressure on this point since 1970 as SDRs worth US$24 billion have been created out of thin air and credited to member nations. The pressure on the IMF has been to have the credits go mainly to the poorer nations rather than mainly to the richer industrialized countries. The pressure has not been successful. Allocations so far have been just in proportion to IMF quotas, which favor the richer trading nations. The IMF did arrange a special oil facility to help with oil-related deficits in 1974–76, raising US$6.9 billion from OPEC nations and from some industrialized countries. The IMF also has a Trust Fund of $3.4 billion, established with the proceeds of sales of one-sixth of the IMF's gold holdings in 1977. The Trust Fund is for special credits to developing nations. Finally, many if not most of the special credit facilities listed in table 25–2 are designed to accommodate the poorer countries rather than the richer ones.

Growth of the world money supply

The least successful aspect of the world financial system's performance has been its inability to provide for growth of international money in line with the needs of world trade. This has been a sore point for at least several hundred years, however, and our current international financial system is better than its predecessors by a large margin even if it is still unsatisfactory.

A gold-based money supply

In the nineteenth century the medium of exchange for most international trade came to be pound-sterling deposits in London banks. Trade was arranged through bills of exchange drawn on these banks and payable at maturity from deposits in these banks. The volume of deposits outstanding was tied to the banks' available cash reserves, which consisted of gold and Bank of England notes. The issue of Bank of England notes was also tied to Bank of England gold holdings, so adequate growth of the money supply depended on adequate growth of Britain's gold holdings. For much of the nineteenth century that growth was not adequate. World gold stocks grew by fits and starts with each new gold discovery, and between those discoveries world monetary growth could occur only if Britain increased its share of the total world gold stock. The result was long periods of falling price levels and slow output growth, particularly in the last quarter of the century. (The falling price level was shown in figure 17–7.) Even now the annual output of gold is less than 3 percent of the existing stock.

The U.S.-dollar glut

Since 1945 the key international currency has been the U.S. dollar. U.S. dollars are supplied to the rest of the world in exchange either for goods sold to U.S. residents or for foreign assets sold to U.S. residents. Both sources generate U.S. Balance of Payments deficits, on Current Account or Capital Account or both. In short, the U.S. receives goods or assets from foreigners in exchange for merely increasing its monetary base and allowing banks to create new U.S.-dollar deposits.

Seigniorage

This ability to get something for nothing is known as *seigniorage* and is enjoyed by the issuers of any money that is not full-bodied, as we discussed in chapter 4. As a measure of the U.S. advantage, external liabilities of the U.S. totalled US$351.8 billion at the start of 1982. U.S. commercial banks had deposit liabilities to foreign nonbank customers of a further $88.6 billion. The total of these two is a rough estimate of the foreign goods, services, and assets bought since 1945 simply by issue of new U.S. dollars. The combined total has been growing at over 17 percent per year since 1975. U.S. external liabilities now exceed the value of Canada's entire annual output.

For a while after 1945 there was a problem of insufficient international money because the U.S. ran huge trade surpluses while other, war-damaged economies were getting back on their feet. The trade surpluses sucked the U.S.-dollar deposits out of the rest of the world in the same way that the trade surpluses of France sucked specie out of the colony of New France in the seventeenth and eighteenth centuries (as described in chapter 4). The rest of the world was left with too little world money to finance trade. Marshall Plan aid from the U.S. to these economies helped to recirculate money with which other nations could buy U.S. goods, and in so doing it lubricated the world trade system.

In the 1950s the supply of U.S. dollars in world trade was sufficient even though world trade grew very rapidly. U.S. Balance of Payments deficits grew to keep pace, mostly in the Capital Account via foreign borrowing in New York.

In the 1960s the United States ran into the gold constraint implied in any version of the gold standard. The U.S. was not on the gold standard domestically; residents were forbidden to hold gold in bullion or specie, and the U.S. money supply could be increased even if official U.S. gold holdings did not increase. Nonresidents could convert their U.S.-dollar assets into gold at $35 per ounce, however, and that promise initially explained a large part of foreigners' willingness to continue holding U.S.-dollar assets. Gradually over the late 1950s and 1960s the volume of U.S.-dollar assets held by nonresidents grew, until it was much larger than the total of U.S. gold reserves. The gold backing of the U.S. dollar began to look shaky even for nonresidents.

The volume of nonresident holdings of U.S.-dollar assets grew because the U.S. economy ran persistent deficits in its Balance of Payments. Its trading partners grew more competitive, and U.S. corporations stepped up their expansion abroad. The U.S. deficits could have been eliminated by devaluation of the U.S. dollar, by restrictive domestic monetary policy, or by trade barriers, but the U.S. government was not willing to allow any of these. Instead, the U.S. waged an expensive war in Vietnam without any major increase in taxes. The results were even larger Balance of Payments deficits and even faster growth of nonresidents' holdings of U.S. dollars. The U.S. government was taking maximum advantage of its seigniorage by fighting the Vietnam war partly with resources of other countries, bought with newly printed world money.

Holders of U.S. dollars did not need to hold their wealth in that form. They could instead use the dollars to buy up U.S. land or the stock of U.S. companies, thereby returning the funds to the U.S. financial system. They could convert the dollars to gold or to their own domestic currency. In the latter case foreign central banks ended up holding the dollars, since under the Bretton Woods system those central banks had to buy up any excess supply of dollars in their foreign exchange markets. More and more of the surplus U.S. dollars came to be held by foreign central banks as private holders became more convinced that the U.S. dollar would have to be devalued.[16] By 1971, U.S. gold reserves were only one-sixth as large as official liabilities of the U.S. to foreigners.

The shift to floating exchange rates and paper money

The crunch came in August 1971 when President Nixon suspended convertibility of the dollar into gold, slapped on a temporary import surcharge, and abandoned any defence of the dollar's value in foreign exchange

---

[16]This caused some protest abroad. The printing of money by the U.S., and the automatic purchase of that money by the Bank of France (as well as by other central banks) in order to defend the U.S.-dollar exchange rate, conferred on the U.S. what General de Gaulle regarded as "an exorbitant privilege." The Bank of France was essentially lending on demand to the U.S., and the loan was being used in part to finance investment abroad by the U.S. As one commentator has put it, "What was to stop the Americans from printing money and buying up France?" Smith, *Paper Money*, 147.

markets. In the Smithsonian Agreement of December 1971 the dollar's value in gold was lowered, while that of several other currencies was raised. By March of 1973 even these measures were not enough, and all major currencies were left to float. Central banks were no longer obligated to buy up unwanted amounts of world money, only to see it devalued months later.

Nixon's action of August 1971 removed the gold constraint from the supply of U.S. dollars to nonresidents. Now there is no explicit limit to the creation of world money. The world has a problem just the opposite of that of the gold-standard system of the previous century. With the U.S. dollar still the main form of world money and with few close substitutes, the U.S. can and does create more world money just by running up large Balance of Payments deficits at the expense of the rest of the world. The rest of the world cannot refuse to accept the U.S. dollars as long as they are the international medium of exchange. Holders can use the dollars to buy up U.S. assets, or exchange them for foreign currencies and force the dollar exchange rate down, or just hold the dollars in Eurodollar deposits (that is, interest-earning near-money deposits) at good interest rates. Most holders have chosen the third alternative, so far, but there were crises in October 1978 and October 1979 when it looked as though foreign holders were going to dump their dollar holdings.

There is a general unwillingness to see the U.S. dollar devalued sharply, because it is the medium of exchange for world trade, but such devaluation is inevitable if the world money supply grows too fast and if the U.S. government is not willing to pursue high-interest-rate policies to attract nonresident holders of U.S.-dollar deposits. From October 1979 to mid-1982 the U.S. pursued a very high interest-rate policy, but the government was unhappy about the domestic effects of such high rates. Furthermore, the United States' major trading partners were also unhappy about the strength of the U.S. dollar that resulted — even those governments that had earlier complained about the U.S. dollar's weakness.

Alternative world moneys

The unsatisfactory state of the world money supply has given rise to a search for better ways of providing it. The problem with using a key currency as the medium of exchange has been that the key-currency country must act against its own short-term self-interest in not exploiting its seigniorage. The U.S. gets only a share of the benefits from proper growth of world money, but all of the benefits of exploiting seigniorage.

In national financial systems without any discipline from a gold standard, the solution to providing a proper domestic money supply has been to have an elected government responsible for providing an adequate money supply and to throw that government out of power if it fails to do so, rather than to entrust the matter to any private group such as bankers. The world's nations have started on a similar route by having the International Monetary Fund issue Special Drawing Rights on the agreement of the world's governments. This is collective action, essentially, by all of the parties who will suffer if the volume of world money is not adequate. So far, however, SDRs are only a limited form of international money, useful only for transactions between central banks.

The solution toward which the world seems to be moving is that suggested by Keynes at the Bretton Woods conference in 1944: a system of paper money created by a world central bank on the agreement of world governments. The value of the paper money would be based on the value of a basket of currencies, and its issue would be subject to no constraints but the consensus of all governments affected. This is a reasonable international approximation of the system Canada has for controlling its domestic money supply, but such an international arrangement is still a long way in the future.

SECTION 4 Summary

The Canadian financial system is embedded in a broader world financial system much as the Canadian economy is embedded in a world economy. There are some obviously international financial institutions that give concrete structure to the world financial system, such as the International Monetary Fund (IMF), the Bank for International Settlements (BIS), and the General Agreement on Tariffs and Trade (GATT).

The rest of the world financial system is more amorphous. Central banks and private commercial banks in each nation play some role internationally by servicing the needs of their customers for foreign exchange and by trading in foreign-currency assets. Canadian banks in particular play a large role abroad relative to their size at home, and they run virtually the whole Canadian foreign exchange market. Even more amorphous is the Eurocurrency market run through banks usually operating out of their home jurisdiction in currencies other than that of the host country. These banks make up a very competitive set of suppliers of short- to long-term deposits and compete equally vigorously for loan customers, usually in syndicates.

The world financial system is a financial system like any other, and its performance can be assessed. The logical criteria are how well it performs its functions of (a) providing a world payments mechanism, (b) transferring surpluses from primary lenders to primary borrowers, and (c) providing neither more nor less money than is needed for world trade. The world financial system scores fairly well in transferring funds and providing a payments mechanism. Transfer of the huge OPEC surpluses of 1974–76 and of 1979–82 to all of the borrowers needing to pay for oil deficits was a sizable achievement even though borrowers' debt levels are too high and some of the credits are questionable.

The major difficulty of the world financial system has been in providing for the right growth of international money. As long as the U.S. dollar is the only key currency, the U.S. is free to increase the world's money supply too fast without suffering all of the consequences, particularly if other nations attempt to hold their exchange rates fixed. That has been the situation for the last two decades, and now there is far more international money than holders — particularly foreign central banks — really want. It is possible that the IMF's Special Drawing Rights will gradually grow to fill much of the U.S. dollar's place in world trade, in which case at least the issue of SDRs will be a collective decision rather than the prerogative of one nation.

Questions for discussion

1. How is the international financial system different from a national financial system, in (a) its roles and (b) its institutions?
2. What is the world money supply, and why is it held?
3. What are Eurobanks, Euroyen, and Eurobonds?
4. Why is the recycling problem for the world financial system more difficult than the domestic recycling problem for a national financial system?
5. In what ways are SDRs money?
6. Why must different nations' monetary policies be co-ordinated under a fixed-exchange-rate system?
7. Who have been the recipients of the benefits of world seigniorage, and how have they come to receive those benefits?
8. Does the United States still receive seigniorage benefits now that the world is operating on a floating-exchange-rate system? Explain.

References

Binhammer, H.H. *Money, Banking and the Canadian Financial System*. 4th ed. Toronto: Methuen, 1982.

Boreham, G.F. *Money and Banking: Analysis and Policy in a Canadian Context*. 2d ed. Toronto: Holt, Rinehart and Winston, 1979, part 7.

Clarke, William M., and George Pulay. *The World's Money: How It Works*. London: Allen and Unwin, 1970.

Clendenning, E. Wayne. *The Eurocurrency Markets and the International Activities of Canadian Banks*. Ottawa: Economic Council of Canada, 1976.

Crockett, Andrew. *International Money: Issues and Analysis*. Sunbury-on-Thames, U.K.: Nelson, 1977.

Meier, Gerald M. *Problems of a World Monetary Order*. 2d ed. New York: Oxford University Press, 1982.

Neave, Edwin H. *Canada's Financial System*. Toronto: Wiley, 1981, chap. 9.

Sampson, Anthony. *The Money Lenders*. New York: Hodder & Stoughton, 1982.

Sarpkaya, S. *The Money Market in Canada*. Toronto: Butterworths, 1980, chap. 3.

Smith, Adam [George J.W. Goodman]. *Paper Money*. New York: Dell, 1981.

GLOSSARY

A

Accelerationist model: Model of aggregate demand and supply behavior in which inflation accelerates or decelerates continually as long as unemployment is not at the natural rate.

Accelerator mechanism: Accelerating and decelerating path of aggregate demand caused by surges of investment demand to build up the capital stock.

Acceptance business: Taking over the management and collection of accounts receivable, either for a fee or by buying the accounts receivable at a discount from face value.

Acceptance company: A firm that buys accounts receivable.

Actuarial reserve: Present value of an insurance company's liabilities to its policyholders.

Aggregate demand (*AD*): Real demand for goods and services during a year; real gross national expenditure, excluding unplanned inventory accumulation.

Aggregate demand multiplier: Rate of change in equilibrium aggregate demand per dollar of change in an exogenous component of aggregate demand.

Amortized value: Recorded value of a bond, calculated in such a way as to spread any capital gain between purchase price and redemption value over the entire lifetime of the bond.

Annuities: Contracts providing for a regular stream of future payments, either for life or for a definite period.

Arbitrage: Interest-sensitive flow of funds from one financial market to another.

Asset-market equilibrium locus, or *LM* curve: A line joining combinations of real income Y and interest rate r at which asset markets are in equilibrium.

Asset portfolio: Collection of assets held.

Assignment rule: Assignment of stabilization policy tools to stabilization policy targets according to each policy tool's comparative advantage in achieving each particular target.

Automatic transfer service, or zero-balance banking: An arrangement under which banks transfer unneeded funds from chequing deposits to earn interest and return them automatically to the chequing deposit to cover cheques written.

B

Balance of Payments: Record of all of a nation's receipts and payments involving foreign currency during a year.

Bankers' acceptances: Large, short-term trade credits whose payment has been guaranteed by a bank.

Bankers' profit: Profit made from the spread between asset yield and debt cost, for the portion of total assets financed by borrowing.

Bank for International Settlements (BIS): Central bankers' bank, mainly co-ordinating collective responses of central banks in advanced industrial economies.

Bank Rate: Minimum rate at which the Bank of Canada will lend to members of the Canadian Payments Association; fixed at 0.25 percent above the weekly Treasury Bill rate.

Barter: Exchange of goods and services directly for other goods and services, without use of any medium of exchange.

Bear market: A market dominated by those expecting falling prices, called *bears*.

Bearer instrument: An asset whose ownership is transferred by passage from hand to hand.

Broad money: Narrow money plus close substitutes for narrow-money assets.

Bull market: A market dominated by those expecting rising prices, called *bulls*.

Buyback: Purchase and resale agreement between a money-market dealer and lenders other than the Bank of Canada.

C

Call option: A contract entitling the holder to buy 100 shares of stock at the strike price on or before the expiry date.

Cambridge equation: $M_d = kPY$, where k is a constant in the short run.

Canada Pension Plan: Mandatory pension plan to which all full-time workers and their employers (outside Quebec) contribute; as of 1984 the rate of contribution was up to 3.6 percent of earnings.

Capacity use: Ratio of actual output to full-capacity output.

Capital Account: Record of all foreign-currency receipts and payments for transactions not involving currently produced goods and services.

Capital consumption, or depreciation: Decrease in value of an asset because of wear and tear.

Capital consumption allowance: An estimate of the decrease in value of real assets due to wear and tear.

Capital gains income: Income or extra wealth received in the form of an increase in the market value of assets held.

Cash reserve assets: Assets that may be used by chartered banks to meet their cash reserve requirement; Canadian coin and Bank of Canada notes, plus deposits in the Bank of Canada.

Cash reserve management: Changing the supply of cash reserve assets (currency and Bank of Canada deposits).

Cash surrender value: Amount to be paid out to each policyholder upon surrender of an insurance policy; approximately equal to the value of the policy reserve for each policy.

Certainty-equivalent approach: Designing policy on the basis of uncertain forecasts of future exogenous variables, as though the forecasts were known with certainty.

Chartered banks: Financial institutions having charters under the federal Bank Act.

Commercial paper: Short-term, nonredeemable loan notes issued by large, well-known corporations with little default risk.

Commodity exchange standard: A monetary system with token money convertible into a commodity that is not itself used as money.

Commodity standard: Monetary system in which the medium of exchange is a commodity with nonmonetary uses.

Common shares: Shares held by ultimate owners of a firm, who share in residual profits of the firm without limit.

Convertible: Exchangeable for common shares at the discretion of the holder, at a set exchange rate.

Cost of forward cover: The cost of buying or selling forward exchange, equal to the difference between forward exchange rate and spot exchange rate.

Cost of insurance protection: The cost to each surviving policyholder of supplementing the policy reserves of deceased policyholders in order to pay their death benefits.

Cost-of-living-adjustment (COLA) **clause:** Clause in collective agreements providing for automatic increase in wage levels in line with changes in the Consumer Price Index.

Covariance: A measure of joint variation of two yields around their respective expected yields; covariance is positive if yields move together, negative if they move in opposite directions.

Covered interest differential: Interest

differential less the cost of forward cover.

Credibility effect: Response of aggregate demand and supply to use of stabilization policy, caused by the public's belief that the policy action will achieve its objectives.

Crowding out: Suppression of other components of aggregate demand by an expansion in one category — especially government spending.

Cumulative preferred shares: Preferred shares whose dividends may be deferred, but not cancelled, if the issuer's profits are not satisfactory.

Current Account: Record of all foreign-currency receipts and payments involving trade in currently produced goods and services (plus transfer payments).

D

Day loan: Loan note issued by money-market dealers to a bank, extendible one day at a time.

Debentures: Bonds that do not have any specific real property pledged as collateral.

Debit float: Amount of cheques deposited but not yet debited from the payors' accounts.

Debt supply: The outstanding stock of debts made available by borrowers at any point of time; also called *supply of financial assets*, or *demand for loanable funds*.

Default risk: Uncertainty over whether the borrower will pay promised values on time and in full.

Defensive operations: Changes in Bank of Canada assets or liabilities undertaken by the Bank just to offset other influences on the monetary base or bank reserves.

Defined-benefit pension plan: A pension plan promising specific pensions at retirement not contingent on the asset value of the pension fund.

Demand for an asset: Amount of an asset that people are willing to hold at any point of time.

Demand-management policy: Use of demand-management tools to achieve desired growth of aggregate demand.

Demand-management tool: Any stabilization policy variable under the government's control that influences aggregate demand.

Depreciation, or capital consumption: Decrease in value of an asset because of wear and tear.

Direct lending: Lending by a saver directly to someone borrowing to finance consumption or real capital formation, rather than to finance purchase of financial assets.

Disintermediation: A shift of asset demand away from debts of intermediaries and toward debts of primary borrowers.

Dynamic efficiency: Allocation of savings to the most productive forms of investment.

Dynamic operations: Changes in Bank of Canada assets or debts undertaken to cause changes in the monetary base or bank reserves.

E

Effective annual interest rate: Annual interest rate including compounding.

Efficient frontier: The upper left edge of the feasible set of combinations of portfolio risk and expected yield.

Efficient-markets hypothesis: Hypothesis that market participants use all available information in arriving at expectations about future asset prices.

Endowment point: The point on a diagram of intertemporal consumption choice whose co-ordinates are the current and future incomes with which the individual is endowed.

Equity: Equal treatment of equals; also, synonym of *wealth*, or *net worth*: total assets less total debt.

Eurobanks: Banks operating in the Eurodollar market.

Eurobond: A bond denominated in a currency other than that of the country in which the bond is issued.

Eurodollar deposit: A deposit denominated in a currency other than that of the country in which the deposit is issued.

Eurodollar, or Eurocurrency, market: Wholesale market for deposits and loans in a currency other than that of the host country (usually U.S. dollars); located in many financial centres.

Excess cash reserves: Cash reserve assets held over and above the cash reserve requirement.

Expectations-augmented Phillips curve: Curve that relates wage inflation to the rate of capacity use and that shifts with changes in expected future inflation.

Expected yield: A weighted average of possible yields, with relative probabilities serving as weights; the midpoint of a probability distribution of possible yields.

F

Factoring and acceptance business: Taking over the management and collection of accounts receivable, either for a fee or by buying the accounts receivable at a discount from face value.

Federal deposit transfers: Transfers of funds between the federal government's deposit in the Bank of Canada and its deposits in the chartered banks.

Fiat money: An item that serves as money because the government says it does.

Fiduciary money: Token money that the holders trust will be convertible into some form of commodity money such as specie.

Finance paper: Short-term, nonredeemable loan notes issued by finance companies, secured by blocks of consumer loans.

Financial Flow Accounts: Record of savings, investment, lending, and borrowing by sectors of the economy.

Fisher effect: Increase in nominal interest rates, caused by expected inflation, by an amount equal to the expected inflation.

Fixed-instalment debt: Debt with a fixed, regular payment blending together interest and principal repayments.

Fix-price markets: Markets in which prices are set, usually by the seller, and are not responsive to demand changes in the short run.

Flex-price markets: Markets in which prices fluctuate to balance supply and demand on a daily basis, as in an auction.

Floating-rate demand loans: Loans with interest payments at a level determined by current interest rates, and with no fixed pattern of principal repayments.

Flow: Rate over a period of time.

Foreign exchange rate: The price of foreign currency (the U.S. dollar, usually) in units of domestic currency.

Foreign exchange risk: A specific form of income risk, the uncertainty being due to quotation of payments in a foreign currency.

Futures market: Market for sale and purchase of contracts for future delivery of specified commodities (or financial assets).

G

General Agreement on Tariffs and Trade (GATT): International code of conduct for trade and capital transactions.

Gresham's Law: Bad money drives out good. *Out* means out of circulation and into other uses.

Gross real investment: Net real investment plus capital consumption allowances.

Gross saving: Net saving plus capital consumption allowances.

H

Hedging: Purchasing an asset or arranging a contract whose yield fluctuations have strong negative correlation with yields on the rest of the asset portfolio.

Human wealth: Capitalized present value of current and expected future real income.

I

Income debentures: Bonds whose interest payments are conditional on satisfactory profits for the issuing company.

Income effect: Effect of a change in real income on quantity demanded, holding relative prices constant.

Income risk: Uncertainty over the stream of future nominal payments to be made by the borrower, other than that due to default risk.

Income velocity of circulation: The number of times the money supply changes hands during a year in a final sale of goods and services.

Incomes policy: Policy to affect wage- and price-setting behavior directly.

Indenture agreement: Agreement between a bond issuer and the bondholders about terms and conditions of a bond issue.

Indirect lending: Lending to a financial intermediary, which then relends the funds to others, and eventually to a primary borrower.

Indirect taxes: Taxes levied on goods or assets, rather than on individuals.

Inflation premium: The extra amount added to the real interest rate to compensate the lender for expected erosion of the purchasing power of principal due to inflation.

Inflation risk: Uncertainty of future purchasing power of known nominal values of assets.

Inflation tax: Reduction in the real value of money holdings each year due to inflation.

Intermediation: Borrowing, and using the funds to buy financial assets; selling one's own debt to lenders in order to buy other debts from borrowers.

International Monetary Fund (IMF): Official international lending agency, creator of Special Drawing Rights.

Investment contract company: Mortgage lending company that raises funds through long-term savings contracts sold to households.

Investment demand: Demand for currently produced real assets — housing, plant, equipment, and inventories.

***IS* curve:** Line joining all combinations of *Y* and *r* at which the goods market is in equilibrium.

J

J curve: Time path of interest rates that first falls and then recovers slightly, tracing out a backwards J pattern when interest rates are plotted over time.

Jobbers: Firms accepting bids and making offers as principals, in order to make a market operate smoothly.

L

Legal tender: Assets that must by law be accepted in payment of debts.

Letters patent: A company charter granted (in the case of banks) by the Minister of Finance rather than by the legislature itself.

Leverage ratio: Ratio of assets to equity; alteratively, ratio of debts to equity.

LIBOR: London Inter-Bank Offer Rate, the rate charged on loans between banks in the Eurocurrency market in London; the benchmark deposit yield in the Eurodollar market.

Liquidity: The property of being realizable at short notice and without significant cost.

Liquidity-preference theory: Theory that expected holding-period yields will be identical except for an increasing liquidity premium added to longer-term yields.

Liquidity risk: Uncertainty about availability of credit in the future.

***LM* curve, or asset-market equilibrium locus:** Line joining combinations of real income *Y* and interest rate *r* at which asset markets are in equilibrium.

Lump sum, immediate annuity: An annuity policy providing for annuity benefit payments starting immediately, paid for in a single payment.

M

M1: Canadian currency and coin outside banks and Canadian-dollar bank demand deposits.

M1A: M1 plus nonpersonal and chequable personal Canadian-dollar notice deposits in banks.

M2: M1A plus other Canadian-dollar notice and personal fixed-term deposits in banks.

M3: M2 plus Canadian-dollar nonpersonal fixed-term deposits in banks, plus residents' foreign-currency deposits held in Canada.

Managed float: Floating exchange rate arrangement in which the central bank intervenes to prevent some or most exchange rate movements.

Mandatory incomes policies: Incomes policies that fix wage and price increases by law or regulation.

Margin deposit: Deposit given to the broker as security for completion of a futures contract.

Marginal rate of substitution of variance for expected yield: The slope of an investor's indifference curves, the absolute ratio of marginal utility of variance to marginal utility of expected yield on a portfolio.

Marginal rate of time preference: Proportional extra marginal utility from consumption now rather than in the next period.

Marginal social cost: The opportunity cost of a particular use of resources.

Marginal social utility: Change in social welfare from a particular use of resources.

Market risk: Uncertainty of the market's future valuation of a known stream of nominal payments receivable in the future.

Medium of exchange: An item regularly accepted in exchange for other goods and services.

Money market: Wholesale market for short-term, liquid assets.

Money-purchase pension plan: A pension plan promising only as large an annuity as the assets of the pension plan will purchase at retirement.

Money-supply multiplier: Ratio of money supply to cash reserve base.

Moral suasion: Use of the central bank's influence to persuade bankers and others to follow particular courses of action.

Mortgage investment company: Mortgage lending company with low leverage, high payout of revenues, and special tax status.

Mutual insurance companies: Insurance companies owned by their participating policyholders, who elect the board of directors.

N

Narrow money: All regularly reported assets that are widely used as media of exchange.

National Capital Account: Table showing the assets held by each sector of the economy at a point in time.

Natural rates of output, unemployment, and capacity use: The rates of output, unemployment, and capacity use occurring in the long run with neither accelerating nor decelerating inflation.

Net capital outflow: Difference between domestic purchases of foreign assets (financial and nonfinancial) and foreign purchases of domestic assets.

Net exports: Total export demand by foreigners, less total import demand by Canadians.

Net Official Monetary Movements: Record of all changes in foreign exchange holdings of the Bank of Canada, the Exchange Fund Account, and the Receiver General for Canada.

Net real investment: Net increase in holdings of real assets.

Net saving, or saving: Change in wealth over any period.

Net worth, or wealth, or equity: Total assets less total debt.

Nominal annual interest rate: Annual interest rate ignoring compounding.

Non-accelerating inflation rate of unemployment (NAIRU): Rate of unemployment at which inflation will not accelerate; same as *natural rate of unemployment*.

Nonsystematic or unsystematic risk: Risk that is unique to a particular asset, not giving rise to high covariances.

Normal distribution: A particular, bell-shaped probability distribution with the largest probabilities in the centre of the distribution.

Numeraire, or unit of account: The good whose value serves as the standard of measurement for values of all other goods and services.

O

Open-market operations: Purchases and sales of government bonds and Treasury Bills by the Bank of Canada.

Open mortgage: A mortgage loan whose principal can be repaid early, in whole or in part, without any extra compensation to the lender.

Opportunity yields: Yields on other assets that could have been held.

Optimal debt:equity ratio: The debt:equity ratio that provides the pair of expected equity yield and variance lying on the equity owner's highest indifference curve.

Optimal policy rule: The announced strategy for use of a policy that minimizes variance of the target variable.

Over-the-counter (OTC) market: The market for stocks not listed on one of the stock exchanges, traded from brokers' offices rather than on the floor of a stock exchange.

P

Paper standard: A monetary system in which token moneys are not convertible into anything of intrinsic value (other than the paper they are printed on).

Participating policies: Insurance policies eligible to receive a partial rebate of premiums if the company's performance is better than was assumed when the premiums were originally set.

Permanent income: Income expected to continue throughout a lifetime.

Permanent insurance: Insurance protection to be continued for life.

Policy dividend: Partial rebate of premium on a participating insurance policy.

Policy reserve: The accumulated value of the surplus premiums contributed by holders of permanent life insurance policies, plus all earnings on that surplus.

Precautionary demand: Demand for money to protect against income shortfalls or unexpected spending needs.

Preferred-habitat theory: Theory that expected holding-period yields will differ by risk premiums that reflect investors' preferences for particular (not necessarily short-term) maturities.

Preferred shares: Shares that have first call on profits for a specified dividend yield, but no more; usually without voting rights, and with provision for redeemability by the firm.

Premiums: Payments made by holders of insurance policies for insurance protection.

Present discounted value: Current equivalent of future values, discounted because of interest not available on later values.

Primary borrowers: Those doing primary borrowing.

Primary borrowing: Borrowing to finance real spending on current output.

Primary lenders: Those doing primary lending.

Primary lending: Lending of money out of current savings.

Primary, or new-issue, markets: Markets in which issuers of debts first sell them to lenders.

Private domestic wealth: National wealth less government wealth and net debt to the rest of the world.

Private markets: Markets in which the terms of each transaction are negotiated privately.

Probability distribution: A graph or schedule showing the distribution of total probability of 1.0 over all possible outcomes.

Public markets: Markets in which prices or yields are posted for all to see.

Purchase and resale agreement (PRA): Sale of a security by a money-market dealer to the Bank of Canada, together with a promise to repurchase it shortly thereafter.

Pure expectations theory: Theory that expected holding-period yields will be identical on all maturities of bond.

Put option: A contract entitling the holder to sell 100 shares of stock at the strike price on or before the expiry date.

Q

***q* ratio:** Ratio of market price of existing real capital assets to their replacement costs.

Quantity Equation: $MV = PT$.

Quebec Pension Plan: Quebec version of the Canada Pension Plan, differing mainly in the investment of contributions.

R

Random-walk hypothesis: Hypothesis that stock-market price changes are random rather than correlated over time.

Real investment: Net increase in holdings of real assets.

Reserve averaging period: Period of time over which the average of bank cash reserve assets must at least equal the minimum legal cash reserve ratio to deposits. Either the first fifteen days of the month or the remaining days in the month.

Retail markets: Small-scale, nonstandardized markets.

Retractable: Redeemable at the discretion of the holder.

Risk averter: One who takes on extra risk only if compensated by the prospect of greater expected yield.

Risk premium: Margin of extra expected yield to compensate for extra riskiness due to either extra covariance or extra variance of an asset's yields.

Risk seeker: One who will give up the prospect of greater expected yield in order to take on greater risk.

S

Saving, or net saving: Change in wealth over any period.

Secondary markets: Markets for buying and selling previously issued financial assets.

Secondary reserve assets: Assets that chartered banks can use to meet the secondary reserve requirement: excess cash reserves, Treasury Bills, and day loans to money-market dealers.

Secondary reserve requirement: Requirement in the Bank Act that banks' holdings of Treasury Bills and day loans and excess cash reserves be at least a minimum ratio (currently 4.5 percent) to their deposits.

Segmented-markets hypothesis: Theory that bonds of different terms to maturity are not close substitutes, so that the bond market is segmented.

Segregated funds: Assets and liabilities relating to special insurance and annuity business involving fewer nominal guarantees by the insurance company.

Seigniorage: The profit from minting coins; in modern times, the profit from creating money.

Sinking fund: A fund built up by the bond issuer to redeem part of the bond issue before final maturity.

Special call loans: Call loans, from banks to investment dealers, that are really callable.

Special Drawing Rights (SDRs): International reserve currency (for central banks only) redeemable in all other currencies.

Specie: Gold or silver coinage.

Speculative motive: Holding money in order to profit from expected price decreases in other assets.

Speculator (in options and futures markets): One who buys options and futures contracts for reasons other than the wish to hedge.

Spot market: Market for immediate delivery of commodities (or financial assets).

Static efficiency: Efficient allocation of resources and distribution of outputs among consumers.

Sterilization: Offsetting of central-bank foreign-exchange transactions with opposite central-bank open-market transactions to prevent changes in the cash reserve base.

Stock: Quantity in existence at a point of time.

Strategy of gradualism: The strategy of stabilizing the economy so that the growth rate of M1 will fall gradually; followed from 1975 to 1982.

Strike price: The buying or selling price agreed on in an option contract.

Substitution effect: Effect of a change in price on quantity demanded, holding real income constant.

Supply of an asset: Amount of an asset in existence; for financial assets, the amount debtors will leave outstanding at any point of time.

Supply-management policy: Use of supply-management tools to control or stabilize the level of costs and prices.

Supply-management tool: Any policy variable that will influence the aggregate supply curve.

Systematic risk: Risk that is common to all or most assets in the financial system, giving rise to high correlation of yields and high covariances.

T

Tax-anticipation note: Short-term loan note issued by a provincial or local government to finance spending in anticipation of tax revenue.

Tax-based incomes policy (TIP): An incomes policy in which adherence to wage and price guidelines is rewarded with tax concessions (or avoidance of tax penalties).

Term insurance: Insurance to be continued only for a specified term (though often renewable thereafter).

Term structure of interest rates: The structure of yields to maturity on assets of different terms to maturity but otherwise identical characteristics.

Terms of trade: Ratio of export prices to import prices.

Tobin's q: Ratio of market value of real capital to its replacement cost.

Token money: An asset with no intrinsic value that is used as a medium of exchange.

Trade credit: Credit extended by suppliers to customers for delayed payment of trade bills.

Transactions demand: Demand for money that will be used to make payment in ordinary transactions.

INDEX

References to tables or figures are indicated in **bold face**.